FOR SEMESTER-I

OSWAL – GURUKUL

Sample Question Papers

ISC CLASS XII

For 2021 Examination

New Specimen Question Paper Released by CISCE in Aug 2021 (Fully Solved)

SCIENCE STREAM

- English I
- English II
- Mathematics
- Computer Science
- Physical Education
- Physics
- Chemistry
- Biology

Paper Pattern Strictly Based on New SQP

Follows the Reduced and Bifurcated Syllabus

Includes Answers with Explanations

BY
PANEL OF AUTHORS

EDITION : 2021

ISBN : 978-93-91184-40-7

PRICE : ₹ 750.00

PRINTED AT : Upkar Printing Unit, Agra

PUBLISHED BY

OSWAL PUBLISHERS

Head Office: 1/12, Sahitya Kunj, M.G. Road, Agra - 282002

Phone   : (0562) 2527771-4, +91 7534077222

E-mail   : info@oswalpublishers.in

Website   : www.oswalpublishers.com

The cover of this book has been designed using resources from Freepik.com

Preface

In accordance with the latest syllabus prescribed by the Council for the Indian Certificate of Secondary Education Examination, New Delhi.

Board examinations are a crucial milestone for every student. In order for them to perform well in the exam, we have introduced a set of Sample Question Papers for the First Semester Examinations. We have designed the book based on the Modified Assessement Plan issued by the Board on August 6, 2021.

The Specimen Question Papers released by the CISCE in August, 2021 have been strictly followed in formulating question papers. The content of the book has been updated according to the Latest Reduced Syllabi issued by the Board on July 19, 2021.

This book comprises Sample Question Papers symmetrically divided among core subjects English-I, English-II, Mathematics, Computer Science, Physical Education, Physics, Chemistry and Biology.

Sample Question Papers caters to the need of all the students with varied academic calibres. The content of this book is designed to focus on topics most likely to be asked in the board examination. Questions are provided with suitable answers and detailed explanation wherever require for better understanding of the topic by the students.

The Sample Question Papers are prepared by subject matter experts to provide best content to the students. It gives the students an insight into how questions are asked in board examinations and what approach should one follow while attempting them.

We hope you will find this book helpful in your preparation for Board examinations. We would advise you to stay calm and manage your time efficiently. Do not get overwhelmed with too many resources and study guides, be selective and choose the best one.

—The Publisher

Easy steps to follow :

Step 1 - In a few clicks, you can completely customize your test

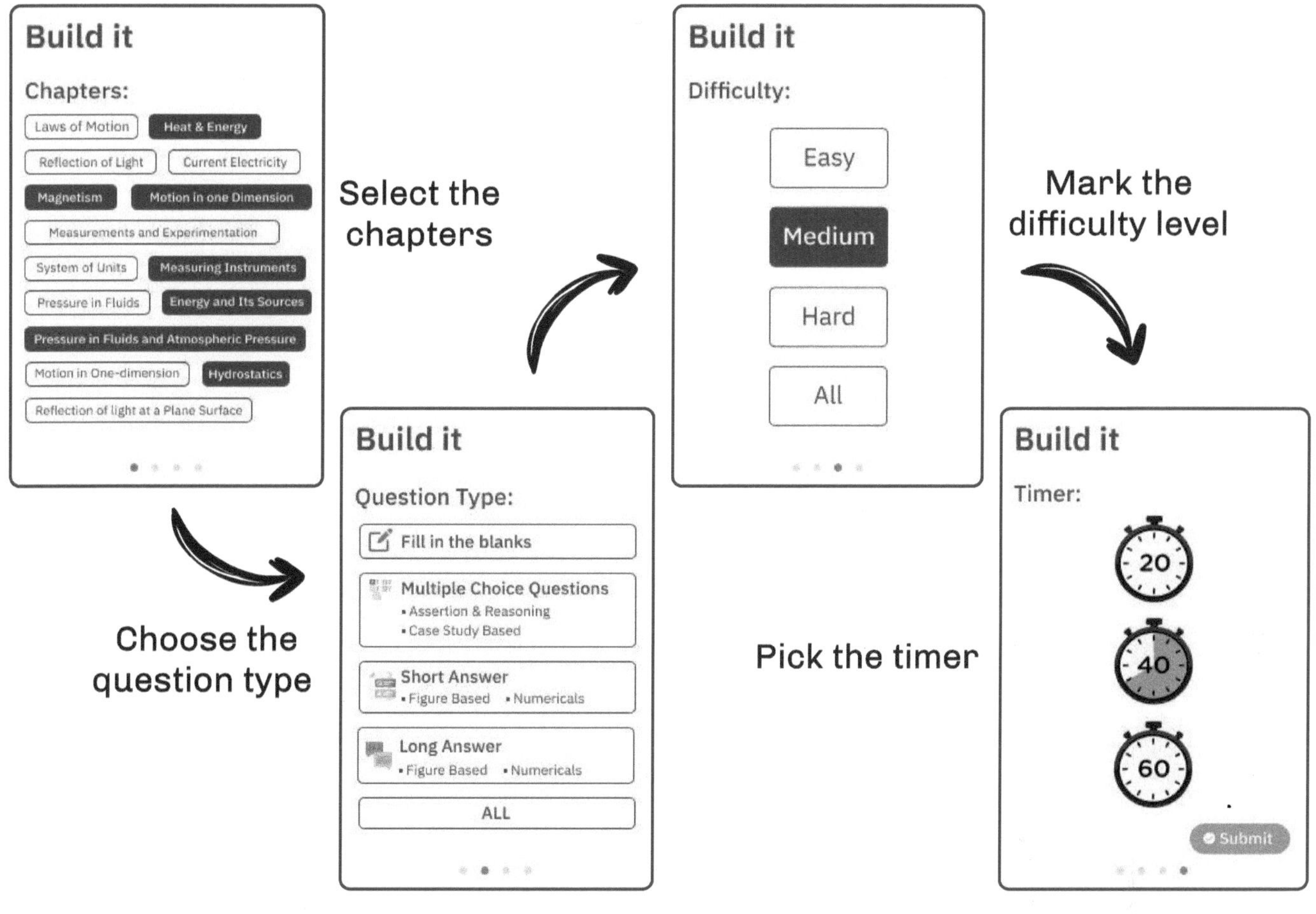

Step 2 - Test is based on the selected question type, chapters, difficulty, time

Step 3 - Click on start and type your answers in the given space

Step 4 - Use insert $\TeX$ equation editor to quickly & accurately insert the difficult math/physics/chem formulas

Step 5 - Skip any question if not sure, proceed to next & submit

Step 6 - You will get your result emailed right away

How to Smartly Approach Tricky MCQs?

Dear Students,

As your exams inch closer to their final date, with the new pattern and exam-style, your way of preparation and approach to the exam has to change too. With the help of this ingenious book, you can time yourself and attempt a mock/practice paper to gauge where you stand.

To help you approach your MCQs smartly, read along for some smart tips you must keep at your fingertips to avoid silly mistakes.

1. Students must read all questions carefully, allowing them to choose the most appropriate answer.
2. Students mustn't be in a rush to tick the correct option, instead apply logic to the reasoning based MCQs.
3. In comprehension-based questions, students should read the passage thoroughly before answering questions. It is important to understand the passage and then select the most suitable option.
4. In numerical-based MCQs, students must take note of the units used in the given data to avoid making mistakes in evaluating the right answer.
5. While choosing the most appropriate answer students should be able to correlate the question with daily life applications and then select the right answer.
6. Students should avoid guesswork while answering MCQs.
7. Diagram-based MCQs should be attempted with utmost care as figures given could be deceptive and one should be able to figure out the gist of the figures.
8. Students should move on to the next question, and not get stuck on one MCQ. These tests are time-specific and have to be attempted in short intervals of time.
9. If two options given are very close to the required answer then try to think of each option in a different perspective and see whether it fits in the same. The answer should be universally acceptable.
10. In the current SQPs published by the Council, we can see Match the Column as a type of MCQ. What the students must be smart about is the way options are given. To avoid making a mistake, have a paper ready to physically match the column to choose the right option.
11. Always use the process of elimination with the given options, instead of jumping to the right answer.
12. Last and foremost important, read your questions multiple times as there are MCQs that require the student to mark two correct answers instead of one. Be mindful of such questions.

Good luck!

Contents

English-I

Specimen Question Paper

English I

Maximum Marks: 80
Time allowed: One and a half hours

General Instructions

*(Candidates are allowed additional **15 minutes** for **only** reading the Paper)*
ALL QUESTIONS ARE COMPULSORY.
The marks intended for questions are given in brackets [ ].
Select the correct option for each of the following questions.

Question 1.

Read the given passage carefully and answer the questions that follow:

I heard the main door creak open directly above our heads.

My first natural **impulse** was to shout, to get help from whoever had come: and then I remembered. Harry had come to this place to _meet_ someone. He didn't know who. He'd gone there trustingly. He'd walked into the boathouse and tried to pick up an envelope and the floor had given way beneath him; and if I hadn't been there with him he would certainly have drowned in the dock.

With doubt but also **awareness** of danger I guessed at an enemy above our heads, not a saviour.

There was silence. Then the creak of a step or two, then the sound of the door being quietly closed. I heard a car door slamming and after that the noise of an engine starting up and being driven away.

No easy exit. The door was solid as a rock. On the wall beside the door, there was a row of three electric switches. I pressed them all without any results from the electric light bulbs along the ceiling. There was also a control box with cables leading to the top of a metal curtain at the level of the river. The arrangement for raising the curtain was a _gear_ designed to turn a rod to wind the metal mesh-up onto it like a _blind_. Without electricity, however, it wasn't going to **oblige**.

'Harry?' I called. 'Sit there and don't worry. I'll come back.'

I slipped into the water and swam a couple of strokes to the curtain. Tried standing up, but the water was much deeper there. Hung onto the wire feeling the tug of the current from the river.

With extreme luck, the curtain wouldn't go all the way down to the river's bed. There must be a gap of at least two or three feet. I took a breath and pulled myself hand over hand down the curtain, seeking to find the bottom of it with my feet: and there was indeed a gap between the bottom edge of the curtain and the mud.

Deep breath. Dived. Came to the end of the wire, felt the mud below. The bottom edge of the curtain was a matter of free links, not a connecting bar. The links could be raised, but only singly, not altogether. I swung down at the bottom, deciding to go head first... praying that the links wouldn't catch on my clothes... head under, push the links up with hands, full strength, take care, don't rush, don't snag clothes, hold onto the wire outside, don't let go, hang on, shoulders through, raise the links, back through, legs... short of breath... lungs hurting... careful, careful... unknown things around my ankles, hampering... had to breathe soon... feet catching... feet... through.

I was through. I came up into the air gasping deeply, panting, aching lungs swelling, feeling a rush of suppressed **terror**, clinging onto the curtain in a shaky *state*.

'Harry?' I called.

'Oh John...' His relief was beyond measure. 'Thank God.'

'Not long now,' I said and heard the **strain** in my own voice too.

I edged along with the curtain in the direction of the shut door and managed to scramble around the boathouse wall and up out of the water to roll at last onto the grassy *bank*. Bitterly cold, shivering violently from several causes, but out.   Adapted from **Longshot** by Dick Francis

(a) (i) Given below are five words from the passage along with four options for each. Choose the option which has a similar meaning in the passage: **[5]**

1. **Impulse**
   - (a) vibration
   - (b) a sudden strong wish
   - (c) whimsical
   - (d) motive

2. **Awareness**
   - (a) knowledge
   - (b) not knowing
   - (c) goods on sale
   - (d) conscience

3. **Terror**
   - (a) fight
   - (b) foreboding
   - (c) uncanny
   - (d) extreme fear

4. **Strain**
   - (a) trouble
   - (b) tiresome
   - (c) anxiety
   - (d) tight

5. **Oblige**
   - (a) be of any help
   - (b) bow down
   - (c) beholden
   - (d) ndebted

(ii) With each of the five words given below, choose the correct sentence that uses the word in a different meaning from that which it carries in the passage.   **[5]**

1. **Meet**
   - (a) The Inter-House Athletic meet of XYZ School had to be postponed due to heavy rains.
   - (b) The two friends had promised to meet at the same spot twenty years later.
   - (c) Some children find it difficult to meet up to the expectations of their parents.
   - (d) After his rude behaviour, it is meet for him to apologise to his father.

2. **Gear**
   - (a) The contestants had to gear up for their performances by 6 o'clock in the evening.
   - (b) The trekker carried his camping gear along with other necessary items.
   - (c) The car went out of control and crashed because its gear systems collapsed.
   - (d) The gearbox broke down and the van came to a standstill.

3. **Blind**
   - (a) The little girl helped the blind beggar to cross the busy road.
   - (b) Mother pulled the blind to keep out the sunlight from the room.
   - (c) Instead of curtains, the Venetian blind looks more appropriate in the office.
   - (d) She has a blind spot where classical music is concerned.

4. **State**
   - (a) The State Electricity Board is responsible for supplying electric current in the whole state.
   - (b) The teacher told the student to state everything in detail in front of the examiner.
   - (c) I was not in the right state of mind to go to the party.
   - (d) In its frozen state water becomes ice.

5. **Bank**

    (a) I had to go to the State Bank of India last week to deposit the money.

    (b) Standing on the riverbank I watched the star-studded sky.

    (c) Shirley is a friend who I can bank on.

    (d) There is a question bank where one can store various types of questions.

(b) Choose the correct option for the question given below: **[10]**

1. What made the narrator think that someone had come?

    (a) The narrator saw someone entering.

    (b) The narrator heard the footsteps of an intruder.

    (c) The narrator heard the main door open directly above their heads.

    (d) The narrator heard the main door shut directly above their heads.

2. Harry had .... gone to meet someone in the boathouse.

    (a) unwisely   (b) trustingly

    (c) foolishly   (d) mistakenly

3. Why did the narrator assume that the intruder was an enemy?

    (a) He had tricked Harry into the boathouse and tried to drown him.

    (b) He had tried to kill Harry.

    (c) He heard the car driving away.

    (d) All of the above.

4. Why was there no easy way out of the boathouse?

    (a) The door was too high and it was locked.

    (b) The door was solid as a rock and there was no electricity.

    (c) There was no electricity so nothing was working. .

    (d) It was difficult to reach the door.

5. Why do you think it was not possible to raise the curtain?

    (a) The metal mesh was far too rusted for it to move.

    (b) The narrator could not operate the gear.

    (c) The gear designed to wind the metal mesh wouldn't work without electricity.

    (d) The curtain was too heavy for the narrator to handle.

6. What did the narrator feel while he was underwater?

    (a) The narrator prayed and tried to remain calm so that he did not make any mistakes.

    (b) The narrator lost his nerves and almost gave up trying.

    (c) The narrator felt at a loss, he did not see any hope of saving his friend, Harry.

    (d) The narrator was so tense that he could not speak.

7. What was his reaction when he came out of the water?

    (a) He was very tired and exhausted and couldn't breathe.

    (b) He was relieved to hear his friend's voice.

    (c) He was feeling bitterly cold.

    (d) He was shivering violently from several causes.

8. How did Harry feel about being rescued?

    (a) He was relieved and happy.   (b) He was too frightened to express himself.

    (c) He was very quiet and scared.   (d) He did not speak a word and that frightened John.

9. How had Harry been trapped in the boathouse?

    (a) He had walked into the boathouse and tried to pick up an envelope when the floor gave way and he fell through.

    (b) He was hit in the head and locked inside.

(c) He had been pushed from the back into the water.

(d) He slipped and fell into the water.

10. Arrange the sequence of events as they occur in the passage.

(i) The narrator dived into the water to reach the end of the curtain.

(ii) He swam a couple of strokes.

(iii) He swung down at the bottom

(iv) He tried standing up hanging on to the wire.

    (a) (iii), (i), (iv), (ii)   (b) (ii), (iv), (i), (iii)

    (c) (i), (ii), (iii), (iv)   (d) (iv), (iii), (ii), (i)

Question 2.

Read the given passage carefully and answer the questions that follow:

A long time ago, it had caused a terrible scandal in noble Lorraine. A young girl, beautiful and rich, Suzanne de Sirmont, had been carried off by a sergeant in the regiment that her father commanded. He was a handsome boy, the son of peasants, but looking good in his dress *uniform*, this soldier who had seduced the daughter of his colonel. No doubt she had seen him, noticed him, fell in love with him while watching the troops march by. But how had he spoken to her, how had they been able to see each other, to talk? How had she dared to make him understand that she loved him? No one ever knew.

No one suspected anything. One night, as the soldier had just finished his enlistment, he disappeared with her. They sought for them, but never found them. They never heard from her again, and they considered her dead.

And I had found her in that **sinister** valley.

Then I said, in my *turn*, "Yes, I remember well. You are Suzanne."

She shook her head yes. Tears fell from her eyes. Then, with a glance at the old man sitting immobile on the doorstep of the **shack**, she told me, "It's him."

And I understood that she still loved him, that she still saw him with seduced eyes.

I asked, "Have you been happy, at least?"

She answered, with a voice that came from the heart, "Oh! Yes, very happy. He has made me very happy. I have never regretted anything."

I contemplated her, sad, surprised, amazed by the power of love! This rich girl had followed this man, this peasant. She had herself become a peasant. She had lived her life without charms, without luxuries, without delicacies of any sort; she had bent herself to his simple habits. And she loved him *still*. She had become **rustic**, in a bonnet and canvas skirt. She ate on an earthenware plate on a crude wooden table, sitting on a cane seat, a gruel of cabbage and potatoes with lard. She lay on a straw mattress by his side.

She had never thought of anything, but him! She had missed neither necklaces, nor fineries, nor elegances, nor soft seats, nor the perfumed warmth of rooms enveloped in curtains, nor the sweetness of **downy** cushions on which to *rest* one's *body*. She had never needed anything but him; as long as he was there, she desired nothing.

She had abandoned life while young, both the world and those who had raised her and loved her. She had come, along with him, to this wild **ravine**. And he had been everything for her, everything one desires, everything one dreams of, everything one constantly waits for, everything one endlessly hopes. He had filled her existence with happiness, from one end to the other. She couldn't have been happier.

And all night, listening to the rough breathing of the old soldier stretched out on his pallet, beside her who had followed him so far, I thought of that strange and simple adventure, of this happiness so complete, made of so little.

And I left with the rising sun, after having shaken hands with the two old people, man and wife."

(519 words)

(a) (i) Given below are five words from the passage along with four options for each. Choose the option which has a similar meaning in the passage: **[5]**

1. **sinister**
   - (a) inful
   - (b) ominous
   - (c) sincere
   - (d) scenic

2. **shack**
   - (a) palace
   - (b) bar
   - (c) hut
   - (d) chib

3. **rustic**
   - (a) simple
   - (b) sophisticated
   - (c) beautiful
   - (d) happy

4. **ravine**
   - (a) house
   - (b) yacht
   - (c) boat
   - (d) valley

5. **downy**
   - (a) lower
   - (b) depressed
   - (c) soft
   - (d) huge

(ii) With each of the five words given below, choose the correct sentence that uses the word in a different meaning from that which it carries in the passage. **[5]**

1. **Uniform**
   - (a) Two well-armed guards stood outside the gate, in a blue medical uniform
   - (b) Ashes and dirt sullied his uniform and made him sneeze.
   - (c) His uniform was trimmed with gold and braid.
   - (d) The rows of houses were uniform in appearance.

2. **Turn**
   - (a) It was her turn to do some studying.
   - (b) He could not turn around as he had a stiff neck.
   - (c) When it was his turn to speak, he became nervous.
   - (d) She was waiting for her turn to offer the bouquet to the chief guest

3. **Still**
   - (a) He looked back and saw the innkeeper still standing by the door.
   - (b) It is still not too late to change our plans.
   - (c) Still waters run deep.
   - (d) Words of praise came more easily to his lips, but he still had trouble accepting praise.

4. **Body**
   - (a) His body shook, and he flung his head back to the sky with a hoarse shout.
   - (b) A legislative body should be composed of two houses.
   - (c) Finding nothing, she spread the blanket and lay down, pulling part of it over her body.
   - (d) His cheekbones were high, his chiselled face matching the chiselled body.

5. **Rest**
   - (a) Why don't you sit down and rest and I'll bring you a piece of pie?
   - (b) About noon they stopped to allow Jim to rest in the shade of a pretty orchard.
   - (c) We had already heard the rest of the story.
   - (d) Being very tired, he decided to go upstairs and rest.

(b) Choose the correct option for the question given below: **[10]**

1. What makes the narrator say that no one suspected anything?
   - (a) No one was in touch with both of them
   - (b) Circumstances did not permit them to meet and interact

  (c) The girl was too shy to express her feelings

  (d) The girl was too shy to express her feelings

2. What makes the narrator understand that the lady was still in love with her husband?

  (a) I had found her in this sinister valley.

  (b) Have you been happy, at least?

  (c) She shook her head. Tears fell from her eyes.

  (d) You are Suzanne.

3. What made the narrator amazed by the power of love?

  (a) The girl had sacrificed all luxuries.   (b) The man appeared to be good for nothing.

  (c) No one had been able to find the couple. (d) The girl hadn't changed her name after marriage.

4. Which of the following statements is correct?

  (a) The narrator was also in love with Suzanne.

  (b) The man does not love his wife anymore.

  (c) Suzanne was troubled on seeing the narrator.

  (d) The narrator wanted to leave as early as possible.

5. What surprised the narrator about the girl the most?

  (a) Suzanne could love a man like the soldier.

  (b) Suzanne had chosen this desolate island to live.

  (c) The soldier had never wanted to return.

  (d) Suzanne had given up a luxurious life.

6. As long as the soldier was with her, she desired…………

  (a) Love   (b) Nothing

  (c) Very little   (d) Food

7. What had the soldier filled Suzanne's life with?

  (a) Love   (b) Jewels

  (c) Peace   (d) Happiness

8. What had lasted between the couple since the beginning of their relationship?

  (a) They still cried together over their past life.

  (b) Suzanne still saw him with seduced eyes.

  (c) Suzanne still wanted her husband to make peace with her parents.

  (d) The husband still wanted Suzanne to make peace with her parents.

9. The narrator remembered Suzanne from the past.

  (a) Yes   (b) No

  (c) May be   (d) Cannot be inferred from the passage

10. Which of the following is true about Suzanne?

  (a) She could have been happier with a little more luxury in life.

  (b) She had a desire to leave the island when had newly reached there.

  (c) She had abandoned life for happiness.

  (d) She sometimes regretted her decision of choosing this man.

Question 3.

Answer sections (a), (b) and (c). In each of the following items, a sentence is given. Select the most appropriate transformation of the given sentence out of the given options: **[10]**

(a) 1. As soon as it starts to rain, the umbrellas go up.

  (a) No sooner does it starts to rain than the umbrellas go up.

  (b) No sooner does it start to rain than umbrellas go up.

    (c) No sooner did it started to rain than the umbrellas go up.

    (d) No sooner does it start to rain than the umbrellas go up.

2.   Save for the old man's help, Johny would have drowned.

    (a) If Johny had not helped, the old man would have drowned.

    (b) Thank God! Johny helped the old man.

    (c) Were it not for the old man's help, Johny would have drowned.

    (d) If the old man had helped, Johny would have drowned.

3.   My aunt said to me, "Will you be able to deliver groceries at my place?"

    (a) My aunt asked me that will I be able to deliver the groceries at her place.

    (b) My aunt asked me whether I would be able to deliver the groceries at her place.

    (c) My aunt asked me whether I would be able to deliver groceries at her place?

    (d) My aunt asked me whether I would be able to deliver groceries at her place.

4.   No other metal is as expensive as gold.

    (a) Only gold is an expensive metal.

    (b) Gold is the most expensive of all metals.

    (c) Gold is more expensive than many other metals.

    (d) Gold is very expensive as a metal

5.   Let him see the picture.

    (a) Let the picture be seen by him.   (b) He must see the picture.

    (c) The picture is seen by him.   (d) He was allowed to see the picture.

6.   With my father's permission, I will go for an excursion.

    (a) If my father permits, I will not go for an excursion.

    (b) If my father permits, I will go for an excursion.

    (c) Unless my father permits, I will go for an excursion.

    (d) Unless my father does not permits, I will not go for an excursion.

7.   They had to spend a night at the platform because the train was delayed.

    (a) If the train were delayed, they had to spend a night at the platform.

    (b) If the train had not been delayed, they would not have had to spend a night at the platform.

    (c) If the train is delayed, they will have to spend a night at the platform.

    (d) If the train had been on time, they would not have to spend a night at the platform.

8.   Walking is the healthiest exercise for the elderly.

    (a) Walking is healthier than many other exercises for the elderly.

    (b) Walking should be made mandatory for the elderly as an exercise.

    (c) No other exercise for the elderly is as healthy as walking.

    (d) Few other exercises for the elderly are as healthy as walking.

9.   You can see the lake from here only on a clear day.

    (a) Only the lake can be seen from here on a clear day.

    (b) Only on a clear day, you can see the lake from here.

    (c) Only on a clear day can you see the lake from here.

    (d) Only if the day is clear, you cannot see the lake from here.

10. He regrets not taking up that job.

    (a) He wishes to take up the job now.

    (b) He wishes he should take the job now.

    (c) He wished to have taken up the job.

    (d) He wishes he had taken up that job.

(b) Choose the most appropriate word to fill in the blank in the given sentences: **[15]**

1. A mini-riot broke __________ as the chief guest arrived.
   - (a) up
   - (b) out
   - (c) into
   - (d) off

2. Sam's house was broken __________ last evening.
   - (a) into
   - (b) up
   - (c) off
   - (d) badly

3. I used to have a good job but then I was __________.
   - (a) put aside
   - (b) laid off
   - (c) put off
   - (d) removed off

4. I need to _______ my phrasal verbs.
   - (a) put on
   - (b) work on
   - (c) keep on
   - (d) hold on

5. You are expected to __________ your homework if you want to escape punishment.
   - (a) break in
   - (b) turn in
   - (c) check in
   - (d) lock in

6. The police took him _______ for more questioning.
   - (a) off
   - (b) in
   - (c) over
   - (d) up

7. She looks very mature so I took her __________ older than she is.
   - (a) for
   - (b) about
   - (c) off
   - (d) in

8. The fantastic dinner more than made _______ for the poor room service.
   - (a) after
   - (b) out
   - (c) off
   - (d) up

9. They ran __________ petrol on the highway.
   - (a) round up
   - (b) out of
   - (c) out for
   - (d) a little

10. If you cannot come, we will have to _______ you.
    - (a) look after
    - (b) do without
    - (c) take on
    - (d) go around

11. When he saw the bear, he __________ in fear.
    - (a) backed up
    - (b) backed away
    - (c) backed down
    - (d) backed back

12. One of the wolves _______ from the pack.
    - (a) broke down
    - (b) broke in
    - (c) broke away
    - (d) broke into

13. The game was __________ because of the bad weather.
    - (a) called over
    - (b) called off
    - (c) called in
    - (d) called up

14. Our plans to go to Tokyo _______ because we could not get a visa.
    - (a) fell out
    - (b) fell through
    - (c) fell in
    - (d) fell over

15. Her uncle _______ yesterday after a short illness.
    - (a) passed out
    - (b) passed over
    - (c) passed away
    - (d) passed on

(c) Choose the correct option to fill in the blank in each sentence: **[15]**

1. If I _______ you were coming, I would have come to the airport.
   - (a) knew
   - (b) would have known
   - (c) had known
   - (d) could know

2. Jason __________ in Moscow since he was born.
   - (a) will be
   - (b) has been
   - (c) could be
   - (d) should be

3. By the time I graduate from school next year, I ________ here for five years.
   - (a) will be
   - (b) should be
   - (c) will have been
   - (d) have been

4. My friend, Darren ________ in Amsterdam now, but he says he'll move soon.
   - (a) is living
   - (b) will be living
   - (c) has ben living
   - (d) should be living

5. By the eighteenth century, English shipping _________ as efficient as the Dutch.
   - (a) will become
   - (b) has become
   - (c) had become
   - (d) is going to become

6. As usual, next year I __________ my vacation in my country house.
   - (a) will spend
   - (b) will have spent
   - (c) have spent
   - (d) am spent

7. We _________ in Norway for nearly 25 years until we moved to Scotland two years ago.
   - (a) were living
   - (b) had been living
   - (c) should have lived
   - (d) lived

8. As soon as you ________ the alarm, press the button.
   - (a) will hear
   - (b) would hear
   - (c) hear
   - (d) heard

9. This time next week I ________ to San Fransisco.
   - (a) will be flying
   - (b) have flown
   - (c) may be flow
   - (d) could have flown

10. I usually __________ after my brother when my parents go out.
    - (a) looked after
    - (b) have look after
    - (c) look after
    - (d) did looked after

11. By the time the troops _________, the war will have ended.
    - (a) will arrive
    - (b) arrived
    - (c) shall arrive
    - (d) arrive

12. I was not surprised to hear that Monica ______ an accident as she is a very reckless driver
    - (a) has
    - (b) had
    - (c) has had
    - (d) had had

13. Hardly had the minister finished his speech when the earthquake _________ the stadium.
    - (a) shook
    - (b) shaken
    - (c) would have shaken
    - (d) did shake

14. Before my trip to Paris two years ago, I _________ to France.
    - (a) have never been
    - (b) would never have been
    - (c) had never been
    - (d) None of these

15. By this time tomorrow, he __________ at his job for a week.
    - (a) will be working
    - (b) will work
    - (c) will have been working
    - (d) has been working

Answers

Question 1.

(a)

(i) 1. (b) a sudden strong wish   **2.** (a) knowledge

   3. (d) extreme fear   **4.** (a) trouble

   5. (a) be of any help

(ii) 1. (d) After his rude behaviour, it is meet for him to apologise to his father.

   2. (a) The contestants had to gear up for their performances by 6 o'clock in the evening.

   3. (a) The little girl helped the blind beggar to cross the busy road.

   4. (a) The State Electricity Board is responsible for supplying electric current in the whole state.

   5. (c) Shirley is a friend who I can bank on.

(b) 1. (c) The narrator heard the main door open directly above their heads.

   2. (b) trustingly

   3. (c) He heard the car driving away.

   4. (b) The door was solid as a rock and there was no electricity.

   5. (c) The gear designed to wind the metal mesh wouldn't work without electricity.

   6. (a) The narrator prayed and tried to remain calm so that he did not make any mistakes.

   7. (d) He was shivering violently from several causes.

   8. (a) He was relieved and happy.

   9. (a) He had walked into the boathouse and tried to pick up an envelope when the floor gave way and he fell through.

  10. (c) (i), (ii), (iii), (iv)

Question 2.

(a)

(i) 1. (b) ominous   **2.** (c) hut

   3. (a) simple   **4.** (d) valley

   5. (c) soft

(ii) 1. (d) The rows of houses were uniform in appearance.

   2. (b) He could not turn around as he had a stiff neck.

   3. (c) Still waters run deep.

   4. (b) A legislative body should be composed of two houses.

   5. (c) We had already heard the rest of the story.

(b) 1. (a) No one was in touch with both of them.

   2. (c) She shook her head. Tears fell from her eyes.

   3. (a) The girl had sacrificed all luxuries.

   4. (d) The narrator wanted to leave as early as possible.

   5. (d) Suzanne had given up a luxurious life.

   6. (b) Nothing

   7. (d) Happiness

   8. (b) Suzanne still saw him with seduced eyes.

   9. (a) Yes

  10. (c) She had abandoned life for happiness.

Question 3.

(a)
1. (d) No sooner does it start to rain than the umbrellas go up.
2. (c) Were it not for the old man's help, Johny would have drowned.
3. (d) My aunt asked me whether I would be able to deliver groceries at her place.
4. (b) Gold is the most expensive of all metals.
5. (a) Let the picture be seen by him.
6. (b) If my father permits, I will go for an excursion.
7. (d) If the train had been on time, they would not have to spend a night at the platform.
8. (c) No other exercise for the elderly is as healthy as walking.
9. (b) Only on a clear day, you can see the lake from here.
10. (d) He wishes he had taken up that job.

(b)
1. (b) out
2. (a) into
3. (b) laid off
4. (b) work on
5. (c) check in
6. (b) in
7. (a) for
8. (d) up
9. (c) out for
10. (b) do without
11. (b) backed away
12. (c) broke away
13. (b) called off
14. (a) fell out
15. (c) passed away

(c)
1. (a) knew
2. (b) has been
3. (d) have been
4. (c) has been living
5. (c) had become
6. (a) will spend
7. (b) had been living
8. (c) hear
9. (a) will be flying
10. (c) look after
11. (d) arrive
12. (c) has had
13. (a) shook
14. (b) would never have been
15. (c) will have been wroking

❑❑

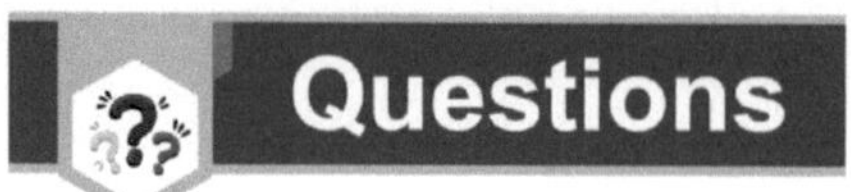

Question 1

Read the given passage carefully and answer the questions that follow:

You never saw such a **commotion** in all your life as when my Uncle Podger undertook to do a job. A picture would be waiting to be put up and Uncle Podger would say: 'Oh, you leave that to me. Don't you worry about that? I'll do all that. Now you go and get me my hammer. You bring me the rule Tom, and I shall want the step – ladder and I had better have a kitchen chair too and Jim, you run round to Mr. Goggles and tell him Pa's kind **regards** and hopes his leg's better and will he lend him his spirit level? And don't you go, Martha, because I shall want somebody to hold me the light, and when the girl comes back, she must go out again for a bit of picture – cord and Tom you come here I shall want you to hand me up the picture.'

And then he would lift up the picture and drop it and it would come out of the frame, and he would try to save the glass and cut himself and then he would spring round the room, looking for his handkerchief. He could not find his handkerchief, because it was in the pocket of the coat he had taken off, and he did not know where he had put the coat. The entire house had to leave off looking for his tools and start looking for his coat, while he would dance round and <u>hinder</u> them. 'Doesn't anybody in the whole house knows where my <u>coat</u> is? Six of you! You can't find a coat!' Then he'd get up and find that he had been sitting on it, and would call out. 'Oh, you can give it up! I've found it myself now.'

When half an hour had been spent in tying up his finger, and a new glass had been got, and the tools, and the ladder, and the chair, and the candle had been brought, he would have another go, the whole family, including the girl and the **charwoman**, standing round in a semi-circle, ready to help.

Two people would have to hold him there, and a fourth would hand him a nail, and a fifth would pass him up the hammer, and he would take hold of the nail, and drop it. "There!' he would say, in an injured tone, 'now the nail's gone'.

We would all have to go down on our knees and grovel for it, while he would stand on the chair, and grunt, and want to know if he was to be kept there all the evening. The nail would be found at last, but by that time he would have lost the hammer. "Where's the hammer? Seven of you gaping round there and you don't know what I did with the hammer?'

We would find the hammer and then he would have lost <u>sight</u> of the mark he had made on the wall. Each of us had to get up on the chair beside him and see if we could find it, and we would each discover it in a different place and he would call us all fools. And he would take the rule, and re-measure and find that he wanted half thirty – one and three-eighths inches from the corner, and would try to do it in his head, and go mad. And we would all try to do it in our heads and all arrive at different results, and the original number would be forgotten, and Uncle Podger would have to measure it again.

He would use a bit of string this time and at the critical moment, when he was leaning over the chair at an angle of forty – five, and trying to reach a point on the wall, the string would slip, and down he would slide on the piano, a really fine musical effect being produced by the **suddenness** with which his head and body struck all the notes at the same time.

At last, Uncle Podger would get the spot fixed again and put the point of the nail on it with his left hand and take the hammer in his right hand. And, with the first blow, he would **smash** his thumb, and <u>drop</u> the hammer with a yell, on somebody's toes.

Aunt Maria would observe that the next time Uncle Podger was going to hammer a <u>nail</u> into the wall; she would go and spend a week with her mother while it was being done. 'You women you make such a fuss over everything,' Uncle Podger would reply. "I like doing a little job of this sort.'

Adapted from Three Men in a Boat (To Say Nothing of the Dog) by Jerome K. Jerome

(a) (i) Given below are five words from the passage along with four options for each. Choose the option which has a similar meaning in the passage:

1. Commotion
   - (a) Occasion
   - (b) Noisy disturbance
   - (c) Working style
   - (d) Ceremony

2. Regards
   - (a) considering someone
   - (b) expressing humour in greetings
   - (c) expressing friendliness in greeting
   - (d) thinking about someone

3. Charwoman
   - (a) a woman employed as a cleaner in house
   - (b) a woman employed as a cook in house
   - (c) a woman employed as a banker in house
   - (d) a woman employed as a physician in house

4. Suddenness
   - (a) rudeness
   - (b) cleanliness
   - (c) smoothness
   - (d) abruptness

5. Smash
   - (a) recall
   - (b) triumph
   - (c) shatter
   - (d) shout

(ii) With each of the five words given below, choose the correct sentence that uses the word in a different meaning from that which it carries in the passage.

1. Hinder
   - (a) She wasn't certain why her chest felt tight enough to hinder her breathing.
   - (b) His anger hindered his professional development.
   - (c) If you pick up a crab and turn it over, you will see just how insignificant is its hinder body.
   - (d) He hindered one way.

2. Coat
   - (a) She shivered in her wool coat, folded the paperwork, and called her sister.
   - (b) She did not recognize the coat of arms on the shield.
   - (c) She was dressed in a long, white fur coat that Katie had no doubt cost more than a small house.
   - (d) She peeled off the thick coat and draped it.

3. Sight
   - (a) No one was in sight.
   - (b) As he turned off, Dean checked the highway in both directions, but there were no other vehicles in sight.
   - (c) Even as a young actress, she always had Hollywood firmly in her sights.
   - (d) There were no people or vehicles in sight.

4. Drop
   - (a) I am not going to drop a pin.
   - (b) She dropped the box on the floor.
   - (c) In the past, impetuous young men would drop out of college and run off to join the army.
   - (d) I drop my bag in the mall.

    5. Nail

        (a) Don't try and hammer nails into the ceiling joists.

        (b) We removed the old nails from the board.

        (c) Tom went to the hardware store to buy another hammer and some nails.

        (d) She is fond of nail polishes.

(b) Choose the correct option for the questions given below:

    1. When Uncle Podger decided to hang the picture, the whole house:

        (a) was satisfied.   (b) felt relieved.

        (c) was in the state of confusion.   (d) both (a) and (b)

    2. What did uncle Podger tell everyone at home?

        (a) to do one's own work.   (b) not to bother.

        (c) not to leave him alone.   (d) to do only his work.

    3. `Pa's' kind regards and hopes his leg's better* shows Uncle's emotions:

        (a) of social concern   (b) of contempt

        (c) of jealously   (d) of revenge

    4. When the girl came back, she was supposed:

        (a) to go out again for a bit of picture.

        (b) to go out again for a bit of picture cord.

        (c) to go out again for shopping.

        (d) to go out again for ordering things.

    5. `Hold the light' means:

        (a) hand him over the light   (b) show him over the light

        (c) take the light   (d) release the light

    6. Which word in the passage mean ``Stairs''?

        (a) penny   (b) spirit level

        (c) step-ladder   (d) undertook

    7. Uncle was a confused character as:

        (a) he kept mum   (b) he had misplaced the hammer

        (c) he did not know anything   (d) he continued to speak to himself

    8. The number of family members was:

        (a) six   (b) seven

        (c) four   (d) five

    9. Uncle Podger shifted his wrong doings:

        (a) On his wife   (b) On himself

        (c) On the entire family   (d) On the maid servant

   10. The hung picture looked `crooked and insecure''. What does the phrase mean?

        (a) Crooked and straight   (b) Unsafe and not aligned

        (c) Unsafe and not straight   (d) Unsafe but straight

Question 2

Read the given passage carefully and answer the questions that follow:

Too many parents these days can't say no. As a result, they find themselves raising 'children' who respond greedily to the advertisements aimed right at them. Even getting what they want doesn't satisfy some kids; they only want more. Now, a growing number of psychologists, educators and parents think it's time to stop the madness and start teaching kids about what's really important : values like hard work, **contentment**, honesty and **compassion**. The struggle to set limits has never been tougher—and the stakes have never been higher. One recent study of adults who were overindulged as children, paints a discouraging picture of their future : when given too much too soon, they grow up to be adults who have difficulty <u>coping</u> with life's disappointments. They also have sense of entitlement that gets in the way of success in the work place and in relationships.

Psychologists say that parents who overindulge their kids, set them up to be more **vulnerable** to future anxiety and depression. Today's parents themselves raised on values of thrift and self-sacrifice, grew up in a culture where 'no' was a household word. Today's kids want much more, partly because there is so much more to want. The oldest members of this generation were born in the late 1980s, just as PCs and video games were making their assault' on the family room. They think of MP3 players and flat screen TV as essential utilities, and they have developed strategies to get them. One survey of teenagers found that when they crave for something new, most expect to ask nine times before their parents give in. By every measure, parents are shelling out record amounts.

Today's parents aren't equipped to deal with the problem. Many of them, raised in the 1960s and 70s, swore they'd act differently from their parents and have closer relationships with their own children. Many even wear the same designer clothes as their kids and listen to the same music. And they work more hours; at the end of a long week, it's tempting to buy peace with 'yes' and not mar precious family time with conflict. Anxiety about the future is another factor. How do well intentioned parents say no to all the sports gear and arts and language lessons they believe will help their kids thrive in an increasingly **competitive** world? Experts agree: too much love won't spoil a child. Too few limits will.

What parents need to find, is a balance between the advantages of an affluent society and the critical life lessons that come from waiting, saving and working hard to achieve goals. That search for balance has to start early. Children need limits on their behaviour because they feel better and more secure when they live within a secured structure.

Older children learn self-control by watching how others, especially parents act. Learning how to overcome challenges is essential to become a successful adult. Few parents ask kids to do. They think their kids are already overburdened by social and **academic** pressures. Every individual can be of service to others, and life has meaning beyond one's own immediate happiness. That means parents eager to teach values have to take a long, hard look at their own. (539 words)

(a) **(i)** Given below are five words from the passage along with four options for each word. Choose the option which has a similar meaning in the passage:

    1. Contentment

      (a) happiness   (b) satisfaction

      (c) tiredness   (d) anger

    2. Compassion

      (a) a strong feeling of sympathy   (b) a strong pitious feeling

      (c) feeling a rage   (d) surprised

    3. Vulnerable

      (a) happy and rejoiceful   (b) pitious and shocked

      (c) weak and easily hurt   (d) strong and powerful

    4. Competitive

      (a) A person's ability to heed   (b) A person's inability to win

      (c) A person's desire to win   (d) A person's desire to surpass others

    5. Academic

      (a) related to education   (b) related to scholarship

      (c) both (a) and (b)   (d) None of these

  (ii) With each of the five words given below, choose the correct sentence that uses the word in a different meaning from that which it carries in the passage.

    1. Pressure

      (a) Tom is under pressure.

      (b) I don't work well under pressure.

      (c) Don't fear pressure, for pressure is what turns rough stones into diamonds.

      (d) Atmospheric pressure changes with distance above or below sea-level.

2. Coping

    (a) May be that was his way of coping with loss of his wife.

    (b) A greater understanding of gender-biases in coping is needed.

    (c) Grant was ill-fitted for coping the difficulties of nation.

    (d) A large coping stone fell onto the car's soft top.

3. Deal

    (a) We have got bigger problems to deal with.

    (b) I really can't deal with that right now.

    (c) They drink a good deal of tea in England.

    (d) We will deal with that when the time comes.

4. Measures

    (a) People should take all necessary measures to avoid such things.

    (b) The government will take all necessary measures to ensure the safety of its citizens.

    (c) We should take measures to guard against the tsunami of social disintegration.

    (d) A meter is a measure of length.

5. Balance

    (a) It is important to keep your life in balance.

    (b) I find it difficult to balance on one foot.

    (c) He helped his daughter balance on her bicycle.

    (d) Our monthly interest is 1.5% of the outstanding balance.

(b) Choose the correct option for the questions given below:

1. What do the psychologists, educators and parents want to teach the children?

    (a) To teach them about treachery.

    (b) To teach them about indiscipline.

    (c) To teach them about the value of life like hard work.

    (d) None of them.

2. What is essential to become a successful adult?

    (a) Learn not to overcome challenges.

    (b) Learn how to overcome challenges.

    (c) Nothing is essential.

    (d) None of the above.

3. Why do children need limits on their behaviour when they line within a secured structure?

    (a) They feel more secure and better.   (b) They feel insecure.

    (c) They feel bored.   (d) They feel delighted.

4. What is the drawback of giving children too much too soon?

    (a) They fail to cope with life's disappointment when they grew up.

    (b) They do not study seriously.

    (c) They become quarrelsome when they grew up.

    (d) None of these.

5. How do elder/older children learn to control their behaviour?

    (a) by seeing their parent's act   (b) by seeing their peers

    (c) by seeing their teachers   (d) by seeing their neighbours

6. Why are parents not able to control their children?

    (a) because of lack of money   (b) because of generation gap

    (c) because of lack of time   (d) because of higher education

7. Why do children of today's generation want more?

    (a) because the items are at cheaper rate.

    (b) because they love buying things.

    (c) because they crave for something new.

    (d) because they can afford it.

8. Why is it necessary to set limits for children?
   - (a) Because they feel better.
   - (b) Because they feel secured to live within a secured structure.
   - (c) Both (a) and (b).
   - (d) None of them.
9. Identify the moral values that parents and teachers want to inculcate in children.
   - (a) Honesty
   - (b) Hardwork
   - (c) Contentment
   - (d) All of these
10. What is the advice of the psychologist for the parents?
   - (a) Do not overindulge their kids.
   - (b) Do not shout on the kids.
   - (c) Do not play with the kids.
   - (d) All of them

Question 3

(a) Answer sections (a), (b) and (c). In each of the following items, a sentence is given. Select the most appropriate transformation of the given sentence out of the given options:

1. That road is narrow. The bus cannot go there.
   - (a) That road is too narrow for the bus to pass.
   - (b) That road is wide enough for the bus to pass.
   - (c) That road is not broad enough for the bus to go there.
   - (d) That road is too narrow.
2. The truth was revealed finally. This brought down the government.
   - (a) The final revelation of the truth brought down the government.
   - (b) The revealed truth brought down the government.
   - (c) The truth, revealed; made the government go down.
   - (d) The final revelation of the truth, made the government go down.
3. He died suddenly. This was a great shock to the family.
   - (a) His sudden demise made everyone shocked in the family.
   - (b) His sudden death was a great shock to the family.
   - (c) His death was a great shock to the family.
   - (d) His sudden death made everyone shocked.
4. They hated the society in which they lived. This made them rebellious.
   - (a) Their hatred for the society in which they lived, made them rebellious.
   - (b) They became rebellious after living in the society which they hated.
   - (c) They were rebellious to the society in which they lived and hated.
   - (d) They got rebellious by living in the society to which they hated.
5. Mr. Johnson was always punctual. This was something he prided himself on.
   - (a) Mr. Johnson was proud of his punctuality.
   - (b) Mr. Johnson's punctuality was something he prided himself on.
   - (c) Mr. Johnson's punctuality made him proud of himself.
   - (d) Mr. Johnson was proud because of his punctuality.
6. This lady is extremely pretty. I have never seen a prettier lady.
   - (a) I have never seen such a pretty lady.
   - (b) I have never seen a pretty lady like her.
   - (c) I have never seen a lady as pretty as her.
   - (d) No one is as pretty as she is.

7. We all enjoyed the story. Our teacher told us the story.
   (a) We all enjoyed the story that our teacher told us.
   (b) We all enjoyed the story told by our teacher.
   (c) The story was enjoyed by all the students.
   (d) The story told by the teacher, was enjoyed by all.

8. Clear your dues. Then you will be given roll numbers.
   (a) You will be only given roll numbers once you clear your dues.
   (b) As soon as you clear your dues, you will be given roll numbers.
   (c) Once the dues are clear, you will be given the roll numbers.
   (d) Roll numbers will be provided after clearing the dues.

9. Joe was so foolish that he believed the old man.
   (a) Joe was foolish to believe the old man.
   (b) Joe was foolish therefore he believed the old man.
   (c) Joe was too foolish to believe the old man.
   (d) Joe was foolish enough to believe the old man.

10. He never admitted that he had stolen my pen.
    (a) At no time, did he admit that he had stolen my pen.
    (b) He never admitted about stealing my pen.
    (c) He did not admit that he had stolen my pen.
    (d) He stole my pen but never admitted it.

(b) Choose the most appropriate word to fill in the blank in the given sentences:

1. Take your books _________ you.
   (a) as far as   (b) along with   (c) all over   (d) in front of

2. His whole life is _________ him.
   (a) on front of   (b) in front of   (c) in between   (d) up front of

3. I have not seen him _________ last Sunday.
   (a) since   (b) before   (c) from   (d) about

4. Mt. Abu is about five thousand feet _________ the sea-level.
   (a) above   (b) along   (c) after   (d) behind

5. He sat _________ me.
   (a) for   (b) into   (c) after   (d) beside

6. Many people have become entrepreneur due to an aptitude _________ business.
   (a) of   (b) in   (c) about   (d) for

7. She began to walk _________ him.
   (a) away from   (b) away of   (c) beside from   (d) beside of

8. He was astonished _________ his failure.
   (a) with   (b) for   (c) in   (d) at

9. They _________ me to accept the offer.
   (a) prevail upon   (b) prevail above   (c) prevail on   (d) prevail in

10. We are _________ a fully funded national strategy on climate change and agriculture.
    (a) calling on   (b) calling to   (c) calling up   (d) calling for

11. Vivek has a strong resemblance _________ his grandfather.
    (a) with   (b) to   (c) from   (d) about

12. Pour the water _________ the jug.
    (a) into   (b) out   (c) before   (d) in

13. We should not compromise _________ safety standards.
    (a) on   (b) with   (c) over   (d) about

14. Other measures to improve food quality are roping _________ branded food providers.
    (a) at   (b) for   (c) from   (d) in

15. She has great affection _________ her grandchildren.
   (a) within   (b) into   (c) against   (d) for

(c) Choose the correct option to fill in the blank in each sentence:

1. Now that I _________ reading *Macbeth*, I shall read *Othello*.
   (a) had finished (b) have been finishing (c) have finished (d) had not finish

2. He _________ a newspaper when I _______ him.
   (a) were reading, see   (b) was reading, saw
   (c) should be reading, sees   (d) will be reading, saw

3. Now that I _________ reading Oliver Twist, I shall read the Bible.
   (a) was reading (b) had reading (c) am finishing (d) have finished

4. We _________ students in this school for the last five years.
   (a) have been (b) were been (c) are being (d) were

5. What _________ you do yesterday in the morning?
   (a) do   (b) does   (c) did   (d) are

6. Since 1900, science _________ rapidly.
   (a) has been progressing   (b) has progressed
   (c) was progressing   (d) was progressive

7. No, Rama is not at home. He _________ just _______ for shopping.
   (a) had, gone (b) has, gone (c) was, going (d) will have, be going

8. They _________ a football match in the evening yesterday. What _______ you do ?
   (a) were playing, do   (b) played, did
   (c) have played, does   (d) are playing, will

9. Having _________ Shyam went out to play.
   (a) finished his work   (b) finish his work
   (c) finishes his work   (d) been finished his work

10. Sheren _________ what you mean. Please explain.
   (a) doesn't understood   (b) does understand
   (c) didn't understand   (d) None of the above

11. I asked him if he _________ a seat.
   (a) has reserved   (b) has been reserving
   (c) reserving   (d) had been reserving

12. The president just _________ the good news.
   (a) announced   (b) is announcing
   (c) has been announced   (d) had announced

13. If I get a scholarship. I _________ to abroad.
   (a) will be going   (b) will have gone
   (c) will go   (d) will have been going

14. Uma finished first, though she _________ late.
   (a) had begun (b) have begun (c) has begun (d) has been beginning

15. When he first _______ her, she _________ as a typist.
   (a) meet, was working   (b) met, was working
   (c) had met, was working   (d) met, were working

Answers

1. (a) (i)   1. (b) Noisy disturbance
      2. (c) expressing friendliness in greeting.
      3. (a) a woman employed as a cleaner in house.
      4. (d) abruptness
      5. (c) shatter

(ii) 1. (c) If you pick up a crab and turn it over, you will see just how insignificant is its hinder body.

   2. (b) She did not recognize the coat of arms on the shield.

   3. (c) Even as a young actress, she always had Hollywood firmly in her sights.

   4. (c) In the past, impetuous young men would drop out of college and run off to join the army.

   5. (d) She is fond of nail polishes.

(b) 1. (c) was in the state of confusion.

   2. (b) not to bother

   3. (a) of social concern

   4. (b) to go out again for a bit of picture cord

   5. (b) show him over the light

   6. (c) step-ladder

   7. (b) he had misplaced the hammer

   8. (b) seven

   9. (c) on the entire family

  10. (b) Unsafe and not aligned

2.(a) (i) 1. (b) satisfaction

   2. (a) a strong feeling of sympathy

   3. (c) weak and easily hurt

   4. (d) A person's desire to surpass others

   5. (c) both (a) and (b)

(ii) 1. (d) A large coping stone fell onto the car's soft top.

   2. (d) Atmospheric pressure changes with distance above or below sea-level.

   3. (c) They drink a good deal of tea in England.

   4. (d) A meter is a measure of length.

   5. (d) Our monthly interest is 1.5% of the outstanding balance.

(b) 1. (c) To teach them about the value of life like hard work

   2. (b) Learn how to overcome challenges

   3. (a) They feel more secure and better

   4. (a) They fail to cope with life's disappointment when they grew up

   5. (a) by seeing their parent's act

   6. (b) because of generation gap

   7. (c) Because they crave for something new

   8. (c) Both (a) and (b)

   9. (d) All of these

  10. (a) Do not overindulge their kids

3. (a) 1. (c) That road is not broad enough for the bus to go there.

   2. (a) The final revelation of the truth brought down the government.

   3. (b) His sudden death was a great shock to the family.

   4. (a) Their hatred for the society in which they lived, made them rebellious.

   5. (b) Mr. Johnson's punctuality was something he prided himself on

   6. (c) I have never seen a lady as pretty as her

   7. (a) We all enjoyed the story that our teacher told us.

   8. (b) As soon as you clear your dues, you will be given roll numbers.

   9. (c) Joe was too foolish to believe the old man.

  10. (a) At no time, did he admit that he had stolen my pen.

(b) 1. (b) along with

   2. (b) in front of

   3. (a) since

   4. (a) above

   5. (d) beside

   6. (d) for

   7. (a) away from

   8. (d) at

   9. (a) prevail upon

  10. (d) calling for

  11. (b) to

  12. (a) into

  13. (a) on

  14. (d) in

  15. (d) for

(c) 1. (c) have finished

   2. (b) was reading, saw

   3. (d) have finished

   4. (a) have been

   5. (c) did

   6. (a) has been progressing

   7. (b) has, gone

   8. (b) played, did

   9. (a) finished his work

  10. (c) didn't understand

  11. (a) has reserved

  12. (a) announced

  13. (c) will go

  14. (a) had begun

  15. (b) met, was working

❑❑

Question 1

Read the given passage carefully and answer the questions that follow:

(1) Have you ever failed at something so miserably that the thought of attempting to do it again was the last thing on your <u>mind</u>?

(2) If your answer is yes, then you should understand that you are not a robot. Unlike robots, we human beings have feelings, emotions, and dreams. We are all meant to grow despite our circumstances and limitations. Flourishing and trying to make our dreams come true feels great when life goes our way. But what happens when it does not? What happens when you fail despite all your hard work? Do you stay down and accept defeat or do you get up again? If you tend to **persevere** and keep going, you have what experts call 'grit'.

(3) Falling down or failing is one of the most agonising, embarrassing, and scary human experiences. But it is also one of the most educational, empowering, and essential parts of living a successful and fulfilling life. Did you know that perseverance (grit) is one of the seven qualities that has been described as the key to personal success and betterment in society? The other six are <u>curiosity</u>, gratitude, optimism, self-control, social intelligence, and **zest**. Thomas Edison is an example of <u>grit</u> for trying more than 1,000 times to invent the light bulb. If you are reading this with the lights on in your room, you will realise the importance of his success. When asked why he kept going despite hundreds of failures, he merely stated that they had not been failures, they were hundreds of attempts towards creating the light bulb. This statement not only revealed his grit but also his **optimism** for looking at the bright side.

(4) Grit can be learnt to help you become more successful. One of the techniques that help is mindfulness. Mindfulness is a practice that makes an individual <u>stay</u> at the moment by bringing awareness of his or her experience without judgement. This practice has been used to quieten the noise of fears and doubts. Through this simple practice of mindfulness, individuals have the ability to stop the self-sabotaging downward spiral of hopelessness, despair, and **frustration**.

(5) What did you do to overcome the <u>negative</u> and self-sabotaging feelings of failure? Reflect on what you did, and try to use those same powerful **resources** to help you today.

Adapted from Three Men in a Boat (To Say Nothing of the Dog) by Jerome K. Jerome

(a) (i) Given below are five words from the passage along with four options for each. Choose the option which has a similar meaning in the passage:

1. Persevere
 (a) persist   (b) disappear
 (c) trending   (d) incomplete

2. Zest
 (a) feeling of pain   (b) feeling of excitement
 (c) feeling of remorse   (d) feeling of distress

3. Optimism
 (a) revenge   (b) negativity
 (c) positivity   (d) nature

    4. Frustration
- (a) disappointed
- (b) elated
- (c) remorsed
- (d) surprised

    5. Resources
- (a) news
- (b) wealth
- (c) energy
- (d) None of them

(ii) With each of the five words given below, choose the correct sentence that uses the word in a different meaning from that which it carries in the passage.

    1. Mind
- (a) It was the last thing on your mind.
- (b) My mind is engaged in during other chores.
- (c) She was fit from mind, body and soul.
- (d) The mind map prepared by Shella is very comprehensive.

    2. Curiosity
- (a) She invented the IT tools out of curiosity.
- (b) Curiosity is the source for discovery.
- (c) He leaned forward as when the curiosity grew further.
- (d) Tobacco was once regarded as a curiosity in Europe.

    3. Grit
- (a) He took out his shoes to remove the small rocks and grit.
- (b) The nature men survived in the harsh conditions due to his grit and patience.
- (c) Grit and determination can lead you to success.
- (d) All of them

    4. Stay
- (a) They wanted to stay at the party.
- (b) You can go with me or stay here.
- (c) You stay here and I'll be back soon.
- (d) There is likely to be a good public library as a stay against boredom.

    5. Negative
- (a) There are two poles in the battery: negative and positive.
- (b) We should eradicate negative feelings and stay positive.
- (c) One should devoid of his negative feelings.
- (d) The new tax was having a negative effect on car sales.

(b) Choose the correct option for the questions given below:

    1. Why are humans not considered as robots?
- (a) Humans have emotions.
- (b) Humans fail at miserable tasks.
- (c) Humans work hard.
- (d) Humans have limitations.

    2. Identify the tone in the following statement, ``Falling down or failing is one of the .... educational, empowering and essential parts of living a successful fulfilling life''?
- (a) Horrifying
- (b) Humorous
- (c) Optimistic
- (d) Solemn

    3. Identify the best suited title of the passage:
- (a) Dreams always come true
- (b) Failure and Grit go Hand in Hand
- (c) Human vs Robots in 21st century
- (d) Falling down and getting up

    4. Why there is a need to practice mindfulness?
- (a) to become more aware in life.
- (b) to work hard during experiments.

    (c) to seek guidance from elders.

    (d) to be in a moment and be aware without judgement.

5. How does mindfulness help?

    (a) It suppresses the noise of fears and doubts.

    (b) It creates and develop awareness.

    (c) It helps one to become more successful.

    (d) It helps to navigate the work.

6. What message is conveyed in the above passage?

    (a) With the help of mindfulness, one can overcome negativity.

    (b) One should live life the king size.

    (c) Social intelligence is important for invention.

    (d) Always aim high.

7. For whom does the words—perseverance and optimism used?

    (a) Abdul Kalam   (b) Issac Newton

    (c) Albert Einstein   (d) Thomas Edison

8. Grit can be learnt to help you become more _____________ .

    (a) successful   (b) intelligent

    (c) patient   (d) intellectual

9. What do you understand by the line ``Falling down or failing is one of the most agonising, embarrassing and scary human experience''?

    (a) Failure can affect our emotions.

    (b) Falling down and getting up is the key to success.

    (c) One should be optimistic and positive.

    (d) Self-control is the key to happiness.

10. Arrange the sequence of events as they occur in the passage.

    (i) Falling down or failing is one of the most agonising, embarrassing, and scary human experiences.

    (ii) We are all meant to grow despite our circumstances and limitations.

    (iii) This practice has been used to quieten the noise of fears and doubts.

    (iv) The other six are _curiosity,_ gratitude, optimism, self-control, social intelligence, and **zest**.

        (a) (iii), (i), (iv), (ii)   (b) (ii), (i), (iv), (iii)

        (c) (i), (ii), (iii), (iv)   (d) (iv), (iii), (ii), (i)

Question 2

Read the given passage carefully and answer the questions that follow:

(1) Maharana Pratap ruled over Mewar only for 25 years. However, he accomplished so much **grandeur** during his reign that his glory surpassed the boundaries of countries and time turning him into an _immortal_ personality. He, along with his kingdom, became a synonym for valour, sacrifice and patriotism. Mewar had been a leading Rajput kingdom even before Maharana Pratap occupied the throne. Kings of Mewar, with the cooperation of their nobles and _subjects,_ had established such traditions in the kingdom, as augmented their magnificence, despite the hurdles of having a smaller area under their command and less population. There did come a few thorny occasions when the flag of the kingdom seemed sliding down. Their flag once again heaved high in the sky, thanks to the gallantry and brilliance of the people of Mewar.

(2) The destiny of Mewar was good in the sense that barring a few kings, most of the rulers were **competent** and patriotic. This glorious tradition of the kingdom almost continued for 1,500 years since its establishment, right from the reign of Bappa Rawal. In fact, only 60 years before Maharana Pratap, Rana Sanga drove the kingdom to the pinnacle of fame. His reputation went beyond Rajasthan and reached Delhi. Two generations before him, Rana Kumbha had given a new stature to the kingdom through victories and developmental work. During his reign, literature and art also progressed extraordinarily. Rana himself was inclined towards writing and his works are read with reverence, even today.

(3) The life of the people of Mewar must have been peaceful and prosperous during the long span of time; otherwise such extraordinary accomplishment in these fields would not have been possible. This is reflected in their art and literature as well as their loving nature. They **compensate** for lack of admirable physique by their firm but pleasant nature. The ambience of Mewar remains lovely, thanks to the cheerful and liberal character of its people.

(4) One may observe astonishing pieces of workmanship, not only in the forts and palaces of Mewar but also in public utility buildings. Ruins of many structures which are <u>still</u> standing tall in their grandeur are testimony to the fact that Mewar was not only the land of the brave but also a seat of art and culture. Amidst aggression and bloodshed, literature and art flourished and **creative** pursuits of literature and artists did not suffer. Imagine, how glorious the period must have been when the Vijaya Stambha, which is the sample of our great ancient architecture even today, was constructed. In the same fort, Kirti Stambha is standing high, reflecting how liberal the then <u>administration</u> was, which allowed people from other communities and kingdoms to come and carry out construction work. It is useless to indulge in the debate, whether the Vijaya Stambha was constructed first or the Kirti Stambha. The fact is that both the <u>capitals</u> are standing side-by-side and reveal the proximity between the king and the subjects of Mewar.

(5) The cycle of time does not remain the same. Whereas, the reign of Rana Sanga was crucial in raising the kingdom to the acme of glory; it also proved to be his nemesis. History took a turn. The fortune of Mewar, the land of the brave, started waning. Rana tried to save the day with his **acumen** which was running against the <u>stream</u> and the glorious traditions for sometime. (565 words)

(a) (i) Given below are five words from the passage along with four options for each word. Choose the option which has a similar meaning in the passage:

1. **Grandeur**
   - (a) famous
   - (b) splendour
   - (c) pride
   - (d) imagination

2. **Competent**
   - (a) proficient
   - (b) competition
   - (c) individualistic
   - (d) egoistic

3. **Compensate**
   - (a) reimburse
   - (b) repay
   - (c) remunerate
   - (d) All of the above

4. **Creative**
   - (a) use of imagination
   - (b) use of confidence
   - (c) use of money
   - (d) use of personality

5. **Acumen**
   - (a) potentiality
   - (b) persona
   - (c) awareness
   - (d) ideas

(ii) With each of the five words given below, choose the correct sentence that uses the word in a different meaning from that which it carries in the passage.

1. **Immortal**
   - (a) He entered the realm of immortal bliss.
   - (b) God is immortal.
   - (c) He will always be one of the immortals of soccer.
   - (d) The cancer cell became immortal in his body.

2. **Subjects**
   - (a) The reign of Mauryans flourished due to kingsmen and subjects.
   - (b) My favourite subjects are Physics and Mathematics.
   - (c) Krishnadeva Raya could establish a large kingdom due to his nobles and subjects.
   - (d) The legislation is applicable only to British subjects.

3. **Capital**
   (a) New Delhi is the capital of India.
   (b) But even as capital, its growth was slow.
   (c) He made the capital of Christendom, the centre of culture.
   (d) We are applying for a business loan because we need capital to fulfill our orders.

4. **Still**
   (a) We are still waiting for our new couch to be deliver.
   (b) Sheena is still teaching in Mumbai.
   (c) Teachers still have an important role in the classroom.
   (d) She stood still with her hair flying in the wind.

5. **Stream**
   (a) I switched boats mid stream and followed the rescue team.
   (b) The stream is flowing above the decided level of the surrouding boundary.
   (c) The Harrach stream enters the mediterranean sea from Bay of Algeers.
   (d) Shweta is from commerce stream.

(b) Choose the correct option for the questions given below:

1. How did Maharana Pratap changed into an immortal being?
   (a) He annexed Mewar and ruled for 25 years.
   (b) He added lot of grandeur and charisma to Mewar.
   (c) He sacrificed and propagated patriotism.
   (d) Both (b) and (c)

2. Identify the difficulty faced by the city of Mewar.
   (a) Lack of friendly cooperation among nobles.
   (b) Traditions and rituals of old kingdom.
   (c) Small area and less population.
   (d) Poverty of subjects.

3. Identify the *Thorny* occasion.
   (a) When the flag of Mewar was hoisted high.
   (b) When the people of Mewar showed gallant.
   (c) When the flag of Mewar was lowered.
   (d) Both (b) and (c).

4. Why is the reign of Mewar kingdom considered lucky?
   (a) Because the nobles were potent enough.
   (b) Because the population was much confident.
   (c) Because the rulers were incompetent.
   (d) All of them

5. Which is the sample work of great architecture?
   (a) Vijaya Stambha   (b) Palace of Mewar
   (c) Port of Mewar   (d) Kirti Stambha

6. Name the earliest King of Mewar.
   (a) Krishnadeva Raya   (b) Bappa Rawal
   (c) Raja of Mewar   (d) Mukul Singh

7. How did Rana Kumbha contributed Mewar's glory?
   (a) Added new stature through victories.
   (b) Flourished art and literature.
   (c) Explored new possibilities in writings.
   (d) All of them

8. How were the people of Mewar?
    (a) pleasant and liberal
    (b) cruel and shrewd
    (c) innocent and modern
    (d) foolish and sharp

9. Which area of Mewar flourished over the time?
    (a) Art
    (b) Science
    (c) Literature
    (d) Both (a) and (c)

10. Arrange the sequence of events as they occur in the passage.
    (i) His reputation went beyond Rajasthan and reached Delhi.
    (ii) Amidst aggression and bloodshed, literature and art flourished and **creative** pursuits of literature and artists did not suffer.
    (iii) There did come a few thorny occasions when the flag of the kingdom seemed sliding down
    (iv) History took a turn.
    (a) (iii), (i), (ii), (iv)
    (b) (ii), (i), (iv), (iii)
    (c) (i), (ii), (iii), (iv)
    (d) (iv), (iii), (ii), (i)

Question 3

(a) Answer sections (a), (b) and (c). In each of the following items, a sentence is given. Select the most appropriate transformation of the given sentence out of the given options:

1. He is a clever man. He won't believe that silly story.
    (a) He is to clever to believe that silly story.
    (b) He is a clever man therefore he won't believe that silly story.
    (c) He is a very clever man so he will not believe that silly story.
    (d) He is not so foolish to believe on that silly story.

2. I heard the song. It brought back memories of my country.
    (a) As soon as I heard the song, the memories of my country came back.
    (b) The memories of my country where brought back while hearing the song.
    (c) As I heard the song, it brought back the memories of my country.
    (d) The memories of my country where brought back while hearing the song.

3. Clear the written test. Only then you will be called for an interview.
    (a) Once you clear the written test, you will be called for an interview.
    (b) You will be called for an interview, once you clear the written test.
    (c) You will be called for an interview only if you clear the written test.
    (d) Clear the written test and get the call for an interview.

4. The typist was clever. We hired the typist.
    (a) The typist being clever, we hired him.
    (b) The typist was clever so we hired him.
    (c) The typist being clever was hired.
    (d) We hired the typist being he was clever.

5. Only graduates can apply for this post.
    (a) Graduates are only eligible for this post.
    (b) Only this post is meant for graduates.
    (c) None other than graduates can apply for the post.
    (d) Only this post can be applied by graduates.

6. We have to study a third language upto class VIII.
    (a) It is compulsory for us to study a third language upto class VIII.

(b) There is no other option than to study a third language upto class VIII.

(c) It is important to study a third language upto class VIII.

(d) All have to study a third language up to class VIII.

7. Hard working students do well in the examination.

   (a) Students only do well if they work hard.

   (b) Students who work hard, do well in the examination.

   (c) Students can work hard and do well in the examination.

   (d) Students do well in the examination, if they work hard.

8. Take the cheque. The cash may not be sufficient.

   (a) The cash may not be sufficient, also take the cheque.

   (b) Since the cash may not be sufficient, so take the cheque.

   (c) Take the cheque if the cash is not sufficient.

   (d) Take cheque and cash both.

9. He always repays whatever he borrows.

   (a) He never borrows and always repay.

   (b) He borrows and he repays.

   (c) He never fails to repay what he borrows.

   (d) He only repays, if he borrows.

10. He is inviting each of his friends.

   (a) All of his friends are invited.

   (b) Each of his friends is being invited by him.

   (c) He has invited all of his friends.

   (d) All of his friends were invited by him.

(b) Choose the most appropriate word to fill in the blank in the given sentence:

1. The people of Iran staged a ___________their king.
   (a) revolt with   (b) revolt to   (c) revolt against   (d) revolt in

2. Our body has a remarkable resistance ___________diseases.
   (a) to   (b) with   (c) at   (d) in

3. He showed great ___________ purpose in bringing the task to completion.
   (a) tenacity for   (b) tenacity at   (c) tenacity of   (d) tenacity in

4. He struggled and gained a victory ___________his enemies.
   (a) with   (b) at   (c) over   (d) between

5. I can't help you, I am ___________ money at present.
   (a) short for   (b) short of   (c) short on   (d) short at

6. He may be slow ___________ understanding.
   (a) to   (b) with   (c) at   (d) for

7. What time did they ___________the hotel?
   (a) get in   (b) arrive in   (c) arrive at   (d) arrive to

8. Autotomy is the ability of an animal to ___________ a part of its body at will to save itself from predators and attackers.
   (a) cast off   (b) cast away   (c) cut of   (d) cut down

9. We judge ourselves by our thought, ___________ others judge us by our actions.
   (a) when   (b) because   (c) whereas   (d) lest

10. The Export Manager is ___________ the Sales Director.
   (a) responsible for   (b) responsible to   (c) responsible by   (d) responsible with

11. He said he was ___________ keeping me waiting.
   (a) sorry for   (b) sorry about   (c) sorry to   (d) sorry at

12. The expected cut in interest will be ___________ industry.

    (a) good at   (b) good with   (c) good for   (d) good by

13. The ministry was ___________ criticism in the paper.

    (a) annoyed about   (b) annoyed with   (c) annoyed for   (d) annoyed by

14. He is ___________ preparing handouts.

    (a) responsible for   (b) responsible to   (c) responsible by   (d) responsible with

15. I am weary ___________ your lame excuses.

    (a) for   (b) in   (c) of   (d) to

(c) Choose the correct option to fill in the blank in each sentence:

1. Sheetal generally ___________ a white suit, but today she ___________ a blue one.

   (a) wears, wore   (b) wears, wearing   (c) has wore, wears   (d) wore, wearing

2. It ___________ that there has been an accident.

   (a) appeared   (b) appears   (c) appearing   (d) has appeared

3. In addition to his advice, he ___________ me.

   (a) helped   (b) is helping   (c) has helped   (d) has been helping

4. The doctor ___________ the patient in the next room.

   (a) had examine   (b) has examined   (c) is examining   (d) was examining

5. My aunt ___________ from Ranchi.

   (a) has just arrived   (b) was arriving

   (c) had been arriving   (d) was arrived

6. If the weather ___________ tomorrow, no planes will take off.

   (a) does not improve   (b) improves

   (c) has not improve   (d) was not improving

7. I want to go to the show, I ___________ a good play for a long time.

   (a) have not seen   (b) was not seen   (c) will be seeing   (d) would have seen

8. To ___________ a diary, is a good habit.

   (a) maintaining   (b) maintain   (c) be maintained   (d) has been maintained

9. I ___________ the minister so far but I ___________ him tomorrow.

   (a) had not met, was meeting   (b) have not met, am meeting

   (c) will have not meet, am meeting   (d) None of them

10. He ___________ us since 1999.

    (a) was visiting   (b) had visited   (c) has been visited   (d) has not visited

11. We ___________ verbs for three weeks.

    (a) have been revising   (b) had been revising

    (c) will be revising   (d) were revising

12. He ___________ there and ran away.

    (a) did not stop   (b) had not stop   (c) was not stopping   (d) was not stopped

13. Two and two ___________ four.

    (a) makes   (b) make   (c) made   (d) making

14. She carried flowers whenever she ___________ the shrine.

    (a) was visiting   (b) has visited   (c) visited   (d) will be visiting

15. Next year we ___________ to Paris.

    (a) will go   (b) would have gone

    (c) will have been going   (d) were to go

Answers

1.(a) (i) 1. (a) persist
2. (b) feeling of excitement
3. (c) positivity
4. (a) disappointed
5. (b) wealth

(ii) 1. (d) The mind map prepared by Shella is very comprehensive.
2. (d) Tobacco was once regarded as a curiosity in Europe.
3. (a) He took out his shoes to remove the small rocks and grit.
4. (d) There is likely to be a good public library as a stay against boredom
5. (a) There are two poles in the battery : negative and positive.

(b) 1. (a) Humans have emotions.
2. (c) Optimistic
3. (d) Falling down and getting up
4. (d) to be in a moment and be aware without judgement
5. (a) It suppresses the noise of fears and doubts
6. (a) With the help of mindfulness, one can overcome negativity
7. (d) Thomas Edison
8. (a) successful
9. (a) Failure can affect our emotions
10. (b) (ii), (i), (iv), (iii)

2.(a) (i) 1. (b) splendour
2. (a) proficient
3. (d) all of the above
4. (a) Use of imagination
5. (c) awareness

(ii) 1. (c) He will always be one of the immortals of soccer.
2. (b) My favourite subjects are Physics and Mathematics
3. (a) New Delhi is the capital of India.
4. (d) She stood still with her hair flying in the wind.
5. (d) Shweta is from commerce stream.

(b) 1. (d) Both (b) and (c)
2. (c) Small area and less population

3. (c) When the flag of Mewar was lowered.
4. (b) Because the population was much confident.
5. (a) Vijaya Stambha
6. (b) Bappa Rawal
7. (d) All of them
8. (a) pleasant and liberal
9. (d) Both (a) and (c)
10. (a) (iii), (i), (ii), (iv)

3. (a) 1. (b) He is a clever man therefore he won't believe that silly story.
2. (a) As soon as I heard the song, the memories of my country came back.
3. (c) You will be called for an interview only if you clear the written test.
4. (b) The typist was clever so we hired him.
5. (c) None other than graduates can apply for the post.
6. (a) It is compulsory for us to study a third language upto class VIII.
7. (b) Students who work hard, do well in the examination.
8. (b) Since the cash may not be sufficient, so take the cheque.
9. (c) He never fails to repay what he borrows.
10. (b) Each of his friends is being invited by him.

(b) 1. (c) revolt against
2. (a) to
3. (c) tenacity of
4. (c) over
5. (b) short of
6. (c) at
7. (c) arrive at
8. (a) cast off
9. (c) whereas
10. (b) responsible to
11. (a) sorry for
12. (c) good for
13. (a) annoyed about

14. (a) responsible for
15. (c) of

(c)
1. (a) wears, wore
2. (b) appears
3. (a) helped
4. (c) is examining
5. (a) has just arrived
6. (a) does not improve
7. (a) have not seen
8. (b) maintain
9. (b) have not met, am meeting
10. (d) has not visited
11. (a) have been revising
12. (a) did not stop
13. (a) makes
14. (c) visited
15. (a) will go

❑❑

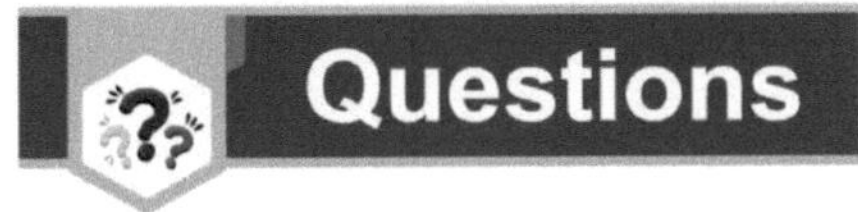

Question 1

Read the given passage carefully and answer the questions that follow:

(1) How often do we remember to treat others as you would like them to treat you? In our quest to get more and more, we forget that the quality of our lives depends on the kind of personalities we have cultivated for ourselves. Genes might play a role when it comes to one's **disposition**, but the major portion of our attitudes and behaviour is influenced by the choices we make. So in the beginning of every year should you resolve to make more money, learn a new language, travel more frequently then you must discontinue to be the same grumpy, impatient soul you always were, should you then not seek to refine your character, focus on nuances like how you treat people, react to challenges and deal with stressful situations? For most people such a course would yield rich results.

(2) According to Mary Thomas, usually our New Year resolutions remain unachieved because we try to achieve the impossible or, sometimes, just add more goals that we wish to accomplish to the list of resolutions, but, strangely, we do not remember much about them during the course of the year as we do not seem to value them enough to complete them. The better option would be to <u>address</u> something fundamental to you, to who you really are, and go ahead with completing them instead of making any drastic resolutions which you will never be able to fulfil. You could resolve to be a better person by having a <u>positive</u> attitude towards people you come across in life. This could involve being nice with the lady who cleans the house, or your colleague who sits near you, but you never interacted with. Another trick is to acknowledge people for the value they add to your personal or professional life. By extending <u>basic</u> courtesies to people around you, you add value to your life and that pays off in the long run.

(3) Sometimes, we know that there is room for improvement as far as our personalities are concerned but we have little or no idea where to make the start. An easy starting point could be to look for opportunities in one's immediate surroundings. One positive starting point could be taking a positive attitude towards life and dispelling all negative thoughts. You could make a positive beginning by being a better person at work. This means treating everyone with respect. You should not only interact politely, but also value each person's ideas however far removed they may be, to your own. After all, your friend's ideas are an integral part of the organization to which both of you belong. Inculcating this habit of making an effort to talk to people you would normally not have to interact with on a daily basis, would make you a better person at the workplace.

(4) Also, you do not have to do something extraordinary to prove your good **intentions**. Just greeting or smiling at your colleagues first thing in the morning could always brighten someone's day. These are simple things that we are taught while growing but tend to forget as we move through life. So essentially, being better is an <u>exercise</u> in learning to be nice, and you will see that playing nice will get your work done better than scolding or **frowning** or passing orders.

(5) A purposeful life should contain skills that lead to practical changes. After all, no people are alike, so why should your ideas be the only right solution? A company, where individual differences are nurtured, information is not **suppressed**, soon becomes a workplace that adds value to its employees, rather than merely extracting work out of them. It makes workers feel intrinsically rewarded. It is, therefore, imperative that co-workers and partners share a camaraderie that **transcends** mere

professional conduct and <u>delivery</u>. Thus, for a person who wishes to remain happy and content, it is as valuable to spend time on nurturing qualities like friendship and consideration as it is on acquiring skills and knowledge.

(a) (i) Given below are five words from the passage along with four options for each. Choose the option which has a similar meaning in the passage:

1. **Disposition**
   - (a) individualism
   - (b) character
   - (c) decision
   - (d) opposition

2. **Intentions**
   - (a) aim
   - (b) importance
   - (c) deeds
   - (d) neglect

3. **Frowning**
   - (a) elated
   - (b) angry
   - (c) disappointed
   - (d) happy

4. **Suppressed**
   - (a) burked
   - (b) repressed
   - (c) restrained
   - (d) all of them

5. **Transcends**
   - (a) surpass
   - (b) more
   - (c) shift
   - (d) change

(ii) With each of the five words given below, choose the correct sentence that uses the word in a different meaning from that which it carries in the passage.

1. **Address**
   - (a) My address is written in my form.
   - (b) His lawyer is going to address the bench.
   - (c) We should address some better references.
   - (d) You should address the queen as ``Your Highness''.

2. **Positive**
   - (a) ``Stay positive and cheerful in your life'', says Dad.
   - (b) The electrons are attracted towards the positive end of the tube.
   - (c) The positive attitude of Meera was appreciable throughout the movie.
   - (d) We should remain positive in all situations.

3. **Basic**
   - (a) Sodium bicarbonate is a basic salt.
   - (b) Kindly extend my basic courtesies to people of your community.
   - (c) The basic amenities of life include food, clothes and shelter.
   - (d) It is the basic truth of life.

4. **Exercise**
   - (a) He was advised to exercise basic yoga movements.
   - (b) ``Your son has done all mathematical exercises'', says teacher.
   - (c) One should exercise good etiquette.
   - (d) He did all the exercises in the gym.

5. **Delivery**
   - (a) The delivery by the person was on time.
   - (b) Her delivery of content was commendable.
   - (c) The doctors worked busily beneath the blinding lights of the delivery room.
   - (d) The delivery man faced problem in figuring my house.

(b) Choose the correct option for the questions given below:

1. Which factor influences our quality of life?
   (a) The personalities we have developed for ourselves.
   (b) The number of promises we make
   (c) The number of new resolutions we create
   (d) The challenges that people give us

2. Why does our New Year Resolution, remain unfulfilled?
   (a) make too many resolutions
   (b) add more goals than what we can accomplish
   (c) get caught up with studies
   (d) feel happy about them

3. How can one add value to his life?
   (a) by earning money
   (b) by becoming a hardworker
   (c) by being nice to the people in surrounding
   (d) both (b) and (c)

4. Workers feel intrinsically rewarded if ....
   (a) they are provided with bonuses
   (b) their work is recognized
   (c) their individual differences are acknowledged
   (d) none of them

5. What will happen if we start to play with people?
   (a) It will not help us at all
   (b) It will make us famous
   (c) It will get our jobs done
   (d) It will reveal our personality

6. Which company becomes a value-added workplace?
   (a) where people do monthly picnics
   (b) where information is not suppressed
   (c) where customers are happy
   (d) where employees complete their monthly targets

7. How can we start improving our personality?
   (a) Looking for opportunity in surrounding
   (b) Start behaving well with friends
   (c) Completing work on time
   (d) All of them

8. What is a purposeful life?
   (a) Life in which you help others
   (b) Life in which you learn to earn money
   (c) Life in which you learn practical skills
   (d) Life in which you develop good habits

9. Individual differences refers to:
   (a) uniqueness of an individual
   (b) specific traits of an individual
   (c) both (a) and (b)
   (d) none of them

10. Arrange the sequence of events as they occur in the passage.
    (i) A purposeful life should contain skills that lead to practical changes.
    (ii) These are simple things that we are taught while growing but tend to forget as we move through life.

     (iii) Genes might play a role when it comes to one's disposition, but the major portion of our attitudes and behaviour is influenced by the choices we make.

     (iv) You could resolve to be a better person by having a positive attitude towards people you come across in life.

     (a) (iii), (iv), (ii), (i)   (b) (ii), (i), (iv), (iii)

     (c) (i), (ii), (iii), (iv)   (d) (iv), (iii), (ii), (i)

Question 2

Read the given passage carefully and answer the questions that follow:

(1) The first Indian woman **physician** Anandibai Joshi, graduated in 1886. Starting from that single figure, about 125 years later, Indian women have started to outnumber men in admissions to medical colleges and the trend continues to grow stronger by the year, particularly over the last five years. During this period, India has produced 4500 more female doctors than male ones.

(2) In India women constituted 51% of the students joining medical colleges, cornering 23,522 seats in 2014-15, compared to 22,934 men. In fact, in the neighbouring countries such as Pakistan and Bangladesh there are much higher portions of women in medical colleges, with figures standing at 70% and 60% respectively.

(3) According,to the medical **journal** Lancet, only 17% of all allopathic doctors and 6% of those in rural areas are women. This is less than one female allopathic doctor per 10,000 population in rural areas, whereas the ratio is 6:5 in urban areas.

(4) According to a paper on women in medicine published in the journal 'Indian **Anthropologist**' by sociologist Dr Mita Bhadra, the gender gap persists at the postgraduation and doctoral levels. The percentage of women doctors here is around one-third of male doctors. She also observed that positions of leadership in academics and administration are still mostly occupied by men.

(5) In Pakistan, though 70% of medical students are women, only 23% of registered doctors were females because a large number of those who graduated never took to practising. The trend of more women joining the medical profession is welcomed in all these countries as female doctors are seen as committed and caring. A paper on women in medicine published by Dr Rakesh Chaddha and Dr Mamta Sood of the psychiatry department of AIIMS noted that medicine has been a male-dominated profession because it demands long working hours that are disadvantageous to women who, even today, struggle to juggle career and family responsibilities.

(6) Earlier, though women were largely restricted to fields such as obstetrics, gynaecology and paediatrics, this is changing now. There has always been a preponderance of women in pre-clinical subjects like anatomy, physiology and biochemistry and **paraclinical** subjects like pharmacology, pathology and **microbiology**, right from the '70s. In departments headed by women, the women faculty was 49% as compared to just 19% in those headed by men, says Dr Chaddha, giving the example of the neurology department at the AIIMS, which saw a lot of women faculty joining when the HOD was a woman. 'It is probably because the head of the department becomes a role model and more women are encouraged to join,' said Dr. Chaddha.

(7) There are skews within the medical profession in most parts of the world with some medical specialties, such as surgery and other disciplines requiring emergency duty with irregular hours being male-dominated. Even in the United Kingdom, though women account for 56% of those opting for medical education, 49% are public health and only 8% are surgeons, according to a Royal College of Physicians expert.

(8) Among the Organization for Economic Co-operation and Development countries (OECD), across ten of them, predominantly from the erstwhile Eastern Bloc, the proportion of female physicians is more than 50%, ranging from a high 73.8% in Estonia to 50.2% in Spain. In two non- OECD countries, Latvia and Lithuania, females accounted for over 74% and 70% of physicians. In contrast, only one in five doctors in Japan and Korea were women. In the United States it is one in three, confirming the fact that the disproportion among women and men doctors is a universal phenomenon.

(a) (i) Given below are five words from the passage along with four options for each word. Choose the option which has a similar meaning in the passage:

1. **Physician**
   - (a) doctor
   - (b) practitioner
   - (c) resource person
   - (d) helper
2. **Journal**
   - (a) periodical
   - (b) publication
   - (c) magazine
   - (d) all of them
3. **Anthropologist**
   - (a) person engaged in study of animals
   - (b) person engaged in study of birds
   - (c) person engaged in study of human
   - (d) person engaged in study of fossils
4. **Paraclinical**
   - (a) providing service related to throat
   - (b) providing resource without direct involvement in care
   - (c) providing service by surgery
   - (d) providing free medical check-up
5. **Microbiology**
   - (a) study of animal
   - (b) study of reptiles
   - (c) study of microbes
   - (d) study of plants

(ii) With each of the five words given below, choose the correct sentence that uses the word in a different meaning from that which it carries in the passage.

1. **Gap**
   - (a) A Gap is a narrow opening between mountain peaks.
   - (b) There is generation gap among parents and children.
   - (c) The gender gap is visible in the statistical report.
   - (d) Maintain gap while you study continuously.

2. **Administration**
   - (a) The administration of the State is managed by CM.
   - (b) Teachers complain that more time is taken up with administration.
   - (c) The university administration took their demands seriously.
   - (d) The inhabitants of the island voted to remain under French administration.

3. **Trend**
   - (a) Coming from Tibetian highlands, the Ghazal Lake has a southern trend to Lake Chad.
   - (b) He follows an old trend in wedding.
   - (c) He was followed by the trend of public opinions.
   - (d) Police is disturbed by the latest trends in driving.

4. **Disciplines**
   - (a) We should discipline ourselves and discharge our duties.
   - (b) There are various disciplines in Biochemistry.
   - (c) She followed the same discipline to that of her sister.
   - (d) Mohan qualified the exam in the toughest discipline of GATE.

5. **Model**
   - (a) Mahatma Gandhi is the role model of young Indian minds.
   - (b) Women entrepreneurs are the role models of today's era.
   - (c) The science model by Rohit won the second prize.
   - (d) The project became a model for others schemes.

(b) Choose the correct option for the questions given below:

1. The female doctors have outnumbered the male doctors by what number in India?
   - (a) 4300
   - (b) 4200
   - (c) 4500
   - (d) 4000

2. What percentage of women are joining medical profession in Pakistan and Bangladesh?
   (a) much lower than the figures in India.
   (b) equal in both the countries.
   (c) same as India's.
   (d) higher than the figures in India.

3. Why do women in medical line are less in number?
   (a) it is a very tedious profession
   (b) it demands long working hours
   (c) women do not enjoy in this field
   (d) women are discouraged by the peers

4. What percentage of females are accounted as the physicians in Lithuania?
   (a) nearly 70%   (b) nearly 74%
   (c) nearly 50%   (d) over 70%

5. Who has occupied the position of leadership in academics and administration?
   (a) women   (b) men
   (c) both men and women   (d) doctors

6. Which subjects are considered under paraclinical in medical science?
   (a) Pharmacology   (b) Pathology
   (c) Microbiology   (d) All of them

7. Name the first Indian physician.
   (a) Dr. Anandibai Joshi   (b) Dr. Anandibai Ben
   (c) Dr. Anandibai Sinha   (d) Dr. Anandibai Sahai

8. Name the medical journal which reported a serious shortage of female doctors in India.
   (a) Lucent   (b) Lancent
   (c) Medical history   (d) Medical filled science

9. Who published `Indian Anthropologist''?
   (a) Dr. Mita Bhadra   (b) Dr. Sunita Chadda
   (c) Dr. Nita Singh   (d) Dr. Sumita Sahai

10. Expand the term OECD.
    (a) Organization for Ecological Council and Department
    (b) Organization for Ecosystem, Climate and Diversity
    (c) Organization for Economic Co-operation and Development
    (d) Organization for Economic Co-operation and Department

Question 3

(a) Answer sections (a), (b) and (c). In each of the following items, a sentence is given. Select the most appropriate transformation of the given sentence out of the given options:

1. He does several activities. None of them succeed.

   (a) He does several activities still none of them succeed.

   (b) He does several activities and none of them succeed.

   (c) He is doing a lot but getting no success.

   (d) He does several activities but succeed in none.

2. None of us should tolerate intellectual dishonesty.

   (a) No one should tolerate intellectual dishonesty.

   (b) Intellectual dishonesty is intolerable.

   (c) Intellectual dishonesty should not be tolerated by any of us.

   (d) Intellectual dishonesty cannot be tolerated.

3. He said to me, "Are you going away tonight?"
    (a) He inquired of me if I was going away that night.
    (b) He inquired if I was going in the night.
    (c) He asked me about my visit tonight.
    (d) He asked whether I was going away that night or not.

4. My old car was slow. My new car is much faster.
    (a) My new car is the fastest.
    (b) My new car is much faster than my old car.
    (c) My old car is slower than the new car.
    (d) My old car was the slowest one.

5. Donald said that it was his sister's fault, but that was unkind.
    (a) It was unkind for Donald to say that it was his sister's fault.
    (b) It was unkind of Donald to say about sister's fault.
    (c) Donald did a fault by saying about his sister.
    (d) Donald should not say such unkind words for his sister.

6. Arundhati said, ``Do you play tennis?"
    (a) Arundhati inquired about my sport.
    (b) Arundhati asked if I could play tennis.
    (c) Arundhati asked me whether I play tennis.
    (d) Arundhati was curious about me playing tennis.

7. Leela said, ``Let me have some coffee."
    (a) Leela wished to have some coffee.
    (b) Leela wished for coffee.
    (c) Leela is craving to have some coffee.
    (d) Leela wished if she could get some coffee.

8. I was right. My father said this.
    (a) My father proved me right
    (b) My father said that I was right.
    (c) My father said that I was not wrong.
    (d) I was right, said by my father.

9. I never thought that they would win the match.
    (a) I didn't believe that they could win the match.
    (b) I didn't think that they could win the match.
    (c) Little did I think that they would win the match.
    (d) Little did I thought of their victory.

10. How selfish he is! No one can imagine.
    (a) No one can imagine his selfishness.
    (b) No one can imagine he is how selfish.
    (c) His selfishness is above one's imagination.
    (d) He is too selfish to be imagined.

(b) Choose the most appropriate word to fill in the blank in the given sentence.

1. His professional ability proves that he is cut _______ for this job.

    (a) out   (b) up   (c) down   (d) for

2. The history of Hindu religion dates back ________ ancient times.

    (a) from   (b) since   (c) to   (d) for

3. Nothing can deter him _____ pursuing his aim of life.
   (a) for   (b) in   (c) to   (d) from
4. No one believes him because he is false _____ heart.
   (a) to   (b) from   (c) of   (d) by
5. The officials have the habit of fawning _____ ministers.
   (a) above   (b) on   (c) at   (d) with
6. The problem of communal harmony cannot be glossed _____ by government.
   (a) over   (b) at   (c) out   (d) on
7. I always meant to ask Indira _____ for dinner, but could never muster the courage.
   (a) with   (b) up   (c) out   (d) over
8. Tony thinks his larynx is acting _____ again.
   (a) up   (b) with   (c) into   (d) for
9. The costume change in the middle of the performance was a last minute add _____ .
   (a) off   (b) upto   (c) on   (d) with
10. The school board agreed _____ look into the student's complaints.
    (a) to   (b) with   (c) in   (d) up
11. I called _____ my boss to let him know I would not come the next day.
    (a) in   (b) with   (c) up   (d) for
12. Our car broke _____ in the middle of nowhere.
    (a) down   (b) up   (c) with   (d) into
13. Sheetal asked _____ a cup of tea.
    (a) to   (b) with   (c) for   (d) nevertheless
14. As children, we were taught to never answer _____ to our teachers, when being told off.
    (a) back   (b) for   (c) into   (d) because
15. It seems Sam's house was broken _____ last evening.
    (a) up   (b) into   (c) for   (d) because

(c) Choose the correct option to fill in the blank in each sentence.
1. Why _____ you _____ your new dress?
   (a) are, not wore   (b) are, not wearing
   (c) have, not been wearing   (d) none of them
2. She _____ since the age of eighteen.
   (a) had driven   (b) was driving   (c) had been driven   (d) has been driving
3. I _____ in Delhi for an year.
   (a) have lived   (b) was living   (c) had been living   (d) had lived
4. My car _____ down yesterday but the mechanic _____ it.
   (a) break, repairing   (b) broke, repaired
   (c) has been broken, repairing   (d) had broken, repaired
5. The Karnataka flight _____ at 4:50 pm.
   (a) will leave   (b) would leave   (c) would have leave   (d) leave
6. Take an umbrella if you are going out, it _____ about to rain.
   (a) has been   (b) was   (c) is   (d) will be
7. An accident _____ place yesterday at Mall Road.
   (a) taken   (b) took   (c) has taken   (d) had taken
8. Do not make noise. The baby _____ in the cradle.
   (a) is sleeping   (b) has been slept   (c) was sleeping   (d) had slept
9. He _____ his meal and is playing in the garden now.
   (a) took   (b) has been taking   (c) has taken   (d) take
10. You cannot go out, till you _____ your homework.
    (a) complete   (b) have completed   (c) has completed   (d) had been completing

11. The hungry child _________ for ten minutes.
    (a) has been crying (b) had been crying   (c) had cried   (d) cried
12. I _________ the minister yet.
    (a) have not meet   (b) have not met
    (c) have not meeting   (d) had met
13. Everybody ____________ a smart boy.
    (a) admires   (b) admire   (c) admired   (d) has admired
14. The policeman ________ me where I was going.
    (a) is asking   (b) asked   (c) has been asking (d) has asked
15. I ________ pity on the old man and gave him five rupees.
    (a) took   (b) was taking   (c) am taking   (d) had been taking

Answers

1.(a) (i) 1. (b) character
    2. (a) aim
    3. (b) angry
    4. (d) all of them
    5. (a) surpass

(ii) 1. (a) My address is written in my form.
    2. (b) The electrons are attracted towards the positive end of the tube.
    3. (a) Sodium bicarbonate is a basic salt.
    4. (b) "Your son has done all mathematical exercises", says teacher.
    5. (c) The doctors worked busily beneath the blinding lights of the delivery room.

(b) 1. (a) The personalities we have developed for ourselves
    2. (b) add more goals than what we can accomplish
    3. (c) by being nice to the people in surrounding
    4. (c) their individual differences are acknowledged
    5. (a) It will not help us at all
    6. (b) where information is not suppressed
    7. (a) Looking for opportunity in surrounding
    8. (c) Life in which you learn practical skills
    9. (c) both (a) and (b)
    10. (a) (iii), (iv), (ii), (i)

2.(a) (i) 1. (a) doctor
    2. (d) all of them
    3. (c) person engaged in study of human

4. (b) providing resource without direct involvement in care
5. (c) study of microbes

(ii) 1. (a) A Gap is a narrow opening between mountain peaks.
    2. (b) Teachers complain that more time is taken up with administration.
    3. (a) Coming from Tibetian highlands, the Ghazal Lake has a southern trend to Lake Chad.
    4. (a) We should discipline ourselves and discharge our duties.
    5. (c) The science model by Rohit won the second prize.

(b) 1. (c) 4500
    2. (d) higher than the figures in India
    3. (b) it demands long working hours
    4. (d) over 70%
    5. (b) men
    6. (d) All of them
    7. (a) Dr. Anandibai Joshi
    8. (b) Lancent
    9. (a) Dr. Mita Bhadra
    10. (c) Organization for Economic Co-operation and Development

3. (a) 1. (a) He does several activities still none of them succeed.
    2. (c) Intellectual dishonesty should not be tolerated by any of us.
    3. (a) He inquired of me if I was going away that night.
    4. (b) My new car is much faster than my old car.

    5. (a) It was unkind for Donald to say that it was his sister's fault.

    6. (c) Arundhati asked me whether I play tennis.

    7. (a) Leela wished to have some coffee.

    8. (b) My father said that I was right.

    9. (c) Little did I think that they would win the match.

  10. (a) No one can imagine his selfishness.

(b) 1. (a) out

  2. (c) to

  3. (d) from

  4. (c) of

  5. (b) on

  6. (a) over

  7. (c) out

  8. (a) up

  9. (c) on

  10. (a) to

  11. (c) up

12. (a) down

13. (c) for

14. (a) back

15. (b) into

(c) 1. (b) are, not wearing

  2. (d) has been driving

  3. (a) have lived

  4. (b) broke, repaired

  5. (a) will leave

  6. (c) is

  7. (b) took

  8. (a) is sleeping

  9. (c) has taken

  10. (b) have completed

  11. (a) has been crying

  12. (b) have not met

  13. (a) admires

  14. (b) asked

  15. (a) took

❑❑

English-II

Specimen Question Paper

English II

Maximum Marks: 80
Time allowed: One and a half hours

General Instructions

*(Candidates are allowed additional **15 minutes** for **only** reading the Paper)*
ALL QUESTIONS ARE COMPULSORY.
The marks intended for questions are given in brackets [ ].
Select the correct option for each of the following questions.

Questions

SECTION-A
THE TEMPEST

1. Choose the correct option given below each question: **[1×10=10]**

   (i) What is Ferdinand doing at the beginning of Act 3 Scene I?

        (a) Cursing Prospero   (b) Gathering wood

        (c) Crying   (d) Plotting to escape

   (ii) Why has Prospero given him this task?

        (a) To punish him.   (b) To humiliate him.

        (c) To test his sincerity in love.   (d) To take revenge.

   (iii) What is Ferdinand willing to become for Miranda?

        (a) King of Naples.   (b) A patient log- man.

        (c) Marry her and become her husband.   (d) To be Prospero's slave for Miranda's sake.

   (iv) What does Ferdinand pray should happen if he speaks false?

        (a) A blight will fall on him

        (b) The Gods will be angry

        (c) His best aspirations may be inverted to mischief.

        (d) Miranda will marry someone else.

   (v) Ferdinand shares a Latin root word to describe Miranda in Act III Scene I. Which word does he use?

        (a) Beautiful   (b) Admired

        (c) Dearest   (d) Royal

   (vi) What does Stephano mean when he says that Caliban has "drown'd his tongue in sack" in Act III Scene II?

        (a) He was drowned in a sack.   (b) He had drunk so much that he could not speak.

        (c) He was lost in thought.   (d) None of the above

   (vii) Which aspect of Caliban's nature is revealed through his words, "bite him to death, I prithee"?

        (a) Savagery   (b) Uncivilised

        (c) Roughness   (d) All of these

(viii) Why does Gonzalo say, "I need must rest me" in Act III Scene III?
    (a) He is feeling sleepy.
    (b) He does not want to go with Antonio and Sebastian and Antonio.
    (c) He is exhausted.
    (d) He wants some time to look around the island.

(ix) To whom is Alonso referring in Act III Scene III, when he says, "he is drown'd"?
    (a) Prospero   (b) Ferdinand   (c) Adrian   (d) Francisco

(x) What do Antonio and Sebastian talk about while Alonso is resting in Act III Scene III?
    (a) About abandoning the King's party
    (b) About making another attempt to murder Alonso.
    (c) About seizing the island for themselves.
    (d) None of the above.

2. Read the lines given below and choose the correct option given after each question: **[1×10=10]**

A. *Miranda:*   *I am a fool*
        To weep at what I am glad of
  Prospero: *Fair encounter*
        Of two most rare affections!

(i) To whom is Miranda speaking?
    (a) Prospero   (b) Ferdinand   (c) Ariel   (d) Alonso

(ii) Of what is Miranda glad?
    (a) Ferdinand reciprocates her love.
    (b) That she can leave the island.
    (c) That her father has not been able to find out about her love.
    (d) That she will be the queen of Naples.

(iii) What do her words reveal about her?
    (a) She is simple.   (b) She is ambitious.
    (c) She is humble.   (d) She is compassionate.

(iv) What is Prospero's reaction to her happiness?
    (a) He is angry with his daughter for not following his commands.
    (b) He is happy with her.
    (c) He decides to punish her for confessing her love to Ferdinand.
    (d) He decides to put obstacles in the way of her love.

(v) Which of the following statements is NOT TRUE about Miranda in the context of the quoted lines?
    (a) She respects her father.   (b) She has a streak of independence in her.
    (c) She is conniving   (d) She has a soft heart.

(vi) What does Prospero mean by "rare affections"?
    (a) Interesting persons   (b) Pure souls
    (c) Unusual emotions   (d) Foolish sentiments

(vii) For what does Prospero go on to ask heaven's blessings?
    (a) For the love that is growing between the young couple.
    (b) For Ferdinand having come to the island.
    (c) For Miranda being so biddable.
    (d) For his efforts on their behalf, to unite the two lovers.

(viii) What does Miranda ask Ferdinand at the end of the scene?
    (a) She asks him to make her his wife.
    (b) She asks him to take her to Naples.
    (c) She asks him to take her away from her father.
    (d) She asks him to finish his task.

(ix) What evidence do we have of Ferdinand's love for Miranda?
   (a) He is willing to do the humble task for her in spite of being a Prince.
   (b) He is willing to elope with her.
   (c) He is willing to make her his wife against.
   (d) He shows the courage to fight Prospero for Miranda's sake.

(x) When do the two plan to meet again?
   (a) The next day
   (b) That evening
   (c) Half an hour later
   (d) They decide to be together.

B. *Antonio:* *I'll believe both*
   And what else does want credit, come to me,

(i) What has Antonio just seen?
   (a) Ariel singing a song.
   (b) Ariel in the shape of a sea nymph.
   (c) Strange shapes bringing in a banquet.
   (d) The fact that their clothes are fresh even after the shipwreck.

(ii) What is Antonio's attitude in these lines?
   (a) Pleasure
   (b) Fear
   (c) Surprise
   (d) Scepticism

(iii) What does Antonio refer to as "both"?
   (a) Ferdinand and Miranda.
   (b) Unicorns and the Phoenix.
   (c) Ariel and Caliban.
   (d) Nymphs and Satyrs.

(iv) How does Gonzalo interpret the sight he has just seen?
   (a) He feels that they are agents of punishment.
   (b) He feels that they are islanders.
   (c) He thinks he has seen a vision.
   (d) He thinks that his eyes are playing tricks with him.

(v) Who is listening to their conversation?
   (a) Ariel
   (b) Caliban
   (c) Prospero
   (d) Ferdinand

(vi) Alonso refers to the "dumb discourse" of the creatures. What does he refer to by these words?
   (a) The signs made by the creatures.
   (b) The dances of the creatures.
   (c) The frightening gestures made by the creatures.
   (d) Their pleasant faces.

(vii) What did the strange creatures bring for Alonso and his group?
   (a) Flowers
   (b) Viands
   (c) Wine
   (d) Stones

(viii) Why does Gonzalo say that Alonso need not fear?
   (a) In their youth they had heard tales of strange people.
   (b) There are many kinds of people inhabiting the earth.
   (c) Since the island is a strange place, they should expect strange things here.
   (d) None of the above

(ix) Why can't the king and his group eat the food brought in?
   (a) They realise that the food is poisoned.
   (b) They find their hunger disappearing.
   (c) Suddenly the food vanishes
   (d) They are warned against eating the food.

(x)   What do you conclude about Gonzalo's nature from his interaction with the others in the scene?

    (a) He is indifferent.

    (b) He is suspicious of everything

    (c) He always speaks against Antonio and Sebastian.

    (d) He tries to find good in everything.

SECTION-B
ECHOES-SHORT STORIES

[1×10=10]

3. (i)   In the short story, *To Build a Fire,* the protagonist travels alone. At what temperature is he warned against travelling alone?

    (a) Thirty-two degrees Fahrenheit   (b) Zero degrees Fahrenheit

    (c) Seventy degrees Fahrenheit below zero   (d) Fifty degrees Fahrenheit below zero

  (ii)   What are we told about Louise Mallard right at the beginning of the story?

    (a) She is ambitious.   (b) She has a weak heart.

    (c) She loves her husband dearly.   (d) She cannot tolerate noise.

  (iii)   What is the term used for the Man in the short story, *To Build a Fire?*

    (a) Novice   (b) Outsider

    (c) Intruder   (d) Chechaquo

  (iv)   What is the breed of the dog which accompanies the man?

    (a) Wolf   (b) Husky

    (c) Great Dane   (d) Alsatian

  (v)   Who had warned the man against travelling alone in such cold weather?

    (a) His mates   (b) Another traveler

    (c) The Old Timer at Sulphur Creek   (d) His dog

  (vi)   What is Jack London's attitude to the Alaskan wilderness in the short story, *To Build A Fire?*

    (a) Horror   (b) Fear

    (c) Wonder   (d) Respect

  (vii)   In the short story, *The Story of an Hour,* what is Mrs. Mallard's immediate reaction to the news of her husband's death?

    (a) She just stared   (b) She went to her room

    (c) She cried   (d) She refused to believe it

  (viii)   In the short story, *The Story of an Hour,* how was the news of her husband's death broken to Mrs. Mallard?

    (a) It was read out from the newspaper   (b) In a straightforward manner

    (c) Gently and with great care   (d) In a roundabout manner

  (ix)   How many characters are there in the short story, *The Story of an Hour?*

    (a) One   (b) Two

    (c) Three   (d) Four

  (x)   Mrs. Mallard, in the short story, *The Story of an Hour* spreads her arms out. Why does she do so?

    (a) To keep her balance   (b) To welcome her future

    (c) To enjoy the cool breeze   (d) To express her love for her husband

4. Read the lines given below and answer the questions by choosing the correct option after each: **[1×10=10]**

At the man's heels trotted a dog, a big native husky, the proper wolf- dog, gray coated and without any visible or temperamental difference from its brother, the wild wolf. The animal was depressed by the tremendous cold.

  (i)   What was unusual about the man's journey?

    (a) The man did not know the region well.

    (b) He did not have the proper clothes for the weather.

(c) He did not have required resources to reach the destination.

(d) He did not have enough food.

(ii) What is the setting of the story?

(a) In Canada

(b) In the Yukon Valley

(c) In Alaska

(d) In the Arctic regions

(iii) What do you conclude about the relation between the Man and the dog?

(a) There was a close bond between the two.

(b) The dog was merely the toil slave of the man.

(c) The dog was too wild to be tamed by the man.

(d) The man completely ignored the dog.

(iv) What was the dog's instinctive response to the tremendous cold?

(a) The dog was used to the cold and enjoyed it.

(b) The dog's instinct told that it was no time for travelling.

(c) The dog expected the man to keep them both warm.

(d) The dog was indifferent to its surroundings.

(v) In what way was the dog protected against the cold?

(a) It did not feel the cold.

(b) It had a thick coat of fur.

(c) It was used to the cold regions.

(d) The Man was there to protect it.

(vi) In what way did the dog come in useful to the Man at one point in the journey?

(a) It helped him to build the fire.

(b) It offered him silent companionship.

(c) It was made to go ahead to ascertain where the dangerous spots were.

(d) It gave the man warmth when the man became numb because of the cold.

(vii) The Man laughs off the advice given to him by the Old Timer. Which attribute of his character does this showcase?

(a) He is able to appreciate humour.

(b) He does not have the intelligence to understand.

(c) He is arrogant and too confident of himself to pay heed to others.

(d) He is not a good listener.

(viii) What did the dog do while the Man had his lunch?

(a) It kept watching the man.

(b) It yearned for food.

(c) It burrowed in the snow.

(d) It kept looking in the direction of the camp.

(ix) Why did the Man have to build a fire before having his lunch?

(a) He wanted to eat his food in comfort.

(b) He had to thaw himself out.

(c) He felt the fire would dispel the cold.

(d) The Old Timer had told him to do so.

(x) What is the theme of this story?

(a) The ignorance of Man

(b) The overconfidence of Man

(c) The conflict between Man and Nature

(d) Nature as an enemy of Man

5. Fill in the missing information from the story *"The Story of an Hour"*. **[1×5=5]**

(i) Mrs. Mallard was informed of her husband's death by……..

(a) Josephine

(b) Richards

(c) the newspapers

(d) Neighbours

(ii) The news of her husband's death was broken gently to her because……..

(a) she loved her husband dearly

(b) she had a weak heart

(c) they wanted to protect her

(d) they didn't want her to faint

(iii) Upon hearing the news, Louise Mallard...........

    (a) broke into a storm of weeping   (b) refused to believe the news

    (c) cried out her husband's name   (d) left the house immediately

(iv) Mrs. Mallard welcomed the future stretching before her because..........

    (a) she could be free to lead a life on her terms

    (b) she could spend as much money she wished.

    (c) she did not need to listen to a man

    (d) she could travel to far off places.

(v) At the end of the story, the reader.........

    (a) understands Louise Mallard's state of mind.

    (b) feels sorry for Louise Mallard.

    (c) empathises with her longing for independence.

    (d) All of the above

SECTION-C

REVERIE–POETRY

6. Choose the correct option after each question: **[1×10=10]**

(i) In the poem, *Crossing the Bar*, which voyage is the poet referring to?

    (a) The voyage from life to death.   (b) The voyage from the known to the unknown.

    (c) The voyage of self-discovery.   (d) The voyage of adventure.

(ii) Which childhood memory is the poet reminded of when he sees the bent birches in the poem, *Birches*?

    (a) Playing in the open countryside.   (b) Swinging on the birch branches.

    (c) Simple games of rural children.   (d) Playing hide and seek in his childhood.

(iii) What does the word 'coppice' mean in the first line of the poem, *The Darkling Thrush*?

    (a) A dense forest.   (b) Shrubs and bushes in the countryside.

    (c) An area of woodland.   (d) Trees.

(iv) In the poem *Birches*, what does the act of swinging symbolize?

    (a) The desire for radical political changes.   (b) The desire to change society.

    (c) The desire to escape reality.   (d) The alteration of hope and despair.

(v) In the poem *Birches*, what happens to the branches when they are bent too far?

    (a) They break   (b) They snap

    (c) They remain bent.   (d) They grow in another direction.

(vi) What does 'clear call' refer to in the poem, *Crossing the Bar*?

    (a) The call of friends.   (b) The call of Life.

    (c) The call of Duty.   (d) The call of Death.

(vii) In which context is the word "embark' used in the poem *Crossing the Bar*?

    (a) To take a ride   (b) To set out on the final journey

    (c) To walk.   (d) To end a journey.

(viii) What is NOT TRUE about the poet's desire about his voyage in *Crossing the Bar*?

    (a) He wants no sadness of farewell.

    (b) He wants a smooth passage.

    (c) He wants people to celebrate his passing.

    (d) He does not want any moaning of the bar.

(ix) What impression does the poet create at the beginning of the poem, *The Darkling Thrush*?

    (a) Of bleakness and desolation.   (b) Of warmth and cheerfulness.

    (c) Of hope and happiness   (d) None of these

(x)   Why had people "sought their household fires" in the poem *The Darkling Thrush*?

    (a) The cold forbidding atmosphere drove them inside.

    (b) They sought the warmth and fellowship of their fellowmen.

    (c) Their household fires were their only source of hope and sustenance.

    (d) All of the above.

7. Read the lines given below and answer the questions that follow by choosing the correct option after each:

[1×10=10]

> *An aged thrush, frail, gaunt and small,*
> *In blast – beruffled plume,*
> *Had chosen thus to fling his soul*
> *Upon the growing gloom*

(i)   What was the poet doing when he heard the thrush?

    (a) He was walking in the woods.   (b) He was leaning on a coppice gate.

    (c) He was looking at the winter sky.   (d) He was looking at the bare branches.

(ii) What did the poet say about the other human beings?

    (a) The human beings were also walking in the woods.

    (b) They had sought the warmth of their household fires.

    (c) They were expressing their sadness about the current situation.

    (d) They were making merry.

(iii) Where was the aged thrush?

    (a) In the woods   (b) Among the leaves.

    (c) Among the bare branches.   (d) Hiding in the bushes.

(iv) Which words does the poet use to describe the bird's song?

    (a) A plaintive lament   (b) Happiness unbounded

    (c) Full-hearted evensong   (d) A dirge

(v)   How does the tone of the poem change with the reference to the bird?

    (a) From sadness to happiness   (b) From negativity to positivity

    (c) From despondency to hope   (d) There is no change

(vi) What does the "growing gloom" symbolize?

    (a) The feeling of sadness   (b) The feeling of despair

    (c) A growing sense of optimism.   (d) A feeling of concern.

(vii) What is meant by "blast- beruffled"?

    (a) Blasted by the wind   (b) Distressed by the blast

    (c) Disturbed by the wind   (d) None of the above

(viii) Why was the poet surprised upon noticing the "aged thrush"?

    (a) The whole area was deserted.

    (b) It was too cold for anyone to be around.

    (c) The thrush was too old and frail to be out in such weather.

    (d) All of the above

(ix) What is the poet's reaction upon listening to the bird's song?

    (a) Happiness.   (b) Surprise and wonder

    (c) Gloominess   (d) Indifference

(x)   Why are the words, "chosen thus" significant in the poem?

    (a) In spite of the gloom and despair, the bird chooses to sing joyously.

    (b) The bird seems to believe that all is not lost.

    (c) Through these words, the poet seems to say that there is hope amidst the gloom.

    (d) All of the above

8. Given below are sentences from the poem *"Crossing the Bar"*.
   Fill in the gaps in the sentences from the options given after each: [1×5=5]
   (i)   Sunset and……….
          (a) darkness   (b) sleep
          (c) call of death   (d) evening star
   (ii)   And one………. for me.
          (a) opportunity   (b) clear call
          (c) more night   (d) more voyage
   (iii) When I …….. to sea?
          (a) set out for   (b) put out
          (c) travel   (d) go out
   (iv)   Too full for…………….
          (a) any sound   (b) sound and foam
          (c) any disturbance   (d) the crashing waves
   (v)   Twilight and ………….
          (a) shadow   (b) sadness
          (c) evening bell   (d) the noises of people

Answers

SECTION-A
THE TEMPEST

1. (i)   (b) Gathering wood   (ii) (c) To test his sincerity in love.
   (iii) (b) A patient log-man   (iv) (c) His best aspirations may be inverted to mischief.
   (v)   (b) Admired   (vi) (b) He had drunk so much that he could not speak.
   (vii) (a) Savagery   (viii) (c) He is exhausted.
   (ix) (b) Ferdinand
   (x)   (b) About making another attempt to murder Alonso.

2. **(A)**
   (i)   (a) Ferdinand   (ii) (a) Ferdinand reciprocates her love.
   (iii) (d) She is compassionate.   (iv) (b) He is happy with her.
   (v)   (c) She is conniving   (vi) (b) Pure souls
   (vii) (a) For the love that is growing between the young couple.
   (viii) (a) She asks him to make her his wife.
   (ix)   (a) He is willing to do the humble task for her in spite of being a Prince.
   (x)   (c) Half an hour later
   (B)
   (i)   (c) Strange shapes bringing in a banquet.
   (ii)   (a) Pleasure
   (iii) (b) Unicorns and the Phoenix.
   (iv)   (b) He feels that they are islanders.
   (v)   (c) Prospero
   (vi)   (a) The signs made by the creatures.
   (vii) (b) Viands
   (viii) (a) In their youth they had heard tales of strange people.
   (ix)   (c) Suddenly the food vanishes
   (x)   (d) He tries to find good in everything.

SECTION-B
ECHOES–SHORT STORIES

3. (i) (d) Fifty degrees Fahrenheit below zero   (ii) (b) She has a weak heart.

(iii) (d) Chechaquo   (iv) (b) Husky

(v) (c) The Old Timer at Sulphur Creek   (vi) (d) Respect

(vii) (c) She cried   (viii) (c) Gently and with great care

(ix) (d) four   (x) (b) To welcome her future

4. (i) (a) The man did not know the region well.

(ii) (b) In the Yukon Valley

(iii) (b) The dog was merely the toil slave of the man.

(iv) (b) The dog's instinct told that it was no time for travelling.

(v) (b) It had a thick coat of fur.

(vi) (c) It was made to go ahead to ascertain where the dangerous spots were.

(vii) (c) He is arrogant and too confident of himself to pay heed to others.

(viii) (a) It kept watching the man.

(ix) (a) He had to thaw himself out.

(x) (c) The conflict between Man and Nature

5. (i) (a) Josephine   (ii) (b) she had a weak heart

(iii) (a) broke into a storm of weeping   (iv) (a) she could be free to lead a life on her terms

(v) (d) All of the above

SECTION-C
REVERIE–POETRY

6. (i) (a) The voyage from life to death.   (ii) (b) Swinging on the birch branches.

(iii) (a) A dense forest.   (iv) (c) The desire to escape reality.

(v) (c) They remain bent.   (vi) (d) The call of Death.

(vii) (d) To end a journey.   (viii) (d) He does not want any moaning of the bar.

(ix) (a) Of bleakness and desolation.

(x) (c) Their household fires were their only source of hope and sustenance.

7. (i) (b) He was leaning on a coppice gate.

(ii) (b) They had sought the warmth of their household fires.

(iii) (c) Among the bare branches.   (iv) (c) Full-hearted evensong

(v) (c) From despondency to hope   (vi) (c) A growing sense of optimism.

(vii) (c) Disturbed by the wind   (viii) (d) All of the above

(ix) (b) Surprise and wonder   (x) (d) All of the above

8. (i) (d) evening star   (ii) (b) clear call

(iii) (b) put out   (iv) (b) sound and foam

(v) (c) evening bell

❑❑

SECTION–A
THE TEMPEST

Question 1

Choose the correct option given below each question:

(i) What does Miranda offer to do for Ferdinand?
- (a) Miranda agrees to Marry Ferdinand
- (b) Miranda cries out of her happiness and reveals name to Ferdinand
- (c) Miranda offers to carry Ferdinand's logs
- (d) Miranda escapes out in silence for Ferdinand's honour

(ii) What does Ariel do in Act III Scene II to lead the men astray and interrupt their plans?
- (a) Becomes invisible
- (b) Beats them
- (c) Ventriloquizes
- (d) Plays music

(iii) Who says, ``I am a fool. To weep at what I am glad of.'' Identify the speaker.
- (a) Brently Mallard
- (b) Miranda
- (c) Richards
- (d) Ferdinand

(iv) ``*This will I tell my master.''* Who is the ``master'' here ?
- (a) Prospero
- (b) Ariel
- (c) Caliban
- (d) Stephano

(v) Who said the following lines and to whom:

Honest lord,

Thou hast said well; for some of you there present

Are worse than devils
- (a) Antonio to himself
- (b) Gonzalo to himself
- (c) Prospero to himself
- (d) Alonso to himself

(vi) *My husband, then* ? Who said this to whom?
- (a) Miranda to Ferdinand
- (b) Miranda to Caliban
- (c) Miranda to Stephano
- (d) Miranda to Prospero

(vii) *As I told thee before, I am subject to a tyrant, a sorcerer.* To whom Caliban says this line?
- (a) Ariel
- (b) Stephano
- (c) Trinculo
- (d) Miranda

(viii) Miranda *addressing* Ferdinand. The word addressing signifies:
- (a) to shout on someone
- (b) to call someone
- (c) to hide someone
- (d) to speak to someone

(ix) Who is afraid of the mysterious music of Ariel's pipe?
- (a) Stephano and Caliban
- (b) Ferdinand and Miranda
- (c) Stephano and Trinculo
- (d) Miranda and Prospero

(x) What does Trinculo say about Caliban?

    (a) Caliban should plot against Ferdinand

    (b) Caliban's eye should be set in tail rather than in his head

    (c) Caliban is the king of the island

    (d) Caliban's mother Sycorax is more beautiful than Miranda

Question 2

Read the lines given below and choose the correct option given after each question.

A. *Miranda: I do not know*

One of my sex; no woman's face remember,

Save, from my glass, mine own, nor have I seen

More than I may call men than you, good friend

(i) Why was Miranda not able to see many faces in her life?

    (a) She was arrogant and didn't like the company.

    (b) She was an introvert.

    (c) She lived with her father alone.

    (d) She hated her family members.

(ii) How has Ferdinand expressed his love for Miranda?

    (a) He worked with her and helped her in chores.

    (b) He was mesmerized by Miranda's beauty.

    (c) He declared his love at first sight.

    (d) He eloped with her.

(iii) How does Miranda respond to Ferdinand's declaration of love to her?

    (a) She starts weeping out of love.

    (b) She runs from the island.

    (c) She denies to Ferdinand.

    (d) She screams out of joy.

(iv) As a reader, what opinion about Miranda's personality can be drawn from her speech?

    (a) She is simple

    (b) She is compassionate

    (c) She is an ambitious woman

    (d) She is indifferent

(v) Who is the architect of this romantic plot in the story?

    (a) Ariel   (b) Ferdinand

    (c) Prospero   (d) Gonzalo

(vi) What does Miranda do when Ferdinand says that he loves her?

    (a) Sneers   (b) Proposes marriage

    (c) Run away   (d) Says nothing

(vii) Ferdinand shares a Latin root word to describe Miranda. Which word does he use?

    (a) Beautiful   (b) Admired

    (c) Dearest   (d) Royal

(viii) Which word in the given extract means—``recollect''?

    (a) Remember   (b) Know

    (c) Call   (d) Friend

(ix) Miranda is the daughter of:

    (a) Stephano   (b) Antonio

    (c) Prospero   (d) Ariel

(x) Who is the hero of this romantic plot?

    (a) Stephano   (b) Ariel

    (c) Ferdinand   (d) Prospero

B. *Trinculo: Servant monster? the folly of this island!*

They say there's but five upon this isle:

We are three of them; if th' other two

be brain'd like us, the state totters.

(i) Who are the ``three of them'' from the given extract?

    (a) Stephano, Ariel and Caliban   (b) Stephano, Caliban and Trinculo

    (c) Caliban, Antonio and Ferdinand   (d) Gonzalo, Stephano and Trinculo

(ii) Who are the ``other two'' in the given extract to which Trinculo refers to ?

    (a) Prospero and Miranda   (b) Caliban and Trinculo

    (c) Prospero and Ariel   (d) Caliban and Gonzalo

(iii) The phrase—``Servant monster'' refers to:

    (a) Ariel   (b) Antonio

    (c) Prospero   (d) Caliban

(iv) Why is Caliban's eye set in his head?

    (a) Because he is an invisible man.

    (b) Because he is an evil monster.

    (c) Because he is half monster and half human.

    (d) Because he is a giant human.

(v) Which character brings out the humor in the given extract?

    (a) Ariel   (b) Trinculo

    (c) Prospero   (d) Gonzalo

(vi) Who wants to be the King of Naples?

    (a) Gonzalo   (b) Caliban

    (c) Sebastian   (d) Antonio

(vii) Who wants to kill Prospero and prepare his murder's plot?

    (a) Antonio   (b) Ariel

    (c) Trinculo   (d) Caliban

(viii) The word `folly' here means:

    (a) fool   (b) wise

    (c) intellectual   (d) angry

(ix) Who want to kill Alonso during his sleep?

    (a) Caliban   (b) Sebastian

    (c) Gonzalo   (d) Prospero

(x) Who is supposed to be disproportionate in shape?

    (a) Alonso   (b) Antonio

    (c) Prospero   (d) Caliban

SECTION–B

ECHOES—SHORT STORIES

Question 3

(i) How, according to London, does the dog know about the danger of the cold?

    (a) It has lived in the cold for considerable time.

    (b) It has studied the land well.

    (c) It has received the knowledge from the man.

    (d) It has inherited sound knowledge of the cold.

(ii) Mrs. Mallard in *The Story of an Hour* suffers from:

    (a) heart disease

    (b) lung disease

    (c) pneumonia

    (d) tuberculosis

(iii) Against whom the man's struggle is, in the short story, *To Build a Fire* ?

    (a) nature

    (b) life's hardships

    (c) women

    (d) his fate

(iv) What is Mrs. Mallard a victim of, in the short story, *The Story of an Hour*?

    (a) existing societal issues, dizziness

    (b) prevalent social norms, values

    (c) loneliness, depression

    (d) harassment, abuse

(v) The Yukon lay a mile wide and hidden under three feet of ice.

From the given line identify the work and the author/poet/writer.

    (a) To build a fire—written by Victorian writer.

    (b) Tempest—written by Victorian writer.

    (c) To Build to Fire—written by American novelist.

    (d) Tempest—written by American novelist.

(vi) Her fancy was running riot along those days ahead of her. Identify the work and author/writer/poet.

    (a) The Story of an Hour—written by feminist author.

    (b) To Build a Fire—written by American novelist.

    (c) The Story of an Hour—written by Victorian writer.

    (d) To Build a Fire—written by feminist author.

(vii) 'He' plunged in among the big spruce trees. Identify 'He'.

    (a) Prospero

    (b) Ferdinand

    (c) The Man

    (d) Richards

(viii) ``She was young, with a fair, calm face, whose lines bespoke repression and even a certain strength''. Who is she ?

    (a) Josephine

    (b) Mrs. Mallard

    (c) Miranda

    (d) Richards' wife

(ix) It was 'he' who had been in the newspaper office when intelligence of the railroad disaster was received. Who is he?

    (a) Louise

    (b) The Man

    (c) Brently Mallard

    (d) Richards

(x) ``*Free ! Body and soul free !*'' Who said this?

    (a) Josephine whispered

    (b) Miranda cried

    (c) Caliban to Trinculo

    (d) Mrs. Mallard whispered

Question 4

Read the lines given below and answer the questions by choosing the correct option after each:

Someone was opening the front door with a latchkey. It was Brently Mallard who entered, a little travel-stained, composedly carrying his grip-sack and umbrella. He had been far from the scene of the accident, and did not even know there had been one. He stood amazed at Josephine's piercing cry; at Richards' quick motion to screen him from the view of his wife.

When the doctors came they said she had died of heart disease–of the joy that kills.

(i) Which literary device is used in ``died of heart disease of the joy that kills''?

    (a) Personification

    (b) Irony

    (c) Simile

    (d) Juxtaposition

(ii) The climax of the story is:
- (a) Brently opening the door
- (b) Mr. Mallard walking through the door
- (c) When doctors said she died of joy
- (d) Richards' quick motion to screen him from the view of his wife

(iii) What is the tone of the story?
- (a) Ironic
- (b) Humorous
- (c) Joyful
- (d) Optimistic

(iv) Identify the veiled hints about Mrs. Mallard from the passage provide.
- (a) Mrs. Mallard was in extreme shock after the demise of her husband
- (b) Mrs. Mallard was the reason of her husband's death
- (c) Mrs. Mallard was unhappy with her married life and she would enjoy complete freedom of body and soul after her husband's death
- (d) Mrs. Mallard was extremely joyous after her husband's death and she was excited to celebrate her freedom.

(v) Who is Richards in the above extract?
- (a) The character whom Mrs. Mallard loved.
- (b) The character who confirmed Brently's death.
- (c) The protagonist of the story.
- (d) The character who killed Brently Mallard.

(vi) What is the irony in the story?
- (a) Involvement of situational and comic irony
- (b) Involvement of verbal irony
- (c) Involvement of comic irony
- (d) Involvement of situational and dramatic irony

(vii) What were the signs of many marriages of the past and present that Mrs. Mallard's marriage showed?
- (a) unhappy
- (b) happy
- (c) satisfactory
- (d) problematic

(viii) A clear and exalted perception enabled her to dismiss the suggestion as trivial. Who is 'her' in the above statement?
- (a) Josephine
- (b) Mrs. Mallard
- (c) Miranda
- (d) Richards' Wife

(ix) ``Go away, I am not making myself ill.'' Who said this to whom?
- (a) Mrs. Mallard to herself
- (b) Mrs. Mallard to Richards
- (c) Mrs. Mallard to Brently
- (d) Mrs. Mallard to Josephine

(x) ``There was something coming to her and she was waiting for it, fearfully.'' What was that which she is afraid from?
- (a) Her survival after husband's death
- (b) She believes it is wrong to be so happy over her husband's death
- (c) She is afraid of loneliness
- (d) She is afraid of her death

Question 5

Fill in the missing information from the story *To Build a Fire*.

(i) ``You were right, old hoss; you were right.'' This line has been said by .... about ....
- (a) Mrs. Mallard, Richards
- (b) The Man, the Sulphur Creek
- (c) Miranda, Ferdinand
- (d) Stephano, Caliban

(ii) Jack London chose to situate his stories ....
- (a) In snowy, sub-freezing world of Yukon
- (b) In the deserted region of Yukon
- (c) In the arid conditions of Japan
- (d) In the busy city life

(iii) The man was not worried, but the dog experienced a vague but menacing .... that caused it to look nervously about.
- (a) monotony
- (b) conscience
- (c) satisfaction
- (d) apprehension

(iv) The man in the short story *To Build a Fire* is travelling with a ....
- (a) cat
- (b) dog
- (c) horse
- (d) camel

(v) He was warned by .... to travel alone in such extreme conditions.
- (a) the dog
- (b) native people of Yukon
- (c) Sulphur Creek
- (d) his boys

SECTION–C
REVERIE—POETRY

Question 6

Choose the correct option after each question:

(i) The beginning of the poem *The Darkling Thrush* reflects:
- (a) motion of amusement
- (b) motion of depression and death
- (c) motion of happiness
- (d) motion of unrealistic world

(ii) What does the ``*act of swinging*'' symbolise in the poem ``Birches''?
- (a) The importance of understanding formal philosophy.
- (b) The importance of scientific truth.
- (c) The desire to escape reality.
- (d) The desire for radical political changes.

(iii) `When I see birches bend to left and right; across the lines of straighter darker trees.' From the given line, identify the poem and the poet/writer.
- (a) Birches—Written by Victorian Writer
- (b) Birches—Written by the recipient of four Pulitzer prizes
- (c) Crossing the Bar—Written by Victorian writer
- (d) Crossing the Bar—Written by the recipient of four Pulitzer Prizes

(iv) Twilight and even bell,

And after that the dark!

Identify the work and the poet.
- (a) Crossing the Bar—Written by Victorian Writer.
- (b) Birches—Written by Victorian Writer.
- (c) Crossing the Bar—Written by an American Novelist.
- (d) The Darkling Thrush—Written by an American Novelist.

(v) Identify the figure of speech used in the line,

``*The tangled bine—stems scored the sky like the strings of broken lyres.*''
- (a) Personification
- (b) Hyperbole
- (c) Metaphor
- (d) Simile

(vi) ``*But such a tide as moving seems asleep.*'' Which figure of speech is used in the given line.
- (a) Assonance
- (b) Personification
- (c) Simile
- (d) Metaphor

(vii) Identify the figure of speech used in the line, ``*They click upon themselves.*''
- (a) Personification
- (b) Assonance
- (c) Onomatopoeia
- (d) Imagery

(viii) Which figure of speech is used in the line `Weakening eye of the day'.

    (a) Alliteration   (b) Symbolism

    (c) Simile   (d) Metaphor

 (ix) Identify the figure of speech in the line, `And there may be no moaning of the bar'.

    (a) Personification   (b) Simile

    (c) Metaphor   (d) Assonance

  (x) How does the poem *Crossing the Bar* begins?

    (a) With sunset and the moon   (b) With sunrise and the morning bliss

    (c) With sunrise and the captivating view   (d) With sunset and the evening star

Question 7

Read the lines given below and answer the questions that follow by choosing the correct option after each:

Often you must have seen them

Loaded with ice a sunny winter morning

After a rain. They click upon themselves

As the breeze rises, and turn many-colored

As the stir cracks and crazes their enamel.

Soon the sun's warmth makes them shed crystal shells

Shattering and avalanching on the snow-crust-

Such heaps of broken glass to sweep away

You'd think the inner dome of heaven had fallen.

  (i) Identify the poem and its poet.

    (a) Birches by Alfred Lord Tennyson

    (b) Crossing the Bar by Thomas Flardy

    (c) Birches by Robert Frost

    (d) Crossing the Bar by Rober Frost

 (ii) ``Cracks and crazes'' shows .... as a literary device.

    (a) onomatopoeia   (b) alliteration

    (c) metaphor   (d) simile

(iii) Choose the best suited option that reveals the closest description of matter of fact or event in the given stanza:

    (a) The process of freezing and thawing of ice

    (b) The process of melting and warmth of sun

    (c) The process of change in season

    (d) The process of appreciating the gift of nature gradually

 (iv) ``A poetic language is used to describe a scientific phenomenon.'' Choose the best appropriate answer.

    (a) Art makes the literal meaning to be more figurative in nature.

    (b) Art makes the reality of the thawing of ice more real.

    (c) Both (a) and (b) are correct

    (d) None of them

  (v) Avalanching refers to:

    (a) Rapid descendance of snow and ice   (b) a man-made disaster

    (c) conversion of water into snow   (d) snowfalling

 (vi) What is the main theme of the poem *Birches* by Robert Frost?

    (a) Inter relationship between human and spirit

    (b) Inter relationship between human and nature

    (c) Inter relationship between imagination and reality

    (d) Inter relationship between men and women

(vii) The poet refers to a colourful/natural phenomenon in the given extract. What is it?

    (a) Ice cubes cracking   (b) The clouds crashing down

    (c) The sun kissed crystals shattering down   (d) A boy riding the branches

(viii) The poet uses a conversational style using `you' several times. Name this type of poem.

    (a) Soliloquy   (b) Dialogue

    (c) Dramatic Monologue   (d) Epic

(ix) ``*When I see birches bend to left and right.*'' The figure of speech used in the line is:

    (a) Assonance   (b) Symbolism

    (c) Alliteration   (d) Metaphor

(x) ``*Life is too much like a pathless wood*''. Which figure of speech is used in the given line.

    (a) Personification   (b) Metaphor

    (c) Simile   (d) Metonymy

Question 8

Given below are sentences from the poem *The Darkling Thrush.*

Fill in the gaps in the sentences from the options given after each:

(i) The Century's .... outleant.

    (a) sharp   (b) corpse

    (c) death   (d) lament

(ii) At once a .... arose.

    (a) rain   (b) voice

    (c) twigs   (d) fires

(iii) And .... dregs made desolate.

    (a) winter   (b) summer

    (c) autumn   (d) hot

(iv) Like .... of broken Lyres.

    (a) strings   (b) thread

    (c) knot   (d) heart

(v) Upon the .... gloom.

    (a) lighted   (b) growing

    (c) ecstatic   (d) carolings

Answers

1. (i) (c) Miranda offers to carry Ferdinand's logs.

  (ii) (d) Plays music

 (iii) (b) Miranda

 (iv) (a) Prospero

  (v) (c) Prospero to himself

 (vi) (a) Miranda to Ferdinand

 (vii) (b) Stephano

(viii)(d) to speak to someone

 (ix) (c) Stephano and Trinculo

  (x) (b) Caliban's eye should be set in tail rather than in his head.

2. (A) (i) (c) She lived with her father alone.

    (ii) (c) He declared his love at first sight.

 (iii) (a) She starts weeping out of love.

 (iv) (a) She is simple

  (v) (c) Prospero

 (vi) (b) Proposes marriage

 (vii) (b) Admired

(viii) (a) Remember

 (ix) (c) Prospero

  (x) (c) Ferdinand

(B) (i) (b) Stephano, Caliban and Trinculo

    (ii) (a) Prospero and Miranda

  (iii) (d) Caliban

  (iv) (c) Because he is half monster and half human.

    (v) (b) Trinculo

    (vi) (c) Sebastian

    (vii) (d) Caliban

    (viii) (a) fool

    (ix) (b) Sebastian

    (x) (d) Caliban

3. (i) (d) It has inherited sound knowledge of the cold

  (ii) (a) heart disease

  (iii) (a) nature

  (iv) (b) prevalent social norms, values

  (v) (c) To Build to Fire—written by American novelist.

  (vi) (a) The Story of an Hour—written by feminist author.

  (vii) (c) The Man

  (viii) (b) Mrs. Mallard

  (ix) (d) Richards

  (x) (d) Mrs. Mallard whispered

4. (i) (b) Irony

  (ii) (b) Mr. Mallard walking through the door

  (iii) (a) Ironic

  (iv) (c) Mrs. Mallard was unhappy with her married life and she would enjoy complete freedom of body and soul after her husband's death.

  (v) (b) The character who confirmed Brently's death

  (vi) (d) Involvement of situational and dramatic irony

  (vii) (a) unhappy

  (viii) (b) Mrs. Mallard

  (ix) (d) Mrs. Mallard to Josephine

  (x) (b) She believes it is wrong to be so happy over her husband's death.

5. (i) (b) The Man, the Sulphur Creek

  (ii) (a) In snowy, sub-freezing world of Yukon

  (iii) (d) apprehension

  (iv) (b) dog

  (v) (c) Sulphur Creek

6. (i) (b) Notion of depression and death

  (ii) (c) The desire to escape reality

  (iii) (b) Birches—Written by the recipient of four Pulitzer prizes

  (iv) (a) Crossing the Bar—Written by Victorian Writer.

  (v) (d) simile

Explanation: A simile is a figure of speech that compares two different things in an interesting way using the word "like' or "as".

  (vi) (b) Personification

Explanation: A personification is a figure of speech in which an idea or thing is given a human attribute and/or feelings or is spoken of as if it were human.

  (vii) (c) Onomatopoeia

Explanation: Onomatopoeia is a figure of speech that describes a sound.

  (viii) (d) Metaphor

Explanation: A metaphor is a figure of speech that is used to make a comparison between two things that aren't alike but do have something in common. Here, the sun is being compared to any.

  (ix) (a) Personification

Explanation: A personification is a figure of speech, in which an idea or thing is govern a human attribute and/or feelings or is spoken of as if it were human.

  (x) (d) With sunset and the evening star.

7. (i) (c) Birches by Robert Frost

  (ii) (b) alliteration.

  (iii) (a) The process of freezing and thawing of ice.

  (iv) (c) Both (a) and (b) are correct.

  (v) (a) Rapid descendance of snow and ice.

  (vi) (c) Inter relationship between imagination and reality.

  (vii) (c) The sun kissed crystals shattering down.

  (viii) (c) Dramatic Monologue.

  (ix) (c) Alliteration

Explanation: It is the repetition of consonant sounds in the same line in quick succession.

  (x) (c) Simile.

Explanation: Simile is a figure of speech in which a similarity between two different objects is explicitly stated using the words 'like' or 'as'.

8. (i) (b) corpse

  (ii) (b) voice

  (iii) (a) winter

  (iv) (a) strings

  (v) (b) growing

❑❑

SECTION–A
THE TEMPEST

Question 1

Choose the correct option given below each question:

(i) How does Prospero acknowledge Miranda and Ferdinand's natural match to be?

    (a) rarest of the rare

    (b) of two most rare affections

    (c) of the heaven's gift

    (d) made for each other

(ii) How does Miranda react when she sees Ferdinand working?

    (a) she feels depressed when she sees him doing tasks

    (b) she feels distressed when she sees him doing tasks

    (c) she feels overjoyed on seeing him working

    (d) she expresses her concern about his ill health

(iii) Prospero says of Miranda as 'infected'. What is she infected with?

    (a) love   (b) cold

    (c) instincts of a poor   (d) some disease

(iv) *Moon calf, speak once in thy life, if thou beest a good moon calf.* For whom, is the 'moon-calf' used?

    (a) Caliban   (b) Stephano

    (c) Trinculo   (d) Ariel

(v) Name the invisible character in *The Tempest*.

    (a) Ferdinand   (b) Prospero

    (c) Stephano   (d) Ariel

(vi) *How does thy honour? Let me lick thy shoe, I'll not serve him, he is not valiant.* Who said the given line and to whom?

    (a) Stephano to Caliban   (b) Trinculo to Caliban

    (c) Caliban to Trinculo   (d) Caliban to Stephano

(vii) *He that dies pays all debts. I defy thee. Mercy upon us !* Who says this line?

    (a) Ariel   (b) Stephano

    (c) Trinculo   (d) Caliban

(viii) *What harmony is this? My good friends, hark!* What ``harmony'' is the speaker talking about?

    (a) banquet   (b) drollery

    (c) strange music   (d) strange shapes

(ix) ``*Give us kind keepers, heavens! What were these?*'' What are ``these'' in the given line?

    (a) drollery   (b) strange shapes

    (c) banquet   (d) magical books

(x) What is 'unicorn' in *The Tempest*?

(a) Name of a bird
(b) Name of a character
(c) Name of Ariel's friend
(d) Name of a mythical animal

Question 2

Read the lines given below and choose the correct option given after each question.

A. *Caliban—``I say, by sorcery he got this isle;*

From me he got it. If thy greatness will

Revenge it on him—for I know thou dar'st

But this thing dare not—

(i) Name the character who got the island by sorcery.

(a) Antonio
(b) Prospero
(c) Alonso
(d) Gonzalo

(ii) Identify the name of Caliban's mother.

(a) Sychoma
(b) Sycorax
(c) Sychilie
(d) Syromace

(iii) How did Prospero capture the island from Caliban?

(a) Through warfare
(b) By murder
(c) Through magic
(d) By killing his mother

(iv) According to Caliban, who should be legal propertier of the island?

(a) Prospero
(b) Antonio
(c) Alonso
(d) Stephano

(v) What is Caliban's plan?

(a) To kill Ferdinand
(b) To kill Prospero
(c) To kill Gonzalo
(d) To kill Stephano

(vi) What did Caliban tell Stephano?

(a) To steal the magical books of Prospero
(b) To steal the wooden logs of Prospero
(c) To save him from his brother
(d) To elope with Miranda

(vii) The speaker Caliban says the above mentioned lines to :

(a) Prospero
(b) Ariel
(c) Trinculo
(d) Stephano

(viii) Why does Stephano beat Trinculo?

(a) Stephano thinks that Trinculo is planning murder against him
(b) Stephano thinks Trinculo is mocking Caliban by calling him liar
(c) Stephano assumes Trinculo is making fun of him by calling him coward
(d) Stephano thinks Trinculo is calling him liar

(ix) Why are Prospero's books important for the plot?

(a) Because without his books, Prospero faints out
(b) Because without his books, Prospero forgets his memory
(c) Because without his books, Prospero has no magical powers
(d) All of the above

(x) Why is Caliban unable to walk in the beginning of the scene?

(a) Caliban is too drunk to walk
(b) Caliban is weak enough
(c) Caliban has met with an accident

    (d) Caliban is disinterested to walk

B. *First to possess his books, for without them He's but a sot, as I am; nor hath not one spirit to command: they all do hate him*

    As rootedly as I, Burn but his books..

(i) Who is the speaker?

    (a) Alonso   (b) Stephano

    (c) Caliban   (d) Gonzalo

(ii) What is Stephano requested to do?

    (a) Steal Prospero's magical books and marry Miranda

    (b) Become the king of the island

    (c) Both (a) and (b)

    (d) None of the above

(iii) The speaker tells to `possess his books'. Why ?

    (a) because without his books he has no knowledge

    (b) because without his books he is dumb

    (c) because without his books he does not have magical powers

    (d) because those are borrowed books and stealing them will make the owner angry

(iv) What does Prospero call his daughter?

    (a) Beautiful   (b) Nonpareil

    (c) Ambitious woman   (d) Brave utensil

(v) To whom does Caliban compare Miranda's beauty?

    (a) to a flower   (b) to his aunt

    (c) to his mother   (d) to moon

(vi) Which time is best suited to assassinate Prospero?

    (a) noon   (b) midnight

    (c) early morning   (d) late evening

(vii) Give the meaning of the word as used in the context of the passage ``rootedly''.

    (a) artificially   (b) superficially

    (c) narrow   (d) deeply

(viii) Which word is close to the meaning of word ``nonpareil''?

    (a) mediocre   (b) incomparable

    (c) usual   (d) worst

(ix) Why is the island known to be enchanted?

    (a) It is haunted

    (b) Many spirits dwell on it

    (c) It is actually a graveyard

    (d) None of the above

(x) Who is Prospero's spirit?

    (a) Caliban   (b) Stephano

    (c) Ariel   (d) Trinculo

SECTION–B

ECHOES — SHORT STORIES

Question 3

(i) What leads to the death of the Man in the short story, *To build a fire*?

    (a) He was shot dead by a stranger

    (b) He met with an accident

(c) His clothes caught fire and he was burnt badly

(d) He was unable to light a fire that could aid his survival

(ii) What happens at the end of the short story, *The Story of an Hour*?

(a) Husband comes back home alive

(b) Husband's dead body was brought home

(c) Mrs. Mallard was happy at the end

(d) Mrs. Mallard and Brently Mallard united at the end

(iii) How does Mrs. Mallard feel after his husband's death?

(a) ``joy that kills''

(b) ``Body and soul free''

(c) ``new spring of life''

(d) ``Bound and depressed''

(iv) Which words in the short story, *To Build a Fire* best suits to describe—It is important to take precautions while travelling against freezing snow.

(a) Imperative

(b) Peremptorily

(c) Intangible

(d) Comparative

(v) *``Day had broken cold and gray''.*

The above given line depict the regions of ...., mentioned in the story of ....

(a) Alaska, Kate Chopin

(b) Yukon, Jack London

(c) Yukon, Thomas Hardy

(d) Yukon, Robert Frost

(vi) What is Jack London's attitude to the Alaskan wilderness in the short story, *To Build a Fire*?

(a) Horror

(b) Respect

(c) Fear

(d) Wonder

(vii) A *chechaquo* to the Yukon. Identify the character.

(a) The Dog

(b) The Old Man

(c) The Lady

(d) The Man

(viii) How does Louise Mallard characterise human relationships in the short story *The Story of an Hour* ?

(a) As a necessity

(b) As a gift

(c) As a puzzle

(d) As a crime

(ix) In what current state does the story *To Build a Fire* take place?

(a) Alaska

(b) The Yukon

(c) North Dakota

(d) New York

(x) What does Louise do after hearing her husband's name in the list of ``killed''?

(a) Kills herself

(b) Gets fainted

(c) Decided to leave the house

(d) Weeps and goes to her room

Question 4

Read the lines given below and answer the questions by choosing the correct option after each:

It was her sister Josephine who told her, in broken sentences; veiled hints that revealed in half concealing. Her husband's friend Richards was there, too, near her. It was he who had been in the newspaper office when intelligence of the railroad disaster was received, with Brently Mallard's name leading the list of "killed." He had only taken the time to assure himself of its truth by a second telegram, and had hastened to forestall any less careful, less tender friend in bearing the sad message.

(i) Where did Mrs Mallard go when she heard the news of her husband's death?

(a) To her room

(b) To bathroom

(c) To prayer-room

(d) To kitchen

(ii) Mrs. Mallard was afflicted with ____________.

(a) Cancer

(b) TB

(c) Heart trouble

(d) Jaundice

(iii) What is Mrs Mallard's response to her husband's death?

(a) Sorrow

(b) Anger

    (c) Sadness   (d) Joy

(iv) What does NOT characterise Mrs Mallard's face?

    (a) Repression   (b) Calmness

    (c) Depression   (d) Strength

(v) What emotion does Louise feel toward her husband?

    (a) Fear   (b) Hatred

    (c) Companionship   (d) Love

(vi) Louise's composure as she descends the stairs can be defined as:

    (a) Prideful vindication   (b) Pretentious

    (c) Tension and apprehensiveness   (d) A Renewed liveliness

(vii) Louise Mallard approaches an awakening after hearing the news of her husband's death. What is the most prominent reoccurring theme?

    (a) Hopefulness   (b) Freedom

    (c) Acceptance   (d) Depression

(viii) What is Mr Mallard's first name?

    (a) John   (b) Brently

    (c) Richards   (d) Charles

(ix) The author's portrayal of the story expects the reader to reflect on the experiences of Louise Mallard with

    (a) Ridicule   (b) Understanding

    (c) Admiration   (d) Ironic detachment

(x) Why was there "feverish triumph" in Mrs. Mallard's eyes?

    (a) because she finally killed her husband

    (b) because she has won a jackpot

    (c) because she was happy to hear her husband's return

    (d) because she finally felt free

Question 5

Fill in the missing information from the story *To Build a Fire*.

(i) The man got wet upto his________.

    (a) knee   (b) waist

    (c) chest   (d) thighs

(ii) The man in the story was a novice who lacked in______.

    (a) Intellect   (b) Knowledge

    (c) Experience   (d) Strength

(iii) The actual temperature of the place was _____ below zero.

    (a) 50 degrees   (b) 107 degrees

    (c) 75 degrees   (d) 80 degrees

(iv) The man built the fire under ______ tree.

    (a) fir   (b) pine

    (c) oak   (d) spruce

(v) In the story, London has used fire as a symbol of _____.

    (a) comfort   (b) life

    (c) power   (d) warmth

SECTION–C

REVERIE—POETRY

Question 6

Choose the correct option after each question:

(i) What is the Sunset compared with in the poem *The Darkling Thrush*?

    (a)   tangled stems of bushes

    (b)   the weakening eye of the day

    (c)   mankind

    (d)   ancient pulse of germ and birth

(ii) In the poem, *The Darkling Thrush* nature can be depressing as hell, as quoted in the line :

    (a)   The weakening eye of the day   (b)   His happy good night air

    (c)   Some blessed hope, where of he knew   (d)   In a full-hearted eversong of joy illimited

(iii) Thomas Hardy has written *The Darkling Thrush* at the turn of what?

    (a)   Sunrise, sunset   (b)   Morning, night

    (c)   century, millennium   (d)   darkness, light

(iv) The line ``Its crypt the cloudy canopy'' has been taken from ...., whose poet is ....

    (a)   Crossing the Bar   :   Alfred Lord Tennyson

    (b)   Birches   :   Thomas Hardy

    (c)   Crossing the Bar   :   Robert Frost

    (d)   The Darkling Thrush :   Thomas Hardy

(v) ``The land's sharp features seemed to be, the Century's corpse outlet.'' Which figure of speech is used in the given line?

    (a)   Simile   (b)   Symbolism

    (c)   Metaphor   (d)   Personification

(vi) Identify the figure of speech used in the line, ``Some blessed hope, whereof he knew And I was unaware''.

    (a)   Assonance   (b)   Enjambment

    (c)   Personification   (d)   Simile

(vii) Which form of poetry is *The Darkling Thrush*?

    (a)   elegy   (b)   pastoral elegy

    (c)   eclogue   (d)   dramatic monologue

(viii) Which is the right place for love according to the given line from the poem `Birches' ?

    .... the right place for love:

    I don't know where its likely to go better.

    (a)   Garden's   (b)   Earth's

    (c)   Beach's   (d)   Heaven's

(ix) ``I'd like to get away from earth awhile and then come back to it and begin over''.

    The following lines are from .... and is written by ....

    (a)   Birches, Robert Frost   (b)   Crossing the bar, Kate Chopin

    (c)   The Story of an Hour, Thomas Hardy   (d)   Birches, Robert Frost

(x) ``When that which drew from out the boundless deep

    Turns again home.''

    The following lines are from ....

    Written by ...., who wrote ....

    (a)   Birches, Alfred Lord Tennyson, In Memorium

    (b)   The Darkling Rush, Jack London, Yukon

    (c)   Crossing The Bar, Alfred Lord Tennyson, In Memorium.

    (d)   Birches, Robert Frost, In Memorium.

Question 7

Read the lines given below and answer the questions that follow by choosing the correct option after each:

I leant upon a coppice gate

    When Frost was spectre-grey,

And Winter's dregs made desolate

The weakening eye of day.
The tangled bine-stems scored the sky
  Like strings of broken lyres,
And all mankind that haunted nigh
  Had sought their household fires.

(i) *"I leant upon a coppice gate"*. What is the meaning of leant upon?

   (a) Bent upon   (b) Laid

   (c) Sat   (d) None of the above

(ii) Coppice means:

   (a) Trees

   (b) Crow

   (c) Bird

   (d) Small woodland area of undergrowth and small trees

(iii) The phrase "spectre- grey means:

   (a) Grey ghost   (b) As grey as spectre

   (c) Grey spectre   (d) Spectre having grey colour

(iv) How did the bine-stem score the sky?

   (a) Like a designed canopy   (b) Like strings of a lyre

   (c) Like strings of broken lyres   (d) Like the design of the logo

(v) Why is the eye of the day weakening?

   (a) Due to the time of the dawn   (b) Due to the time of twilight

   (c) Due to the bad weather of the day   (d) Due to the season of winter

(vi) In *The Darkling Thrush*, when the poet is lost in his thoughts, he suddenly hears a shrill happy note of a/an ....

   (a) trees   (b) piano

   (c) Thrush   (d) birds

(vii) The above lines have been taken from the poem .... written by ....

   (a) The Darkling Thrush, Thomas Hardy   (b) Birches, Robert Frosts

   (c) Crossing the Bar, Kate Chopin   (d) Birches, Thomas Hardy

(viii) ``*And all mankind that haunted nigh*" the phrase haunted nigh refers to:

   (a) Deserted recently   (b) Become victims

   (c) Reside nearby   (d) Out of the house

(ix) Who comprises the death-lament of the dead century?

   (a) The thrush   (b) The wind

   (c) The cloudy sky   (d) The poetic persona

(x) ``*His crypt the cloudy canopy*". Here the word crypt means:

   (a) mansion   (b) cover

   (c) vault or dome   (d) manuscript

Question 8

Given below are sentences from the poem *Crossing the Bar*.

Fill in the gaps in the sentences from the options given after each.

(i) And one clear .... for me!

   (a) call   (b) moaning

   (c) morning   (d) tide

(ii) When I put out to ....

   (a) river   (b) sea

   (c) home   (d) god

(iii) I hope to see my .... face to face.
    (a) Pilot   (b) Survivor
    (c) God   (d) Protector

(iv) When I have .... the bar.
    (a) Cross   (b) Crost
    (c) Crossing   (d) Turned

(v) Too full for .... and foam.
    (a) noise   (b) time
    (c) place   (d) sound

Answers

1. (i) (b) of two most rare affections
  (ii) (b) she feels distressed when she sees him doing tasks
  (iii) (a) love
  (iv) (a) Caliban
  (v) (d) Ariel
  (vi) (d) Caliban to Stephano
  (vii) (b) Stephano
  (viii) (c) strange music
  (ix) (b) strange shapes
  (x) (d) Name of a mythical animal

2. (A) (i) (b) Prospero
    (ii) (b) Sycorax
    (iii) (c) Through magic
    (iv) (d) Stephano
    (v) (b) To kill Prospero
    (vi) (a) To steal the magical books of Prospero
    (vii) (d) Stephano
    (viii) (b) Stephano thinks Trinculo is mocking Caliban by calling him liar
    (ix) (c) Because without his books, Prospero has no magical powers
    (x) (a) Caliban is too drunk to walk

  (B) (i) (c) Caliban
    (ii) (c) Both (a) and (b)
    (iii) (c) because without his books he does not has magical powers
    (iv) (b) Nonpareil
    (v) (c) to his mother
    (vi) (a) noon
    (vii) (d) deeply
    (viii) (b) incomparable
    (ix) (b) Many spirits dwell on it
    (x) (c) Ariel

3. (i) (d) He was unable to light a fire that could aid his survival
  (ii) (a) Husband comes back home alive
  (iii) (b) ``Body and Soul free''
  (iv) (a) Imperative
  (v) (b) Yukon, Jack London
  (vi) (b) Respect
  (vii) (d) The Man
  (viii) (c) As a puzzle
  (ix) (a) Alaska
  (x) (d) Weeps and goes to her room

4. (i) (a) To her room
  (ii) (c) Heart trouble
  (iii) (d) Joy
  (iv) (c) Depression
  (v) (d) Love
  (vi) (a) Prideful vindication
  (vii) (b) Freedom
  (viii) (b) Brently
  (ix) (b) Understanding
  (x) (d) because she finally felt free

5. (i) (a) knee
  (ii) (c) Experience
  (iii) (c) 75 degrees
  (iv) (d) spruce
  (v) (b) life

6. (i) (b) the weakening eye of the day.
  (ii) (a) The weakening eye of the day.
  (iii) (c) century, millennium.
  (iv) (d) The Darkling Thrush : Thomas Hardy.
  (v) (b) Symbolism

    Explanation: It is applied only to a phrase or a word that represents any event or any object which in turn depicts something, or suggests a range of reference, or beyond imagination or itself.

(vi) (c) Personification

Explanation: Here, hope is personified. Personification is a figure on speech where any non-living entity or any feeling is compared to a Human. Here, hope is regarded as a sentient being.

(vii) (a) elegy

Explanation: An elegy is a poem written to lament the death of a poem.

(viii)(b) Earth's

(ix) (a) Birches, Robert Frost

(x) (c) Crossing The Bar, Alfred Lord Tennyson, In Memoriam

7. (i) (b) Laid

(ii) (d) Small woodland area of undergrowth and small trees

(iii) (b) As grey as spectre

(iv) (c) Like strings of broken lyres

(v) (d) Due to the season of winter

(vi) (c) Thrush

(vii) (a) The Darkling Thrush, Thomas Hardy

(viii) (c) Reside nearby

(ix) (b) The wind

(x) (c) vault or dome

8. (i) (a) call

(ii) (b) sea

(iii) (a) pilot

(iv) (b) crost

(v) (d) sound

❑❑

SECTION–A

THE TEMPEST

Question 1

Choose the correct option given below each question:

(i) What title does Stephano assume in Act III, Scene II ?

(a) King of the Island   (b) Lord of the Island

(c) Lord of the Tempest   (d) King of Naples

(ii) Whom did Prospero bring to the isolated island for punishing?

(a) Alonso, Antonio and Sebastian   (b) Ariel, Alonso and Sebastian

(c) Alonso, Trinculo and Gonzalo   (d) Antonio, Stephano and Trinculo

(iii) Who was the honest and trusted advisor to king Alonso of Naples?

(a) Trinculo   (b) Stephano

(c) Gonzalo   (d) Ariel

(iv) Who is referred to as the ``old lord'' in the Scene III of Act III in The Tempest :

(a) Alonso   (b) Gonzalo

(c) Antonio   (d) Sebastian

(v) Why is Gonzalo feeling dizziness?

(a) He is tired while searching for Prospero   (b) He has not eaten anything from many days

(c) He met with an accident and fainted   (d) He is tired while searching for Ferdinand

(vi) Who is the father of Ferdinand?

(a) Alonso   (b) Gonzalo

(c) Prospero   (d) Antonio

(vii) What are `unicorns' referred to?

(a) Wild animals of forest

(b) Non-existent animal with single horn on head

(c) Non-existent animal with a horse body

(d) Both (b) and (c)

(viii) What is `phoenix' referred to?

(a) Normal bird found in nature   (b) Mythical bird from Arabian legend

(c) Mythical bird with colourful feathers   (d) None of them

(ix) Sebastian says ``*A living drollery!*'' What does ``drollery'' mean?

(a) Car race   (b) Circus

(c) Puppet show   (d) Zoo show

(x) What did Sebastian call as the `living drollery'?

(a) floating mirrors   (b) magical books

(c) dancing strange shapes   (d) dancing wooden logs

Question 2

Read the lines given below and choose the correct option given after each question.

A. *Stephano: How now shall this be compassed?*
Canst thou bring me to the party?
Caliban: Yes, yea, my Lord : I'll yield him thee asleep,
Where thou mayst knock a nail into his head.

(i) Who is Stephano in the story ?
    (a) Miranda's fiance   (b) Prospero's slave
    (c) Alonso's butler   (d) Prospero's disciple

(ii) What is the ``this'' that is to be ``compassed'' ?
    (a) `This' refers to purpose of Stephano
    (b) `This' refers to Stephano being the king of the island
    (c) Both (a) and (b)
    (d) None of them

(iii) ``I'll yield him thee sleep''. For whom is Caliban speaking this statement ?
    (a) Gonzalo   (b) Alonso
    (c) Prospero   (d) Trinculo

(iv) A phrase 'pied ninny' is used in the scene. Who uses the phrases?
    (a) Caliban   (b) Prospero
    (c) Trinculo   (d) Alonso

(v) Who is called as ``a pied ninny'' ?
    (a) Caliban   (b) Trinculo
    (c) Prospero   (d) Alonso

(vi) What does the phrase ``a pied ninny'' mean?
    (a) a fool without stripped clothes   (b) a fool one eye
    (c) a fool with stripped clothes   (d) a fool who is drowsy

(vii) A phrase 'Scurvy patch' is referred. What exactly does the phrase mean?
    (a) evil clown   (b) diseased clown
    (c) dizzy clown   (d) clown with magical powers

(viii) What is the plan in the mind of Ariel during her presence in the scene?
    (a) wants to elope with Miranda
    (b) wants to settle dispute between Prospero and Angles
    (c) wants to cause quarrel between Stephano and Trinculo
    (d) wants to cause quarrel between Miranda and Ferdinand

(ix) What does Ariel do to execute her plan?
    (a) ventriloquizes   (b) pinches
    (c) plays music   (d) shows magic

(x) Whom does Caliban plan to kill?
    (a) Miranda   (b) Prospero
    (c) Alonso   (d) Antonio

B. *Gonzalo: Faith, sir, you need not fear.*
When we were boys,
Who would believe that there were mountaineers
Dewlapp'd like bulls, whose throats had hanging at 'em
Wallets of flesh?

(i) Who all are resting in the given extract?
    (a) Gonzalo   (b) Alonso
    (c) Both (a) and (b)   (d) None of them

    (ii) What kind of people do exist according to Gonzalo?
- (a) People with their heads in their chests
- (b) People with one eye
- (c) People with two heads
- (d) People with no head

    (iii) Identify the magical incident that did not happen in the scene.
- (a) Thunder
- (b) Lightening
- (c) Banquet disappears
- (d) Landslides

    (iv) In which form does Ariel clap his wings on table?
- (a) Monster
- (b) Harpy
- (c) Evil
- (d) Invisible man

    (v) What is the meaning of *harpy* in context with the extract?
- (a) a strange looking bird
- (b) a strange looking animal
- (c) an instrument
- (d) a magical sign

    (vi) How does Ariel address the characters in the given extract?
- (a) Three evil monsters
- (b) Three miserable souls
- (c) Three men of sin
- (d) Three invisible men

    (vii) Which option best describes the island?
- (a) An island without inhabitants
- (b) An island with evil spirits
- (c) An island with dense forest
- (d) An island with sparse population

    (viii) Give the meaning of the word 'mountaineer'.
- (a) Mountain-dweller
- (b) Mountain-adviser
- (c) Mountain-traveller
- (d) All of these

    (ix) What does ``Dewlapp'd'' mean?
- (a) lumps of flesh around the neck
- (b) lumps of flesh around the hand
- (c) piece of flesh near cheeks
- (d) a gland in body

    (x) How has destiny played with Gonzalo and Alonso?
- (a) Presented them in front of their good luck charm
- (b) Surprised them with ample food
- (c) Thrown them on a desolated island
- (d) Gifted them with a box of treasure

SECTION–B

ECHOES—SHORT STORIES

Question 3

    (i) What does Josephine believe that Louise is doing behind the closed door?
- (a) Looking at photographs
- (b) Making herself ill
- (c) Killing herself
- (d) Gets fainted

    (ii) What fact did not worry the man?
- (a) The thought that they will float down to the village
- (b) dark day due to absence of sun
- (c) that he will be killed by animals
- (d) that he was alone in the forest

    (iii) What does the dog in the short story, *To build a fire* represent?
- (a) Intellect
- (b) Instinct
- (c) Experience
- (d) Knowledge

    (iv) How many matches does the man light at once?
- (a) 100
- (b) 10
- (c) 50
- (d) 70

    (v) What is the synonym of the word 'repression' as used in the line, ``*She was young with a fair, calm face, whose lines bespoke repression*''?
- (a) Constraint
- (b) Possession
- (c) Incontinence
- (d) Discretion

(vi) What does the man frequently do with his hands to warm them up?

    (a) He rubs them against the dog's fur   (b) He blows on them

    (c) He builds a fire   (d) He beats them against his legs

(vii) Which difficulties made no impression on the man?

    (a) not finding the correct path   (b) travelling in the forest

    (c) far reaching trail, tremendous cold   (d) mysterious puzzles

(viii) According to Mrs. Mallard, how did her husband use to treat her?

    (a) He used to oppress Mrs. Mallard

    (b) He always looked her with love and care

    (c) He was jealous and possessive towards Mrs. Mallard

    (d) He was mean and uncaring

(ix) *"She knew that she would weep again."* Why do you think she will weep again?

    (a) As she will see her husband's corpse

    (b) As she will come to know that her husband is not dead

    (c) She will weep for her freedom

    (d) She will weep because of her isolation

(x) How many characters are there in the short story, *The Story of an Hour.*

    (a) One   (b) Two

    (c) Three   (d) Four

Question 4

Read the lines given below and answer the questions by choosing the correct option after each:

"Go away. I am not making myself ill." No; she was drinking in a very elixir of life through that open window. Her fancy was running riot along those days ahead of her.

(i) To whom was she speaking these lines to?

    (a) Mr. Mallard   (b) Josephine

    (c) Richards   (d) Her inner thoughts

(ii) What was Josephine doing?

    (a) She was hesitating to knock the door.

    (b) She was happy with the freedom of Mrs. Mallard

    (c) Josephine was trying to console Mrs. Mallard by gaining admission through the locked door.

    (d) None of the above

(iii) What does the open window symbolize?

    (a) the freedom and opportunities that await Mrs. Mallard after her husband has died

    (b) Mrs. Mallard's sadness and heartbreak at the loss of her husband

    (c) tragedy and anguish

    (d) a hope that her husband will return

(iv) What does the metaphor "drinking in a very elixir of life" infer in the story?

    (a) She was breathing in a draught of fresh air with a sense of freedom

    (b) She was drinking alcohol

    (c) She was digesting her sorrows

    (d) She was enjoying herself

(v) Choose a word which is similar in meaning to the word "riot."

    (a) Pacification   (b) Upheaval

    (c) Sobriety   (d) Quiescence

(vi) Who breaks the news of Mr. Mallard's death to Louise?

    (a) Brently   (b) Josephine

    (c) Richards   (d) Roberts

(vii) What might Mrs. Mallard's ailment symbolize?
    (a) her inability to see things as they are
    (b) her inability to filter out less important things in life
    (c) her unhappiness and troubling emotions
    (d) her inability to remember things

(viii) In what season does the short story, *The Story of an Hour* occur?
    (a) Summer   (b) Spring
    (c) Winter   (d) Autumn

(ix) What does Mrs Mallard see when she is by herself looking out the window?
    (a) Scenes of spring and new life   (b) Scenes of death and decay
    (c) Scenes of an indifferent world   (d) Scenes of violence and chaos

(x) "The delicious breath of rain was in the air" is an example of?
    (a) Allusion   (b) Personification
    (c) Metaphor   (d) Simile

Question 5

Fill in the missing information from the story *The Story of an Hour*.

(i) The most desired thing to Mrs. Mallard was________.
    (a) love   (b) wealth
    (c) freedom   (d) happiness

(ii) The theme of the story is ________.
    (a) self-identity   (b) time is precious
    (c) relationships   (d) women empowerment

(iii) The fact that Louise had a heart condition ________ her death from a heart attack.
    (a) paradox   (b) double entendres
    (c) foreshadows   (d) flashbacks

(iv) ___________ is used as a literary device at the end of the story when the doctor claims Mrs. Mallard "died of heart disease- of the joy that kills".
    (a) Personification   (b) Irony
    (c) Simile   (d) Juxtaposition

(v) *"She sat with her head thrown back upon the cushion of the chair, quite motionless, except when a sob came up into her throat and shook her, as a child who has cried itself to sleep."* The figurative language used here is ______.
    (a) Motif   (b) Simile
    (c) Personification   (d) Hyperbole

SECTION–C

REVERIE —POETRY

Question 6

Choose the correct option after each question:

(i) Which of the following establishes the settling of *The Darkling thrush*?
    (a) ``frost was spectre grey''      (b) ``a coppice gate''
    (c) ``strings of broken lyres''   (d) household fires

(ii) What bends the birches to stay down ?
    (a) Heavy drops of rain   (b) Strong currents of wind
    (c) A storm of freezing rain   (d) A stormy weather

(iii) "spectre-grey" foreshadows which of the following moments in the poem?
    (a) "some blessed hope"   (b) "the century's corpse outleant"
    (c) "little cause for carolings"   (d) "shrunken hard and dry"

(iv) The poet says earlier *"So was I once myself a swinger of birches."* What quality of his is the poet referring to?

    (a) poise   (b) care

    (c) balance   (d) all of the above

(v) Identify the type of figurative language that these lines exhibit: *"It's when I'm weary of considerations, / And life is too much like a pathless wood / Where your face burns and tickles with the cobwebs / Broken across it, and one eye is weeping".*

    (a) Metaphor   (b) Imagery

    (c) Simile   (d) Alliteration

(vi) What is one thing that the act of swinging might symbolize?

    (a) The importance of scientific truth.

    (b) The desire to escape reality.

    (c) The desire for radical political changes.

    (d) The importance of understanding formal philosophy.

(vii) As the boy climbs up the tree, he is climbing towards:

    (a) another tree   (b) snowy hills

    (c) heaven   (d) home

(viii) Poet says he wants to be a birch swinger because:

    (a) he does not want to return to earth

    (b) he is frustrated with worldly life

    (c) he wants to preserve the fragile and difficult balance of life

    (d) there is no other pastime that can occupy his interest

(ix) In the poem, *Crossing the Bar*, the line 'moving seems asleep' means:

    (a) walking in sleep

    (b) wants to die in sleep

    (c) disturbed sleep

    (d) crossing silently and peacefully

(x) Which expression brings out the best meaning of the line 'bourne of Time and Place'?

    (a) born within time and place

    (b) beyond the limits of thought and action

    (c) boundary of life on earth

    (d) bounded by mortal aspirations

Question 7

Read the lines given below and answer the questions that follow by choosing the correct option after each:

The land's sharp features seemed to be
    The Century's corpse outleant,
His crypt the cloudy canopy
    The wind his death-lament
The ancient pulse of germ and birth
    Was Shrunken hard and dry,
And every spirit upon earh
    Seemed fervourless as I

(i) Which of the following is not an example of alliteration?

    (a) ``winter's dregs made desolate''       (b)  ``the century's corpse outleant''

    (c) ``his crypt the cloud canopy''         (d)  ``in blast-beruffled plume''

(ii) The season highlighted in the poem *The Darkling Thrush* is :

    (a) winter   (b) summer

    (c) spring   (d) rainy season

(iii) *The wind its death lament.* This line provides a valid description of:

    (a) Delight and Hope   (b) Death and Sadness

    (c) Death and revival of life   (d) Hope and victory

(iv) The line ``The ancient pulse of germ and birth'' in the poem signify:

    (a) The aura of life   (b) The origin of life

    (c) The sad conditions of life   (d) None of them

(v) Which expression matches the word fervourless used in the stanza.

    (a) hard and rigid   (b) full of passion

    (c) devoid of passion   (d) full of confidence

(vi) What is the dominant theme in this stanza?

    (a) Hostility   (b) Pessimism

    (c) Passion   (d) Randomness

(vii) What is the metaphor of the given line?

``The land is sharp features seemed to be

The century's corpse outleant.''

    (a) harsh barren landscape symbolizing death of the 19th century

    (b) loss of the 19th century values the modern life

    (c) loss of the energy and zeal of natural elements

    (d) both (a) and (b)

(viii) The word crypt signify:

    (a) The vault or chamber   (b) The realistic condition

    (c) The sad denusi   (d) The deserted soul

(ix) Where was the poet standing when the song burst on him?

    (a) In the courtyard of his house   (b) At the forest gate

    (c) On the street   (d) At the cross road

(x) Which of the following is not an example of visual imagery?

    (a) ``the bleak twigs overhead''       (b)  ``weakening eye of day''

    (c) ``wind his death lament''       (d)  ``the cloudy canopy''

Question 8

Given below are the sentences: from *Birches*

Fill in the gaps in the sentences from the option given after each:

(i) I like to think some boys been .... them.

    (a) swaying   (b) hanging

    (c) swinging   (d) healing

(ii) Some boy too far from town to learn ....

    (a) baseball   (b) football

    (c) hockey   (d) chess

(iii) One by one he subdued his .... trees.

    (a) mother's   (b) father's

    (c) brother's   (d) granny's

(iv) Broken across it, and one eye is ....

    (a) weeping

    (b) crying

    (c) both (a) and (b)

    (d) none of them

(v) Earth's the right place for ....

    (a) living

    (b) love

    (c) birth

    (d) birches

Answers

1. (i) (b) Lord of the Island

  (ii) (a) Alonso, Antonio and Sebastian

  (iii) (c) Gonzalo

  (iv) (b) Gonzalo

  (v) (d) He is tired while searching for Ferdinand.

  (vi) (a) Alonso

  (vii) (d) Both (b) and (c)

  (viii) (b) Mythical bird from Arabian legend.

  (ix) (c) Puppet show

  (x) (c) dancing strange shapes

2. (A) (i) (c) Alonso's butler

  (ii) (c) Both (a) and (b)

  (iii) (c) Prospero

  (iv) (a) Caliban

  (v) (b) Trinculo

  (vi) (c) a fool with stripped clothes

  (vii) (b) diseased clown

  (viii) (c) wants to cause quarrel between Stephano and Trinculo

  (ix) (a) ventriloquizes

  (x) (b) Prospero

  (B) (i) (c) Both (a) and (b)

  (ii) (a) People with their heads in their chests

  (iii) (d) Landslides

  (iv) (b) Harpy

  (v) (a) a strange looking bird

  (vi) (c) Three men of sin

  (vii) (a) An island without inhabitants

  (viii) (a) Mountain-dweller

  (ix) (a) lumps of flesh around the neck

  (x) (c) Thrown them on a desolated island

3. (i) (b) Making herself ill

  (ii) (b) dark day due to absence of sun

  (iii) (b) Instinct

  (iv) (d) 70

  (v) (a) Constraint

  (vi) (d) He beats them against his legs

  (vii) (c) far-reaching trial, tremendous cold

  (viii) (b) He always looked her with love and care

  (ix) (a) As she will see her husband's corpse

  (x) (b) Four

4. (i) (b) Josephine

  (ii) (c) Josephine was trying to console Mrs. Mallard by gaining admission through the locked door.

  (iii) (a) the freedom and opportunities that await her after her husband has died

  (iv) (a) She was breathing in a draught of fresh air with a sense of freedom

  (v) (b) Upheaval

  (vi) (b) Josephine

  (vii) (c) her unhappiness and troubling emotions

  (viii) (b) Spring

  (ix) (a) Scenes of spring and new life

  (x) (b) Personification

5. (i) (c) freedom

  (ii) (a) self-identity

  (iii) (c) foreshadows

  (iv) (b) Irony

  (v) (b) Simile

6. (i) (b) ``a coppice gate''

  (ii) (c) A storm of freezing rain

  (iii) (b) "the century's corpse outleant"

  (iv) (d) all of the above

  (v) (b) Imagery

  (vi) (b) The desire to escape reality.

  (vii) (c) heaven

  (viii) (c) he wants to preserve the fragile and difficult balance of life

  (ix) (d) crossing silently and peacefully

  (x) (b) beyond the limits of thought and action

7. (i) (b) ``the century corpse outleant''
   (ii) (a) winter
   (iii) (b) Death and Sadness
   (iv) (a) The aura of life
   (v) (c) devoid of passion
   (vi) (b) pessimism
   (vii) (d) both (a) and (b)
   (viii) (a) The vault or chamber
   (ix) (b) At the forest gate
   (x) (c) ``wind his death lament''

8. (i) (c) swinging
   (ii) (a) baseball
   (iii) (b) father's
   (iv) (a) weeping
   (v) (b) love

□□

Mathematics

Specimen Question Paper

Mathematics

Maximum Marks: 80
Time allowed: One and a Half hours

General Instructions

(Candidates are allowed additional 15 minutes for only reading the paper.)
The Question paper consists of three sections A, B and C.
Candidates are required to attempt **all** questions from Section A and all questions **either** from
Section B **OR** Section C.
The marks intended for questions or parts of questions are given in brackets [ ].
Select the correct option for each of the following questions.

Questions

SECTION A (64 Marks)

(Answer all Questions)

Question 1. [2]

The function $f: R \to R$ defined by $f(x) = \sin(3x + 2)$, $\forall\, x \in R$ is:
(a) One-One   (b) Onto
(c) Neither one-one nor onto   (d) one-one but not onto

Question 2. [2]

What will be the Principal value of $\operatorname{cosec}^{-1}\left(-\sqrt{2}\right)$?

(a) $\dfrac{3\pi}{4}$ (b) $-\dfrac{\pi}{6}$ (c) $\dfrac{\pi}{4}$ (d) $-\dfrac{\pi}{4}$

Question 3. [2]

If set A contains 5 elementes and set B contains 6 elements, then the number of one-one onto mappings from A to B is :
(a) 720   (b) 120   (c) 0   (d) none of these

Question 4. [2]

If $\alpha \le 2 \sin^{-1} x + \cos^{-1} x \le \beta$, then (α, β) is :

(a) $(0, \pi)$ (b) $\left(-\dfrac{\pi}{2}, \dfrac{\pi}{2}\right)$

(c) $\left(-\dfrac{3\pi}{2}, \dfrac{\pi}{2}\right)$ (d) None of these

Question 5. [2]

Let A be the set of all students of a boy's school. Then the relation R in A is defined by :
$R = \{(a, b) : a$ is sister of $b\}$ is
(a) an equivalence relation   (b) symmetric relation
(c) an empty relation   (d) a universal relation

Question 6. [2]

$\forall\, x \in R,\ \cot^{-1}(-x) =$
(a) $\pi - \cot^{-1} x$ (b) $-\tan^{-1} x$ (c) $-\cot^{-1} x$ (d) $\pi + \cot^{-1} x$

Question 7. [2]

The value of $\begin{vmatrix} 1 & \log_a b \\ \log_b a & 1 \end{vmatrix}$ is :

(a) $1 - \log ab$

(b) $1 - \dfrac{\log b}{\log a}$

(c) 0

(d) $\log ab - 1$

Question 8. [2]

From the matrix equation AB = AC, it can be concluded that B = C provided :

(a) A is singular matrix

(b) A is non-singlular matrix

(c) A is a symmetric matrix

(d) A is a skew symmetric matrix

Question 9. [2]

What is the transpose of a column matrix.

(a) Zero matrix   (b) Diagonal matrix   (c) Column matrix   (d) Row matrix

Question 10. [2]

What is the multiplicative inverse of matrix A is ?

(a) A

(b) A^2

(c) $|A|$

(d) $\dfrac{adj\ A}{|A|}$

Question 11. [2]

If A and B are two non singular matrices, and AB exists, then $(AB)^{-1}$ is :

(a) $A^{-1} B^{-1}$

(b) $B^{-1} A^{-1}$

(c) AB

(d) None of these

Question 12. [2]

If $\Delta = \begin{vmatrix} a & b & c \\ x & y & z \\ p & q & r \end{vmatrix}$, then $\begin{vmatrix} ka & kb & kc \\ kx & ky & kz \\ kp & kq & kr \end{vmatrix}$ is :

(a) Δ (b) $k\Delta$ (c) $3k\Delta$ (d) $k^3\Delta$

Question 13. [2]

If $y = t^2$ and $t = x + 3$ then $\dfrac{dy}{dx}$ is equal to :

(a) $(x + 3)^2$ (b) $2\,(x + 3)$ (c) $2t$ (d) $2\,(x + 3)^2$

Question 14. [2]

The set of points, where the function $f(x) = x\,|x|$ is differentiable in :

(a) $(-\infty, \infty)$

(b) $(-\infty, 0) \cup (0, \infty)$

(c) $(0, \infty)$

(d) $[0, \infty]$

Question 15. [2]

If $\sin^{-1} x + \sin^{-1} y = \dfrac{\pi}{2}$, then $\dfrac{dy}{dx}$ is equal to :

(a) $\dfrac{x}{y}$ (b) $-\dfrac{x}{y}$ (c) $\dfrac{y}{x}$ (d) $-\dfrac{y}{x}$

Question 16. [2]

The value of $\lim\limits_{x \to 0} \dfrac{\log(1+x)}{x}$ is equal to :

(a) e (b) 0 (c) 1 (d) -1

Question 17. [2]

What will be value of x for the determinant equation $\begin{vmatrix} 3 - x & 6 & 3 \\ -6 & 3 - x & 3 \\ 3 & 3 & 3 - x \end{vmatrix} = 0$?

(a) 6 (b) 3 (c) 0 (d) -6

Question 18. [2]

Any tangent to the curve $y = 3x^7 + 5x + 3$.

(a) is parallel to x-axis

(b) is parallel to y-axis

(c) makes an acute angle with x-axis

(d) makes on obtuse angle with y-axis

Question 19. [2]

The second derivation of $y = x^3 - 5x^2 + x$ is :

(a) $10x - 5$

(b) $6x - 10$

(c) $3x^2 - 10x$

(d) $3x^2 - 10x + 1$

Question 20. [2]

What will be the derivative of $\sin^{-1}\left(\dfrac{2x}{1+x^2}\right)$ with repect to $\cos^{-1}\left(\dfrac{1-x^2}{1+x^2}\right)$?

(a) -1

(b) 1

(c) 2

(d) 4

Question 21. [4×2]

Ramu purchased 5 pens, 3 bags and 1 instrument box and paid ₹16. From the same shop Venkat purchased 2 pens, 1 bag and 3 instrument boxs and paid ₹19 while Gopi purchased 1 pen, 2 bag and 4 instrument boxes and paid ₹25.

Using the concept of Matrices and Determinants to answer the following questions by choosing the correct option:

(i) If x, y & z repectively denotes the cost of pen, bag and instrument box then which of the following is true?

(a) $5x + 3y + z = 16$

(b) $2x + y + 3z = 19$

(c) $x + 2y + 4z = 25$

(d) All of these

(ii) If $A = \begin{pmatrix} 5 & 3 & 1 \\ 2 & 1 & 3 \\ 1 & 2 & 4 \end{pmatrix}$, $|A|$ is :

(a) -22

(b) 22

(c) 0

(d) 20

(iii) If $A = \begin{pmatrix} 5 & 3 & 1 \\ 2 & 1 & 3 \\ 1 & 2 & 4 \end{pmatrix}$ and $adj\, A = \begin{pmatrix} -2 & x & 8 \\ -5 & 19 & -13 \\ 3 & -7 & y \end{pmatrix}$ then missing value of x and y are :

(a) $x = -10$ & $y = -1$

(b) $x = 10$ & $y = -1$

(c) $x = -10$ & $y = 1$

(d) $x = 10$ & $y = 1$

(iv) The cost of one pen is :

(a) ₹2

(b) ₹5

(c) ₹1

(d) ₹3

Question 22. [4×2]

A Norman window is constructed by adjoining a semicircle to the top of an ordinary rectangular window as shown in the figure given below. The total perimeter of the window is 10 m.

Based on the above information answer the following by choosing the correct option:

(i) If the length and breadth of the rectangle portion of the window is y and x respectively (as shown in the figure above) then the relation betwen the variable is :

(a) $y = \dfrac{20 + (\pi - 2)x}{4}$

(b) $y = \dfrac{20 - (\pi + 2)x}{2}$

(c) $y = \dfrac{20 - (\pi + 4)x}{4}$

(d) $y = \dfrac{20 - (\pi + 2)x}{4}$

(ii) Let A be the area of the Norman window which admits the sunlight. Then A expressed in terms of x is:

(a) $A = 5x + \dfrac{\pi}{4}x^2 - 2x^2$

(b) $A = 5x + \dfrac{\pi}{8}x^2 - \dfrac{1}{2}x^2$

(c) $A = 5x - \dfrac{\pi}{8}x^2 - \dfrac{1}{2}x^2$

(d) $A = 5x - \dfrac{\pi}{2}x^2 - \dfrac{1}{4}x^2$

(iii) For the maximum value of A what will be the radius of the semicircle?

(a) $\dfrac{10}{2+\pi}$

(b) $\dfrac{10}{\pi-2}$

(c) $\dfrac{10}{4+\pi}$

(d) $\dfrac{20}{4-\pi}$

(iv) For maximum value of A, the length of the rectangle represented by y will be equal to :

(a) $\dfrac{10}{4+\pi}$

(b) $\dfrac{10}{\pi-2}$

(c) $\dfrac{20}{4+\pi}$

(d) $\dfrac{20}{4-\pi}$

Question 23. [4×2]

Consider the mapping $f : A \to B$ is defined by $f(x) = \dfrac{x-1}{x-2}$ such that $f(x)$ is one-one onto. Based on the above information, answer the following questions by choosing the correct options.

(i) Domain of $f(x)$ is:

(a) $R - \{2\}$

(b) R

(c) $R - \{1, 2\}$

(d) $R - \{0\}$

(i) Range of $f(x)$ is:

(a) $R - \{2\}$ (b) R (c) $R - \{1\}$ (d) $R - \{0\}$

(i) If $g(x) = 2f(x) - 1$, then $g(x)$ in terms of x is :

(a) $\dfrac{x+2}{x}$

(b) $\dfrac{x+1}{x-2}$

(c) $\dfrac{x-2}{x}$

(d) $\dfrac{x}{x-2}$

(i) A function $f(x)$ is said to be one-one if :

(a) $f(x_1) = f(x_2) \Rightarrow x_1 = x_2$

(b) $f(-x_1) = f(-x_2) \Rightarrow -x_1 = x_2$

(c) $f(x_1) = f(x_2) \Rightarrow -x_1 = x_2$

(d) $-f(x_1) = f(x_2) \Rightarrow x_1 = x_2$

SECTION B (16 Marks)

(Answer all Questions)

Question 24. [2]

What will be the value of m if the vector $2\hat{i} + m\hat{j} + \hat{k}$ is perpendicular to $2\hat{i} - \hat{j} + 3\hat{k}$?

(a) 7   (b) 0   (c) 1   (d) −1

Question 25. [2]

What will be the angle between the two lines $\dfrac{-x+2}{-2} = \dfrac{y-1}{7} = \dfrac{z+3}{-3}$ and $\dfrac{x+2}{-1} = \dfrac{2y-8}{4} = \dfrac{z-5}{4}$?

(a) $\dfrac{\pi}{2}$ (b) $\dfrac{\pi}{4}$ (c) 0   (d) π

Question 26. [2]

What are the direction ratios of the line passing through two points $(-2, 4, 5)$ and $(1, 2, 3)$?

(a) $< 1, 2, 3 >$ (b) $< -3, 2, 2 >$ (c) $< 2, 4, 5 >$ (d) $< 0, -1, 4 >$

Question 27. [2]

The equation of the line passing $(1, -1, 0)$ and parallel to the line $\dfrac{x-1}{1} = \dfrac{y+2}{-2} = \dfrac{z+1}{-1}$ is :

(a) $\dfrac{x-1}{1} = \dfrac{y+1}{-2} = \dfrac{z}{-1}$

(b) $\dfrac{x-1}{2} = \dfrac{y+2}{-1} = \dfrac{z+1}{-3}$

(c) $\dfrac{x-6}{1} = \dfrac{y-2}{-2} = \dfrac{z+1}{3}$

(d) $\dfrac{x-2}{-2} = \dfrac{y+2}{-2} = \dfrac{z+3}{-1}$

Question 28. [4×2]

The given figure shown as air plant holder which is in the shape of a tetrahedron. Let A(1, 1, 1) B(2, 1, 3), C(3, 2, 2) & D(3, 3, 4) are the vertices of air plant holder. Based on the above information answer the following questions.

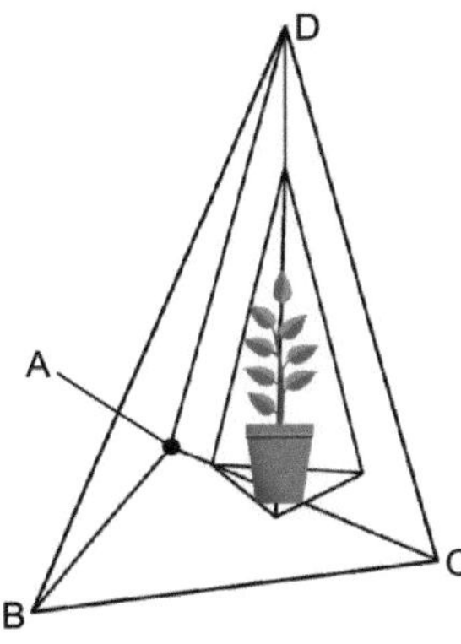

(i) The vector of $\overrightarrow{AB}$ is :

(a) $-\hat{i} - 2\hat{k}$

(b) $2\hat{i} + \hat{k}$

(c) $\hat{i} + 2\hat{k}$

(d) $-2\hat{i} - \hat{k}$

(ii) The vector of $\overrightarrow{AC}$ is :

(a) $2\hat{i} - \hat{j} - \hat{k}$

(b) $2\hat{i} + \hat{j} + \hat{k}$

(c) $-2\hat{i} - \hat{j} + \hat{k}$

(d) $\hat{i} + 2\hat{j} + \hat{k}$

(iii) Area of $\triangle ABC$ is :

(a) $\dfrac{\sqrt{11}}{2}$ Sq. units

(b) $\dfrac{\sqrt{14}}{2}$ Sq. units

(c) $\dfrac{\sqrt{13}}{2}$ Sq. units

(d) $\dfrac{\sqrt{17}}{2}$ Sq. units

(iv) The unit vector along the $\overrightarrow{AB}$ is :

(a) $\dfrac{-2\hat{i} - \hat{k}}{\sqrt{5}}$

(b) $\dfrac{-\hat{i} - 2\hat{k}}{\sqrt{5}}$

(c) $\dfrac{2\hat{i} + \hat{k}}{\sqrt{5}}$

(d) $\dfrac{\hat{i} + 2\hat{k}}{\sqrt{5}}$

SECTION C (16 Marks)
(Answer all Questions)

Question 29. [2]

A company sells its product for ₹20 per unit. Fixed for the company is ₹45,000 and variable costs is estimated to run 25% of total revenue. If x denotes number of units produced, then what will be the total cost function?

(a) $45000 + 5x$

(b) $15000 + 4x$

(c) $45000 + 2x$

(d) $4500 + 20x$

Question 30. [2]

The demand function for a certain commodity is given by $p = 4000 - 100x$. What will be the total revenue from sale of 3 units?

(a) 11,100

(b) 1000

(c) 4500

(d) 2000

Question 31.

A company sells x packets of biscuits each day at ₹10 a packet. The cost of manufacturing these packets is ₹5 per packet plus a fixed daily overhead cost of ₹700. What will be the profit function?

(a) $6x - 400$ (b) $5x - 700$ (c) $10x - 500$ (d) $5x - 10$

Question 32.   [2]

The cost function of a firm is given by $(x) = 3x^2 - 2x + 6$. The average cost of the firm at $x = 3$ is:

(a) 11   (b) 17   (c) 9   (d) 27

Question 33.   [4×2]

The demand function for a certain product is represented by the equation: $p = ax^2 + bx + c$ where x is the number of units demanded and p is the price per unit.

(i) The revenue function R(x) is :

(a) $ax^3 + bx^2 + cx$ (b) $ax + b + \dfrac{c}{x}$

(c) $ax^3 + bx^2 + cx + d$ (d) $2ax + b$

(ii) The marginal revenue MR(x) is :

(a) $a - \dfrac{c}{x^2}$ (b) $3ax^2 + 2bx + c$

(c) $3ax^3 + 2bx^2 + c$ (d) $2a$

(iii) The slope of the marginal revenue is :

(a) 0 (b) $6ax + 2b$

(c) $\dfrac{2c}{x^3}$ (d) $9ax^2 + 4bx$

(iv) Values of x, for which marginal revenue increases is :

(a) $x > \dfrac{-b}{3a}$ (b) $x < \dfrac{-b}{3a}$

(c) $x = \dfrac{-b}{3a}$ (d) $x \le \dfrac{-b}{3a}$

SECTION A

1. (c) Neither one-one nor onto.

Explanation: Let
$$h(x) = \sin x$$
$$g(x) = 3x + 2$$

$g(x)$ is one-one and onto $\forall\ x \in R$

but $\sin x$ is an occilatry function

$h(x)$ is not one-one

$h(x)$ is not onto

$(hog)\ x$ is also not one-one onto

hence $f(x)$ is neither one-one nor onto.

2. (d) $-\dfrac{\pi}{4}$

Explanation: $\because\ \text{cosec}^{-1} : R - (-1, 1) \to \left[\dfrac{\pi}{2}, 0\right] \cup \left[0, \dfrac{\pi}{2}\right]$ is a bijection.

$\therefore \operatorname{cosec}^{-1} x$ represents an angle is $\left[-\dfrac{\pi}{2}, 0\right] \cup \left[0, \dfrac{\pi}{2}\right]$ whose cosecant is x.

$\Rightarrow \operatorname{cosec}^{-1}\left(-\sqrt{2}\right)$ = An ange in $\left[\dfrac{-\pi}{2}, 0\right] \cup \left[0, \dfrac{\pi}{2}\right]$ whose cosecant is $\left(\sqrt{2}\right)$

$\Rightarrow \operatorname{cosec}^{-1}\left(-\sqrt{2}\right) = \dfrac{\pi}{4}$

3. (c) 0

Explanation: Let A = {a, b, c, d, e} and B {1, 2, 3, 4, 5, 6,}

It we try to make one-one function from A to B, then its range has five element. So, it will not be into. If we try to make onto function from A to B, then at least one element of A has at least two of set B which contradicts one-one mapping.

Hence, it is not possible to create a function with one-one onto.

$\therefore$ Numbers of one-one onto mapping from A to B = 0.

4. (a) $(0, \pi)$

Explanation: $\alpha \le 2\sin^{-1} x + \cos^{-1} x \le \beta$ (given)

$$\because \qquad -\dfrac{\pi}{2} \le \sin^{-1} x \le \dfrac{\pi}{2}$$

$$\Rightarrow \qquad \dfrac{\pi}{2} - \dfrac{\pi}{2} \le \sin^{-1} x + \dfrac{\pi}{2} \le \dfrac{\pi}{2} + \dfrac{\pi}{2}$$

$$\Rightarrow \qquad 0 \le \sin^{-1} x + \dfrac{\pi}{2} \le \pi$$

$$\Rightarrow \qquad 0 \le \sin^{-1} x + \sin^{-1} x + \cos^{-1} x \le \pi$$

$$\Rightarrow \qquad 0 \le 2\sin^{-1} x + \cos^{-1} x \le \pi$$

Hence, $(\alpha, \beta) \to (0, \pi)$

5. (c) an empty relation

Explanation: Given, R = {(a, b) : a is sister of b}

Since, it is a boy's school

$\Rightarrow$ These are no girls students in the school

It means, there can not be sister of any student of the school.

$\therefore$ R = ϕ i.e. an empty relation.

6. (a) $\pi - \cot^{-1} x$

Explanation: Let $\qquad\qquad \cot^{-1}(-x) = \theta \Rightarrow -x = \cot\theta$

$$\Rightarrow \qquad x = -\cot\theta$$

$$\Rightarrow \qquad x = \cot(\pi - \theta)$$

$$\Rightarrow \qquad \cot^{-1} x = \pi - \theta$$

$$\Rightarrow \qquad \theta = \pi - \cot^{-1} x$$

$$\Rightarrow \qquad \cot^{-1}(-x) = \pi - \cot^{-1} x$$

7. (c) 0

Explanation: $\begin{vmatrix} 1 & \log_a b \\ \log_b a & 1 \end{vmatrix} = 1 - \log_a b . \log_b a$

$$= 1 - \log_a b . \dfrac{1}{\log_a b}$$

$$= 1 - 1 = 0$$

8. (b) A is non-singular matrix

    Explanation: Given, $\qquad AB = AC$

    $\Rightarrow \qquad A^{-1}AB = A^{-1}AC$

    $\Rightarrow \qquad IB = IC$

    For A^{-1} exist, $B = C$ *i.e.* A is non-singular.

9. (d) Row matrix

    Explanation: Transpose of a column matrix = Row matrix.

10. (c) $\dfrac{adj\ A}{|A|}$

    Explanation: Multiplication inverse of matrix $A = A^{-1}$

    and, $A^{-1} = \dfrac{adj\ A}{|A|}$

11. (b) $B^{-1}A^{-1}$

    Explanation: $(AB)^{-1} = B^{-1}A^{-1}$

12. (d) $k^3\Delta$

    Explanation: $\Delta = \begin{vmatrix} a & b & c \\ x & y & z \\ p & q & r \end{vmatrix}$

    $\therefore \begin{vmatrix} ka & kb & kc \\ kx & ky & kz \\ kp & kq & kr \end{vmatrix} = k.k.k \begin{vmatrix} a & b & c \\ x & y & z \\ p & q & r \end{vmatrix} = k^3\Delta$

13. (b) $2(x + 3)$

    Explanation: $y = t^2$ and $t = x + 3$

    $$\frac{dy}{dt} = 2t \text{ and } \frac{dt}{dx} = 1 \qquad\qquad \text{[Diff. w.r. to } t]$$

    $$\therefore \qquad \frac{dy}{dx} = \frac{dy}{dt} \times \frac{dt}{dx} = 2t \times 1 = 2t$$

    $$= 2(x + 3)$$

14. (a) $(-\infty, \infty)$

    Explanation: We know that,

    $$f(x) = \begin{cases} x^2 & x \geq 0 \\ -x^2 & x < 0 \end{cases}$$

    Now, LHD at $x = 0 = \lim\limits_{h \to 0} \dfrac{f(0-h) - f(0)}{-h} = \lim\limits_{h \to 0} \dfrac{f(-h)}{-h} = \dfrac{h^2}{-h} = 0$

    RHD at $x = 0 \ \lim\limits_{h \to 0} \dfrac{f(0+h) - f(0)}{h} = \lim\limits_{h \to 0} \dfrac{f(h)}{h} = \dfrac{h^2}{h} = 0$

    $\therefore$ (LHD at $x = 0$) = (RHD at $x = 0$)

    So, $f(x)$ is differentiable at $x = 0$

    $\Rightarrow$ It is differential for all, *i.e.* $(-\infty, \infty)$

    $\therefore$ option (A) is correct.

15. (b) $-\dfrac{x}{y}$

    Explanation: $\sin^{-1} x + \sin^{-1} y = \dfrac{\pi}{2}$

    $$\sin^{-1} x = \frac{\pi}{2} - \sin^{-1} y = \cos^{-1} y$$

$$\Rightarrow \qquad \cos^{-1}\sqrt{1-x^2} = \cos^{-1} y$$

$$\Rightarrow \qquad \sqrt{1-x^2} = y \qquad \text{...(i)}$$

Diff. w.r. to x

$$\frac{1}{2}\cdot\frac{-2x}{\sqrt{1-x^2}} = \frac{dy}{dx}$$

$$\frac{-x}{\sqrt{1-x^2}} = \frac{dy}{dx} \ \text{ or } \ \frac{dy}{dx} = -\frac{x}{y} \qquad \text{[From eq ...(i)]}$$

16. (c) 1

Explanation: $\displaystyle\lim_{x\to 0}\frac{\log(1+x)}{x}$

Using L' Hospital rule

$$= \lim_{x\to 0}\frac{\dfrac{d}{dx}\log(1+x)}{\dfrac{d}{dx}x}$$

$$= \lim_{x\to 0}\frac{1}{1+x} = \frac{1}{1+0} = 1$$

17. (b) 3

Explanation: $\begin{vmatrix} 3-x & 6 & 3 \\ -6 & 3-6 & 3 \\ 3 & 3 & 3-x \end{vmatrix} = 0$

If $\qquad\qquad x = 3$, then

L.H.S. $\begin{vmatrix} 0 & 6 & 3 \\ -6 & 0 & 3 \\ 3 & 3 & 0 \end{vmatrix} = \begin{vmatrix} 0 & 0 & 3 \\ -6 & -6 & 3 \\ 3 & 3 & 0 \end{vmatrix}\ c_2 \to (c_2 - 2c_3)$

$$= 0 \ \text{R.H.S.}$$

Hence, option (b) is correct.

18. (c) makes an acute angle with x-axis

Explanation: $y = 3x^7 + 5x + 3$

$$\frac{dy}{dx} = 21x^6 + 5 \qquad\qquad (\text{Diff. w.r. to } x)$$

Slope, $\qquad\qquad m = 21x^6 + 5$

$\because \qquad\qquad x^6 > 0$

$\Rightarrow \qquad\qquad 21x^6 + 5 > 0$

$\Rightarrow \qquad\qquad m > 0 \ \text{or} \ \tan\theta > 0$

it mean θ will lie $\left(0, \dfrac{\pi}{2}\right)$

$\Rightarrow$ it makes an acute angle with x-axis.

19. (b) $6x - 10$

Explanation: $\qquad\qquad y = x^3 - 5x^2 + x$

Diff. w.r. to x

$$\frac{dy}{dx} = 3x^2 - 10x + 1$$

Again, Diff. w.r. to x,

$$\frac{d^2y}{dx^2} = 6x - 10$$

20. (b) 1

Explanation: Let $u = \sin^{-1}\left(\dfrac{2x}{1+x^2}\right)$ and $v = \cos^{-1}\left(\dfrac{1-x^2}{1+x^2}\right)$

Let $x = \tan\theta \Rightarrow \theta = \tan^{-1} x$

$$u = \sin^{-1}\left(\frac{2\tan\theta}{1+\tan^2\theta}\right) \quad \text{and} \quad v = \cos^{-1}\left(\frac{1-\tan^2\theta}{1+\tan^2\theta}\right)$$

$$u = \sin^{-1}\sin 2\theta \qquad \text{and} \quad v = \cos^{-1}\cos 2\theta$$

$$u = 2\theta \qquad \text{and} \quad v = 2\theta$$

$$\therefore \qquad u = 2\tan^{-1}x \qquad \text{and} \quad v = 2\tan^{-1}x$$

$$\frac{du}{dx} = \frac{2}{1+x^2} \qquad \text{and} \ \frac{dv}{dx} = \frac{2}{1+x^2}$$

$$\therefore \ \frac{du}{dv} = \frac{du}{dx} \times \frac{dx}{dv} = \frac{2}{1+x^2} \times \frac{1+x^2}{2} = 1$$

21. (i) (d) All of these

(ii) (a) – 22

Explanation:

$$A = \begin{bmatrix} 5 & 3 & 1 \\ 2 & 1 & 3 \\ 1 & 2 & 4 \end{bmatrix}$$

$$|A| = 5\,(4-6) - 3\,(8-3) + 1\,(4-1)$$
$$|A| = -10 - 15 + 3 = -22$$

(iii)(a) $x = -10$ & $y = -1$

Explanation: $A = \begin{bmatrix} 5 & 3 & 1 \\ 2 & 1 & 3 \\ 1 & 2 & 3 \end{bmatrix}$ and $adj\ A = \begin{bmatrix} -2 & x & 8 \\ -5 & 19 & -13 \\ 3 & -7 & y \end{bmatrix}$ ...(i)

$c_{11} = 4 - 6 = -2$, $c_{12} = -(8-3) = -5$, $c_{13} = 4-1 = 3$

$c_{21} = -(12-2) = -10$, $c_{22} = 20-1 = 19$, $c_{23} = -(10-3) = -7$

$c_{31} = 9-1 = 8$, $c_{32} = -(15-2) = -13$, $c_{33} = 5-6 = -1$

$$\therefore adj\ A = \begin{bmatrix} -2 & -5 & 3 \\ -10 & 19 & -7 \\ 8 & -13 & -1 \end{bmatrix}^{T} = \begin{bmatrix} -2 & -10 & 8 \\ -5 & 19 & -13 \\ 3 & -7 & -1 \end{bmatrix}$$

compare with given $adj\ A$ from eq ...(i),

we have, $x = -10$ and $y = -1$

(iv)(c) ₹1

Explanation: Let cost of one pen = x

cost of one bag = y

cost of one instrument = z

So,
$$5x + 3y + z = 16$$
$$2x + y + 3z = 19$$

$$x + 2y + yz = 25$$

$$A = \begin{bmatrix} 5 & 3 & 1 \\ 2 & 1 & 3 \\ 1 & 2 & 4 \end{bmatrix}$$

From (ii) and (iii) part

$$A^{-1} = \frac{-1}{22} \begin{bmatrix} -2 & -10 & 8 \\ -5 & 19 & -13 \\ 3 & -7 & -1 \end{bmatrix}$$

$$A^{-1} B = \begin{bmatrix} x \\ y \\ z \end{bmatrix}$$

$$\frac{1}{-22} \begin{bmatrix} -2 & -10 & 8 \\ -5 & 19 & -13 \\ 3 & -7 & -1 \end{bmatrix} = \begin{bmatrix} 16 \\ 19 \\ 25 \end{bmatrix} = \begin{bmatrix} x \\ y \\ z \end{bmatrix}$$

$$\frac{-1}{22} \begin{bmatrix} -32 - 190 + 200 \\ -80 + 361 + 325 \\ 48 - 133 - 25 \end{bmatrix} = \begin{bmatrix} x \\ y \\ z \end{bmatrix}$$

$$\frac{-1}{22} \begin{bmatrix} -22 \\ -44 \\ -110 \end{bmatrix} = \begin{bmatrix} x \\ y \\ z \end{bmatrix}$$

$$\begin{bmatrix} 1 \\ 2 \\ 5 \end{bmatrix} = \begin{bmatrix} x \\ y \\ z \end{bmatrix}$$

$$x = 1 \quad y = 2 \quad z = 5$$

cost of one pen = ₹1.

22. (i) (d) $y = \dfrac{20 - (\ne + 2)x}{4}$

Explanation: According to question,

$$\text{Total perimeter } = 10 \text{ m}$$
$$\pi r + x + 2y = 10$$
$$\Rightarrow \quad \pi \frac{x}{2} + x + 2y = 10 \qquad \left[\because r = \frac{x}{2} \right]$$
$$\Rightarrow \quad \pi r + 2x + 4y = 20$$
$$\Rightarrow \quad 4y = 20 - (\pi + 2)x$$
$$\Rightarrow \quad y = \frac{20 - (\pi + 2)x}{4}$$

(ii) (c) $A = 5x - \dfrac{\pi}{8}x^2 - \dfrac{1}{2}x^2$

Explanation:

$$\text{Total Area } = \frac{1}{2}\pi r^2 + x.y$$

$$A = \frac{1}{2}\pi.\left(\frac{x}{2}\right)^2 + x.\frac{20 - (\pi + 2)x}{4}$$

$$A = \pi . \frac{x^2}{8} + 5x - \pi . \frac{x^2}{4} - \frac{x^2}{2}$$

$$A = 5x - \frac{\pi}{8} x^2 - \frac{1}{2} x^2$$

(iii)(c) $\dfrac{10}{4+\pi}$

Explanation: For maximum value,

$$\frac{dA}{dx} = 5 - x - \frac{\pi x}{4}$$

Putting $\dfrac{dA}{dx} = 0$

$$5 - x \frac{\pi x}{4} = 0 \Rightarrow x = \frac{20}{\pi+4}$$

and $\dfrac{d^2 A}{dx^2} = -1 - \dfrac{\pi}{4} < 0$

$\therefore \quad \dfrac{d^2 A}{dx^2} < 0$ at $x = \dfrac{20}{\pi+4}$

Hence, A is maximum, when $x = \dfrac{20}{\pi+4}$

and radius, $\dfrac{x}{2} = \dfrac{10}{\pi+4}$

(iv)(a) $\dfrac{10}{\pi+4}$

Explanation: We have,

$$y = 5 - x \left(\frac{\pi}{4} + \frac{1}{2} \right)$$

$$y = 5 - \frac{20}{\pi+4} \times \frac{\pi+2}{4}$$

$$y = 5 - 5 . \frac{\pi+2}{\pi+4} = \frac{5\pi+20-5\pi-10}{\pi+4}$$

$$y = \frac{10}{\pi+4}$$

23. (i) (a) R – {2}

Explanation: Domain of $f(x)$ = R – {2}

(ii) (c) R – {1}

Explanation: $f(x) = \dfrac{x-1}{x-2}$

Let $y = \dfrac{x-1}{x-2}$

$$yx - 2y = x - 1$$
$$yx - x = 2y - 1$$
$$x(y-1) = 2y - 1$$
$$x = \frac{2y-1}{y-1}$$

Hence $\quad$ Range = R – {1}

(iii)(d) $\dfrac{x}{x-2}$

Explanation:
$$g(x) = 2f(x) - 1$$
$$= 2.\dfrac{x-1}{x-2} - 1 = \dfrac{2x-2-x+2}{x-2}$$
$$= \dfrac{x}{x-2}$$

(iv)(a) $f(x_1) = f(x_2) \Rightarrow x_1 = x_2$

Explanation: A function $f(x)$ is said to be one-one if :
$$f(x_1) = f(x_2) \Rightarrow x_1 = x_2$$

SECTION B

24. (a) 7

Explanation: $\because$ vector $2\hat{i} + m\hat{j} + \hat{k}$ is perpendicular to $2\hat{i} - \hat{j} + 3\hat{k}$

$\therefore \qquad (2\hat{i} + m\hat{j} + \hat{k}).(2\hat{i} - \hat{j} + 3\hat{k}) = 0$

$\Rightarrow \qquad 2.2 + m.(-1) + 1.3 = 0$

$\Rightarrow \qquad 4 - m + 3 = 0$ or $m = 7$

25. (a) $\dfrac{\pi}{2}$

Explanation: Angle between the pair of lines

$$\cos\theta = \left| \dfrac{a_1a_2 + b_1b_2 + c_1c_2}{\sqrt{a_1^2 + b_1^2 + c_1^2}\,\sqrt{a_2^2 + b_2^2 + c_2^2}} \right|$$

Here, $a_1 = 2$, $b_1 = 7$, $c_1 = -3$ and $a_2 = -1$, $b_2 = 2$, $c_2 = 4$

Now, $\qquad a_1a_2 + b_1b_2 + c_1c_2 = 2 \times (-1) + 7 \times 2 + (-3) \times 4$

$\therefore \qquad \cos\theta = 0 = \cos\dfrac{\pi}{2}$

$$\theta = \dfrac{\pi}{2}$$

26. (b) $< -3, 2, 2 >$

Explanation: Direction Ratio of the line $AB = \overrightarrow{AB}$

$$\overrightarrow{AB} = (-2-1)\hat{i} + (4-2)\hat{j} + (5-3)\hat{k}$$

$$\overrightarrow{AB} = 3\hat{i} + 2\hat{j} + 2\hat{k}$$

$\therefore \qquad$ Direction Ratio $= (-3, 2, 2)$

A (1, 2, 3)   B (−2, 4,5)

27. (a) $\dfrac{x-1}{1} = \dfrac{y-1}{-2} = \dfrac{z}{-1}$

Explanation: Direction Ratio of the line $\dfrac{x-1}{1} = \dfrac{y+2}{-2} = \dfrac{z+1}{-1}$

are 1, – 2 and –1. Direction ratios parallel line are $1k$, $-2k$, $-1k$.

$\therefore$ Equation of the line passing through (x_1, y_1, z_1) and parallel to the given line is

$$\frac{x - x_1}{a} = \frac{y - y_1}{b} = \frac{z - z_1}{c}$$

$$\Rightarrow \frac{x-1}{k} = \frac{y+1}{-2k} = \frac{z}{-k} \text{ or } \frac{x-1}{1} = \frac{y+1}{-2} = \frac{z}{-1} = k$$

$\therefore$ option (a) is correct.

28. (i) (c) $\hat{i} + 2\hat{k}$

Explanation:

$$\vec{AB} = \text{P.V. of } \vec{B} - \text{P.V. of } \vec{A}$$
$$= (2-1)\hat{i} + (1-1)\hat{j} + (3-1)\hat{k}$$
$$= \hat{i} + 2\hat{k}$$

(ii) (b) $2\hat{i} + \hat{j} + \hat{k}$

Explanation:

$$\vec{AC} = \text{P.V. of } \vec{C} - \text{P.V. of } \vec{A}$$
$$= (3-1)\hat{i} + (2-1)\hat{j} + (2-1)\hat{k}$$
$$= 2\hat{i} + \hat{j} + \hat{k}$$

(iii) (b) $\dfrac{\sqrt{14}}{2}$ Sq. units

Explanation: Area of $\Delta ABC = \dfrac{1}{2} \times |\vec{u}|$, where $\vec{u}$ = orthoral vector

$$\vec{u} = \vec{AB} \times \vec{AC}$$

$$= \begin{vmatrix} \hat{i} & \hat{j} & \hat{k} \\ 1 & 0 & 2 \\ 2 & 1 & 1 \end{vmatrix} \hat{i}[-2] - \hat{j}[-3] + \hat{k}[1] - 2\hat{i} + 2\hat{j} + \hat{k} \text{ or } <-2, 3, 1>$$

$$|\vec{u}| = \sqrt{(-2)^2 + 3^2 + 1^2} = \sqrt{4+9+1} = \sqrt{14}$$

$\therefore$
$$\Delta = \frac{|\vec{u}|}{2} = \frac{\sqrt{14}}{2} \text{ Sq. units}$$

(iv) (d) $\dfrac{\hat{i} + 2\hat{k}}{\sqrt{5}}$

Explanation: Unit vector along the $\vec{AB} = \dfrac{\vec{AB}}{\sqrt{a_1^2 + b_1^2 + c_1^2}}$

$$= \frac{\hat{i} + 2\hat{k}}{\sqrt{1^2 + 0 + 2^2}} = \frac{\hat{i} + 2\hat{k}}{\sqrt{5}}$$

SECTION C

29. (a) $45000 + 5x$

Explanation: Given, Price per unit $= ₹20$

Total no. of units $= x$

$$\therefore \quad \text{Total revenue, } R(x) = P.x = 20x$$
$$\therefore \quad \text{Total cost function} = 45000 + 25\% \text{ of } R(x)$$
$$= 45000 + \frac{25}{100} \times 20x$$
$$= 45000 + 5x$$

30. (a) 11,100

Explanation: Demand function, $P = 4000 - 100x$

Total no. of units, $x = 3$

$$\text{Revenue,} \qquad R = Px$$
$$= (4000 - 100x)\, x$$
$$= 4000x - 100x^2$$
$$\text{at } x = 3, \qquad R = 4000 \times 3 - 100 \times 9$$
$$= 12000 - 900$$
$$= 11100$$

31. (b) $5x - 700$

Explanation: Total revenue, $\quad R(x) = 10x$

cost function, $\qquad C(x) = 700 + 5x$

$$\therefore \qquad \text{Profit function} = R(x) - C(x)$$
$$= 10x - (700 + 5x)$$
$$= 5x - 700$$

32. (c) 9

Explanation: $\qquad c(x) = 3x^2 - 2x + 6$

$$\therefore \qquad \text{Average cost} = \frac{c(x)}{x} = \frac{3x^2 - 2x + 6}{x} = 3x - 2 + \frac{6}{x}$$

At $x = 3$,

$$\text{Average cost} = 3 \times 3 - 2 + \frac{6}{3}$$
$$= 7 + 2$$
$$= 9$$

33. (i) (a) $ax^3 + bx^2 + cx$

Explanation: $\qquad$ Demand function $P = ax^2 + bx + c$

$$\text{Revenue function} = Px$$
$$R(x) = (ax^2 + bx + c)x = ax^3 + bx^2 + cx$$

(ii) (b) $3ax^2 + 2bx + c$

Explanation: For marginal revenue (MR)

$$\frac{dR}{dx} = \frac{d}{dx}(ax^3 + bx^2 + cx) = 3ax^2 + 2bx + c$$

(iii)(b) $6ax + 2b$

Explanation: The slope of the marginal revenue

$$\frac{d}{dx}(MC) = \frac{d}{dx}(3ax^2 + 2bx + c)$$
$$= 6ax + 2b$$

(iv)(b) $x < \dfrac{-b}{3a}$

Explanation: According to question,

$$6ax + 2b > 0$$
$$6ax > -2b$$
$$x > \frac{-2b}{6a} \text{ or } \frac{-b}{3a}$$

❑❑

Sample Paper

Mathematics

Questions

SECTION–A
(Answer all Questions)

Question 1

Check whether the relation R defined in the set A of all the newspapers in an auditorium of a library given by R = {(a, b) : a and b have the equal number of pages} is:

(a) Reflexive   (b) Symmetric   (c) Transitive   (d) All of these

Question 2

Given that $f : x \to 3x - 5$ and $g : x \to x^3$ for all $x \in R$. The value of $f[g(x) + 5]$ is:

(a) $3x^3 + 10$ (b) $3x + 10$ (c) $3x^3 + 15$ (d) $3x^2$

Question 3

Find the value of $\sin\left(\cos^{-1}\dfrac{3}{5}\right)$.

(a) $\dfrac{5}{3}$ (b) $\dfrac{5}{4}$ (c) $\dfrac{4}{5}$ (d) $\dfrac{3}{4}$

Question 4

Find the domain of the function defined by $f(x) = \sin^{-1}\sqrt{x - 1}$.

(a) $[0, \infty]$ (b) $[-1, 1]$

(c) $[0, 1]$ (d) $[1, 2]$

Question 5

Find the minimum value of n for which $\cos^{-1}\left(\dfrac{n}{2}\right) > \dfrac{\pi}{6}$, $n \in N$ is valid.

(a) 1   (b) 2   (c) 3   (d) 4

Question 6

Let A be the set of all human beings in a city at a particular time. Then the relation R in A is defined by R = {(x, y) : x is father of y} is:

(a) an equivalence relation   (b) a universal relation

(c) symmetric relation   (d) None of these

Question 7

If A_{ij} be the co-factors for the determinant $\begin{vmatrix} 1 & 0 & -2 \\ 3 & -1 & 2 \\ 4 & 5 & 6 \end{vmatrix}$, then evaluate $A_{13} + A_{21}$.

(a) 9   (b) 12   (c) 15   (d) 0

Question 8

''A matrix of order 2 × 3 is equal to the another matrix of order 3 × 2''. This statement is:

(a) True   (b) False

(c) True for some values   (d) None of these

Question 9

If $A = \begin{bmatrix} -1 & 4 \\ 2 & 1 \end{bmatrix}$, find A^2.

(a) $\begin{bmatrix} -1 & 2 \\ 4 & 1 \end{bmatrix}$ (b) $\begin{bmatrix} 2 & 1 \\ 4 & -1 \end{bmatrix}$ (c) $\begin{bmatrix} 1 & -1 \\ 4 & 2 \end{bmatrix}$ (d) $\begin{bmatrix} 9 & 0 \\ 0 & 9 \end{bmatrix}$

Question 10

If A be any square matrix, then $A + A'$ is:

(a) skew symmetric   (b) symmetric   (c) Both (a) and (b)   (d) None of these

Question 11

If A and B be two non-singular matrices of the same type, then

(a) adj (AB) = (adj B)(adj A)   (b) adj (AB) = (adj A) + (adj B)

(c) adj (AB) = (adj B) – (adj A)   (d) None of these

Question 12

Evaluate: $\begin{vmatrix} 6 & 2 & 6 \\ -3 & -1 & -3 \\ 1 & 4 & 12 \end{vmatrix}$

(a) – 12   (b) – 8   (c) 0   (d) 48

Question 13

If $y = t^3 + 3t^2$ and $t = 4x - 5$, find $\dfrac{dy}{dx}$.

(a) $12(4x - 5)(4x - 3)$ (b) $6(4x - 5)^2$ (c) $2(4x - 3)$ (d) $4(x + 3)$

Question 14

Find the value of $\lim\limits_{x \to 0} \dfrac{1 - \cos x}{x^2}$.

(a) 1   (b) $\dfrac{1}{2}$ (c) 2   (d) $\dfrac{3}{2}$

Question 15

Differentiate $y = \sin^2 x$ with respect to x.

(a) $2 \sin x$ (b) $\cos^2 x$ (c) $\sin 2x$ (d) $\cos 2x$

Question 16

What will be the value of $\dfrac{dy}{dx}$ if $y = \cos^{-1}(\sin x)$?

(a) $\cos x$ (b) x (c) – 1   (d) 0

Question 17

The value of $\lim\limits_{x \to 0} \dfrac{\sin x}{x}$ is equal to:

(a) e (b) 0   (c) 1   (d) – 1

Question 18

Find the slope of the tangent to the curve $y = 3x^2 - 2x - 1$ at $x = 2$.

(a) 10   (b) 8   (c) 6   (d) 4

Question 19

The second derivative of $y = 4x^3 - 5x + 7$ is:

(a) $24x$ (b) $12x^2 - 5$ (c) $3x^2 - 5$ (d) $12x - 5$

Question 20

If $\tan^{-1} a + \tan^{-1} b + \tan^{-1} c = \pi$, the value of $a + b + c$ is:

(a) 0   (b) 1   (c) abc (d) None of these

Question 21

Ansh bought 5 pens, 3 pencils and 1 geometry boxes. From the same shop Rajat bought 2 pens, 1 pencil and 3 geometry boxes. Yuvan bought 1 pen, 2 pencils and 4 geometry boxes. Ansh, Rajat and Yuvan paid ₹ 16, ₹ 19 and ₹ 25 respectively for their items.

Using the concept of matrices and determinants to answer the following questions by choosing the correct option:

(i) If x, y and z be the cost of pen, pencil and geometry box, which equation(s) is/are true?

   (a) $5x + 3y + z = 16$ (b) $2x + y + 3z = 19$ (c) $x + 2y + 4z = 25$ (d) All of these

(ii) If $A = \begin{vmatrix} 1 & 2 & 4 \\ 2 & 1 & 3 \\ 5 & 3 & 1 \end{vmatrix}$, the value of $|A|$ is:

   (a) 0   (b) 10   (c) 20   (d) 22

(iii) If $A = \begin{vmatrix} 5 & 3 & 1 \\ 2 & 1 & 3 \\ 1 & 2 & 4 \end{vmatrix}$ and adj $A = \begin{vmatrix} -2 & -10 & 8 \\ -5 & y & -13 \\ x & -7 & -1 \end{vmatrix}$, find the values of x and y.

   (a) $(-3, -19)$ (b) $(3, 19)$ (c) $(3, -19)$ (d) $(-3, 19)$

(iv) Find the cost of one geometry box.

   (a) ₹ 5   (b) ₹ 3   (c) ₹ 2   (d) ₹ 1

Question 22

An iron bridge in form of a trapezium is placed to cross over a railway track 10 m wide.

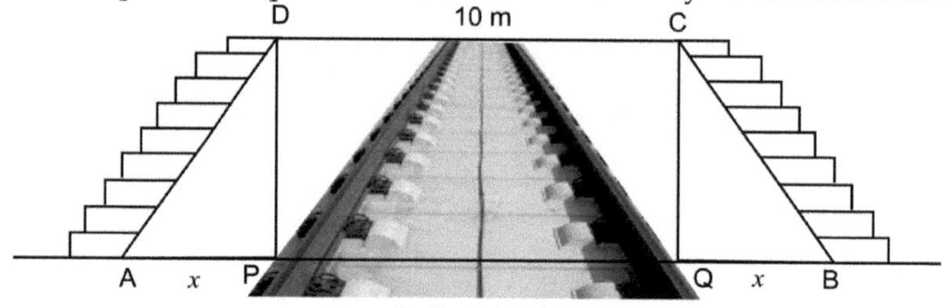

(i) Find the value of DP if AP = QB = x m and AD = BC = 10 m.

   (a) $(100 + x^2)$ m   (b) $(x^2 - 100)$ m   (c) $\sqrt{x^2 - 100}$ m   (d) $\sqrt{100 - x^2}$ m

(ii) If S is the area of trapezium, find the value of S.

   (a) $(10 + x)\sqrt{100 - x^2}$ (b) $(x + 10)(100 - x^2)$ (c) $(100 - x)\sqrt{100 + x^2}$ (d) $x^2 - 100$

(iii) Find the value of x at which first derivative of S = 0.

   (a) 0   (b) 5   (c) 10   (d) 15

(iv) For which possible value of x, S(x) has maximum value.

   (a) 0   (b) -5 (c) 5   (d) 10

Question 23

For the function $f(x) = \begin{cases} |x - 3| & , x \geq 1 \\ \dfrac{1}{4}(x^2 - 6x + 13) & , x < 1 \end{cases}$

Answer the following questions:

(i) R.H.D. of $f(x)$ at $x = 1$ is:

   (a) -1 (b) 0   (c) 1   (d) 2

(ii) L.H.D. of $f(x)$ at $x = 1$ is:

   (a) -1 (b) 0   (c) 1   (d) 2

(iii) $f(x)$ is not differentiable at:

   (a) $x = 1$ (b) $x = 2$ (c) $x = 3$ (d) $x = 4$

(iv) The value of $f'(-1)$ is :

   (a) -2 (b) -1 (c) 1   (d) 2

SECTION–B

(Answer all Questions)

Question 24

What will be the value of m if the vector $m\hat{i} - 3\hat{j} + 2\hat{k}$ is perpendicular to $2\hat{i} - 6\hat{k}$?

(a) 6 (b) 8 (c) 4 (d) 12

Question 25

If $|\vec{a}| = 5$, find the value of $6\vec{a} - 5\vec{a}$.

(a) 2 (b) 4 (c) 1 (d) 5

Question 26

The sum of the squares of the direction cosines of a line is:

(a) 0 (b) 1 (c) 2 (d) Can't say

Question 27

The direction ratios of a line are $-2, -1$ and 2. What are its direction cosines?

(a) $\dfrac{-2}{3}, \dfrac{-1}{3}, \dfrac{2}{3}$ (b) $\dfrac{-2}{5}, \dfrac{-1}{5}, \dfrac{2}{5}$ (c) $\dfrac{1}{3}, \dfrac{1}{6}, \dfrac{1}{9}$ (d) None

Question 28

The given figure shows a prism whose base is a shape of triangle. Let the vertices of the base triangle are A(1, 4, 2), B(– 2, 1, 2) and C(2, – 3, 4). Based on the above information answer the following questions.

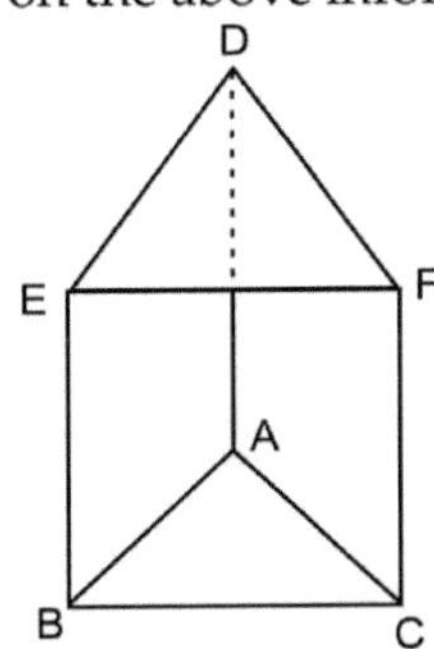

(i)   The vector of $\vec{BC}$ is:

(a) $-3\hat{i} + 2\hat{j} + \hat{k}$ (b) $4\hat{i} - 4\hat{j} + 2\hat{k}$ (c) $4\hat{i} + 4\hat{j} - 2\hat{k}$ (d) None of these

(ii) The vector of $\vec{AB}$ is:

(a) $2\hat{i} - 2\hat{k}$ (b) $-(3\hat{i} + 3\hat{j})$ (c) $2\hat{i} - 3\hat{j}$ (d) $4\hat{k}$

(iii) Area of $\triangle ABC$ is:

(a) $10\sqrt{2}$ sq. unit (b) $16\sqrt{2}$ sq. unit (c) $18\sqrt{2}$ sq. unit (d) $9\sqrt{2}$ sq. unit

(iv) The unit vector along the $\vec{BC}$ is:

(a) $\dfrac{1}{6}(4\hat{i} - 4\hat{j} + 2\hat{k})$ (b) $\dfrac{1}{6}(4\hat{i} + 2\hat{k})$ (c) $\dfrac{1}{6}(4\hat{i} - 4\hat{j})$ (d) None of these

SECTION–C

(Answer all Questions)

Question 29

A company produced an item with ₹ 4000 fixed costs. The variable cost is estimated to 25% of the total revenue when it is sold at a rate of ₹ 3 per unit. Find the total variable cost.

(a) $\dfrac{3x}{4}$ (b) $\dfrac{21x}{10}$ (c) $\dfrac{16}{5}x$ (d) $\dfrac{42}{10}x$

Question 30

Given the total cost function for x units of an item as $C(x) = \dfrac{1}{2}x^2 + 5x - 6$. Find marginal cost.

(a) $x^2 - 6$ (b) $2x - 6$ (c) $x + 5$ (d) None of these

Question 31

The demand function of a certain commodity is given by $p = 1500 - 5x - x^2$. Find marginal revenue at $x = 20$.

(a) ₹ 100   (b) ₹ 150   (c) ₹ 200   (d) ₹ 250

Question 32

Let, the cost function $C(x) = 20000 + 400x$ and the rvenue function $R(x) = x(3400 - 100x)$. Find the break-even values.

(a) $(40, 50)$ (b) $(35, 45)$ (c) $(20, 10)$ (d) $(15, 10)$

Question 33

Given the total function for x units of a commodity as $C(x) = x^3 + 3x^2 - 5x + 6$.

(i) The average cost (AC) is:

(a) $x^2 + 3x + \dfrac{6}{x} - 5$ (b) $x^3 + \dfrac{3}{x} + 6x - 5$ (c) $x^3 + 5x + \dfrac{3}{x} - 6$ (d) None of these

(ii) The marignal cost (MC) is :

(a) $6x^2 + 3x - 5$ (b) $3x^2 + 6x - 5$ (c) $5x^2 + 3x - 6$ (d) $5x^2 + 6x - 3$

(iii) The marginal average cost (MAC) is:

(a) $\dfrac{2x}{3} + 3 - \dfrac{16}{x^2}$ (b) $\dfrac{6}{x^2} - 3 + \dfrac{2}{3}x$ (c) $2x - \dfrac{6}{x^2} + 3$ (d) None of these

(iv) Slope of the marginal cost function is:

(a) $6x + 1$ (b) $5x + 1$ (c) $5(x + 1)$ (d) $6(x + 1)$

Answers

1. (d) All of these

   Explanation: Given, A = {All newspaper is an auditorium}

   R = {(a, b) : a and b have the equal no. of pages}

   Reflexive : $(a, a) \in R \Rightarrow R$ is reflexive on A

   Symmetric : $(a, b) = (b, a) \in R$
   $\Rightarrow R$ is symmetric on A.

   Transitivity : $(a, b) \in R$ and $(b, c) \in R \Rightarrow (a, c) \in R$
   $\Rightarrow R$ is transitive on A.

2. (a) $3x^3 + 10$

   Explanation: $f[g(x) + 5] = f(x^3 + 5)$
   $$= 3(x^3 + 5) - 5$$
   $$= 3x^3 + 15 - 5$$
   $$= 3x^3 + 10$$

3. (c) $\dfrac{4}{5}$

   Explanation:

   Let $\cos^{-1}\dfrac{3}{5} = \theta$

   $\Rightarrow \cos\theta = \dfrac{3}{5}$

$\therefore \quad \sin\theta = \sqrt{1 - \dfrac{9}{25}}$

$$= \dfrac{4}{5}$$

$\Rightarrow \quad \theta = \sin^{-1}\dfrac{4}{5}$

$\therefore \quad \cos^{-1}\dfrac{3}{5} = \sin^{-1}\dfrac{4}{5}$

Now, $\sin\left(\cos^{-1}\dfrac{3}{5}\right) = \sin\sin^{-1}\dfrac{4}{5} = \dfrac{4}{5}$

4. (d) $[1, 2]$

   Explanation: $\because$ Domain of $\sin^{-1}x = [-1, 1]$

   and domain of $\sqrt{x} = [0, \infty)$

   $\therefore$ Domain of $\sin^{-1}\sqrt{x - 1} = 0 \le \sqrt{x - 1} \le 1$
   $$= 0 \le x - 1 \le 1$$
   $$= 1 \le x \le 2 \ i.e. \ [1, 2]$$

5. (b) 2

   Explanation: $\cos^{-1}\left(\dfrac{n}{2}\right) > \dfrac{\pi}{6}$

$$\Rightarrow \qquad \frac{n}{2} > \cos\frac{\pi}{6}$$

$$\Rightarrow \qquad \frac{n}{2} > \frac{\sqrt{3}}{2}$$

or $n > 1.7$

$\Rightarrow$ Minimum value will be 2.

6. (d) None of these

Explanation: A = {All human beings in a city}

R = $\{x, y\} : x$ is father of y

Reflexive: x can not be a father of himself

$\Rightarrow$ R is not reflexive.

Symmetric: If x is father of y, then y cannot be father of x.

$\Rightarrow$ R is not symmetric.

Transitive: In case of father, $x \to y$, $y \to z$

$\Rightarrow x \to z$

$\Rightarrow$ R is not transitive.

$\therefore$ Option (d) is correct.

7. (a) 9

Explanation: $\begin{vmatrix} 1 & 0 & -2 \\ 3 & -1 & 2 \\ 4 & 5 & 6 \end{vmatrix}$

Here, $\qquad A_{13} = (-1)^{1+3}\begin{vmatrix} 3 & -1 \\ 4 & 5 \end{vmatrix} = +19$

$$A_{21} = (-1)^{2+1}\begin{vmatrix} 0 & -2 \\ 5 & 6 \end{vmatrix} = -10$$

$\therefore \qquad A_{13} + A_{21} = 19 - 10 = 9$

8. (b) False.

9. (d) $\begin{bmatrix} 9 & 0 \\ 0 & 9 \end{bmatrix}$

Explanation: A = $\begin{bmatrix} -1 & 4 \\ 2 & 1 \end{bmatrix}$

$$A^2 = A.A = \begin{bmatrix} -1 & 4 \\ 2 & 1 \end{bmatrix}\begin{bmatrix} -1 & 4 \\ 2 & 1 \end{bmatrix}$$

$$= \begin{bmatrix} 1+8 & -4+4 \\ -2+2 & 8+1 \end{bmatrix}$$

$$= \begin{bmatrix} 9 & 0 \\ 0 & 9 \end{bmatrix}$$

10. (b) symmetric

Explanation: A + A′ will be symmetric matrix.

11. (a) adj (AB) = (adj B)(adj A)

Explanation: From property

$$\text{adj (AB)} = \text{(adj B).(adj A)}$$

12. (c) 0

Explanation:

$$\begin{vmatrix} 6 & 2 & 6 \\ -3 & -1 & -3 \\ 1 & 4 & 12 \end{vmatrix} = 3\begin{vmatrix} 6 & -2 & 2 \\ -3 & -1 & -1 \\ 1 & 4 & 4 \end{vmatrix} = 0$$

(Since, two rows/columns be identical, then result is zero.)

13. (a) $12(4x - 5)(4x - 3)$

Explanation: $\qquad y = t^3 + 3t^2$

$$\frac{dy}{dt} = 3t^2 + 6t$$

and $\qquad t = 4x - 5$

and $\qquad \frac{dt}{dx} = 4$

$\therefore \qquad \dfrac{dy}{dx} = \dfrac{dy}{dt} \cdot \dfrac{dt}{dx}$

$$= (3t^2 + 6t).4$$

$$= 12t(t + 2)$$

$$= 12(4x - 5)(4x - 3)$$

14. (b) $\dfrac{1}{2}$

Explanation: $\displaystyle\lim_{x \to 0} \frac{1 - \cos x}{x^2}$

Since, this is $\dfrac{0}{0}$ form. So, apply L'Hospital rule.

$$= \lim_{x \to 0} \frac{\dfrac{d}{dx}(1 - \cos x)}{\dfrac{d}{dx}(x^2)}$$

$$= \lim_{x \to 0} \frac{\sin x}{2x}$$

$$= \frac{1}{2}\lim_{x \to 0} \frac{\sin x}{x}$$

$$= \frac{1}{2}\left[\because \lim_{h \to 0}\frac{\sinh}{h} = 1\right]$$

15. (c) $\sin 2x$

Explanation: $\qquad y = \sin^2 x$

Differentiating w.r. to x,

$$\frac{dy}{dx} = \frac{d}{dx}(\sin^2 x)$$

$$= 2\sin x \frac{d}{dx}(\sin x)$$

$$= 2\sin x.\cos x$$

$$= \sin 2x$$

16. (c) -1

Explanation: $\qquad y = \cos^{-1}(\sin x)$

$$y = \cos^{-1}\left[\cos\left(\frac{\pi}{2} - x\right)\right]$$

$$= \frac{\pi}{2} - x$$

Differentiating w.r. to x,

$$\frac{dy}{dx} = \frac{d}{dx}\left(\frac{\pi}{2} - x\right)$$

$$= 0 - 1 = -1$$

17. (c) 1

Explanation: $\lim\limits_{x \to 0} \dfrac{\sin x}{x}$

$\because$ It is a $\dfrac{0}{0}$ form. So, apply L'Hospital rule,

$$= \lim_{x \to 0} \frac{\dfrac{d}{dx}(\sin x)}{\dfrac{d}{dx}(x)}$$

$$= \lim_{x \to 0} \frac{\cos x}{1}$$

$$= \frac{1}{1} = 1$$

18. (a) 10

Explanation:

$$y = 3x^2 - 2x - 1$$

$$\frac{dy}{dx} = \frac{d}{dx}(3x^2 - 2x - 1)$$

$$\frac{dy}{dx} = 6x - 2$$

Now, $\left(\dfrac{dy}{dx}\right)_{x=2} = 6 \times 2 - 2 = 10$

19. (a) $24x$

Explanation: $\quad y = 4x^3 - 5x + 7$

Differentiating w.r. to x,

$$\frac{dy}{dx} = \frac{d}{dx}(4x^3 - 5x + 7)$$

$$= 12x^2 - 5$$

Again, differentiating w.r.t to x,

$$\frac{d^2 y}{dx^2} = \frac{d}{dx}(12x^2 - 5)$$

$$= 24x$$

20. (c) abc

Explanation: $\because \tan^{-1}a + \tan^{-1}b = \tan^{-1}\dfrac{a+b}{1-ab}$

Now, $(\tan^{-1}a + \tan^{-1}b) + \tan^{-1}c$

$$= \tan^{-1}\frac{a+b}{1-ab} + \tan^{-1}c$$

$$\Rightarrow \tan^{-1}\frac{\dfrac{a+b}{1-ab} + c}{\left(1 - \dfrac{a+b}{1-ab}\right) \times c}$$

$$\Rightarrow \tan^{-1}\frac{(a+b+c-abc)/(1-ab)}{c(1-ab-a-b)/(1-ab)}$$

$\because \tan^{-1}a + \tan^{-1}b + \tan^{-1}c = \pi$

$$\Rightarrow \tan^{-1}\frac{a+b+c-abc}{c(1-ab-a-b)} = \pi$$

$$\Rightarrow \frac{a+b+c-abc}{c(1-ab-a-b)} = \tan \pi = 0$$

$$\Rightarrow \quad a + b + c - abc = 0$$

or $\quad a + b + c = abc$

21. (i) (d) All of these.

(ii) (d) 22

Explanation:

$$|A| = \begin{vmatrix} 1 & 2 & 4 \\ 2 & 1 & 3 \\ 5 & 3 & 1 \end{vmatrix}$$

$$= 1(1 - 9) - 2(2 - 15) + 4(6 - 5)$$

$$= -8 + 26 + 4 = 22$$

(iii) (b) (3, 19)

Explanation:

$\because$ A is non-singular. The system has the unique solution *i.e.* $X = A^{-1}B$

$\Rightarrow A_{11} = -2$, $A_{12} = -5$, $A_{13} = 3$, $A_{21} = -10$, $A_{22} = 19$, $A_{23} = -7$, $A_{31} = 8$, $A_{32} = -13$,

$A_{33} = -1$

$$A = \begin{vmatrix} -2 & -10 & 8 \\ -5 & 19 & -13 \\ 3 & -7 & -1 \end{vmatrix}$$

$\therefore \quad$ adj $A = \begin{vmatrix} -2 & -10 & 8 \\ -5 & 19 & -13 \\ 3 & -7 & -1 \end{vmatrix}$

Hence, $x = 3$ and $y = 19$.

(iv) (a) ₹ 5

Explanation: Now,

$$A^{-1} = \frac{\text{adj } A}{|A|} = \frac{1}{-22}\begin{vmatrix} -2 & -10 & 8 \\ -5 & 19 & -13 \\ 3 & -7 & -1 \end{vmatrix}$$

$|A| = -22$

$$= \begin{bmatrix} -\dfrac{2}{-22} & \dfrac{-10}{-22} & \dfrac{8}{-22} \\ \dfrac{-5}{-22} & \dfrac{19}{-22} & \dfrac{-13}{-22} \\ \dfrac{3}{-22} & \dfrac{-7}{-22} & \dfrac{-1}{-22} \end{bmatrix}$$

$\because \quad X = A^{-1}B$

$$\begin{bmatrix} x \\ y \\ z \end{bmatrix} = \begin{bmatrix} \dfrac{2}{22} & \dfrac{10}{22} & -\dfrac{8}{22} \\ \dfrac{5}{22} & \dfrac{-19}{22} & \dfrac{13}{22} \\ \dfrac{-3}{22} & \dfrac{7}{22} & \dfrac{1}{22} \end{bmatrix}\begin{bmatrix} 16 \\ 19 \\ 25 \end{bmatrix}$$

$$\begin{bmatrix} x \\ y \\ z \end{bmatrix} = 22 \begin{bmatrix} \dfrac{1}{22} \\ \dfrac{2}{22} \\ \dfrac{5}{22} \end{bmatrix} \text{ or } \begin{bmatrix} 1 \\ 2 \\ 5 \end{bmatrix}$$

$\therefore$ Cost of one geometry box $z = 5$.

22. (i) (d) $\sqrt{100 - x^2}$ m

Explanation: From figure,

In $\triangle$ADP,
$$DP^2 = AD^2 - AP^2$$
$$DP^2 = 100 - x^2$$
$$DP = \sqrt{100 - x^2} \text{ m}$$

(ii) (a) $(10 + x)\sqrt{100 - x^2}$

Explanation:

Area of trapezium $= \dfrac{1}{2}(DC + AB) \times DP$

$$S = \dfrac{1}{2}(10 + 10 + 2x) \times \sqrt{100 - x^2}$$

$$S = (10 + x)\sqrt{100 - x^2}$$

(iii) (b) 5

Explanation: Differentiating w.r. to x,

$$\dfrac{dS}{dx} = (10 + x)\dfrac{d}{dx}\sqrt{100 - x^2} + \sqrt{100 - x^2}$$

$$\dfrac{d}{dx}(10 + x)$$

$$\dfrac{dS}{dx} = (10 + x)\cdot\dfrac{-2x}{2\sqrt{100 - x^2}} + \sqrt{100 - x^2}$$

$\because \dfrac{dS}{dx} = 0$

$$\Rightarrow \dfrac{-x(10 + x) + (100 - x^2)}{\sqrt{100 - x^2}} = 0$$

$$\Rightarrow -x(10 + x) + (10 + x)(10 - x) = 0$$

$$\Rightarrow -x + 10 - x = 0$$

$$\Rightarrow 2x = 10 \text{ or } x = 5$$

(iv) (c) 5

Explanation: At $x = 5$, $S(x)$ will be the maximum.

23. (i) (a) -1

Explanation:
$$f(x) = \begin{cases} x - 3, & x \geq 3 \\ 3 - x, & 1 \leq x < 3 \\ \dfrac{1}{4}(x^2 - 6x + 13), & x < 1 \end{cases}$$

$$Rf'(1) = \lim_{h \to 0} \dfrac{f(1 + h) - f(1)}{h}$$

$$\Rightarrow \lim_{h \to 0} \dfrac{3 - (1 + h) - 2}{h}$$

$$\Rightarrow \lim_{h \to 0} \dfrac{-h}{h} = -1$$

(ii) (a) -1

Explanation:
$$Lf'(1) = \lim_{h \to 0} \dfrac{f(1 - h) - f(1)}{-h}$$

$$= \lim_{h \to 0} \dfrac{-1}{4h}[(1 - h)^2 - 6(1 - h) + 13]$$

$$= \lim_{h \to 0} \dfrac{-1}{4h}(h^2 + 4h)$$

$$= 0 - 1 = -1$$

(iii) (c) $x = 3$

Explanation: $\because$ R.H.D. $= 1$ at $x = 3$
and L.H.D. $= -1$ at $x = 3$
$\therefore f(x)$ is non-differentiable at $x = 3$

(iv) (a) -2

Explanation:
$$f'(x) = \dfrac{d}{dx}\left[\dfrac{x^2}{4} - \dfrac{3x}{2} + \dfrac{13}{4}\right]$$

$$f'(x) = \dfrac{x}{2} - \dfrac{3}{2}$$

$$\therefore \quad f'(-1) = \dfrac{-1}{2} - \dfrac{3}{2} = \dfrac{-4}{2} = -2$$

24. (a) 6

Explanation: $\because$ Two vectors are perpendicular to each other,

$$\therefore \quad \vec{A}.\vec{B} = 0$$

$$(m\hat{i} - 3\hat{j} + 2\hat{k}).(2\hat{i} - 6\hat{k}) = 0$$

$$\Rightarrow 2m - 12 = 0$$

$$\Rightarrow 2m = 12 \text{ or } m = 6$$

25. (d) 5

Explanation: $|\vec{a}| = 5$

$$|6\vec{a}| = 6|\vec{a}| = 6 \times 5 = 30$$

and $|5\vec{a}| = 5|\vec{a}| = 5 \times 5 = 25$

$$\therefore 6\vec{a} - 5\vec{a} = 30 - 25 = 5$$

26. (b) 1

Explanation: If l, m, n be the direction cosines of a line, then $l^2 + m^2 + n^2 = 1$

27. (a) $\dfrac{-2}{3}, \dfrac{-1}{3}, \dfrac{2}{3}$

Explanation: The direction cosines are

$$l = \frac{a}{\sqrt{a^2 + b^2 + c^2}}$$

$$= \frac{-2}{\sqrt{4 + 1 + 4}}$$

$$= \frac{-2}{3}$$

$$m = \frac{b}{\sqrt{a^2 + b^2 + c^2}}$$

$$= \frac{-1}{\sqrt{9}} = \frac{-1}{3}$$

$$n = \frac{c}{\sqrt{a^2 + b^2 + c^2}}$$

$$= \frac{2}{\sqrt{9}} = \frac{2}{3}$$

28. (i) (b) $4\hat{i} - 4\hat{j} + 2\hat{k}$

Explanation:

$$\vec{BC} = \text{P.V. of } \vec{C} - \text{P.V. of } \vec{B}$$

$$= (+2\hat{i} - 3\hat{j} + 4\hat{k}) - (-2\hat{i} + \hat{j} + 2\hat{k})$$

$$= 4\hat{i} - 4\hat{j} + 2\hat{k}$$

(ii) (b) $-(3\hat{i} + 3\hat{j})$

Explanation:

$$\vec{AB} = \text{P.V. of } \vec{B} - \text{P.V. of } \vec{A}$$

$$= (-2\hat{i} + \hat{j} + 2\hat{k}) - (\hat{i} + 4\hat{j} + 2k)$$

$$= -3\hat{i} - 3\hat{j}$$

(iii) (d) $9\sqrt{2}$ sq. unit

Explanation:

$$\text{Area of } \Delta = \frac{1}{2}\left|(\vec{AB} \times \vec{AC})\right|$$

$$= \frac{1}{2}[(-3\hat{i} - 3\hat{j}) \times (\hat{i} - 7\hat{j} + 2\hat{k})]$$

$$\vec{AB} \times \vec{AC} = -6\hat{i} + 6\hat{j} + 24\hat{k}$$

$$|\vec{AB} \times \vec{AC}| = \sqrt{36 + 36 + 576}$$

$$= \sqrt{648} = 18\sqrt{2}$$

$$\therefore \quad \Delta = \frac{1}{2} \times 18\sqrt{2} = 9\sqrt{2} \text{ sq. unit}$$

(iv) (a) $\dfrac{1}{6}(4\hat{i} - 4\hat{j} + 2\hat{k})$

Explanation:

$$\text{Answer} = \frac{\vec{BC}}{|\vec{BC}|}$$

$$= \frac{4\hat{i} - 4\hat{j} + 2\hat{k}}{\sqrt{16 + 16 + 4}}$$

$$= \frac{1}{6}(4\hat{i} - 4\hat{j} + 2\hat{k})$$

29. (a) $\dfrac{3x}{4}$

Explanation: Let, the total no. of units $= x$

Fixed cost $= ₹\ 4,000$

Total revenue $= ₹\ 3x$

$\therefore$ Variable cost $= 25\%$ of total revenue

$$= \frac{25}{100} \times 3x = \frac{3x}{4}$$

30. (c) $x + 5$

Explanation: $\quad C(x) = \dfrac{1}{2}x^2 + 5x - 6$

$\therefore$ Marginal cost (MC) $= \dfrac{dC}{dx}$

$$= \frac{d}{dx}\left[\frac{1}{2}x^2 + 5x - 6\right]$$

$$= x + 5$$

31. (a) ₹ 100

Explanation:

Revenue function $R = px$

$$R = (1500 - 5x - x^2)x$$

$$R = 1500x - 5x^2 - x^3$$

$\therefore$ Marginal revenue, $MR = \dfrac{dR}{dx}$

$$= \frac{d}{dx}(1500x - 5x^2 - x^3)$$

$$= 1500 - 10x - 3x^2$$

At $x = 20, MR = 1500 - 10 \times 20 - 3 \times (20)^2$

$$= 1500 - 200 - 1200$$

$$= 1500 - 1400 = ₹\ 100$$

32. (c) $(20, 10)$

Explanation: For break-even values,

$$R(x) = C(x)$$

$$x(3400 - 100x) = 20000 + 400x$$

$$\Rightarrow \quad 3400x - 100x^2 = 20000 + 400x$$

$$\Rightarrow \quad 100x^2 - 3000x + 20000 = 0$$

$$\Rightarrow \quad x^2 - 30x + 200 = 0$$

$$\Rightarrow \quad (x - 20)(x - 10) = 0$$

$$\text{or} \quad x = 20, 10$$

33. (i) (a) $x^2 + 3x + \dfrac{6}{x} - 5$

Explanation: $C(x) = x^3 + 3x^2 - 5x + 6$

The average cost (AC) = $\dfrac{C(x)}{x}$

$$= x^2 + 3x - 5 + \dfrac{6}{x} - 5$$

(ii) (b) $3x^2 + 6x - 5$

Explanation:

Marginal cost (MC) = $\dfrac{d}{dx}C(x)$

$$= \dfrac{d}{dx}(x^3 + 3x^2 - 5x + 6)$$

$$= 3x^2 + 6x - 5$$

(iii) (c) $2x - \dfrac{6}{x^2} + 3$

Explanation:

Marginal Average Cost (MAC) = $\dfrac{d}{dx}(AC)$

$$= \dfrac{d}{dx}\left[x^2 + 3x - 5 + \dfrac{6}{x} \right]$$

$$= 2x + 3 - \dfrac{6}{x^2} \text{ or } 2x - \dfrac{6}{x^2} + 3$$

(iv) (d) $6(x + 1)$

Explanation: Slope of the marginal cost

$$= \dfrac{d}{dx}(MC)$$

$$= \dfrac{d}{dx}(3x^2 + 6x - 5)$$

$$= 6x + 6 = 6(x + 1)$$

Questions

SECTION–A

(Answer all Questions)

Question 1

Relation R in the set A = {1, 2, 3, ..., 14} is defined as R = {$(x, y) : 3x - y = 0$}. Determine the relation R.

(a) Reflexive   (b) Symmetric   (c) Transitive   (d) None of these

Question 2

The function $f : R \to R$ defined by $f(x) = x^2 + 1$, $\forall\, x \in R$ is:

(a) one-one   (b) onto

(c) neither one-one nor onto   (d) None

Question 3

Evaluate: $\tan^{-1}\left(\tan \dfrac{3\pi}{4} \right)$

(a) $\dfrac{3\pi}{4}$ (b) $\dfrac{\pi}{4}$ (c) $-\dfrac{\pi}{4}$ (d) $-\dfrac{3\pi}{4}$

Question 4

If $\tan^{-1}x + \tan^{-1}y = \dfrac{\pi}{4}$ and $xy < 1$, then what will be the value of $x + y + xy$?

(a) 1   (b) 0   (c) 3   (d) None of these

Question 5

Find the minimum value of n for which $\sin^{-1}\left(\dfrac{n}{\pi} \right) > \dfrac{\pi}{2}$, $n \in N$ is valid.

(a) 0   (b) 1   (c) 2   (d) 4

Question 6

If $f(x) = x^2 - 1$ and $g(x) = \sqrt{x}$, find the value of $fog(x)$.

(a) $\sqrt{x^2 - 1}$ (b) $x - 1$ (c) $x^{3/2}$ (d) None of these

Question 7

If M_{ij} be the minors for the determinant $\begin{vmatrix} 2 & -2 & 3 \\ 1 & 4 & 5 \\ 2 & 1 & -3 \end{vmatrix}$, then find $M_{11} + M_{32} + M_{33}$.

(a) 0   (b) 4   (c) 12   (d) -1

Question 8

A square matrix in which the diagonal elements are all equals, all other elements being zeroes, is called:

(a) Row matrix   (b) Column matrix   (c) Scalar matrix   (d) None of these

Question 9

The product of an $m \times p$ and $p \times n$ matrices is an:

(a) $m \times p$ matrix   (b) $p \times n$ matrix   (c) $m \times n$ matrix   (d) None of these

Question 10

A square matrix is said to be symmetric if:

(a) $a_{ij} = a_{ji}$ (b) $a_{ij} > a_{ji}$ (c) $a_{ij} \neq a_{ji}$ (d) $a_{ij} < a_{ji}$

Question 11

Let $A = \begin{bmatrix} 2 & 5 \\ 4 & 10 \end{bmatrix}$ is singular. Find A^{-1}.

(a) $\begin{bmatrix} 1 & 2 \\ 4 & 8 \end{bmatrix}$ (b) $\begin{bmatrix} 10 & 1 \\ 40 & 1 \end{bmatrix}$ (c) $\begin{bmatrix} 10 & 4 \\ 5 & 2 \end{bmatrix}$ (d) No inverse exists

Question 12

If $\Delta = \begin{vmatrix} 0 & ab^2 & ac^2 \\ a^2b & 0 & bc^2 \\ a^2c & b^2c & 0 \end{vmatrix}$, then find the value of Δ.

(a) 0 (b) $2abc$ (c) $a^2b^2c^2$ (d) $2a^3b^3c^3$

Question 13

If $y = 3t^2$ and $t = x^2 + 5$, then $\dfrac{dy}{dx}$ is equal to:

(a) $6t$ (b) $12x(x^2 + 5)$ (c) $12x$ (d) $12(x^2 + 5)$

Question 14

The function f is defined by

$$f(x) = \left. \begin{matrix} x^2 & \text{when } x \neq 1 \\ 2 & \text{when } x = 1 \end{matrix} \right\}$$

Then, at $x = 1$, the function $f(x)$ will be:

(a) Continuous   (b) Discontinuous   (c) Both (a) and (b)   (d) None of these

Question 15

Find $\dfrac{dy}{dx}$ if $y = \log(\tan x)$:

(a) $\operatorname{cosec} x \sec x$ (b) $\cot x$ (c) $\sec^2 x$ (d) None of these

Question 16

Let $y = \sin^{-1} \dfrac{x}{a}$. What will be the value of $\dfrac{dy}{dx}$ at $x = a$?

(a) 1 (b) ∞ (c) 0 (d) $\dfrac{\pi}{2}$

Question 17

The value of $\lim\limits_{x \to \frac{\pi}{4}} \dfrac{1 - \tan x}{\cos 2x}$ is equal to:

(a) -1 (b) 1 (c) 0 (d) e

Question 18

Find the slope of the tangent to the curve $y = \sin^2 x$ at $x = \dfrac{\pi}{4}$.

(a) -1 (b) 1 (c) 0 (d) $\dfrac{1}{2}$

Question 19

The second derivative of $y = 5x^3 - 7x^2 + 2x$ is:

(a) $2(15x - 7)$ (b) $15x^2 - 14x + 2$ (c) $5x + 2$ (d) None of these

Question 20

Find the value of $\sin(\tan^{-1}a + \cot^{-1}a)$.

(a) 0 (b) 1 (c) -1 (d) ∞

Question 21

Saumya purchased 1 scale and 2 erasers and paid ₹ 5. From the same place, Vaishnavi purchased 1 eraser and 2 pens and paid ₹ 8 while Drashti purchased 2 scales and 1 pen and paid ₹ 5.

Using the concept of matrices and determinants to answer the following questions by choosing the correct option:

(i) If x, y and z respectively represent the cost of scale, eraser and pen. Which equation(s) is/are true?

    (a) $x + 2y = 5$ (b) $x + 2z = 5$ (c) $2y + z = 8$ (d) None of these

(ii) If $A = \begin{vmatrix} 1 & 2 & 0 \\ 0 & 1 & 2 \\ 2 & 0 & 1 \end{vmatrix}$, find the value of $|A|$.

    (a) 15   (b) 12   (c) 9   (d) 0

(iii) Find the cost of one scale.

    (a) ₹ 1   (b) ₹ 2   (c) ₹ 3   (d) ₹ 5

(iv) If $A = \begin{vmatrix} 1 & 2 & 0 \\ 0 & 1 & 2 \\ 2 & 0 & 1 \end{vmatrix}$ and adj $A = \begin{vmatrix} 1 & -2 & x \\ 4 & 1 & -2 \\ y & 4 & 1 \end{vmatrix}$, find x and y is:

    (a) $(4, -2)$ (b) $(1, 1)$ (c) $(4, 4)$ (d) $(-2, -2)$

Question 22

In a fiber glass factory, a rectangular sheet of fiber 45 cm by 24 cm is to be made into a box without top by cutting off square from each corner and folding up flaps.

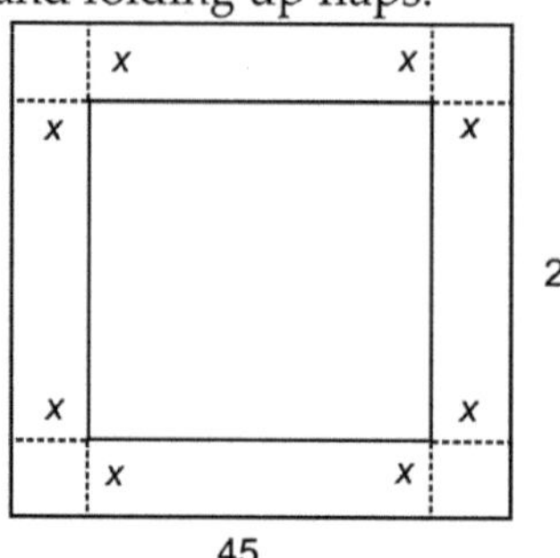

(i) Find the volume of the fiber box.

    (a) $4x^2 - 138x + 1080$ (b) $4x^3 + 138x^2 - 1080x$

    (c) $4x^3 - 138x^2 + 1080x$ (d) $4x^2 + 70x - 300$

(ii) For what value of x at which 2nd derivative of V will be zero? (Approx. value)

    (a) 6   (b) 14   (c) $\dfrac{23}{2}$ (d) $\dfrac{15}{2}$

(iii) What is maximum volume of box?

    (a) 2450 cm^3 (b) 2250 cm^3 (c) 1850 cm^3 (d) 1500 cm^3

(iv) For what value of x at which $V'(x) = 0$?

    (a) 3   (b) -3 (c) 5   (d) -5

Question 23

Using the CHAIN rule, find the derivative of functions w.r. to x in the following:

(i) $\dfrac{d}{dx}(\cos \sqrt{x})$

    (a) $-\sin \sqrt{x}$ (b) $\dfrac{-\sin \sqrt{x}}{2\sqrt{x}}$ (c) $\dfrac{\cos \sqrt{x}}{x}$ (d) $\dfrac{1}{2}\cos x$

(ii) $\sqrt{\dfrac{1 - \cos x}{1 + \cos x}}$

    (a) $\sec^2 \dfrac{x}{2}$ (b) $-\sec^2 \dfrac{x}{2}$ (c) $\dfrac{1}{2}\sec^2 \dfrac{x}{2}$ (d) $-\dfrac{1}{2}\sec^2 \dfrac{x}{2}$

(iii) $\cos^{-1}(\sqrt{\cos x})$

(a) $\dfrac{\sin x}{\sqrt{\cos x}}$ (b) $\dfrac{\sin \sqrt{x}}{\cos \sqrt{x}}$ (c) $\dfrac{1}{2}$ (d) $\dfrac{\sin x}{2\sqrt{\cos x}(\sqrt{1-\cos x})}$

(iv) $x = at^2$ and $y = 2at$

(a) 1 (b) $\dfrac{1}{t}$ (c) 2 (d) $\dfrac{2}{t}$

SECTION–B

(Answer all Questions)

Question 24

Find the acute angle between two lines whose direction ratios are $1, 2, 2$ and $\sqrt{2}, 0, \sqrt{2}$ respectively.

(a) $\dfrac{\pi}{2}$ (b) $\dfrac{\pi}{3}$ (c) $\dfrac{\pi}{4}$ (d) $\dfrac{\pi}{6}$

Question 25

Find the angle between the two lines $\dfrac{x-2}{3} = \dfrac{y+1}{-2} = \dfrac{z-2}{0}$ and $\dfrac{x-1}{2} = \dfrac{y-5}{3} = \dfrac{z-4}{7}$.

(a) $\dfrac{\pi}{6}$ (b) $\dfrac{\pi}{2}$ (c) $\dfrac{\pi}{3}$ (d) $\dfrac{\pi}{4}$

Question 26

Find the direction ratios of the line passing through the two points A(3, 2, – 1) and B(1, 3, 2).

(a) $<-2, 1, 3>$ (b) $<2, -1, 3>$ (c) $<2, 1, 3>$ (d) $<-1, -2, 3>$

Question 27

Find the vector equation of the line joining the points $\hat{i} + 2\hat{j} + 3\hat{k}$ and $\hat{i} - \hat{j} + \hat{k}$. ($\lambda = 1$).

(a) $\hat{i} + \hat{j} + \hat{k}$ (b) $-\hat{i} + \hat{j} - \hat{k}$ (c) $-\hat{i} - \hat{j} - \hat{k}$ (d) $\hat{i} - \hat{j} + \hat{k}$

Question 28

Based on the scalar triple product, find the answers of the following questions:

(i) $[\hat{i}\ \hat{j}\ \hat{k}] = ?$

(a) -1 (b) 1 (c) 0 (d) 2

(ii) If $\vec{a} = \hat{i} + \hat{j} + \hat{k}$, $\vec{b} = \hat{i} - \hat{j} + \hat{k}$, $\vec{c} = \hat{i} - \hat{j} - \hat{k}$, find $[\vec{a}\ \vec{b}\ \vec{c}]$.

(a) 1 (b) 2 (c) 4 (d) None of these

(iii) The value of $\hat{i}.(\hat{j} \times \hat{k}) + (\hat{i} \times \hat{k}).\hat{j}$ is:

(a) 0 (b) 1 (c) -1 (d) 2

(iv) Find the value of λ which makes $\lambda\hat{i} - \hat{j} + \hat{k}, 2\hat{i} + \hat{j} - \hat{k}$ and $-\hat{i} + \hat{j} + \hat{k}$ coplanar.

(a) -2 (b) -1 (c) 0 (d) 2

SECTION–C

(Answer all Questions)

Question 29

The cost of manufacturing of certain commodity consists of ₹ 4500 as overheads, ₹ 25 per commodity as the cost of the material and the labour costs ₹ 10 x for x items produced. Find the total cost function.

(a) $4500 + 35x$ (b) $4500 + 25x$ (c) $4500 + 15x$ (d) None of these

Question 30

Given the total cost function for x units of an item as $C(x) = \dfrac{1}{3}x^3 - 5x^2$, find the marginal cost.

(a) $x(x + 10)$ (b) $x(x - 10)$ (c) $x^2 - 10$ (d) $x - 10$

Question 31

The demand function of a certain item is given by $p = 1700 - 7x - \dfrac{1}{3}x^2$. Find the marginal revenue at $x = 10$.

(a) 1460   (b) 1360   (c) 1260   (d) 1110

Question 32

The cost function, $C(x) = 37500 + 500x$ and the revenue function $R(x) = (4500 - 100x)x$. Find the break-even values.

(a) (25, 15)   (b) (35, 20)   (c) (40, 25)   (d) None of these

Question 33

A surgical equipment manufacturer is planning production of a new equipment. For the beginning the fixed cost for setting up the new production line is ₹ 5 lakh. Variable cost for producing each equipment is ₹ 50. The sales department projects that 15000 units can be sold in the first year at the rate of ₹ 100 each. Based on the above information, answer the following questions:

(i) Express the cost function $C(x)$.

     (a) $45000 + x$ (b) $500000 + 50x$ (c) $5000 + 50x$ (d) None of these

(ii) Evaluate the revenue function $R(x)$ for the total revenue from the sale of x units.

     (a) $50x$ (b) $100x$ (c) $150x$ (d) $200x$

(iii) Find the profit function $P(x)$.

     (a) $50(x - 10000)$ (b) $50x - 10000$ (c) $50x + 1000$ (d) None of these

(iv) Determine the break-even point.

     (a) 2500   (b) 5000   (c) 8000   (d) 10000

Answers

1. (d) None of these

     Explanation:
$$A = \{1, 2, 3, ..., 14\}$$
$$R = \{(x, y) : 3x - y = 0\}$$
$$= \{(1, 3), (2, 6), (3, 9), (4, 12)\}$$

     Reflexive: Since (x, x) or $(y, y) \notin R$

     $\Rightarrow$ R is not reflexive.

     Symmetric: Since $(1, 3) \in R$ but $(3, 1) \notin R$

     $\Rightarrow$ R is not symmetric.

     Transitivity: There is no such pair who follow transitivity.

     $\therefore$ Option (d) is correct.

2. (c) neither one-one nor onto

     Explanation: $f : R \to R$ s.t. $f(x) = x^2 + 1$

     Let A and B be two sets of real numbers.

     Let $x_1, x_2 \in A$ s.t. $f(x_1) = f(x_2)$

     $\Rightarrow \qquad x_1^2 + 1 = x_2^2 + 1$

     or $\qquad x_1^2 = x_2^2$

     $\Rightarrow (x_1 - x_2)(x_1 + x_2) = 0$

     $\Rightarrow x_1 = x_2$ or $x_1 = -x_2$

     It means, f is many-one function.

     Now, $\qquad y = x^2 + 1$

     $\Rightarrow \qquad x = \sqrt{y - 1}$

$\Rightarrow$ There is no such element for which y has its pre image.

$\Rightarrow f$ is not onto.

3. (c) $-\dfrac{\pi}{4}$

     Explanation: $\tan^{-1}\left(\tan\dfrac{3\pi}{4} \right)$

$$= \tan^{-1}\left[\tan\left(\pi - \dfrac{\pi}{4} \right) \right]$$

$$= \tan^{-1}\left[-\tan\dfrac{\pi}{4} \right]$$

$$= -\dfrac{\pi}{4}$$

4. (a) 1

     Explanation:

$$\tan^{-1} x + \tan^{-1} y = \dfrac{\pi}{4}$$

$$\tan^{-1}\left(\dfrac{x + y}{1 - xy} \right) = \dfrac{\pi}{4}$$

$$\dfrac{x + y}{1 - xy} = \tan\dfrac{\pi}{4} = 1$$

     $\Rightarrow$

     $\Rightarrow \qquad x + y = 1 - xy$

or $\quad x + y + xy = 1$

5. (d) 4

Explanation: $\sin^{-1}\left(\dfrac{n}{\pi}\right) > \dfrac{\pi}{2}$

$\Rightarrow \qquad \dfrac{n}{\pi} > \sin\dfrac{\pi}{2}$ or 1

$\Rightarrow \qquad n > \pi$ or 3.14

$\therefore$ Minimum value of $n = 4$

6. (b) $x - 1$

Explanation:
$$f(x) = x^2 - 1;$$
$$g(x) = \sqrt{x}$$
$$(fog)(x) = f\,[g(x)]$$
$$= f(\sqrt{x})$$
$$= (\sqrt{x})^2 - 1 = x - 1$$

7. (a) 0

Explanation: $\begin{vmatrix} 2 & -2 & 3 \\ 1 & 4 & 5 \\ 2 & 1 & -3 \end{vmatrix}$

$$M_{11} = \begin{vmatrix} 4 & 5 \\ 1 & -3 \end{vmatrix} = -17;$$

$$M_{32} = \begin{vmatrix} 2 & 3 \\ 1 & 5 \end{vmatrix} = 7;$$

$$M_{33} = \begin{vmatrix} 2 & -2 \\ 1 & 4 \end{vmatrix} = 10$$

$\therefore \quad M_{11} + M_{32} + M_{33} = -17 + 7 + 10$
$$= -17 + 17 = 0$$

8. (c) Scalar matrix.

9. (c) $m \times n$ matrix

Explanation: $A_{m \times p} \times B_{p \times n} = AB_{m \times n}$

10. (a) $a_{ij} = a_{ji}$

Explanation: For a symmetric, $a_{ij} = a_{ji}$.

11. (d) No inverse exists

Explanation: $A = \begin{bmatrix} 2 & 5 \\ 4 & 10 \end{bmatrix}$

$$|A| = 20 - 20 = 0$$

$\Rightarrow A^{-1}$ doesn't exist.

12. (d) $2a^3b^3c^3$

Explanation:

$$D = \begin{vmatrix} 0 & ab^2 & ac^2 \\ a^2b & 0 & bc^2 \\ a^2c & b^2c & 0 \end{vmatrix}$$

$$= a^2b^2c^2 \begin{vmatrix} 0 & a & a \\ b & 0 & b \\ c & c & 0 \end{vmatrix}$$

$$= a^2b^2c^2[-a(0 - bc) + a(bc - 0)]$$
$$= a^2b^2c^2 \times 2abc = 2a^3b^3c^3$$

13. (b) $12x(x^2 + 5)$

Explanation: $y = 3t^2 \quad$ and $\quad t = x^2 + 5$

$\dfrac{dy}{dt} = 6t$ and $\dfrac{dt}{dx} = 2x$

$\therefore \qquad \dfrac{dy}{dx} = \dfrac{dy}{dt} \times \dfrac{dt}{dx}$

$$= 6t \times 2x$$
$$= 12tx = 12x\,(x^2 + 5)$$

14. (b) Discontinuous

Explanation:

$$\lim_{x \to 1} f(x) = \lim_{x \to 1} (x^2)$$
$$= (1)^2 = 1$$

and $\qquad f(1) = 2$

$\because \ \lim_{x \to 1} f(x) \neq f(1)$

$\Rightarrow f$ is discontinuous at $x = 1$

15. (a) $\operatorname{cosec} x \sec x$

Explanation: $y = \log(\tan x)$

Differentiating w.r. to x,

$$\dfrac{dy}{dx} = \dfrac{d}{dx}[\log(\tan x)]$$

$$= \dfrac{1}{\tan x} \dfrac{d}{dx}\tan x$$

$$= \dfrac{1}{\tan x} \cdot \sec^2 x$$

$$= \dfrac{\cos x}{\sin x} \cdot \dfrac{1}{\cos^2 x}$$

$$= \operatorname{cosec} x \sec x$$

16. (b) ∞

Explanation:

$$y = \sin^{-1}\dfrac{x}{a}$$

$$\dfrac{dy}{dx} = \dfrac{1}{\sqrt{1 - \dfrac{x^2}{a^2}}}$$

$$= \dfrac{a}{\sqrt{a^2 - x^2}}$$

$$\left(\dfrac{dy}{dx}\right)_{x=a} = \dfrac{a}{\sqrt{a^2 - a^2}} = \infty$$

17. (b) 1

Explanation: $\lim\limits_{x \to \frac{\pi}{4}} \dfrac{1 - \tan x}{\cos 2x}$

$\because$ It is $\dfrac{0}{0}$ form apply L'Hospital rule,

$$= \lim_{x \to \frac{\pi}{4}} \frac{\dfrac{d}{dx}(1 - \tan x)}{\dfrac{d}{dx}\cos 2x}$$

$$= \lim_{x \to \frac{\pi}{4}} \frac{-\sec^2 x}{-2\sin 2x}$$

$$= \frac{\sec^2 \dfrac{\pi}{4}}{2\sin \dfrac{\pi}{2}}$$

$$= \frac{2}{2 \times 1} = 1$$

18. (b) 1

Explanation: $y = \sin^2 x$

Differentiating w.r. to x,

$$\frac{dy}{dx} = \frac{d}{dx}(\sin^2 x)$$

$$= 2\sin x \cos x$$
$$= \sin 2x$$

$$\therefore \left(\frac{dy}{dx}\right)_{x = \frac{\pi}{4}} = \sin 2 \times \frac{\pi}{4}$$

$$= \sin \frac{\pi}{2} = 1$$

19. (a) $2(15x - 7)$

Explanation: $y = 5x^3 - 7x^2 + 2x$

$$y' = \frac{d}{dx}(5x^3 - 7x^2 + 2x)$$

$$y' = 15x^2 - 14x + 2$$

$$y'' = \frac{d}{dx}(5x^2 - 14x + 2)$$

$$= 30x - 14 \text{ or } 2(15x - 7)$$

20. (b) 1

Explanation: $\sin(\tan^{-1}a + \cot^{-1}a)$

$$\because \quad \tan^{-1}x + \cot^{-1}x = \frac{\pi}{2}$$

$$\therefore \qquad \sin \frac{\pi}{2} = 1$$

21. (i) (a) $x + 2y = 5.$

(ii) (c) 9

Explanation: $|A| = 1(1 - 0) - 2(0 - 4) = 1 + 8 = 9$

(iii) (a) ₹ 1

Explanation: $A_{11} = 1, A_{12} = 4, A_{13} = -2; A_{21} = -2,$
$A_{22} = 1, A_{23} = 4, A_{31} = 4, A_{32} = -2, A_{33} = 1$

$$\therefore \qquad \text{adj } A = \begin{vmatrix} 1 & -2 & 4 \\ 4 & 1 & -2 \\ -2 & 4 & 1 \end{vmatrix}$$

Now $\qquad X = A^{-1}B$

$$\Rightarrow \quad \begin{bmatrix} x \\ y \\ z \end{bmatrix} = \frac{1}{9}\begin{bmatrix} 1 & -2 & 4 \\ 4 & 1 & -2 \\ -2 & 4 & 1 \end{bmatrix}\begin{bmatrix} 5 \\ 8 \\ 5 \end{bmatrix}$$

$$\begin{bmatrix} x \\ y \\ z \end{bmatrix} = \begin{bmatrix} 1 \\ 2 \\ 3 \end{bmatrix}$$

$$\Rightarrow x = 1, y = 2, z = 3$$

$\therefore$ The cost of 1 scale = ₹ 1

(iv) (a) $(4, -2)$

Explanation: From the previous part (iii)
$x = 4$ and $y = -2$

22. (i) (c) $4x^3 - 138x^2 + 1080x$

Explanation:

$$\text{Volume (V)} = (45 - 2x)(24 - 2x)x$$
$$= (4x^2 - 138x + 1080)x$$
$$= 4x^3 - 138x^2 + 1080x$$

(ii) (c) $\dfrac{23}{2}$

Explanation:

$$\frac{dV}{dx} = 12x^2 - 276x + 1080$$

$$\text{and } \frac{d^2V}{dx^2} = 24x - 276$$

According to question,
$$24x - 276 = 0$$

$$x = \frac{276}{24} = \frac{23}{2}$$

(iii) (a) 2450 cm^3

Explanation: $\because \dfrac{dV}{dx} = 0$

$$12x^2 - 276x + 1080 = 0$$
$$x^2 - 23x + 90 = 0$$
$$(x - 18)(x - 5) = 0$$

or $\qquad x = 18, 5$

For the max. volume, put $x = 5$

$$V = (45 - 2x)(24 - 2x)x$$
$$V_{x = 5} = 35 \times 14 \times 5$$
$$= 2450 \text{ cm}^3$$

(iv) (c) 5

Explanation: From previous part (iii) $x = 5$.

23. (i) (b) $\dfrac{-\sin \sqrt{x}}{2\sqrt{x}}$

Explanation:

$$\frac{d}{dx}(\cos \sqrt{x}) = -\sin \sqrt{x} \, \frac{d}{dx}\sqrt{x}$$

$$= -\sin\sqrt{x} \cdot \frac{1}{2\sqrt{x}}$$

$$= \frac{-\sin\sqrt{x}}{2\sqrt{x}}$$

(ii) (c) $\dfrac{1}{2}\sec^2\dfrac{x}{2}$

Explanation:

$$\sqrt{\frac{1-\cos x}{1+\cos x}} = \frac{1-\cos x}{\sin x}$$

$$= \operatorname{cosec} x - \cot x$$

[After multiplying $\sqrt{1-\cos x}$ in numerator and denominator]

$$\therefore \quad \frac{dy}{dx} = \tan\left(\frac{x}{2}\right)\operatorname{cosec} x$$

$$= \frac{\sin\left(\dfrac{x}{2}\right)}{\cos\dfrac{x}{2}\left(2\sin\left(\dfrac{x}{2}\right)\text{or}\left(\dfrac{x}{2}\right)\right)}$$

$$= \frac{1}{2}\sec^2\left(\frac{x}{2}\right)$$

(iii) (d) $\dfrac{\sin x}{2\sqrt{\cos x}(\sqrt{1-\cos x})}$

Explanation: $\dfrac{d}{dx}\left[\cos^{-1}(\sqrt{\cos x})\right]$

$$= \frac{-1}{\sqrt{1-\cos x}}\frac{d}{dx}\sqrt{\cos x}$$

$$= \frac{-1}{\sqrt{1-\cos x}} \cdot \frac{1}{2\sqrt{\cos x}}\frac{d}{dx}\cos x$$

$$= \frac{\sin x}{2\sqrt{\cos x}\sqrt{1-\cos x}}$$

(iv) (b) $\dfrac{1}{t}$

Explanation: $x = at^2$ and $y = 2at$

$$\frac{dx}{dt} = 2at \text{ and } \frac{dy}{dt} = 2a$$

$$\therefore \quad \frac{dy}{dx} = \frac{dy}{dt} \cdot \frac{dt}{dx}$$

$$= 2a \cdot \frac{1}{2at} = \frac{1}{t}$$

24. (c) $\dfrac{\pi}{4}$

Explanation: $\cos\theta = \dfrac{\Sigma a_1 a_2}{\sqrt{\Sigma a_1^2}\cdot\sqrt{\Sigma a_2^2}}$

$$\cos\theta = \frac{1\times\sqrt{2}+2\times0+2\times\sqrt{2}}{\sqrt{1^2+2^2+2^2}\cdot\sqrt{(\sqrt{2})^2+(0)^2+(\sqrt{2})^2}}$$

$$\cos\theta = \frac{\sqrt{2}+2\sqrt{2}}{3\times2}$$

$$= \frac{3\sqrt{2}}{3\times2} = \frac{1}{\sqrt{2}}$$

$$\cos\theta = \cos\frac{\pi}{4} \implies \theta = \frac{\pi}{4}$$

25. (b) $\dfrac{\pi}{2}$

Explanation:

Angle, $\cos\theta = \dfrac{\vec{a}\cdot\vec{b}}{|\vec{a}|\cdot|\vec{b}|}$

$$\cos\theta = \frac{3\times2-2\times3+0\times7}{\sqrt{3^2+(-2)^2}\cdot\sqrt{2^2+3^2+7^2}} = 0$$

$$\theta = \cos\frac{\pi}{2} \text{ or } \theta = \frac{\pi}{2}$$

26. (a) $<-2, 1, 3>$

Explanation: Direction ratios of the line $AB = \vec{AB}$

$$\vec{AB} = (1-3)\hat{i}+(3-2)\hat{j}+(2+1)\hat{k}$$

$$\vec{AB} = -2\hat{i}+\hat{j}+3\hat{k}$$

$\therefore$ Direction ratios $= <-2, 1, 3>$

27. (d) $\hat{i}-\hat{j}+\hat{k}$

Explanation: Using formula,

$$\vec{r} = \vec{a}+\lambda(\vec{b}-\vec{a})$$

$$\vec{r} = (\hat{i}+2\hat{j}+3\hat{k})+\lambda[(\hat{i}-\hat{j}+\hat{k})-(\hat{i}+2\hat{j}+3\hat{k})]$$

$$\vec{r} = (\hat{i}+2\hat{j}+3\hat{k})+1(-3\hat{j}-2\hat{k})$$

$$\vec{r} = \hat{i}-\hat{j}+\hat{k}$$

28. (i) (b) 1

Explanation:

$$[\hat{i}\ \hat{j}\ \hat{k}] = (\hat{i}\times\hat{j}).\hat{k}$$

$$= \hat{k}.\hat{k} \qquad [\because \hat{i}\times\hat{j}=\hat{k}]$$

$$= 1 \qquad [\because \hat{k}.\hat{k}=1]$$

(ii) (c) 4

Explanation:

$$[\vec{a}\ \vec{b}\ \vec{c}] = \begin{vmatrix} 1 & 1 & 1 \\ 1 & -1 & 1 \\ 1 & -1 & -1 \end{vmatrix}$$

$$= 1(1+1)-1(-1-1)+1(-1+1)$$

$$= 2+2+0 = 4$$

(iii) (a) 0

Explanation:
$$\hat{i}.(\hat{j}\times\hat{k})+(\hat{i}\times\hat{k}).\hat{j}$$
$$= \hat{i}.\hat{i}+[-(\hat{k}\times\hat{i})].\hat{j}$$
$$= \hat{i}.\hat{i}-(\hat{k}\times\hat{i}).\hat{j}$$
$$= \hat{i}.\hat{i}-\hat{j}.\hat{j} = 1-1 = 0$$

(iv) (a) -2

Explanation: Since, the given vectors will be coplanar, if
$$[\vec{a}\ \vec{b}\ \vec{c}] = 0$$
$$\begin{vmatrix} \lambda & -1 & 1 \\ 2 & 1 & -1 \\ -1 & 1 & 1 \end{vmatrix} = 0$$
$$\Rightarrow \quad \lambda(1+1)+1(2-1)+1(2+1) = 0$$
$$\Rightarrow \quad 2\lambda+1+3 = 0$$
$$\Rightarrow \quad \lambda = \frac{-4}{2} = -2$$

29. (a) $4500 + 35x$

Explanation: Total cost function
$$= \text{Fixed cost} + \text{total cost of material}$$
$$= 4500 + (25\times x + 10x)$$
$$= 4500 + 35x$$

30. (b) $x(x-10)$

Explanation: $C(x) = \dfrac{1}{3}x^3 - 5x^2$

$\therefore$ Marginal cost (MC) $= \dfrac{dC}{dx}$
$$= \frac{d}{dx}\left(\frac{1}{3}x^3 - 5x^2\right)$$
$$= x^2 - 10x \text{ or } x(x-10)$$

31. (a) 1460

Explanation: Revenue function, $R = px$
$$R = \left(1700 - 7x - \frac{1}{3}x^2\right)x$$
$$R = 1700x - 7x^2 - \frac{1}{3}x^3$$

Marginal Revenue, MR $= \dfrac{dR}{dx}$
$$= \frac{d}{dx}\left(1700x - 7x^2 - \frac{1}{3}x^3\right)$$
$$= 1700 - 14x - x^2$$

At, $x = 10$
$$MR = 1700 - 14\times10 - (10)^2$$
$$= 1700 - 240$$
$$= 1460$$

32. (a) (25, 15)

Explanation: For break-even values,
$$C(x) = R(x)$$
$$37500 + 500x = (4500 - 100x)\,x$$
$$\Rightarrow \quad 37500 + 500x = 4500x - 100x^2$$
$$\Rightarrow 100x^2 - 4000x + 37500 = 0$$
$$\Rightarrow \quad x^2 - 40x + 375 = 0$$
$$\Rightarrow \quad (x-25)(x-15) = 0$$
$$x = 25,\ 15$$

33. (i) (b) $500000 + 50x$

Explanation: Let x be the no. of surgical units sold. Then the cost function is
$$C(x) = 500000 + 50x$$

(ii) (b) $100x$

Explanation: Revenue function,
$$R(x) = P.x = 100x$$

(iii) (a) $50(x - 10000)$

Explanation:
Profit function, $P(x) = R(x) - C(x)$
$$P(x) = 100x - (50x + 500000)$$
$$P(x) = 50x - 500000$$
$$P(x) = 50(x - 10000)$$

(iv) (d) 10000

Explanation: According to question,
Total cost = Total revenue
$$500000 + 50x = 100x$$
$$\Rightarrow \quad 50x = 500000$$
$$\Rightarrow \quad x = 10000$$

❑❑

Questions

SECTION–A

(Answer all Questions)

Question 1

Let A be the set of straight lines in a plane. Then the relation R in A is defined by:

$$R = \{(x, y) : x \perp y\} \text{ is}$$

(a) Symmetric
(b) Reflexive
(c) Transitive
(d) None

Question 2

The function $F : N \to N$ is defined by $f(x) = 10x$ is:

(a) Injective
(b) Surjective
(c) Both (a) and (b)
(d) None

Question 3

If $f(x) = 5x^2 + 2$ and $g(x) = (x + 4)^{-1}$, then the value of $(fog)(2)$ is:

(a) $1\dfrac{5}{36}$
(b) $1\dfrac{4}{37}$
(c) $2\dfrac{5}{36}$
(d) $2\dfrac{4}{37}$

Question 4

If $\alpha \le 2 \tan^{-1}x + \cot^{-1}x \le \beta$, then (α, β) is:

(a) $(0, \pi)$
(b) $\left(-\dfrac{\pi}{2}, \dfrac{\pi}{2}\right)$
(c) $\left(-\dfrac{3\pi}{2}, \dfrac{\pi}{2}\right)$
(d) None

Question 5

Let $A = \{a, b, c\}$ and $B = \{1, 2, 3\}$. Find f^{-1} of the function $f = \{(a, 3), (b, 2), (c, 1)\}$ while $f : A \to B$.

(a) $\{a, 2b, 3c\}$
(b) $\{(3, a), (2, b), (1, c)\}$
(c) $\{(1, a), (2, b), (3, c)\}$
(d) None

Question 6

$\forall\ x \in R$, the value of $\cos^{-1}(-x)$ is:

(a) $\pi + \cos^{-1}(-x)$
(b) $\pi - \cos^{-1}x$
(c) $-\cos^{-1}x$
(d) $\sin^{-1}x$

Question 7

The value of $\begin{vmatrix} -1 & \sin^2 \theta \\ 1 & \cos^2 \theta \end{vmatrix}$ is:

(a) 0
(b) 1
(c) -1
(d) 2

Question 8

The value of $\sin^{-1}\left[\cos\left(\dfrac{13\pi}{5}\right)\right]$ is:

(a) $-\dfrac{\pi}{10}$
(b) $-\dfrac{\pi}{2}$
(c) $\dfrac{\pi}{2}$
(d) $\dfrac{\pi}{10}$

Question 9

Determine the value of k for which $\begin{vmatrix} k & k \\ 4k & 2k \end{vmatrix} = -8$.

(a) 0 (b) -2 (c) 2 (d) ± 2

Question 10

Find the area of the triangle whose vertices are $(b, a + c)$, $(c, a + b)$ and $(a, b + c)$.

(a) 0 (b) $a^2 - b^2$ (c) $ab + bc + ca$ (d) abc

Question 11

Let $a_{ij} = \begin{cases} 1, & \text{if } i = j \\ 0, & \text{if } i \neq j \end{cases}$

Then, A square matrix $A = [a_{ij}]_{m \times n}$ is called :

(a) Identity matrix (b) Unit matrix (c) (a) or (b) (d) None

Question 12

Find the values of x and y which satisfy the following matrix equation.

$$\begin{bmatrix} x+5 & x+5y \\ 4z & 7+t \end{bmatrix} = \begin{bmatrix} 9 & 19 \\ 10 & 8 \end{bmatrix}$$

(a) $(2, 4)$ (b) $(-1, 1)$ (c) $(-3, -1)$ (d) $(4, 3)$

Question 13

Find the points on the curve $y = x^3 - \dfrac{15}{2}x^2 + 18x - 10$ whose gradient is 0.

(a) $(2, 4)$ (b) $(4, -2)$ (c) $(1, 1)$ (d) None

Question 14

Find the value of the following:

$$\sin^{-1}(1) + \sec^{-1}\left(\frac{1}{4}\right) + \csc^{-1}\left(\frac{1}{4}\right)$$

(a) $\dfrac{\pi}{2}$ (b) π (c) $\dfrac{\pi}{3}$ (d) $\dfrac{\pi}{6}$

Question 15

What will be the value of $\tan^{-1}(x^2 + x + 1) - \cot^{-1}(x + 1)$?

(a) $\sin^{-1}x$ (b) $\cos^{-1}x$ (c) $\cot^{-1}x$ (d) $\tan^{-1}x$

Question 16

Find the value of $\lim\limits_{x \to 0} \dfrac{\tan x - x}{x}$.

(a) 1 (b) -1 (c) 0 (d) None

Question 17

If $y = 4 \cos 2x + 5 \sin 2x$, then find the value of $y_2 + 4y$.

(a) 0 (b) 1 (c) 2 (d) 5

Question 18

Evaluate: $\begin{vmatrix} y+z & z & y \\ z & z+x & x \\ y & x & x+y \end{vmatrix}$

(a) $x + y + z$ (b) $4xyz$ (c) $2x + y + z$ (d) 0

Question 19

Let $y = \dfrac{1}{3}x^3 - \dfrac{11}{2}x^2 + 25x + 11$. Find the second derivative of the function y at $x = 6$.

(a) 1 (b) 2 (c) 10 (d) 11

Question 20

Differentiate $\cos^{-1}\left(\dfrac{1-x^2}{1+x^2}\right)$ w.r. to $\tan^{-1}\left(\dfrac{3x-x^3}{1-3x^2}\right)$.

(a) $\dfrac{1}{3}$ (b) $\dfrac{2}{3}$ (c) $\dfrac{1}{2}$ (d) $\dfrac{1}{5}$

Question 21

Let $\begin{bmatrix} 3 & 1 & 1 \\ 2 & -1 & -1 \\ -1 & -1 & 1 \end{bmatrix}\begin{bmatrix} x \\ y \\ z \end{bmatrix} = \begin{bmatrix} 3 \\ 2 \\ 1 \end{bmatrix}$ is represent in the form of AX = B. Based on the above equations, find the answers of the following questions:

(i) The value of $|A|$ is:

    (a) 5   (b) 7   (c) -5 (d) -10

(ii) Find the form of adj A.

    (a) $\begin{vmatrix} -2 & -2 & 0 \\ -1 & 4 & 5 \\ -3 & 2 & -5 \end{vmatrix}$ (b) $\begin{vmatrix} -1 & -1 & 0 \\ -2 & 4 & 5 \\ 3 & 2 & 5 \end{vmatrix}$ (c) $\begin{vmatrix} -1 & 4 & 5 \\ -2 & -1 & 3 \\ 1 & 2 & 3 \end{vmatrix}$ (d) None

(iii) Find A^{-1}.

    (a) $\begin{bmatrix} 1/10 & 2/10 & 3/10 \\ -1 & 1 & 1/10 \\ 5/10 & 1 & 1 \end{bmatrix}$ (b) $\begin{bmatrix} +2/10 & +2/10 & 0 \\ +1/10 & -4/10 & -5/10 \\ +3/10 & -2/10 & +5/10 \end{bmatrix}$

    (c) $\begin{bmatrix} 1 & 2 & 3 \\ -1 & -2 & 1 \\ -1/2 & 1/2 & 3/10 \end{bmatrix}$ (d) None

(iv) Find the value of x, y and z.

    (a) $x = 1, y = -1, z = 1$ (b) $x = y = -1, z = 2$ (c) $x = 0, y = z = 2$ (d) None

Question 22

In a dressing table, the mirror is in the form of a rectangle, surmounted by a semi-cricle. The total perimeter of such mirror is 30 m.

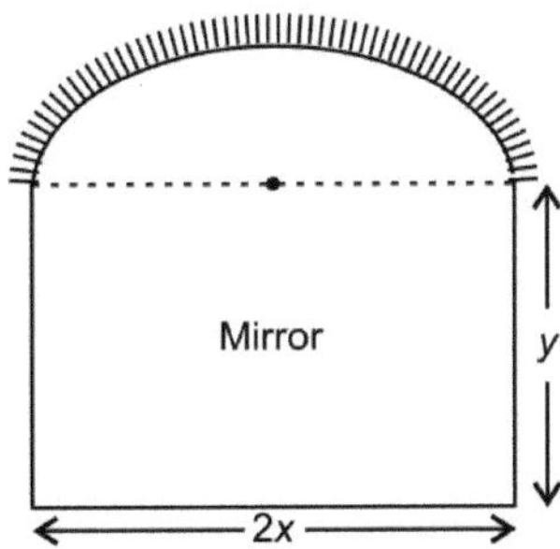

Based on the above information answer the following questions:

(i) Find the relation between x and y.

    (a) $(2+\pi)x + 2y = 30$ (b) $(\pi - 2)x + y = 60$ (c) $(2+\pi)x - 2y = 30$ (d) $(\pi - 2)x + 2y = 60$

(ii) Find the area in terms of x.

    (a) $A = 60 - 2x^2 + \dfrac{1}{2}x$ (b) $A = 30x - 2x^2 - \dfrac{\pi x^2}{2}$

    (c) $A = 60x - \dfrac{\pi x^2}{2} + 3x$ (d) None of these

(iii) For the maximum value of A, the radius of the semicircle is:

    (a) $\dfrac{20}{\pi + 4}$ (b) $\dfrac{20}{\pi - 4}$ (c) $\dfrac{30}{\pi + 4}$ (d) $\dfrac{-30}{\pi - 4}$

(iv) For the maximum value of A, the value of Y will be:

(a) $\dfrac{10}{\pi+4}$ (b) $\dfrac{15}{\pi+4}$ (c) $\dfrac{20}{\pi+4}$ (d) $\dfrac{30}{\pi+4}$

Question 23

Consider the mapping $f : A \to B$ is defined by $f(x) = \dfrac{x^2 - x}{x^2 + 2x}$ such that $f(x)$ is one-one.

Based on this information, answer the following questions:

(i) Domain of $f(x)$ is :

(a) $R - \{0, -2\}$ (b) R (c) $R - \{0\}$ (d) $R - \{1, 2\}$

(ii) Range of $f(x)$ is:

(a) $R - \{1, 2\}$ (b) R (c) $R - \left\{1, -\dfrac{1}{2}\right\}$ (d) None of these

(iii) If $g(x) = 2f(x) + 1$, then $g(x)$ in terms of x is:

(a) $\dfrac{2x}{x+3}$ (b) $\dfrac{2x+3}{x}$ (c) $\dfrac{x+2}{3x}$ (d) $\dfrac{3x}{x+2}$

(iv) A function $f(x)$ is said to be one-one if:

(a) $f(x_1) = f(x_2) \Rightarrow x_1 = x_2$ (b) $-f(x_1) = f(x_2) \Rightarrow x_1 = x_2$
(c) $f(-x_1) = f(-x_2) \Rightarrow x_1 = x_2$ (d) None of these

SECTION–B

(Answer all Questions)

Question 24

What will be the value of m if the vector $\hat{i} - 3\hat{j} + m\hat{k}$ is perpendicular to $4\hat{i} + 2\hat{j} + \hat{k}$?

(a) 0 (b) 1 (c) 2 (d) 3

Question 25

The angle between the two lines $\dfrac{x-5}{1} = \dfrac{y-4}{2} = \dfrac{z+2}{-2}$, $\dfrac{x-3}{2} = \dfrac{y+6}{2} = \dfrac{3z-6}{3}$ is:

(a) $\cos^{-1}\left(\dfrac{2}{3}\right)$ (b) $\cos^{-1}\left(\dfrac{2}{9}\right)$ (c) $\cos^{-1}\left(\dfrac{4}{9}\right)$ (d) $\cos^{-1}\left(\dfrac{4}{3}\right)$

Question 26

What are the direction ratios of the line passing through two points $(3, -2, -5)$ and $(3, -2, 6)$?

(a) <0, 0, 11> (b) <3, 4, 1> (c) <6, -4, 1> (d) None of these

Question 27

The equation of the line passing through the point $(2, -1, 3)$ and parallel to the line $\dfrac{x-3}{3} = \dfrac{y+5}{-5} = \dfrac{z+2}{-2}$ is:

(a) $\dfrac{x-2}{3} = \dfrac{y+1}{-5} = \dfrac{z-3}{-2}$ (b) $\dfrac{x-3}{2} = \dfrac{y+5}{-1} = \dfrac{z+2}{3}$

(c) $\dfrac{x+3}{-2} = \dfrac{y-1}{5} = \dfrac{z-2}{2}$ (d) None of these

Question 28

Let $\vec{a} = 5\hat{i} - 4\hat{j} + 3\hat{k}, \ \vec{b} = \hat{i} + 2\hat{j} - \hat{k}, \ \vec{c} = 2\hat{i} + \hat{j} + \hat{k}$.

Based on this information answer the following questions:

(i) The value of $\vec{c} . \vec{a}$ is:

(a) 7 (b) 9 (c) 11 (d) 15

(ii) The value of $|\vec{a}|$ is:

(a) $2\sqrt{5}$ (b) $5\sqrt{2}$ (c) $\sqrt{5}$ (d) $\sqrt{2}$

(iii) The value of $\vec{a} \cdot \vec{b}$ is:

(a) -6 (b) 6 (c) 5 (d) 3

(iv) The value of $|\vec{c}|$ is:

(a) $\sqrt{3}$ (b) $\sqrt{5}$ (c) $\sqrt{6}$ (d) 1

SECTION–C
(Answer all Questions)

Question 29

Ansh sells a product for ₹ 10 per unit. Fixed costs for him is ₹ 5,000 and variable costs is estimated to run 25% of total revenue. If x shows the no. of units produced, then what will be the total cost function?

(a) $5000 + \dfrac{5}{2}x$ (b) $5000 + 10x$ (c) $5000 + 25x$ (d) None

Question 30

The demand function for a certain item is given by $p = 5000 - 200x$. What will be the total revenue from the sale of 5 units?

(a) 20000 (b) 25000 (c) 15000 (d) 10000

Question 31

A manufacturing company sells m packets of shoes each day at ₹ 200 a packet. The cost of manufacturing these packets is ₹ 100 per packet plus a fixed daily overhead cost of ₹ 450. What will be the profit function?

(a) $450 + 100\,m$ (b) $100\,m - 450$ (c) $450\,m$ (d) $100\,m$

Question 32

The cost function of a firm is given by $f(x) = 5x^3 - 20x$. The average cost of the firm at $x = 5$ is:

(a) 90 (b) 100 (c) 105 (d) 125

Question 33

The demand function for a certain product is represented by the equation: $p = x^2 + 5x + 6$ where x is the number of units demanded and p is the price per unit.

(i) The revenue function $R(x)$ is:

(a) $x^3 + 5x^2 + 6x$ (b) $2x + 5$ (c) $x^2 - 5x - 6$ (d) None

(ii) The marginal revenue $MR(x)$ is:

(a) $1 - \dfrac{6}{x^2}$ (b) $3x^2 + 10x + 6$ (c) $3x^3 + 10x^2 + 6$ (d) $2x^2 + 5$

(iii) The slope of the marginal revenue is:

(a) $5(x + 2)$ (b) $2(3x + 5)$ (c) $10x + 7$ (d) None

(iv) Values of x, for which marginal revenue increases is:

(a) $x = \dfrac{5}{3}$ (b) $x = -\dfrac{5}{3}$ (c) $x > \dfrac{-5}{3}$ (d) None

Answers

1. (a) Symmetric

   Explanation: If $x \perp y \Rightarrow y \perp x$

   $\Rightarrow (x, y)$ and $(y, x) \in R$

   i.e., R is symmetric.

2. (a) Injective

   Explanation: For injective, the function should be one-one.

   Let $x_1, x_2 \in N$. Then we have,

   $$f(x_1) = f(x_2)$$

$\Rightarrow \qquad 10x_1 = 10x_2$

$\Rightarrow \qquad x_1 = x_2 \; " \; x_1, x_2 \in N$

$\therefore f(x)$ is injective.

Now, Range of $f(x)$ = Multiplies of 5 " x in the domain.

But, co-domain = N

$\Rightarrow \qquad$ Range $\neq$ Codomain

$\therefore f(x)$ is not surjective.

3. (c) $2\dfrac{5}{36}$

Explanation: $f(x) = 5x^2 + 2;\ g(x) = (x+4)^{-1} = \dfrac{1}{x+4}$

$$\therefore\quad (fog)(x) = f[g(x)]$$
$$= f\left(\dfrac{1}{x+4}\right)$$
$$= 5\left(\dfrac{1}{x+4}\right)^2 + 2$$

$$\therefore\quad (fog)(2) = 5\left(\dfrac{1}{2+4}\right)^2 + 2$$
$$= \dfrac{5}{36} + 2$$
$$= \dfrac{77}{36} \text{ or } 2\dfrac{5}{36}$$

4. (a) $(0, \pi)$

Explanation: $\alpha \le 2\tan^{-1}x + \cot^{-1}x \le B$ (Given)

Since, $-\dfrac{\pi}{2} \le \tan^{-1}x \le \dfrac{\pi}{2}$

$$\Rightarrow \dfrac{\pi}{2} - \dfrac{\pi}{2} \le \tan^{-1}x + \dfrac{\pi}{2} \le \dfrac{\pi}{2} + \dfrac{\pi}{2}$$
$$\Rightarrow \quad 0 \le \tan^{-1}x + \tan^{-1}x + \cot^{-1}x \le \pi$$
$$\Rightarrow \quad 0 \le 2\tan^{-1}x + \cot^{-1}x \le \pi$$

So, $(\alpha, \beta) \to (0, \pi)$

5. (b) $\{(3, a), (2, b), (1, c)\}$

Explanation: $A = \{a, b, c\},\ B = \{1, 2, 3\}$

$F = \{(a, 3), (b, 2), (c, 1)\}$

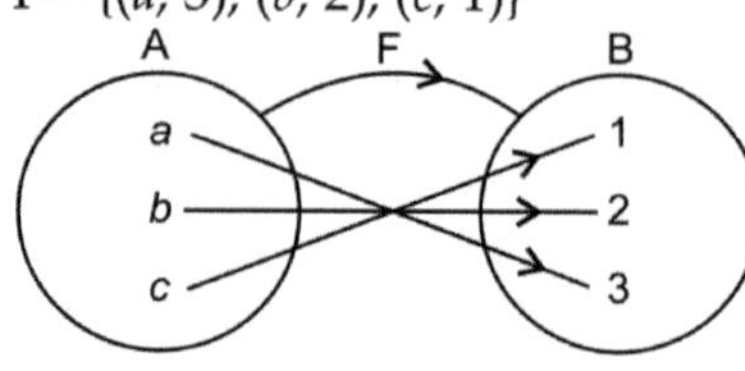

Since, as per the figure, $f : A \to B$ is bijective.

So, its inverse exists.

$$\therefore\quad F^{-1} = \{(3, a), (2, b), (1, c)\}$$

6. (b) $\pi - \cos^{-1}x$

Explanation: Let $\cos^{-1}(-x) = \theta$
$$\Rightarrow \qquad x = -\cos\theta$$
$$\Rightarrow \qquad x = \cos(\pi - \theta)$$
$$\Rightarrow \qquad \cos^{-1}x = \pi - \theta$$
$$\text{or} \qquad \theta = \pi - \cos^{-1}x$$

7. (c) -1

Explanation:
$$\begin{vmatrix} -1 & \sin^2\theta \\ 1 & \cos^2\theta \end{vmatrix} = -\cos^2\theta - \sin^2\theta$$
$$= -(\cos^2\theta + \sin^2\theta)$$
$$= -1 \quad [\because \cos^2\theta + \sin^2\theta = 1]$$

8. (a) $-\dfrac{\pi}{10}$

Explanation: $\sin^{-1}\left[\cos\left(\dfrac{13\pi}{5}\right)\right]$

$$= \sin^{-1}\left[\cos\left(2\pi + \dfrac{3\pi}{5}\right)\right]$$
$$= \sin^{-1}\left[\cos\dfrac{3\pi}{5}\right] \qquad [\because \cos(2n\pi + \theta) = \cos\theta]$$
$$= \sin^{-1}\left[\cos\left(\dfrac{\pi}{2} + \dfrac{\pi}{10}\right)\right]$$
$$= \sin^{-1}\left[-\sin\left(\dfrac{\pi}{10}\right)\right]$$
$$= \sin^{-1}\sin\left(-\dfrac{\pi}{10}\right)$$
$$= -\dfrac{\pi}{10}$$

9. (d) ± 2

Explanation:
$$\begin{vmatrix} k & k \\ 4k & 2k \end{vmatrix} = -8$$
$$\Rightarrow k^2 \begin{vmatrix} 1 & 1 \\ 4 & 2 \end{vmatrix} = -8$$
$$\Rightarrow \quad k^2(2 - 4) = -8 \text{ or } -2k^2 = -8$$
$$\Rightarrow k^2 = 4 \text{ or } k = \pm 2$$

10. (a) 0

Explanation:
$$\text{Area of } \Delta = \dfrac{1}{2}\begin{vmatrix} b & c+a & 1 \\ c & a+b & 1 \\ a & b+c & 1 \end{vmatrix}$$
$$= \dfrac{1}{2}\begin{vmatrix} b & b+c+a & 1 \\ c & c+a+b & 1 \\ a & a+b+c & 1 \end{vmatrix} \quad C_2 \to C_1 + C_2$$
$$= \dfrac{1}{2}(a+b+c)\begin{vmatrix} b & 1 & 1 \\ c & 1 & 1 \\ a & 1 & 1 \end{vmatrix}$$
$$= \dfrac{1}{2}|(a+b+c)\times 0|$$
$$= \dfrac{1}{2}\times 0 = 0$$

11. (c) (a) or (b)

Explanation: Identity or unit matrix.

12. (d) $(4, 3)$

Explanation: By the principle of equality of matrices,

$$\begin{bmatrix} x+5 & x+5y \\ 4z & 7+t \end{bmatrix} = \begin{bmatrix} 9 & 19 \\ 10 & 8 \end{bmatrix}$$

$\Rightarrow x + 5 = 9 \qquad$ and $\qquad x + 5y = 19$

$\Rightarrow x = 4 \qquad$ and $\qquad 4 + 5y = 19$

$$5y = 19 - 4 = 15$$
$$y = 3$$

Hence, $(x, y) = (4, 3)$

13. (a) (2, 4)

Explanation:

$$y = x^3 - \frac{15}{2}x^2 + 18x - 10$$

Differentiation w.r. to x,

$$\frac{dy}{dx} = \frac{d}{dx}\left(x^3 - \frac{15}{2}x^2 + 18x - 10 \right)$$

$$\frac{dy}{dx} = 3x^2 - 15x + 18$$

Here, gradient $\left(\dfrac{dy}{dx} \right) = 0$

$\Rightarrow \qquad\qquad 3x^2 - 15x + 18 = 0$

$\Rightarrow \qquad\qquad x^2 - 5x + 6 = 0$ or $x = 3, 2$

Hence, at $x = 3$, $y = 27 - \dfrac{135}{2} + 54 - 10 = \dfrac{7}{2}$

at $x = 2$, $y = 8 - 30 + 36 - 10 = 4$

$\therefore \qquad\qquad (x, y) = (2, 4)$

14. (b) π

Explanation: $\sin^{-1}(1) + \sec^{-1}\left(\dfrac{1}{4}\right) + \mathrm{cosec}^{-1}\left(\dfrac{1}{4}\right)$

$\because \qquad \sec^{-1}x + \mathrm{cosec}^{-1}x = \dfrac{\pi}{2}$

and $\qquad\qquad \sin\dfrac{\pi}{2} = 1$

$\Rightarrow \qquad\qquad \dfrac{\pi}{2} + \dfrac{\pi}{2} = \pi$

15. (d) $\tan^{-1}x$

Explanation: $\tan^{-1}(x^2 + x + 1) - \cot^{-1}(x + 1)$

$= \tan^{-1}(x^2 + x + 1) - \tan^{-1}\dfrac{1}{x+1}$

$= \tan^{-1}\left(\dfrac{x^2 + x + 1 - \dfrac{1}{x+1}}{1 + \dfrac{x^2 + x + 1}{x+1}} \right)$

$= \tan^{-1}x$

16. (c) 0

Explanation: $\lim\limits_{x \to 0} \dfrac{\tan x - x}{x}$

$= \lim\limits_{x \to 0} \dfrac{\tan x}{x} - \lim\limits_{x \to 0} \dfrac{x}{x}$

$= \lim\limits_{x \to 0} \dfrac{\dfrac{d}{dx}(\tan x)}{\dfrac{d}{dx}(x)} - 1 \qquad\qquad \left[\because \dfrac{0}{0} \text{ form} \right]$

$= \lim\limits_{x \to 0} \dfrac{\sec^2 x}{1} - 1$

$= \sec^2 0 - 1 = 1 - 1 = 0$

17. (a) 0

Explanation: $y = 4\cos 2x + 5\sin 2x \qquad ...(i)$

Differentiation w.r. to x,

$$y_1 = -4 \times 2\sin 2x + 5 \times 2\cos 2x$$

Again, differentiation w.r. to x,

$$y_2 = -4 \times 2 \times 2\cos 2x - 5 \times 2 \times 2\sin 2x$$
$$y_2 = -4(4\cos 2x + 5\sin 2x) \quad \text{[From eq. (i)]}$$
$$y_2 = -4y \text{ or } y_2 + 4y = 0$$

18. (b) $4xyz$

Explanation: $\begin{vmatrix} y+z & z & y \\ z & z+x & x \\ y & x & x+y \end{vmatrix}$

Using, $C_1 \to C_1 - (C_2 + C_3)$

$$\begin{vmatrix} 0 & z & y \\ -2x & z+x & x \\ -2x & x & x+y \end{vmatrix}$$

Using, $R_2 \to R_2 - R_3$

$$\begin{vmatrix} 0 & z & y \\ 0 & z & -y \\ -2x & x & x+y \end{vmatrix} = -2x(-yz - yz)$$

$$= -2x(-2yz) = 4xyz$$

19. (a) 1

Explanation: $y = \dfrac{1}{3}x^3 - \dfrac{11}{2}x^2 + 25x + 11$

Differentiation w.r. to x,

$$\frac{dy}{dx} = x^2 - 11x + 25$$

Again, differentiation w.r. to x,

$$\frac{d^2 y}{dx^2} = 2x - 11$$

and $\left[\dfrac{d^2 y}{dx^2} \right]_{x=6} = 2 \times 6 - 11$

$$= 12 - 11 = 1$$

20. (b) $\dfrac{2}{3}$

Explanation: Let $u = \cos^{-1}\left(\dfrac{1-x^2}{1+x^2} \right)$

and $v = \tan^{-1}\left(\dfrac{3x - x^3}{1 - 3x^2} \right)$

and say, $x = \tan\theta \Rightarrow \theta = \tan^{-1}x$

$$u = \cos^{-1}\left(\frac{1-\tan^2\theta}{1+\tan^2\theta}\right)$$

and $$v = \tan^{-1}\left(\frac{3\tan\theta - \tan^3\theta}{1-3\tan^2\theta}\right)$$

$u = \cos^{-1}\cos 2\theta$ and $\quad v = \tan^{-1}\tan 3\theta$

$u = 2\theta \qquad\qquad$ and $\qquad v = 3\theta$

$u = 2\tan^{-1}x \qquad$ and $\qquad v = 3\tan^{-1}x$

$\therefore \quad \dfrac{du}{dx} = \dfrac{2}{1+x^2}$ and $\dfrac{dv}{dx} = \dfrac{3}{1+x^2}$

Now $\quad \dfrac{du}{dv} = \dfrac{du}{dx} \times \dfrac{dx}{dv}$

$$= \frac{2}{1+x^2} \times \frac{1+x^2}{3} = \frac{2}{3}$$

21. (i) (d) -10

Explanation: $|A| = \begin{vmatrix} 3 & 1 & 1 \\ 2 & -1 & -1 \\ -1 & -1 & 1 \end{vmatrix}$

$$= 3(-1-1) - 1(2-1) + 1(-2-1)$$

$$= -6 - 1 - 3 = -10$$

(ii) (a) $\begin{vmatrix} -2 & -2 & 0 \\ -1 & 4 & 5 \\ -3 & 2 & -5 \end{vmatrix}$

Explanation: $A_{11} = -2, A_{12} = -1, A_{13} = -3,$
$A_{21} = -2,$

$A_{22} = 4, A_{23} = 2, A_{31} = 0, A_{32} = 5, A_{33} = -5$

$\therefore \qquad \text{adj } A = \begin{bmatrix} -2 & -2 & 0 \\ -1 & 4 & 5 \\ -3 & 2 & -5 \end{bmatrix}$

(iii) (b) $\begin{bmatrix} +2/10 & +2/10 & 0 \\ +1/10 & -4/10 & -5/10 \\ +3/10 & -2/10 & +5/10 \end{bmatrix}$

Explanation:

$$A^{-1} = \frac{\text{adj } A}{|A|}$$

$$= \begin{bmatrix} -2/-10 & -2/-10 & 0 \\ -1/-10 & 4/-10 & 5/-10 \\ -3/-10 & 2/-10 & -5/-10 \end{bmatrix}$$

$$= \begin{bmatrix} 2/10 & 2/10 & 0 \\ 1/10 & -4/10 & -5/10 \\ 3/10 & -2/10 & 5/10 \end{bmatrix}$$

(iv) (a) $x = 1, y = -1, z = 1$

Explanation: $X = A^{-1}B$

$$X = \begin{bmatrix} +2/10 & +2/10 & 0 \\ +1/10 & -4/10 & -5/10 \\ +3/10 & -2/10 & +5/10 \end{bmatrix}\begin{bmatrix} 3 \\ 2 \\ 1 \end{bmatrix}$$

$\therefore x = 1, y = -1, z = 1$

22. (i) (a) $(2+\pi)x + 2y = 30$

Explanation: Total perimeter = 30

$$y + 2x + y + \pi.x = 30$$

$$2x + 2y + \pi x = 30$$

$$(2+\pi)x + 2y = 30$$

(ii) (b) $A = 30x - 2x^2 - \dfrac{\pi x^2}{2}$

Explanation: Area = Area of rectangle + Area of semicircle

$$A = 2x \times y + \frac{1}{2}\pi x^2$$

$$A = 2xy + \frac{1}{2}\pi x^2$$

$$A = x[30 - (2+\pi)x] + \frac{1}{2}\pi x^2$$

$$A = 30x - 2x^2 - \pi x^2 + \frac{1}{2}\pi x^2$$

$$A = 30x - 2x^2 - \frac{1}{2}\pi x^2$$

(iii) (c) $\dfrac{30}{\pi+4}$

Explanation: $\dfrac{dA}{dx} = 30 - 4x - \pi x$

For max or min, $\dfrac{dA}{dx} = 0$

$$\Rightarrow \quad 30 - 4x - \pi x = 0$$

$$\Rightarrow \quad x = \frac{30}{\pi+4}$$

and $\dfrac{d^2A}{dx^2} = -4 - \pi = -\text{ve}$

$\therefore$ A is maximum when $x = \dfrac{30}{\pi+4}$

(iv) (d) $\dfrac{30}{\pi+4}$

Explanation: $2y = 30 - (2+\pi)x$

$$2y = 30 - (2+\pi)\cdot\frac{30}{\pi+4}$$

$$2y = 30\left[\frac{\pi+4-2-\pi}{\pi+4}\right] \text{ or } y = \frac{30}{\pi+4}$$

23. (i) (a) $R - \{0, -2\}$

Explanation: $f(x) = \dfrac{x^2 - x}{x^2 + 2x} = \dfrac{x - 1}{x + 2}$

$\therefore$ Domain of $f(x) = R - \{0, -2\}$

(ii) (c) $R - \left\{1, -\dfrac{1}{2}\right\}$

Explanation: Range of $f(x) = R - \left\{1, -\dfrac{1}{2}\right\}$

(iii) (d) $\dfrac{3x}{x + 2}$

Explanation: $g(x) = 2f(x) + 1$

$$= 2 \cdot \dfrac{x - 1}{x + 2} + 1$$

$$= \dfrac{2x - 2 + x + 2}{x + 2}$$

$$= \dfrac{3x}{x + 2}$$

(iv) (a) $f(x_1) = f(x_2) \Rightarrow x_1 = x_2$

Explanation: $f(x_1) = f(x_2)$

$\Rightarrow \qquad x_1 = x_2$

As, $\dfrac{x_1 - 1}{x_1 + 2} = \dfrac{x_2 - 1}{x_2 + 2}$

$\Rightarrow x_1 x_2 - x_2 + 2x_1 - 2 = x_1 x_2 - x_1 + 2x_2 - 2$

$\Rightarrow 2x_1 + x_1 = 2x_2 + x_2$

$\Rightarrow 3x_1 = 3x_2$ or x_1 or x_2

24. (c) 2

Explanation: Since, both vectors are perpendicular to each other.

So, $(\hat{i} - 3\hat{j} + m\hat{k}).(4\hat{i} + 2\hat{j} + \hat{k}) = 0$

$\Rightarrow \qquad 1.4 + (-3).2 + m.1 = 0$

$\Rightarrow \qquad 4 - 6 + m = 0$

$\Rightarrow \qquad m = 2$

25. (c) $\cos^{-1}\left(\dfrac{4}{9}\right)$

Explanation:

$$\cos\theta = \left|\dfrac{a_1 a_2 + b_1 b_2 + c_1 c_2}{\sqrt{a_1^2 + b_1^2 + c_1^2} \cdot \sqrt{a_2^2 + b_2^2 + c_2^2}}\right|$$

Here, $a_1 = 1$, $a_2 = 2$, $b_1 = 2$, $b_2 = 2$, $c_1 = 2$, $c_2 = 1$

$\therefore \qquad \cos\theta = \left|\dfrac{1 \times 2 + 2 \times 2 + (-2) \times 1}{\sqrt{1 + 4 + 4} \cdot \sqrt{4 + 4 + 1}}\right|$

$\cos\theta = \left|\dfrac{2 + 4 - 2}{3 \times 3}\right| = \left|\dfrac{4}{9}\right|$

$\Rightarrow \qquad \theta = \cos^{-1}\left(\dfrac{4}{9}\right)$

26. (a) $\langle 0, 0, 11 \rangle$

Explanation: Direction ratios

$= \langle (3 - 3), (-2 + 2), (6 + 5) \rangle$

$= \langle 0, 0, 11 \rangle$

27. (a) $\dfrac{x - 2}{3} = \dfrac{y + 1}{-5} = \dfrac{z - 3}{-2}$

Explanation: Equation of the line

$\Rightarrow \dfrac{x - x_1}{a} = \dfrac{y - y_1}{b} = \dfrac{z - z_1}{c}$

$\Rightarrow \dfrac{x - 2}{3} = \dfrac{y + 1}{-5} = \dfrac{z - 3}{-2}$

28. (i) (b) 9

Explanation:

$\vec{c} \cdot \vec{a} = (2\hat{i} + \hat{j} + \hat{k}).(5\hat{i} - 4\hat{j} + 3\hat{k})$

$= 2.5 + 1.(-4) + 1.3$ As $(i.i = 1)$

$= 10 - 4 + 3 = 9$

(ii) (b) $5\sqrt{2}$

Explanation: $|\vec{a}| = \sqrt{(5)^2 + (-4)^2 + 3^2} = \qquad =$

$= \sqrt{50} = 5\sqrt{2}$

(iii) (a) -6

Explanation: $\vec{a} \cdot \vec{b} = (5\hat{i} - 4\hat{j} + 3\hat{k}).(\hat{i} + 2\hat{j} - \hat{k})$

$= 5.1 + (-4).2 + 3.(-1)$

$= 5 - 8 - 3 = -6$

(iv) (c) $\sqrt{6}$

Explanation: $|\vec{c}| = \sqrt{2^2 + 1^2 + 1^2}$

$= \sqrt{4 + 1 + 1} = \sqrt{6}$

29. (a) $5000 + \dfrac{5}{2}x$

Explanation: Given,

Price per unit = ₹ 10

Total units = x

$\therefore$ Total revenue $R(x) = P.x = 10x$

$\therefore$ Total cost function $C(x)$

$= 5000 + 25\%$ of $R(x)$

$= 5000 + \dfrac{25}{100} \times 10x$

$= 5000 + \dfrac{5}{2}x$

30. (a) 20000

Explanation: Demand function, $P = 5000 - 200x$

Total no. of units, $x = 5$

$\therefore \qquad$ Revenue, $R(x) = P.x$

$= (5000 - 200x)x$

$= 5000x - 200x^2$

At $x = 5$, $R(5) = 5000 \times 5 - 200 \times 25$

$$= 25000 - 5000$$
$$= 20000$$

31. (b) 100 m–450

Explanation: Total revenue, $R(m) = 200\,m$

Cost function, $C(m) = 450 + 100m$

$\therefore$ Profit function $= R(m) - C(m)$

$$= 200\,m - (450 + 100\,m)$$
$$= 100\,m - 450$$

32. (c) 105

Explanation: $f(x) = 5x^3 - 20x$

$$\text{Average cost} = \frac{f(x)}{x}$$
$$= \frac{5x^3 - 20x}{x}$$
$$= 5x^2 - 20$$

At $x = 5$,

$$\text{Average cost} = 5 \times (5)^2 - 20$$
$$= 125 - 20$$
$$= 105$$

33. (i) (a) $x^3 + 5x^2 + 6x$

Explanation: Demand function,
$$p = x^2 + 5x + 6$$

Revenue function,
$$R(x) = p.x$$
$$R(x) = (x^2 + 5x + 6).x$$
$$R(x) = x^3 + 5x^2 + 6x$$

(ii) (b) $3x^2 + 10x + 6$

Explanation: For marginal revenue (MC)
$$\frac{dR}{dx} = \frac{d}{dx}(x^3 + 5x^2 + 6x)$$
$$= 3x^2 + 10x + 6$$

(iii) (b) $2(3x + 5)$

Explanation:

Slope, $\dfrac{d}{dx}(\text{MC}) = \dfrac{d}{dx}(3x^2 + 10x + 6)$

$$= 6x + 10 = 2(3x + 5)$$

(iv) (c) $x > \dfrac{-5}{3}$

Explanation: For increasing condition:
$$6x + 10 > 0$$
$$\Rightarrow \qquad 6x > -10$$
$$\Rightarrow \qquad x > \frac{-10}{6} \text{ or } \frac{-5}{3}$$

$\square\square$

SECTION–A
(Answer all Questions)

Question 1

The function $f : R \rightarrow R$ defined by $f(x) = 4x + 3$ is:

(a) one-one   (b) many-one   (c) onto   (d) bijective

Question 2

Let $A = \{1, 2, 3\}$ and R be the function defined as $R = \{(1, 1), (2, 2), (3, 3), (1, 2), (2, 3), (1, 3)\}$. Then R is:

(a) reflexive but not symmetric   (b) reflexive but not transitive

(c) symmetric but not transitive   (d) symmetric but not reflexive

Question 3

If $f(x) = \dfrac{3x + 2}{5x - 3}$, then $(fof)(x)$ is:

(a) x (b) $2x - 3$ (c) $-x$ (d) $3x - 2$

Question 4

The principal value of $\cos^{-1}\left(-\dfrac{1}{2}\right)$ is:

(a) $-\dfrac{\pi}{3}$ (b) $\dfrac{2\pi}{3}$ (c) $\dfrac{5\pi}{6}$ (d) $\dfrac{\pi}{3}$

Question 5

The value of the expression $2\sec^{-1} 2 + \sin^{-1}\left(\dfrac{1}{2}\right)$ is:

(a) $\dfrac{\pi}{3}$ (b) $\dfrac{\pi}{6}$ (c) $\dfrac{5\pi}{6}$ (d) $\dfrac{2\pi}{9}$

Question 6

Let T be the set of triangles in a plane and let R be a relation defined as $R = \{(T_1, T_2) : T_1 \text{ is congruent to } T_2\}$. Then R is:

(a) reflexive   (b) symmetric   (c) transitive   (d) equivalence

Question 7

If $P = \begin{bmatrix} x+2 & 2x+3 \\ x-1 & 3 \end{bmatrix}$ is a symmetric matrix, then value of x is:

(a) 1   (b) -2 (c) -4 (d) 3

Question 8

The value of $\begin{vmatrix} \sin 60° & \sin 90° \\ \cos 90° & \cos 30° \end{vmatrix}$ is:

(a) 1   (b) $\dfrac{3}{4}$ (c) $\dfrac{1}{2}$ (d) $\dfrac{3}{2}$

Question 9

Which of the following is a row matrix?

(a) $[1\ 2\ 3]$ (b) $\begin{bmatrix} 1 \\ 2 \\ 3 \end{bmatrix}$ (c) $\begin{bmatrix} 1 & 0 \\ 0 & 1 \end{bmatrix}$ (d) $\begin{bmatrix} 0 & 0 \\ 0 & 0 \end{bmatrix}$

Question 10

If $A = \begin{bmatrix} a & b \\ b & a \end{bmatrix}$ and $A^2 = \begin{bmatrix} \alpha & \beta \\ \beta & \alpha \end{bmatrix}$, then $(\alpha + \beta) =$

(a) $a^2 - b^2$ (b) $(a - b)^2$ (c) $(a + b)^2$ (d) $a^2 + b^2$

Question 11

The point on the curve $y = x^3 - 3x^2 + 3x$ where the tangent to the curve is parallel to x-axis is:

(a) $(0, 2)$ (b) $(1, 1)$ (c) $(-2, 0)$ (d) $(3, 4)$

Question 12

If $A = \begin{bmatrix} 1 & 3 \\ 5 & 7 \end{bmatrix}$ and $B = \begin{bmatrix} -1 & 9 \\ 7 & 2 \end{bmatrix}$, then $(AB)^T$ is:

(a) $\begin{bmatrix} -1 & 35 \\ 27 & 14 \end{bmatrix}$ (b) $\begin{bmatrix} 0 & 12 \\ 12 & 14 \end{bmatrix}$ (c) $\begin{bmatrix} 26 & 13 \\ 58 & 49 \end{bmatrix}$ (d) $\begin{bmatrix} 20 & 44 \\ 15 & 59 \end{bmatrix}$

Question 13

If $x = \log t$ and $y = \sin t$, then $\dfrac{dy}{dx} = ?$

(a) $t \cos t$ (b) $\dfrac{\cos t}{t}$ (c) $t \sec t$ (d) $\dfrac{\sin t}{\log t}$

Question 14

If $y = (x + \sqrt{x^2 - 1})^m$, then $(x^2 - 1)\left(\dfrac{dy}{dx}\right)^2 = ?$

(a) m^2 (b) $m^2 y^2$ (c) y (d) y^2

Question 15

If the matrix $\begin{bmatrix} 3-x & 2 & 2 \\ 2 & 4-x & 1 \\ -2 & -4 & -1-x \end{bmatrix}$ is singular, then the value(s) of x is/are:

(a) $0, 1, 2$ (b) $-1, 3, 4$ (c) $-4, 3, 7$ (d) $0, 3, 3$

Question 16

If $\begin{vmatrix} 2x & 5 \\ 8 & x \end{vmatrix} = \begin{vmatrix} 6 & -2 \\ 7 & 3 \end{vmatrix}$, then the value(s) of x is/are :

(a) $3, 3$ (b) ± 3 (c) ± 6 (d) $3, 6$

Question 17

If the function given by $f(x) = \begin{cases} ax + 1, & x \le 3 \\ bx + 3, & x > 3 \end{cases}$ is continuous at $x = 3$, then the relation between a and b is:

(a) $a = b + \dfrac{2}{3}$ (b) $a = b$ (c) $3a = b$ (d) $a + b = \dfrac{1}{3}$

Question 18

The function $f(x) = x^3 - 3x^2 + 4x, \ x \in R$ is increasing on:

(a) $(0, \infty)$ (b) $(-\infty, 3)$ (c) R (d) $(-\infty, 0)$

Question 19

The points of local maxima and local minima of the function $f(x) = x^3 - 3x + 3$, are:

(a) ± 1 (b) $0, 1$ (c) $-1, 0, 1$ (d) $1, 3$

Question 20

The derivative of x^x with respect to $x \log x$ is:

(a) $\dfrac{x^x}{1+\log x}$ 　　　 (b) $\dfrac{x^x \log x}{1+\log x}$ 　　　 (c) $x \log x$ 　　　 (d) x^x

Question 21

Trigonometric functions are many-one functions, so they are many-one, and hence their inverse does not exist. But if we restrict their domain and range, then their inverse may exist.

Based on the above information, answer the following questions:

(i) If $\sin^{-1}(2x\sqrt{1-x^2}) = ?$

(a) $2 \sin^{-1} x$ 　　　 (b) $\dfrac{2}{\sin^{-1} x}$ 　　　 (c) $-2\cos^{-1} x$ 　　　 (d) $-2\sec^{-1} x$

(ii) $\tan^{-1}\dfrac{1}{2} + \tan^{-1}\dfrac{2}{11} = ?$

(a) $\tan^{-1}\dfrac{14}{13}$ 　　　 (b) $\tan^{-1}\dfrac{3}{4}$ 　　　 (c) $\tan^{-1}\dfrac{1}{11}$ 　　　 (d) $\tan^{-1}\dfrac{13}{22}$

(iii) The value of $\cos(\sec^{-1}x + \csc^{-1}x)$, $|x| \geq 1$, is:

(a) 1 　　　 (b) 0 　　　 (c) -1 　　　 (d) $\dfrac{1}{2}$

(iv) If $\cos^{-1}\{\sin(\cos^{-1}x)\} = \dfrac{\pi}{6}$, then the value(s) of x are:

(a) $\pm\dfrac{1}{\sqrt{2}}$ 　　　 (b) ± 1 　　　 (c) $\pm\dfrac{1}{2}$ 　　　 (d) $0, 1$

Question 22

Consider a closed right circular cylinder of given surface area and maximum volume.

Based on the above information, answer the following questions by choosing the correct option.

(i) If r, h are the radius and height, respectively of the cylinder, then the height of the cylinder in terms of its radius is:

(a) $h = \dfrac{S}{2\pi r}$ 　　　 (b) $h = \dfrac{S+2\pi r}{\pi r^2}$ 　　　 (c) $h = \dfrac{S-2\pi r^2}{2\pi r}$ 　　　 (d) $h = \dfrac{Sr}{2\pi}$

(ii) Volume of the cylinder, as a function of radius is:

(a) $\dfrac{1}{2}Sr - \pi r^3$ 　　　 (b) $\dfrac{1}{2}Sr$ 　　　 (c) $S - 2\pi r$ 　　　 (d) $\dfrac{S+2\pi r}{\pi r^2}$

(iii) The volume of the cylinder will be maximum if:

(a) $r = h$ 　　　 (b) $r = 2h$ 　　　 (c) $r = \dfrac{1}{3}h$ 　　　 (d) $r = \dfrac{1}{2}h$

(iv) Maximum volume of the cylinder is:

(a) πr^3 　　　 (b) $2\pi r^3$ 　　　 (c) $\dfrac{\pi}{2r}$ 　　　 (d) $\dfrac{\pi}{r}$

Question 23

The sum of three numbers is 6. If we multiply third number by 3 and add second number to it, we get 11. By adding first and third numbers, we get double of the second number.

Based on the above information, answer the following questions by choosing the correct answer.

(i) Let x, y, z be the three numbers respectively. Then the linear equations representing the given conditions are:

(a) $x + y + z = 6;\ x + 3y = 11;\ x - 2y + z = 0$ 　　　 (b) $x + y + z = 6;\ y + 3z = 11;\ x - 2y + z = 0$

(c) $x + y + z = 6;\ x + 3z = 11;\ x + 2y + z = 0$ 　　　 (d) $x + y + z = 6;\ y + 3z = 11;\ x + 2y + z = 0$

(ii) Let AX = B be the matrix form of given conditions. Then adj A =

(a) $\begin{bmatrix} 7 & 3 & -1 \\ -3 & 0 & 3 \\ 2 & -3 & 1 \end{bmatrix}$ 　(b) $\begin{bmatrix} -7 & -3 & 1 \\ 3 & 0 & -3 \\ -2 & 3 & -1 \end{bmatrix}$ 　(c) $\begin{bmatrix} -7 & 3 & -2 \\ -3 & 0 & 3 \\ 1 & -3 & -1 \end{bmatrix}$ 　(d) $\begin{bmatrix} 7 & -3 & 2 \\ 3 & 0 & -3 \\ -1 & 3 & 1 \end{bmatrix}$

(iii) Inverse of matrix A is:

(a) $\dfrac{1}{9}\begin{bmatrix} 7 & 3 & -1 \\ -3 & 0 & 3 \\ 2 & -3 & 1 \end{bmatrix}$ 　(b) $\dfrac{1}{9}\begin{bmatrix} -7 & 3 & -2 \\ -3 & 0 & 3 \\ 1 & -3 & -1 \end{bmatrix}$ 　(c) $\dfrac{1}{9}\begin{bmatrix} 7 & -3 & 2 \\ 3 & 0 & -3 \\ -1 & 3 & 1 \end{bmatrix}$ 　(d) Does not exist

(iv) The values of x, y, z respectively are:

(a) 1, 3, 2 　　(b) 1, 2, 3 　　(c) 3, 1, 2 　　(d) 2, 1, 3

SECTION–B
(Answer all Questions)

Question 24

If $\vec{a}$ and $\vec{b}$ are two vectors such that $|\vec{a}| = 2, |\vec{b}| = 3$ and $\vec{a}.\vec{b} = 3$, then the angle between $\vec{a}$ and $\vec{b}$ is:

(a) $\dfrac{\pi}{2}$ 　　(b) $\dfrac{\pi}{6}$ 　　(c) $\dfrac{\pi}{4}$ 　　(d) $\dfrac{\pi}{3}$

Question 25

The direction cosines of the line $\dfrac{2x-5}{4} = \dfrac{y+4}{3} = \dfrac{6-z}{6}$ are:

(a) $\dfrac{2}{7}, \dfrac{3}{7}, -\dfrac{6}{7}$ 　(b) $\dfrac{4}{\sqrt{61}}, \dfrac{3}{\sqrt{61}}, \dfrac{6}{\sqrt{61}}$ 　(c) $\dfrac{4}{\sqrt{61}}, \dfrac{3}{\sqrt{61}}, -\dfrac{6}{\sqrt{61}}$ 　(d) $\dfrac{2}{7}, \dfrac{3}{7}, \dfrac{6}{7}$

Question 26

If the lines $\dfrac{1-x}{3} = \dfrac{y-2}{2k} = \dfrac{z-3}{2}$ and $\dfrac{x-1}{3k} = \dfrac{y-5}{1} = \dfrac{6-z}{5}$ are perpendicular to each other, then the value of k is:

(a) $\dfrac{2}{3}$ 　　(b) $-\dfrac{4}{9}$ 　　(c) $-\dfrac{10}{7}$ 　　(d) $\dfrac{19}{4}$

Question 27

The shortest distance between the lines $\dfrac{x-8}{3} = \dfrac{y+9}{-16} = \dfrac{z-10}{7}$ and $\dfrac{x-15}{3} = \dfrac{y-29}{8} = \dfrac{z-5}{-5}$ is:

(a) 7.44 units 　(b) 8.39 units 　(c) 6.47 units 　(d) 5.24 units

Question 28

The coordinates of houses of four friends, abtilesh, Bharat, Charlie and Divit are given as A(1, – 1, 2), B(2, 1, – 1), C(3, – 1, 2) and D(2, 3, 1) respectively.

Based on the above information, answer the following questions by choosing the correct option.

(i) The position vector $\vec{BC}$ is:

(a) $\hat{i}+2\hat{j}+3\hat{k}$ 　(b) $-\hat{i}+2\hat{i}-3\hat{k}$ 　(c) $\hat{i}-2\hat{j}+3\hat{k}$ 　(d) $\hat{i}+2\hat{j}-3\hat{k}$

(ii) The magnitude of vector $\vec{BC}$ is:

(a) $\sqrt{13}$ units 　(b) $\sqrt{14}$ units 　(c) $\sqrt{12}$ units 　(d) $\sqrt{11}$ units

(iii) The projection of $\vec{A}$ on $\vec{C}$ is:

(a) $\dfrac{8}{\sqrt{14}}$ 　　(b) $\dfrac{7}{\sqrt{14}}$ 　　(c) $\dfrac{5}{\sqrt{14}}$ 　　(d) $\dfrac{11}{\sqrt{14}}$

(iv) The cross product of vectors $\vec{D}$ and $\vec{A}$ is:

(a) $7\hat{i}+3\hat{j}+5\hat{k}$ 　(b) $7\hat{i}-3\hat{j}+5\hat{k}$ 　(c) $7\hat{i}+3\hat{j}-5\hat{k}$ 　(d) $7\hat{i}-3\hat{j}-5\hat{k}$

SECTION–C

(Answer all Questions)

Question 29

The revenue function of a commodity is given by R(x) = $10x^2 - 17x + 43$. Its marginal revenue function is:

(a) $20x - 17$ (b) $10x - 17 + \dfrac{43}{x}$ (c) $\dfrac{10}{3}x^3 - \dfrac{17}{2}x^2 + 43x$ (d) None of these

Question 30

For manufacturing a certain item, the fixed cost is ₹ 6500 and cost of producing each unit is ₹ 12. If the number of units produced is x, then the average cost function is:

(a) $12x + 6500$ (b) $12x^2 + 6500x$ (c) $12 + \dfrac{6500}{x}$ (d) $6x^2 + 6500x$

Question 31

If the demand function of a commodity is $p = 100 - x$ and x is the number of units demanded, then the revenue function is:

(a) $100x - \dfrac{x^2}{2}$ (b) $100 - x$ (c) $\dfrac{100}{x} - 1$ (d) $100x - x^2$

Question 32

If the price of a commodity is fixed at ₹ 15, x is the number of units demanded and its cost function is C(x) = $2x + 26$, then the break-even point is:

(a) $x = 1$ (b) $x = 2$ (c) $x = 5.5$ (d) $x = -5.5$

Question 33

Given the total cost function for x units of a commodity is C(x) = $\dfrac{1}{3}x^3 - 5x^2 + 30x - 15$.

Based on the above information, answer the following questions by choosing the correct answer.

(i) The cost of 3 units of the commodity is:

    (a) 9   (b) 25   (c) 42   (d) 17

(ii) The average cost function is:

    (a) $\dfrac{2}{3}x^2 - 10x + 30$ (b) $\dfrac{1}{3}x^4 - 5x^3 + 30x^2 - 15x$

    (c) $\dfrac{1}{3}x^2 - 5x + 30 - \dfrac{15}{x}$ (d) $\dfrac{1}{12}x^4 - \dfrac{5}{3}x^3 + 15x^2 - 15x$

(iii) The marginal cost function is:

    (a) $\dfrac{2}{3}x^2 - 5x + 30$ (b) $x^2 - 10x + 30$

    (c) $\dfrac{1}{3}x^2 - 5x + 30 - \dfrac{15}{x}$ (d) $\dfrac{1}{12}x^4 - \dfrac{5}{3}x^3 + 15x^2 - 15x$

(iv) The slope of average cost function is:

    (a) $x^2 - 10x + 30$ (b) $\dfrac{2}{3}x - 5 + \dfrac{15}{x^2}$ (c) $\dfrac{2}{3}x^2 - 5x + 30$ (d) $\dfrac{1}{3}x^2 - 5x + 30 - \dfrac{15}{x}$

Answers

1. (d) bijective

    Explanation: We have, $f(x) = 4x + 3$

    To check one-one:

    Let $f(x)_1 = f(x_2)$ for any $x_1, x_2 \in$ R

    Then, $4x_1 + 3 = 4x_2 + 3$

$\Rightarrow$ $x_1 = x_2$

i.e., $f(x_1) = f(x_2)$

$\Rightarrow$ $x_1 = x_2$

$\therefore f(x)$ is one-one.

To check onto:

Let $\qquad y = f(x),\ y \in R$

$\Rightarrow \qquad y = 4x + 3$

$\Rightarrow \qquad x = \dfrac{y-3}{4}$

So, for any $y \in R$, we have $x \in R$.

$\therefore f(x)$ is onto.

Since, $f(x)$ is one-one as well as onto, so it is a bijective function.

2. (a) reflexive but not symmetric.

Explanation:

We have, $\quad R = \{(1, 1), (2, 2), (3, 3), (1, 2), (2, 3),$
$\qquad\qquad\qquad\qquad\qquad\qquad\qquad (1, 3)\}$

Reflexive:

$\because (1, 1), (2, 2), (3, 3) \in R$

$\therefore R$ is reflexive.

Symmetric:

$(1, 2) \in R$ but $(2, 1) \notin R$.

$\therefore R$ is not symmetric.

Transitive:

For $(1, 2), (2, 3) \in R$

$\Rightarrow (1, 3) \in R$

$\therefore R$ is transitive.

3. (a)

Explanation:

$$f(x) = \frac{3x+2}{5x-3}$$

$\therefore \quad (f \circ f)(x) = f\{f(x)\}$

$$= \frac{3(f(x)) + 2}{5\{f(x)\} - 3}$$

$$= \frac{3\left(\dfrac{3x+2}{5x-3}\right) + 2}{5\left(\dfrac{3x+2}{5x-3}\right) - 3}$$

$$= \frac{9x + 6 + 10x - 6}{15x + 10 - 15x + 9}$$

$$= \frac{19x}{19} = x$$

4. (b) $\dfrac{2\pi}{3}$

Explanation:

Let $\cos^{-1}\left(-\dfrac{1}{2}\right) = y$

$\Rightarrow \qquad \cos y = -\dfrac{1}{2}$

$$= -\cos\frac{\pi}{3}$$

$$= \cos\left(\pi - \frac{\pi}{3}\right) = \cos\frac{2\pi}{3}$$

$\because$ The principal value branch of $\cos^{-1}$ is $(0, \pi)$

$\therefore \qquad \cos y = \cos\dfrac{2\pi}{3}$

$\Rightarrow \qquad y = \cos^{-1}\left(-\dfrac{1}{2}\right) = \dfrac{2\pi}{3}$

5. (c) $\dfrac{5\pi}{6}$

Explanation:

$$2\sec^{-1} 2 + \sin^{-1}\frac{1}{2} = 2 \times \frac{\pi}{3} + \frac{\pi}{6}$$

$$= \frac{2\pi}{3} + \frac{\pi}{6}$$

$$= \frac{4\pi + \pi}{6} = \frac{5\pi}{6}$$

6. (d) equivalence

Explanation: We have, $R = \{(T_1, T_2) : T_1$ is congruent to $T_2\}$

Reflexive: Since every triangle is congruent to itself.

$\therefore (T_1, T_2) \in R \Rightarrow R$ is reflexive.

Symmetric: Let $(T_1, T_2) \in R \Rightarrow T_1$ is congruent to T_2.

We can also say that T_2 is congruent to T_1.

$\Rightarrow (T_2, T_1) \in R \Rightarrow R$ is symmetric.

Transitive: Let $(T_1, T_2) \in R$ and $(T_2, T_3) \in R$

$\Rightarrow T_1$ is congruent to T_2 and T_2 is congruent to T_3.

$\Rightarrow T_1$ is congruent to T_3.

$\Rightarrow (T_1, T_3) \in R \Rightarrow R$ is transitive.

Since, R is reflexive, symmetric and transitive, So R is an equivalence relation.

7. (c) -4

Explanation: Since, P is a symmetric matrix.

$\therefore P^T = P$

$$\Rightarrow \begin{bmatrix} x+2 & 2x+3 \\ x-1 & 3 \end{bmatrix}^T = \begin{bmatrix} x+2 & 2x+3 \\ x-1 & 3 \end{bmatrix}$$

$$\begin{bmatrix} x+2 & x-1 \\ 2x+3 & 3 \end{bmatrix} = \begin{bmatrix} x+2 & 2x+3 \\ x-1 & 3 \end{bmatrix}$$

$\Rightarrow x - 1 = 2x + 3 \Rightarrow x = -4$

8. (b) $\dfrac{3}{4}$

Explanation:

$$\begin{vmatrix} \sin 60° & \sin 90° \\ \cos 90° & \cos 30° \end{vmatrix} = \begin{vmatrix} \dfrac{\sqrt{3}}{2} & 1 \\ 0 & \dfrac{\sqrt{3}}{2} \end{vmatrix}$$

$$= \frac{\sqrt{3}}{2} \times \frac{\sqrt{3}}{2} - 1 \times 0$$

$$= \frac{3}{4}$$

9. (a) [1 2 3]

Explanation: Matrix having only one row, is called a row matrix.

10. (c) $(a + b)^2$

Explanation:

$$\because \qquad A = \begin{bmatrix} a & b \\ b & a \end{bmatrix}$$

$$\therefore \quad A^2 = A.A = \begin{bmatrix} a & b \\ b & a \end{bmatrix}\begin{bmatrix} a & b \\ b & a \end{bmatrix}$$

$$= \begin{bmatrix} a^2 + b^2 & ab + ba \\ ba + ab & b^2 + a^2 \end{bmatrix}$$

$$= \begin{bmatrix} a^2 + b^2 & 2ab \\ 2ab & a^2 + b^2 \end{bmatrix}$$

But $\qquad A^2 = \begin{bmatrix} \alpha & \beta \\ \beta & \alpha \end{bmatrix}$ (Given)

$$\therefore \quad \begin{bmatrix} a^2 + b^2 & 2ab \\ 2ab & a^2 + b^2 \end{bmatrix} = \begin{bmatrix} \alpha & \beta \\ \beta & \alpha \end{bmatrix}$$

$$\Rightarrow \alpha = a^2 + b^2;\ \beta = 2ab$$

$$\therefore \qquad \alpha + \beta = (a^2 + b^2) + 2ab$$

$$= (a + b)^2$$

11. (b) (1, 1)

Explanation:

Given curve is,

$$y = x^3 - 3x^2 + 3x$$

$\therefore$ Tangent to the curve,

$$\frac{dy}{dx} = 3x^2 - 6x + 3$$

$$= 3(x - 1)^2$$

$\because$ Tangent is parallel to x-axis

$$\therefore \qquad \frac{dy}{dx} = \tan 0° = 0$$

$$\Rightarrow 3(x - 1)^2 = 0$$

$$\Rightarrow \qquad x = 1$$

For $x = 1$,

$$y = (1)^3 - 3(1)^2 + 3(1) = 1$$

$\therefore$ The required point is (x, y) i.e., (1, 1)

12. (d) $\begin{bmatrix} 20 & 44 \\ 15 & 59 \end{bmatrix}$

Explanation:

$$AB = \begin{bmatrix} 1 & 3 \\ 5 & 7 \end{bmatrix}\begin{bmatrix} -1 & 9 \\ 7 & 2 \end{bmatrix}$$

$$= \begin{bmatrix} -1 + 21 & 9 + 6 \\ -5 + 49 & 45 + 14 \end{bmatrix}$$

$$= \begin{bmatrix} 20 & 15 \\ 44 & 59 \end{bmatrix}$$

$$\text{So,} \quad (AB)^T = \begin{bmatrix} 20 & 15 \\ 44 & 59 \end{bmatrix}^T$$

$$= \begin{bmatrix} 20 & 44 \\ 15 & 59 \end{bmatrix}$$

13. (a) $t \cos t$

Explanation:

$\because\ x = \log t$ and $y = \sin t$

$$\therefore \qquad \frac{dx}{dt} = \frac{1}{t}$$

and $\qquad \dfrac{dy}{dt} = \cos t$

Now, $\qquad \dfrac{dy}{dx} = \dfrac{dy/dt}{dx/dt}$

$$= \frac{\cos t}{1/t} = t \cos t$$

14. (b) $m^2 y^2$

Explanation:

$$y = (x + \sqrt{x^2 - 1})^m \qquad\qquad ...(i)$$

$$\therefore \quad \frac{dy}{dx} = m(x + \sqrt{x^2 - 1})^{m-1}$$

$$\times \left[1 + \frac{1}{2}(x^2 - 1)^{-1/2} \times (2x) \right]$$

$$= m(x + \sqrt{x^2 - 1})^{m-1}\left[1 + \frac{x}{\sqrt{x^2 - 1}} \right]$$

$$= \frac{m(x + \sqrt{x^2 - 1})^{m-1}(\sqrt{x^2 - 1} + x)}{\sqrt{x^2 - 1}}$$

$$= \frac{m(x + \sqrt{x^2 - 1})^m}{\sqrt{x^2 - 1}}$$

$$\text{So,}\ (x^2 - 1)\left(\frac{dy}{dx} \right)^2$$

$$= (x^2 - 1) \times \left[\frac{m(x + \sqrt{x^2 - 1})^m}{\sqrt{x^2 - 1}} \right]^2$$

$$= m^2[(x + \sqrt{x^2 - 1})^m]^2$$

$$= m^2 y^2 \qquad\qquad \text{[Using (i)]}$$

15. (d) 0, 3, 3

Explanation:

Since, the given matrix is singular,

$$\therefore \quad \begin{vmatrix} 3-x & 2 & 2 \\ 2 & 4-x & 1 \\ -2 & -4 & 1-x \end{vmatrix} = 0$$

$\Rightarrow (3-x)[(4-x)(-1-x)-(-4)] - 2[2(-1-x)$
$\qquad\qquad - (-2)] + 2[-8-(-2)(4-x)] = 0$
$\Rightarrow (3-x)[-4+x-4x+x^2+4] - 2[-2-2x+2]$
$\qquad\qquad\qquad + 2[-8+8-2x] = 0$
$\Rightarrow (3-x)(x^2-3x)+4x-4x = 0$
$\Rightarrow 3x^2-9x-x^3+3x^2 = 0$
$\Rightarrow -x^3+6x^2-9x = 0$
$\Rightarrow x^3-6x^2+9x = 0$
$\Rightarrow x(x^2-6x+9) = 0$
$\Rightarrow x(x^2-6x+9) = 0$
$\Rightarrow x(x^2-3x-3x+9) = 0$
$\Rightarrow x(x(x-3)-3(x-3)) = 0$
$\Rightarrow x= 0, 3, 3$

16. (c) ± 6

Explanation:

$$\begin{vmatrix} 2x & 5 \\ 8 & x \end{vmatrix} = \begin{vmatrix} 6 & -2 \\ 7 & 3 \end{vmatrix}$$

$\Rightarrow \qquad 2x^2-40 = 18+14 = 32$
$\Rightarrow \qquad\qquad 2x^2 = 72$
$\Rightarrow \qquad\qquad x^2 = 36$
$\Rightarrow \qquad\qquad x = \pm 6$

17. (a) $a = b + \dfrac{2}{3}$

Explanation:

Since $f(x)$ is continuous at $x = 3$.
$\therefore \qquad f(3) = $ R.H.L. At $x = 3$
$\Rightarrow \quad a(3)+1 = \lim_{x\to 0} b(3+h)+3$
$\Rightarrow \qquad 3a+1 = 3b+3$
$\Rightarrow \qquad 3a = 3b+2$
or $\qquad\qquad a = b+\dfrac{2}{3}$

18. (c) R

Explanation:

$\qquad f(x) = x^3-3x^2+4x$
$\therefore \quad f'(x) = 3x^2-6x+4$
$\qquad\qquad = (3x^2-6x+3)+1$
$\qquad\qquad = 3(x-1)^2+1$
Now, for any value of $x \in$ R,
$\qquad\qquad (x-1)^2 \geq 0$
$\Rightarrow \qquad 3(x-1)^2 \geq 0$
$\Rightarrow \quad 3(x-1)^2+1 \geq 1$
i.e., $\quad 3(x-1)^2+1 > 0$

or $\qquad\qquad f'(x) > 0$
$\therefore\ f(x)$ is increasing on R.

19. (a) ± 1

Explanation:

$\qquad f(x) = x^3-3x+3$
To find the points of local maxima/minima.
Put $\qquad f'(x) = 0$
$\Rightarrow \qquad\qquad 3x^2-3 = 0$
$\Rightarrow \qquad\qquad 3(x^2-1) = 0$
$\Rightarrow \qquad\qquad x = \pm 1$
$\therefore$ The points of local maxima and local minima
are ± 1.

20. (d) x^x

Let $\qquad u = x^x$ and $v = x \log x$
Now, $\quad u = x^x$
$\Rightarrow \quad \log u = \log(x^x) \qquad$ [Taking log on both sides]
$\Rightarrow \quad \log u = x \log x$
Differentiating w.r.t. x, we get
$$\frac{1}{u} \times \frac{du}{dx} = x \times \frac{1}{x} + \log x \times 1$$
$$= 1 + \log x$$
$\Rightarrow \qquad \dfrac{du}{dx} = u[1+\log x]$
$$= x^x(1+\log x) \qquad\qquad ...(i)$$
and $\qquad v = x \log x$
$\Rightarrow \qquad \dfrac{dv}{dx} = x \times \dfrac{1}{x} + \log x \times 1$
$$= 1 + \log x \qquad\qquad ...(ii)$$
So, $\qquad \dfrac{du}{dv} = \dfrac{du/dx}{dv/dx}$
$$= \frac{x^x(1+\log x)}{1+\log x} = x^x$$

21. (i) (a) $2 \sin^{-1} x$

Explanation:

Let $x = \sin\theta$

Then, $\sin^{-1}(2x\sqrt{1-x^2})$

$= \sin^{-1}(2\sin\theta\sqrt{1-\sin^2\theta})$

$= \sin^{-1}(2\sin\theta\cos\theta)$

$= \sin^{-1}(\sin 2\theta) = 2\theta$

$$[\because \sin 2\theta = 2\sin\theta\cos\theta]$$

$$\left[\begin{array}{l} \because x = \sin\theta \\ \Rightarrow \theta = \sin^{-1}x \end{array}\right]$$

$= 2\sin^{-1}x$

(ii) (b) $\tan^{-1}\dfrac{3}{4}$

Explanation:

$$\tan^{-1}\frac{1}{2}+\tan^{-1}\frac{2}{11} = \tan^{-1}\left(\frac{\dfrac{1}{2}+\dfrac{2}{11}}{1-\dfrac{1}{2}\times\dfrac{2}{11}}\right)$$

$$= \tan^{-1}\left(\frac{\dfrac{11+4}{22}}{\dfrac{22-2}{22}}\right)$$

$$= \tan^{-1}\left(\frac{15}{20}\right)$$

$$= \tan^{-1}\left(\frac{3}{4}\right)$$

(iii) (b) 0

Explanation:

$$\cos(\sec^{-1}x + \operatorname{cosec}^{-1}x)$$

$$= \cos\left(\frac{\pi}{2}\right)=0$$

$$\left[\because \sec^{1}x+ \operatorname{cosec}^{-1}x=\frac{\pi}{2}\right]$$

(iv) (c) $\pm\dfrac{1}{2}$

Explanation :

We have, $\cos^{-1}\{\sin(\cos^{-1}x)\}=\dfrac{\pi}{6}$

$$\Rightarrow \sin(\cos^{-1}x) = \cos\frac{\pi}{6}=\frac{\sqrt{3}}{2}$$

$$\Rightarrow \sin(\sin^{-1}\sqrt{1-x^2}) = \frac{\sqrt{3}}{2}$$

$$\Rightarrow \sqrt{1-x^2} = \frac{\sqrt{3}}{2} \qquad [\because \sin(\sin^{-1}\theta)=\theta]$$

$$\Rightarrow 1-x^2 = \frac{3}{4} \qquad \text{[Squaring both sides]}$$

$$\Rightarrow x^2 = \frac{1}{4}$$

$$\Rightarrow x = \pm\frac{1}{2}$$

22. (i) (c) $h=\dfrac{S-2\pi r^2}{2\pi r}$

Explanation :

T.S.A. of closed cylinder, $S = 2\pi rh + 2\pi r^2$

$$\Rightarrow \qquad h = \frac{S-2\pi r^2}{2\pi r}$$

(ii) (a) $\dfrac{1}{2}Sr-\pi r^3$

Explanation:

Volume of closed cylinder, V

$$= \pi r^2 h$$

$$= \pi r^2\left(\frac{S-2\pi r^2}{2\pi r}\right) \text{ [Using part (i)]}$$

$$= \frac{1}{2}Sr-\pi r^3$$

(iii) (d) $r=\dfrac{1}{2}h$

Explanation:

Volume of cylinder will be maximum, if

$$\frac{dV}{dr}=0$$

$$\Rightarrow \quad \frac{d}{dr}\left(\frac{1}{2}Sr-\pi r^3\right)=0$$

$$\Rightarrow \quad \frac{S}{2}-3\pi r^2=0$$

$$\Rightarrow \qquad S=6\pi r^2$$

$$\Rightarrow \quad 2\pi rh+2\pi r^2=6\pi r^2$$

$$\Rightarrow \qquad 2\pi rh=4\pi r^2$$

$$\Rightarrow \qquad h=2r \qquad [\because r\neq 0]$$

$$\text{or} \qquad r=\frac{h}{2}$$

(iv) (b) $2\pi r^3$

Explanation :

Maximum volume of the cylinder

$$= \pi r^2 h$$

$$= \pi r^2(2r)\left[\text{From part (iii) } r=\frac{h}{2}\Rightarrow h=2r\right]$$

$$= 2\pi r^3$$

23. (i) (b) $x+y+z=6;\ y+3z=11;\ x-2y+z=0$

Explanation: According to the question,

$$x+y+z=6 \qquad \qquad \text{...(A)}$$

$$\text{Also,} \qquad 3z+y=11$$

$$\Rightarrow \qquad 0x+y+3z=11 \qquad \text{...(B)}$$

$$\text{And,} \qquad x+z=2y$$

$$\Rightarrow \qquad x-2y+z=0 \qquad \text{...(C)}$$

(ii) (d) $\begin{bmatrix} 7 & -3 & 2 \\ 3 & 0 & -3 \\ -1 & 3 & 1 \end{bmatrix}$

Explanation : Equations $x+y+z=6$, $y+3z=11$ and $x-y+z=0$ in matrix form can be written as

$$\begin{bmatrix} 1 & 1 & 1 \\ 0 & 1 & 3 \\ 1 & -2 & 1 \end{bmatrix}\begin{bmatrix} x \\ y \\ z \end{bmatrix}=\begin{bmatrix} 6 \\ 11 \\ 0 \end{bmatrix}$$

$$\Rightarrow \quad AX = B$$

$$\therefore \quad A = \begin{bmatrix} 1 & 1 & 1 \\ 0 & 1 & 3 \\ 1 & -2 & 1 \end{bmatrix}$$

Cofactors of matrix A are,

$A_{11} = 7; A_{12} = 3; A_{13} = -1$

$A_{21} = -3; A_{22} = 0; A_{23} = 3$

$A_{31} = 2; A_{32} = -3; A_{33} = 1$

$$\therefore \quad adj\, A = \begin{bmatrix} 7 & 3 & -1 \\ -3 & 0 & 3 \\ 2 & -3 & 1 \end{bmatrix}^{T}$$

$$= \begin{bmatrix} 7 & -3 & 2 \\ 3 & 0 & -3 \\ -1 & 3 & 1 \end{bmatrix}$$

(iii) (c) $\dfrac{1}{9}\begin{bmatrix} 7 & -3 & 2 \\ 3 & 0 & -3 \\ -1 & 3 & 1 \end{bmatrix}$

Explanation : $A^{-1} = \dfrac{1}{|A|}(Adj\,A)$

$$\because \quad |A| = 1(1+6) - 1(0-3) + 1(0-1)$$

$$= 7 + 3 - 1 = 9 \neq 0$$

$$\therefore \quad A^{-1} \text{ exist.}$$

$$\text{So,} \quad A^{-1} = \dfrac{1}{9}\begin{bmatrix} 7 & -3 & 2 \\ 3 & 0 & -3 \\ -1 & 3 & 1 \end{bmatrix}$$

(iv) (b) 1, 2, 3

Explanation :

From part (ii), we have

$$AX = B$$

$$\Rightarrow \quad X = A^{-1}B$$

$$= \dfrac{1}{9}\begin{bmatrix} 7 & -3 & 2 \\ 3 & 0 & -3 \\ -1 & 3 & 1 \end{bmatrix}\begin{bmatrix} 6 \\ 11 \\ 0 \end{bmatrix}$$

$$\Rightarrow \quad X = \begin{bmatrix} x \\ y \\ z \end{bmatrix} = \begin{bmatrix} 1 \\ 2 \\ 3 \end{bmatrix}$$

$$\therefore \quad x = 1, y = 2, z = 3$$

24. (d) $\dfrac{\pi}{3}$

Explanation :

We know, $\quad \vec{a}\cdot\vec{b} = |\vec{a}||\vec{b}|\cos\theta$

$$\Rightarrow \quad 3 = 2 \times 3 \times \cos\theta$$

$$\Rightarrow \quad \cos\theta = \dfrac{1}{2} = \cos\dfrac{\pi}{3}$$

$$\Rightarrow \quad \theta = \dfrac{\pi}{3}$$

25. (a) $\dfrac{2}{7}, \dfrac{3}{7}, -\dfrac{6}{7}$

Explanation :

Given line is, $\dfrac{2x-5}{4} = \dfrac{y+4}{3} = \dfrac{6-z}{6}$

$$\Rightarrow \quad \dfrac{x-5/2}{2} = \dfrac{y+4}{3} = \dfrac{z-6}{-6}$$

$\therefore$ Direction ratios of the line = <2, 3, – 6>

$\therefore$ Direction cosines of this line

$$= \dfrac{2}{\sqrt{2^2+3^2+(-6)^2}}, \dfrac{3}{\sqrt{2^2+3^2+(-6)^2}},$$

$$\dfrac{-6}{\sqrt{2^2+3^2+(-6)^2}}$$

$$= \dfrac{2}{7}, \dfrac{3}{7}, -\dfrac{6}{7}$$

26. (c) $-\dfrac{10}{7}$

Explanation :

Given equations of lines can be written as

$$\dfrac{x-1}{-3} = \dfrac{y-2}{2k} = \dfrac{z-3}{2}$$

and $\dfrac{x-1}{3k} = \dfrac{y-5}{1} = \dfrac{z-6}{-5}$

Since, the two lines are perpendicular,

$$\therefore \quad (-3)(3k) + (2k)(1) + (2)(-5) = 0$$

$$\Rightarrow \quad -9k + 2k - 10 = 0$$

$$\Rightarrow \quad -7k - 10 = 0$$

$$\Rightarrow \quad k = -\dfrac{10}{7}$$

27. (a) 7.44 units

Explanation :

Here, $(x_1, y_1, z_1) = (8, -9, 10)$, $<a_1, b_1, c_1> = <3, -16, 7>$,

$(x_2, y_2, z_2) = (15, 29, 5)$ and $<a_2, b_2, c_2> = <3, 8, -5>$

Now, Shortest distance

$$= \dfrac{\begin{vmatrix} x_2-x_1 & y_2-y_1 & z_2-z_1 \\ a_1 & b_1 & c_1 \\ a_2 & b_2 & c_2 \end{vmatrix}}{\sqrt{(a_1b_2-a_2b_1)^2+(b_1c_2-b_2c_1)^2+(a_1c_2-a_2c_1)^2}}$$

$$= \dfrac{\begin{vmatrix} 15-8 & 29-(-9) & 5-10 \\ 3 & -16 & 7 \\ 3 & 8 & -5 \end{vmatrix}}{\sqrt{\begin{aligned}(3\times8-3\times(-16))^2+((-1)\times5-8\times7)^2 \\ +(3\times(-5)-3\times6)^2\end{aligned}}}$$

$$= \frac{\begin{vmatrix} 7 & 38 & -5 \\ 3 & -16 & 7 \\ 3 & 8 & -5 \end{vmatrix}}{\sqrt{(72)^2 + (-136)^2 + (36)^2}}$$

$$= \frac{1}{\sqrt{24976}} [7(80 - 56) - 38(-15 - 21)$$

$$- 5(24 + 48)]$$

$$= \frac{1}{158.03}(168 + 1368 - 360)$$

$$= \frac{1176}{158.03} = 7.44 \text{ units}$$

28. (i) (c) $\hat{i} - 2\hat{j} + 3\hat{k}$

Explanation :

$$\vec{BC} = \text{Position vector of } \vec{C}$$

$$- \text{Position vector of } \vec{B}$$

$$= (3\hat{i} - \hat{j} + 2\hat{k}) - (2\hat{i} + \hat{j} - \hat{k})$$

$$= \hat{i} - 2\hat{j} + 3\hat{k}$$

(ii) (b) $\sqrt{14}$

From part (i), we have

$$\vec{BC} = \hat{i} - 2\hat{j} + 3\hat{k}$$

$$\therefore \text{ Magnitude of } \vec{BC} = |BC|$$

$$= \sqrt{1^2 + (-2)^2 + 3^2}$$

$$= \sqrt{14}$$

(iii) (a) $\dfrac{8}{\sqrt{14}}$

Explanation :

$$\text{Projection of } \vec{A} \text{ on } \vec{C} = \frac{\vec{A}.\vec{C}}{|\vec{C}|}$$

$$= \frac{(\hat{i} - \hat{j} + 2\hat{k}).(3\hat{i} - \hat{j} + 2\hat{k})}{\sqrt{3^2 + (-1)^2 + 2^2}}$$

$$= \frac{3 + 1 + 4}{\sqrt{14}} = \frac{8}{\sqrt{14}}$$

(iv) (d) $7\hat{i} - 3\hat{j} - 5\hat{k}$

Cross product of $\vec{\Delta}$ and $\vec{A}$

$$= \begin{vmatrix} \hat{i} & \hat{j} & \hat{k} \\ 2 & 3 & 1 \\ 1 & -1 & 2 \end{vmatrix}$$

$$= \hat{i}(6 + 1) - \hat{j}(4 - 1) + \hat{k}(-2 - 3)$$

$$= 7\hat{i} - 3\hat{j} - 5\hat{k}$$

29. (a) $20x - 17$

Explanation :

Given, Revenue function,

$$R(x) = 10x^2 - 17x + 43$$

$\therefore$ Marginal revenue, MR

$$= \frac{d}{dx}R(x)$$

$$= \frac{d}{dx}(10x^2 - 17x + 43)$$

$$= 20x - 17$$

30. (c) $12 + \dfrac{6500}{x}$

Explanation :

Fixed cost = ₹ 6500 and variable cost = ₹ 12x

$\therefore$ Cost function = Fixed cost + Variable cost

$$\Rightarrow \qquad C(x) = 6500 + 12x$$

$\therefore$ Average cost function

$$= \frac{C(x)}{x} = \frac{6500}{x} + 12$$

31. (d) $100x - x^2$

Explanation :

Demand function, $p = 100 - x$

Quantity $= x$

$\therefore$ Revenue function, $R(x) = px$

$$= (100 - x)x$$

$$= 100x - x^2$$

32. (b) $x = 2$

Explanation :

Price of a commodity = ₹ 15

$\therefore$ Price of x commodity = ₹ 15x

Also, cost function, $C(x) = 2x + 26$

We know, at break-even points,

$$\text{Cost function} = \text{Revenue function}$$

$$\Rightarrow \qquad 2x + 26 = 15x$$

$$\Rightarrow \qquad 13x = 26$$

$$\Rightarrow \qquad x = 2$$

33. (i) (a) 9

Explanation :

$$C(x) = \frac{1}{3}x^3 - 5x^2 + 30x - 15$$

At $x = 3$,

$$C(3) = \frac{1}{3}(3)^3 - 5(3)^2 + 30(3) - 15$$

$$= 9 - 45 + 60 - 15$$

$$= 9$$

Thus, the cost of 3 units is ₹ 9.

(ii) (c) $\dfrac{1}{3}x^2 - 5x + 30 - \dfrac{15}{x}$

Explanation :

Average cost function, $AC = \dfrac{C(x)}{x}$

$$= \dfrac{1}{3}x^2 - 5x + 30 - \dfrac{15}{x}$$

(iii) (b) $x^2 - 10x + 30$

Explanation :

Marginal cost function, MC

$$= \dfrac{d}{dx}\{C(x)\}$$

$$= \dfrac{d}{dx}\left(\dfrac{1}{3}x^3 - 5x^2 + 30x - 15\right)$$

$$= x^2 - 10x + 30$$

(iv) (b) $\dfrac{2}{3}x - 5 + \dfrac{15}{x^2}$

Explanation :

Slope of average cost function

$$= \dfrac{d}{dx}(AC)$$

By putting the value of AC from Q. 33(ii)

$$= \dfrac{d}{dx}\left(\dfrac{1}{3}x^2 - 5x + 30 - \dfrac{15}{x}\right)$$

$$= \dfrac{2}{3}x - 5 + 0 - \left(-\dfrac{15}{x^2}\right)$$

$$= \dfrac{2}{3}x - 5 + \dfrac{15}{x^2}$$

❑❑

SECTION–A

(Answer all Questions)

Question 1

If set A contain 3 elements and set B contain 2 elements, then the number of one-one mappings from A to B is:

(a) 5 (b) 6 (c) 1 (d) 2

Question 2

If $3 \tan^{-1}x + \cot^{-1}x = \pi$, then the value of x is:

(a) 1 (b) 2 (c) 3 (d) 4

Question 3

If $f(x) = 8x^3$ and $g(x) = x^{1/3}$, the gof is:

(a) x (b) $\dfrac{x}{2}$ (c) $8x$ (d) $2x$

Question 4

Let R be the relation in the set A of human beings be defined by $R = \{(x, y) : x$ is exactly 7 cm taller than $y\}$. Then the relation R is:

(a) reflexive and symmetric but not transitive

(b) symmetric and transitive but not reflexive

(c) neither reflexive nor symmetric nor transitive

(d) an equivalence relation

Question 5

The value of $\sec^2 (\tan^{-1} 2) + \csc^2 (\cot^{-1} 3)$ is:

(a) 5 (b) 15 (c) 6 (d) 1

Question 6

The $f : N \to N$ given by $f(x) = 2x$ is:

(a) one-one and onto

(b) onto but not one-one

(c) one-one but not onto

(d) neither one-one nor onto

Question 7

The value of $\begin{vmatrix} a & b & c \\ a+2x & b+2y & c+2z \\ x & y & z \end{vmatrix}$ is:

(a) $(a + b + c)$ (b) $x + y + z$ (c) $ax + by + cz$ (d) 0

Question 8

If $A = \begin{bmatrix} 3 & -2 \\ 4 & -2 \end{bmatrix}$, I is an identity matrix of order 2 and $A^2 = KA - 2I$, then the value of K is:

(a) 1 (b) -1 (c) 2 (d) -2

Question 9

If $x^3 + y^3 = 3axy$, then $\dfrac{dy}{dx} = ?$

(a) $\dfrac{x^2 + ay}{y^2 + ax}$
(b) $\dfrac{x^2 - ay}{y^2 - ax}$
(c) $\dfrac{ay - x^2}{y^2 - ax}$
(d) $\dfrac{x^2 - ay}{y^2 + ax}$

Question 10

If $A = \begin{bmatrix} \cos\alpha & -\sin\alpha \\ \sin\alpha & \cos\alpha \end{bmatrix}$ and $A + A^T = I_2$, then the value of α is:

(a) $\dfrac{\pi}{2}$
(b) $\dfrac{\pi}{6}$
(c) $\dfrac{\pi}{4}$
(d) $\dfrac{\pi}{3}$

Question 11

The inverse of matrix $P = \begin{bmatrix} 2 & -3 \\ -1 & 2 \end{bmatrix}$ is:

(a) $\begin{bmatrix} 2 & 3 \\ 1 & 2 \end{bmatrix}$
(b) $\begin{bmatrix} -2 & 3 \\ 1 & -2 \end{bmatrix}$
(c) $\begin{bmatrix} -2 & -1 \\ -3 & -2 \end{bmatrix}$
(d) $\begin{bmatrix} 2 & 1 \\ 3 & 2 \end{bmatrix}$

Question 12

If A is a square matrix of order 3, then $|kA|$ is equal to:
(a) $k|A|$
(b) $k^2|A|$
(c) $k^3|A|$
(d) $3k|A|$

Question 13

The function $f(x) = |x - 5|$ is:
(a) continuous as well as differentiable at $x = 5$
(b) continuous but not differentiable at $x = 5$
(c) differentiable but not continuous at $x = 5$
(d) both continuous and differentiable at $x = 5$

Question 14

If $F(x) = \begin{bmatrix} \cos x & -\sin x & 0 \\ \sin x & \cos x & 0 \\ 0 & 0 & 1 \end{bmatrix}$, then $F(x).F(y) =$

(a) $F(x.y)$
(b) $F(x - y)$
(c) $F(x + y)$
(d) $F\left(\dfrac{x}{y}\right)$

Question 15

If $e^y (x + 1) = 1$, then $\dfrac{d^2 y}{dx^2} = ?$

(a) y
(b) $\dfrac{dy}{dx}$
(c) $-y^2$
(d) $\left(\dfrac{dy}{dx}\right)^2$

Question 16

If $Y = \begin{bmatrix} 3 & 2 \\ 1 & 4 \end{bmatrix}$ and $2X + Y = \begin{bmatrix} 1 & 0 \\ -3 & 2 \end{bmatrix}$, then the matrix X is:

(a) $\begin{bmatrix} -1 & -1 \\ -2 & -1 \end{bmatrix}$
(b) $\begin{bmatrix} 1 & 2 \\ 3 & 7 \end{bmatrix}$
(c) $\begin{bmatrix} 1 & 1 \\ -2 & -1 \end{bmatrix}$
(d) $\begin{bmatrix} -1 & 2 \\ 3 & -7 \end{bmatrix}$

Question 17

The equation of tangent to the curve $y = \dfrac{x - 7}{(x - 2)(x - 3)}$ at the point where it cut x-axis is:

(a) $x - 20y - 7 = 0$
(b) $20x - y - 7 = 0$
(c) $20x + y - 7 = 0$
(d) $x + 20y - 7 = 0$

Question 18

The derivative of $\tan^{-1}\left(\dfrac{\sqrt{1 + x^2} - 1}{x}\right)$ w.r.t. x is:

(a) $\dfrac{1-x^2}{1+x^2}$ (b) $\dfrac{1}{2(1+x^2)}$ (c) $\dfrac{2x}{\sqrt{1+x^2}-1}$ (d) $\dfrac{2x}{(1+x^2)^{3/2}}$

Question 19

The values of k in the function $f(x) = kx^3 + 5$, so that $f(x)$ is strictly decreasing, are:

(a) $k < 0$ (b) $k > 0$ (c) $k \geq 0$ (d) $k \leq 0$

Question 20

The minimum value of the function $f(x) = (2x - 1)^2 + 7$ is:

(a) $\dfrac{1}{2}$ (b) 3 (c) 7 (d) Does not exist

Question 21

Consider the following matrices:

$$A = \begin{bmatrix} 1 & 2 & 3 \\ 2 & 3 & 1 \end{bmatrix}, \; B = \begin{bmatrix} 9 & -2 \\ -1 & 1 \\ 4 & 3 \end{bmatrix}, \; C = \begin{bmatrix} 2 & 3 & 4 \\ 4 & 6 & 8 \\ 6 & 9 & 12 \end{bmatrix}, \; D = \begin{bmatrix} \alpha & \beta \\ \gamma & -\alpha \end{bmatrix}$$

(i) The order of product matrix AB is:

(a) 2×3 (b) 2×2 (c) 3×2 (d) Does not exist

(ii) AB = ?

(a) $\begin{bmatrix} -19 & 9 \\ 19 & 4 \end{bmatrix}$ (b) $\begin{bmatrix} -19 & 9 \\ 19 & -4 \end{bmatrix}$ (c) $\begin{bmatrix} 19 & 9 \\ 19 & 2 \end{bmatrix}$ (d) Does not exist

(iii) The main diagonal elements of matrix C are:

(a) 2, 6, 12 (b) 4, 6, 4 (c) 2, 8, 6 (d) 4, 4, 9

(iv) If $D^2 = I_2$, then which of the following relation is correct?

(a) $\beta^2 + \alpha\gamma = 1$ (b) $\alpha^2 + \beta\gamma = 1$ (c) $\alpha^2 - \beta^2 - \gamma^2 = 1$ (d) $\alpha^2 + \beta^2 + \gamma^2 = 1$

Question 22

Given the sum of the perimeters of a square and a circle.

(i) If x be the side of the square and r be the radius of the circle. Then the radius of the circle in terms of side of square is:

(a) $r = \dfrac{P - 2\pi}{4x}$ (b) $r = P - 4x$ (c) $r = \dfrac{P - 4x}{2\pi}$ (d) $r = \dfrac{P + 2\pi}{4x}$

(ii) The sum of areas of square and circle as a function of x is:

(a) $x^2 + \left(\dfrac{P - 2\pi}{4x}\right)^2$ (b) $x^2 + \dfrac{(P - 4x)^2}{4\pi}$ (c) $x^2 + (P - 4x)^2$ (d) $x^2 + \left(\dfrac{P + 2\pi}{4\pi}\right)^2$

(iii) The sum of areas of square and circle will be least if:

(a) $x = 2r$ (b) $x = r$ (c) $r = 2x$ (d) $r = x + 2$

(iv) Least sum of areas of the square and the circle is:

(a) $x^2 + r^2$ (b) $4x^2$ (c) $(\pi + 4)x^2$ (d) $(\pi + 4)r^2$

Question 23

Let $f : \{1, 3, 4\} \rightarrow \{1, 2, 5\}$ and $g = \{1, 2, 5\} \rightarrow \{1, 3\}$ be given by $f = \{(1, 2), (3, 5), (4, 1)\}$ and $g = \{(1, 3), (2, 3), (5, 1)\}$.

(i) The function f is:

(a) one-one but not onto (b) onto but not one-one
(c) neither one-one nor onto (d) both one-one and onto

(ii) The function g is :

(a) one-one but not onto (b) onto but not one-one
(c) neither one-one nor onto (d) both one-one and onto

(iii) The value of $fog(2)$ is:

(a) 5   (b) 1   (c) 3   (d) does not exist

(iv) The value of $gof(1)$ is:

(a) 1   (b) 5   (c) 3   (d) does not exist

SECTION–B

(Answer all Questions)

Question 24

If $|\vec{a}| = 3, |\vec{b}| = 5, |\vec{c}| = 7$ and $(\vec{a} + \vec{b} + \vec{c}) = 0$, then the angle between $\vec{a}$ and $\vec{b}$ is:

(a) $\dfrac{\pi}{6}$ (b) $\dfrac{\pi}{4}$ (c) $\dfrac{\pi}{3}$ (d) $\dfrac{\pi}{2}$

Question 25

The equation of a line passing through a point $(-1, 2, 3)$, which is parallel to the line $\dfrac{x-3}{2} = \dfrac{y-3}{4} = \dfrac{z+4}{5}$ is:

(a) $\dfrac{x-1}{2} = \dfrac{y+2}{4} = \dfrac{z+3}{5}$

(b) $\dfrac{x+1}{2} = \dfrac{y-2}{4} = \dfrac{z-3}{5}$

(c) $\dfrac{x-1}{-3} = \dfrac{y+2}{-3} = \dfrac{z+3}{-4}$

(d) $\dfrac{x+1}{3} = \dfrac{y-2}{3} = \dfrac{z-3}{4}$

Question 26

The values of p and q so that the point $(p, q, 1)$ lies on the line $\dfrac{x}{-1} = \dfrac{y-2}{2} = \dfrac{z+1}{-1}$ are:

(a) $p = 1, q = -1$ (b) $p = -1, q = 1$ (c) $p = -2, q = 2$ (d) $p = 2, q = -2$

Question 27

The vector form of equation of the line $\dfrac{x-3}{2} = \dfrac{y+5}{3} = \dfrac{z-7}{4}$ is:

(a) $(3\hat{i} - 5\hat{j} + 7\hat{k}) + \lambda(2\hat{i} + 3\hat{j} + 4\hat{k})$

(b) $(2\hat{i} + 3\hat{j} + 4\hat{k}) + \lambda(3\hat{i} - 5\hat{j} + 4\hat{k})$

(c) $(3\hat{i} - 5\hat{j} + 7\hat{k}) + \lambda(\hat{i} + 2\hat{j} - 3\hat{k})$

(d) $(2\hat{i} + 3\hat{j} + 4\hat{k}) + \lambda(5\hat{i} - 2\hat{j} + 11|\hat{k}|)$

Question 28

Consider the vectors $\vec{a} = 3\hat{i} - \hat{j} - 2\hat{k}, \vec{b} = \hat{i} + \lambda\hat{j} - 3\hat{k}, \vec{c} = 3\hat{i} + 5\hat{j} - 7\hat{k}, \vec{d} = 2\hat{i} + 5\hat{j} + 10\hat{k}$.

(i) If the vectors $\vec{a}$ and $\vec{b}$ are perpendicular, then the value of λ:

(a) 9   (b) 1   (c) 4   (d) -1

(ii) If $\vec{c}$ and $\vec{d}$ represents the diagonals of a parallelogram, then the area of the parallelogram is:

(a) 95.84 sq. units   (b) 31.94 sq. units   (c) 47.92 sq. units   (d) 76.35 sq. units

(iii) The scalar triple product of $\vec{a}, \vec{c}, \vec{d}$ is:

(a) 433   (b) 694   (c) 153   (d) 289

(iv) If $\vec{a} \times \vec{c} = 17\hat{i} + 15\hat{j} + 18\hat{k}$, the sine of angle between the vectors $\vec{a}$ and $\vec{c}$ is:

(a) $\sqrt{\dfrac{432}{1171}}$ (b) $\sqrt{\dfrac{842}{1573}}$

(c) $\sqrt{\dfrac{838}{1162}}$ (d) $\sqrt{\dfrac{492}{1437}}$

SECTION–C

(Answer all Questions)

Question 29

If the total cost function of a firm for x units of commodity is $C(x) = 4x^2 - \dfrac{7}{2}x + 3$, then the marginal cost function is:

(a) $4x - \dfrac{7}{2} + \dfrac{3}{x}$

(b) $4 - \dfrac{3}{x^2}$

(c) $8x - \dfrac{7}{2}$

(d) $4x^2 - \dfrac{7}{2}x$

Question 30

The demand function is $x = \dfrac{24 - 2p}{3}$ where x is the number of units demanded and p is the price per unit. Then the revenue function, $R(x)$ is:

(a) $\dfrac{24x - 2px}{3}$

(b) $12x - \dfrac{3}{2}x^2$

(c) $12 - \dfrac{3}{2}x$

(d) $6x^2 - \dfrac{4}{3}px^2$

Question 31

If the cost function of a firm is given by $C(x) = 3x^3 + 2x^2 - 9x$, then average cost function at $x = 2$ is:

(a) 7
(b) 9
(c) 11
(d) 13

Question 32

A firm has a cost function $C(x) = \dfrac{x^3}{3} - 7x^2 + 27x - 30$ and the demand function is $p = 100 - x$. So, the profit function, $f(x)$ is:

(a) $x^2 - 14x + 27$

(b) $\dfrac{x^4}{3} - 7x^3 + 27x^2 - 30x$

(c) $\dfrac{x^3}{3} - 14x^2 - 27x + 30$

(d) $-\dfrac{x^3}{3} + 6x^2 + 73x + 30$

Question 33

The total revenue received from the sale of x units of a product is given by $R(x) = 24 - 5x + x^2$.

(i) The average revenue function is:

  (a) $24x - 10x^2 + \dfrac{x^3}{3}$

  (b) $2x - 5$

  (c) $\dfrac{24}{x} - 5 + x$

  (d) $-\dfrac{24}{x^2} - 5x + \dfrac{x^2}{2}$

(ii) The marginal revenue function is:

  (a) $2x - 5$

  (b) $24x - 10x^2 + \dfrac{x^3}{3}$

  (c) $\dfrac{24}{x} - 5 + x$

  (d) $-12x^2 - 5x + \dfrac{x^2}{2}$

(iii) The average revenue function at $x = 1$ is:

  (a) 20

  (b) $\dfrac{37}{3}$

  (c) -3

  (d) $-\dfrac{37}{2}$

(iv) Revenue received from the sale of 11th item is:

  (a) ₹ 90
  (b) ₹ 74
  (c) ₹ 52
  (d) ₹ 16

Answers

1. (b) 6

Explanation: Here, $m = 3$ and $n = 2$

$\therefore$ Number of one-one mappings $= {}^mP_n = {}^3P_2$

$= \dfrac{3!}{(3-2)!} = 6$

2. (a) 1

Explanation:

$$3\tan^{-1}x + \cot^{-1}x = \pi$$
$$\Rightarrow 2\tan^{-1}x + \tan^{-1}x + \cot^{-1}x = \pi$$

$$\left[\because \tan^{-1}x + \cot^{-1}x = \frac{\pi}{2}\right]$$

$$\Rightarrow \quad 2\tan^{-1}x = \pi - \frac{\pi}{2}$$

$$\Rightarrow \quad \tan^{-1}x = \frac{\pi}{4}$$

$$\Rightarrow \quad x = \tan\left(\frac{\pi}{4}\right) = 1$$

3. (d) $2x$

Explanation:

$$f(x) = 8x^3 \text{ and } g(x) = x^{1/3}$$
$$\therefore \quad gof = g\{f(x)\}$$
$$= g(8x^3)$$
$$= (8x^3)^{1/3}$$
$$= \{(2x)^3\}^{1/3}$$
$$= 2x$$

4. (c) neither reflexive nor symmetric nor transitive

Explanation: $R = \{(x, y) : x$ is exactly 7 cm taller than $y\}$

Reflexive: Since, one human being cannot be 7 cm taller than himself.

$\therefore$ For any $x \in A$, $(x, x) \in R$.

$\therefore$ R is not reflexive.

Symmetric: Let $(x, y) \in R$, $x, y \in A$

$\therefore$ x is 7 cm taller than y.

$\Rightarrow y$ is 7 cm shorter than x.

$\Rightarrow (y, x) \in R$

$\therefore$ R is not symmetric.

Transitive: Let $(x, y) \in R$ and $(y, z) \in R$

$x, y, z \in A$

$\therefore$ x is 7 cm taller than y and y is 7 cm taller than z

$$x - y = 7 \text{ and } y - z = 7$$
$$\Rightarrow \quad x - z = 14 \neq 7$$
$$\therefore \quad (x, z) \in R$$

$\therefore$ R is not transitive.

$\therefore$ R is neither reflexive nor symmetric nor transitive.

5. (b) 15

Explanation: We have,

$\sec^2(\tan^{-1} 2) + \text{cosec}^2(\cot^{-1} 3)$

$= (1 + \tan^2(\tan^{-1} 2)) + (1 + \cot^2(\cot^{-1} 3))$

$$\left[\begin{array}{l}\because \sec^2\theta = 1 + \tan^2\theta \\ \text{cosec}^2\theta = 1 + \cot^2\theta\end{array}\right]$$

$= 2 + \{\tan(\tan^{-1} 2)\}^2 + \{\cot(\cot^{-1}3)\}^2$

$$\left[\begin{array}{l}\because \tan(\tan^{-1}\theta) = \theta \\ \cot(\cot^{-1}\theta) = \theta\end{array}\right]$$

$= 2 + (2)^2 + (3)^2$

$= 15$

6. (c) one-one but not onto

Explanation: We have, $f : N \to N$, $f(x) = 2x$

To check one-one: Let $x_1, x_2 \in N$ such that $f(x_1) = f(x_2)$.

$$\Rightarrow \quad 2x_1 = 2x_2$$
$$\Rightarrow \quad x_1 = x_2$$

$\therefore$ $f(x)$ is one-one.

To check onto: Let $y = f(x)$, $y \in N$

$$\Rightarrow \quad y = 2x$$
$$\Rightarrow \quad x = \frac{y}{2}$$

Here, for odd values of $y \in N$, so there is pre-image of $x \in N$.

$\therefore$ $f(x)$ is not onto.

7. (d) 0

Explanation: We have,

$$\begin{vmatrix} a & b & c \\ a+2x & b+2y & c+2z \\ x & y & z \end{vmatrix}$$

$$= \begin{vmatrix} a & b & c \\ 2x & 2y & 2z \\ x & y & z \end{vmatrix}$$

$$[\text{Applying } R_2 \to R_2 - R_1]$$

$$= 2\begin{vmatrix} a & b & c \\ x & y & z \\ x & y & z \end{vmatrix}$$

$$[\text{Taking 2 common from } R_2]$$

$= 2 \times 0 \quad [\because R_2 \text{ and } R_3 \text{ are identical}]$

$= 0$

8. (a) 1

Explanation:

$$A = \begin{bmatrix} 3 & -2 \\ 4 & -2 \end{bmatrix}$$

$$\therefore \quad A^2 = A.A = \begin{bmatrix} 3 & -2 \\ 4 & -2 \end{bmatrix}\begin{bmatrix} 3 & -2 \\ 4 & -2 \end{bmatrix}$$

$$= \begin{bmatrix} 9-8 & -6+4 \\ 12-8 & -8+4 \end{bmatrix}$$

$$= \begin{bmatrix} 1 & -2 \\ 4 & -4 \end{bmatrix}$$

Now, it is given that

$$A^2 = kA - 2I$$

$$\Rightarrow \begin{bmatrix} 1 & -2 \\ 4 & -4 \end{bmatrix} = k\begin{bmatrix} 3 & -2 \\ 4 & -2 \end{bmatrix} - 2\begin{bmatrix} 1 & 0 \\ 0 & 1 \end{bmatrix}$$

$$= \begin{bmatrix} 3k & -2k \\ 4k & -2k \end{bmatrix} - \begin{bmatrix} 2 & 0 \\ 0 & 2 \end{bmatrix}$$

$$= \begin{bmatrix} 3k-2 & -2k \\ 4k & -2k-2 \end{bmatrix}$$

$$\Rightarrow -2k = -2 \Rightarrow k = 1$$

9. (c) $\dfrac{ay - x^2}{y^2 - ax}$

Explanation: $x^3 + y^3 = 3axy$

Differentiating w.r.t. x, we get

$$3x^2 + 3y^2 \cdot \frac{dy}{dx} = 3a\left[x \cdot \frac{dy}{dx} + y.1 \right]$$

$$\Rightarrow \quad x^2 + y^2 \frac{dy}{dx} = ax\frac{dy}{dx} + ay$$

$$(y^2 - ax)\frac{dy}{dx} = ay - x^2$$

$$\Rightarrow \quad \frac{dy}{dx} = \frac{ay - x^2}{y^2 - ax}$$

10. (d) $\dfrac{\pi}{3}$

Explanation: Given $A + A^T = I_2$

$$\Rightarrow \begin{bmatrix} \cos\alpha & -\sin\alpha \\ \sin\alpha & \cos\alpha \end{bmatrix} + \begin{bmatrix} \cos\alpha & -\sin\alpha \\ \sin\alpha & \cos\alpha \end{bmatrix}^T = \begin{bmatrix} 1 & 0 \\ 0 & 1 \end{bmatrix}$$

$$\Rightarrow \begin{bmatrix} \cos\alpha & -\sin\alpha \\ \sin\alpha & \cos\alpha \end{bmatrix} + \begin{bmatrix} \cos\alpha & +\sin\alpha \\ -\sin\alpha & \cos\alpha \end{bmatrix} = \begin{bmatrix} 1 & 0 \\ 0 & 1 \end{bmatrix}$$

$$\Rightarrow \begin{bmatrix} 2\cos\alpha & 0 \\ 0 & 2\cos\alpha \end{bmatrix} = \begin{bmatrix} 1 & 0 \\ 0 & 1 \end{bmatrix}$$

$$\Rightarrow 2\cos\alpha = 1 \Rightarrow \cos\alpha = \frac{1}{2} = \cos\frac{\pi}{3}$$

$$\Rightarrow \alpha = \frac{\pi}{3}$$

11. (a) $\begin{bmatrix} 2 & 3 \\ 1 & 2 \end{bmatrix}$

Explanation: We have, $P = \begin{bmatrix} 2 & -3 \\ -1 & 2 \end{bmatrix}$

$$\therefore \quad |P| = 4 - 3 = 1 \neq 0$$

$$\therefore \quad P^{-1} \text{ exist.}$$

Cofactors of matrix P are

$$P_{11} = 2, \; P_{12} = 1, \; P_{21} = 3; \; P_{22} = 2$$

$$\therefore \quad \text{adj } P = \begin{bmatrix} 2 & 1 \\ 3 & 2 \end{bmatrix}^T = \begin{bmatrix} 2 & 3 \\ 1 & 2 \end{bmatrix}$$

So, $\quad P^{-1} = \dfrac{1}{|P|}(\text{adj } P)$

$$= \frac{1}{1}\begin{bmatrix} 2 & 3 \\ 1 & 2 \end{bmatrix}$$

$$= \begin{bmatrix} 2 & 3 \\ 1 & 2 \end{bmatrix}$$

12. (c) $k^3 |A|$

Explanation: Since, A is a square matrix of order 3

$$\therefore \quad |kA| = k^3 |A|$$

13. (b) continuous but not differentiable at $x = 5$

Explanation: We have,

$$f(x) = |x-5| = \begin{cases} -(x-5), & x \leq 5 \\ x-5, & x > 5 \end{cases}$$

$\because$ Modulus functions are continuous every where,

$\therefore$ $f(x)$ is continuous at $x = 5$.

Differentiating at $x = 5$:

$$\text{L.H.D.} = \lim_{h \to 0} \frac{f(5-h) - f(5)}{-h}$$

$$= \lim_{h \to 0} \frac{[5-(5-h)] - [-(5-5)]}{-h}$$

$$= \lim_{h \to 0} \frac{h}{-h} = -1$$

$$\text{R.H.D.} = \lim_{h \to 0} \frac{(5+h) - f(5)}{h}$$

$$= \lim_{h \to 0} \frac{[(5+h)-5] - [-(5-5)]}{h}$$

$$= \lim_{h \to 0} \frac{h}{h} = 1$$

$\because \quad$ L.H.D. $\neq$ R.H.D.

$\therefore$ $f(x)$ is not differentiable at $x = 5$.

14. (c) $F(x + y)$

Explanation: We have,

$$F(x) = \begin{bmatrix} \cos x & -\sin x & 0 \\ \sin x & \cos x & 0 \\ 0 & 0 & 1 \end{bmatrix}$$

$$\therefore \quad F(x).F(y) = \begin{bmatrix} \cos x & -\sin x & 0 \\ \sin x & \cos x & 0 \\ 0 & 0 & 1 \end{bmatrix}$$

$$\begin{bmatrix} \cos y & -\sin y & 0 \\ \sin y & \cos y & 0 \\ 0 & 0 & 1 \end{bmatrix}$$

$$= \begin{bmatrix} \cos x\cos y - \sin x\sin y & -\cos x\sin y - \sin x\cos y & 0 \\ \sin x\cos y + \cos x\sin y & -\sin x\sin y + \cos x\cos y & 0 \\ 0 & 0 & 1 \end{bmatrix}$$

$$= \begin{bmatrix} \cos(x+y) & -\sin(x+y) & 0 \\ \sin(x+y) & \cos(x+y) & 0 \\ 0 & 0 & 1 \end{bmatrix}$$

$$= F(x + y)$$

15. (d) $\left(\dfrac{dy}{dx}\right)^2$

Explanation: We have,

$$e^y(x + 1) = 1$$

Differentiating w.r.t. x, we get

$$(x+1)\left(e^y \cdot \frac{dy}{dx}\right) + e^y(1) = 0$$

$$e^y(x+1)\frac{dy}{dx} + e^y = 0$$

$$\Rightarrow \quad 1 \cdot \frac{dy}{dx} + e^y = 0 \qquad [\because e^y(x+1) = 1]$$

$$\Rightarrow \quad \frac{dy}{dx} = -e^y \qquad \text{...(i)}$$

$$\frac{d^2y}{dx^2} = -e^y \cdot \frac{dy}{dx}$$

$$\Rightarrow \quad \frac{d^2y}{dx^2} = \frac{dy}{dx} \cdot \frac{dy}{dx} \qquad [\text{Using (i)}]$$

$$\Rightarrow \quad \frac{d^2y}{dx^2} = \left(\frac{dy}{dx}\right)^2$$

16. (a) $\begin{bmatrix} -1 & -1 \\ -2 & -1 \end{bmatrix}$

Explanation:

We have, $\quad 2X + Y = \begin{bmatrix} 1 & 0 \\ -3 & 2 \end{bmatrix}$

$$\Rightarrow \quad 2X + \begin{bmatrix} 3 & 2 \\ 1 & 4 \end{bmatrix} = \begin{bmatrix} 1 & 0 \\ -3 & 2 \end{bmatrix}$$

$$\Rightarrow \quad 2X = \begin{bmatrix} 1 & 0 \\ -3 & 2 \end{bmatrix} - \begin{bmatrix} 3 & 2 \\ 1 & 4 \end{bmatrix}$$

$$= \begin{bmatrix} -2 & -2 \\ -4 & -2 \end{bmatrix}$$

$$\Rightarrow \quad X = \frac{1}{2}\begin{bmatrix} -2 & -2 \\ -4 & -2 \end{bmatrix}$$

$$= \begin{bmatrix} -1 & -1 \\ -2 & -1 \end{bmatrix}$$

17. (a) $x - 20y - 7 = 0$

Explanation: Given equation of curve is,

$$y = \frac{x-7}{(x-2)(x-3)}$$

$$= \frac{x-7}{x^2 - 5x + 6} \qquad \text{...(i)}$$

On x-axis, y-coordinate is zero.

$$\therefore \quad 0 = \frac{x-7}{x^2 - 5x + 6} \Rightarrow x - 7 = 0 \Rightarrow x = 7$$

So, a point on the tangent to the curve is $(7, 0)$.

Now, differentiating in w.r.t. x, we get

$$\frac{dy}{dx} = \frac{(x^2 - 5x + 6)(1) - (x-7)(2x-5)}{(x^2 - 5x + 6)^2}$$

$$\Rightarrow \left(\frac{dy}{dx}\right)_{x=7}$$

$$= \frac{[(7)^2 - 5(7) + 6] - (7-7)[2(7) - 5]}{[(7)^2 - 5(7) + 6]^2}$$

$$= \frac{20 - 0}{(20)^2} = \frac{1}{20}$$

$$\therefore \text{Slope of tangent, } m = \frac{1}{20}$$

We know, equation of the line with slope m and passing through a point (x_1, y_1) is

$$(y - y_1) = m(x - x_1)$$

$$\Rightarrow \quad y - 0 = \frac{1}{20}(x - 7)$$

$$\Rightarrow \quad 20y = x - 7$$

$$\Rightarrow \quad x - 20y - 7 = 0$$

18. (b) $\dfrac{1}{2(1 + x^2)}$

Explanation:

Let $x = \tan\theta \Rightarrow \theta = \tan^{-1}x$ \qquad ...(i) so, $\tan^{-1}\left(\dfrac{\sqrt{1+x^2}-1}{x}\right)$

$= \tan^{-1}\left(\dfrac{\sqrt{1+\tan^2\theta}-1}{\tan\theta}\right)$

$= \tan^{-1}\left(\dfrac{\sec\theta-1}{\tan\theta}\right)$

$= \tan^{-1}\left(\dfrac{1-\cos\theta}{\sin\theta}\right)$

$= \tan^{-1}\left(\dfrac{2\sin^2\dfrac{\theta}{2}}{2\sin\dfrac{\theta}{2}\cos\dfrac{\theta}{2}}\right)$

$= \tan^{-1}\left(\tan\dfrac{\theta}{2}\right)$

$= \dfrac{\theta}{2} = \dfrac{1}{2}\tan^{-1}x$ [Using (i)]

Now, the derivative of $\dfrac{1}{2}\tan^{-1}x$ w.r.t. x is

$\dfrac{d}{dx}\left(\dfrac{1}{2}\tan^{-1}x\right) = \dfrac{1}{2}\left(\dfrac{1}{1+x^2}\right)$

$\qquad\qquad\qquad = \dfrac{1}{2(1+x^2)}$

19. (a) $k < 0$

Explanation:

$\qquad f(x) = kx^3 + 5$

$\therefore \qquad f'(x) = 3kx^2$

For $f(x)$ to be strictly decreasing.

$\qquad f'(x) < 0$

$\Rightarrow \qquad 3kx^2 < 0$

$\Rightarrow \qquad 3k < 0$ $[\because x^2 \geq 0]$

$\Rightarrow \qquad k < 0$

20. (c) 7

Explanation:

We have, $\quad f(x) = (2x-1)^2 + 7$

$\because$ For any value of x,

$\qquad (2x-1)^2 \geq 0$

$\Rightarrow \quad (2x-1)^2 + 7 \geq 7$

$\Rightarrow \qquad f(x) \geq 7$

$\therefore$ Minimum value of $f(x)$ is 7.

21. (i) (b) 2×2

Explanation: 2×2

$[A]_{2\times3}\,[B]_{3\times2} = [AB]_{2\times2}$

(ii) (c) $\begin{bmatrix} 19 & 9 \\ 19 & 2 \end{bmatrix}$

Explanation:

$AB = \begin{bmatrix} 1 & 2 & 3 \\ 2 & 3 & 1 \end{bmatrix}\begin{bmatrix} 9 & -2 \\ -1 & 1 \\ 4 & 3 \end{bmatrix}$

$\quad = \begin{bmatrix} 9-2+12 & -2+2+9 \\ 18-3+4 & -4+3+3 \end{bmatrix}$

$\quad = \begin{bmatrix} 19 & 9 \\ 19 & 2 \end{bmatrix}$

(iii) (a) 2, 6, 12

Explanation: 2, 6, 12

For any square matrix A, the elements a_{ij}, $i = j$ are called its main diagonal elements.

(iv) (b) $\alpha^2 + \beta\gamma = 1$

Explanation:

$D^2 = D.D = \begin{bmatrix} \alpha & \beta \\ \gamma & -\alpha \end{bmatrix}\begin{bmatrix} \alpha & \beta \\ \gamma & -\alpha \end{bmatrix}$

$= \begin{bmatrix} \alpha^2+\beta\gamma & \alpha\beta-\beta\alpha \\ \alpha\gamma-\alpha\gamma & \gamma\beta+\alpha^2 \end{bmatrix}$

$= \begin{bmatrix} \alpha^2+\beta\gamma & 0 \\ 0 & \alpha^2+\beta\gamma \end{bmatrix}$

$\because \quad D^2 = I_2$ [Given]

$\therefore \quad \begin{bmatrix} \alpha^2+\beta\gamma & 0 \\ 0 & \alpha^2+\beta\gamma \end{bmatrix} = \begin{bmatrix} 1 & 0 \\ 0 & 1 \end{bmatrix}$

$\alpha^2 + \beta\gamma = 1$, which is the required relation between α, β and γ.

22. (i) (c) $r = \dfrac{P-4x}{2\pi}$

Explanation: Let P be the sum of perimeters of the square and the circle.

$\therefore \qquad P = 4x + 2\pi r$

$\Rightarrow \qquad r = \dfrac{P-4x}{2\pi}$

(ii) (b) $x^2 + \dfrac{(P-4x)^2}{4\pi}$

Explanation: Let $A(x)$ be the sum of areas of the square and the circle.

$\because \qquad A(x) = x^2 + \pi r^2$

$\qquad = x^2 + \pi\left(\dfrac{P-4x}{2\pi}\right)^2$

$\qquad\qquad\qquad$ [From part (i)]

$\qquad = x^2 + \dfrac{(P-4x)^2}{4\pi}$

(iii) (a) $x = 2r$

Explanation: From part (ii), we have

$$A(x) = x^2 + \frac{(P-4x)^2}{4\pi}$$

$$\therefore \quad A'(x) = 2x + \frac{2(P-4x)(-4)}{4\pi}$$

$$= 2x - \frac{2}{\pi}(P-4x)$$

For maximum/minimum value,

Put $\quad A'(x) = 0$

$$\Rightarrow \quad 2x - \frac{2}{\pi}(P-4x) = 0$$

$$\Rightarrow \quad 2x = \frac{2}{\pi}(P-4x)$$

$$= \frac{2}{\pi} \cdot 2\pi r \quad \text{[Using part (i)]}$$

$$x = 2r$$

Also, $\quad A''(x) = 2 - \frac{2}{\pi}(-4)$

$$= 2 + \frac{8}{\pi} > 0$$

$\therefore$ $A(x)$ will be least if $x = 2r$.

(iv) (d) $(\pi + 4)r^2$

Explanation: From part (ii), we have
$$A(x) = x^2 + \pi r^2$$
$$= (2r)^2 + \pi r^2$$
$$= (4 + \pi)r^2$$

23. (i) (d) both one-one and onto

Explanation: We have, $f : \{1, 3, 4\} \to \{1, 2, 5\}$ and $f(x) = \{(1, 2), (3, 5), (4, 1)\}$

We observe that each value of x in domain has a unique value.

$\therefore$ $f(x)$ is one-one.

Also, each value of $f(x)$ in co-domain has its pre-image in domain.

$\therefore$ $f(x)$ is onto.

(ii) (b) onto but not one-one

Explanation: We have, $g : \{1, 2, 5\} \to \{1, 3\}$ and $g(x) = \{(1, 3), (2, 3), (5, 1)\}$.

We observe that elements 1, 2 in domain has a same image *i.e.*, 3 in co-domain.

$\therefore$ $g(x)$ is not one-one.

And, every element in co-domain has some pre-image in domain.

$\therefore$ $g(x)$ is onto.

(iii) (a) 5

Explanation: $fog(2) = f\{g(2)\} = f(3) = 5$

(iv) (c) 3

Explanation: $gof(1) = g\{f(1)\} = g(2) = 3$

24. (c) $\dfrac{\pi}{3}$

Explanation:

We have, $\quad \vec{a} + \vec{b} + \vec{c} = 0$

$$\Rightarrow \quad \vec{c} = -(\vec{a} + \vec{b})$$

$$\Rightarrow \quad |\vec{c}|^2 = |-(a+b)|^2$$

[Squaring both sides]

$$\Rightarrow \quad |\vec{c}|^2 = |\vec{a}|^2 + |\vec{b}|^2 + 2\vec{a}.\vec{b}$$

$$\Rightarrow \quad |\vec{c}|^2 = |\vec{a}|^2 + |\vec{b}|^2 + 2|\vec{a}||\vec{b}|\cos\theta$$

$$\Rightarrow \quad (7)^2 = (3)^2 + (5)^2 + 2 \times 3 \times 5 \cos\theta$$

$$\Rightarrow \quad \cos\theta = \frac{49-34}{30} = \frac{15}{30}$$

$$= \frac{1}{2} = \cos\frac{\pi}{3}$$

$$\Rightarrow \quad \theta = \frac{\pi}{3}$$

25. (b) $\dfrac{x+1}{2} = \dfrac{y-2}{4} = \dfrac{z-3}{5}$

Explanation: The required line is parallel to the line $\dfrac{x-3}{2} = \dfrac{y-3}{4} = \dfrac{z+4}{5}$

$\therefore$ Direction ratios of the required line $= <2, 4, 5>$

So, equation of line through $(-1, 2, 3)$ with direction ratios $<2, 4, 5>$ is

$$\frac{x-(-1)}{2} = \frac{y-2}{4} = \frac{z-3}{5}$$

i.e., $\quad \dfrac{x+1}{2} = \dfrac{y-2}{4} = \dfrac{z-3}{5}$

26. (d) $p = 2, q = -2$

Explanation: Since, $(p, q, 1)$ lies on the line
$$\frac{x}{-1} = \frac{y-2}{2} = \frac{z+1}{-1}$$

$\therefore \quad \dfrac{p}{-1} = \dfrac{q-2}{2} = \dfrac{1+1}{-1}$

$$\Rightarrow \quad \frac{p}{-1} = \frac{2}{-1} ; \frac{q-2}{2} = \frac{2}{-1}$$

$$\Rightarrow p = 2, q = -4 + 2 = -2$$

27. (a) $(3\hat{i} - 5\hat{j} + 7\hat{k}) + \lambda(2\hat{i} + 3\hat{j} + 4\hat{k})$

Explanation: The vector form of equation of line $\dfrac{x - x_1}{a} = \dfrac{y - y_1}{b} = \dfrac{z - z_1}{c}$ is

$$r = (x_1\hat{i} + y_1\hat{j} + z_1\hat{k}) + \lambda(a\hat{i} + b\hat{j} + c\hat{k})$$

$$\Rightarrow r = (3\hat{i} - 5\hat{j} + 7\hat{k}) + \lambda(2\hat{i} + 3\hat{j} + 4\hat{k})$$

28. (i) (a) 9

Explanation: Since, $\vec{a}$ and $\vec{b}$ are perpendicular to each other,

$$\therefore \qquad \vec{a} \cdot \vec{b} = 0$$

$$\Rightarrow (3\hat{i} - \hat{j} - 2\hat{k}).(\hat{i} + \lambda\hat{j} - 3\hat{k}) = 0$$

$$\Rightarrow \qquad 3 - \lambda + 6 = 0$$

$$\Rightarrow \qquad \lambda = 9$$

(ii) (c) 47.92 sq. units

Explanation: Since, $\vec{c}$ and $\vec{d}$ are diagonals of a parallelogram

$\therefore$ Area of the parallelogram

$$= \frac{1}{2} |\vec{c} \times \vec{d}|$$

$$= \frac{1}{2} \begin{vmatrix} i & j & k \\ 3 & 5 & -7 \\ 2 & 5 & 10 \end{vmatrix}$$

$$= \frac{1}{2} |\hat{i}(50 + 35) - \hat{j}(30 + 14) + \hat{k}(15 - 10)$$

$$= \frac{1}{2} |85\hat{i} - 44\hat{j} + 5\hat{k}|$$

$$= \frac{1}{2}\sqrt{(85)^2 + (-44)^2 + (5)^2}$$

$$= \frac{1}{2} \times 95.84 = 47.92 \text{ sq. units}$$

(iii) (d) 289

Explanation: Scalar triple product of $\vec{a}, \vec{c}, \vec{d} = (\vec{a} \times \vec{c}) \cdot \vec{d}$

$$= \begin{vmatrix} \hat{i} & \hat{j} & \hat{k} \\ 3 & -1 & -2 \\ 3 & 5 & -7 \end{vmatrix}.(2\hat{i} + 5\hat{j} + 10\hat{k})$$

$$= [\hat{i}(7 + 10) - \hat{j}(-21 + 6) + \hat{k}(15 + 3)]$$

$$(2\hat{i} + 5\hat{j} + 10\hat{k})$$

$$= (17\hat{i} + 15\hat{j} + 18\hat{k}).(2\hat{i} + 5\hat{j} + 10\hat{k})$$

$$= 17(2) + 15(5) + 18(10)$$

$$= 289$$

(iv) (c) $\sqrt{\dfrac{838}{1162}}$

Explanation: We know,

$$\vec{a} \times \vec{c} = |\vec{a}| |\vec{c}| \sin\theta$$

where, θ is the angle between $\vec{a}$ and $\vec{c}$

$\therefore$ Required sine of angle between $\vec{a}$ and $\vec{c}$

$$= \frac{|\vec{a} \times \vec{c}|}{|\vec{a}| |\vec{c}|}$$

$$= \frac{\sqrt{(17)^2 + (15)^2 + (18)^2}}{\sqrt{(3)^2 + (-1)^2 + (-2)^2} \cdot \sqrt{(3)^2 + (5)^2 + (-7)^2}}$$

[Using part (iii)]

$$= \frac{\sqrt{838}}{\sqrt{14}\sqrt{83}} = \sqrt{\frac{838}{1162}}$$

29. (c) $8x - \dfrac{7}{2}$

Explanation:

$$C(x) = 4x^2 - \frac{7}{2}x + 3$$

$\therefore$ Marginal cost function $= \dfrac{d}{dx}\{C(x)\}$

$$= \frac{d}{dx}\left(4x^2 - \frac{7}{2}x + 3\right)$$

$$= 8x - \frac{7}{2}$$

30. (b) $12x - \dfrac{3}{2}x^2$

Explanation:

Demand function, $x = \dfrac{24 - 2p}{3}$

$$\Rightarrow \qquad p = \frac{24 - 3x}{2}$$

Now, revenue function $R(x) = \text{price} \times \text{quantity}$

$$= \frac{24 - 3x}{2} \times x$$

$$= 12x - \frac{3}{2}x^2$$

31. (a) 7

Explanation:

$$C(x) = 3x^3 + 2x^2 - 9x$$

$$\therefore \text{ Average cost function, } A(x) = \frac{C(x)}{x}$$

$$= \frac{3x^3 + 2x^2 - 9x}{x}$$

$$= 3x^2 + 2x - 9$$

At $x = 2$,

$$A(2) = 3(2)^2 + 2(2) - 9$$

$$= 7$$

32. (d) $-\dfrac{x^3}{3} + 6x^2 + 73x + 30$

Explanation:

Cost function, $C(x) = \dfrac{x^3}{3} - 7x^2 + 27x - 30$

and, Demand function, $p = 100 - x$

$\therefore$ Revenue function, $R(x) =$ Price × Quantity

$$= (100 - x) \times x$$

$$= 100x - x^2$$

Now, Profit function,

$$P(x) = R(x) - C(x)$$

$$= 100x - x^2 - \left(\frac{x^3}{3} - 7x^2 + 27x - 30 \right)$$

$$= -\frac{x^3}{3} + 6x^2 + 73x + 30$$

33. (i) (c) $\dfrac{24}{x} - 5 + x$

Explanation:

$$R(x) = 24 - 5x + x^2$$

$\therefore$ Average revenue function,

$$AR(x) = \frac{R(x)}{x}$$

$$= \frac{24 - 5x + x^2}{x}$$

$$= \frac{24}{x} - 5 + x$$

(ii) (a) $2x - 5$

Explanation : Marginal revenue function,

$$MR(x) = \frac{d}{dx}\{R(x)\}$$

$$= \frac{d}{dx}(24 - 5x + x^2)$$

$$= 2x - 5$$

(iii) (a) 20

Explanation:

From part (i), we have

$$AR(x) = \frac{24}{x} - 5 + x$$

$$\therefore \qquad AR(1) = \frac{24}{1} - 5 + 1$$

$$= 20$$

(iv) (d) ₹ 16

Explanation:

Revenue received from the sale of 11th item
= Revenue received from the sale of 11 items – Revenue received from the sale of 10 items

$$= R(11) - R(10)$$

$$= [24 - 5(11) + (11)^2] - [24 - 5(10) + (10)^2]$$

$$= 90 - 74$$

$$= 16$$

Computer Science

Specimen Question Paper

Computer Science

Maximum Marks: 70
Time allowed: One and a Half hours

General Instructions

*(Candidates are allowed additional **15 minutes** for **only** reading the paper.)*
ALL QUESTIONS ARE COMPULSORY
The marks intended for questions are given in brackets [ ].
Select the correct option for each of the following questions.

Questions

1. The law which represents the Boolean equation A + B = B + A is: [1]
   - (a) Associative Law
   - (b) Distributive Law
   - (c) Commutative Law
   - (d) Absorption Law

2. The dual of the Boolean equation $(X+Y) \cdot 1 = X+Y$ is: [1]
   - (a) $X+Y+0$
   - (b) $X \cdot Y + 0 = X \cdot Y$
   - (c) $(X \cdot Y) + 1 = X \cdot Y$
   - (d) $(X+Y) + 0 = X \cdot Y$

3. If A=1, B=0, C=0 and D=1, then the maxterm will be: [1]
   - (a) AB'C'D
   - (b) A'BCD'
   - (c) A+B'+C'+D
   - (d) A'+B+C+D'

4. The compliment of the Boolean expression $F(P,Q,R) = (P + Q + R)$ is: [1]
   - (a) P'Q'R'
   - (b) P' + Q' + R'
   - (c) P + (Q'+R')
   - (d) (P+Q) + R'

5. The propositional operator => represents: [1]
   - (a) Conjunction
   - (b) Implication
   - (c) Disjunction
   - (d) Negation

6. Encoders are used for: [1]
   - (a) Adding two bits
   - (b) Converting Decimal to Binary
   - (c) Converting Binary to Decimal
   - (d) Data transmission

7. NAND gate is formed by the combinations of: [1]
   - (a) AND gate and OR gate
   - (b) OR gate and NOT gate
   - (c) NAND gate and NOT gate
   - (d) AND gate and NOT gate

8. The combinational circuit which adds two binary bits is: [1]
   - (a) Full Adder
   - (b) Decoder
   - (c) Half Adder
   - (d) Multiplexer

9. The Quad group in a Karnaugh's map eliminates: [1]
   - (a) One variable
   - (b) Four variables
   - (c) Three Variables
   - (d) Two variables

10. The proposition (a <=> b) is represented by: **[1]**

    (a) a'b' + ab   (b) (a'+b') · (a+b)

    (c) (a+b)'   (d) (a·b)'

11. If the input in a decoder is A'BC'D, then the decimal equivalent output will be: **[2]**

    (a) 8   (b) 10

    (c) 5   (d) 6

12. A matrix MAT[10][15] is stored in the memory in Row Major Wise with each element requiring 2 bytes of storage. If the base address at MAT[1][2] is 2215, then the address of MAT[3][7] will be: **[2]**

    (a) 2285   (b) 2315

    (c) 2319   (d) None of the above

13. With reference to the given proposition ~P => Q , answer the following questions:

    (a) the converse of the proposition is: **[1]**

        (i)   Q => ~P   (ii)   ~Q => P

        (iii) ~Q => ~P   (iv) ~P => ~Q

    (b) the contra-positive of the proposition is: **[1]**

        (i)   ~P => Q   (ii)   Q => P

        (iii) ~Q => P   (iv)   Q => ~P

14. The reduced expression for the Boolean expression $F(X,Y,Z) = \Sigma(0,1,2,3,4,5,6,7)$ is: **[2]**

    (a) XY' + X'Y   (b) 1

    (c) 0   (d) None of these

15. What is the output of the code given below? **[2]**

```java
int i,j;
for( i=1; i<=5;i++);
    for(j=i+1;j<1;j++);
        System.out.print(i + "+" + j) ;
```

    (a) 67   (b) 1 + 2

    (c) 6 + 7   (d) 12

16. What is the output of the statement given below? **[2]**

```java
System.out.print(Integer.parseInt("234")+'A');
```

    (a) 234 + 65   (b) 234A

    (c) 299   (d) ERROR

17. What is the output of the statement given below? **[2]**

```java
System.out.print('A'+'1'+'C');
```

    (a) 65 + 1 + 66   (b) 10 + 1 + 67

    (c) 181   (d) 65 + 49 + 67

18. The basic logic gate that represents the simplification of the Boolean expression **A.(A'+B). (A+B)** is: **[2]**

    (a) OR gate   (b) NOT gate

    (c) AND gate   (d) None of these

19. What is the conditional statement to check for the Non-boundary elements in a double dimensional array of 'M' number of rows and 'N' number of columns? The row index is represented by 'r' and the column index is represented by 'c'. **[2]**

    (a) (r>0 || r<M-1 && c>0 || c<N-1)   (b) (r>0 && r<M-1 || c>0 && c<N-1)

    (c) (r>0 && r<M-1 && c>0 && c<N-1)   (d) (r>0 || r<M-1 || c>0 || c<N-1)

20. The proposition ~(a ∧ b) V (~a => b) is a: **[2]**

    (a) Contradiction   (b) Contingency

    (c) Tautology   (d) Implication

21. Reduce the given Boolean function $F(A,B,C,D) = \Sigma(0,2,4,8,9,10,12,13)$ by using 4-variable Karnaugh map and answer the following questions:

(a) What will be the least number of groups and their types formed for reduction? **[1]**

    (i)   6 pairs   (ii)   2 quad and 2 pairs

    (iii) 1 quad and 3 pairs   (iv) 3 quads

(b) The reduced expression of the Boolean function given above is: **[2]**

    (i) $ACD' + B'D' + BD$ (ii) $(A+C'+D').(B'+D').(A+C')$

    (iii) $C'D' + AC' + B'D'$ (iv) $(C+D'). (B'+D').(A+B+D)$

22. A school intends to select candidates for an Inter school competition as per the criteria given below:

- The student has participated in an earlier competition and is very creative

Or

- The student is very creative and has excellent general awareness, but has not participated in any competition earlier

Or

- The student has excellent general awareness and has won prize in an inter -house competition

The inputs are:

Inputs	
A	Participated in a competition earlier
B	Is very creative
C	Won prize in an inter house competition
D	Has excellent general awareness

(In all the above cases 1 indicates yes and 0 indicates no).

Output: X [1 indicates yes and 0 indicates no for all cases].

Draw the truth table for the inputs and outputs given above and answer the following questions:

(a) The POS expression for X(A,B,C,D) will be: **[2]**

    (i) $F(A,B,C,D) = \Sigma(3, 5, 7, 11, 12, 13, 14, 15)$ (ii) $F(A,B,C,D) = \pi(3, 5, 7, 11, 12, 13, 14, 15)$

    (iii) $F(A,B,C,D) = \pi(0, 1, 2, 4, 6, 8, 9, 10)$ (iv) $F(A,B,C,D) = \Sigma(0, 1, 2, 4, 6, 8, 9, 10)$

(b) The maximum input combinations for the above truth table will be: **[1]**

    (i)   24   (ii)   16

    (iii) 8   (iv)   4

23. Reduce the given Boolean function $F(A,B,C,D) = \pi(3,4,5, 6, 7, 11,13,15)$ by using 4-variable Karnaugh map and answer the following questions:

(a) What will be the least number of groups and their types formed for reduction? **[1]**

    (i)   6 pairs   (ii)   3 quads

    (iii) 1 quad and 3 pairs   (iv) 2 quad and 3 pairs

(b) The reduced expression of the Boolean function given above is: **[2]**

    (i) $(B+C).(B+D).(A'+D)$ (ii) $BC + BD + A'D$

    (iii) $AB' + C'D' + B'D'$ (iv) $(A+B').(C'+D').(B'+D')$

24.

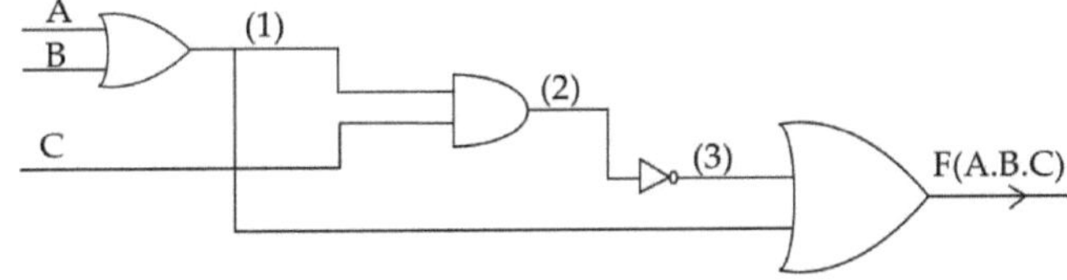

From the logic diagram given above, where A,B and C are inputs and F is the output, answer the following questions:

(a) The expression at (1) is: **[1]**

    (i) $A.B$ (ii) $A' + B'$

    (iii) $A + B'$ (iv) $A + B$

(b) The expression at (3) is: [1]

    (i)   A+B.C′   (ii)   ((A+B)′.C)′

    (iii) ((A+B).C)′   (iv)   (A+B).C

(c) The final expression F(A,B,C) is: [1]

    (i)   F=((A+B)′.C)′ + (A+B)   (ii)   F= (A+B)′.(C+A+B)

    (iii) F=((A+B).C)′ + (A+B)   (iv)   F= (AB + C)′ +(A+B)

25. Given the Boolean expression F = (P + R) · (P·Q + Q·R′), identify:

(a) The complement of the expression: [2]

    (i)   P′R′ + (P′+Q′).(Q′+R)   (ii)   (P′+R′) . (P′+Q′) + (Q+R′)

    (iii) P′R′ .(PQ′ + Q′R)   (iv)   (P+R)′ .(P′+Q).(Q′+R)

(b) The law used: [1]

    (i)   Distributive Law   (ii)   De Morgan Law

    (iii) Associative Law   (iv)   Idempotent Law

26. With reference to the program code given below, answer the questions that follow:

```
void fun(int n)
{ int i,f,;
for( i=1,f=1;i<=n;i++,f*=i);
System.out.print(f);
}
```

(a) What is the output of the method **fun()** when the value of n=4? [2]

    (i)   24   (ii)   72

    (iii) 120   (iv)   ERROR

(b) What is the method **fun()** performing? [1]

    (i)   Checking for Prime Numbers   (ii)   Product of odd numbers

    (iii) Factors of a number   (iv)   Finding the factorial

27. With reference to the program code given below, answer the questions that follow:

```
int test(int n)
    { if(n==1) return 0;
        for (int i=2;i<=(int)(Math.sqrt(n));i++)
        if( n%i==0)
        return 0;
        return 1;
    }
```

(a) What will the method **test()** return when the value of n=9? [2]

    (i)   1   (ii)   true

    (iii) 0   (iv)   Error

(b) What is the method **test()** performing? [1]

    (i)   Prime number/Composite number   (ii)   Armstrong number

    (iii) Palindrome number   (iv)   Perfect number

28. With reference to the program code given below, answer the questions that follow:

```
void dimen(int n[ ][ ])
{ int p=0;
    for (int i=0;i<n.length;i++)
    for(int j=0;j<n[0].length;j++)
    { if(i==0 ||i==n.length-1 || j==0 || j==n[0].length-1)
```

```
        p=p+n[i][j];
    }
  System.out.print(p);
}
```

(a) What will be the output of the method **dimen()** when the value of n[ ][ ] ={{2,3,7},{1,5,9},{10,-3,8}} ? **[2]**

    (i)   42   (ii)   33

    (iii) 5   (iv) 37

(b) What is the method **dimen( )** performing? **[1]**

    (i)   Finding the product of the boundary elements

    (ii)   Finding the sum of the non-boundary elements

    (iii) Finding the sum of the boundary elements

    (iv) Finding the sum of the matrix elements

29. With reference to the program code given below, answer the questions that follow:

```
void single(int x[])
{ int w=1;
   for(int y=0;y<x.length;y++)
     { if(x[y]%2==0 && x[y]>0)
        w=w*x[y];
     }
   System.out.print(w);
}
```

(a) What will be the output of the method **single()** when the value of x[] = {10,2,9,-6,5,6} ? **[2]**

    (i)   120   (ii)   45

    (iii) 720   (iv) 18

(b) What is the method **single( )** performing? **[1]**

    (i)   Sum of the positive odd elements   (ii)   Product of the even elements

    (iii) Product of the positive even elements   (iv)   Sum of the positive even elements

30. With reference to the program code given below, answer the questions that follow:

```
int solve(int a, int b)
  { int i,l=0;
     for(i=1;i<=a*b;i++)
     { if(i%a==0&& i%b==0)
        { l=i; break;}
     }
   return l;
  }
```

(a) What will be the output of the method **solve()** when the value of a=8 and b=12? **[2]**

    (i)   4   (ii)   96

    (iii) 0   (iv) 24

(b) What is the method **solve( )** performing? **[1]**

    (i)   HCF of 'a' and 'b'   (ii)   Prime Factors of 'a' and 'b'

    (iii) LCM of 'a' and 'b'   (iv)   None of these

31. The following program code checks if the positive integer 'N' is a palindrome number by returning true or false. There are some places in the code marked as ?1?, ?2?, ?3?, ?4? and ?5? which are to be replaced by a statement/expression so that the code works properly.

boolean Palindrome(int N)

```java
{ int rev = ?1? ;
   int num = N;
   while (num>0)
   { int f = num/10;
       int s = ?2? ;
       int digit = num - ?3? ;
       rev = ?4? + digit;
       num /= ?5?;
   }
   if(rev == N)
       return true;
   else
       return false;
}
```

Answer the following question:

(a) What is the statement or expression at ?1? [1]

    (i)   –1   (ii) 0

    (iii) 10   (iv) 2

(b) What is the statement or expression at ?2? [1]

    (i)   s *10   (ii) f /10

    (iii) rev   (iv) f *10

(c) What is the statement or expression at ?3? [1]

    (i)   s   (ii) rev

    (iii) f   (iv) digit * 10

(d) What is the statement or expression at ?4? [1]

    (i)   s * 10   (ii) rev *10

    (iii) f   (iv) rev

(e) What is the statement or expression at ?5? [1]

    (i)   1   (ii) 100

    (iii) 10   (iv) rev

32. The following program code sorts a single dimensional array in ascending order using **Insertion Sort technique**. There are some places in the code marked as **?1?, ?2?, ?3?, ?4?** and **?5?** which are to be replaced by a statement/expression so that the code works properly.

```java
void insertionSort(int array[])
{ int n = ?1?;
   for (int j = 1; j < n; j++)
   {
       int key = ?2?;
       int i = j-1;
       while ( (i > -1) && ( array [i] > ?3? ) )
       {
           array [i+1] = ?4?;
           i--;
       }
       ?5? = key;
   }
```

Answer the following question:

(a) What is the statement or expression at ?1?   [1]

   (i) array.length()   (ii) array.length

   (iii) length   (iv) −1

(b) What is the statement or expression at ?2?   [1]

   (i) j   (ii) array[j+1]

   (iii) array[j]   (iv) 0

(c) What is the statement or expression at ?3?   [1]

   (i) key   (ii) array[j]

   (iii) i+1   (iv) n

(d) What is the statement or expression at ?4?   [1]

   (i) j+1   (ii) key

   (iii) array[j]   (iv) array[i]

(e) What is the statement or expression at ?5?   [1]

   (i) array[i+1]   (ii) i+1

   (iii) j   (iv) array[i]

1. (c) Commutative Law

   Explanation: According to Commutative law , (A+B) = (B+A)

2. (b) $X \cdot Y + 0 = X \cdot Y$

   Explanation: According to the principle of Duality, the dual form of a Boolean expression can be found by replacing each AND ($\bullet$) to OR(+) , each OR (+) with AND ($\bullet$). Also replacing each zero(0) with one(1) and one(1) with zero (0).

3. (d) $A'+B+C+D'$

   Explanation: As per the Maxterm, 1 means variable in the complement form and 0 means variable in the normal form.

4. (a) $P'Q'R'$

   Explanation: Here we can use the DeMorgan's law. In short, we can replace OR(+) to AND ($\bullet$) and replace AND ($\bullet$) to OR(+). Also convert the normal variable to the complement form and complement form to normal.

5. (b) Implication

   Explanation: '$\rightarrow$' represents the implication

6. (b) Converting Decimal to Binary

   Explanation: Encoders can be used to convert decimal to binary format (In the syllabus we discuss about the decimal to binary encoder).

7. (d) AND gate and NOT gate

   Explanation: NAND means negation of AND , so it is the combination of NOT gate and AND gate.

8. (c) Half Adder

   Explanation: Half adders are used for adding two binary bits whereas full adders used for adding three binary bits.

9. (d) Two variables

   Explanation: Quad group eliminates two variables , octet eliminates three variables and pair removes one variable.

10. (a) a'b' + ab

   Explanation: If you form the SOP (sum of products) of the equivalent connective , then it is **a'.b' + a.b**

11. (c) 5

Explanation: A′.B.C′.D is equal to 0101 which is equal to 5.

12. (a) 2285

Explanation: The formula we use here is row major wise .

Address of MAT[I][J] = B + W * ((I – LR) * N + (J – LC)) From the question, B = 2215 , W= 2 , I = 3, J = 7, LR = 1, LC= 2, N is the number of columns= 15.

Calculation :

= 2215 + 2x(15x(3-1) + (7-2))

= 2215 +2x35

= 2215 + 70

= 2285

13. (a) (i) $Q \Rightarrow \sim P$

Explanation: The given proposition is $\sim P \to Q$ so converse is $Q \to \sim P$

(b) (iii) $\sim Q \Rightarrow P$

Explanation: The contrapositive of the proposition is $\sim Q \to P$.

14. (b) 1

Explanation: If we draw the Karnaugh Map of the given expression, we get an octet, reducing an octet means eliminating 3 elements. So 1 is the answer as it is the SOP.

15. (c) 6 + 7

Explanation: The value of i is 6 and j loop will execute only where j= i+1 (7).

16. (c) 299

Explanation: Integer.parseInt("234")+ 'A' = 234 + 65 (ASCII value of A) = 299.

17. (c) 181

Explanation: ASCII value of 'A' = 65 ASCII value of '1'= 49 ASCII value of 'C' = 67. So sum of all these ASCII values is 65+ 49+ 67=181.

18. (c) AND gate

Explanation: $\quad$ A.(A′+B).(A+B) = (A.A′ + A.B).(A+B)

$\qquad\qquad\qquad\qquad$ = (0 + A.B).(A+ B)

$\qquad\qquad\qquad\qquad$ = A.B.A + A.B.B = A. B

19. (b) (r>0 && r<M-1 || c>0 && c<N-1)

Explanation: To access the non boundary elements the condition for rows is r > 0 & r< M-1 and the condition for columns is c>0 &c < N-1.

20. (c) Tautology

Explanation: The expression is :

$\sim$(a ∧ b) V ($\sim$a => b)

a	b	a^b	~(a^b)	~a	~a => b	~(a ∧ b) V (~a => b)
0	0	0	1	1	0	1
0	1	0	1	1	1	1
1	0	0	1	0	1	1
1	1	1	0	0	1	1

So , $\sim$(a ∧ b) V ($\sim$a => b) will give always True , which means it is a tautology.

21. (a) (iv) 3 quads

(b) (iii) C′.D′ + A.C′ + B′.D′

Explanation: F (A, B, C, D) = ss(0, 2, 4, 8, 9, 10, 12, 13)

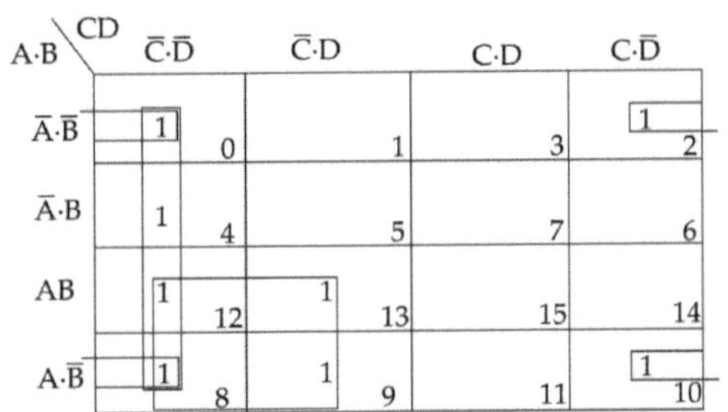

Quad 1 (0, 4, 12, 8) = $\overline{C}\cdot\overline{D}$

Quad 2 (8, 9, 12, 13) = $A\cdot\overline{C}$

Quad 3 (0, 2, 8, 10) = $\overline{B}\cdot\overline{D}$

22. (a) (iii) $F(A,B,C,D) = \pi(0, 1, 2, 4, 6, 8, 9, 10)$

Explanation: The POS expression for X(A,B,C,D).

(b) (ii) 16

Explanation: as there are 4 inputs, there will be 2^4 (16) input combinations.

A	B	C	D	X(output)
0	0	0	0	0
0	0	0	1	0
0	0	1	0	0
0	0	1	1	1
0	1	0	0	0
0	1	0	1	1
0	1	1	0	0
0	1	1	1	1
1	0	0	0	0
1	0	0	1	0
1	0	1	0	0
1	0	1	1	1
1	1	0	0	1
1	1	0	1	1
1	1	1	0	1
1	1	1	1	1

$X(A,B,C,D) = \pi(0,1,2,4,6,8,9,10)$

23. (a) (ii) 3 quads

(b) (iv) (A+B').(C'+D').(B'+D')

Explanation:

There will be 3 quads

Quad 1 (3, 7, 5, 11)

Quad 2 (4, 5, 7, 6)

Quad 3 (5, 7, 13, 15)

24. (a) (iv) A+B

    (b) (iii) $((A+B).C)'$

    (c) (iii) $F=((A+B).C)' + (A+B)$

25. (a) (i) $P'R' + (P'+Q').(Q'+R)$

          Explanation: Applying the DeMorgan's law

$$F = (P + R) \cdot (P{\cdot}Q + Q{\cdot}R')$$
$$= ((P+R).\ (P.Q+Q.R'))'$$
$$= ((P+R)' + (P.Q +Q.R')') \ (\text{De-morgan's law})$$
$$= P'.R' + (P.Q)'.(Q.R')'$$
$$= P'.R' + (P'+Q')(Q'+R)$$

    (b) (ii) De Morgan Law

26. (a) (iii) 120

          Explanation: n = 4 , f = f*i. The final value of i is 5 and f= 24 (4 factorial). The value of f will be updated as f= 24 *5= 120.

    (b) (iv) Finding the factorial

27. (a) (iii) 0

          Explanation: When n= 9, the iterative values of 'i' are, 2 and 3, so it returns 0

    (b) (i) Prime number/Composite number

          Explanation: as it will return 1 for prime number and 0 for composite number.

28. (a) (iv) 37

          Explanation: 37 it is the sum of the boundary elements of the 2 dimensional array.

    (b) (iii) Finding the sum of the boundary elements

29. (a) (i) 120

          Explanation: The method single() checks two conditions inside the for loop. One is the condition of even number and other is checking the condition of greater than zero or not. The answer is 120. The initial value of w= 1, as the loop executes , it becomes 10,20 (10 × 2)and finally 120(20 × 6)

    (b) (iii) Product of the positive even elements

          Explanation: It calculates the product of the positive even numbers.

30. (a) (iv) 24

          Explanation: 24. Here a= 8 and b= 12. So the for loop executes from 0 to 96 (8 × 12). It satisfies the condition i%a ==0 and i%b==0 only when iterative value of 'i ' is 24.

    (b) (iii) LCM of 'a' and 'b'

          Explanation: method solve() calculates the LCM of a and b.

31. (a) (ii) 0

          Explanation: i.e int rev=0 (here we initialise the value of rev)

    (b) (iv) f *10

          Explanation: So, int s= f*10;

    (c) (i) s

          Explanation: so int digit= num- s

    (d) (ii) rev *10

          Explanation: so rev= rev*10 + digit;

    (e) (iii) 10

          Explanation: so num/= 10 (num= num/10, for eliminating the last digit from num and eventually num becomes zero.)

32. (a) (ii) array.length

    (b) (iii) array[j]

          Explanation: int key = array [j]

    (c) (i) key

          Explanation: array[i]> key

    (d) (iv) array[i]

          Explanation: array [i+1] = array [i]

    (e) (i) array[i+1]

          Explanation: array [i+1] = key

❑❑

1 Sample Paper

Computer Science

 **Questions**

1. The gates that are called Universal gates are:
   (a) NAND and AND   (b) OR and AND   (c) NAND and NOR   (d) None

2. The law which represents the Boolean equation $(A + B)' = A'.B'$ is:
   (a) Associative Law   (b) Distributive Law   (c) De-Morgan's Law   (d) Absorption Law

3. $((X)')'$ gives:
   (a) X' (b) X   (c) X.X   (d) None

4. If $P = 0, Q = 0, R = 0$ and $S = 1$, then the minterm will be:
   (a) P'Q'RS   (b) PQRS   (c) P'Q'R'S   (d) $P' + Q' + R' + S$

5. The number of quads in the Karnaugh map of the boolean expression $F = \pi(0, 1, 3, 5, 9, 14)$ will be:
   (a) 4   (b) 8   (c) 16   (d) 12

6. The expression $F = P'Q + PQ'R + P$ reduces to:
   (a) $P + Q$ (b) $P' + Q$ (c) $P + Q'$ (d) $P' + Q'$

7. If both the inputs are High the output of XOR gate will be:
   (a) High   (b) Low   (c) No output   (d) None of these

8. A multiplexor allows
   (a) Addition of bits   (b) Selection of signals   (c) Multiplication of bits   (d) None of these

9. The combinational circuit which adds three binary bits is:
   (a) Full Adder   (b) Decoder   (c) Half Adder   (d) Multiplexer

10. The output of the circuit given below is:

    (a) $A.B' + C.(A + B.D)$ (b) $A' + B + C'A'.D$ (c) $A + B'.C' + (B + C)'$ (d) $ABC' + (A + B + C)'$

11. $A.A' + A$ gives
    (a) A   (b) 0   (c) 1   (d) A'

12. A device that converts an applied signal to a coded digital bit stream is:
    (a) Multiplexer   (b) Decoder   (c) Encoder   (d) Adder

13. (i) An array M[20][40] is stored in memory along the row. The address of M [15][19] , if the M[0][0] is at address 1000 and each element occupies 4 bytes is:

    (a) 2000   (b) 2200   (c) 3476   (d) None

  (ii) What will be the total memory occupied by the array elements?

    (a) 3200   (b) 3400   (c) 1600   (d) 800

14. The Expression $A.A'=0$ is a

    (a) Tautology   (b) Fallacy   (c) Disjunction   (d) None

15. The reduced expression for $F(A, B, C, D)= \Sigma(0, 1, 2, 5, 7, 8, 9, 10, 13, 15)$ is

    (a) $BD + C'D + B'D'$ (b) $B + D' + C'D'$ (c) $BD + (C + D) + BD'$ (d) None

16. The following code on execution prints:

```
int n = 25792, s = 0;
while (n > 0)
{
    d = n%10;
    if (d%2 == 0)
    s = s + d;
    else
    s = s – d;
    n = n/10;
}
System.out.println(s+"");
```

    (a) –17   (b) –19   (c) 17   (d) 19

17. The import statement(s) to make the following code execute properly is __________

```
public static void main(String [] args)
{
    try
    {
        int n;
        Scanner sc=new Scanner(System.in);
        n=sc.nextInt();
    }
    catch(IOException e)
    {}
}
```

    (a) import java.lang;   (b) import java.util.* ; , import java.io.IOException;

    (c) import java.awt.*; , import java.net.*;   (d) None of these

18.

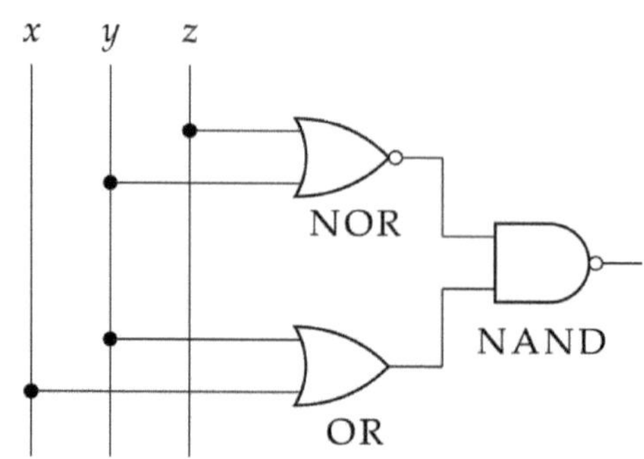

The output produced from the above circuit is:

(a) $(xy' + z') + xz'$

(b) $((y + z)' . (x + y))'$

(c) $(xyz' + xy' + z')'$

(d) None

19. The boolean function reduces to:
$$F(A, B, C, D) = \Sigma(0, 1, 3, 5, 7, 8, 9, 11, 13, 15)$$

(a) $B'C' + D$ (b) $BC + D'$ (c) $B'C' + D$ (d) None

20. The expression $F(x,y,z) = x'y'z + xy'z'$ is a

(a) Canonical expression

(b) Canonical SOP expression

(c) Canonical POS expression

(d) Not a Canonical expression

21. (i) Given the $p \to q$ then the contrapositive is:

(a) $q \to p$

(b) $\sim q \to \sim p$

(c) $\sim p \to \sim q$

(d) $\sim p \to q$

(ii) The expression $A'+B'$ can also be written as:

(a) $(A.B)'$

(b) $(A+B)'$

(c) $A'.B$

(d) $A.B'$

22. Answer the questions with respect to solution of the expression $F(A,B,C,D) = \Sigma(2, 3, 4, 5, 7, 8, 10, 13, 15)$, while solving it using K-Maps.

(i) How many quads are possible in the solution of above K-Map?

(a) 4 (b) 2 (c) 1 (d) 0

(ii) How many pairs can be made while solving the above expression

(a) 1 (b) 2 (c) 3 (d) 4

23. An array M[10][40] is stored in memory along the column. The element M[0][0] is at location 500 with each element occupying 2 bytes.

(i) Find the address of M[5][15]

(a) 820 (b) 810 (c) 800 (d) None

(ii) Find the total memory occupied by the elements of the array.

(a) 900 Bytes

(b) 910 Bytes

(c) 1000 Bytes

(d) 800 Bytes

24. Given the circuit diagram

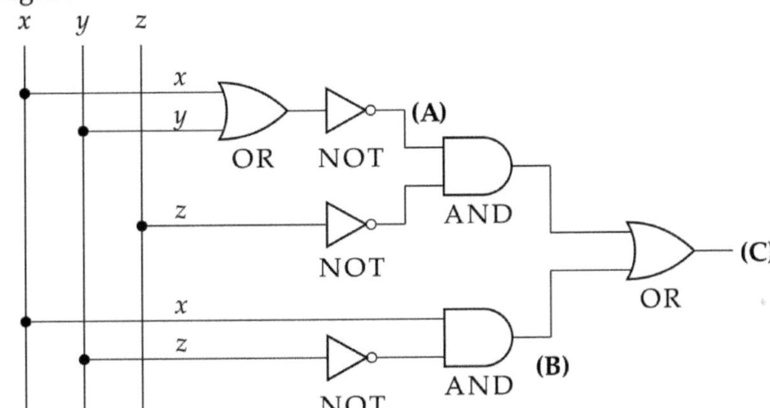

(i) Identify the output at (A)

(a) $(X + Y)'$ (b) $(X.Y)'$ (c) XY (d) None

(ii) Identify the output at (B)

(a) $(X + Y)'$ (b) $(X.Y)'$ (c) XZ' (d) None

(iii) Find the final output of the circuit at (C)

(a) $(X + Y)'Z + XZ'$

(b) $(X.Y)' + Z'$

(c) XY

(d) None

25. A boolean function $F(x,y,z)$ gives the following outputs:

X	Y	Z	F
0	0	0	1
0	0	1	1
0	1	0	0
0	1	1	0
1	0	0	0
1	0	1	1
1	1	0	1
1	1	1	1

(i) The canonical SOP expression is:

(a) X'Y'Z' + X'Y'Z + XY'Z + XYZ' + XYZ

(b) XY'Z' + X'Y'Z + XY'Z + XYZ' + XYZ

(c) X'Y'Z' + XYZ + XY'Z + XYZ' + XYZ

(d) None

(ii) The number of maxterms are:

(a) 1   (b) 2   (c) 3   (d) None

26. Given the expression

$$F(P,Q,R) = (P + Q)' + PQ' + (P + Q)R'$$

(i) The dual of the expression is

(a) (P + Q)' . (P + Q') . (P + Q) + R'

(b) (P.Q) . (P+Q')' . (P.Q) + R'

(c) (P.Q)' . (P + Q') . (P.Q) + R'

(d) None

(ii) If P = 1, Q = 1 and R = 0 , the output of the expression is:

(a) 1   (b) 0   (c) Error   (d) No output

27. Answer questions with respect to the following code:

```
int Sumdig(int num)
{
    s = 0;
    while (num>0)
    {
        d = num%10;
        if (d%2 == 0)
        s = s + d;
        else
        s = s - d;
        num = num/10;
    }
    return s;
}
```

(i) What will be the value of r if the function is called as
r = Sumdig(5678)?

(a) 2   (b) 3   (c) 4   (d) –2

(ii) How many times will the loop execute?

(a) 3   (b) 2   (c) 4   (d) 1

28. Given the code

```
void rev(int num)
{
    r = 0;
    while (num>0)
    {
        d = num%10;
        r = r*10 + d;
        num=num/10;
    }
}
```

(i) What is the function rev( ) doing?

(a) Finding sum of the digits of the number   (b) Reversing the number

(c) Adding the even digits   (d) Adding the odd digits

(ii) What will be the output of the function , if it is called with 678?

(a) 678   (b) 876   (c) 786   (d) None

29. Answer questions with respect to the code given below:

```
public void factorial( int n)
{
    if (n==1)
    return 1;
    else
    return n* factorial (____________) ;
}
```

(i) What kind of function is the above function?

(a) Redundant   (b) Recursive   (c) Reiterative   (d) None

(ii) What will be the statement in the blank?

(a) n   (b) n + 1   (c) n – 1   (d) n*2

30. The function prime() checks whether a number is prime or not

```
protected void prime( int number)
{
    int a=0,count=0;
    for (a=1;a<=number;a++)
    {
        if (number %a==0)
        count = ____________;
    }
    if (count= = ____________)
    System.out.println("Prime");
    else
    System.out.println("Composite");
}
```

(i) The statements/words/numbers that are required for correct execution of the code is/are:

(a) count+1 , 2   (b) count+2, >2   (c) count+3 , 2   (d) None

(ii) What is the access specifier of the function?

(a) private   (b) protected   (c) public   (d) default

31. Write answers with respect to the following code given below:

```
class myclass
{
        private void sumarray(int ar[])
        {
            int i, s=0;
            for (i=0;i<ar.length;i++)
            if (i%2==0)
            s=s+ar[i];
            System.out.println("Sum"+____________);
        }
}
```

(i) What is the return type of the function?

    (a) int   (b) float   (c) boolean   (d) None

(ii) Where is the function accessible?

    (a) Own class   (b) Package   (c) Subclasses   (d) Everywhere

(iii) What kind of parameter is the function receiving?

    (a) Array   (b) Single integer   (c) A String   (d) None

(iv) What is the function doing?

    (a) Function sum of all the members   (b) Finding sum of members at even indexes
    (c) Finding sum of even elements   (d) Finding sum of odd elements

(v) What should be the contents of the blank?

    (a) i   (b) s   (c) a   (d) None

32. Given the following code , that checks whether a number is automorphic or not. Fill in the blanks for proper execution of the code.

(An automorphic number is one which is found at its square. Example 25 , 252 = 625 , 625 has 25 at its end.)

```
import java. ____________ // Blank 1
public void main()
{
    int num , sq, d,t;
    Scanner sc = new ____________; // Blank 2
    num= sc. ____________// Blank 3
    t=num;
    sq=(int)Math.pow(num,2);
    while (num>0)
    {
        num=num/10;
        c=c+1;
    }
    if (sq%(int)Math.pow(10, ____________)== ____________) // Blank 4 and // Blank 5
    System.out.println("Automorphic");
    else
    System.out.println("Not Automorphic");
}
```

(i) Requirement for // Blank 1

    (a) lang   (b) util.*
    (c) util.Date   (d) awt

(ii) Requirement for // Blank 2

    (a) Scanner(System.out);   (b) Scanner(System.in);

    (c) Scanner(System.err);   (d) None

(iii) Requirement for // Blank 3

    (a) nextLine ();   (b) next( );

    (c) nextInt( );   (d) nextFloat ( );

(iv) Requirement for // Blank 4

    (a) c   (b) num   (c) d   (d) sq

(v) Requirement for // Blank 5

    (a) t   (b) c   (c) sq   (d) num

Answers

1. (c) NAND and NOR

2. (c) De- Morgan's Law

3. (b) X

   Explanation: Involution Law

4. (c) P'Q'R'S

5. (c) 16

6. (a) P + Q

   Explanation:

$$P'Q + PQ'R + P = P'Q + P(Q'R + 1)$$
$$= P'Q + P.1$$
$$= P + P'Q$$
$$= P + Q \qquad \text{(3rd Distributive Law)}$$

7. (b) Low

8. (b) Selection of signals

9. (a) Full Adder

10. (a) A.B' + C.(A + B.D)

11. (a) A

   Explanation: A.A' = 0 + A gives A

12. (c) Encoder

13. (i) (c) 3476

     Explanation: Address calculation in Row major order

$$Aij = Base + Width (nc(I - Lr) + (J - Lc))$$

     So, $1000 + 4(40 \times (15 - 0) + (19 - 0)) = 1000 + 4 \times 619$
$$= 3476$$

   (ii) 3200

     Explanation : No. of elements in the array $40 \times 20 = 800$, Size of each element 4 Bytes, so total memory occupied = $800 \times 4 = 3200$

14. (b) Fallacy

15. (a) BD + C'D + B'D'

    Explanation: Since the given boolean expression has 4 variables, so we draw a 4×4 K Map. We fill the cells of K Map in accordance with the given boolean function.

Then, we form the groups in accordance with the above rules.

Then, we have—

CD AB	$\overline{C}\,\overline{D}$	$\overline{C}D$	CD	$C\overline{D}$
$\overline{A}\,\overline{B}$	1 0	1 1	3	1 2
$\overline{A}B$	4	1 5	1 7	6
AB	12	1 3	1 15	14
$A\overline{B}$	1 8	1 9	11	1 10

Now,

$$F(A, B, C, D) = (A'B + AB)(C'D + CD) + (A'B' + A'B + AB + AB')\,C'D$$
$$+ (A'B' + AB')(C'D' + CD')$$
$$= BD + C'D + B'D'$$

16. (a) –17

Explanation: The code extracts each digit and checks for its divisibility by 2 , if it is, then it adds the digit else subtracts. Hence:
$$2 - 9 - 7 - 5 + 2 = -17$$

17. (b) import java.util.* ; , import java.io.IOException;

Explanation: To use Scanner class java.util.* and java.io.IOException for Exceptions.

18. (b) ((y+z)' . (x+y))'

Explanation: y and z go to a NOR gate so (y + z)' , x and y go to a OR gate so (x + y) , both join to a NAND gate so output is ((y + z)' . (x + y))'

19. (a) B'C' + D

Explanation: Since the given boolean expression has 4 variables, so we draw a 4 × 4 K Map.

We fill the cells of K Map in accordance with the given boolean function. Then, we form the groups in accordance with the above rules.

Then, we have—

CD AB	$\overline{C}\,\overline{D}$	$\overline{C}D$	CD	$C\overline{D}$
$\overline{A}\,\overline{B}$	1 0	1 1	1 3	2
$\overline{A}B$	4	1 5	1 7	6
AB	12	1 13	1 15	14
$A\overline{B}$	1 8	1 9	1 11	10

Now,

$$F(A, B, C, D) = (A'B' + A'B + AB + AB')(C'D + CD) + (A'B' + AB')(C'D' + C'D)$$
$$= D + B'C'$$

Thus, minimized boolean expression is:
$$F(A, B, C, D) = B'C' + D$$

20. (d) Not a Canonical expression

    Explanation: Since it comprises both of maxterms and minterms, it is not a canonical expression.

21. (i) (b) $\sim q \rightarrow \sim p$

    (ii) (a) (A.B)′

      Explanation : De Morgan's 2nd Law (A.B)′ = A′+B′

22. (i) (c) 1

    (ii) (c) 3

      Explanation: The figure explains the plotting and the number of quads and pairs.

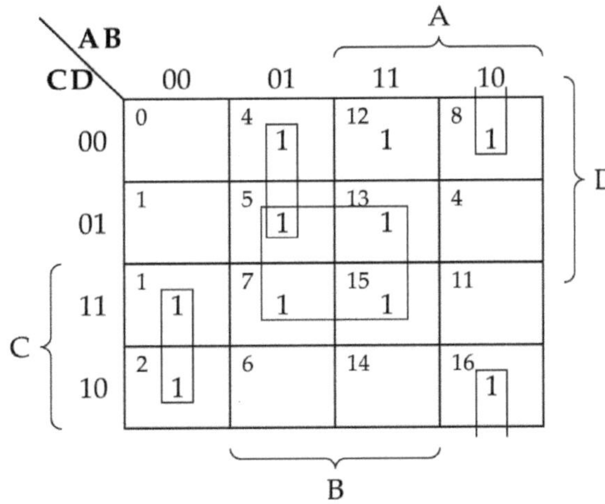

23. (i) (b) 810

    (ii) (d) 800 Bytes

      Explanation: Formula for address calculation in column major order is

      (A)   Aij = Base + Width(nr(J – Lc) + (I – Lr))

      Here

      $500 + 2 \times (10 \times (15 - 0) + (5 - 0))$

$$= 500 + 310$$
$$= 810$$

      (B) Total number of elements are:

$$10 \times 40 = 400$$

      Total memory occupied $= 400 \times 2$

$$= 800 \text{ Bytes}$$

24. (i) (a) (X+Y)′

    (ii) (c) XZ′

    (iii) (a) (X+Y)′Z + XZ′

25. (i) (a) X′Y′Z′ + X′Y′Z + XY′Z + XYZ′ + XYZ

    (ii) (c) 3

      Explanation: Minterms are found at the rows where the output is 0 and maxterms are found at the rows where output is 1. While writing minterms 0 is written as X′ and 1 is written as X.

26. (i) (c) (P.Q)′ . (P+Q′) . (P.Q)+R′

      Explanation: Dual is obtained by converting + to . , . to + , 1 to 0 , 0 to 1 , Hence the solution.

    (ii) (a) 1

      Explanation:

      $(1 + 1)′ + 1.1′ + (1 + 1).0′ = 0 + 0 + 1 = 1$

27. (i) (a) 2

Explanation: The function extracts each digit of the number and either adds or subtracts the digit from s, depending on whether the digit is even or odd. Hence:

$$6 + 8 - 5 - 7 = 2$$

(i) (c) 4 Times

Explanation: Since the number is a 4 digit number , the loop will execute for 4 times.

28. (i) (b) Reversing the number.

(ii) (d) None

Explanation: There is no print statement.

29. (i) (b) Recursive

Explanation: The function is calling itself again and again in the last statement.

(ii) (c) n – 1

30. (i) (a) count+1, 2

Explanation: The count is to be increased whenever a number % a == 0 that is a factor is found, hence count=count +1.

The condition for being prime is number of factors is equal to 2

(ii) (b) protected

31. (i) (d) None

Explanation: The function is returning void.

(ii) (a) Own class

Explanation: The function is Private.

(iii) (a) Array

(iv) (b) Finding sum of members at even indexes

(v) (b) s

32. (i) (b) util.*

(ii) (b) Scanner(System.in);

(iii) (c) nextInt( );

(iv) (a) c

(v) (a) t

Explanation for questions (iv) and (v): The code finds the square of the number input and then counts the number of digits in the original number and then extracts that many digits from the back of the square.

❑❑

Questions

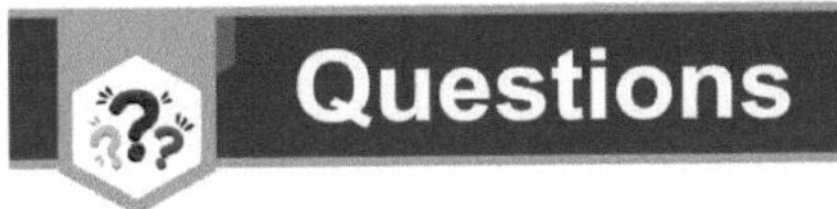

1. The absorption law states that:
   (a) $X.X = X$ (b) $X + X = X$ (c) $((X)')' = X$ (d) $X + XY = X$

2. If the inputs to a NAND gate are True and False the output will be:
   (a) True   (b) False   (c) 12   (d) 0

3. The law that states that $A + BC = (A + B)(A + C)$ is:
   (a) De-Morgan's law   (b) Involution law
   (c) Distributive Law   (d) None

4. The formulae to find the number of Quads in a Karnaugh map where n is the number of variables:
   (a) 2^{n-1} (b) 2^{n+1} (c) 2^{n+2} (d) 2^{n}

5. Maxterms are:
   (a) Sum terms   (b) Product terms
   (c) Combination of sum and product terms   (d) None of these

6. The expression $F = ((A + B')(B + C))B$ reduces to:
   (a) BC   (b) ABC   (c) A   (d) AB

7. Simplification of the expression $(AB)' + (A + B)'$ gives:
   (a) 1   (b) 0   (c) A'+B'   (d) A'

8. A Decoder performs:
   (a) Addition of bits   (b) Selection of signals
   (c) Converts encoded signals to its original form   (d) None of these

9. The combinational circuit which adds two binary bits is:
   (a) Full Adder   (b) Decoder   (c) Half Adder   (d) Multiplexer

10. The number of Minterms possible for 3 inputs is:
    (a) 7   (b) 8   (c) 9   (d) 1

11. Determine the values of A, B, C and D that make the sum term equal to zero:
    (a) $A = 1, B = 0, C = 1, D = 0$ (b) $A = 0, B = 1, C = 1, D = 0$
    (c) $A = 1, B = 0, C = 0, D = 1$ (d) $A = 1, B = 0, C = 1, D = 1$

12.

The output of the above circuit is:
(a) $(X+Y)' . (X . Y)$ (b) $(X.Y')' . (X' + Y)$ (c) $(X.Y)' . (X + Y)$ (d) $(X'.Y)' . (X' + Y')$

13. (i)   The simplification of $Y = AB' + (A' + A)C$.
   (a) $AB' + C$ (b) A   (c) 1   (d) $A'B + C$
   13. (ii)

   (ii) The simplification of $(A+A')C + BBC$ is :
   (a) C   (b) B   (c) AB   (d) AB'

14. The expression $Y = (A + B)(B + C)(C + A)$ is a:
   (a) SOP expression   (b) POS expression
   (c) Neither SOP nor POS   (d) None of these

15. An array P[30][20] is stored in memory in row major order. The address of P [15][10] , if the base address is 200 and each element occupies 8 bytes is:
   (a) 2000   (b) 2680   (c) 3220   (d) None

16. Which of the following expression is not in POS form?
   (a) $(X + Y)(X' + Y')$ (b) $(X + Y).XY$ (c) $X(X + Y) + XYZ$ (d) Both (b) and (c)

17. From the truth table given below the POS expression is:

A	B	C	Output
0	0	0	0
0	0	1	1
0	1	0	0
0	1	1	1
1	0	0	0
1	0	1	0
1	1	0	1
1	1	1	0

   (a) $(A + B + C)(A + B' + C)(A' + B + C)(A' + B + C')(A' + B' + C')$
   (b) $(ABC)(AB'C)(A'BC)(A'BC')(A'B'C')$
   (c) $(A + B' + C)(A' + B + C)(A' + B + C')(A' + B' + C')$
   (d) None of the above

18. The reduction of the boolean function $F (a, b, c, d) = \Sigma(0, 1, 2, 4, 5, 6, 8, 9, 12, 13, 14)$ using K-Map gives:

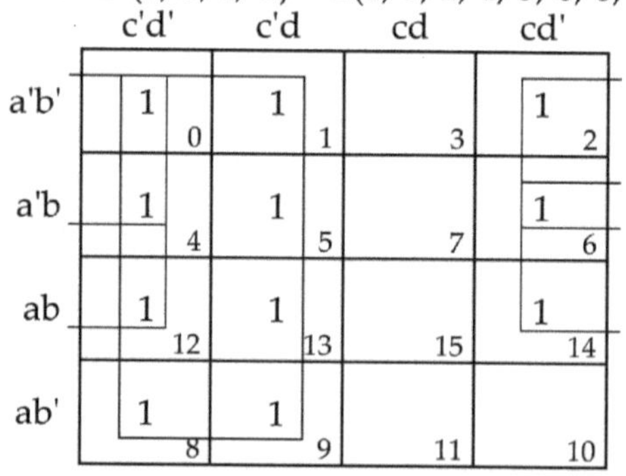

	c'd'	c'd	cd	cd'
a'b'	1 (0)	1 (1)	(3)	1 (2)
a'b	1 (4)	1 (5)	(7)	1 (6)
ab	1 (12)	1 (13)	(15)	1 (14)
ab'	1 (8)	1 (9)	(11)	(10)

   (a) $c' + a'd' + bd'$ (b) $b' + a' + d' + bd'$ (c) $a' + (c + d') + bd'$ (d) $(a + c)' + (b + d')$

19. $Z = \Sigma A, B, C(1, 3, 6, 7)$ will form a .... variable map
   (a) 4   (b) 2   (c) 1   (d) 3

20. The contra positive of $p \rightarrow q$ is
   (a) $\neg q \rightarrow \neg p$ (b) $\neg p \rightarrow \neg q$ (c) $p \rightarrow q$ (d) None

21. (i)   The following code on execution prints:

```
public void main()
{
        boolean p1=true;
        boolean p2=false;
        if (p1)
```

```java
        System.out.println(p2);
        else
        System.out.println(p1);
    }
```

    (a) true   (b) false   (c) boolean   (d) None

(ii)

```java
    public void main()
    {
        String str="Sweets and Snacks";
        System.out.println(str.lastIndexOf('S') + str.firstIndexOf('s'));
    }
```

The output of the code if the function is called will be :

    (a) 19   (b) 20   (c) Error   (d) None of these

22. (i) The import statement(s) to make the following code execute properly is ....

```java
    public static void main(String [] args)
    {
        int n;
        Scanner sc=new Scanner(System.in);
        n=sc.nextInt();
        d=d.getDate();
    }
}
```

    (a) import java.io;
    (b) import java.util.Date ; , import java.util.Scanner;
    (c) import java.net.*;
    (d) None of the above

(ii) An array when passed to a function , the call type is:

    (a) By value   (b) By reference
    (c) By address   (d) None

23. (i) Which of the following is true about the concrete class?

    (a) All methods are defined   (b) There are no methods
    (c) It has a fixed class name   (d) It has no class name

(ii) How many values can a function in java return to the calling function ?

    (a) 1   (b) 2   (c) 3   (d) 4

24. Given the boolean function:

$$F (A, B, C, D) = \Sigma(0, 1, 2, 3, 12, 13, 14, 15)$$

  (i) How many quads will it have?

    (a) 2   (b) 3   (c) 1   (d) No quads

  (ii) Reducing the expression using K-map gives:

    (a) $A + B + A'B'$ (b) $AB + A'B'$ (c) $A'B + AB'$ (d) $AB' + AB$

  (iii) The combination that reduces the largest number of variables in a Karnaugh map is :

    (a) Pairs   (b) Quads   (c) Octets   (d) None

25. A logical function M for three inputs A, B and C, where $M = F (A, B, C)$ is such that the output is 0 (zero), if the majority of inputs are zero (0) and one (1) if the majority of inputs are one (1).

  (i) How many minterms will be there?

    (a) 1   (b) 3   (c) 4   (d) None

  (ii) What is the SOP expression?

    (a) $ABC' + ABC + A'B'C' + ABC$ (b) $A'BC + AB'C + ABC' + ABC$
    (c) $A'BC' + AB'C' + ABC' + ABC'$ (d) $A'BC + A'B'C + AB'C' + ABC'$

26. Given the following code:

```
void function1(int ar[ ])
{
    for (i=0;i<ar.length;i++)
    {
        if ( ar[i] >10)
        ar[i]=ar[i-1];
        else
        ar[i]=ar[i]*2;
    }
    for (i=0;i<ar.length;i++)
    System.out.print(ar[i]+" ");
}
```

If the function is called with an input array [9,10,11,2]:

(i) How many times will the for loop execute?

    (a) 5 Times   (b) 4 Times   (c) 3 Times   (d) None

(ii) What will be the output of the code?

    (a) 17, 18, 21, 20   (b) 19, 20, 21, 20   (c) 18, 20, 20, 20   (d) None

27.
```
class myclass( )
{
    public void show(int n1,int n2) //f1
    { }
    public void show(int p,float q) //f2
    { }
    public void show( int x,int y , int z) //f3
    { }
}
```

(i) Which OOPs concept is illustrated by functions f1, f2, f3?

    (a) Inheritance   (b) Abstraction   (c) Encapsulation   (d) Polymorphism

(ii) Statements to call f2 and f3 respectively with an object ob of the class are:

    (a) ob.show(10,20); , ob.show(10,5,6);   (b) ob.show(10,20,5); , ob.show(10,5,6);

    (c) Both (a) and (b)   (d) ob.show(10,20.5); , ob.show(10,5,6);

28.
```
String s="Quadratic equations";
System.out.println(s.substring(2,7) ); //Line1
System.out.println(s.lastIndexOf('a') +s.length()); //Line2
```

(i) The output of Line1

    (a) uadra   (b) adrat   (c) drat   (d) Quad

(ii) The output of Line2 is:

    (a) 33   (b) 32   (c) 31   (d) 29

29. Given below is a function that finds whether a number is a Perfect number or not.

(A perfect number is one whose sum of factors other than itself is equal to the number. Ex: 6 = 1 + 2 + 3)

```
private void checknumber(int num)
{
    int s=0,a;
    for (a=1;a ___________;a=a+1) //Blank1
```

```
    {
        if (num%a==0)
        s=s+___________; // Blank2
    }
    if (s==num)
    System.out.println("Perfect Number ");
    else
    System.out.println("Not a perfect number ");
}
```

(i) For which of the following numbers the code will print "Perfect Number"?

   (a) 6   (b) 17   (c) 18   (d) 16

(ii) What will be the values of blank1 and blank 2 respectively?

   (a) <= num, s   (b) <num, a   (c) a, s   (d) num, a

30. The code for finding the number of words in a sentence is given below.

```
int words(String sen)
{
    int i=0,count=1;
    while(i++<sen.length())
    {   ch=sen___________(i);
        if (ch==' ')
        count++;
    }
    return count;
}
```

(i) What should be the access specifier of the function to make it available in subclasses?

   (a) private   (b) protected   (c) default   (d) package

(ii) Which java function should be used in the blank?

   (a) indexOf( )   (b) lastIndexOf()   (c) charAt()   (d) charat()

31. The following java code has some errors:

```
Protected void Editcode(int num) //Line1
{
    String s; //Line2
    static int p; //Line3
    Scanner sc=newobject Scanner();//Line4
    if (num=50) //Line5
    print("Fifty"); //Line6
}
```

(i) Which of the variable is a class variable?

   (a) s   (b) p   (c) sc   (d) num

(ii) Error in Line2 is:

   (a) String should be string   (b) No error

   (c) String should be word   (d) Both (a) and (c)

(iii) Error in Line4 is:

   (a) newobject should be createobject   (b) newobject should be object

   (c) newobject should be new   (d) None

(iv) Error in Line 5 is:

    (a) = should be = =   (b) No error   (c) = should be = = =   (d) None of these

(v) Error in Line 6 is:

    (a) print should be show   (b) print should be display

    (c) print should be System.out.println   (d) None

32. Given the following code that displays each word of the String passed as a parameter to the function, in separate lines. Fill in the blanks to complete the code.

```
public void wordfinder(String sen)
{
    String word="";
    char ch;
    senlength=___(1)___;
    for(i=0;i<senlength; ___(2)___)
    {
        ch=sen.___(3)___;
        if (ch !=' ')
        word=word+ ___(4)___;
        else
        {
            System.out.println(___(5)___);
            word="";
        }
    }
}
```

(i) Requirement for // (1)

    (a) len(sen)   (b) sen.length();   (c) length(sen)   (d) None

(ii) Requirement for // (2)

    (a) i++   (b) i = i + 2   (c) i   (d) i = i – 1

(iii) Requirement for // (3)

    (a) nextLine ();   (b) charAt( );   (c) substring( );   (d) char( );

(iv) Requirement for // (4)

    (a) ch   (b) sen   (c) word   (d) None

(v) Requirement for // (5)

    (a) sen   (b) ch   (c) i   (d) word

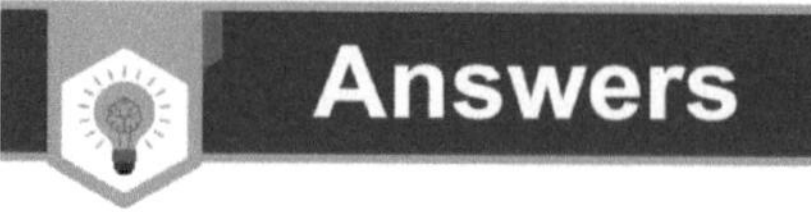

Answers

1. (d) $X + XY = X$

2. (a) True

3. (c) Distributive Law

4. (d) 2^n

5. (a) Sum Terms

6. (d) AB

  Explanation:

$$((A+B')(B+C))B = (AB + AC + BB' + B'C)B$$
$$= (ABB + ABC + 0 + BB'C)$$
$$= AB + ABC + 0 + 0 \qquad \text{(Since } BB' = 0)$$
$$= AB(1 + BC) \qquad \text{(Since } BB = B)$$
$$= AB$$

7. (c) $A' + B'$

  Explanation:

$$(AB)' + (A + B)' = (A' + B') + (A + B)'$$
$$\text{(Since } (A + B)' = A'.B' - \text{De Morgan;s Law)}$$
$$= (A' + B') + A'B'$$
$$= (A' + B' + A')(A' + B' + B')$$
$$= (A' + B')(A' + B')$$
$$= A' + B'$$

8. (c) Converts encoded signals to its original form

9. (c) Half Adder

10. (b) 8

11. (a) $A = 1, B = 0, C = 1, D = 0$

12. (c) $(X.Y)' . (X + Y)$

13. (i) (a) $AB' + C$

  Explanation:

$$Y = AB' + (A' + A)C$$
$$= AB' + 1.C$$
$$= AB' + C \text{(Since 1.C = C)}$$

  (ii) (a) C

  Explanation :

$$(A + A')C + BBC = (1).C + BC \qquad \text{(Since } A + A' = 1, B . B = B)$$
$$= C + BC$$
$$= C(1 + B) \qquad \text{(Since } 1 + B = 1)$$
$$= C.1$$
$$= C$$

14. (b) POS Expression

  Explanation: It is carrying all maxterms

15. (b) 2680

  Explanation: Address calculation in Row major order

$$A_{ij} = \text{Base} + \text{Width}(n_c(I - L_r) + (J - L_c))$$
$$\text{So,} \quad 200 + 8(20 \times (15 - 0) + (10 - 0)) = 200 + 2480$$
$$= 2680$$

16. (d) Both (b) and (c)

17. (a) $(A + B + C)(A + B' + C)(A' + B + C)(A' + B + C')(A' + B' + C')$

  Explanation: Taking the rows that have the output column as 0 , and finding the product of the maxterms.

18. (a) $c' + a'd' + bd'$

  Explanation:

From Octet (0, 1, 4, 5, 12, 13, 8, 9):

Rows representing the Octet: 1 (Both variables a and b are in opposite form. Hence, they get cancelled.)

Columns representing the Octet:
$$c'd' + c'd = c'$$
$$\text{Term Obtained} = c'$$

From quad (0,2,4,6):

Rows representing the quad:
$$a'b' + a'b = a'$$

Columns representing the quad:
$$c'd' + cd' = d'$$
$$\text{Term Obtained} = a'd'$$

From quad (4, 6, 12, 14):

Rows representing the quad:
$$a'b + ab = b$$

Columns representing the quad:
$$c'd' + cd' = d'$$
$$\text{Term Obtained} = bd'$$
$$\text{Simplified expression} = c' + a'd' + bd'$$

19. (d) 3

20. (a) $\neg q \to \neg p$

21. (i) (b) false

    Explanation: p1 is true, so if (p1) is true, so its prints p2 which is false, hence output is false.

  (ii) (c) Error

    Explanation : There is no function called firstIndexOf()

22. (i) (b) import java.util.Date ; , import java.util.Scanner;

    Explanation: To use Scanner class java.util.Scanner and java.io.IOException for Exceptions.

  (ii) (b) By reference

23. (i) (a) All methods are defined

    Explanation: A concrete class is one whose all the methods are defined and whose objects can be created, hence option (a).

  (ii) (a) 1

    Explanation : In java a function returns only 1 value

24. (i) (a) 2

    Explanation: The Karnaugh map diagram shows it.

  (ii) (b) AB + A'B'

    Explanation:

	C'D'	C'D	CD	CD'
A'B'	1 (0)	1 (1)	1 (3)	1 (2)
A'B	(4)	(5)	(7)	(6)
AB	1 (12)	1 (13)	1 (15)	1 (14)
AB'	1 (8)	1 (9)	(11)	(10)

From Quad (0,1,3,2):

Rows representing the quad: A'B'

Columns representing the quad: 1 (Both variables C and D are in opposite form. Hence, they get cancelled.)

Term Obtained = A'B'

From quad (12,13,15,14):

Rows representing the quad: AB

Columns representing the quad: 1 (Both variables C and D are in opposite form. Hence, they get cancelled.)

Term Obtained = AB

Simplified expression = AB + A'B'

(iii) (c) Octets

Explanation : In octets 3 variables are removed.

25. (i) (c) 4

Explanation: The rows where the output is 1 are the minterms, The truth table shows that there are 4 rows with output 1.

(ii) (b) A'BC + AB'C + ABC' + ABC

A	B	C	F (Output)	Minterms
0	0	0	0	
0	0	1	0	
0	1	0	0	
0	1	1	1	A'BC
1	0	0	0	
1	0	1	1	AB'C
1	1	0	1	ABC'
1	1	1	1	ABC

Explanation: SOP expression is formed by adding the minterms, hence the expression.

26. (i) 4 Times

Explanation: The array has 4 elements , so the loop will execute for 4 times.

(ii) (c) 18,20,20,20

Explanation: The first 2 elements are not more than 10, so they are getting doubled as per the code in else part, the other 2 elements of the array are > 10, so they are getting the previous elements of the array.

27. (i) (d) Polymorphism

Explanation: Multiple functions with same name but different signature.

(ii) (d) ob.show(10, 20.5); , ob.show(10, 5, 6);

Explanation: f2() takes an int and a float, f3() takes 3 ints.

28. (i) (b) adrat

Explanation: substring(2, 7) returns characters from index 2 to 6

(ii) (b) 32

Explanation: lastIndexOf('a') returns the index of last occurance of 'a' and length() returns the number of characters in the string.

29. (i) (a) 6

(ii) (b) < num, a

Explanation: The code loops to find sum of factors of the number other than itself . Hence the loop has to go to < num, wherever a is a factor, it is to be added to s.

30. (i) (b) protected

(ii) (c) charAt()

31. (i) (b) p

(ii) (b) No error

    (iii) (c) newobject should be new

    (iv) (a) = should be = =

    (v) (c) print should be System.out.println

32. (i) (b) sen.length();

    (ii) (a) i++

    (iii) (b) charAt( );

    (iv) (a) ch

    (v) (d) word

        Explanation: The code extracts each character from the String and checks if it is a space or not, if not space concats the character with word, when space is found the word is printed and emptied.

❑❑

1. The NAND gate can be used to make:
   (a) NOT gate (b) AND gate (c) OR gate (d) All of these

2. The XNOR gate gives the outputs opposite to:
   (a) XOR (b) NAND (c) OR (d) None of these

3. The law that states that $P + P'Q = P + Q$ is:
   (a) Involution law (b) De-Morgan's law
   (c) Third Distributive Law (d) None

4. The function F=(0,1,2,3,4,5,6) when simplified using K-Maps will make:
   (a) 2 squares (b) 3 squares (c) 8 squares (d) 12 squares

5. If x=0 , y=1 , z= 1 the minterm will be:
   (a) x'yz (b) xyz (c) x'y'z' (d) None of these

6. The complement of $(A + B).(B + C).(A + C)$ is:
   (a) $A.B + B'.C' + A'.C'$ (b) $A'.B' + B'.C' + A'.C'$
   (c) $A'.B' + B.C + A.C$ (d) $A'.B' + B' + C' + A' + C'$

7. The output of the logic circuit diagram at point (i) is

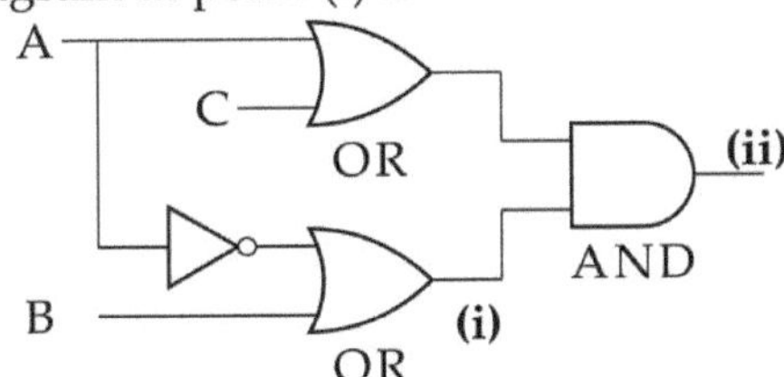

   (a) $(A + B)$ (b) $(A + B')$ (c) $A' + B$ (d) $A'+B'$

8. The output at point (ii) with respect to diagram in Question 7 is:
   (a) $(A + C).(A' + B)$ (b) $(A' + C').(A' + B)$ (c) $(A + C').(A + B')$ (d) None of these

9. The simplification of $XY + YZ + Y Z'$ gives:
   (a) Y (b) $(X + Y')$ (c) $(Y + Z)X'$ (d) $Y'Z' + X$

10. The number of minterms possible for 3 inputs is:
   (a) 7 (b) 8 (c) 9 (d) 1

11. Determine the SOP expression for the POS expression $F(X, Y, Z) = \pi(4, 5, 6, 7)$
   (a) $XYZ' + XY'Z + X'Y'Z' + X'YZ$ (b) $X'Y'Z' + X'Y'Z + X'YZ' + X'YZ$
   (c) $X'Y'Z + X'YZ + XYZ' + X'YZ$ (d) None of these

12. The complement of $XY'Z + XY + YZ'$ is
   (a) $(X' + Y + Z').(X' + Y').(Y' + Z)$ (b) $(X + Y' + Z').(X + Y').(Y' + Z)$
   (c) $(X' + Y + Z').(X + Y).(Y' + Z)$ (d) $(X' + Y + Z').(X' + Y).(Y + Z')$

13. (i) The POS of the expression $F(A, B) = (A + B).A'$ is:

    (a) $(A' + B').(A' + B).(A' + B')$ (b) $(A + B').(A' + B').(A' + B')$

    (c) $(A + B).(A + B).(A + B')$ (d) $(A + B).(A' + B).(A' + B')$

  (ii) The below symbol represents a :

    (a) Adder   (b) Multiplexer   (c) XNOR gate   (d) XOR gate

14. How many NAND gates are required to make an OR gate?

    (a) 1   (b) 2

    (c) 3   (d) OR cannot be made from NAND

15. A boolean function $F(P,Q,R)$ gives the output as High if any two inputs are high. What will be the canonical SOP expression for the function?

    (a) $PQR + PQ'R + PQR'$ (b) $PQR + PQR + PQR'$ (c) $PQR + PQR + PQR$ (d) $P'QR + PQ'R + PQR'$

16. The simplification of the expression $F(P, Q) = (P \wedge Q) \vee (P \wedge {\sim}Q)$ gives:

    (a) Q   (b) P   (c) P' (d) Q'

17. Given the statements:

Debarati's mother Paramita told that the statements

I will give you a chocolate if you score more than 95 in any of the subjects Maths , Science.

If the marks of Debarati in Maths is given by M and marks of science is given by S then which of the statements match with her mother's commitment.

    (a) $M'.S$ (b) $S' + M$ (c) $M + S$ (d) $M.S$

18. Given the statements

M: Do Good.

N: Good will come back to you.

The statement: If you do not do good, good will not come back to you, is represented by:

    (a) $({\sim}M) \Rightarrow ({\sim}N)$ (b) $(M) \Rightarrow ({\sim}N)$ (c) $({\sim}M) \Rightarrow (N)$ (d) None of these

19. The contrapositive of: If it rains, then you will not play.

    (a) If you will not play then it will rain.   (b) If it doesn't rain then you will play.

    (c) If you will play then it will not rain.   (d) None

20. The output of the circuit is:

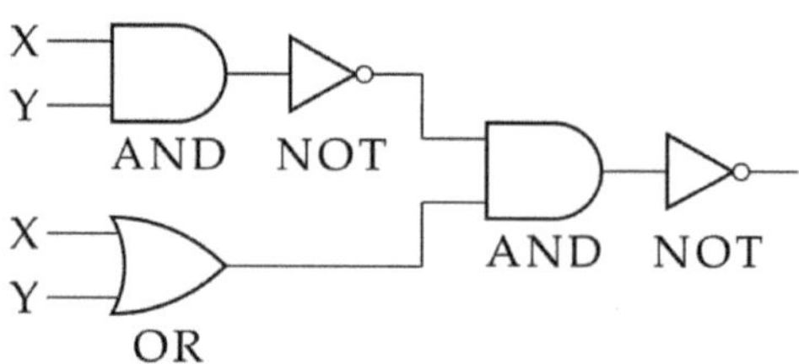

    (a) $((X+Y)' . (X+Y))'$ (b) $((X'.Y)' . (X'.Y))'$ (c) $((X.Y)' . (X+Y))'$ (d) None

21. (i) An array P[15][10] is stored in memory in row major order. The address of P [10][7], if the base address is 1400 and each element occupies 8 bytes is:

    (a) 2000   (b) 2256   (c) 3410   (d) None

  (ii) While sending a 2 dimensional array to a function , which statement is correct?

    (a) Both the row and column sizes of the array , in the formal parameter has to be specified .

    (b) The array name has to be same in actual and formal parameters.

    (c) The array name in the actual and formal parameters must be different

    (d) The array name in actual and formal parameters can be same or different.

22. (i) What does a constructor function do?

    (a) Deallocates memory   (b) Initialises an object

    (c) Deletes an object   (d) None

(ii) A constructor should optimally be :

   (a) private   (b) public

   (c) Can be private or public   (d) None

23. Given the code:

```java
class sample
{
    int x,y;
    public sample() //F1
    {
        x=0;
        y=0.0;
    }
    public sample(int p, float q) // F2
    {
        x=p; y=q;
    }
}
```

  (i) What kind of functions are functions F1 and F2?

    (a) Class function   (b) Data function   (c) Constructor function (d) Static function

  (ii) What kind of constructor is F2?

    (a) Non parameterized   (b) parameterized

    (c) Default   (d) Package

24. With respect to the JAVA code given below answer the questions that follow:

```java
class Employee
    int eno;
    String ename;
    private void getEmployee()
    {
    }
    public void showEmployee()
    {
    }
```

  (i) What is the access specifier of the data member eno?

    (a) private   (b) protected   (c) default   (d) None of these

  (ii) Where is the function getEmployee() accessible?

    (a) Own class   (b) Subclasses

    (c) Package and Subclasses   (d) Package and own class.

  (iii) How many values can the function showEmployee() of class Employee return?

    (a) 1   (b) 2   (c) 0   (d) 4

25.

```java
public void show()
{
    int i,p=0,q=1,s=0;
    System.out.println(p + " " + q);
    for(i=0;i<10;i++)
    {
        s=p+q;
        System.out.print(" " + s);
```

```
        p=q;
        q=s;
    }
}
```

(i) How many numbers will the code print?

    (a) 10   (b) 9   (c) 8   (d) 12

(ii) What is the code doing?

    (a) Adding some numbers   (b) Showing prime numbers between 0 and 10

    (c) Displaying the Fibonacci series   (d) None of these

26. (i) Which of the following is not true about Constructor functions?

    (a) They have same name as class

    (b) They cannot be static

    (c) They are inherited

    (d) They are called automatically when object is created

  (ii) Which of the following is not true about static methods?

    (a) They are also called class methods   (b) They can only access static data members

    (c) They are called by class name   (d) They are created by the keyword interface

27. Given the code to find sum of even and odd factors of a number

```
public void sum(int num)
{
    for(i=1;i<=num;i++)
    {
        if (num%i==0)
        if (i%2==0)
        s1=s1+____________;
        else
        s2=s2 +____________;
    }
}
```

(i) The variables to be declared are:

    (a) i,s2   (b) s1,s2   (c) s1   (d) i,s1,s2

(ii) The blanks will need

    (a) num   (b) sum   (c) i   (d) None

28. (i) The function that modifies its parameters is called a:

    (a) Virtual function (b) Pure function   (c) Impure function   (d) None

  (ii) Static functions can access:

    (a) Static data members   (b) Non static data members

    (c) Both static and non static data members   (d) None

29. (i) A User Defined Function in java can have .... number of parameters.

    (a) 2   (b) 3   (c) 4   (d) Any number

  (ii) A user defined function in Java can return .... number of values.

    (a) 2   (b) 3   (c) 1   (d) None

30. Given the function:

```
public int callitself(int n)
{
    if (n==1)
    return 1;
    else
```

```
        return n*callitself(n-1);
}
```

(i) The function callitself(n) gives output ...., if it is called as callitself(6).

    (a) 120   (b) 720   (c) 320   (d) 400

(ii) What kind of function is it?

    (a) Constructive   (b) Additive   (c) Recursive   (d) None

31. Given the code to find number of lowercase vowels in a message , fill up the blanks to complete working of the code:

```
import java.util.*;
void main()
{
    String msg;
    int count=0;
    msg=sc.____________; //Blank 1
    i=0;
    while(i++<msg.____________( )) // Blank 2
    {
        ch=____________.charAt(i); //Blank 3
        if (ch=='a' || ch=='e' || ch=='i' || ch=='o' ____________) //Blank 4
            ____________; // Blank 5
    }
    System.out.println("Number of lowercase vowels"+count);
}
```

(i) Requirement for // Blank 1

    (a) nextLine()   (b) nextInt()   (c) length()   (d) nextFloat();

(ii) Requirement for // Blank 2

    (a) substring(0,3)   (b) reverse()   (c) length()   (d) None

(iii) Requirement for // Blank 3

    (a) ch   (b) sc   (c) i   (d) msg

(iv) Requirement for // Blank 4

    (a) || ch=='u'   (b) ch==' '   (c) ch=='.'   (d) None

(v) Requirement for // Blank 5

    (a) i++   (b) ch++   (c) count++   (d) None

32. Given below the code to check whether a number is a Palprime number or not . Find the errors in the code.

(A Palprime number is a number that is both palindrome and prime)

```
public void main( )
{
    int n,temp,count=0,d;
    Scanner sc=new Scanner(System.in);
    n=sc.nextInt();
    temp=n ;
    while (n>0)
    {
        d=n%10;
        rev=rev*10+d;
        n=n/10;
    }
    if (rev= =n) //Line1
```

```
    {
        for (i=1;i<=n;i++)
        {
            if (n%i= =1) //Line2
            count--; //Line3
        }
        if (count= =3) //Line4
        print("Palprime"); //Line5
        else
        System.out.println("Not Palprime");
    }
}
```

(i)   Correction in Line1 is:
    (a) rev= =i   (b) rev= =0   (c) rev= =temp   (d) rev= =d

(ii) Correction in Line2 is:
    (a) n%i= =0   (b) n%i= =3   (c) n%i= =4   (d) n%i= =' '

(iii) Correction in Line3 is:
    (a) count=count+2   (b) count++   (c) count=count+9   (d) None

(iv) Correction in Line4 is:
    (a) count= =10   (b) count= =11   (c) count= =2   (d) None

(v)   Correction in Line5 is:
    (a) System.out.println("Palprime");   (b) Show("Palprime");
    (c) Display("Palprime");   (d) View("Palprime");

Answers

1. (d) All of these
2. (a) XOR
3. (c) Third Distributive Law
4. (c) 8 squares
5. (a) x'yz
6. (b) A'.B' + B'.C' + A'.C'

    Explanation:

$$\begin{aligned}
\text{Complement of } (A + B).(B + C).(A + C) &= ((A + B).(B + C).(A + C))' \\
&= (A + B)' + ((B + C).(A + C))' \\
&= (A + B)' + (B + C)' + (A + C)' \\
&= A'.B' + B'.C' + A'.C'
\end{aligned}$$

7. (c) A' + B
8. (a) (A + C).(A' + B)
9. (a) Y

    Explanation:

$$\begin{aligned}
XY + YZ + Y\,Z' &= XY + Y(Z + Z') \\
&= XY + Y(\text{Since } Z + Z' = 1) \\
&= Y(X + 1) \\
&= Y(\text{Since } X + 1 = 1)
\end{aligned}$$

10. (b) 8

11. (b) X′Y′Z′ + X′Y′Z+ X′YZ′ + X′YZ

Explanation:

$$\pi(4, 5, 6, 7) = \Sigma(0, 1, 2, 3)$$
$$= 000 + 001 + 010 + 011$$
$$= X′Y′Z′ + X′Y′Z + X′YZ′ + X′YZ$$

12. (a) (X′ + Y + Z′).(X′ + Y′).(Y′ + Z)

Explanation: Complement of

$$XY′Z + XY + YZ′ = (XY′Z + XY + YZ′)′$$
$$= (XY′Z)′.(XY)′.(YZ′)′$$
$$= (X′ + Y + Z′).(X′ + Y′).(Y′ + Z)$$

13. (i) (d) (A + B).(A′ + B).(A′ + B′)

Explanation:

$$(A + B).A′ = (A + B).(A′ + BB′)$$
$$= (A + B).(A′ + B).(A′ + B′)$$

(ii) (c) XNOR gate

14. (c) 3

15. (d) P′QR + PQ′R + PQR′

Explanation: Forming the truth table:

P	Q	R	Output	Minterms
0	0	0	0	
0	0	1	0	
0	1	0	0	
0	1	1	1	P′QR
1	0	0	0	
1	0	1	1	PQ′R
1	1	0	1	PQR′
1	1	1	0	

Therefore SOP expression: P′QR + PQ′R + PQR′

16. (b) P

Explanation: Forming the Truth Table

P	Q	~Q	P^Q	P^~Q	(P^Q) v (P^~Q)
0	0	1	0	0	0
0	1	0	0	0	0
1	0	1	0	1	1
1	1	0	1	0	1

The columns of P and (P ^ Q) v (P ^ ~Q) have the same entries. Hence simplified expression is P.

17. (c) M + S

Explanation: Mother has given the condition that if she gets the required marks in any one of the subjects, hence the condition is an OR condition.

18. (a) (~M) $\Rightarrow$ (~N)

19. (c) If you will play then it will not rain.

20. (c) ((X.Y)′ . (X+Y))′

21. (i) (b) 2256

Explanation: Address calculation in Row major order

$$A_{ij} = \text{Base} + \text{Width}(n_c(I - L_r) + (J - L_c))$$
$$\text{So,} \quad 1400 + 8(10 \times (10 - 0) + (7 - 0)) = 1400 + 856$$
$$= 2256$$

(ii) (d) The array name in actual and formal parameters can be same or different.

22. (i) (b) Initialises an object

    (ii) (b) public

        Explanation : If constructor is private , objects of the class cannot be created.

23. (i) (c) Constructor function

        Explanation: Constructor function has name same as class.

    (ii) (b) parameterized

        Explanation: The function is taking parameters as input, so it is parameterized constructor.

24. (i) (c) default

        Explanation: The default access specifier is package/default.

    (ii) (a) Own class

        Explanation: The function getEmployee() is a private function and private functions are accessible only in own class.

    (iii) (c) 0

        Explanation : The return type of the function is void.

25. (i) (d) 12

        Explanation: The code print p, q separately and the for loop goes from 0 to 9 that is 10 times, so a total of 12 times.

    (ii) (c) Displaying the Fibonacci series.

        Explanation: The code prints p(0), q(1) and then in a loop prints p + q and swapping p to q and q to s, thereby printing 0 1 1 2 3 5 8 13….. which is the fibonacci series.

26. (i) (c) They are inherited

    (ii) (d) They are created by the keyword interface

27. (i) (d) i,s1,s2

    (ii) (c) i

28. (i) (c) Impure function

    (ii) (a) Static data members

29. (i) (d) Any number

    (ii) (c) 1

30. (i) (b) 720

        Explanation: The function callitself is a recursive function that returns its parameter and calls itself again and again until it receives parameter as 1. So when called with 6 it returns $6 \times 5 \times 4 \times 3 \times 2 \times 1 = 720$

    (ii) (c) Recursive

31. (i) (a) nextLine()

    (ii) (c) length()

    (iii) (d) msg

    (iv) (a) || ch=='u'

    (v) (c) count++

        Explanation: The code extracts each character from the string and checks whether it is a lowercase vowel or not and then increases the count.

32. (i) (c) rev==temp

    (ii) (a) n%i==0

    (iii) (b) count++

    (iv) (c) count= =2

    (v) (a) System.out.println("Palprime");

Sample Paper

Computer Science

Questions

1. $A + BC = (A + B)(A + C)$ is stated by the law:
   - (a) Absorption
   - (b) Distributive
   - (c) De Morgan's
   - (d) None

2. Which of the following are derived gates?
   - (a) NAND
   - (b) NOR
   - (c) XOR
   - (d) All of these

3. Given the function $F(A, B, C) = \pi(0, 1, 2, 5, 7, 11)$ what is the error in the statement?
   - (a) It cannot have maxterms
   - (b) It cannot have a value 5
   - (c) 3 Variable function cannot have the maxterm 11
   - (d) None

4. What is the shorthand form representation of $(X' + Y' + Z')$?
   - (a) M_7
   - (b) M_8
   - (c) m_8
   - (d) m_7

5. How many NAND gates are required to make a NOT gate?
   - (a) 1
   - (b) 2
   - (c) 3
   - (d) 4

6. $(A + B)(A' + B')$ reduces to
   - (a) $A'B' + AB'$
   - (b) $(A + B') + A'B$
   - (c) $AB' + A'B$
   - (d) $AB' + A' + B$

7. If $A = 1, B = 0, C = 1, D = 0$, what is the value of $F(A, B, C) = AB'C + (B + C)' + BC'$?
   - (a) 1
   - (b) 0
   - (c) A
   - (d) B

8. The dual of $P.Q' + (P + Q')' + R'Q$ is :
   - (a) $(P + Q) . (P.Q) + R + Q$
   - (b) $(P.Q') . (P.Q')' + R + Q$
   - (c) $(P + Q) . (P.Q)' + R' + Q$
   - (d) $(P + Q') . (P.Q')' . (R' + Q)$

9. The output of the circuit given below is:

   - (a) $A'BC$
   - (b) $A'B$
   - (c) $(A' + B)C$
   - (d) $A'(B + C)$

10. Simplification of the expression $F = (AB)' + (A + B)'$ is:
    - (a) $(AB)'$
    - (b) $(A + B)$
    - (c) $(A + B)'$
    - (d) None

11. Simplification of the K-Map given by $F(A, B, C, D) = \Sigma(3, 7, 11, 15)$ gives :
    - (a) AB'
    - (b) $A + C'D'$
    - (c) CD
    - (d) $A' + C'$

12. The below truth table represents :

X	Y	Output
1	1	1
1	0	0
0	1	0
0	0	1

   (a) NOR   (b) XNOR   (c) XOR   (d) NAND

13. (i) The statement A ⊕ B represents which relation between A and B?

   (a) NOT   (b) NAND   (c) NOR   (d) XOR

   (ii) Which operator gives the reverse of the operation shown in (i)?

   (a) NAND   (b) XNOR   (c) AND   (d) NOT

14. The simplification of the expression $F(a, b, c)\ (a' + a).b.c + abc' + a.b.(c + c')$ gives :

   (a) $(a + b')$ (b) $a'.b'$ (c) b   (d) None

15. How many NOR gates will be required to make an AND gate?

   (a) 3   (b) 2

   (c) 1   (d) AND cannot be made by NOR

16. Which among the following is not an applications of Multiplexer?

   (a) Data transmission   (b) Routing of signals

   (c) Telephone exchange   (d) Encoding of signals

17. The operator that creates a new object and allocates memory for it is:

   (a) delete   (b) create   (c) new   (d) newobject

18. Radha wants a data member of her class "Toys" to be available in all child classes, the access specifier she should use is __________ .

   (a) private   (b) protected   (c) extends   (d) inherits

19. The keyword that represents the current object is:

   (a) now   (b) this   (c) current   (d) None

20. Reducing the expression $F(A,B,C,D) = \pi(0,1,2,4,5,6,8,10)$ using Karnaugh map gives:

   (a) $(A' + C')(A + D)(B + D)$ (b) $(A' + C)(A' + D')(B + D)$

   (c) $(A + C)(A + D)(B + D)$ (d) $(A + C')(A' + D')(B' + D')$

21. (i) What is the output at position x?

   (a) $B + D$ (b) BD' (c) $B.D$ (d) None

   (ii) Which gate is required at position G to get the output as shown in the diagram?

   (a) XOR   (b) XNOR   (c) NOR   (d) None

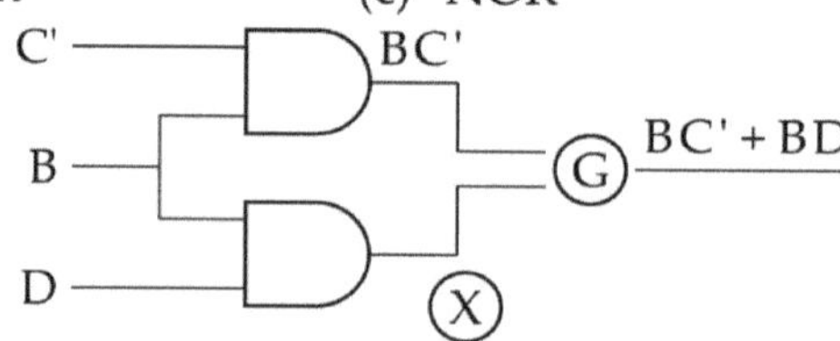

22. The reduction of the expression $F(U, V, W, Z) = \pi(0, 1, 3, 5, 6, 7, 10, 14, 15)$ using Karnaugh map :

   (i) How many quads will be formed?

   (a) 1   (b) 2   (c) 3   (d) 4

   (ii)

   (a) $(U' + Z').\ (V + W).\ (U + V + W).\ (U' + W' + Z)$

   (b) $(U + Z').\ (V' + W).\ (U' + V' + W').\ (U' + W' + Z)$

   (c) $(U + Z').\ (V' + W').\ (U' + V + W).\ (U + W + Z')$

   (d) $(U + Z').\ (V' + W').\ (U + V + W).\ (U' + W' + Z)$

23. Answer the questions while solving the reduction problem using Karnaugh map

$$F(A, B, C, D) = \Sigma(0, 1, 4, 8, 10, 12, 14)$$

   (i) What will be the reduced expression?

     (a) A′B′ + B′C + A′C′D′   (b) A′B′ + B′C′ + ACD

     (c) A′B′ + BC + A′C′D′   (d) AB + B′C′ + A′C′D′

  (ii) How many pairs will be formed?

     (a) 2   (b) 1   (c) 3   (d) None

24. (i) The keyword to inherit a class from another class is:

     (a) extend   (b) interface   (c) extends   (d) import

  (ii) Java does not support .... kind of inheritance

     (a) Single   (b) Multilevel   (c) Multiple   (d) Hierarchical

 (iii) If multiple functions with same name, signature exist in both base and child class:

     (a) Base class function gets higher priority   (b) Child class function gets higher priority

     (c) Error occurs   (d) None

25. (i) A boolean function $F(A, B, C) = A′BC + ABC′ + A′B′C′$ is given, what will be the shorthand form of it?

     (a) $m_3 + m_6 + m_0$ (b) $m_2 + m_6 + m_0$ (c) $m_3 + m_7 + m_0$ (d) $m_3 + m_8 + m_1$

  (ii) What kind of expression is it?

     (a) Canonical SOP   (b) Canonical POS   (c) Canonical PSP   (d) None

26. (i) Which package needs to be imported to use the substring() function?

     (a) Math   (b) Swing   (c) Util   (d) No import required

  (ii) The keyword that creates a package is:

     (a) pack   (b) bundle   (c) package   (d) None of these

27. (i) Given

```
str = "computerscience";
System.out.println(str.substring(0, 6) + str.length()); returns :
```

     (a) comput14   (b) compute15   (c) comput15   (d) None

  (ii) System.out.println(str.indexOf('u') + str.lastIndexOf('e') + str.length(); returns :

     (a) 29   (b) 11   (c) 22   (d) 33

28. Given the code below :

```
class Calc {
    int p, q;
    static int a = 0;
    static int product(int x, int y) {
        return x * y;
    }
    public static void main(String[] args) {
        Calc obj = new Calc();
        int ans = Calc. product(5, 3);
        System. out. println(ans);
    }
}
```

   (i) Which are the class variables?

     (a) p, q   (b) a   (c) x, y   (d) None

  (ii) A statement that calls the static method is :

     (a) obj. product(5, 3);   (b) product(5, 3);

     (c) Calc. product(5, 3);   (d) obj. product(5);

29. In the given code, find errors :

```
Class errorclass //L1
{
      int p, q; //L2
      static void show() //L3
      {
          p = q = 10; //L4
      }
      //L5
```

  (i) The lines that have error are :

    (a) L5, L4, L1   (b) L5   (c) L4   (d) L1, L2

 (ii) What are the errors in Line L1 and L4?

    (a) L1: Class → class, L4 : Invalid access of non static member by a static method.

    (b) No errors

    (c) L1: class → class, L4 → No error

    (d) L4 → p = q = 0;

30. public void main()

```
{
      int myarr[] = {10, 20, 30, 40, 50};
      int i;
      for (i = 0;i<myarr.length;i = i + 2)
      if (myarr[i]>20)
      myarr[i] = myarr[i] + 10;
      else
      myarr[i] = myarr[i] %2;
      for(i = 0;i<myarr.length;i + + )
      System.out.print(myarr[i] + " ");
}
```

  (i) How many times will the first for loop execute?

    (a) 2 times   (b) 5 times   (c) 3 times   (d) 4 times

 (ii) What will be the output of the code?

    (a) 20, 30, 0, 0, 0   (b) 0, 0, 40, 50, 60   (c) 20, 30, 40, 50, 60   (d) None of these

31. Fill in the blanks w.r.t the code for checking of whether a number is special number or not. (Special number : A number whose sum of factorials of the digits is equal to the number Ex : 145 = 1! + 4! + 5! = 1 + 24 + 120 = 145)

```
import java.util.Scanner;
public void main()
{
      int num, fact = 1, d, sum = 0, i;
      Scanner sc = new Scanner(System.in);
      num = sc.nextInt();
      t = num;
      while(___(i)___>0)
      {
          d = num%10;
          i = 1;
          fact = ___(ii)___;
          while(i + + < = d)
          fact = fact*___(iii)___;
```

```
        sum = sum + ___(iv)___ ;
        num = num/10;
    }
    if (___(v)___ = = t)
    System.out.println("Special number ");
    else
    System.out.println("Not a Special number ");
}
```

(i)   The statement at (i) will be
    (a) d   (b) *   (c) num   (d) None

(ii) The statement at (ii) will be
    (a) 2   (b) 1   (c) 3   (d) 0

(iii) The statement at (iii) will be
    (a) i   (b) j   (c) 2   (d) None

(iv) The statement at (iv) will be
    (a) sum   (b) d   (c) fact   (d) i

(v)   The statement at (v) will be
    (a) sc   (b) sum   (c) num   (d) d

32. Fill in the blanks w.r.t the code for checking of whether a number is Neon number or not (A neon number is one whose sum of digits of the square is equal to the number. Ex : $9^2 = 81 = 8 + 1 = 9$)

```
import java.util. ___?1?___ ;
public void main()
{
    int num, sq = 0, d, sum = 0;
    Scanner sc = new Scanner(System.in);
    ___?2?___ = sc.nextInt();
    sq = num*num;
    while(___?3?___ >0)
    {
        d = sq ___?4?___ ;
        sum = sum + d;
        sq = sq/10;
    }
    if (___?5?___ = = num)
    System.out.println("Neon number ");
    else
    System.out.println("Not a Neon number ");
}
```

(i)   The statement at ?1? will be
    (a) Scanner   (b) *   (c) awt   (d) Both (a) and (b)

(ii) The statement at ?2? will be
    (a) sum   (b) num   (c) sq   (d) d

(iii) The statement at ?3? will be
    (a) sq   (b) sum   (c) d   (d) None

(iv) The statement at ?4? will be
    (a) //10   (b) /100   (c) %10   (d) *10

(v)   The statement at ?5? will be
    (a) num   (b) d   (c) sq   (d) sum

Answers

1. (b) Distributive

2. (d) All of these

3. (c) 3 Variable function cannot have the maxterm 11

   Explanation: Maximum value for 3 Variable map is 7.

4. (a) M_7

   Explanation: $(X' + Y' + Z')$ means $(111) = M_7$

5. (a) 1

6. (c) $AB' + A'B$

   Explanation:
   $$(A + B)(A' + B') = AA' + AB' + A'B + BB'$$
   $$= 0 + AB' + A'B + 0 \qquad \text{(Since } AA' = 0)$$
   $$= AB' + A'B$$

7. (a) 1

   Explanation: $AB'C + (B + C)' + BC' = 1.0'.1 + (0 + 1)' + 0.1'$
   $$= 1 + 0 + 0 = 1$$

8. (d) $(P + Q') . (P.Q')' . (R' + Q)$

   Explanation : Dual is formed by changing all . to +, + to ., 1 to 0, 0 to 1

9. (a) $A'BC$

10. (a) $(AB)'$

    Explanation:
    $$(AB)' + (A + B)' = A' + B' + A'.B' \text{ (De Morgan's law)}$$
    $$= A'(1 + B') + B'$$
    $$= A' + B'$$
    $$= (AB)'$$

11. (c) CD

    Explanation :

		C'D' 00	C'D 01	CD 11	CD' 10
A'B'	00	0	0	1	0
A'B	01	0	0	1	0
AB	11	0	0	1	0
AB'	10	0	0	1	0

    Quad(3, 7, 11, 15) = CD

12. (b) XNOR

    Explanation : The output of XNOR is High if the number of high inputs are even.

13. (i) (d) XOR

    (ii) (b) XNOR

14. (c) b

    Explanation :
    $$(a' + a).b.c + abc' + a.b.(c + c') = 1.b.c + abc' + a.b$$
    $$= bc + bc' + ab$$
    $$= b(c + c') + ab$$
    $$= b + ab$$
    $$= b(a + 1) = b$$

15. (a) 3

16. (d) Encoding of signals

17. (c) new

18. (b) protected

19. (b) this

20. (c) $(A + C)(A + D)(B + D)$

Explanation:

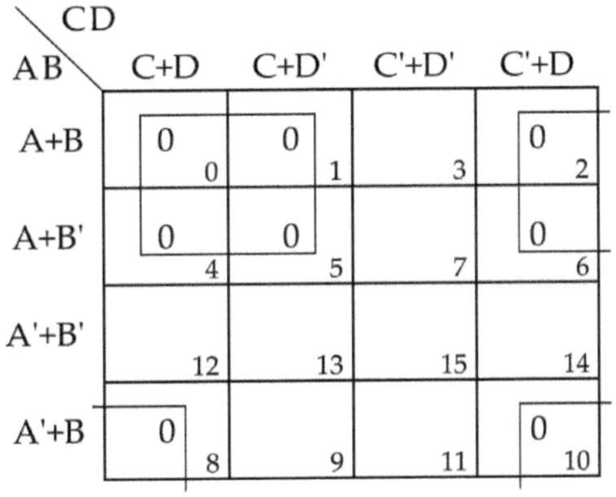

CD \ AB	C+D	C+D'	C'+D'	C'+D
A+B	0 (0)	0 (1)	(3)	0 (2)
A+B'	0 (4)	0 (5)	(7)	0 (6)
A'+B'	(12)	(13)	(15)	(14)
A'+B	0 (8)	(9)	(11)	0 (10)

Quad1(0,1,4,5) gives A+C
Quad2(0,1,2,6) gives A+D
Quad3(0,2,8,10) gives (B+D)
Hence reduced expression:

$$(A + C)(A + D)(B + D)$$

21. (i) (c) B.D

Explanation : B and D are connected to an AND gate, hence B.D

(ii) (d) None

Explanation : We have BC' + BD, + means an OR, so an OR gate is required.

22. (i) (b) 2

(ii) (d) $(U + Z'). (V' + W'). (U + V + W). (U' + W' + Z)$

Explanation :

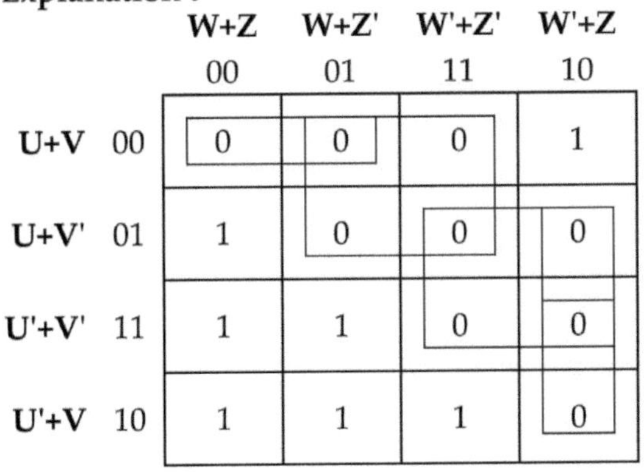

	W+Z (00)	W+Z' (01)	W'+Z' (11)	W'+Z (10)
U+V 00	0	0	0	1
U+V' 01	1	0	0	0
U'+V' 11	1	1	0	0
U'+V 10	1	1	1	0

Quad1 (1, 3, 5, 7) = $(U + Z')$
Quad2 (6, 7, 14, 15) = $(V' + W')$
Pair1(0, 1) = $(U + V + W)$
Pair2(10, 14) = $(U' + W' + Z)$
Reduced expression : $(U + Z'). (V' + W'). (U + V + W). (U' + W' + Z)$

23. (i) (a) $A'B' + B'C + A'C'D'$

 (ii) (b) 1

 Explanation :

		A'B' 00	A'B 01	A B 11	A B' 10
C'D'	00	1	1	0	0
C'D	01	1	0	0	0
CD	11	1	0	0	1
CD'	10	1	0	0	1

Quad1(0, 4, 8, 12) = A'B'

Quad2(8, 10, 12, 14) = B'C

Pair1(0, 1) = A'C'D'

24. (i) (c) extends

 (ii) (c) Multiple

 (iii) (b) Child class function gets higher priority

 Explanation : According to the principle of Function overriding.

25. (i) (a) $m_3 + m_6 + m_0$

 Explanation :

$$A'BC + ABC' + A'B'C' = 011 + 110 + 000$$
$$= m_3 + m_6 + m_0$$

 (ii) (a) Canonical SOP

 Explanation : All the terms are minterms and expressed in Sum form.

26. (i) (d) No import required

 (ii) (c) package

27. (i) (c) comput15

 Explanation : substring() function extracts a part of a string from start index to end index-1, length() function returns the number of characters in a string.

 (ii) (d) 33

 Explanation : The indexOf() function returns the index of first occurrence of a character, whereas lastIndexOf() returns the index of the last occurrence of a character, length() returns the length of a string.

28. (i) (b) a

 (ii) (c) Calc. product(5, 3);

 Explanation : Static methods are called using class name and not object names.

29. (i) (a) L5, L4, L1

 (ii) (a) L1: Class $\rightarrow$ class, L4 : Invalid access of non static member by a static method.

 Explanation : L1: Class $\rightarrow$ class, L4 : Invalid access of non static member by a static method, L5 : class should end with a }

30. (i) (c) 3 times

 Explanation : The array has 5 elements and the loop is progressing by 2, so 3 times.

(ii) (b) 0, 0, 40, 50, 60

> **Explanation :** 1st 2 elements are < 20 hence the modulus 2 is stored in those places, last 3 are > 20, so they are incremented by 10.

31. (i) (c) num

   (ii) (b) 1

   (iii) (a) i

   (iv) (c) fact

   (v) (b) sum

> **Explanation :** The code inputs the number and in the outer loop extracts each digit. The inner loop finds the factorial of each digit and sums up. Finally the sum is matched with the original number whose copy is in t.

32. (i) (d) Both (a) and (b)

   (ii) (b) num

   (iii) (a) sq

   (iv) (c) %10

   (v) (d) sum

> **Explanation :** The code inputs the number and stores the square in sq, then extracts each digit of the square and sums them. Finally it compares the sum with the original number.

❑❑

Sample Paper

Computer Science

Questions

1. Sarita wants a data member of her class "Travel" to be available in all child classes, the access specifier she should use is __________ .
   - (a) private
   - (b) protected
   - (c) extends
   - (d) inherits

2. What can be the return types of a constructor?
   - (a) int
   - (b) float
   - (c) No return type
   - (d) boolean

3. Given the function $F(P, Q, R) = \pi(1, 3, 5, 7)$, what are the minterms?
   - (a) (0, 2, 4, 6)
   - (b) (1, 2, 3, 4)
   - (c) (1, 3, 4, 6)
   - (d) None of these

4. Reducing the expression $F(A, B, C, D) = \pi(0, 1, 2, 4, 5, 6, 8, 10)$ gives :
   - (a) $(A' + C')(A + D)(B + D)$
   - (b) $(A + C)(A' + D')(B + D)$
   - (c) $(A + C)(A + D)(B + D)$
   - (d) $(A + C)(A' + D)(B' + D)$

5. The complement of $(A + B).(B + C).(A + C)$ is:
   - (a) $(A + B') + B.C + A'.C'$
   - (b) $A'.B' + B'.C' + A'.C'$
   - (c) $A.B + B.C + A.C$
   - (d) $(A' + B') + B'.C' + A'.C'B$

6. The output of the expression $X + X'$ will be always:
   - (a) Low
   - (b) High
   - (c) 1
   - (d) Both (b) and (c)

7. An expression $F(P, Q, R)$ gives output High if only the number of high inputs are even. How many minterms will it have?
   - (a) 1
   - (b) 2
   - (c) 3
   - (d) 4

8. Converting the $F(M, N) = (M + N).M'$ expression into canonical POS form gives :
   - (a) $(M + N).(M' + N).(M' + N')$
   - (b) $(M + N).(M' + N)$
   - (c) $(M + N).(M'.N).(M + N)$
   - (d) $(M' + N').(M + N').(M + N)$

9. If the output of a Boolean expression is always False then it is called :
   - (a) Contingency
   - (b) Involution
   - (c) Proposition
   - (d) Fallacy

10. How many constructor functions can a class have?
    - (a) 1
    - (b) 2
    - (c) 3
    - (d) Multiple

11. A half adder has .... number of inputs.
    - (a) 2
    - (b) 3
    - (c) 4
    - (d) None

12. The expression $F(A, B, C) = ABC + A'BC + AB'C$ in shorthand form is :
    - (a) $m_2 + m_3 + m_5$
    - (b) $m_7 + m_1 + m_5$
    - (c) $m_7 + m_3 + m_9$
    - (d) $m_7 + m_3 + m_5$

13. (i) If $P = 1, Q = 0, R = 0$ and $S = 1$ then the maxterm in short form is :
    - (a) M_1
    - (b) M_9
    - (c) M_2
    - (d) M_4

    (ii) If in function $F(P,Q,R,S)$, $P = 0, Q = 1, R = 1, S = 0$ then the minterm will be :
    - (a) m_6
    - (b) m_7
    - (c) m_8
    - (d) m_9

14. Which statement about a constructor is False :

(a) It initializes data members

(b) It can be static

(c) It has name same as class

(d) It is automatically called

15. The expression $F(A, B, C, D) = (x + a)^n = \Sigma(1, 3, 5, 7, 9, 11, 13, 15)$ reduces to :

(a) A   (b) B   (c) D   (d) C

16. The below truth table represents :

X	Y	Output
1	1	0
1	0	1
0	1	1
0	0	0

(a) NOR   (b) XNOR   (c) XOR   (d) NAND

17. Which of the following is not an access specifier in java?

(a) private

(b) default

(c) package

(d) All are access specifiers

18. The default value of a static integer variable of a class is :

(a) 1   (b) 0   (c) NULL   (d) 10

19. Which one of the following is not true?

(a) A class containing abstract methods is called an abstract class.

(b) Abstract methods should be implemented in the derived class.

(c) An abstract class cannot have non-abstract methods.

(d) A class must be qualified as 'abstract' class, if it contains one abstract method.

20. The keyword that creates a constant in java is :

(a) now   (b) new   (c) final   (d) constant

21. With respect to java library packages :

(i) Which package is imported by default in java?

    (a) lang   (b) io   (c) util   (d) net

(ii) Which package needs to be imported for the getDate() function usage?

    (a) util   (b) Scanner   (c) IOException   (d) net

22. With respect to Exceptions in java :

(i) The block that executes irrespective of whether exception occurs or not?

    (a) try   (b) catch   (c) finally   (d) None of these

(ii) The exception that occurs if, we try to access an array more than its size is :

    (a) FileNotFoundException

    (b) IoException

    (c) ArrayOutofBoundsException

    (d) None of these

23. On reduction of the expression $F(U, V, W, Z) = \pi(1, 3, 5, 6, 7, 14, 15)$ using Karnaugh map :

(i) How many quads will be formed?

    (a) 1   (b) 2   (c) 3   (d) 4

(ii) What will be the reduced expression?

    (a) $(U + Z).(V + W')$

    (b) $(U + Z').U$

    (c) $(U + Z').(V' + W').(U' + V + W)$

    (d) $(U + Z').(V' + W')$

24. (i) The java run time system automatically calls this method while garbage collection:

    (a) finalizer()   (b) finalize()   (c) finally()   (d) finalized()

(ii) An overloaded method consists of:
   (a) The same method name with different types of parameters
   (b) The same method name with different number of parameters
   (c) The same method name and same number and type of parameters with different return type
   (d) Both (a) and (b) above

(iii) The block in java that handles the exception in a code is:
   (a) try   (b) catch   (c) finally   (d) final

25. (i) All exception types are subclasses of the built-in class:
   (a) Exception   (b) RuntimeException   (c) Error   (d) Throwable

(ii) When an overridden method is called from within a subclass, it will always refers to the version of that method defined by the
   (a) Super class   (b) Subclass
   (c) Compiler will choose randomly   (d) Interpreter will choose randomly

26. Given the code :

```
public void main()
{
    String str = "The agra fort is a heritage building";
    int count = 0;
    for(int i = 0;i<str. _________ ; i + + )
    {
        if (str.charAt(i) = = 'a')
        count = count + 2;
    }
    System.out.println(count + "");
}
```

(i) What will be the content of the blank, if the loop is supposed to iterate through every character of the string?
   (a) len   (b) length()   (c) data()   (d) None

(ii) What will be the output of the code?
   (a) 6   (b) 7   (c) 8   (d) 10

27. Answer the questions with respect to the code given below:

```
public void stringshow()
{
    String mystr = "We went to Varanasi last year";
    int i;
    String word = "";
    for(int i = 0;i<mystr.length(); i + + )
    {
        if (str.charAt(i)! = ' ')
        word = word + str.charAt(i)
        else
        if(word.length()>5)
        {   System.out.print(word + " ");
            word = ""; }
    }
}
```

(i) How many times the loop will execute?
   (a) 27   (b) 29   (c) 30   (d) 31

(ii) What will be the output of the code?

    (a) went to   (b) last year   (c) Varanasi   (d) None of these

28. An array T[30][20] is stored in memory in column major order. Each element occupies 4 bytes and the base address is 3000.

  (i) How many bytes will the array occupy?

    (a) 1200 Bytes   (b) 800 Bytes   (c) 1000 Bytes   (d) 2400 Bytes

 (ii) What will be the address of T[10][10]?

    (a) 4240   (b) 2240   (c) 3240   (d) None

29. Given the code below :

```
class newclass
{
    int x = 0;
    private void calculate()
    {}
    public void newclass(int p) //Line1
    {
        _________ ) //Line2
    }
}
```

  (i) What replacement is to be done to make the function calculate() accessible to all classes of the same package and own class only?

    (a) Instead of private → public   (b) Instead of private → default

    (c) Instead of private → protected   (d) None

 (ii) What is the error in Line1. What should be the contents of the blank in Line2 to initialize the data member?

    (a) void should not be there in declaration, x = p;

    (b) No error, p = x;

    (c) int should be there in declaration instead of void, x = p;

    (d) String should be there in declaration instead of void, x = 0;

30. Given the code, find errors :

```
class int //Line1
{
    public void incorrect()//Line2
    {
        int p = 10, s = 20, n; //Line3
        n = sc.nextLine(); //Line4
        While(n! = 0) : //Line5
        {
            if (n = = 0) //Line6
            s = 20; //Line7
        }
    }
}
```

  (i) The error in Line1 is

    (a) class name cannot be int   (b) class should be class

    (c) ; is missing   (d) No error

 (ii) The lines that have error is/are :

    (a) Line1, Line4   (b) Line1, Line3   (c) Line1, Line4, Line5   (d) No Error

31. Fill in the blanks w.r.t the code for checking of whether the sum of digits of a number is a prime number or not.

```java
import java.util.Scanner;
public void main()
{
    int num, d, sum = 0, i, count = 0;
    Scanner sc = new Scanner(System.in);
    num = sc.nextInt();
    while(   ?1?   >0)
    {
        d = num%10;
        sum =    ?2?
        num = num/10;
    }
    for (i = 1;i< =    ?3?   ;i + + )
    if (sum%i = = 0)
    count = count +    ?4?   ;
    if (   ?5?   = = 2)
    System.out.println("Sum of digits is prime ");
    else
    System.out.println("Sum of digits is not prime ");
}
```

(i) What is the statement or expression at ?1?

    (a) d   (b) i   (c) num   (d) None

(ii) What is the statement or expression at ?2?

    (a) sum + i   (b) d   (c) sum + d   (d) sum + num

(iii) What is the statement or expression at ?3?

    (a) i   (b) sum   (c) 5   (d) None

(iv) What is the statement or expression at ?4?

    (a) 1   (b) 2   (c) i   (d) 3

(v) What is the statement or expression at ?5?

    (a) i   (b) sum   (c) num   (d) count

32. Given the following class University, fill in the blanks to complete the code .

class name :   University

Data members:

Studroll   integer

Studname   String

Sem1marks   float

Sem2marks   float

Total float

Perc float

Member functions:

getUniversity() – To input student roll, name and marks in 2 semesters and calculate total, percentage (Formula : Perc = (Sem1 + Sem2)/2) showUniversity() – To display student name, total and percentage.

```
class University
{
    int studroll;
    __?1?__ studname ;
    float sem1marks;
    float sem2marks;
    float perc, total;
    public void __?2?__
    {
        __?3?__ sc = new Scanner(System.in);
        studroll = sc.nextInt();
        studname = sc.nextLine();
        sem1marks = sc.nextFloat();
        sem2marks = sc.nextFloat();
        total = (sem1marks + sem2marks);
        perc = __?4?__ ;
    }
    public void __?5?__
    {
        System.out.println("Name :", studname)
        System.out.println("Total :", total);
        System.out.println("Percentage:", perc);
    }
}
```

(i)   The statement or expression at ?1? is:

    (a) int   (b) float   (c) boolean   (d) String

(ii) The statement or expression at ?2? is:

    (a) showUniversity() (b) University()   (c) Studroll   (d) getUniversity()

(iii) The statement or expression at ?3? is:

    (a) int   (b) float   (c) Scanner   (d) util

(iv) The statement or expression at ?4? is:

    (a) (sem1marks + sem2marks)/2   (b) (sem1marks + sem2marks)

    (c) (sem1marks + sem2marks) %2   (d) None

(v)   The statement or expression at ?5? is:

    (a) showUniversity( )   (b) display()

    (c) System.out.println()   (d) getUniversity()

Answers

1. (b) protected
2. (c) No return type

    Explanation : Constructor does not return anything, not even void.
3. (a) (0, 2, 4, 6)

4. (c) $(A + C)(A + D)(B + D)$

Explanation :

	C+D	C+D'	C'+D'	C'+D
A+B	0 (0)	0 (1)	(3)	0 (2)
A+B'	0 (4)	0 (5)	(7)	0 (6)
A'+B'	(12)	(13)	(15)	(14)
A'+B	0 (8)	(9)	(11)	0 (10)

$$\text{Quad1}(0, 1, 4, 5) = (A + C)$$
$$\text{Quad2}(0, 4, 2, 6) = (A + D)$$
$$\text{Quad3}(0, 2, 8, 10) = (B + D)$$

Hence simplified expression: $(A + C)(A + D)(B + D)$

5. (b) $A'.B' + B'.C' + A'.C'$

Explanation : Complement of $(A + B).(B + C).(A + C)$
$$= [(A + B).(B + C).(A + C)]'$$
$$= (A + B)' + [(B + C).(A + C)]'$$
$$= (A + B)' + (B + C)' + (A + C)'$$
$$= A'.B' + B'.C' + A'.C'$$

6. (d) Both (b) and (c)

Explanation : $X + X'$ is always 1 + so output will be always High or 1.

7. (d) 4

Explanation :

P	Q	R	Output
1	1	1	0
1	1	0	1
1	0	1	1
1	0	0	0
0	1	1	1
0	1	0	0
0	0	1	0
0	0	0	1

8. (a) $(M + N).(M' + N).(M' + N')$

Explanation :
$$(M + N).M' = (M + N).(M' + NN')$$
$$= (M + N).(M' + N).(M' + N')$$

9. (d) Fallacy

10. (d) Multiple

11. (a) 2

Explanation : A half adder is a combinational circuit with 2 inputs and 2 outputs.

12. (d) $m_7 + m_3 + m_5$

Explanation :
$$ABC + A'BC + AB'C = 111 + 011 + 101 = m_7 + m_3 + m_5$$

13. (i) (b) M_9

(ii) (a) m_6

Explanation : 0110 converted to decimal gives 6, hence m_6

14. (b) It can be static

15. (c) D

Explanation :

		C'D' 00	C'D 01	CD 11	CD' 10
A'B'	00	0	1	1	0
A'B	01	0	1	1	0
AB	11	0	1	1	0
AB'	10	0	1	1	0

Octet (1, 3, 5, 7, 9, 11, 13, 15) = D

16. (c) XOR

Explanation : The output of XOR is High if the number of high inputs are odd.

17. (d) All are access specifiers

18. (b) 0

19. (c) An abstract class cannot have non-abstract methods.

20. (c) final

21. (i) (a) lang

    (ii) (a) util

22. (i) (c) finally

    (ii) (c) ArrayOutofBoundsException

23. (i) (b) 2

    (ii) (d) $(U + Z')$. $(V' + W')$

Explanation :

		W+Z 00	W+Z' 01	W'+Z' 11	W'+Z 10
U+V	00	1	0	0	1
U+V'	01	1	0	0	0
U'+V'	11	1	1	0	0
U'+V	10	1	1	1	1

Quad1 (1, 3, 5, 7) = $(U + Z')$

Quad2 (6, 7, 14, 15) = $(V' + W')$

Reduced expression : $(U + Z').(V' + W')$

24. (i) (b) finalize()

    (ii) (d) Both (a) and (b) above

    (iii) (b) catch

25. (i) (d) Throwable

    (ii) (b) Subclass

26. (i) (b) length()

Explanation : To extract each character the loop should go up to the last character of the string, so length() function is used to traverse the entire length.

(ii) (c) 8

Explanation : The loop extracts each character and increases count by 2 if the character is 'a'. Since there are 4 a's the count will be 2.

27. (i) (b) 29

Explanation : Since the loop is extracting each character it will execute for the entire length of the string, which is 29.

(ii) (c) Varanasi

Explanation : The loop extracts each character and forms words. Then checks if the length of the word is more than 5, prints it. Since there is only one such word, the output is "Varanasi".

28. (i) (d) 2400 Bytes

Explanation :

Total number of elements = 30 × 20

= 600, each element occupies 4 bytes, 600 × 4

= 2400 Bytes

(ii) (a) 4240

Explanation : Address calculation in column major order

$$A_{ij} = \text{Base} + \text{Width}(n_r(J - L_c) + (I - L_r))$$

So, $3000 + 4(30 \times (10 - 0) + (10\text{-}0)) = 3000 + 1240$

$= 4240$

29. (i) (b) Instead of private → default

Explanation : Since default or package access specifier makes the members accessible to all classes of the same package.

(ii) (a) void should not be there in declaration, x = p;

Explanation : Constructor has no return type, the parameterized constructor initializes data members with its parameters, so x = p.

30. (i) (a) Class name cannot be int.

(ii) (c) Line1, Line4, Line5

Explanation : Line1: int cannot be class name, Line4 : sc – Scanner object not defined, Line 5 : While should be while, the loop statement should not end with a.

31. (i) (c) num

(ii) (c) sum + d

(iii) (b) sum

(iv) (a) 1

(v) (d) count

Explanation : The code inputs the number and extracts each of the digits and sums them. Now it checks whether the sum is a prime number by finding the count of its factors.

32. (i) (d) String

(ii) (d) getUniversity()

(iii) (c) Scanner

(iv) (a) (sem1marks + sem2marks)/2

(v) (a) showUniversity( )

❑❑

Physical Education

Specimen Question Paper

Physical Education

Maximum Marks: 70
Time allowed: One and a half hours

Question 1 [1]

Physical development for the Romans was:
(a) Military motive
(b) All round development
(c) Recreational motive
(d) None of these

Question 2 [1]

In which country developed the concept of all round development?
(a) Rome
(b) Germany
(c) Denmark
(d) Greece

Question 3 [1]

Per Henrick Ling had established The Royal Institute of Gymnastics, where students were trained in three different phases. Which of following is not one of the phases?
(a) Medical Gymnastics
(b) Educational Gymnastics
(c) Military Gymnastics
(d) Professional Gymnastics

Question 4 [1]

Which God was honoured by the Greeks in their famous Olympian festival?
(a) Poseidon
(b) Zeus
(c) Aphrodite
(d) Apollo

Question 5 [1]

In which year did India host the biggest games festival : The Asian Games?
(a) 1948
(b) 1950
(c) 1951
(d) 1954

Question 6 [1]

During which period were Arrow shooting, Chariot racing and Hunting prevalent in India?
(a) Vedic Period
(b) Medieval Period
(c) Ancient Period
(d) Indus Valley Civilisation

Question 7 [1]

Physical education develops qualities like- Patience, ____________, Sympathy and Tolerance.
(a) Rebellious
(b) Co-operation
(c) Jealousy
(d) Ruthlessness

Question 8 [1]

Games spd sports are a means of:
(a) National and International integration
(b) Increasing the divide
(c) Starting street fights
(d) Initiating political protests

Question 9 [1]

Which of the following traits reflects personality development?

(a) Helpfulness (b) Team spirit (c) Both (a) and (b) (d) None of them

Question 10 [1]

Sports _______ people of all castes, creed and religion.

(a) Unite (b) Differentiates (c) Divide (d) Distance

Question 11 [1]

Games and Sports develop individuals by:

(a) Increasing Physical activity levels (b) Promoting healthy attitude and behaviour
(c) Both (a) and (b) (d) None of them

Question 12 [1]

Sports in the present time aim at:

(a) Living a fuller life (b) Earning a livelihood
(c) All round development of human beings (d) Just as a pass time activity

Question 13 [1]

Which method is used to draw the fixture of a single league tournament?

(a) Cyclic method (b) Tabular method (c) Staircase method (d) All of these

Question 14 [1]

Who developed Interval training Method?

(a) Woldemar Gerschler and Dr. Hans Reindell (b) Dr. Harre and Dr. Martin
(c) Gosta Holmer (d) Dr. V. Aaken

Question 15 [1]

When and where was Netaji Subhash National Institute of Sports founded?

(a) Banglore 1962 (b) Kolkata 1961
(c) Thiruvananthapuram 1962 (d) Patiala 1961

Question 16 [1]

_____________ tournament is set up to provide an opportunity for a second chance in a tournament for those participants who lose their first match.

(a) Single league (b) Double league
(c) Double counter league (d) Single counter league

Question 17 [1]

Who founded the Indian Olympic Association (IOA) in 1927?

(a) Eric Brandon (b) Sir B P Nair (c) Sir Dorabji Tata (d) John Brown

Question 18 [1]

Isotonic contraction, which means equal tension, is known as:

(a) Eccentric contraction (b) Static contraction
(c) Concentric contraction (d) Dynamic contraction

Question 19 [1]

When an isotonic exercise is performed against resistance the load remains:

(a) Constant (b) Variable (c) Static (d) Oscillating

Question 20 [1]

Which of the following is not an objective of the sports training?

(a) Technique development (b) Aerobic endurance training
(c) Physical fitness (d) Tactical development

Question 21 [1]

What is the rate of speed, at which physical activity is performed, known as?

(a) Work-load (b) Exercise volume (c) Load stimulus (d) Intensity

Question 22 [1]

Which of the following techniques stresses on "programmed phase of work and recovery"?

(a) Interval training (b) Continuous method

(c) Fartlek training (d) Acceleration runs

Question 23 [1]

What is the central core of circuit training?

(a) Exercise intensity (b) Exercise density

(c) Exercise volume (d) Exercise continuity

Question 24 [1]

Players particularly benefit from warming exercise because:

(a) The cardio-respiratory system gets ready for the ensuing action

(b) They gain a lot with little effort

(c) Running incorporates only a limited range of movements

(d) This accelerates their peripheral blood supply

Question 25 [1]

Circuit training method was developed by:

(a) G.D. Sondhi and Mr. Dorabji Tata (b) Dr. D.G. Noehrem

(c) Mr. Dorabji Tata (d) R.E. Morgan and G.T. Adamson

Question 26 [1]

Which of the following is not a type of strength training?

(a) Maximum strength (b) Knock-out strength

(c) Explosive strength (d) Strength endurance

Question 27 [1]

Which of the following rules is not related to weight training?

(a) Concentrating on the muscles during exercise.

(b) Maintaining a good rhythm during exercise.

(c) Resting between the sets for 30 to 60 seconds.

(d) Not warming up and stretching before the workouts.

Question 28 [1]

What is the advantage of Cooling Down?

(a) Abnormal blood circulation.

(b) Efficient work of the bodily system to work efficiently.

(c) Increases in level of Adrenaline in the blood.

(d) Proper supply of blood and oxygen to muscles.

Question 29 [1]

Which of the following is not a component of Physical fitness?

(a) Agility (b) Anaerobic capacity

(c) Lexibility (d) Muscle composition

Question 30 [1]

Which of the following is not a Weight Training exercise?

(a) Shoulder press (b) Bench press (c) Running (d) Triceps press

Question 31 [1]

Fartlek, which means "speed play" is a variation of:

(a) Fast continuous method (b) Interval method

(c) Acceleration runs (d) Circuit training

Question 32 [1]

Which of the following in an incorrect method of training?

(a) Interval training method (b) Continuous method

(c) Explosive strength method (d) Fartlek method

Question 33 [1]

What does full form of LNIPE stand for:
(a) Lakshmibai National Institute of Physical Education.
(b) Lakshmibai National University of Physical Education.
(c) Lakshmi National Institute of Physical Education.
(d) Lakshmibai National College of Physical Education.

Question 34 [1]

In which year was the LNIPE founded?
(a) 1957   (b) 1958   (c) 1857   (d) 1956

Question 35 [1]

Give the full form of YMCA:
(a) Young Men's Christian Authority   (b) Young Men's Christian Association
(c) Youth Men's Christian Association   (d) Youth Men's Challenge Association

Question 36 [1]

Who founded the YMCA college of Physical Education?
(a) Mr. Harry Crowe Buck   (b) Ministry of Youth Affairs and Sports
(c) Rev. J.H. Messmore   (d) SAI

Question 37 [1]

IOA stands for:
(a) International Olympic Authority   (b) Indian Olympic Authority
(c) Indian Olympic Association   (d) International Olympic Association

Question 38 [1]

Which one of the following option is not a purpose of the IOC?
(a) To ensure the regular celebration of the Olympic games.
(b) To lead the fight against doping in sports.
(c) Development of sports for all.
(d) To not take action to strengthen the unity of the Olympic movement.

Question 39 [1]

When was International Olympic Committee formed?
(a) 26 June 1896   (b) 27 June 1896   (c) 26 June 1898   (d) 25 June 1894

Question 40 [1]

What does NSNIS stand for?
(a) Netaji Sports National Institute of Survey   (b) Netaji Subhas National Institute of Sports
(c) New Sports National Institute of Sports   (d) Netaji Subhas National Indian Sports

Question 41 [1]

Where is the permanent headquarter of IOC located?
(a) In Atlanta (U.S.A)   (b) In Lausanne (Switzerland)
(c) In Beijing (China)   (d) In Stockholm (Sweden)

Question 42 [1]

The Olympic motto consists of Latin words:
(a) Situs, Altius, and Forties   (b) Citeus, Altius and Forties
(c) Citius, Altius, and Fortius   (d) None of these

Question 43 [1]

What does the Olympic flag consist of?
(a) A Green background with no border and Olympic symbol in the centre.
(b) A Red background with no Olympic symbol.
(c) A White background with no border and Olympic symbol in the centre.
(d) None of the above.

Question 44 [1]

When was Sports Authority of India formed?

(a) 1982　　　　(b) 1984　　　　(c) 1983　　　　(d) 1988

Question 45 [1]

Who is the first president of IOA?

(a) Sir Dorabji Tata　　　　(b) G.D Sodhi

(c) Raja Bhalender Singh　　　　(d) Suresh Kalmadi

Question 46 [1]

Which of the following pairs is not correct?

(a) NSNIS -1961　　　　(b) YMCA -1920　　　　(c) SAI -1984　　　　(d) IOA -1999

Question 47 [1]

Who is the Father of Modern Olympics games?

(a) Demetrius Vikelas　　　　(b) Le Marques Samaranch

(c) Baron Pierre de Cubertin　　　　(d) Ferenc Kemeny

Question 48 [1]

The Five rings of the Olympic flag are in five different colours. They are red, green, yellow, blue and __________.

(a) Orange　　　　(b) Indigo　　　　(c) Black　　　　(d) Violet

Question 49 [1]

In which year was the first summer Olympics held?

(a) 1896　　　　(b) 1897　　　　(c) 1904　　　　(d) 1908

Question 50 [1]

Which type of tournament is best if there are a large number of teams participating?

(a) Round robin　　　　(b) Challenge　　　　(c) Combination　　　　(d) Elimination

Question 51 [1]

League – Cum – Knock Out is a part of:

(a) Knock Out tournament　　　　(b) Round Robin tournament

(c) Combination tournament　　　　(d) Consolation tournament

Question 52 [1]

Which of the following pairs is incorrect?

(a) AIFF - All India football federation　　　　(b) AITA - All India tennis Association

(c) BAI - Badminton Association of India　　　　(d) HI - India Hockey

Question 53 [1]

Which of the following is not a correct statement about intramurals?

(a) They are recreational sports.

(b) They provide opportunities for every individual.

(c) They are played inside the campus.

(d) They are the competitions with other schools.

Question 54 [1]

Which of the following is not a merit of tournament?

(a) Tournament tests your skills.

(b) In team games, all players do not get equal chance.

(c) Tournament helps one to overcome fears.

(d) Culture exchange.

Question 55 [1]

(I) The team in upper half would be n/2

(II) The teams in lower half would be n/2

With reference to the above formulae, which is the formula for the Single Knock – Out for even number of teams?

(a) Only I　　　　(b) Only II　　　　(c) Both (I) and (II)　　　　(d) None of the two

Question 56 [1]

Which one of the following is not a type of tournament?

(a) Olympic tournaments   (b) Combination tournament

(c) Knock-out   (d) Round robin tournament

Question 57 [1]

_____________ activities are organised amongst the students outside the walls of an institution.

(a) Recreational   (b) Amateurs   (c) Extramural   (d) Intramural

Question 58 [1]

Which statement is incorrect about professional sports persons?

(a) They play for money.   (b) They play out of compulsion.

(c) They train full time.   (d) They view sports as a leisure activity.

Question 59 [1]

Which of the following is not a major international tournament?

(a) National games   (b) Asian games   (c) Olympic games   (d) FIH World cup

Question 60 [1]

Which of the following trophies is not related to cricket?

(a) Ranji Trophy   (b) B. C. Roy Trophy

(c) Irani Trophy   (d) Vijay Hazare Trophy

Question 61 [1]

What is the exact duration of Olympic games?

(a) 18 days   (b) 17 days   (c) 15 days   (d) 16 days

Question 62 [1]

Which of the following game is popularly played in the Commonwealth countries?

(a) Hockey   (b) Horse polo   (c) Cricket   (d) Lawn Tennis

Question 63 [1]

The other name of League Tournament is:

(a) Round Robin Tournament   (b) Challenge Tournament

(c) Knock Out Tournament   (d) Combination Tournament

Question 64 [1]

Which of the given procedures is followed to avoid competing in the initial round?

(a) Bye   (b) Seeding   (c) Special Seeding   (d) Fixture

Question 65 [1]

How many byes are given for 21 teams on the knockout basis?

(a) 11   (b) 17   (c) 18   (d) 15

Question 66 [1]

Which of the following is not an objective of Intramural tournament?

(a) Learning a variety of games & skill.   (b) To help in overall development.

(c) To achieve high performance.   (d) To provide recreation.

Question 67 [1]

Which of the following competitions is organized for the student of a school, within the school boundaries?

(a) Inter – state   (b) Intramural   (c) Extramural   (d) None of these

Question 68 [1]

Tournaments help in:

(a) Development of Social qualities.   (b) Development of Sports skills.

(c) Selection of players.   (d) All of these.

Question 69 [1]

The objective of a tournament is:
(a) To find out the best team.
(b) To provide a source of recreation for the public.
(c) To learn new skills.
(d) All of the above.

Question 70 [1]

Bye is a privilege given in
(a) Team sports (b) Individual sports (c) Both (a) and (b) (d) None of these

Answers

1. (a) Military motive
2. (b) Germany
3. (d) Professional Gymnastics
4. (b) Zeus
5. (c) 1951
6. (c) Ancient Period
7. (b) Co-operation
8. (a) National and International integration.
9. (c) Both (a) and (b)
10. (a) Unite
11. (c) Both (a) and (b)
12. (c) All round development of human beings.
13. (d) All of these
14. (a) Woldemar Gerschler and Dr. Hans Reindell
15. (d) Patiala 1961
16. (b) Double league
17. (c) Sir Dorabji Tata
18. (c) Concentric contraction
19. (a) Constant
20. (b) Aerobic endurance training
21. (d) Intensity
22. (a) Interval training
23. (a) Exercise intensity
24. (a) The cardio-respiratory system gets ready for the ensuing action.
25. (d) R.E. Morgan and G.T. Adamson
26. (b) Knock-out strength
27. (d) Not warming up and stretching before the workouts.
28. (d) Proper supply of blood and oxygen to muscles.
29. (c) Lexibility
30. (c) Running
31. (a) Fast continuous method
32. (a) Interval training method
33. (a) Lakshmibai National Institute of Physical Education.
34. (a) 1957
35. (b) Young Men's Christian Association.
36. (a) Mr. Harry Crowe Buck
37. (c) Indian Olympic Association
38. (d) To not take action to strengthen the unity of the Olympic movement.
39. (d) 25 June 1894
40. (b) Netaji Subhas National Institute of Sports
41. (b) Lausanne (Switzerland)
42. (c) Citius, Altius, and Fortius
43. (c) A White background with no border and Olympic symbol in the centre.
44. (b) 1984
45. (a) Sir Dorabji Tata
46. (d) IOA -1999
47. (a) Demetrius Vikelas
48. (c) Black
49. (a) 1896
50. (d) Elimination
51. (c) Combination tournament
52. (d) HI - India Hockey
53. (d) They are the competitions with other schools.

54. (a) Tournament tests your skills.

55. (c) Both (I) and (II)

56. (a) Olympic tournaments

57. (c) Extramural

58. (d) They view sports as a leisure activity.

59. (a) National games

60. (b) B. C. Roy Trophy

61. (d) 16 days

62. (c) Cricket

63. (a) Round Robin Tournament

64. (a) Bye

65. (a) 11

66. (c) To achieve high performance.

67. (b) Intramural

68. (d) All of these

69. (d) All of the above.

70. (c) Both (a) and (b)

❑❑

Question 1

Who define for first time that Physical education is a big muscles activities?

(a) C.A.Bucher

(b) R.J.B.Nash

(c) C.C.Cowell

(d) D. Oberteuffer

Question 2

In a knock-out tournament, the teams directly play from third round, its mean the team get:

(a) Bye

(b) Seeding

(c) Special seeding

(d) None of these

Question 3

A competition held among various teams in a particular activity according to a fixed schedule, its known as:

(a) Planning

(b) League

(c) Bye

(d) Fixture

Question 4

In which type of tournament the former champions keep their titles they are defeated by an opponent?

(a) Knockout

(b) League

(c) League-cum-knock out

(d) Challenge tournament

Question 5

If the competition are conducted between the two different institution, its known as:

(a) Inter-school

(b) Inter-section

(c) Extramural

(d) All of these

Question 6

In which year IAO was formed?

(a) 1957

(b) 1972

(c) 1927

(d) 1827

Question 7

A league tournament also known as _________ tournament.

(a) Elimination

(b) Knock-out

(c) Round robin

(d) Combination

Question 8

Who was the first president of IOC?

(a) ThomasBach

(b) Demetrios Vikelas

(c) Pierre de Coubertin

(d) Hippocrates

Question 9

For the teaching of physical education in elementary school, for that which qualification is basically needed?

(a) Only knowing the fundamental movements is enough

(b) Must be Graduate

(c) Must be completed B.P.Ed.

(d) Must be completed M.P.Ed.

Question 10

In a knock-out tournament there are 16 teams, then how many teams will play in lower half?

(a) 10 (b) 8 (c) 9 (d) 6

Question 11

If there is 7 teams in a knock -out tournament, then how many round will be there?

(a) 5 (b) 7 (c) 2 (d) 4

Question 12

Which team will get third bye in knock-out tournament ?

(a) The last team of the lower half (b) The first team of the lower half
(c) The first team of the upper half (d) The third team of the upper half

Question 13

Among the following which one is related to Berger system ?

(a) Knock-out tournament (b) League tournament
(c) Combination tournament (d) Consolation tournament

Question 14

The team or player get opportunity to play directly from the second round, its known as:

(a) Seeded teams (b) Special seeded teams
(c) Bye teams (d) Schedule teams

Question 15

A team has already defeated in the knock-out tournament, but again the team is consider for play and got 3rd position ,this type tournament is known as:

(a) Consolation type-I (b) Consolation type-II
(c) Combination (d) Both (a) and (b)

Question 16

In a knock-out tournament there are 21 teams, then how many special seeding teams will recognize by the organizing committee?

(a) 4 (b) 2 (c) 8 (d) 6

Question 17

Which one is the academic wing of SAI ?

(a) NSNIS (b) SNISN (c) MSAI (d) IOA

Question 18

If there is 17 teams in a knock-out tournament, then how many match will be there?

(a) 15 (b) 16 (c) 12 (d) 13

Question 19

For teaching physical education in senior secondary school, which qualification the person needs?

(a) C.P.Ed. (b) B.P.Ed. (c) D.P.Ed. (d) M.P.Ed.

Question 20

Aim of physical education is __________

(a) Social Development (b) Mental Development
(c) Physical Development (d) Wholesome Development

Question 21

A person has physically, mentally, socially, neuromuscular, nutritionally and emotionally developed ,so the person fulfill the __________.

(a) Aim of the physical education (b) Aim of the adaptive physical education
(c) Objectives of physical education (d) Objectives of adaptive physical education

Question 22

Elimination tournament means:

(a) Knock-out tournament

(b) League tournament

(c) Combination tournament

(d) Consolation tournament

Question 23

A school has to conduct a inter class tournament, it is a example of:

(a) Extramural

(b) Intermural

(c) Intramural

(d) All of these

Question 24

Which objectives of physical education develops the friendly behaviour in society?

(a) Mental development

(b) Physical development

(c) Social development

(d) Neuromuscular development

Question 25

If there is 7 teams in a league tournament, so how many bye will be there?

(a) 1

(b) 2

(c) 0

(d) 3

Question 26

The person can easily manage his/her distress, if the person is _________.

(a) Development of health

(b) Mentally development

(c) Physically development

(d) Emotionally development

Question 27

Who was the president of IOA in 1928?

(a) Sir Dorabji Tata

(b) Dr. Noehren

(c) Maharaja Bhupindra Singh

(d) Milkha Singh

Question 28

In which type of method the fixture is look like a ladder?

(a) Cyclic

(b) Staircase

(c) Tabular

(d) None of these

Question 29

In which year LNIPE was established?

(a) 1957, August

(b) 1857, July

(c) 1975, June

(d) 1857, May

Question 30

Which one is the pertinent to administration related career?

(a) The Director of sports

(b) Teaching in High school

(c) Dietitian

(d) Rehabilitation

Question 31

The word recreation mean:

(a) Enjoyment activity with pleasure

(b) High intensity running

(c) Leisure

(d) Gymnastics

Question 32

Calculate the total number of matches in third round in upper-half, if 28 teams will played in knock-out:

(a) 2

(b) 3

(c) 4

(d) 8

Question 33

Which one is relevant to health related career in physical education?

(a) Diet and nutrition

(b) Doctor

(c) Physiotherapist

(d) Occupational therapist

Question 34

_________is a large contest of many rounds among various teams.

(a) Bye

(b) Fixture

(c) Tournament

(d) Schedule

Question 35

Where is the NSNIS head quarter situated?

(a) Delhi   (b) Patiala   (c) Uttar Pradesh   (d) Rajasthan

Question 36

Which types of exercise recreate energy?

(a) Recreation   (b) Sports   (c) Games   (d) None of these

Question 37

Which one is the objective of tournament ?

(a) To find the best team   (b) To develop the captainship qualities
(c) To develop the leadership qualities   (d) None of these

Question 38

Which team will get first bye in knock-out tournament ?

(a) The last team of the lower half   (b) The first team of the lower half
(c) The first team of the upper half   (d) The third team of the upper half

Question 39

Which one is the formula to calculate single league tournament ?

(a) $N(N-1)/2$ (b) $N(N-1)$ (c) $(N-1)$ (d) none of these

Question 40

Which one is comes under the Big five personality factors ?

(a) Openness   (b) Physique   (c) Emotion   (d) Intellect

Question 41

In which one personality's behavior is extrovert ?

(a) Ectomorph   (b) Mesomorph   (c) Endomorph   (d) Asthenic

Question 42

It is the ability to resist the fatigue means:

(a) Endurance   (b) Speed   (c) Strength   (d) Flexibility

Question 43

Who define the body types and personality according to morphological and psychic aspects ?

(a) Ernest Kretschmer   (b) Hippocrates   (c) W. H.Sheldon   (d) E.L.Thorndike

Question 44

The method in which there will be no change in the length of the muscle is known as:

(a) Isometric method   (b) Isotonic method
(c) Isokinetic method   (d) Fartlek method

Question 45

Who gave explain about Ectomorph body type and their personality?

(a) Ernest Kretschmer   (b) Hippocrates   (c) W. H. Sheldon   (d) E.L. Thorndike

Question 46

Which one is comes under personality traits ?

(a) Openness   (b) Consciousness   (c) Agreeableness   (d) Physique

Question 47

According to Hippocrates the types of personality or body types are:

(a) 3   (b) 4   (c) 5   (d) 2

Question 48

Who define the body types and personality according to three germs layer of embryonic development ?

(a) Ernest Kretschmer   (b) Hippocrates
(c) W. H. Sheldon   (d) Sigmund Faren Horney

Question 49

Name of the ability which help to over come the resistance with speed is known as:

(a) Maximum strength (b) Explosive strength
(c) strength endurance (d) Static strength

Question 50

What is strength?

(a) an ability to act against a resistance (b) a capacity to do work for prolong time
(c) it is ability of bones (d) it is ability of tendon

Question 51

Who was developed Isokinetic Exercises?

(a) J.J. Perrine (b) Harre (c) Crow and Crow (d) C.A.Bucher

Question 52

In Isometric muscles contraction , the person work is:

(a) displacement (b) speed
(c) range of movements (d) work done in zero

Question 53

Sticking to the fitness programme is known as:

(a) Fitness (b) Exercise adherence (c) Performance (d) Training

Question 54

Which one is the example of Isotonic exercise?

(a) Push-ups (b) Pull-ups
(c) Pushing against the wall (d) Both (a) and (b)

Question 55

In a knock-out tournament there are 21 teams and 4 teams are recognised for special seeding teams, so how many byes teams will be there?

(a) 15 (b) 11 (c) 10 (d) 12

Question 56

Which one is the example of Isometric muscles contraction?

(a) Gymnastic (b) Weight lifting (c) both (a) and (b) (d) None of these

Question 57

If the total number of team is 8 in a league tournament ,so how many bye teams will get bye?

(a) 0 (b) 1 (c) 2 (d) 3

Question 58.

In which year Indian Red cross Society was formed?

(a) 1947 (b) 1946 (c) 1938 (d) 1944

Question 59

Which one is the example of Isokinetic exercise?

(a) Running (b) Jumping (c) Swimming (d) Walking

Question 60

If there is 36 teams which type of tournament the organizer should choose for completing the tournament as early as possible?

(a) league (b) knock-out (c) combination (d) consolation

Question 61

Which one is the example of Isokinetic machine?

(a) cybex (b) treadmill (c) Shift roller (d) Cable machine

Question 62

In Isometric muscle contraction ,the muscle length is:

(a) Decreasing (b) Increasing (c) Remain same (d) None of these

Question 63

Pull-up is the example of:

(a) Isokinetic muscles contraction

(b) Isometric muscles contraction

(c) Isotonic muscles contraction

(d) Static muscles contraction

Question 64

In which type of exercise the work done is zero?

(a) Isometric muscles contraction

(b) Isotonic muscles contraction

(c) Isokinetic muscles contraction

(d) None of these

Question 65

Who developed Isometric exercises?

(a) Muller and Hettinger

(b) J.J. Perrine

(c) Harre

(d) Crow and Crow

Question 66

________ is a state of complete physical, mental and social well-being and not merely an absence of disease or infirmity.

(a) Health   (b) Age   (c) Growth   (d) None of these

Question 67

Which type of fixture is made in combination tournament?

(a) League

(b) Knock-out

(c) Berger system

(d) All of these

Question 68

If 9 teams participate in a double league tournament such as in the FIFA, how many matches will be played in the first phase of league ?

(a) 72   (b) 42   (c) 63   (d) 81

Question 69

Extramural encompasses the activities which are performed ________ the wall of the institute or school.

(a) Outside   (b) Inside   (c) On   (d) Both (a) and (b)

Question 70

Muller and Hettinger developed ___________.

(a) Isometric muscles contraction

(b) Isotonic muscles contraction

(c) Isokinetic muscles contraction

(d) Static muscles contraction

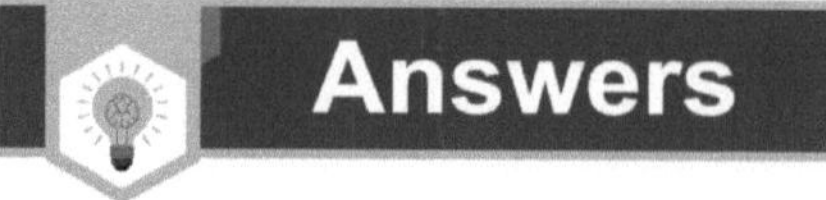

Answers

1. (b) R.J.B.Nash

2. (c) Special seeding

3. (d) Fixture

4. (d) Challenge tournament

5. (d) All of these

6. (c) 1927

7. (c) Round robin

8. (b) Demetrios Vikelas

9. (a) Only knowing the fundamental movements is enough

10. (b) 8

Explanation: Total Number of teams = 16

$$\text{No. of teams in Upper half} = \frac{N}{2}$$

$$= \frac{16}{2} = 8$$

$$\text{No. of teams in Lower Half} = \frac{N}{2}$$

$$= \frac{16}{2} = 8$$

11. (b) 7

12. (b) The first team of the lower half

13. (b) League tournament

14. (c) Bye teams

15. (d) Both (a) and (b)

16. (a) 4

17. (a) NSNIS

18. (b) 16

   Explanation: Total Number of teams = 17.

   No. of Matches = (N – 1)

   = (17 – 1)

   = 16

19. (d) M.P.Ed.

20. (d) Wholesome Development

21. (c) Objectives of physical education

22. (a) Knock-out tournament

23. (c) Intramural

24. (c) Social development

25. (a) 1

26. (a) Emotionally development

27. (c) Maharaja Bhupindra Singh

28. (b) Staircase

29. (a) 1957, August

30. (a) The Director of sports

31. (a) Enjoyment activity with pleasure

32. (c) 4

33. (a) Diet and nutrition

34. (c) Tournament

35. (b) Patiala

36. (a) Recreation

37. (a) To find the best team

38. (a) The last team of the lower half

39. (a) N(N – 1)/2

40. (a) Openness

41. (a) Ectomorph

42. (a) Endurance

43. (a) Ernest Kretschmer

44. (a) Isometric method

45. (c) W. H. Sheldon

46. (d) Physique

47. (b) 4

48. (c) W. H. Sheldon

49. (c) strength endurance

50. (a) an ability to act against a resistance

51. (a) J.J. Perrine

52. (d) Work done in zero

53. (b) Exercise adherence

54. (d) (a) and (b)

55. (a) 15

56. (c) both (a) and (b)

57. (a) 0

58. (b) 1946

59. (c) Swimming

60. (b) knock-out

61. (a) cybex

62. (c) Remain same

63. (c) Isotonic muscles contraction

64. (a) Isometric muscles contraction

65. (a) Muller and Hettinger

66. (a) Health

67. (d) All of these

68. (a) 72

   Explanation:

   Number of teams = 9   [Double league]

   Number of matches = N (N – 1)

   = 9 (9 – 1)

   = 9 × 8

   = 72

69. (a) Outside

70. (a) Isometric muscles contraction

2 Sample Paper

Physical Education

Questions

Question 1

What was the exact time duration of ancient Olympics?

(a) 5 days   (b) 16 days   (c) 15 days   (d) 20 days

Question 2

In which year the boxing game was included in Olympics?

(a) 720 B.C   (b) 688 B.C   (c) 724 B.C   (d) 648 B.C

Question 3

In which body types have strong digestive system?

(a) Ectomorph   (b) Extrovert   (c) Endomorph   (d) Both (b) and (c)

Question 4

The term sociology was first time used by __________.

(a) Auguste Compte   (b) Karl Max   (c) William Sheldon   (d) None of these

Question 5

__________believed that music is for the soul and exercise for the body.

(a) Rome   (b) Greece   (c) Athenians   (d) None of them

Question 6

Who is basically known as social scientist?

(a) Auguste Compte   (b) Newton   (c) C.A.Bucher   (d) K. John

Question 7

Which one of the following is scientific study about the culture and society ?

(a) Physiology   (b) Psychology   (c) Sociology   (d) Ontology

Question 8

__________ is the theory of sociology?

(a) Surplus energy theory   (b) recreational theory

(c) Play theory   (d) symbolic interaction theory

Question 9

The study of relationship between the people in group is known as:

(a) Sociology   (b) Kinesiology   (c) Histology   (d) Biology

Question 10

Which is mainly for speed work which probably helps avoid injuries?

(a) Repetition   (b) Interval   (c) Continuous   (d) None of these

Question 11

Man is animal who can not live with out __________.

(a) Society   (b) play   (c) game   (d) socialisation

Question 12

The leader who serve the needs of the society by innate qualities, is known as __________.

(a) Born leader   (b) Made leader   (c) Autocratic leader   (d) Democratic leader

Question 13

The people who become leaders through the process of teaching, learning and observation ,they known as:

(a) Born leader	(b) Made leader	(c) Autocratic leader	(d) Democratic leader

Question 14

Which one is the example of relative strength ?

(a) body weight is 100 kg and can lift 12 kg weight

(b) body weight is 95 kg and can lift 65 kg weight

(c) body weight is 80 kg and can lift 100 kg weight

(d) both (a) and (c)

Question 15

which one is the example of explosive strength?

(a) standing broad jump	(b) 600 meter run

(c) lifting 100 kg weight	(d) 4×10 meter shuttle run

Question 16

Long jump is the example of:

(a) maximum strength	(b) strength endurance	(c) explosive strength	(d) static strength

Question 17

An athlete doing bicep curl exercise for prolong time with the weight of 8 lbs dumbbell with 80% intensity, it is known as:

(a) maximum strength	(b) explosive strength	(c) strength endurance	(d) None of these

Question 18

__________is said to be the place where ball games like cricket and football had originated.

(a) Germany	(b) England	(c) Australia	(d) New Zealand

Question 19

Which one is not an example of principles of sports training?

(a) Principle of continuity	(b) Principle of Uninterrupted training

(c) Principle of interrupted training	(d) Principle of variety

Question 20

Principle of progression is related to:

(a) aims of sports training	(b) objective of sports training

(c) principle of sports training	(d) ethics of sports training

Question 21

Through the help of warming-up the athlete can __________.

(a) reduces the blood lactic acid	(b) avoid injuries

(c) both (a) and (b)	(d) decrease the metabolic rate

Question 22

An athlete prepares himself with some jogging, running, stretching and rotational exercises doing before the events, it is known as:

(a) Limbering down	(b) cooling down	(c) warming-up	(d) Oxygen dept

Question 23

Which one is not the principle of warming-up

(a) complex to simple	(b) simple to complex

(c) exercise for all the parts of the body	(d) none of these

Question 24

After the moderate exercise the body comes to its normal state, its known as:

(a) warming-up	(b) warming-down	(c) both (a) and (b)	(d) rest stage

Question 25

The fartlek method was developed by:

(a) Gosta and Holmer (b) J.J. Pierre (c) Krestchmer (d) William

Question 26

The _________ of training was followed in ancient India.

(a) Gurukul system (b) Interval (c) Continuous (d) Both (a) and (b)

Question 27

Who developed circuit training ?

(a) R.E.Morgan (b) G.T.Anderson (c) both a and b (d) J.B.Nash

Question 28

What is the main drawback of continuous training method?

(a) Does not improve speed or agility (b) No drawback
(c) Flexibility decreases (d) None of these

Question 29

In fartlek training method the maximum heart rate falls in:

(a) 140-160 beats/minute (b) 180 beats/minute
(c) 160-180 beats/minute (d) 120-110 beats/minute

Question 30

In interval training method maximum heart rate is fall in:

(a) 140-160 beats/minute (b) 180 beats/minute
(c) 160-180 beats/minute (d) 120-110 beats/minute

Question 31

Exercise _________ muscles and different organs of the body.

(a) Strengthens (b) Weakens
(c) Decreases bone density (d) None of them

Question 32

Which training method was developed in Sweden?

(a) Fartlek (b) Continuous (c) Interval (d) Circuit

Question 33

In which type of training method the trainer uses multiple training Stations ?

(a) Fartlek method (b) Variable pace method
(c) Circuit training method (d) None of these

Question 34

Match the following:

(a) Explosive strength (i) Endurance
(b) Continuous method (ii) To over come resistance with speed
(c) Post Iso-metric method (iii) Coordinative abilities
(d) Help to do movement (iv) Flexibility
(a) a – iv, b – iii, c – ii, d – i (b) a – ii, b – i, c – iii, d – iv
(c) a – ii, b – i, c – iv, d – iii (d) a – i, b – ii, c – iv, d – iii

Question 35

Match the following:

(a) Isometric method (i) Heart rate 140-180 beats /minute
(b) Fartlek method (ii) Speed
(c) Circuit training (iii) Length of muscle remains same
(d) Pace run method (iv) To exercise without any break
(a) a – iv, b – iii, c – ii, d – i (b) a – i, b – iii, c – ii, d – iv
(c) a – iii, b – i, c – ii, d – iv (d) a – iii, b – i, c – iv, d – ii

Question 36

Which type of muscles fiber is responsible for fartlek training ?

(a) slow twitch   (b) fast twitch   (c) red muscles fiber   (d) both (a) and (c)

Question 37

Which type of muscles fiber is responsible for speed ability ?

(a) white muscles fiber   (b) fast twitch   (c) red muscles fiber   (d) both (a) and (b)

Question 38

A multinational company recruit a physical instructor , in their company , this is because __________.

(a) Industrial recreation   (b) Sports facilities management

(c) Human management   (d) Supervised the company's work

Question 39

Through the help of industrial recreation the national or multinational companies are tried to provide their employees to __________.

(a) Recreation   (b) Sports opportunities

(c) Physically and mentally fit   (d) All of these

Question 40

In which year NSNIS was formed ?

(a) 1961   (b) 1916   (c) 1954   (d) 1964

Question 41

Where is IOC head quarter present?

(a) Switzerland   (b) Mali   (c) Brazil   (d) France

Question 42

India won gold medal in which Olympics year and where ?

(a) 1980, Moscow   (b) 1932, Los Angeles   (c) 1948, London   (d) 1928, Amsterdam

Question 43

What was motto of 2020, Tokyo Olympics ?

(a) Citius, altius, fortius   (b) Faster, Higher, Stronger and together

(c) Citius, altius, forties and una   (d) Both (b) and (c)

Question 44

Which one is not related to sports industry?

(a) T-shirt   (b) Track-suit   (c) Sports footwear   (d) Book Publishing

Question 45

In which year volley ball game was included in Olympic Games?

(a) 1964   (b) 1952   (c) 1940   (d) 1932

Question 46

In which year Khelo India Programme was launched ?

(a) 2012-2013   (b) 2015-2016   (c) 2017-2018   (d) 2019-2020

Question 47

Sports and __________ help to develop the ability to control various emotions like fear, pleasure, hope, wonder, anger, etc.

(a) Music   (b) Games   (c) Both (a) and (b)   (d) None of these

Question 48

Benefits of Health run is __________.

(a) Enhance the Stamina (b) Running rout   (c) Schedule   (d) Running tips

Question 49

Sports day is celebrated on __________ in India.

(a) 29 May   (b) 29 April   (c) 29 July   (d) 29 August

Question 50

Which festival is celebrated for Major Dhyan Chand's birth in India ?

(a) National Sports Day

(b) International sports day

(c) World sports day

(d) National Eradication day

Question 51

What is the intensity of the speed in intensive Interval method ?

(a) 80-90%   (b) 100-110%   (c) 60-65%   (d) 40-50%

Question 52

Which time duration is fall in short interval method ?

(a) 2 minutes-8 minutes

(b) 15 seconds-2 minutes

(c) 8 minutes-15 minutes

(d) none of these

Question 53.

___________ helps an individual to develop the attitude of competition against themselves for their betterment.

(a) Science   (b) Humanities   (c) Physical education   (d) None of these

Question 54

___________of muscle becomes faster as the viscosity is lowered.

(a) Rate of contraction   (b) Rate of relaxation   (c) Stroke volume   (d) None of these

Question 55

In which warm up athletes are prepared mentally for the activity?

(a) Psychological Warm Up

(b) Physiological warm up

(c) Cooling down

(d) All of these

Question 56

Who spend time behind the scenes coordinating all business-related activities for the team that employs them?

(a) Sports managers   (b) Media manager   (c) Physio   (d) None of these

Question 57

Who is the present president of FINA?

(a) Husain Al- Musallam

(b) Barron Pierre de Coubertin

(c) Thomas Bach

(d) None of these

Question 58

In which year the Indian Olympic Association came into existence?

(a) 1958   (b) 1927   (c) 1989   (d) 2000

Question 59

What has emerged both as a lucrative business opportunity and a sustainable career choice?

(a) Fitness   (b) Gym training   (c) Games   (d) None of these

Question 60

Netaji Subhash National Institute of Sports (NSNIS) was established in which year?

(a) 1958   (b) 1959   (c) 1960   (d) 1961

Question 61

___________ is preparing the athletes mentally and physically to adjust to the sudden increase in the movement.

(a) Warming up   (b) Cooling down   (c) Both (a) and (b)   (d) None of these

Question 62

Which is not a interval training method ?

(a) Intensive Interval method

(b) Extensive Interval method

(c) Continuous method

(d) both (a) and (b)

Question 63

__________ come with inherent risks.
- (a) Competitions
- (b) Tournaments
- (c) Performance
- (d) None of these

Question 64

__________ are the 'third team' on the field.
- (a) Sports officials
- (b) Media managers
- (c) Team players
- (d) All of these

Question 65

Which time duration is fall in medium interval method ?
- (a) 2 minutes – 8 minutes
- (b) 15 seconds-2 minutes
- (c) 8 minutes-15 minutes
- (d) none of these

Question 66

Which among the following is the function of IOA?
- (a) Deciding the organisation of the National Games.
- (b) Maintaining liaison between the Government of India and member federations or associations.
- (c) Protecting the amateur status of sportsmen.
- (d) All of these

Question 67

__________ College of Physical Education was founded by Harry Crowe Buck.
- (a) YMCA
- (b) NSNIS
- (c) LCCPE
- (d) LNUPE

Question 68

"A series of contests in which many contestants compete and the one that prevails through the final round or that finishes with the best record is declared the winner." This definition of competition was given by:
- (a) Farlex
- (b) Merriam-Webster
- (c) Cambridge English Dictionary
- (d) Collins English Dictionary

Question 69

Which of the following is not the positive influence of media?
- (a) Promote healthy active lifestyles and showcases the sport's positive values.
- (b) Present a positive and inspiring role model seeing good sportspeople on TV and in newspapers makes them a role model for people to look up to.
- (c) Motivate people to take part.
- (d) Undermine people's confidence and careers.

Question 70

What is the name of the way of keeping the better players or teams apart in the early stages of a cup or 'knockout' competition?
- (a) Seeding
- (b) Bye
- (c) Standby
- (d) None of these

Answers

1. (a) 5 days
2. (b) 688 B.C
3. (d) both (b) and (c)
4. (a) Auguste Compte
5. (c) Athenians
6. (a) Auguste Compte
7. (c) Sociology
8. (d) symbolic interaction theory
9. (a) Sociology
10. (a) Repetition
11. (a) Society
12. (a) Born leader
13. (b) Made leader
14. (d) both (a) and (c)
15. (a) standing broad jump
16. (c) explosive strength
17. (c) strength endurance

18. (b) England
19. (c) Principle of interrupted training
20. (c) principle of sports training
21. (c) both (a) and (b)
22. (c) warming-up
23. (b) simple to complex
24. (b) warming-down
25. (a) Gosta and Holmer
26. (a) Gurukul system
27. (c) both (a) and (b)
28. (a) Does not improve speed or agility
29. (c) 160-180 beats/minute
30. (b) 180 beats/minute
31. (a) Strengthens
32. (a) Fartlek
33. (c) circuit training method
34. (c) a – ii, b – i, c – iv, d – iii
35. (d) a – iii, b – i, c – iv, d – ii
36. (d) both (a) and (c)
37. (d) both (a) and (b)
38. (a) Industrial recreation
39. (d) All of these
40. (a) 1961
41. (a) Switzerland
42. (a) 1980, Moscow
43. (d) both (b) and (c)

44. (d) Book Publishing
45. (a) 1964
46. (c) 2017-2018
47. (b) Games
48. (a) Enhance the Stamina
49. (d) 29 August
50. (a) National Sports Day
51. (a) 80-90%
52. (b) 15 seconds-2 minutes
53. (c) Physical education
54. (a) Rate of contraction
55. (a) Psychological Warm Up
56. (a) Sports managers
57. (c) 8 minutes-15 minutes
58. (b) 1927
59. (a) Fitness
60. (a) 1958
61. (a) Warming up
62. (c) Continuous method
63. (a) Competitions
64. (a) Sports officials
65. (a) 2 minutes-8 minutes
66. (d) All of these
67. (a) YMCA
68. (a) Farlex
69. (d) Undermine people's confidence and careers.
70. (a) Seeding

❑❑

Physics

Specimen Question Paper

Physics

Maximum Marks: 70
Time allowed: One and a Half hours

General Instructions

*(Candidates are allowed **15 minutes** for **only** reading the paper)*
ALL QUESTIONS ARE COMPULSORY.
The marks intended for questions are given in brackets [ ].
Select the correct option for each of the following questions.

Questions

Question 1.

The ratio of forces between two small spheres having a constant charge 'q' when placed in air to when placed in a medium of dielectric constant K, is: **[1]**

(a) $1 : K$ (b) $K : 1$ (c) $1 : K^2$ (d) $K^2 : 1$

Question 2.

When a soap bubble is given a positive charge, then its radius: **[1]**

(a) Decreases

(b) Increases

(c) Remains unchanged

(d) Nothing can be predicted as information is insufficient

Question 3.

Four charges are arranged at the corners of a square ABCD , as shown in the adjoining figure. The force on the charge 'Q' kept at the centre O is: **[1]**

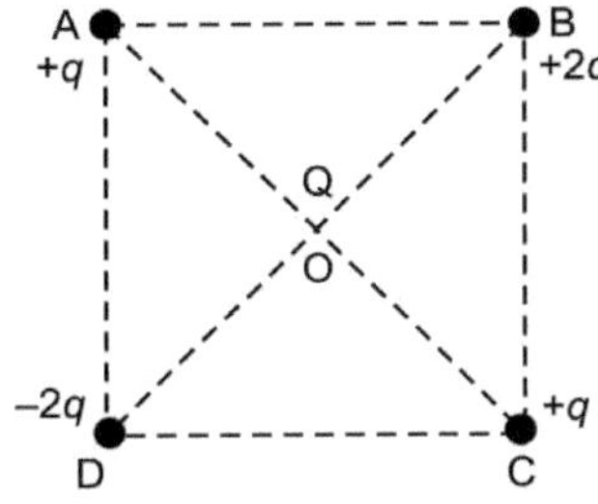

Figure 1

(a) Zero   (b) Along the diagonal AC

(c) Along the diagonal BD   (d) Perpendicular to side AB

Question 4.

The surface charge density of a conductor, in the absence of another conductor: **[1]**

(a) Is proportional to the charge on the conductor and its surface area

(b) Inversely proportional to the charge and directly proportional to the surface area

(c) Directly proportional to the charge and inversely proportional to the surface area

(d) Inversely proportional to the charge and the surface area

Question 5.

Which of the following is not the characteristic of resonance in an LCR series circuit? **[1]**

(a) $X_L = X_C$

(b) $\omega L = \dfrac{1}{\omega C}$

(c) $2\pi fL = 2\pi fC$

(d) $f_0 = \dfrac{1}{2\pi}\sqrt{\dfrac{1}{LC}}$

Question 6.

A graph showing variation in impedance Z of a series LCR circuit, with frequency f of alternating emf applied to it is shown below. What is the minimum value of this impedance? **[1]**

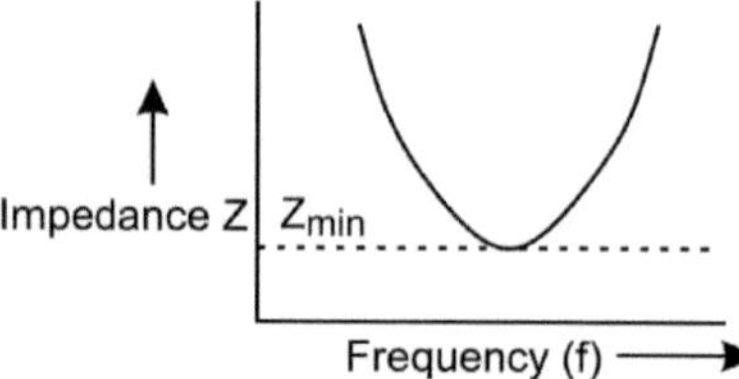

Figure 2

(a) R

(b) $Z = \sqrt{R^2 + (X_L - X_C)^2}$

(c) Z_{min}

(d) $X_L = X_C$

Question 7.

An electric dipole of moment $\vec{p}$ is placed in a uniform electric field $\vec{E}$. It has maximum (negative) potential energy when the angle between $\vec{p}$ and $\vec{E}$ is: **[1]**

(a) $\dfrac{\pi}{2}$

(b) Zero

(c) π

(d) $\dfrac{3\pi}{2}$

Question 8.

A charge placed at a distance from a short electric dipole in the end-on position experiences a force F. If the distance is halved, then the force will become: **[1]**

(a) 4 F

(b) 8 F

(c) $\dfrac{F}{4}$

(d) $\dfrac{F}{8}$

Question 9.

In **figure 3** given below, Electric field intensity 'E' at a point P, at a perpendicular distance 'r' from an infinitely long line charge X'X having linear charge density λ is given by: **[1]**

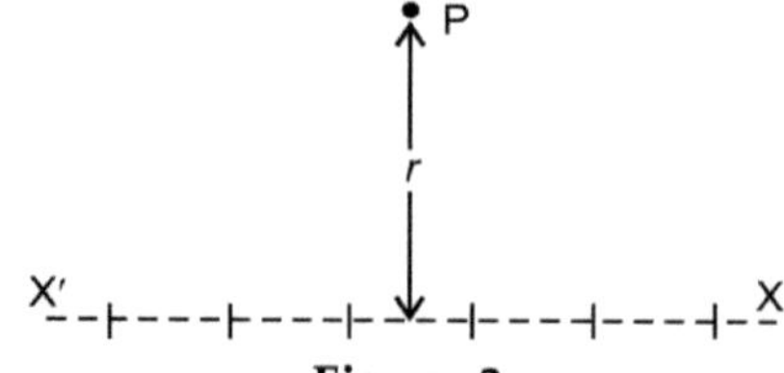

Figure 3

(a) $E = \left(\dfrac{1}{4\pi\varepsilon_0}\right)\dfrac{2\lambda}{r^2}$

(b) $E = \left(\dfrac{1}{4\pi\varepsilon_0}\right)\dfrac{2\lambda}{r}$

(c) $E = \left(\dfrac{1}{4\pi\varepsilon_0}\right)\dfrac{\lambda}{r^2}$

(d) $E = \left(\dfrac{1}{4\pi\varepsilon_0}\right)\dfrac{\lambda}{r}$

Question 10.

Three capacitors, each of capacitance C, are connected in series. Their equivalent capacitance is C_s. The same three capacitors are now connected in parallel. Their equivalent capacitance becomes C_p. The ratio of C_p to C_s is: **[1]**

(a) $9:1$ (b) $1:9$ (c) $3:1$ (d) $1:3$

Question 11.

Note: There is a discrepancy in board's questions,the correct question should be:

The charges $q_1 = 3\mu C$, $q_2 = 4\mu C$ and $q_3 = -7\mu C$ are placed on the circumference of a circle of radius 1.0 m as shown in the figure below. What is the value of charge q_4 placed on the same circle if the potential at the centre is 0? **[1]**

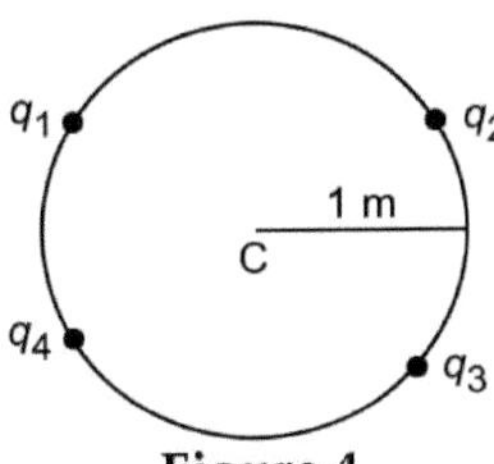

Figure 4

(a) $-4\mu C$ (b) $-3\mu C$ (c) $7\mu C$ (d) 0

Question 12.

Three equal charges of $5.0\mu C$ each, are placed at the three vertices of an equilateral triangle of side 5.0cm each. The electrostatic potential energy of the system of charges is: **[1]**

(a) $13.5\,J$ (b) $17.5\,J$ (c) $27\,J$ (d) $15\,J$

Question 13.

Note: There is a discrepancy in board's questions,the correct question should be:

Three capacitors $C_1 = 3\mu F$, $C_2 = 6\mu F$ and $C_3 = 10\mu F$ are connected to a 50V battery as shown in the figure below: **[1]**

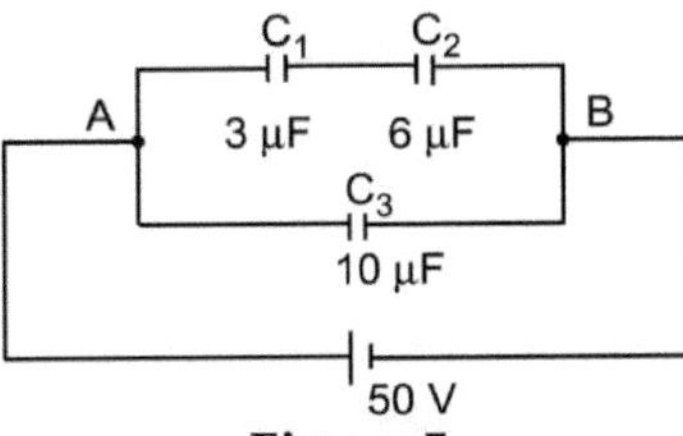

Figure 5

The equivalent capacitance of the circuit between point A and B and the charge on C_1 are...

(a) $12\mu F, 150\mu C$ (b) $4.75\mu F, 100\mu C$ (c) $12\mu F, 100\mu C$ (d) $4.75\mu F, 150\mu C$

Question 14.

A substance behaves like a magnet only if there are: **[1]**

(a) at least some tiny current loops within the magnet   (b) stationary charges within the magnet

(c) magnet within the magnet   (d) none of these

Question 15.

A straight long wire is turned into a loop of radius R = 10 cm, as shown in **figure 6** below. If a current I = 16 A is passed through the wire, then the magnetic field at the centre of the loop is: **[1]**

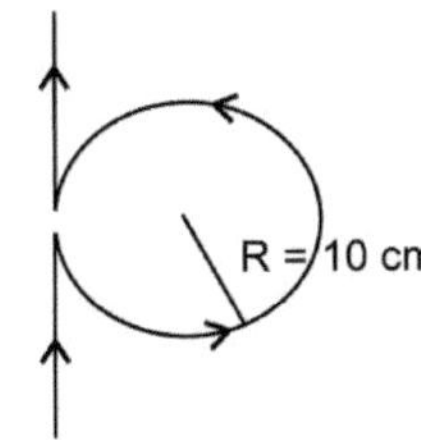

Figure 6

(a) $3.4 \times 10^{-5}\,T$ (b) $6.8 \times 10^{-5}\,T$ (c) $1.7 \times 10^{-5}\,T$ (d) $5.1 \times 10^{-5}\,T$

Question 16.

The current in the circuit shown in **figure 7** below, will be: [1]

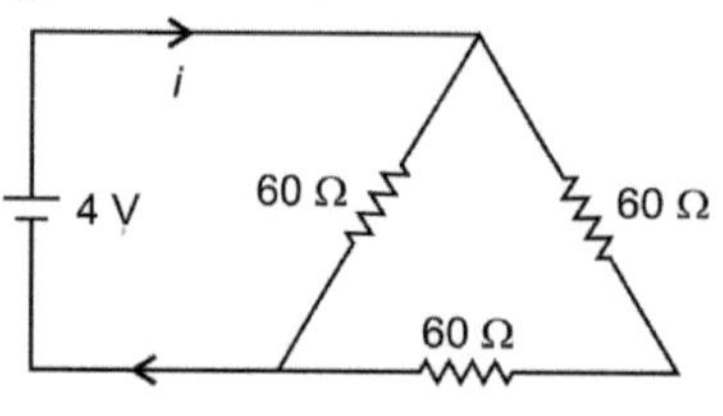

Figure 7

   (a) 1/45 A   (b) 1/15 A

   (c) 1/10 A   (d) 1/5 A

Question 17.

A cell of e.m.f. E is connected to an external resistance R. The potential difference across cell is V. The internal resistance of cell will be: [1]

   (a) $\dfrac{(E-V)R}{E}$ (b) $\dfrac{(E-V)R}{V}$

   (c) $\dfrac{(V-E)R}{V}$ (d) $\dfrac{(V-E)R}{E}$

Question 18.

The **figure 8** given below shows currents in a part of an electric circuit. The current i is: [1]

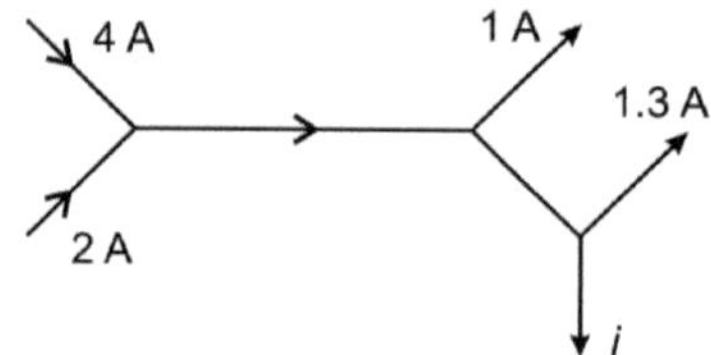

Figure 8

   (a) 1.7 A   (b) 3.7 A

   (c) 2.7 A   (d) 4.7 A

Question 19.

n identical cells each of e.m.f. E and internal resistance r are connected in parallel. An external resistance R is connected in series to this combination. The current through R is: [1]

   (a) $\dfrac{nE}{R+nr}$ (b) $\dfrac{nE}{nR+r}$

   (c) $\dfrac{E}{R+nr}$ (d) $\dfrac{nE}{R+r}$

Question 20.

The circuit shown in **figure 9** below is used to compare the e.m.f. of two cells E_1 and E_2 where $E_2 > E_1$. The null point is at C when the galvanometer is connected to E_1. When the galvanometer is connected to E_2, the null point will be: [1]

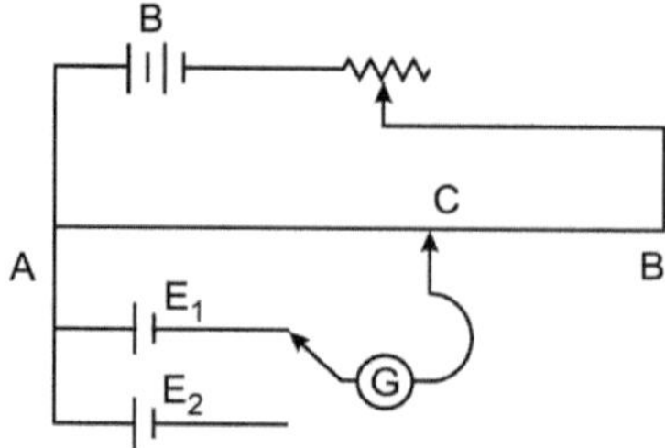

Figure 9

   (a) To the left of C   (b) To the right of C

   (c) At C itself   (d) Nowhere on AB

Question 21.

Figure 10 given below shows a graph of emf 'ε' generated by an ac generator verses time. What is the frequency of the emf? [1]

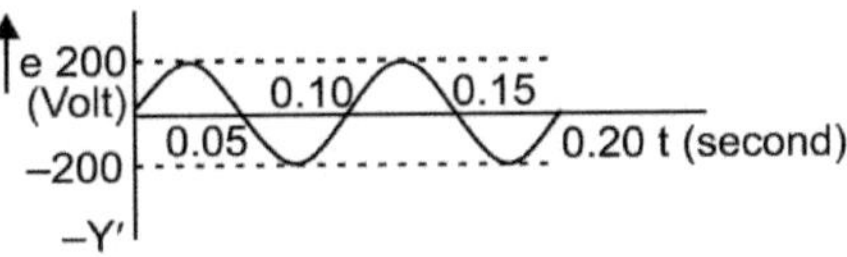

Figure 10

(a) 10 Hz (b) 0.10 Hz

(c) 20 Hz (d) 50 Hz

Question 22.

If m, e, τ and n respectively represent the mass, charge, average relaxation time and density of the electron, then what will be the resistance of a wire of length l and area of cross-section A? [1]

(a) $\dfrac{ml}{ne^2\tau A}$

(b) $\dfrac{m\tau^2 A}{ne^2\tau l}$

(c) $\dfrac{ne^2\tau A}{2ml}$

(d) $\dfrac{ne^2 A}{2m\tau l}$

Question 23.

The drift velocity of a current carrying conductor is v. What will be the drift velocity if the current flowing through the wire is doubled? [1]

(a) $v/4$ (b) $v/2$ (c) $2v$ (d) $4v$

Question 24.

The resistance of a wire is 10 Ω. It is stretched so that its length becomes four times. What will be the new resistance of the wire? [1]

(a) 40 Ω (b) 160.0 Ω

(c) 120 Ω (d) 80.0 Ω

Question 25.

What is the angle between the current element $\overrightarrow{dl}$ and the magnetic flux density $\overrightarrow{B}$ at point 'P' in the **figure 11** given below? [1]

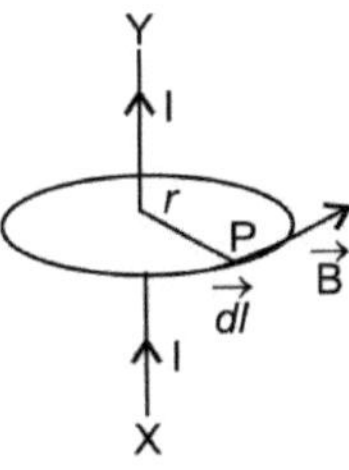

Figure 11

(a) Parallel to each other (b) Perpendicular to each other

(c) Normal to each other (d) Any angle between them is possible

Question 26.

An A.C. generator generating an e.m.f of ε = 300 sin (100π) t is connected to a series combination of 16μF capacitor, 1 H inductor and 100 Ω resistor. What is the frequency of A.C.? [1]

(a) 100 Hz (b) 50 Hz

(c) 300 Hz (d) 25 Hz

Question 27.

Four identical cells each having an e.m.f. of 4 V are connected in parallel. What will be the e.m.f. of this combination? [1]

(a) 1 V (b) 16 V (c) 1/4 V (d) 4 V

Question 28.

A 2 volt battery, a 15 Ω resistor and a potentiometer of 100 cm length, all are connected in series. If the resistance of potentiometer wire is 5 Ω, then the potential gradient of the potentiometer wire is: **[1]**

(a) 0.005 V/cm

(b) 0.05 V/cm

(c) 0.02 V/cm

(d) 0.2 V/cm

Question 29.

The potential gradient along the length of a uniform wire is 20 volt/metre. B and C are the two points at 40 cm and 70 cm point on a meter scale fitted along the wire. What is the potential difference between B and C? **[1]**

(a) 6 V

(b) 0.4 V

(c) 0.6 V

(d) 4 V

Question 30.

In an experiment of meter bridge, a null point is obtained at the centre of the bridge wire. When a resistance of 5 is connected in one gap, what is the value of resistance in the other gap? **[1]**

(a) 10 Ω

(b) 5 Ω

(c) 1/5 Ω

(d) 500 Ω

Question 31.

What is the locus of an electron, projected perpendicular to a uniform magnetic field? **[1]**

(a) Circle

(b) Right bisector

(c) Parabola

(d) Straight line

Question 32.

Which of the following is the right expression to define the magnetic field B? **[1]**

(a) $\vec{F} = q(\vec{v} \times \vec{B})$

(b) $\vec{F} = B(\vec{I} \times \vec{l})$

(c) $\dfrac{\vec{F}}{l} = \dfrac{\mu_0}{2\pi} \dfrac{l^2}{a}$

(d) $B = \mu_0 ni$

Question 33.

What is the SI (base unit) unit of permeability? **[1]**

(a) $kg\, ms^{-2}\, A^{-2}$

(b) $kg\, m^2 s^{-2}\, A^{-2}$

(c) $kg\, m^2 s\, A^{-2}$

(d) $kg\, ms^2\, A^{-2}$

Question 34.

The loss of power in a transformer can be reduced by: **[1]**

(a) Increasing the number of turns in primary.

(b) Using solid core made of steel.

(c) Increasing ac voltage applied to primary.

(d) Using a laminated core of soft iron.

Question 35.

Which is the most harmful radiation entering the atmosphere of earth from outer space? **[1]**

(a) X - Rays

(b) Visible rays

(c) Gamma radiations

(d) Radio waves

Question 36.

Radio waves and gamma waves are both transverse in nature and electromagnetic in character and have the same speed in vacuum. In what respects are they different? **[1]**

(a) Frequency

(b) Wavelength

(c) Both (a) and (b)

(d) None of these

Question 37.

Which of the following groups belongs only to the electromagnetic spectrum? **[1]**

(a) alpha rays, beta rays, gamma rays

(b) ultra-sonic rays, radio waves, infra red rays

(c) gamma rays, cathode rays, X-rays

(d) X-rays, radio waves, infra red rays

Question 38.

Which electromagnetic radiation has wavelength greater than that of X-rays and smaller than that of visible light? **[1]**

(a) Radio waves
(b) Microwaves
(c) Infra Red Rays
(d) Ultra Violet Rays

Question 39.

A parallel plate capacitor of plate area A = 600 cm^2 and plate separation d = 2.0 mm is connected to a d.c. source of 200 V. **[2]**

(i) What is the magnitude of the uniform electric field E between the plates?

(a) $E = 1.0 \times 10^5$ V/m,
(b) $E = 1.0 \times 10^7$ V/m,
(c) $E = 0.5 \times 10^5$ V/m,
(d) $E = 0.5 \times 10^7$ V/m,

(ii) What is the charge density σ on any one of the two plates?

(a) $\sigma = 8.85 \times 10^{-7}$ C/m^2
(b) $\sigma = 8.85 \times 10^{-9}$ C/m^2
(c) $\sigma = 4.45 \times 10^{-7}$ C/m^2
(d) $\sigma = 4.45 \times 10^{-9}$ C/m^2

Question 40.

A torch bulb rated as 4.5 W, 1.5 V is connected as shown in **figure 12** given below. **[2]**

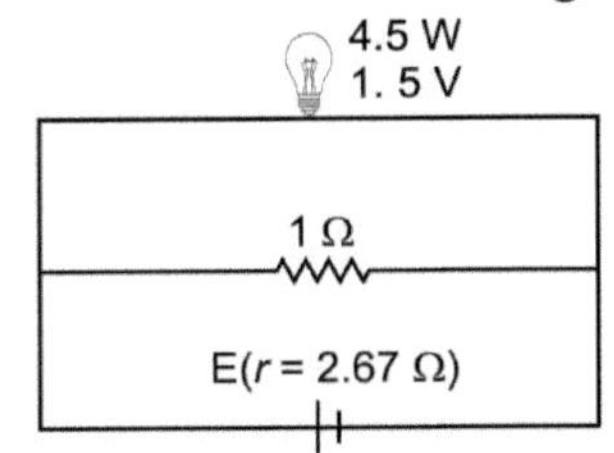

Figure 12

(i) What should be the e.m.f. of the cell required to make this bulb glow at full intensity?

(a) 4.5 V
(b) 1.5 V
(c) 2.67 V
(d) 13.5 V

(ii) What is the current passing through 1 Ω resistor?

(a) 4.5 A
(b) 1.5 A
(c) 2.67 A
(d) 13.5 A

Question 41.

The specific resistance of manganin is 50×10^{-8} Ω m. **[2]**

(i) The resistance of a cube of length 50 m will be:

(a) 10^{-6} Ω
(b) 2.5×10^{-5} Ω
(c) 10^{-8} Ω
(d) 50×10^{-8} Ω

(ii) The specific resistance of the combination of two cubes of length 50 m in series will be:

(a) 10^{-6} Ω m
(b) 2.5×10^{-5} Ω m
(c) 2×10^{-6} Ω m
(d) 50×10^{-8} Ω m

Question 42.

A metallic rod CD rests on a thick metallic wire PQRS with arms PQ and RS parallel to each other, at a distance l = 50 cm, as shown in **figure 13** below. A uniform magnetic field B = 0.1T acts perpendicular to the plane of this paper, pointing inwards into the plane. (*i.e.*, away from the reader). **[2]**

The rod is now made to slide towards right, with a constant velocity of v = 5.0 m/s.

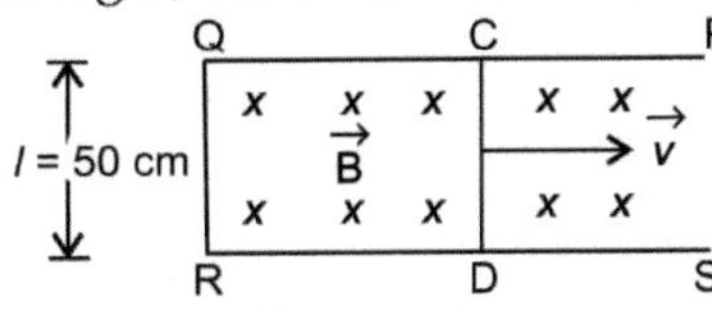

Figure 13

  (i) How much emf is induced between the two ends of the rod CD?

    (a) 25.0 V   (b) 0.25 V

    (c) 2.50 V   (d) .025 V

 (ii) What is the direction in which the induced current flows?

    (a) Along 'CQRDC'   (b) Along the direction of motion of the conductor

    (c) Along 'CDRQC'   (d) Against the direction of motion of the conductor

Question 43.

Study the diagram given below: **[2]**

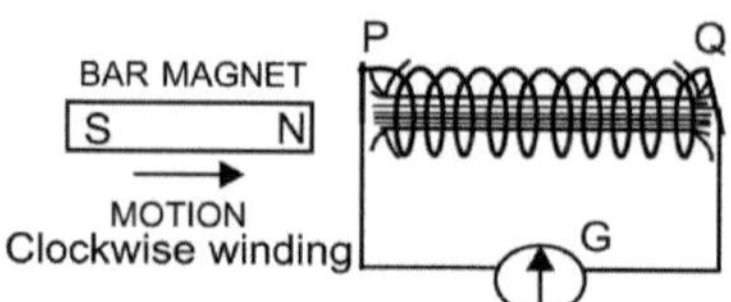

Figure 14

  (i) The direction of the current at end 'P' will be:

    (a) Anti clockwise   (b) Clockwise

    (c) Towards the magnet   (d) Away from the magnet

 (ii) The magnetic poles induced at the end 'Q' of the coil will be:

    (a) North pole   (b) South pole

    (c) Anti clockwise   (d) No pole

Question 44.

The resistance of a galvanometer is 50 Ω. It is converted into a voltmeter or an ammeter.

Calculate the resistance of the voltmeter and ammeter to an accuracy of 2sf. Only with the mention below in the subparts.   **[2]**

  (i) A voltmeter using a 10 k Ω resistor is:

    (a) 10050 Ω (b) 10.050 k Ω

    (c) 10000 Ω (d) 10 k Ω

 (ii) An ammeter using a 10 m Ω resistor is:

    (a) 50 Ω (b) 10 m Ω

    (c) 0.0999 Ω (d) 50. 0999 Ω

Question 45.

Two bulbs B_1 and B_2 are connected in series with an source of emf 250 V as shown in the **figure 15** below. The labels on the bulbs read 250 V, 80 W and 250 V, 100 W respectively.   **[3]**

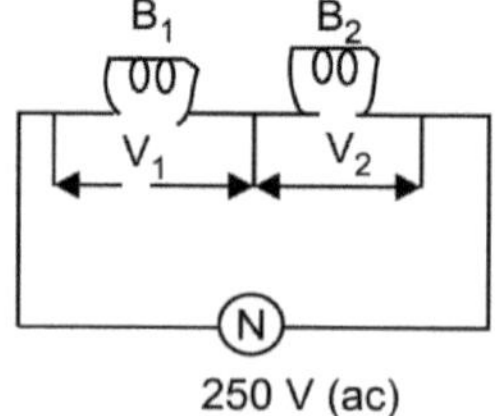

Figure 15

  (i) What will be the ratio of the resistance of the bulbs R_1/R_2?

    (a) 1.4 A   (b) 2.2 A

    (c) 2.0 A   (d) 1.8 A

 (ii) What will be the ratio of the power consumed (P1/P2) when connected in series?

    (a) 5 : 4   (b) 4 : 5

    (c) 1: 1   (d) 5 : 3

(iii) What is the ratio of the pd across the bulbs (V_1/V_2)?

    (a) 5 : 4   (b) 4 : 5   (c) 1 : 1   (d) 5 : 3

Question 46.

A 2 µF capacitor, 100 Ω resistor and 8 H inductor are connected in series with an ac source. At a certain frequency of about 40 Hz for this ac source, the current drawn in the circuit is maximum. If the peak value of e.m.f. of the source is 200V: **[3]**

(i) What is the peak value of current in the circuit?

    (a) 1.4 A   (b) 2.2 A

    (c) 2.0 A   (d) 1.8 A

(ii) What is the phase relation between voltages across inductor and resistor?

    (a) $\pi/2$ radian   (b) $\pi/3$ radian

    (c) $\pi/4$ radian   (d) π radian

(iii) What is the phase difference between voltages across inductor and capacitor?

    (a) $\pi/2$ radian   (b) $\pi/3$ radian

    (c) $\pi/4$ radian   (d) π radian

Question 47.

Given below is a neat, labelled diagram to obtain balancing condition of Wheatstone bridge. **[3]**

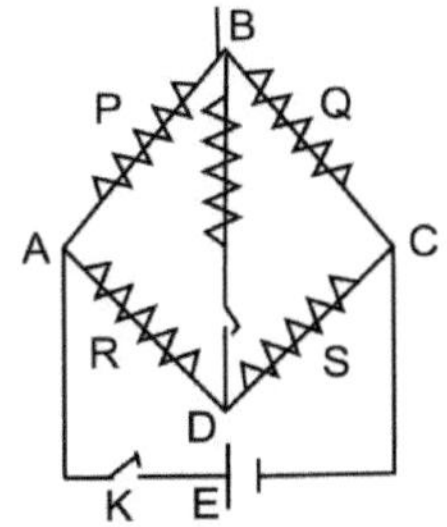

Figure 16

(i) Why is the key 'K' pressed before the key K_1?

    (a)   There is no such requirement

    (b)   To avoid a back emf in the closed loops

    (c)   There is no current till the key 'K' is pressed

    (d)   None of these

(ii) What is the relation between the potential at 'B' and 'D', when the bridge is balanced?

    (a) $V_B > V_D$ (b) $V_B < V_D$

    (c) $V_B = V_D$ (d) $V_B \geq V_D$

(iii) What is the galvanometer current when the bridge is balanced?

    (a) I_g flows from 'B' to 'D'   (b) I_g flows from 'D to 'B'

    (c) I_g has no significance in this case   (d) $I_g = 0$

Question 48.

Figure 17 shows a right-angled isosceles triangle PQR having its base equal to 'a'. A current of 1.0 A is passing downwards along a thin straight wire cutting the plane of a paper normally as shown at Q. Likewise, a similar wire carries an equal current moving normally upwards at R. Assume the wire is to be infinitely long. **[3]**

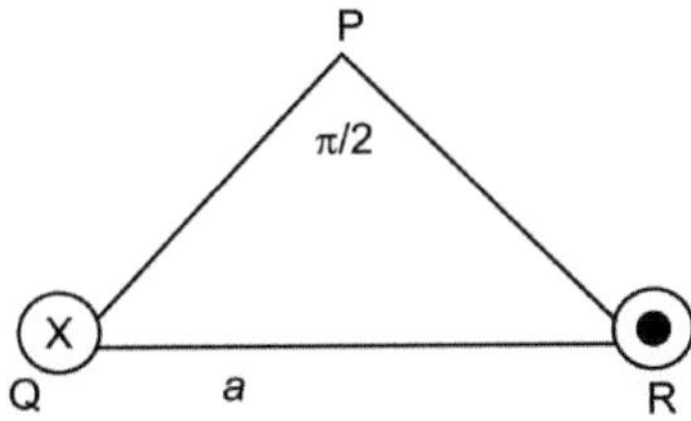

Figure 17

(i) The magnitude and the direction of the magnetic induction B at P due to wire at 'Q':

(a) $B = \dfrac{\mu_0}{\sqrt{2}} \dfrac{I}{\pi a}$ acting along PQ

(b) $B = \dfrac{\mu_0}{\sqrt{2}} \dfrac{I}{\pi a}$ acting along PR

(c) $B = \dfrac{\mu_0}{\sqrt{2}} \dfrac{I}{\pi a}$ towards the mid-point of QR

(d) $B = \dfrac{\mu_0}{\pi} \dfrac{I}{a}$ towards the mid-point of QR

(ii) The magnitude and the direction of the magnetic induction B at P due to wire at 'R':

(a) $B = \dfrac{\mu_0}{\sqrt{2}} \dfrac{I}{\pi a}$ acting along PQ

(b) $B = \dfrac{\mu_0}{\sqrt{2}} \dfrac{I}{\pi a}$ acting along PR

(c) $B = \dfrac{\mu_0}{\sqrt{2}} \dfrac{I}{\pi a}$ towards the mid-point of QR

(d) $B = \dfrac{\mu_0}{\pi} \dfrac{I}{a}$ towards the mid-point of QR

(iii) The net magnitude and the direction of the magnetic induction B at P:

(a) $B = \dfrac{\mu_0}{\sqrt{2}} \dfrac{I}{\pi a}$ acting along PQ

(b) $B = \dfrac{\mu_0}{\sqrt{2}} \dfrac{I}{\pi a}$ acting along PR

(c) $B = \dfrac{\mu_0}{\sqrt{2}} \dfrac{I}{\pi a}$ towards the mid-point of QR

(d) $B = \dfrac{\mu_0}{\pi} \dfrac{I}{a}$ towards the mid-point of QR

Question 49.

An alternating e.m.f of 100 V is applied to a circuit containing a resistance of 40 Ω and an inductance L in series. The current is found to lag behind the voltage by an angle $a = \tan^{-1}\frac{3}{4}$. **[4]**

(i) The inductive reactance in this case is:

(a) 40 Ω

(b) 30 Ω

(c) 50 Ω

(d) $10\sqrt{5}$ Ω

(ii) The impedance of the circuit is:

(a) 40 Ω

(b) 30 Ω

(c) 50 Ω

(d) $10\sqrt{5}$ Ω

(iii) The current flowing through the circuit is:

(a) 2.5 A

(b) 3.33 A

(c) 2.0 A

(d) $10\sqrt{5}$ A

(iv) If the inductance has a value of 0.096 H, and π = 3.14, the approximate frequency of the applied e.m.f.

(a) 40 Hz   (b) 50 Hz   (c) 30 Hz   (d) None of these

Question 50.

The teacher of Priti's school took the students on a study trip to a power generating station, located nearly 250 km away from the city. The teacher explained that electrical energy is transmitted over such a long distance to their city, in the form of alternating current (a.c.) raised to a high voltage. At the receiving end in the city, the voltage is reduced to operate the devices. As a result, the power loss is reduced. Priti listened to the teacher and asked questions about how the ac is converted to a higher or lower voltage. **[4]**

(i) What is the device used to change the alternating voltage to a higher or lower value?

(a) Transformer

(b) Rectifier

(c) Ammeter

(d) Voltmeter

(ii) What is the cause for power dissipation in the device referred to above?

(a) Hysteresis

(b) Eddy current

(c) Flux loss

(d) All of these

(iii) In the device used above, what is the relation between the power output and power input for an ideal case?

(a) Power output is less than power input

(b) Power output is greater than power input

(c) Power output is equal to power input

(d) It depends upon the situation

(iv) What source input should be used in this device?

    (a)   AC source   (b)   DC source

    (c)   Half wave rectifier   (d)   Full wave rectifier

Answers

1. (b) $K : 1$

Explanation: Let two small spheres having a constant charge q place d in air at a distance r, then the force acting between them is given by

$$F_{air} = \frac{1}{4\pi\varepsilon_0} \cdot \frac{q^2}{r^2}$$

When both changes placed in a medium of dielectric constant K, then

$$F_{medium} = \frac{1}{4\pi\varepsilon_0 K} \cdot \frac{q^2}{r^2}$$

$$\therefore \quad \frac{F_{air}}{F_{medium}} = \frac{K}{1}$$

2. (b) Increases

Explanation: The positive charge is uniformely distributed on the soap bubble it causes repulsive force between charge particles distributed on the bubble due to electrostatic force between them. Hence, its radius increases.

3. (c) Aong the diagonal BD

Explanation: The net force acting on O

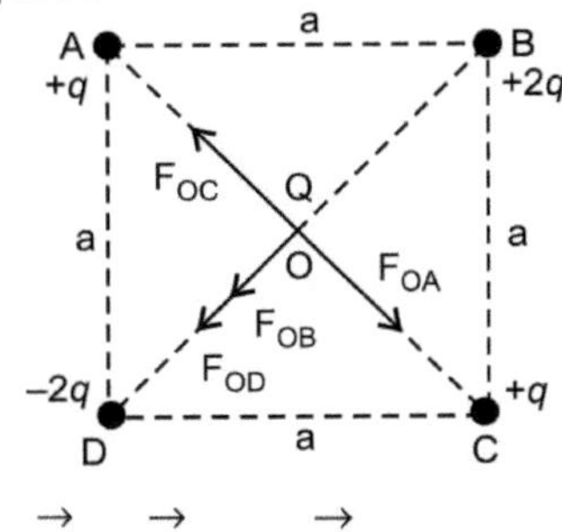

$$\vec{F} = \vec{F}_{OB} + \vec{F}_{OD}$$

F_{OC} and F_{OA} are equal and opposite to each other. So, they will cancel out.

$$\therefore \quad F = \frac{1}{4\pi\varepsilon} \cdot \frac{(2q)Q}{\left(\frac{a\sqrt{2}}{2}\right)^2} + \frac{1}{4\pi\varepsilon} \cdot \frac{(+2q)Q}{\left(\frac{a\sqrt{2}}{2}\right)^2}$$

$$= \frac{1}{4\pi\varepsilon} \cdot \frac{8q.Q}{a^2} \quad \text{Along the diagonal BD}$$

4. (c) Directly proportional to the charge and inversely proportional to surface area.

Explanation: The surface charge density of a conductor is given by

$$\sigma = \frac{q}{A}$$

Where q is the charge on the conductor of area A.

5. (c) $2\pi f L = 2\pi f C$

Explanation: At resonance, $X_L = X_C$

$$\therefore \qquad \omega L = \frac{1}{\omega C}$$

$$\omega^2 = \frac{1}{LC}$$

$$(2\pi f_0)^2 = \frac{1}{LC}$$

$$f_0 = \frac{1}{2\pi}\sqrt{\frac{1}{LC}}$$

6. (a) R

Explanation: The impedance of LCR circuit is given by.

$$Z = \sqrt{R^2 + (X_L - X_C)^2}$$

Value of Z will be minimum if, $\qquad X_L = X_C$

$$\therefore \qquad Z_{min} = R$$

7. (b) Zero

Explanation: $\qquad\qquad\qquad\qquad U = -pE\cos\theta$

Maximum ($-ve$) potential energy $U_{max} = -pE$ when $\cos\theta = 1$ and $\theta = 0°$ (zero)

8. (b) 8 F

Explanation: Electic field due to electric dipole at charge q placed at a distance r in an axial point is,

$$E = \frac{q}{4\pi\varepsilon_0} \cdot \frac{2p}{r^3}$$

$\therefore$ Force on charged particle having charge q placed at a distance r,

$$F = qE = \frac{q}{4\pi\varepsilon_0} \cdot \frac{2p}{r^3}$$

$$F \propto \frac{1}{r^3}$$

If distance is halved then,

new force

$$F' = \frac{1}{4\pi\varepsilon_0} \cdot \frac{2pq}{\left(\frac{1}{2}r\right)^3}$$

$$= \frac{1}{4\pi\varepsilon_0} \cdot \frac{2pq}{(r^3)} \cdot 8 = 8\,F$$

9. (b) $E = \dfrac{1}{4\pi\varepsilon_0} \cdot \dfrac{2\lambda}{r}$

Explanation: Using Gauss's law of electrostatic

$$\oint E.dA = \frac{q_{enc}}{\varepsilon_0}$$

$$E.2\pi rl = \frac{q}{\varepsilon_0} = \frac{\lambda l}{\varepsilon_0} \text{, where } \lambda \text{ is line charge density}$$

$$E = \frac{1}{4\pi\varepsilon_0}\cdot\frac{2\lambda}{r}$$

10. (a) $9:1$

Explanation: When three capacitors connected in series,

$$\frac{1}{C_s} = \frac{1}{C}+\frac{1}{C}+\frac{1}{C} = \frac{3}{C}$$

$$C_s = \frac{C}{3}$$

Now same three capacitors are connected in parallel

$$\therefore \qquad C_p = C + C + C = 3\,C$$

$$\frac{C_p}{C_s} = \frac{3C}{C/3} = 9:1$$

11. (d) 0

Explanation: $q_1 = 3\mu C$, $q_2 = 4\mu C$, $q_3 = -7\mu C$, $q_4 = ?$, $V = 0$

$$V = V_1 + V_2 + V_3 + V_4$$

$$0 = \frac{1}{4\pi\varepsilon_0}\frac{1}{r}\,[q_1 + q_2 + q_3 + q_4] \qquad\qquad [\because \text{At centre, } V = 0]$$

$$0 = \frac{1}{4\pi\varepsilon_0}\left[\frac{3\mu C + 4\mu C - 7\mu C + q_4}{r}\right]$$

$$q_4 = 0C$$

12. (a) $13.5\,J$

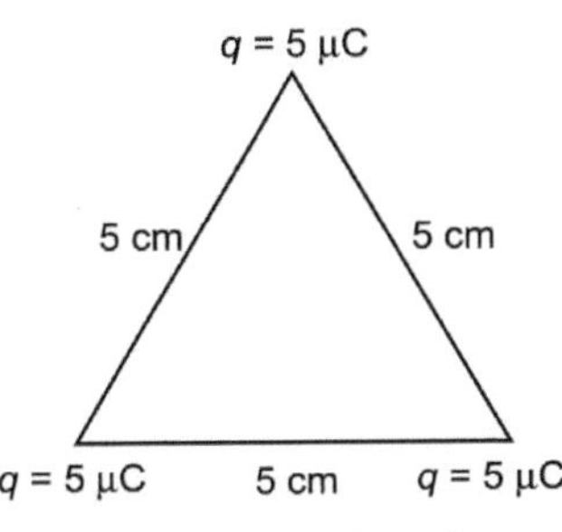

Explanation:

$$U = \frac{1}{4\pi\varepsilon_0}\left(\frac{3q^2}{r}\right)$$

$$= 9\times10^9 \times \frac{(3\times5\times10^{-6}\times5\times10^{-6})}{5\times10^{-2}} = 13.5\,J$$

13. (c) $12\mu F$, $100\mu C$

Explanation: $C_1 = 3\mu F$, $C_2 = 6\mu F$ and $C_3 = 10\mu F$

C_1 and C_2 are connected in series

$$\therefore \qquad C_s = \frac{C_1 C_2}{C_1 + C_2} = \frac{3\mu F.6\mu F}{9\mu F} = 2\mu F$$

C_s and C_3 are connected in parallel

$$\therefore \qquad C_p = C_s + C_3 = 2\mu F + 10\mu F = 12\mu F$$

The charge Q on $C_s = C_s V$

$$= 2\mu F.50\ V = 100\mu C$$

The charge on C_1 is $100\mu C$

14. (a) At least some tiny current loops within the magnet

Explanation: A current carrying conductor produces magnetic field around it. Magnetic field can be produced by current.

15. (b) 6.8×10^{-5} T

Explanation: Magnetic field $\vec{B} = \vec{B_1} - \vec{B_2}$

Where $\vec{B_1}$ is magnetic field due to straight wire at centre of loop in inward direction and $\vec{B_2}$ is the magnetic field at a centre of loop due to current loop in outward direction. So direction of B_1 and B_2 are opposite to each other.

$\therefore$

$$\vec{B} = \frac{\mu_0}{4\pi}.\frac{2i}{R} - \frac{\mu_0 i}{2R}$$

$$= \frac{\mu_0 i}{2R}\left[\frac{1}{\pi}-1\right]$$

$$= \frac{4\pi \times 10^{-7} \times 16}{2 \times 10^{-1}} \times \left[\frac{1}{3.14}-1\right]$$

$$= 6.8 \times 10^{-5}\ T\ \text{(outword direction)}$$

16. (c) $\dfrac{1}{10}$ A

Explanation:

$$R_s = 60 + 60 = 120\ \Omega$$

R_s and $R_3 = 60\ \Omega$ connected in parallel

$$R_p = \frac{R_s R_3}{R_s + R_3} = \frac{120 \times 60}{120 + 60} = \frac{120 \times 60}{180} = 40\ \Omega$$

$$i = \frac{V}{R} = \frac{4}{40} = \frac{1}{10}\ A$$

17. (b) $\left(\dfrac{E-V}{V}\right)R$

Explanation:

$$\frac{V}{R} = \frac{E}{R+r}$$

$$\frac{R+r}{R} = \frac{E}{V}$$

$$1 + \frac{r}{R} = \frac{E}{V}$$

$$r = \left(\frac{E}{V}-1\right)R = \left(\frac{E-V}{V}\right)R$$

18. (b) 3.7A

Explanation:

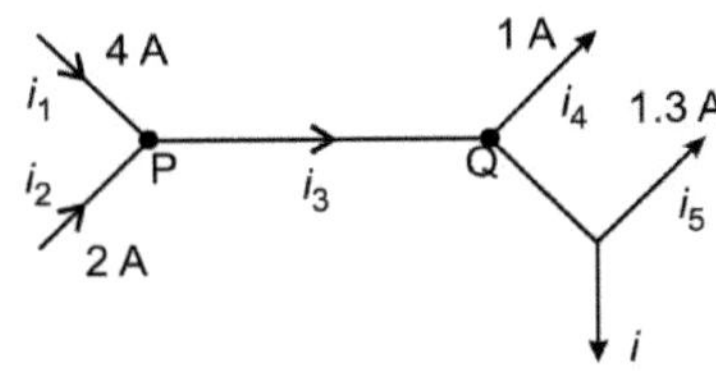

By applying KCL at node P, $i_1 + i_2 = i_3$

$$i_3 = 4 + 2 = 6A$$

Again by applying KCL at node Q, $i_3 = i_4 + i_5 + i$

$$6 = 1 + 1.3 + i$$

$$4.7 = i$$

$$i = 3.7A$$

19. (b) $\dfrac{nE}{nR + r}$

Explanation: n identical cells each of e.mf. E and internal resistance r are in parallel and connected in series with R.

Then, $i = \dfrac{E}{R + \dfrac{r}{n}}$ $\left[\because \dfrac{1}{r_{\text{total}}} = \dfrac{1}{r} + \dfrac{1}{r} + \dfrac{1}{r} \dots n \text{ times} = \dfrac{n}{r}, r_{\text{total}} = \dfrac{r}{n} \right]$

$$i = \dfrac{nE}{nR + r}$$

20. (b) To the right of C

Explanation: We know that, in potentiometer

$$\dfrac{E_1}{l_1} = \dfrac{E_2}{l_2} = \text{Constant} \qquad \dots(i)$$

In Case 1,

Let $AC = l_1$ (When galvonometer is connected to E_1)

In Case 2, E_2 is connected with galvonometer

$\because$ By equation (i),

$$E_1 l_2 = E_2 l_1 = \text{Constant}$$

Given, $E_2 > E_1$

$\therefore$ $l_2 > l_1$

$\therefore$ $l_2 > AC$

21. (a) 10 Hz

Explanation: Time period $= 0.1$ sec.

Frequency of the emf is given by

$$f = \dfrac{1}{T} = \dfrac{1}{0.1} = 10 \text{ Hz}$$

22. (a) $\dfrac{ml}{ne^2 \tau A}$

Explanation: We know that,

The current, $i = \dfrac{ne^2 A \tau V}{ml}$

By comparing, $i = \dfrac{V}{R}$

$$R = \dfrac{ml}{ne^2 A\tau}$$

23. (c) $2v$

Explanation:

$$i = neAv_d$$

$$v_d \propto i$$

If current is doubled then v_d will become double.

24. (b) $160\,\Omega$

Explanation: $\qquad R = 10\,\Omega$

If it streched four times, then length become increase fourth time but volume remains constant.

$\therefore \qquad$

$$\pi r_1^{\,2} l_1 = \pi r_2^{\,2} l_2$$

$$\dfrac{l_2}{l_1} = \dfrac{r_1^{\,2}}{r_2^{\,2}} \qquad \qquad \text{...(i)}$$

Now, $\qquad R = \rho\,\dfrac{l}{A} \qquad\qquad$ Where ρ is specific resistances

$$\dfrac{R_1}{R_2} = \dfrac{l_1}{l_2}\cdot\dfrac{A_2}{A_1} = \dfrac{l_1}{l_2}\cdot\dfrac{\pi r_2^{\,2}}{\pi r_1^{\,2}} = \dfrac{l_1}{l_2}\times\dfrac{l_1}{l_2} \qquad \text{[By using (i)]}$$

$$= \dfrac{l_1^{\,2}}{l_2^{\,2}}$$

$$R_2 = \dfrac{l_2^{\,2}}{l_1^{\,2}}\times R_1 = (4)^2\,R_1 = 16\,R_1 = 160\,\Omega$$

25. (a) Parallel to each other

Explanation: The current element dl and magnetic flux density $\vec{B}$ at any point P are always tangential to each other.

26. (b) 50 Hz

Explanation:

By comparing,

$$\varepsilon = 300 \sin (100\pi)t$$

$$\varepsilon = \varepsilon_0 \sin \omega t$$

$$\omega = 100\pi$$

$$2\pi f = 100\pi$$

$$2f = 100$$

$$f = 50\text{ Hz}$$

27. (d) 4V

Explanation: In the parallel combination potential difference or emf are same. The combined emf is 4 volt.

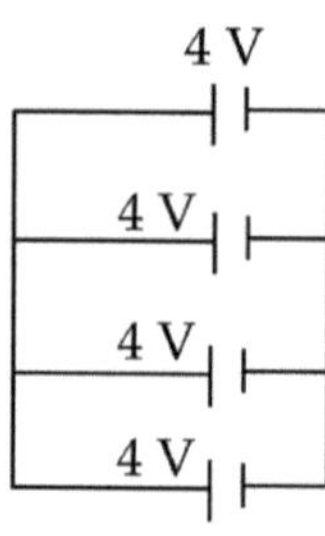

28. (a) 0.005 V/cm

Explanation:

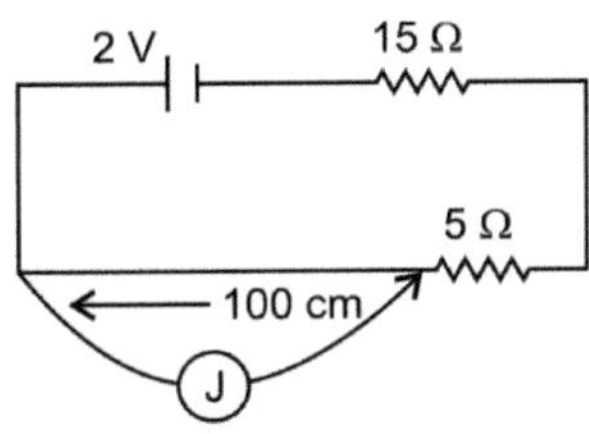

The voltage across the potentiometer, $E = \dfrac{2}{15+5} \times 5 = \dfrac{10}{20} = 0.5$ V

Potential gradient, $K = \dfrac{E}{l} = \dfrac{0.5}{100} = 0.005$ V/cm

29. (a) 6 V

Explanation: $K = 20$ V/m

Two points at 40 cm and 70 cm point on meter scale fitted along the wire. Let potential difference between B and C is E′

$\because \qquad K = \dfrac{E}{l} = 20$ V/m

$\therefore \qquad E' = Kl' = 20 \times (0.70 - 0.40) = 20 \times 0.3 = 6$ V

30. (b) $5\,\Omega$

Explanation: A null point is obtained at the centre of the bridge.

$\therefore \qquad \dfrac{R_1}{R_2} = \dfrac{l}{100-l} = \dfrac{50}{100-50} = \dfrac{50}{50} = 1$

$R_2 = R_1 = 5\,\Omega$

31. (a) Circle

Explanation: When an electron projected perpendicular to a uniform magnetic field it moves along a circular path.

32. (a) $\vec{F} = q(\vec{v} \times \vec{B})$

Explanation: When a charge particle moving in a magnetic field, there is a force actng on a particle *i.e.,*

$F = q(\vec{v} \times \vec{B})$.

33. (a) kg. m.sec.$^{-2}$.A^{-2}

Explanation: We know that the force per unit length acting between two wire.

$\dfrac{F}{l} = \dfrac{\mu_0}{4\pi} \cdot \dfrac{2I_1 I_2}{r}$

$\mu_0 = \dfrac{F.4\pi.r}{l.2I_1 I_2} = \dfrac{kg.\dfrac{m}{sec^2}.m}{m.A.A} = kg.\,m.sec.^{-2}.A^{-2}$

34. (d) Laminated core of soft iton.

Explanation: Due to the constantly changing magnetic field. There is a loss of current in the core. This current is known as eddy current. To reduce eddy current losses, we use a laminated core of soft iron.

35. (c) gamma radiation

Explanation: The most harmful radiation entering the atmosphere of earth from outer space is UV radiation or gamma radiations.

36. (c) Both (a) and (b)

   Explanation: The frequency and wavelength of radiowave and gamma wave are different.

37. (d) X-ray, radiowaves, infra-red rays.

   Explanation: In eletromagnetic spectrum, the group of rays are radiowave, infra-red, visible rays, UV-rays, X-ray and gamma rays.

38. (d) Ultra Violet Rays

   Explanation: $\lambda_{X\text{-ray}} < \lambda_{UV} < \lambda_{Visible}$

39. (i) (a) 1×10^5 V/m

   Explanation:

$$A = 600 \text{ cm}^2 = 6 \times 10^{-2} \text{ m}^2$$
$$d = 2 \times 10^{-3} \text{ m}$$
$$V = 200 \text{ V}$$

By

$$V = E.d \text{ [where E is electric field]}$$
$$E = \frac{V}{d}$$
$$= \frac{200}{2 \times 10^{-3}} = 10^5 \text{ V/m}$$

   (ii) (a) 8.05×10^{-7} c/m^2

   Explanation:

$$E = \frac{\sigma}{\varepsilon_0}$$

$\therefore$

$$\sigma = E\varepsilon_0$$
$$= 10^5 \times 8,85 \times 10^{-12} = 8.85 \times 10^{-7} \text{ c/m}^2$$

40. (i) (d) 13.5 V

   Explanation: P = 4.5, V = 1.5 V, R′ = 1Ω

Resistance of bulb,

$$R = \frac{V^2}{P} = \frac{(1.5)^2}{4.5} = 0.5 \ \Omega$$

$$\frac{1}{R''} = \frac{1}{R} + \frac{1}{R'} = 2 + 1 \quad \Rightarrow R'' = \frac{1}{3} = 0.33 \ \Omega$$

$$R_{total} = r + R'' = 2.67 + 0.33 = 3 \ \Omega$$

$$\frac{E}{r + R''} = \frac{V}{R''} \quad \Rightarrow \frac{E}{3\,\Omega} = \frac{1.5}{1/3} \quad \Rightarrow E = 13.5 \text{ V}$$

   (ii) (b) 1.5 A

   Explanation: Voltage across 1Ω resister $V_{1\Omega}$ = 1.5 V

$$i = \frac{V}{R'} = \frac{1.5}{1} = 1.5 \text{ A}$$

41. (i) (c) $10^{-8} \ \Omega$

   Explanation:

$$R = \rho \frac{l}{A}$$

$$= 50 \times 10^{-8} \times \frac{50}{50 \times 50} = 10^{-8} \ \Omega$$

   (ii) (d) $50 \times 10^{-8} \ \Omega$ m

   Explanation: Specific resistance does not depend upon area and length. Therefore, the value will remain constant *i.e.*, $50 \times 10^{-8} \ \Omega$ m.

42. (i) (b) 0.25 V

Explanation:
$$e = Bvl$$
$$= 0.1 \times 5 \times 0.5 = 0.25 \text{ Volt}$$

(ii) (c) Along CDRQC

Explanation: By using fleming's right hand rule, the direction of induced current is clockwise.

43. (i) (a) Anti-clockwise

Explanation: The motion of magnet is towards the coil PQ. The point P will become north pole which opposes the relative motion between coil and magnet. Therefore, anti-clockwise current will flow at P.

(ii) (b) South pole

Explanation: The magnetic poles induced at P and Q are north pole and South pole respectively.

44. (i) (a) 10050 Ω

Explanation: Galvanometer resistance = 50 Ω

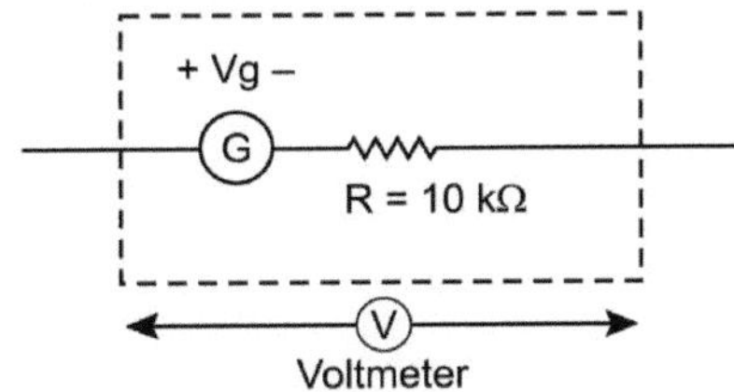

A voltmeter can be formed by connecting a high resistance in the series with Galvonometer.

$$\frac{V_g}{G} = \frac{V - V_g}{R} \qquad \text{where V is voltage of voltmeter}$$

Resistance of voltmeter is $R_V = G + R$
$$= 50 + 10000 = 10050 \text{ Ω}$$

(ii) (d) 10 m Ω

Explanation: Ammeter can be formed by connecting galvonometer with very low resistance in parallel.

$$\frac{1}{R_A} = \frac{1}{R} + \frac{1}{G}$$

$$= \frac{100}{1} + \frac{1}{10000} = \frac{1000000 + 1}{10000}$$

Resistance of ammeter, $\quad R_A = \dfrac{10000}{1000001} = 0.0099 \text{ Ω} \simeq 10 \text{ m Ω}$

45. (i) (a) 5 : 4

Explanation:
$$R_1 = \frac{V_1^2}{P_1}, \ R_2 = \frac{V_2^2}{P_2}$$

$$\frac{R_1}{R_2} = \left(\frac{V_1}{V_2}\right)^2 \cdot \frac{P_2}{P_1}$$

$$= \left(\frac{250}{250}\right)^2 \times \frac{100}{80} = \frac{5}{4}$$

(ii) (b) $4 : 5$

Explanation:
$$\frac{P_1}{P_2} = \left(\frac{V_1}{V_2}\right)^2 \frac{R_2}{R_1} = \frac{4}{5}$$
$[\because R_1 : R_2 = 5 : 4]$

(iii)(c) $1 : 1$

Explanation: $V_1 = V_2 = 250$ Volt

46. (i) (c) 2.0 A

Explanation: In LCR Circuit, $Z = \sqrt{R^2 + (X_L - X_C)^2}$

$$= \sqrt{(100)^2 + \left(2\pi f L - \frac{1}{2\pi f C}\right)^2}$$

$$= \sqrt{10000 + \left(6.28 \times 40 \times 8 - \frac{1}{6.28 \times 40 \times 2 \times 19^{-6}}\right)^2}$$

$$= \sqrt{10000 + 19^2} = 101.78 \ \Omega$$

$$i_0 = \frac{V_0}{Z} = \frac{200}{101.70} = 1.96 \text{ A} \sim 2 \text{ A}$$

(ii) (a) $\dfrac{\pi}{2}$ radian

Explanation: Inductor is leading by $\dfrac{\pi}{2}$ to resistor.

(iii)(d) π radian

Explanation: There is phase difference of π between inductor and capacitor.

47. (i) (a) There is no current till key 'K' is pressed.

Explanation: If K is open then there is no current flow in the bridge.

(ii) (c) $V_B = V_D$

Explanation: When the bridge is balanced the potential at B and D are same.

$$V_B = V_D$$

(iii)(d) $I_g = 0$

Explanation: At balanced condition, there is no current flow through Galvonometer (BD).

i.e., $\qquad I_g = 0$

48. (i) (b) $B = \dfrac{\mu_0}{\sqrt{2}} \cdot \dfrac{i}{\pi a}$ acting along PR

Explanation: Let $\qquad PQ = PR = x$

$$\sqrt{2x^2} = a$$

$$\sqrt{2}x = a$$

$$x = \frac{a}{\sqrt{2}}$$

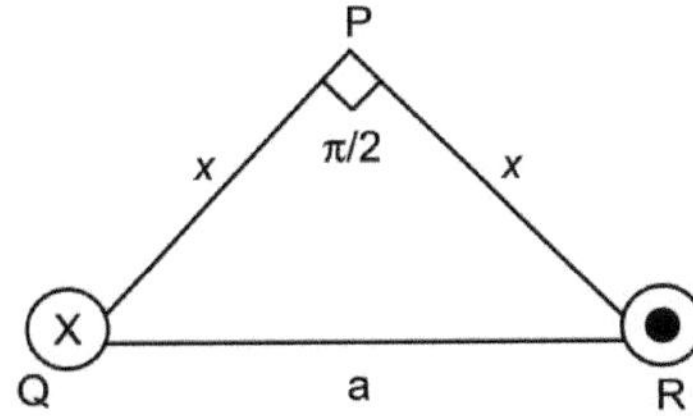

Magnetic field B at P due to wire Q, $B = \dfrac{\mu_0}{4\pi} \cdot \dfrac{2i}{\dfrac{a}{\sqrt{2}}}$

$$= \dfrac{\mu_0}{\sqrt{2}\,\pi} \cdot \dfrac{i}{a} \text{ acting along PR}$$

(ii) (a) $B = \dfrac{\mu_0}{\sqrt{2}\,\pi} \cdot \dfrac{i}{a}$ acting along PQ

Explanation: Magnetic field B due to wire R, at point P

$$B = \dfrac{\mu_0}{\sqrt{2}\pi} \cdot \dfrac{i}{a} \text{ acting along PQ}$$

(iii)(d) $B = \dfrac{\mu_0}{\sqrt{2}\pi} \cdot \dfrac{i}{a}$ towards the mid-point of QR

Explanation: Magnetic field at P,

$$B_{net} = \sqrt{B_{PQ}^2 + B_{PR}^2} = \sqrt{2}B \qquad [\because B_{PQ} = B_{PR} = B]$$

$$B = \dfrac{\mu_0}{\pi} \cdot \dfrac{i}{a} \text{ towards the mid-point of QR}$$

49. (i) (b) 30 Ω

    Explanation: $\qquad X_L = \omega L = 2\pi f L$

In LR circuit, resistance and inductance are connected in series.

$\therefore \qquad \tan a = \dfrac{3}{4} = \dfrac{X_L}{R} \qquad \left(\because \tan a = \dfrac{V_L}{V_R} = \dfrac{IX_L}{IR} \right)$

$$X_L = \dfrac{3}{4}\,R = \dfrac{3}{4} \times 40 = 30\ \Omega$$

(ii) (c) 50 Ω

Explanation: Impedance of the circuit, $Z = \sqrt{R^2 + X_L^2}$

$$= \sqrt{40^2 + 30^2} \qquad (\because X_L = 30\ \Omega)$$

$$= 50\ \Omega$$

(iii)(c) 2.0 A

Explanation: $\qquad$ Current flow, $I = \dfrac{V}{Z} = \dfrac{100}{50} = 2\ A \qquad (\because Z = 50\ \Omega)$

(iv)(b) 50 Hz

Explanation: $\qquad L = 0.096\ H$

Calculated, $X_L = 30\ \Omega$

$$2\pi f L = 30$$

$$2 \times 3.14 \times f \times 0.096 = 30$$

$$f = \dfrac{30}{2 \times 3.14 \times 0.096} = 49.76\ Hz = 50\ Hz$$

50. (i) (a) Transformer

    Explanation: A transformer is used to change the AC voltage to higher to lower value or lower to higher value.

(ii) (d) All of these

    Explanation: A transformer's output power is always slightly less than the input power. There is power dissipation in the transformer due to hysteresis losses, eddy current and flux losses.

(iii)(c) Power output is equal to power input

    Explanation: Power input = Power output

In ideal case, effeciency should be 1

i.e.
$$\eta = 1 = \frac{P_{out}}{P_{in}}$$

(iv)(a) AC source

    Explanation: A transformer is generally operated on AC. If converted AC voltage to higher to lower value and viva-versa.

❑❑

 Questions

Question 1
Charge present in 2.0 mole of a neutral Hydrogen (H_2) gas is:
(a) 0.5432×10^7 C (b) 5.432×10^{11} C (c) 0.3853×10^6 C (d) 38.53×10^{11} C

Question 2
A copper wire is stretched to make it 0.5% longer. The percentage increase in resistance will be:
(a) 1 (b) 2 (c) 5 (d) 10

Question 3
The magnetic flux through a coil perpendicular to the plane is varying according to the relation
$$\phi = (5t^3 + 4t^2 + 2t - 5) \text{ Wb}$$
If the resistance of the coil is 5Ω, then the induced current through the coil at $t = 1s$, is:
(a) 1A (b) 2A (c) 5A (d) 10A

Question 4
Which one of the following is the property of a monochromatic, plane electromagnetic wave in free space?
(a) Electric and magnetic fields are in the same phase.
(b) The energy contribution of both electric and magnetic fields are not equal.
(c) The speed of the wave is B/E.
(d) All of the above.

Question 5
The force between two point charges placed in a material medium of dielectric constant ε_r is F. If the material is removed, then the force between them becomes:

(a) εF (b) $\varepsilon_r F$ (c) $\dfrac{F}{\varepsilon_r}$ (d) $\dfrac{\varepsilon}{F}$

Question 6
A potential difference of 600 volt is applied across the plates of a parallel plate capacitor placed in a magnetic field. The separation between the plates is 2 mm. An electron projected vertically upward, parallel to the plates, with a velocity of 3×10^6 m/s moves undeflected between the plates. The magnitude of the magnetic field in the region between the capacitor plates is:
(a) 0.1 T (b) 1 T (c) 10 T (d) 2T

Question 7
If two parallel wires carrying currents of equal magnitude and flowing in the same direction then they will exert:
(a) an attractive force on each other (b) a repulsive force on each other
(c) no force on each other (d) a rotational torque on each other

Question 8
The time period of a charged particle undergoing a circular motion in a uniform magnetic field depends on:
(a) mass (b) charge (c) magnetic field (d) all of these

Question 9
Two bulbs with ratings 200 V – 100 W and 200 V – 200 W are joined in series and are connected to a power supply of 220 V. The total power consumed by them will be:

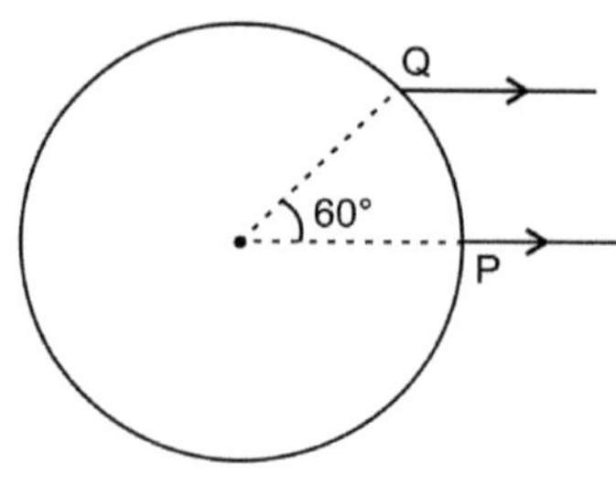

(a) 66.61 W (b) 98.37 W (c) 80.67 W (d) Zero

Question 10

The resistance of a bulb filament is 100 Ω at a temperature of 100°C and 200 Ω at 400°C. Then, the temperature coefficient of the material of the filament is :

(a) $0.005°C^{-1}$ (b) $0.003°C^{-1}$ (c) $0.001°C^{-1}$ (d) $0.3°C^{-1}$

Question 11

A uniform wire is bent in the form of a circle. The resistance of the wire is 36 Ω. The effective resistance across the point P and Q will be:

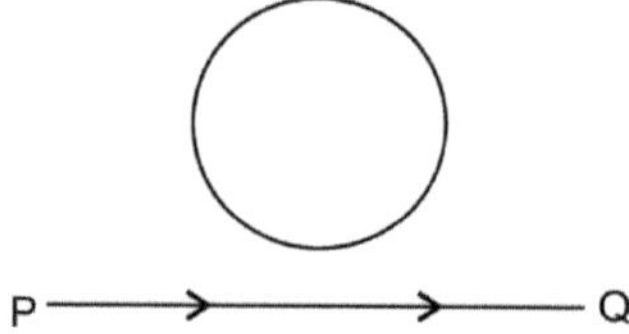

(a) 15 Ω (b) 10 Ω (c) 25 Ω (d) 5 Ω

Question 12

In a potentiometre experiment, the balancing with a cell is at length 250 cm. On shunting the cell with a resistance of 2 Ω, the balancing length becomes 100 cm. The internal resistance of the cell is:

(a) 1 Ω (b) 2 Ω (c) 3 Ω (d) 5 Ω

Question 13

The angle between the dipole moment and electric field at any point on the equatorial plane is:

(a) 45° (b) 90° (c) 60° (d) 180°

Question 14

Two infinitely long parallel plates of equal areas 7 cm², are separated by a distance of 1 cm. One of the plates have a charge of + 10 nC while the while the other has – 10 nC. If $\varepsilon_0 = \dfrac{10^{-9}}{49\pi}$ F/m^{-1}, then the magnitude of electric field between the plates is:

(a) 7π kV m^{-1} (b) 7 kV m^{-1} (c) 5π kV m^{-1} (d) 70π kV m^{-1}

Question 15

An alternating voltage of 220 V, 50 Hz frequency is applied across a capacitor of capacitance 5 μF. The impedance of the circuit is:

(a) $\dfrac{\pi}{2000}$ Ω (b) $2000\,\pi$ (c) $\dfrac{2000}{\pi}$ Ω (d) $\dfrac{1000}{\pi}$

Question 16

An electron moves along the line PQ which lies in the same plane at a circular loop of conducting wire as shown in the figure. Then choose the correct option from the following:

(a) The direction of induced current will be clockwise

(b) The direction of induced current will be anticlockwise

(c) No current will be induced

(d) The current will change direction as the electron pass by.

Question 17

A circuit PQRS is held perpendicular in a magnetic field of magnitude 5×10^{-2} T extending over the region ABCD and directed into the plane of the paper. The circuit PQRS is pulled out of the field at a uniform speed of 0.1 ms^{-1} for 2.0 s. The current in the 5 Ω resistor during this time will be :

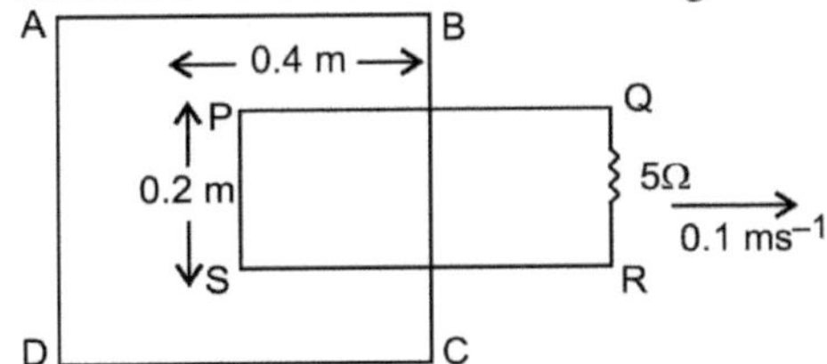

(a) 0.1 mA from S to Q   (b) 0.2 mA from Q to R   (c) 0.1 mA from Q to S   (d) 0.2 mA from S to Q

Question 18

A LC parallel resonant circuit:

(a) have zero impedance.

(b) have very high impedance.

(c) have a very high value of current.

(d) have resistance of very low value.

Question 19

The effective resistance between A and B when each resistance is of 4 Ω, is:

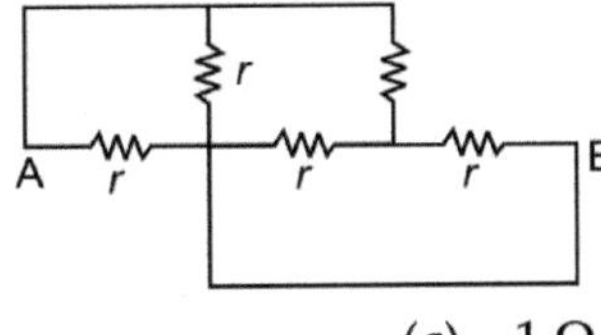

(a) 2 Ω (b) 3 Ω (c) 1 Ω (d) 8 Ω

Question 20

Which of the following statements is incorrect:

(a) Kirchoff's first law represents conservation of charge

(b) Kirchoff's second law represents conservation of energy

(c) In a balanced wheatstone bridge, if the cell and the galvanometer are exchanged, the null point is disturbed.

(d) Wheatstone bridge is the most sensitive when all the four resistance are of the same order of magnitude

Question 21

A battery of emf 8V with internal resistance 1 Ω is charged by a 136 V dc supply using a series resistance of 15 Ω. The terminal voltage of the battery is:

(a) 16 V   (b) 8 V   (c) 32 V   (d) 48 V

Question 22

A metre-bridge is set up with null deflection in the galvanometer. The value of unknown resistance R is:

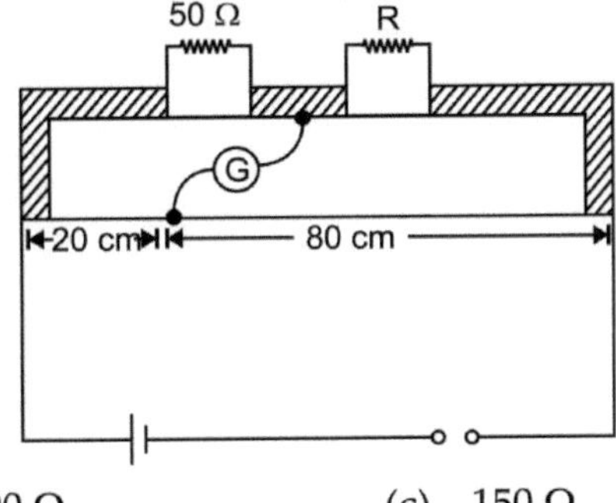

(a) 200 Ω (b) 100 Ω (c) 150 Ω (d) 110 Ω

Question 23

A copper wire has a resitance of 20 Ω and an area of cross-section 1 mm^2. A potential difference of 10 V is applied across the wire. If number of electrons per cubic metre in copper is 5×10^{28} electrons, then the drift speed of electrons will be:

(a) 0.0625×10^{-6} ms^{-1} (b) 62.5×10^{8} ms^{-1}

(c) 0.0625×10^{-3} ms^{-1} (b) 625 ms^{-1}

Question 24

The value of current I in the given circuit shown in figure, is :

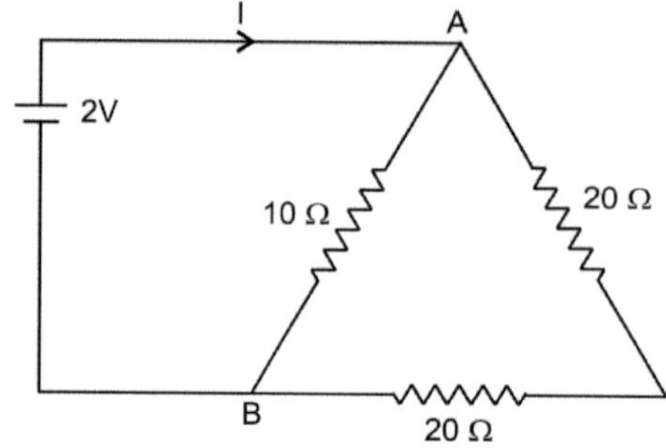

(a) 1 A   (b) 0.25 A   (c) 1.25 A   (d) 2A

Question 25

A circular coil of radius 20 cm and 100 turns carries current 2A. The magnetic moment of the coil is:

(a) 25.12 Am^{-2} (b) 2.5 Am^{2} (c) 25 Am^{2} (d) 0.2151 Am^{2}

Question 26

Shunt resistance required to allow 5% of the main current through the galvanometer of resistance 55 Ω is about:

(a) $2\,\Omega$ (b) $3\,\Omega$ (c) $1\,\Omega$ (d) $5\,\Omega$

Question 27

Two conducting spheres A and B having radius x and y respectively are at the same potential. The ratio of the surface charge densities of A and B is:

(a) $\dfrac{y^2}{x^2}$ (b) $\dfrac{x^2}{y^2}$ (c) $\dfrac{x}{y}$ (d) $\dfrac{y}{x}$

Question 28

Angle between the equipotential surface and electric lines of force is:

(a) 180°   (b) 0°   (c) 90°   (d) 60°

Question 29

The total energy stored in the condenser system shown in the figure will be:

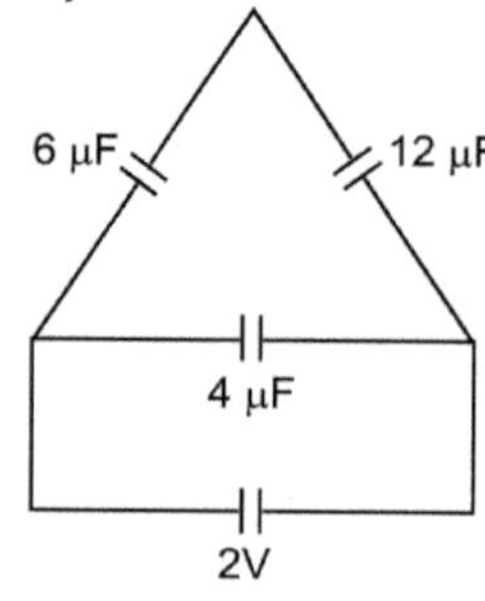

(a) 6 μJ   (b) 8 μJ   (c) 32 μJ   (d) 16 μJ

Question 30

Three charges placed at the vertex of an equilateral triangle is shown in the given figure. The electostatic potential energy is zero, for Q equal to:

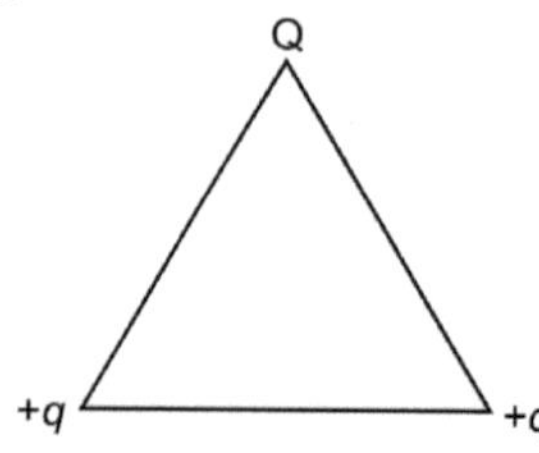

(a) $\dfrac{q}{2}$ (b) $2q$ (c) $-\dfrac{q}{2}$ (d) $-2q$

Question 31

If the direction of electric and magnetic field vectors of a plane electromagnetic wave are along positive y-direction and positive Z-direction, then the wave propagates a long:

(a) positive x-direction   (b) negative x-direction   (c) positive z-direction   (d) negative y-direction

Question 32

Which of the following is not an electromagnetic wave?

(a) Sound wave   (b) Radio waves   (c) Infrared waves   (d) Gamma rays

Question 33

The part of the electromagnetic spectrum having maximum wavelength is:

(a) Infrared waves   (b) Ratio waves   (c) X-rays   (d) Micro waves

Question 34

Consider the following types of electromagnetic waves:

(i) Green light   (ii) Gamma rays   (iii) Micro waves   (iv) X-rays

Which of the following sequences arranges these in the correct order of increasing wavelengths?

(a) (ii), (iv), (i), (iii)   (b) (i), (ii), (iii), (iv)   (c) (iv), (iii), (ii), (i)   (d) (i), (ii), (iv), (iii)

Question 35

An infinite line charge produce a field of magnitude 27×10^5 N/C at a distance of 4 cm. The linear charge density is:

(a) $6\ \mu C/m$ (b) $3\ \mu C/m$ (c) $8\ \mu C/m$ (d) $10\ \mu C/m$

Question 36

The nature of Gaussian surface involved in Gauss law of electrostatic is:

(a) Vector   (b) Scalar   (c) Electrical   (d) Magnetic

Question 37

An electron have an acceleration of 3.5 m/s^2 under the action of a given coulomb force. Then, the magnitude of the acceleration of a proton under the action of same force is nearly.

(a) 1.6×10^{19} ms^{-2} (b) 1.6×10^{-19} ms^{-2} (c) 1.9×10^{19} ms^{-2} (d) 1.9×10^{-19} ms^{-2}

Question 38

Potential at point O in the given network of resistances is:

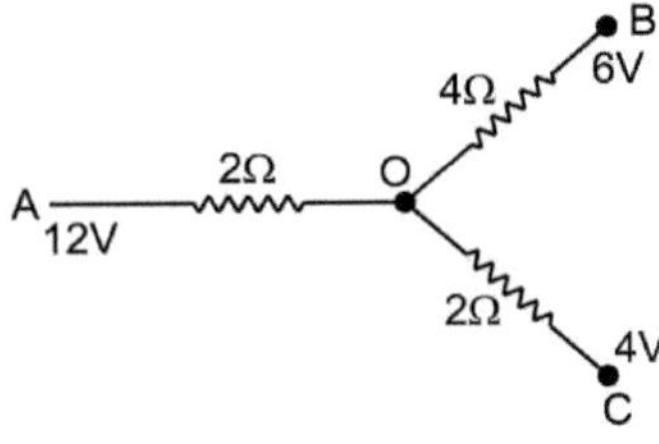

(a) 6.6 V   (b) 8 V   (c) 7.6 V   (d) 10 V

Question 39

A potentiometer wire of length 10 m and resistance 20 Ω is connected in series with a 20 V battery and an external resistance 40 Ω. A secondary cell of emf ε in the secondary circuit is balanced by 200 cm long potentiometer wire.

(i) What will be the current in the wire?

(a) $\dfrac{1}{2}$ A   (b) $\dfrac{1}{3}$ A   (c) 1A   (d) 2A

(ii) What is the emf ε of the cell?

(a) $\dfrac{1}{2}$ V   (b) $\dfrac{1}{3}$ V   (c) $\dfrac{4}{3}$ V   (d) $\dfrac{3}{4}$ V

Question 40

Two hollow concentric spheres S_1 and S_2 enclosing charges q and $2q$ is shown in figure.

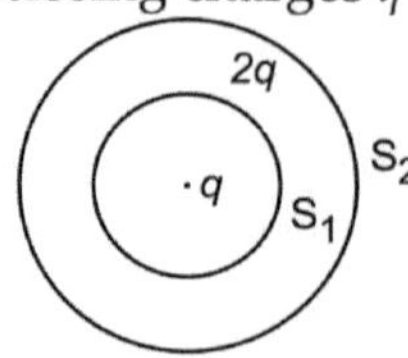

(i) What is the ratio of the electric flux through S_1 and S_2?

    (a) $1:2$ (b) $1:3$ (c) $1:1$ (d) $2:1$

(ii) If a medium of dielectric constant 3 is introduced in the space inside S_1 in place of air, then flux through S_1, is:

    (a) $\dfrac{Q}{\varepsilon_0}$ (b) $\dfrac{3Q}{\varepsilon_0}$ (c) $\dfrac{Q}{3\varepsilon_0}$ (d) $\dfrac{\varepsilon_0}{3Q}$

Question 41

A battery of emf 5V and internal resistance 0.1 Ω is connected to a resistor of 0.9 Ω as shown in figure.

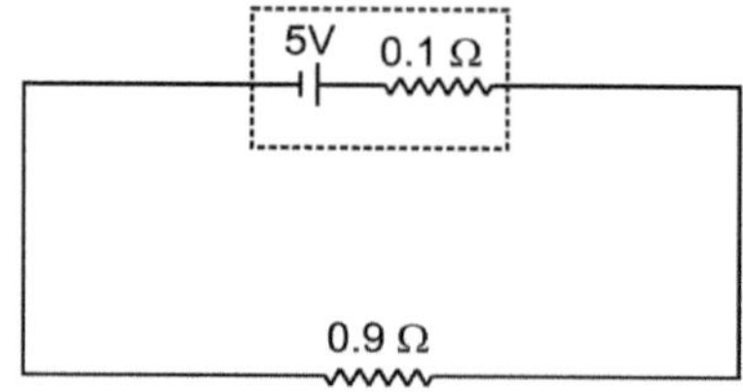

(i) What is the power generated by the cell?

    (a) 20 W   (b) 25 W   (c) 5 W   (d) 15 W

(ii) What is the rate at which energy is dissipated in the internal resistance?

    (a) 2.5 W   (b) 25 W   (c) 20 W   (d) 0.25 W

Question 42

A proton, a deuteron and an α-particle are moving with same momentum in a uniform magnetic field.

(i) What is the ratio of magnetic forces acting on them in the given order ?

    (a) $1:1:1$ (b) $2:1:1$ (c) $1:2:1$ (d) $1:1:2$

(ii) What is the ratio of their speeds in the given order?

    (a) $2:4:1$ (b) $1:4:2$ (c) $1:2:4$ (d) $4:2:1$

Question 43

A conductor of length 4.0 cm is placed parallel to a conductor of length 2.0 m near its centre at a distance 2.0 cm apart. The conductors carry currents 4.0 A and 2.0 A respectively in the same direction.

(i) What is the magnitude of magnetic field produced by the longer conductor?

    (a) 2×10^{-5} T   (b) 1×10^{-5} T   (c) 2×10^{-7} T   (d) 1×10^{-7} T

(ii) What is the total force experienced by the shorter conductor?

    (a) 1.2×10^{-6} N   (b) 3.0×10^{-8} N   (c) 3.0×10^{-7} N   (d) 3.2×10^{-6} N

Question 44

In the given circuit, current is to be measured, where the ammeter shown is a galvanometer with resistance 50 Ω.

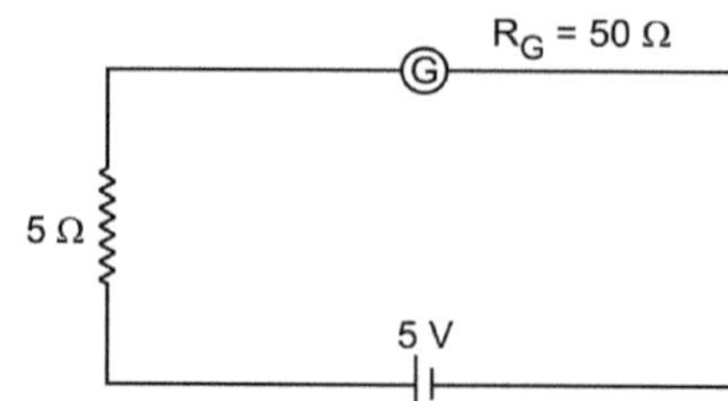

(i) What is the value of current measured by the galvanometer?

    (a) $\dfrac{1}{5}$ A   (b) $\dfrac{1}{2}$ A   (c) $\dfrac{1}{11}$ A   (d) $\dfrac{1}{10}$ A

(ii) What is the value of current if the galvanometer with resistance 50 Ω is converted to an ammeter by a shunt resistance r_S = 0.02 Ω?

    (a) 99 A   (b) 0.99 A   (c) 9 A   (d) 90 A

Question 45

A potential difference of 220 V is maintained across a 10,000 Ω rheostat AB. A volt meter V have a resistance of 5000 Ω and a point C is at one fourth of the distance from A to B.

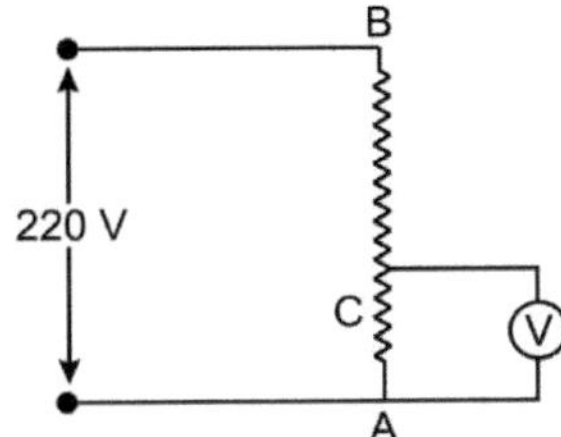

(i) What is the resistance between A and C ?

    (a) 2500 Ω   (b) 2000 Ω   (c) 3000 Ω   (d) 200 Ω

(ii) What is the effective resistance between points A and C?

    (a) 1100 Ω   (b) 2100 Ω   (c) 1666.7 Ω   (d) 2000 Ω

(iii) What is the reading in the voltmeter ?

    (a) 10 V   (b) 4 V   (c) 20 V   (d) 40 V

Question 46

An LCR series circuit with L = 100 mH, C = 100 μF and R = 120 Ω is connected to an ac source of emf, $\varepsilon = (30\ V) \sin (100\ S^{-1})t$, as shown in figure.

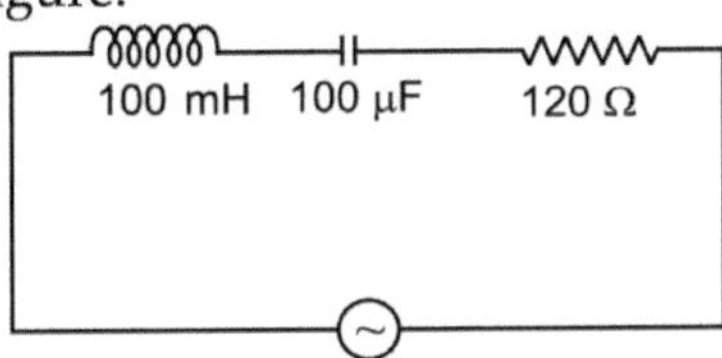

(i) What are the inductive and capacitive reactances?

    (a) 10 Ω, 100 Ω   (b) 10 Ω, 20 Ω   (c) 20 Ω, 100 Ω   (d) 10 Ω, 10 Ω

(ii) What is the impedance of the circuit?

    (a) 100 Ω   (b) 150 Ω   (c) 200 Ω   (d) 110 Ω

(iii) What is the value of peak current in the circuit?

    (a) 0.1 A   (b) 1 A   (c) 0.2 A   (d) 2A

Question 47

In the circuit shown in figure emf of the cell = 5V and each resistance = 7Ω.

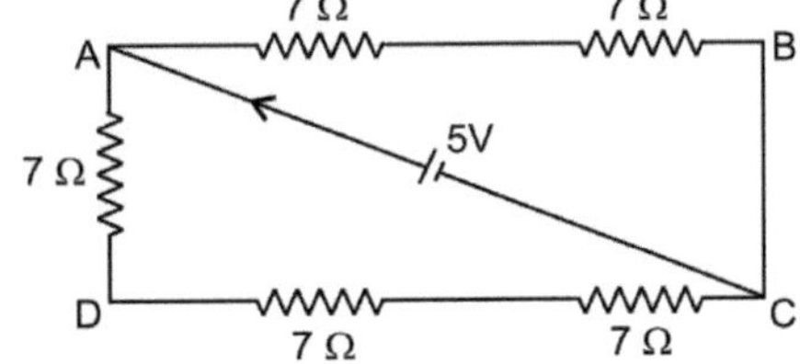

(i) The equivalent resistance of the circuit is:

    (a) $\dfrac{2}{21}\Omega$ (b) $\dfrac{21}{2}\Omega$ (c) 21 Ω   (d) $\dfrac{2}{11}\Omega$

(ii) Potential difference between A and B is:

    (a) $\dfrac{10}{3}V$ (b) $\dfrac{3}{10}V$ (c) $\dfrac{100}{3}V$ (d) $\dfrac{3}{100}V$

(iii) Potential difference between A and D is:

    (a) $\dfrac{5}{3}V$ (b) $\dfrac{3}{5}V$ (c) $\dfrac{50}{3}V$ (d) $\dfrac{3}{50}V$

Question 48

A circular coil of 100 turns and radius 20 cm is placed in a uniform magnetic field of 0.1 T normal to the plane of the coil. Current in the coil is 5 A.

(i) What is the torque on the coil?

    (a) 2 Nm   (b) zero   (c) 5 Nm   (d) 10 Nm

(ii) What is the total force on the coil?

    (a) zero   (b) 2 N   (c) 5 N   (d) 10 N

(iii) If the coil is made up of copper wire of cross-sectional area 10^{-5} m^2 and the free electron density in copper is 10^{29} m^{-3}, then what is the average force on each electron in the coil due to the magnetic field?

    (a) 5×10^{-10} N   (b) 5×10^{-20} N   (c) 5×10^{-15} N   (d) 5×10^{-25} N

Question 49

The electricity reaches our homes by passing through a network of various stags which includes generation, transmission and distribution of electric power. Electricity is generated in power plants using coal, water, wind, sun or even nuclear elements as source. This electricity is then converted into high voltage and transmitted to large substations using high voltage overhead lines. Substations further transmits electricity to a distribution network, where voltage is reduced to a safe and standard value. A transformer is a device which is used extensively in the power system to step up or step down voltage at different stages during generation and transmission of electric power.

(i) The core of a transformer is usually made of:

    (a) Steel   (b) Copper   (c) Soft iron   (d) Aluminium

(ii) Quantity that remains unchanged in a transformer is :

    (a) Voltage   (b) Current   (c) Frequency   (d) None of these

(iii) The core of a transformer is laminated to reduce:

    (a) flux leakage   (b) hysteresis   (c) copper loss   (d) eddy current

(iv) A transformer works on the principle of:

    (a) mutual induction   (b) magnetic effect of current

    (c) self induction   (d) chemical effect of current

Question 50

Mutual inductance is the main operating principle of various electrical machines such as generators, motors and transformers. Mutual induction is the interaction between the fields of two circuits, where change in the current in one circuit induces an emf in the other circuit.

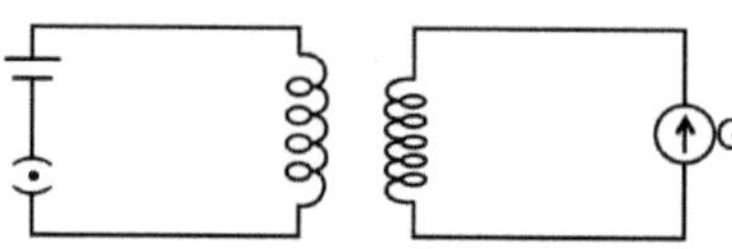

(i) How does the mutual inductance of a pair of coils change when the distance between the coils is increased?

    (a) increases   (b) decreases

    (c) remains same   (d) first increases then decreases

(ii) How does the mutual inductance of a pair of coils change when the number of turns in each coil is decreased?

    (a) increases   (b) decreases

    (c) remains same   (d) first increases then decreases

(iii) How does the mutual inductance of a pair of coils change when a thin iron sheet is placed between the two coils, other factors remaining the same?

    (a) increases   (b) decreases

    (c) remains same   (d) first increases then decreases

(iv) What is the coefficient of mutual inductance, when the magnetic flux changes by 3×10^{-2} Wb and change in current is 0.02 A?

    (a) 3.0 H   (b) 1 H   (c) 2.0 H   (d) 1.5 H

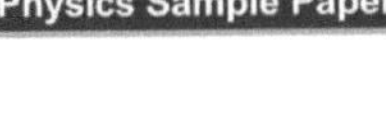

Answers

1. (c) 0.3853×10^6 C

Explanation: 2.0 mole of H_2 gas contains $2.0 \times 6.02 \times 10^{23}$ molecules

Each H_2 molecule contains 2 electrons/protons,

$$\therefore \quad n = 2 \times 2.0 \times 6.02 \times 10^{23}$$
$$= 24.08 \times 10^{23}$$
$$\therefore \quad q = ne$$
$$= 24.08 \times 10^{23} \times 1.6 \times 10^{-19}$$
$$= 0.3853 \times 10^6 \text{ C}$$

2. (a) 1

Explanation: $R = \rho \dfrac{l}{A}$

where ρ is a constant.

Let length of wire = L

Area of cross section = A

and Resistance = R

So, after increase new length = L

Area of cross section = A′

New resistance = R′

$$L' = L + 0.5\% \text{ of } L$$
$$= 1.005L$$

But, the volume remains same,

So, $\quad A' = \dfrac{A}{1.005}$

New resistance R′

$$= \dfrac{\rho \times 1.005 \times L}{A / 1.005}$$

$$= (1.005)^2 . R \qquad \left[\because R = \dfrac{\rho l}{A} \right]$$

$$\% \text{ charge} = \dfrac{R' - R}{R} \times 100$$

$$= \dfrac{(1.010)R - R}{R} \times 100\%$$

$$= 1\%$$

3. (c) 5A

Explanation: $\varepsilon = \dfrac{d\phi}{dt}$

$$= \dfrac{d}{dt}(5t^3 + 4t^2 + 2t - 5)$$

$$= 15t^2 + 8t + 2$$

At $t = 1s$,

$$|\varepsilon| = 15(1)^2 + 8(1) + 2$$
$$= 25 \text{ V}$$

Given, resistance of the coil, $R = 5\,\Omega$

$$\therefore \quad \text{Induced current, } I = \dfrac{|\varepsilon|}{R} = \dfrac{25}{5} = 5A$$

4. (a) Electric and magnetic fields are in the same phase.

Explanation: The energy is equally divided between electric and magnetic field in a electromagnetic wave. The speed of the electromagnetic wave is E/B.

5. (b) $\varepsilon_r F$

Explanation: Force between two point charges q_1 and q_2 placed in a material medium of dielectric constant ε_r at a distance r, is given by

$$\text{or} \qquad F = \dfrac{1}{4\pi\varepsilon_0 r} \left(\dfrac{q_1 q_2}{r^2} \right) . \dfrac{1}{\varepsilon_r} \qquad ...(i)$$

$$\left[\because F = \dfrac{1}{4\pi\varepsilon_0 r} \left(\dfrac{q_1 q_2}{r^2} \right) \right]$$

When the material is removed, $\qquad$ [Using (i)]

$$F' = F \times \varepsilon_r = F.\varepsilon_r$$

6. (a) 0.1 T

Explanation: Electric field intensity between the plates,

$$E = \dfrac{V}{d}$$

$$= \dfrac{600}{2 \times 10^{-3}}$$

$$= 3 \times 10^5 \text{ Vm}^{-1}$$

For an electron to remain undeflected, force due to magnetic field should be equal to the force due to the electric field.

$$\therefore \qquad Bev = eE$$

$$\text{or} \qquad B = \dfrac{E}{v} = \dfrac{3 \times 10^5}{3 \times 10^6} = 0.1 \text{ T}$$

7. (a) an attractive force on each other

Explanation: An attractive force occurs when two parallel wires carry currents in same direction.

8. (d) all of these

Explanation: $T = \dfrac{2\pi m}{qB}$

i.e., time depends on mass, charge and magnetic field.

9. (c) 80.67 W

Explanation: $P = \dfrac{V^2}{R}$

For first bulb, $100 = \dfrac{(200)^2}{R_1} \Rightarrow R_1 = 400\,\Omega$

For second bulb, $200 = \dfrac{(200)^2}{R_2} \Rightarrow R_2 = 200\ \Omega$

When the two bulbs connected in series, equivalent resistance is

$$R = R_1 + R_2 = 600\ \Omega$$

$\therefore$ Total power consumed

$$= \dfrac{(220)^2}{600} = 80.67\ \text{W}$$

10. (b) $0.003°C^{-1}$

Explanation: $T_1 = 100°C$, $T_2 = 400°C$

$R_{T_1} = 100\ \Omega$ and $R_{T_2} = 200\ \Omega$

Temperature coefficient,

$$\alpha = \dfrac{R_{T_2} - R_{T_1}}{R_{T_1}(T_2 - T_1)}$$

$$= \dfrac{200 - 100}{100(400 - 100)}$$

$$= \dfrac{100}{100 \times 300} = 0.003°C^{-1}$$

11. (d) $5\ \Omega$

Explanation: Let R be the resistance of total length of the circular wire, *i.e.*, R = 36 Ω.

Resistance of arc PQ, $R_1 = \dfrac{R}{6} = 6\Omega$

Resistance of rest of the circular wire,

$$R_2 = \dfrac{R - R_1}{6}$$

$$= 36 - 6$$

$$= 30\ \Omega$$

Now R_1 and R_2 are in parallel between points P and Q.

$\therefore$ Effective resistance between P and Q is,

$$R_{PQ} = \dfrac{6 \times 30}{6 + 30} = 5\Omega$$

12. (c) $3\ \Omega$

Explanation: Internal resistance of the cell is

$$r = R\left(\dfrac{l_1 - l_2}{l_2}\right)$$

$$= 2\left(\dfrac{250 - 100}{100}\right) = 3\Omega$$

13. (d) $180°$

Explanation: The direction of electric field at any point on the equatorial line is opposite to the dipole moment. Thus, angle between $\vec{p}$ and $\vec{E}$ is $180°$.

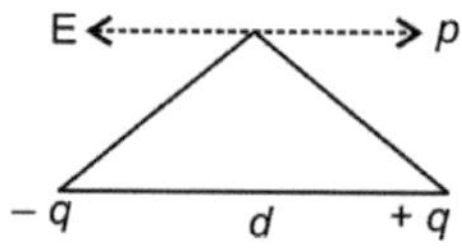

14. (a) $7\pi\ \text{kV m}^{-1}$

Explanation: $A = 7\ cm^2$, $d = 1\ cm$, $q = 10\ nC$

Electric field between the plates,

$$E = \dfrac{q}{\varepsilon_0 A}$$

$$= \dfrac{10 \times 10^{-9}}{\dfrac{10^{-9}}{49\pi} \times (7 \times 10^{-4})}$$

$$= 7\pi \times 10^5$$

$$= 7\pi\ \text{kV m}^{-1}$$

15. (c) $\dfrac{2000}{\pi}\ \Omega$

Explanation: Impedance of capacitor, $X_C = \dfrac{1}{\omega C}$

or $\quad X_C = \dfrac{1}{2\pi f C}$

$$= \dfrac{1}{2\pi \times 50 \times 5 \times 10^{-6}}$$

$$= \dfrac{2000}{\pi}\ \Omega$$

16. (d) The current will change direction as the electron pass by.

Explanation: If electron is moving from left to right, the flux linked with will first increase and then decrease as the electron passes by. So the induced current in the loop will be first move anticlock wise and will charge direction as the electron passes by.

17. (b) 0.2 mA from Q to R

Explanation: $\phi = Blx$

$$|\varepsilon| = \dfrac{d\phi}{dt} = Bl\left(\dfrac{dx}{dt}\right)$$

$$\varepsilon = 5 \times 10^{-2} \times 0.2 \times 0.1$$

$$= 1 \times 10^{-3}\ \text{V}$$

Current, $i = \dfrac{\varepsilon}{R} = \dfrac{10^{-3}}{5} = 0.2 \times 10^{-3} = 0.2\ \text{mA}$

The direction of current will be clockwise *i.e.*, from Q to R through the 5 Ω resistor.

18. (b) have very high impedance.

Explanation: LC parallel resonant circuit has a very high impedance and hence a very low value of current.

19. (c) $1\ \Omega$

Explanation: Here, all resistances are connected in parallel.

$$\therefore \quad \frac{1}{R_{AB}} = \frac{1}{r} + \frac{1}{r} + \frac{1}{r} + \frac{1}{r} = \frac{4}{r}$$

or $\quad R_{AB} = \dfrac{r}{4} = \dfrac{4}{4} = 1\,\Omega$

20. (c) In a balanced wheatstone bridge, if the cell and the galvanometer are exchanged, the null point is disturbed.

21. (a) 16 V

Explanation: Effective emf in the circuit,
$\varepsilon = 136\,V - 8V = 128\,V$

Total resistance of the circuit $= R + r = 15 + 1$
$= 16\,\Omega$

$\therefore$ Current in the circuit during charging

$$I = \frac{\varepsilon}{R + r}$$

$$= \frac{128\,V}{16\,\Omega} = 8A$$

Now, terminal voltage of the battery during charging,

$$V = \varepsilon_b + Ir$$
$$= 8V + Ir$$
$$= 8V + 8A \times (1\,\Omega)$$
$$= 8V + 8V$$
$$= 16\,V$$

22. (a) $200\,\Omega$

Explanation: Balance condition for a meter bridge

$$\frac{S}{R} = \frac{l}{100 - l}$$

$$\Rightarrow \quad \frac{50}{R} = \frac{20}{80}$$

or $\quad R = \dfrac{80 \times 50}{20} = 200\,\Omega$

23. (c) $0.0625 \times 10^{-3}\ ms^{-1}$

Explanation: $I = neAv_d$

or $\quad \dfrac{V}{R} = neAv_d$

or $\quad v_d = \dfrac{V}{neAR}$

$$= \frac{10}{5 \times 10^{28} \times 1.6 \times 10^{-19} \times 10^{-6} \times 20}$$

$$= 0.0625 \times 10^{-3}\ ms^{-1}$$

24. (b) 0.25 A

Explanation: Effective resistance of the circuit,

$$R = \frac{10 \times 40}{10 + 40} = 8\,\Omega$$

Current, $I = \dfrac{V}{R} = \dfrac{2}{8} = 0.25\ A$

25. (a) $25.12\ Am^{-2}$

Explanation:
$$M = NIA = NI \times \pi r^2$$
$$= 100 \times 2 \times 3.14\,(20 \times 10^{-2})^2$$
$$= 25.12\ Am^{-2}$$

26. (b) $3\,\Omega$

Explanation:

$$S = \frac{I_g G}{(I - I_g)}$$

$$= \frac{0.05\,I \times 55}{(I - 0.05\,I)}$$

$$= \frac{0.05 \times 55}{0.95}$$

$$= 2.89\,\Omega$$

$$\simeq 3\,\Omega$$

27. (d) $\dfrac{y}{x}$

Explanation: Given that, potential of A = potential of B

$$\therefore \quad \frac{1}{4\pi\varepsilon_0}\frac{Q_1}{x} = \frac{1}{4\pi\varepsilon_0}\frac{Q_2}{y}$$

or $\quad \dfrac{Q_1}{x} = \dfrac{Q_2}{y}$

Surface charge density $\sigma = \dfrac{\theta}{4\pi r^2}$

or $\quad \dfrac{4\pi x^2 \sigma_1}{x} = \dfrac{4\pi y^2 \sigma_2}{y}$

or $\quad x\sigma_1 = y\sigma_2$

or $\quad \dfrac{\sigma_1}{\sigma_2} = \dfrac{y}{x}$

28. (c) $90°$

Explanation: Angle between an equipotential surface and electric lines of force is $90°$.

29. (d) $16\ \mu J$

Explanation: $6\ \mu F$ and $12\ \mu F$ are in series,

$$C' = \frac{6 \times 12}{6 + 12}$$

$$C' = 4\ \mu F$$

C' is in parallel with $4\ \mu F$

$\therefore \quad C_{eq} = (4 + 4)\ \mu F = 8\ \mu F$

Total energy stored in the condenser system

$$E = \frac{1}{2}C_{eq}V^2$$

$$= \frac{1}{2} \times 8 \times 10^{-6} \times (2)^2$$

$$= 16 \times 10^{-6} = 16\ \mu J$$

30. (c) $-\dfrac{q}{2}$

Explanation: Electrostatic potential energy of the system of charges is:

$$U = \frac{1}{4\pi\varepsilon_0}\left[\frac{Qq}{r}+\frac{Qq}{r}+\frac{q^2}{r}\right]$$

$$= \frac{1}{4\pi\varepsilon_0 r}[2Qq+q^2)$$

Given that, $U = 0$

$\therefore \quad 2Qq + q^2 = 0$

or $\qquad Q = -\dfrac{q}{2}$

31. (a) positive x-direction

Explanation: In electromagnetic wave, the direction of wave propagation is along $\vec{E}\times\vec{B}$

$i.e.\,(+\hat{j})\times(+\hat{k}) = \hat{i}$

It will always be positive in x direction $= \hat{i}$

32. (a) Sound wave

Explanation: Sound waves are mechanical waves which requires medium to travel whereas EM waves do not require any medium and can travel through vacuum.

33. (b) Ratio waves

Explanation: Radio waves have minimum frequency and hence have maximum wavelength in the electromagnetic spectrum.

34. (a) (ii), (iv), (i), (iii)

Explanation: In the order of increasing wavelengths, the rays are Gamma rays, X-rays, Green light and micro waves.

35. (a) $6\ \mu C/m$

Explanation: $E = 27\times10^5$ N/C, $r = 4$ cm $= 4\times10^{-2}$ m

For infinite line charge,

$$E = \frac{\lambda}{2\pi\varepsilon_0 r}$$

$$\Rightarrow \quad \lambda = 2\pi\varepsilon_0 Er = \frac{EXr}{2\left(\dfrac{1}{4\pi\varepsilon_0}\right)}$$

$$\Rightarrow \quad \lambda = \frac{27\times10^5\times4\times10^{-2}}{2\times9\times10^9}$$

$$= 6\times10^{-6}\ C/m$$

$$= 6\ \mu C/m$$

36. (c) Electrical

Explanation: Gaussian surface has a direction outwards the enclosed path and it obeys vector algebra rules. Thus, it is a vector in nature.

37. (c) $\simeq 1.9\times10^{19}$ ms^{-2}

Explanation: Acceleration of the electron,

$$a_e = \frac{F}{m_e}$$

Acceleration of the proton, $a_p = \dfrac{F}{m_p}$

For the same coulombic force,

$$\frac{a_P}{a_e} = \frac{m_e}{m_p}$$

or $\qquad a_p = \dfrac{a_e m_e}{m_p}$

$$= \frac{3.5\times10^{22}(\text{ms}^{-2})\times9.1\times10^{-31}(\text{kg})}{(1.67\times10^{-27}\text{kg})}$$

$$= 19.07\times10^{18}\ \text{ms}^{-2}$$

$$\simeq 1.9\times10^{19}\ \text{ms}^{-2}$$

38. (c) 7.6 V

Explanation: Using Kirchoff's current law,

$$I_A = I_B + I_C$$

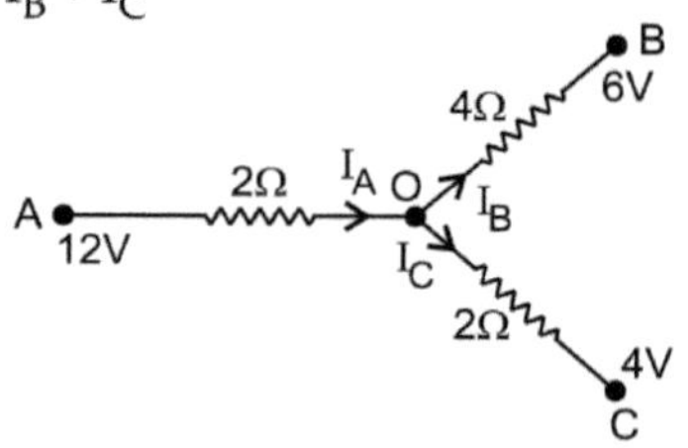

$$\frac{V_O - V_O}{O_{AO}} = \frac{V_O - V_B}{R_{OB}} + \frac{V_O - V_C}{R_{OC}}$$

$$\frac{12 - V_0}{2} = \frac{V_0 - 6}{4} + \frac{V_0 - 4}{2}$$

$$5V_0 = 38$$

$\therefore\ \ V_0 = 7.6$ V

39. (i) (b) $\dfrac{1}{3}$ A

Explanation:

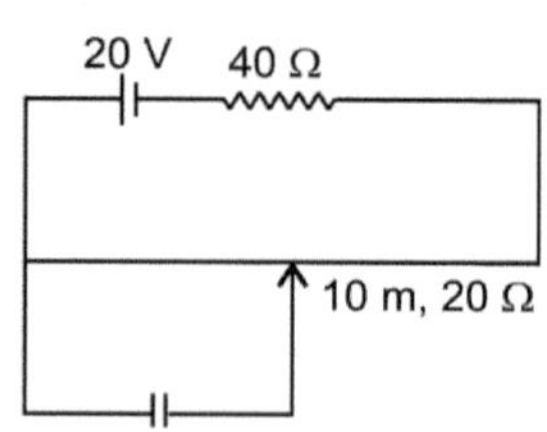

$$i = \frac{20}{(40+20)} = \frac{20}{60} = \frac{1}{3}\text{ A}$$

(ii) (c) $\dfrac{4}{3}$ V

Explanation: Resistance of 200 cm length of wire

$$R = \frac{20}{10}\times2.0 = 4\Omega$$

$$\varepsilon = iR = \frac{1}{3}\times4 = \frac{4}{3}\text{ V}$$

40. (i) (b) $1:3$

Explanation: By Gauss's theorem,

Flux through S_1, $\phi_1 = \dfrac{q}{\varepsilon_0}$

Flux through S_2, $\phi_2 = \dfrac{2q+q}{\varepsilon_0} = \dfrac{3q}{\varepsilon_0}$

$\therefore \quad \dfrac{\phi_1}{\phi_2} = \dfrac{q/\varepsilon_0}{3q/\varepsilon_0} = \dfrac{1}{3}$

(ii) (c) $\dfrac{Q}{3\varepsilon_0}$

Explanation: Flux through S, when a medium of dielectric constant k is introduced in the space inside S_1

$$\phi_1' = \oint \vec{E}.\overrightarrow{dS} = \oint \dfrac{\vec{E}}{k}\overrightarrow{dS}$$

$$= \dfrac{1}{k}\oint \vec{E}.\overrightarrow{dS}$$

$$= \dfrac{1}{k}\cdot\dfrac{q}{\varepsilon_0}$$

Given that, $k = 3$,

$\therefore \qquad \phi_1' = \dfrac{q}{3\varepsilon_0}$

41. (i) (b) 25 W

Explanation: Current through the circuit,

$$i = \dfrac{E}{R+r}$$

$$i = \dfrac{5V}{(0.9\Omega + 0.1\Omega)}$$

Power generated by the cell, $P = E.i$

$$= 5V \times 5A$$
$$= 25 \text{ W}$$

(ii) (a) 2.5 W

Explanation: Rate at which energy is dissipated in the internal resistance $= i^2 r$

$$= (5)^2 \times 0.1 \ \Omega$$
$$= 2.5 \text{ W}$$

42. (i) (b) $2:1:1$

Explanation: Force on a charged particle due to a given field $= Bqv$

$\therefore \quad F = Bq\left(\dfrac{p}{m}\right)$, where p is momentum

or $\quad F = Bp\left(\dfrac{q}{m}\right)$

B and p are same for all the particles.

$\therefore \qquad F \propto \dfrac{q}{m}$

$\therefore \qquad F_p : F_d : F_\alpha = \dfrac{1}{1} : \dfrac{1}{2} : \dfrac{2}{4}$

$$= 2:1:1$$

(ii) (d) $4:2:1$

Explanation: Velocity, $v = \dfrac{p}{m} = \dfrac{\text{momentum}}{\text{mass}}$

$\therefore \qquad v \propto \dfrac{1}{m}$

$\therefore \qquad v_\alpha : v_d : v_p = \dfrac{1}{4} : \dfrac{1}{2} : \dfrac{1}{1}$

$$= 1:2:4$$

or $\qquad v_p : v_d : v_\alpha = 4:2:1$

43. (i) (a) 2×10^{-5} T

Explanation: As the two conductors are of different lengths, thus the longer conductor can be considered to be of infinite length. Therefore, magnetic field produced by it at a distance 2.0 cm from the shortes conductor, will be,

$$B = \dfrac{\mu_0 I_2}{2\pi r}$$

$$= \dfrac{4\pi \times 10^{-7} \times 2}{2\pi \times 0.02} \text{ T}$$

$$= 2 \times 10^{-5} \text{ T}$$

(ii) (d) 3.2×10^{-6} N

Explanation: Force on the shorter conductor due to the magnetic field of longer conductor will be,

$$F = BI_1 l_1 = 2 \times 10^{-5} \times 4 \times 4 \times 10^{-2} \text{ N}$$
$$= 3.2 \times 10^{-6} \text{ N}$$

44. (i) (c) $\dfrac{1}{11}$ A

Explanation: The ammeter shown is a galvanometer with resistance $R_G = 50 \ \Omega$

$\therefore$ Current in the circuit,

$$I = \dfrac{5}{55} = \dfrac{1}{11} \text{ A}$$

(ii) (b) 0.99 A

Explanation: When, the galvanometer is converted into ammeter by using a shunt resistance, the equivalent resistance of ammeter is:

$$R_{eq} = \dfrac{R_G r_S}{r_S + R_G}$$

$$= \dfrac{50 \times 0.02}{0.02 + 50} \simeq 0.02 \ \Omega$$

Total resistance in the circuit,

$$R = 5 + 0.02 = 5.02 \ \Omega$$

Hence current $I = \dfrac{5}{5.02} = 0.99$ A

45. **(i)** **(a)** 2500 Ω

Explanation: For a linear rheostat, R ∝ length

$$\therefore \qquad \frac{R_{AC}}{R_{AB}} = \frac{AC}{AB}$$

where, $R_{AB} = 10,000\ \Omega$ and $AC = \dfrac{1}{4}AB$

$$\therefore\ R_{AC} = 10,000 \times \frac{1}{4} = 2500\ \Omega$$

(ii) **(c)** 1666.7 Ω

Explanation: As the resistance $R_{AC} = 2500\ \Omega$ is in parallel with the voltmeter of resistance 5000 Ω therefore, the effective resistance between points A and C will be:

$$R'_{AC} = \frac{2500 \times 5000}{2500 + 5000} = 1666.7\ \Omega$$

(iii) **(d)** 40 V

Explanation: Resistance between points B and C

$$R_{BC} = R_{AB} - R_{AC} = 10,000\ \Omega - 2500\ \Omega$$
$$= 7500\ \Omega$$

R_{BC} and R'_{AC} are in series, thus voltmeter reading will be

$$V_{AC} = \frac{R'_{AC}V_{AB}}{(R_{BC} + R'_{AC})}$$

$$= \frac{1666.7 \times 220}{(7500 + 1666.7)}$$

$$= 40\ V$$

46. **(i)** **(a)** 10 Ω, 100 Ω

Explanation: Here, $\omega = 100$ rad s^{-1}

Inductive reactance, $X_L = \omega L$
$$= 100 \times 100 \times 10^{-3}$$
$$= 10\ \Omega$$

Capacitive reactance,

$$X_C = \frac{1}{\omega C}$$

$$= \frac{1}{100 \times 100 \times 10^{-6}}$$

$$= 100\ \Omega$$

(ii) **(b)** 150 Ω

Explanation: Impedance of the LCR circuit is:

$$Z = \sqrt{R^2 + (X_L - X_C)^2}$$

$$= \sqrt{(120)^2 + (10 - 100)^2}$$

$$Z = \sqrt{(120)^2 + (-90)^2}$$

$$= 150\ \Omega$$

(iii) **(c)** 0.2 A

Explanation: Peak current, $I_0 = \dfrac{\varepsilon_0}{Z} = \dfrac{30\ V}{150\ \Omega}$

$$= 0.2\ A$$

47. **(i)** **(b)** $\dfrac{21}{2}\Omega$

Explanation: ABC and ADC are in parallel.

$$R_{ABC} = 21\ \Omega$$
$$\text{and} \qquad R_{ADC} = 21\ \Omega$$

$$\therefore \qquad \frac{1}{R_{eq}} = \frac{1}{21}\Omega + \frac{1}{21}\Omega$$

$$\Rightarrow \frac{21}{2}\ \Omega$$

(ii) **(a)** $\dfrac{10}{3}V$

Explanation: Current in the circuit,

$$I = \frac{V}{R} = \frac{5}{21/2}$$

$$= \frac{10}{21}A$$

Thus, current in equally distributed in the two branches.

$$V_{AB} = iR_{AB}$$
$$\text{or} \qquad V_{AB} = \frac{5}{21} \times 14$$

$$= \frac{10}{3}\ V$$

(iii) **(a)** $\dfrac{5}{3}V$

Explanation: $\qquad V_{AD} = i \times R_{AD}$

$$= \frac{5}{21} \times 7 = \frac{5}{3}\ V$$

48. **(i)** **(b)** zero

Explanation: Magnetic field is normal to the plane of the coil, so condition of minimum torque occurs.

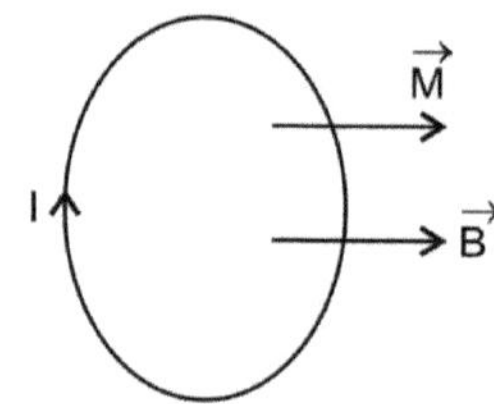

Torque on the coil, $\tau = NIBA \sin \theta$

Here $\theta = 0°$, $\therefore\ \tau = 0$

(ii) **(a)** zero

Explanation: Force on every element of the coil is cancelled by the force on corresponding element.

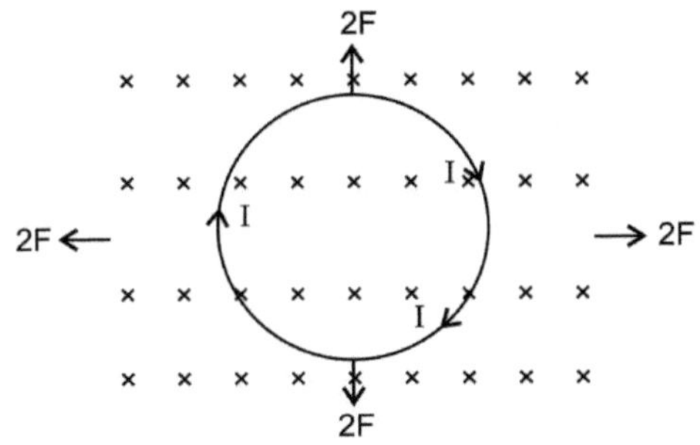

Net force is zero.

(iii) (d) 5×10^{-25} N

Explanation: To calculate force on each electron, let us find the drift velocity.

We know that, $i = neAv_d$

$$\therefore \quad v_d = \frac{i}{neA}$$

$$= \frac{5}{10^{29} \times 1.6 \times 10^{-19}} \times 10^{-5}$$

or $\quad v_d = 3.125 \times 10^{-5}$ ms^{-1}

Now, force $F = qv_d B$

$$= 1.6 \times 10^{-19} \times 3.125 \times 10^{-5} \times 0.1$$

$$= 5 \times 10^{-25} \text{ N}$$

49. (i) (c) Soft iron

Explanation: The core of a transformer is usually made of soft iron.

(ii) (c) Frequency

Explanation: A transformer does not change the frequency of the AC supply.

(iii) (d) eddy current

Explanation: The core of a transformer is laminated to reduce eddy currents.

(iv) (a) mutual induction

Explanation: The transformer works on the principle of mutual induction.

50. (i) (b) decreases

Explanation: The mutual inductance of two coils decreases when the distance between them is increased. This is because, the flux passing from one coil to another, decreases.

(ii) (b) decreases

Explanation: Mutual inductance,

$$M = \frac{\mu_0 N_1 N_2 A}{l}$$

i.e., $\qquad M \propto N_1 N_2$

Thus, when the number of turns N_1 and N_2 in the two coils is decreased, the mutual inductance are decreased.

(iii) (a) increases

Explanation: When an iron sheet is placed between the two coils, the mutual inductance increases because $M \propto$ permeability (μ).

(iv) (d) 1.5 H

Explanation: As $\phi = MI$

$$\therefore \qquad \Delta\phi = M\Delta I$$

or $\qquad M = \dfrac{\Delta\phi}{\Delta I}$

$$= \frac{3 \times 10^{-2}}{0.02} = 1.5 \text{H}$$

❑❑

Question 1

Which of the following is the property of charge?

(a) Two types of charge.

(b) Quantization of charge.

(c) Total charge conservation.

(d) All of these.

Question 2

Choose the incorrect statement for the electric field lines.

(a) Field lines starts from positive charges and end at negative charges.

(b) Field lines can be considered to be continuous curves without any breaks in a charge free region.

(c) Two field lines can never intersect each other.

(d) Electric field lines can form closed loops.

Question 3

Two point charges $+ 6\ \mu C$ and $- 6\ \mu C$ are placed at A and B, 20 cm apart as shown in the figure. The electric field at C, 20 cm apart from both A and B, is :

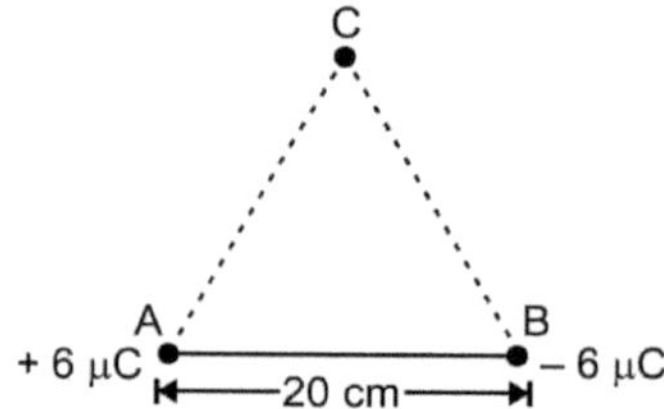

(a) 1.35×10^4 N/C

(b) 1.35×10^6 N/C

(c) 0.35×10^2 N/C

(d) 0.35×10^6 N/C

Question 4

Electric flux through a surface element $\overrightarrow{dS} = 4\hat{i}$ placed in an electric field $\overrightarrow{E} = (5\hat{i} + 4\hat{j} + 9\hat{k})$, is :

(a) 20 units

(b) 40 units

(c) 16 units

(d) 36 units

Question 5

An AC source of voltage $E = 30 \sin 100\ t$ is connected across a resistance 30 Ω. The RMS value of current in the circuit will be:

(a) $\dfrac{1}{2}$ A

(b) 1 A

(c) $\dfrac{1}{\sqrt{2}}$ A

(d) $\sqrt{2}$ A

Question 6

An electron is moving in straight line near a conducting circular loop. The direction of induced current if any in the loop is :

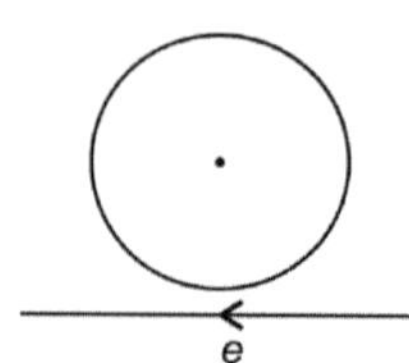

(a) Zero

(b) Clockwise

(c) Anticlockwise

(d) Variable

Question 7

The mutual electrostatic potential energy between two point charges of 12 and 5 microcoulombs, placed 10 cm apart in air, is:

(a) 5.4 J　　　　(b) 2. 8 J　　　　(c) 3. 6 J　　　　(d) 4. 8 J

Question 8

An electric dipole of moment $\vec{p}$ is placed in an uniform electric field $\vec{E}$. Then

(i) the torque on the dipole is $\vec{p} \times \vec{E}$.

(ii) the potential energy of the system is $\vec{p} \cdot \vec{E}$.

(iii) the resultant force on the dipole is zero.

(a) (i), (ii) and (iii) are correct.

(b) (i) and (iii) are correct and (ii) is wrong.

(c) only (ii) is correct.

(d) (i) and (ii) are correct and (iii) is wrong.

Question 9

A network of six identical capacitors, each of capacity 2 µF, is made as shown in figure. The equivalent capacitance between the points A and B is:

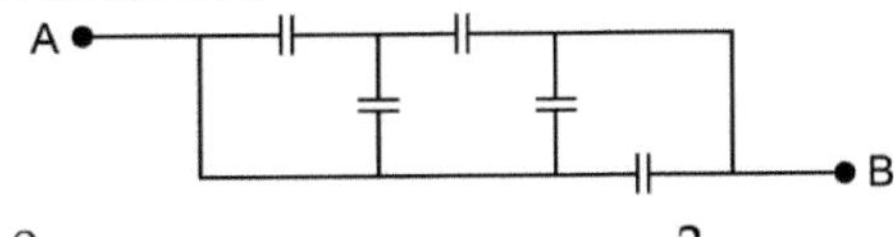

(a) $\dfrac{4}{3}$ µF　　　　(b) $\dfrac{8}{3}$ µF　　　　(c) $\dfrac{2}{3}$ µF　　　　(d) $\dfrac{3}{4}$ µF

Question 10

The electrical potential V at any point x, y, z (all in metres) in space is given by $V = 8x^2$ V. The electric field (in V/m) at points (1m, 0, 2m) is given by

(a) $8\,\hat{i}$　　　　(b) $16\,\hat{i}$　　　　(c) $-16\,\hat{i}$　　　　(d) $-8\,\hat{i}$

Question 11

A uniform electric field in the plane of the paper is as shown in the figure, where A, B, C, D are the points on the circle and V_1, V_2, V_3, V_4 are the potentials at the respective points. Then,

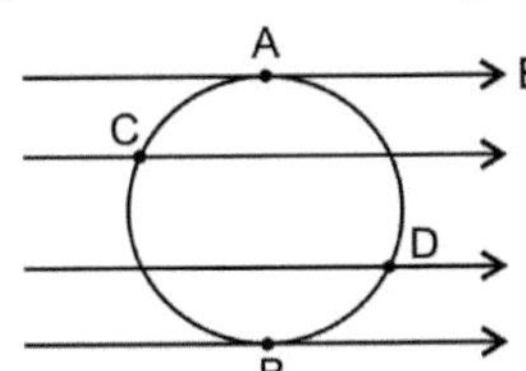

(a) $V_A = V_C$, $V_B > V_D$　　(b) $V_A = V_B$, $V_C > V_D$　　(c) $V_A = V_C$, $V_B = V_D$　　(d) $V_A > V_C$, $V_B > V_D$

Question 12

Two point charges q and $-q$ separated by a distance $2x$ constitute a electric dipole. Then, direction of the axis of this dipole is:

(a) from positive charge to negative charge

(b) perpendicular to the line joining the two charges drawn at the centre and pointing in upward direction

(c) perpendicular to the line joining the two charges drawn at the centre and pointing in downward direction

(d) from negative charge to positive charge.

Question 13

Three concentric metallic spherical shells of radii $r, 2r, 3r$ are given charges q_1, q_2, q_3 respectively. If the surface charge density on the outer surfaces of the shells are equal, then the ratio of the charges given to the shells is:

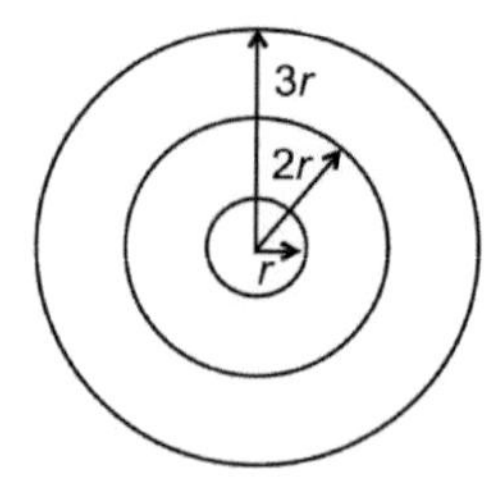

(a) $1:3:5$ (b) $1:2:4$ (c) $1:5:2$ (d) $1:1:1$

Question 14

The magnetic field due to a current in a straight wire segment of length L at a point on its perpendicular bisector at a distance r ($r \gg L$).

(a) decreases as $\dfrac{1}{r}$ (b) decreases as $\dfrac{1}{r^3}$ (c) decreases as $\dfrac{1}{r^2}$ (d) increases as r^2

Question 15

A straight wire of length 100 cm carrying a current of 5A is suspended in mid-air by a uniform magnetic field of 0.5 T, as shown in figure. Then the mass of the wire is (Take, $g = 10$ ms^{-2}).

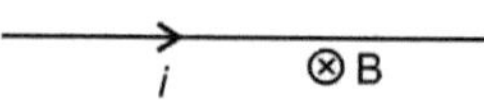

(a) 100 gm   (b) 25 gm   (c) 150 gm   (d) 250 gm

Question 16

Five conductors carrying currents are meeting at a point O, as shown in figure. The value of current I in the fifth conductor is:

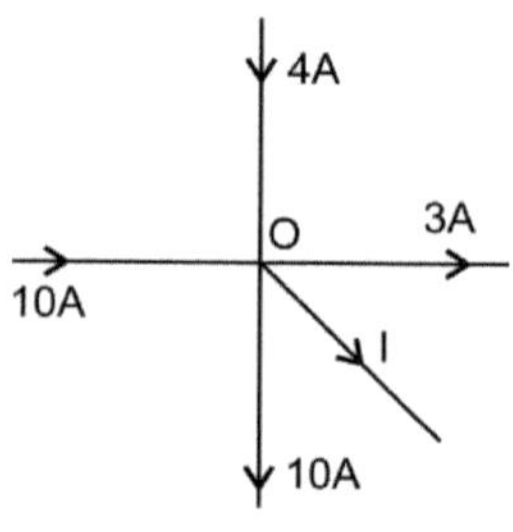

(a) 2 A   (b) 10 A   (c) 1 A   (d) 5 A

Question 17

Three resistances P, Q and R each of resistance 5 Ω and an unknown resistance S form the four arms of a Wheatstone bridge circuit. When a resistance of 10 Ω is connected in parallel to S, the bridge gets balanced. The value of S is:

(a) 10 Ω   (b) 5 Ω   (c) 20 Ω   (d) 2 Ω

Question 18

A cell of fractional internal resistance and emf 5 V is connected in a series combination of three resistances 1 Ω, 1 Ω and 3 Ω, as shown in figure. Then, the potential difference across 3 Ω resistance is :

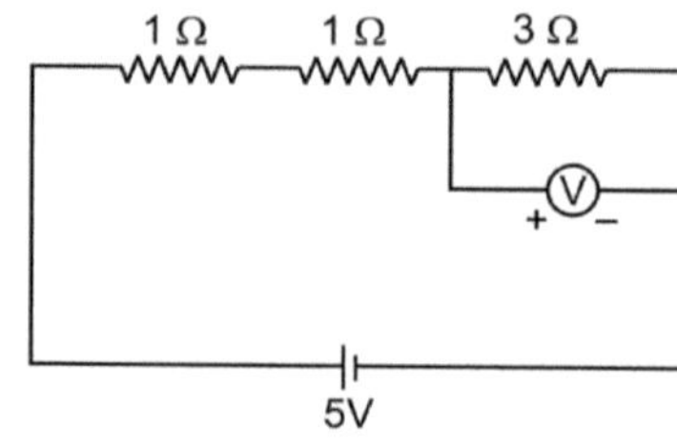

(a) 2V   (b) 3V   (c) 1V   (d) 5V

Question 19

The fractional increase in resistivity per unit increase in temperature is:

(a) drift velocity   (b) conductivity

(c) resistivity   (d) temperature coefficient of resistivity

Question 20

The resistance across P and Q shown in the figure, will be :

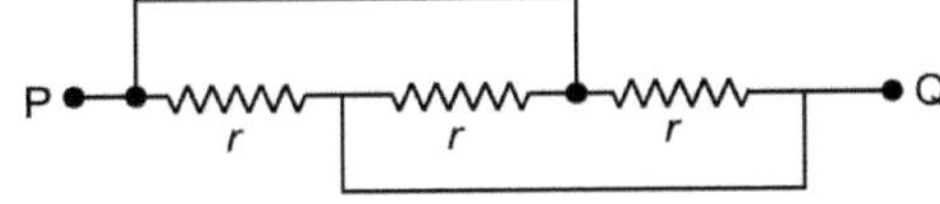

(a) $\dfrac{r}{3}$

(b) $\dfrac{r}{2}$

(c) $2r$

(d) $3r$

Question 21

A series LCR circuit consist of a capacitor of capacitive reactance 30 Ω, a non-inductive resistor of 42 Ω and a coil of inductive reactance 90 Ω and resistances 38 Ω. The circuit is connected across a 200 V, 50 Hz line as shown in figure. The power disssipated in the coil is:

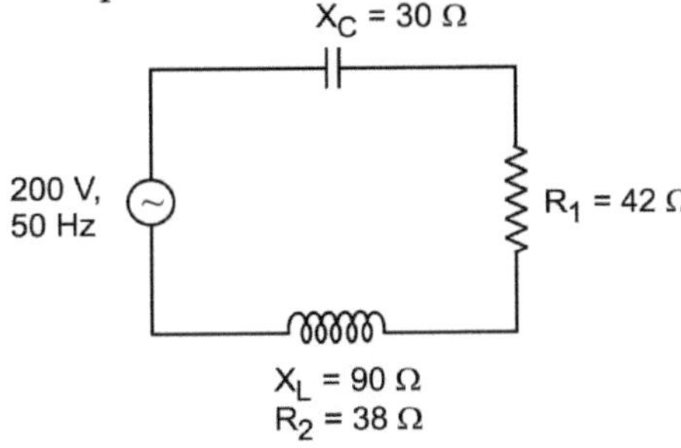

(a) 152 W

(b) 178 W

(c) 144 W

(d) 160 W

Question 22

A wire of certain cross-section carrying a current of 2 ampere. The number of electrons flowing through the wire is:

(a) 2.25×10^{19}

(b) 6.25×10^{19}

(c) 1.25×10^{19}

(d) 0.25×10^{19}

Question 23

The graph between voltage and current across a conductor that follows ohm's law is:

(a) Parabola

(b) Eclipse

(c) Straight line

(d) Sine-curve

Question 24

Two bulbs connected across a 110 V supply have resistances in the ratio 5 : 9. The ratio of brightness of the light from them is :

(a) 9 : 5

(b) 5 : 9

(c) 1 : 1

(d) 1 : 2

Question 25

Two long parallel conductors PQ and RS are separated by a certain distance. M is the mid-point between them, as shown in figure. Net magnetic field at M is B. If current 2A is switched off, then field at M will becomes

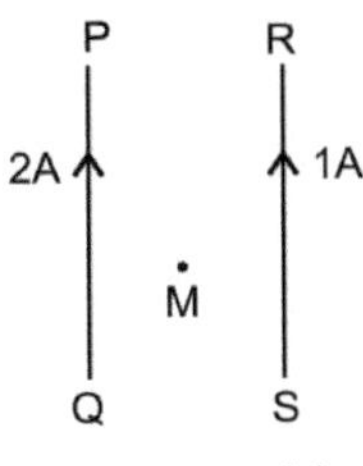

(a) 2B

(b) 3B

(c) B/2

(d) B

Question 26

In an AC generator, if the plane of its armature is perpendicular to the applied magnetic field, then:

(a) magnetic flux is zero.

(b) emf is maximum.

(c) magnetic flux is maximum.

(d) both magnetic flux and emf are zero.

Question 27

Magnitude of drift velocity per unit electric field is called

(a) Mobility

(b) Resistivity

(c) Conductivity

(d) Current density

Question 28

A cell can be balanced against 100 cm and 80 cm of a potentiometer wire, respectively with and without being short circuited through a resistance 10 Ω. The internal resistance of the cell is:

(a) $1.5\,\Omega$ (b) $2.5\,\Omega$ (c) $3.5\,\Omega$ (d) $2.0\,\Omega$

Question 29

Two resistances are connected in two gaps of a metre bridge. The balance point is 20 cm from the zero end. A resistance of 10 Ω is connected in series with the resistance of smaller value out of the two. Now, if the null point shifts to 40 cm, then the value of smaller resistance will be :

(a) $6\,\Omega$ (b) $3\,\Omega$ (c) $9\,\Omega$ (d) $10\,\Omega$

Question 30

Two wires of same material having same length but their area of cross-section are in the ratio of $2:1$. They are joined in series. If the resistance of the thicker wire is 15 Ω, then the total resistance of the combination will be :

(a) $30\,\Omega$ (b) $25\,\Omega$ (c) $40\,\Omega$ (d) $45\,\Omega$

Question 31

Ampere's circuital law can be derived from:

(a) Biot-Savart law   (b) Gauss law   (c) Coulomb's law   (d) Ohm's law

Question 32

Magnetic moment and angular velocity is related as:

(a) $M \propto \omega$ (b) $M \propto \sqrt{\omega}$ (c) $M \propto \omega^2$ (d) $M \propto \dfrac{1}{\omega}$

Question 33

A 2m long solenoid having 1000 turns produces a flux density of 3.14×10^{-3} T. Current in the solenoid will be:

(a) $1\,A$ (b) $2\,A$ (c) $5\,A$ (d) $10\,A$

Question 34

Two similar circular loops carry equal currents in the same direction. If we move the coils apart, the electric current will

(a) remain same in both.   (b) increase in both.

(c) decrease in both.   (d) increase in one but decrease in the second.

Question 35

The direction of propagation of electromagnetic wave is along

(a) $\vec{E}\cdot\vec{B}$ (b) $\vec{E}\times\vec{B}$ (c) $\vec{B}\times\vec{E}$ (d) none of these

Question 36

Which of the following phenomena proved the transverse nature of EM waves?

(a) Interference   (b) Dispersion   (c) Diffraction   (d) Polarization

Question 37

The electromagnetic radiation used to study the crystal structure is:

(a) UV rays   (b) X-rays   (c) IR radiation   (d) Microwaves

Question 38

X-rays, gamma rays and microwaves travelling in vacuum have:

(a) same frequency and same velocities.

(b) same frequency and same velocities.

(c) same velocity and different wavelengths.

(d) same frequency and different velocities.

Question 39

Two resistors of resistances 200 kΩ and 1 MΩ respectively form a potential divider with outer junctions maintained at potentials of $+3V$ and $-15V$.

(i) The potential difference across 1 MΩ resistor is:

(a) $14.4\,V$ (b) $15\,V$ (c) $25\,V$ (d) $28.2\,V$

(ii) The potendial difference across 200 kΩ resistor is:

    (a) zero   (b) 15 V   (c) 3 V   (d) 5 V

Question 40

A capacitor of capacitance 1 μF is charged by a battery, and the energy stored is U.

(i) If the capacitor is charged to 30 V, the energy stored U, is :

    (a) 450 μJ   (b) 150 μJ   (c) 300 μJ   (d) 500 μJ

(ii) If the battery is disconnected and the capacitor is connected to another capacitor of 2 μF, then the energy loss by the system will be :

    (a) 450 μJ   (b) 100 μJ   (c) 300 μJ   (d) 350 μJ

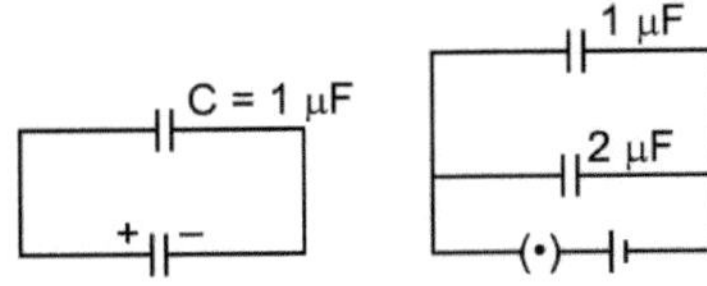

Question 41

A wire of resistance 20 Ω is stretched to thrice its original length.

(i) What is the change in the resistivity of the wire?

    (a) doubled   (b) remains same   (c) halved   (d) quadrupled

(ii) What is the value of new resistance?

    (a) 120 Ω   (b) 140 Ω   (c) 180 Ω   (d) 100 Ω

Question 42

An electron travels in a circular path of radius 10 cm in a magnetic field of 5×10^{-3} T.

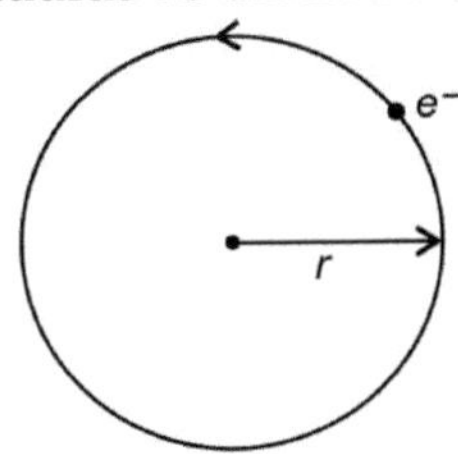

(i) What is the speed of the electron?

    (a) 87×10^7 m/s   (b) 8.7×10^7 ms^{-1} (c) 8.7×10^9 ms^{-1} (d) 0.87×10^9 ms^{-1}

(ii) What is the potential difference through which the electron must be accelerated to acquire this speed?

    (a) 12 kV   (b) 14 kV   (c) 21.5 kV   (d) 12.5 kV

Question 43

A rectangular coil of sides 8 cm and 6 cm having 1000 turns and carrying a current of 200 mA is placed in a uniform magnetic field of 0.2 T directed along positive X-axis?

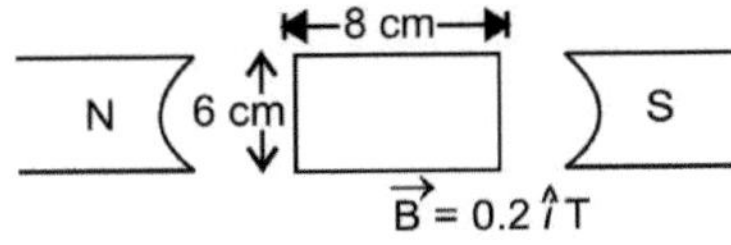

(i) What is the magnitude of magnetic dipole moment?

    (a) 0.96 Am^2 (b) 1.96 Am^2 (c) 9.6 Am^2 (d) 19.6 Am^2

(ii) What is the maximum torque the coil can experience?

    (a) 19.2 Nm   (b) 1.92 Nm   (c) 192 Nm   (d) 0.192 Nm

Question 44

A current of 100 μA deflects the coil of a moving coil galvanometer through 30°.

(i) What should be the current to cause the rotation through π/10 radian?

    (a) 120 μA   (b) 60 μA   (c) 180 μA   (d) 30 μA

(ii) What is the sensitivity of the galvanometer?

    (a) 0.3 deg μA^{-1} (b) 0.1 deg μA^{-1} (c) 0.2 deg μA^{-1} (d) 2 deg μA

Question 45

A potentiometer wire of length 1 m is connected to a driver cell of emf 2.5 V as shown in figure. When a cell of emf 1.5 V is used in the secondary circuit, the balance point is found to be at 60 cm. On replacing this cell and using a cell of unknown emf, the balance point shifts to 80 cm.

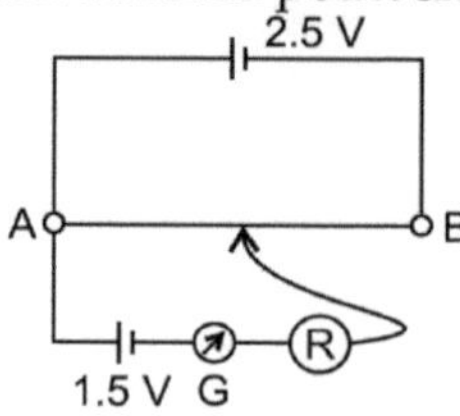

(i) What is the unknown emf of the cell?

    (a) 2V   (b) 3V   (c) 1V   (d) 5V

(ii) What is the position of balance point if we replace the driver cell with a cell of emf 1 V?

    (a) 60 cm   (b) 40 cm   (c) 100 cm   (d) cannot be obtained

(iii) The high resistance R, used in the secondary circuit will affect the balance point by:

    (a) shifting it by 60 cm.   (b) shifting it by 80 cm.

    (c) shifting it by 40 cm.   (d) no effect on balance point.

Question 46

A rectangular coil of wire has dimensions 0.2 m × 0.1 m. The coil has 2000 turns. The coil rotates in a magnetic field about an axis parallel to its length and perpendicular to the magnetic field of 0.02 Wb m^{-2}. The speed of rotation of the coil is 4200 rpm.

(i) What is the angular frequency of rotation of the coil?

    (a) $100\,\pi$ rad s^{-1} (b) $170\,\pi$ rad s^{-1} (c) $140\,\pi$ rad s^{-1} (d) $200\,\pi$ rad s^{-1}

(ii) What is the maximum value of induced emf in the coil?

    (a) 3000 V   (b) 3520 V   (c) 3200 V   (d) 3430 V

(iii) What is the instantaneous value of induced emf when the plane of the coil has rotated through an angle of 30° from the initial position?

    (a) 1700 V   (b) 1720 V   (c) 1760 V   (d) 1520 V

Question 47

A 8 V battery of negligible internal resistance is connected across a uniform wire AB of length 100 cm. The positive terminal of another battery of emf 3V and internal resistance 1 Ω is joined to the point A as shown in figure. Take the potential at point B to be zero.

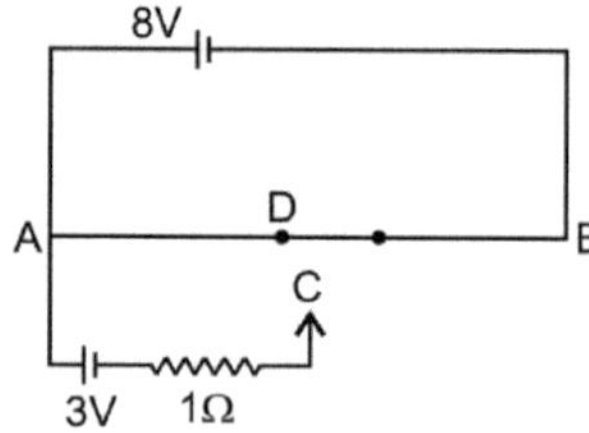

(i) What is the potential at point C?

    (a) 5 V   (b) 8 V   (c) 3 V   (d) 10 V

(iii) At which point D of the wire AB, the potential of the wire is equal to the potential at C?

    (a) 20 cm from A   (b) 62.5 cm from A   (c) 62.5 cm from B   (d) 55.5 cm from B

(iii) If the points C and D are connected by a resistor 1 Ω, what will be the current through 1 Ω resistor?

    (a) 5A   (b) 4A   (c) 2A   (d) zero

Question 48

A long straight wire AB carries a current 5A. A proton P travels with a speed of 5×10^6 m/s in a direction parallel to the wire and opposite to the direction of current in the wire. Proton P is moving at a distance 0.2 m away from the wire.

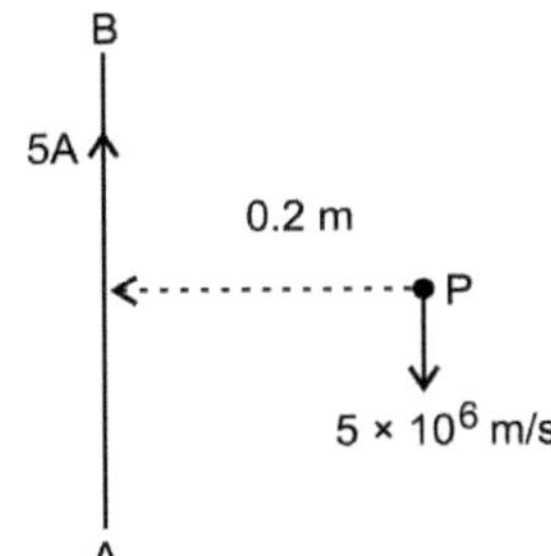

(i)   What is the magnitude of magnetic field at point P due to the current in the wire AB?

   (a) 2×10^{-6} T   (b) 5×10^{-6} T   (c) 10^{-8} T   (d) 3×10^{-6} T

(ii)   What is the force which the magnetic field of current exerts on the proton?

   (a) 8×10^{-18} N   (b) 4×10^{-19} N   (c) 4×10^{-18} N   (d) 2×10^{-19} N

(iii)   What is the direction of force acting on the proton?

   (a) towards right into the plane of paper   (b) towards left out of the plane of paper

   (c) towards right out of the plane of paper   (d) towards left into the plane of paper

Question 49

A sinusoidal voltage of peak value 210 V and angular frequency 300 /s is applied to a series LCR circuit. Given that R = 5Ω, L = 25 mH and C = 1000 μF.

(i)   Calculate the inductive reactance.

   (a) 7 Ω   (b) 7.5 Ω   (c) 5 Ω   (d) 10 Ω

(ii)   Calculate the capacitive reactance.

   (a) 2.3 Ω   (b) 3.3 Ω   (c) 3.5 Ω   (d) 4.3 Ω

(iii)   Calculate the total impedance of the circuit.

   (a) 6.5 Ω   (b) 5 Ω   (c) 6 Ω   (d) 7 Ω

(iv)   What is the phase difference between the voltage across the source and the current?

   (a) 180°   (b) 78.1°   (c) 30°   (d) 81.6°

Question 50

There are two main types of backup generators viz., AC generators and DC generators. An AC generator creates an alternating current that periodically reverses direction. But in a DC generator, a direct current flows in one direction. AC generators are commonly used to power smaller electrical appliances. They are cost effective and requires lower maintenance.

(i)   AC generator converts

   (a) Mechanical energy to electrical energy.   (b) Electrical energy to mechanical energy.

   (c) Electrical energy to heat energy.   (d) Mechanical energy to heat energy.

(ii)   What replacement is required to convert an AC generator to a DC generators?

   (a) Armature with coil

   (b) Slip rings with split rings

   (c) Concave magnet with horse-shoe magnet

   (d) None of these

(iii)   AC generators works on the principle of :

   (a) Electrochemical effect   (b) Electromechanical effect

   (c) Electromagnetic Induction   (d) None of the above

(iv)   In AC generators, the slip rings are made up of:

   (a) Wood   (b) Rubber   (c) Metal   (d) Clay

Answers

1. (d) All of these

Explanation: There are only two types of charge : positive and negative. Like charges repel each other whereas unlike charges attract each other.

Charge is quantized according to the principle of quantization of electric charge.

According to principle of conservation of charges, the charges can not be created nor destroyed but they can only be transferred from one body to the other.

2. (d) Electric field lines can form closed loops.

Explanation: Electric field lines can not form closed loops as they are conservative in nature.

3. (b) 1.35×10^6 N/C

Explanation: Electric field at C due to charge at point A,

$$\vec{E_1} = \frac{1}{4\pi\varepsilon_0} \cdot \frac{6\times10^{-6}}{(0.2)^2} \text{ (Along AC)}$$

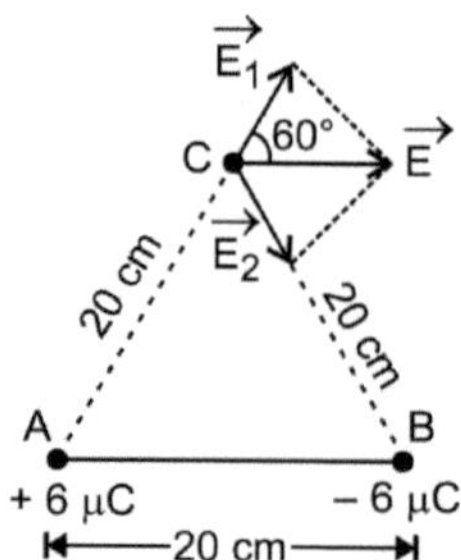

Electric field at C due to the charge at B,

$$\vec{E_2} = -\frac{1}{4\pi\varepsilon_0} \cdot \frac{6\times10^{-6}}{(0.2)^2} \text{ (Along CB)}$$

By symmetry the vertical components will cancel out and horizontal components will add, and we can see that $|\vec{E_1}| = |\vec{E_2}|$

$$\therefore \quad E = 2\,E_1\cos 60° = E_1$$

$$\text{or} \quad E = \frac{1}{4\pi\varepsilon_0} \times \frac{6\times10^{-6}}{(0.2)^2}$$

$$= 9 \times 10^9 \times \frac{6\times10^{-6}}{(0.2)^2}$$

$$= 1.35 \times 10^6 \text{ N/C}$$

4. (a) 20 units

Explanation: $\vec{E} = 5\hat{i} + 4\hat{j} + 9\hat{k}$ and $d\vec{S} = 4\hat{i}$

Electric flux, $\quad d\phi = \vec{E}.d\vec{S}$

$$= (5\hat{i} + 4\hat{j} + 9\hat{k}).(4\hat{i})$$

$$= 20 \text{ units}$$

5. (c) $\frac{1}{\sqrt{2}}$ A

Explanation: $E_0 = 30$ V and $R = 30\,\Omega$

$$I_0 = \frac{E_0}{R} = \frac{30\text{ V}}{30\,\Omega} = 1 \text{ V}$$

RMS value of current in the circuit, $I_{rms} = \dfrac{I_0}{\sqrt{2}}$

$$\therefore \quad I_{rms} = \frac{1}{\sqrt{2}} \text{ A}$$

6. (d) Variable

Explanation: Here, the electron is moving from right to left, the flux linked with the loop will first increase and then decrease as the electron passes by. So, the induced current in the loop will be first clockwise and will change direction (*i.e.,* anticlockwise) as the electron passes by.

7. (a) 5.4 J

Explanation: Here, $q_1 = 12 \times 10^{-6}$ C, $q_2 = 5 \times 10^{-6}$ C and $r = 10 = 0.1$ m

$$U = \frac{1}{4\pi\varepsilon_0} \cdot \frac{q_1 q_2}{r}$$

$$= 9\times10^9 \times \frac{12\times10^{-6} \times 5\times10^{-6}}{(0.1)}$$

$$= 5.4 \text{ J}$$

8. (b) (i) and (iii) are correct and (ii) is wrong.

Explanation: In a uniform electric field $\vec{E}$, dipole experiences a torque $\vec{\tau}$ given by $\vec{\tau} = \vec{p} \times \vec{E}$ but experiences no force.
The potential energy of the dipole in a uniform electric field $\vec{E}$ is $U = -\vec{p}.\vec{E}$

9. (b) $\dfrac{8}{3}$ μF

Explanation:

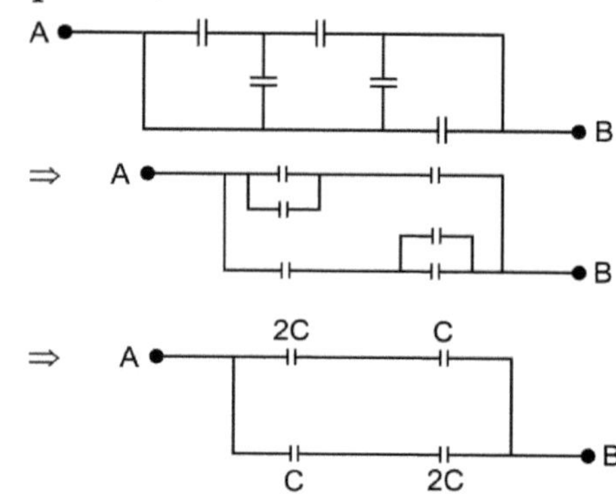

$$\Rightarrow \qquad \frac{1}{2C}+\frac{1}{C}=\frac{1}{C'}$$

$$\Rightarrow \qquad C'=\frac{2C}{3}$$

$$C_{eq}=2\times\frac{2C}{3}=\frac{4}{3}\times 2 \qquad (\because C=2\mu F)$$

$$=\frac{8}{3}\mu F$$

10. (c) $-16\,\hat{i}$

Explanation: Given that,
$$V=8x^2$$
$$E_x=-\frac{\partial V}{\partial x}=-16x$$

$E_y=E_z=0$ as V is independent of y and z.

For $x=1$ m, $\vec{E}=-16\hat{i}$ V/m

11. (b) $V_A=V_B$, $V_C>V_D$

Explanation: In the direction of electric field, electrical potential decreases.
$$\therefore \qquad V_C>V_A=V_B>V_D$$
or $\qquad V_C>V_D$, $V_A=V_B$

12. (d) from negative charge to positive charge.

Explanation: By convention, the direction of axis of an electric dipole is from negative charge to the positive charge.

13. (a) $1:3:5$

Explanation: Charge density, $\sigma=\dfrac{\text{Charge}}{\text{Area}}$

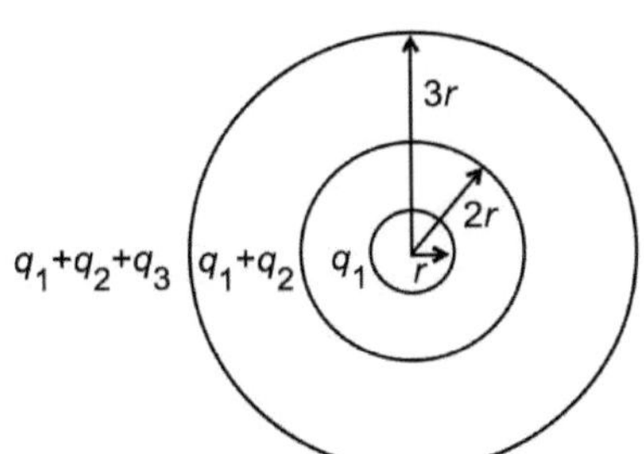

$$\therefore \qquad \frac{q_1}{4\pi r^2}=\frac{q_1+q_2}{4\pi(4r^2)}$$

$$=\frac{q_1+q_2+q_3}{4\pi(9r^2)}$$

or $\qquad q_1=\dfrac{q_1+q_2}{4}$

or $\qquad 3q_1=q_2$

$$\frac{q_1+q_2+q_3}{9}=\frac{q_1}{1}$$

$$\Rightarrow \qquad 8q_1-q_2=q_3$$
$$\Rightarrow \qquad 8q_1-3q_1=q_3$$
$$\Rightarrow \qquad 5q_1=q_3$$

$$\therefore \qquad \frac{q_1}{1}=\frac{q_2}{3}=\frac{q_3}{5}$$

$$\therefore\ q_1:q_2:q_3=1:3:5.$$

14. (c) decreases as $\dfrac{1}{r^2}$

Explanation: From Biot-Savart's law,
$$dB=\frac{\mu_0}{4\pi}\frac{Idl}{r^2}$$
i.e., $\qquad dB\propto\dfrac{1}{r^2}$

15. (d) 250 gm

Explanation: For mid-air suspension,

Weight of wire = Force exerted by magnetic field

$$mg=Bil\sin\theta$$

or $\qquad m=\dfrac{Bil\sin\theta}{g}$

$$=\frac{0.5\times5\times1\times\sin90°}{10}$$

$$=0.25\text{ kg}$$

$$=250\text{ gm}$$

16. (c) 1 A

Explanation: According to Kirchoff's first law,
$$10+4+(-3)+(-10)-I=0$$
or $\qquad I=1A$

17. (a) $10\,\Omega$

Explanation: The given wheatstone bridge circuit is shown in figure.

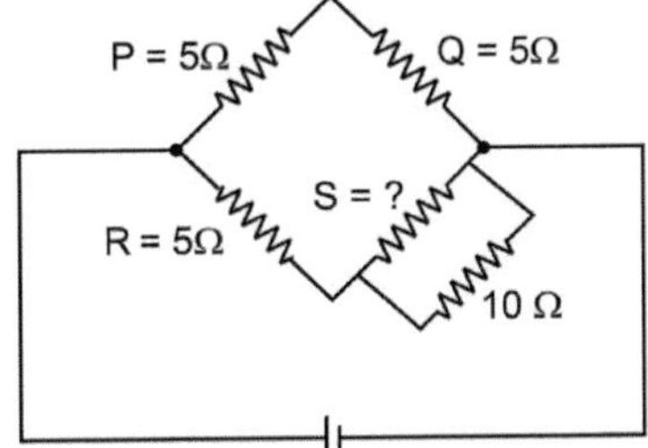

For the bridge to get balanced,

$$\frac{P}{Q}=\frac{R}{\dfrac{S(10\,\Omega)}{S+10\,\Omega}}$$

$$\therefore \qquad \frac{5\Omega}{5\Omega}=\frac{5\,\Omega}{\dfrac{S(10\,\Omega)}{S+10\,\Omega}}$$

or $\qquad \dfrac{S(10\,\Omega)}{S+10\,\Omega}=5\,\Omega$

or $\qquad S=10\,\Omega$

18. (b) 3V

Explanation: V = 5V

Equivalent resistance, $R_{eq} = 1 + 1 + 3 = 5\Omega$

Using Ohm's law, $V = IR_{eq}$

$$\therefore \quad I = \frac{V}{R_{eq}} = \frac{5}{5} = 1\,A$$

Potential drop across 3 Ω resistor $= IR_3$
$$= (1A) \times (3\,\Omega)$$
$$= 3V$$

19. (d) temperature coefficient of resistivity

Explanation: Temperature coefficient of resistivity is defined as the fractional increase in resistivity per unit increase in temperature.

20. (a) $\dfrac{r}{3}$

Explanation: The equivalent circuit diagram is :

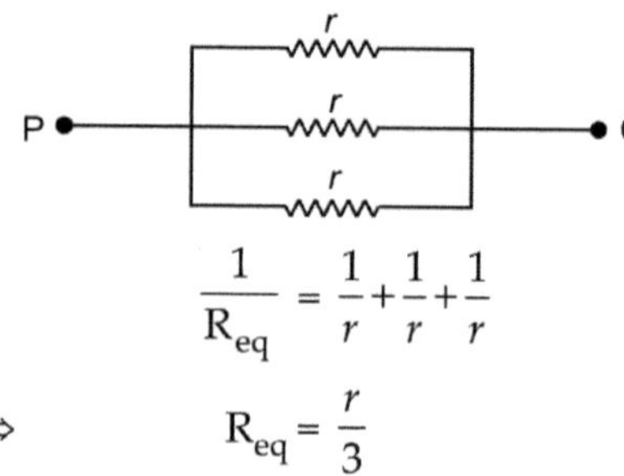

$$\frac{1}{R_{eq}} = \frac{1}{r} + \frac{1}{r} + \frac{1}{r}$$

$$\Rightarrow \qquad R_{eq} = \frac{r}{3}$$

21. (a) 152 W

Explanation: Impedance of the circuit,
$$Z = \sqrt{(R_1 + R_2)^2 + (X_L - X_C)^2}$$
$$= \sqrt{(42 + 38)^2 + (90 - 30)^2}$$
$$= \sqrt{(80)^2 + (60)^2}$$
$$= 100\ \Omega$$

Current in the circuit, $I = \dfrac{V}{Z} = \dfrac{200\ V}{100\ \Omega} = 2A$

Power dissipated in the coil,
$$P = I^2 R_2 = (2A)^2 \times (38\ \Omega)$$
$$= 152\ W$$

22. (c) 1.25×10^{19}

Explanation: $\quad I = \dfrac{ne}{t}$

or $\qquad \dfrac{n}{t} = \dfrac{I}{e} = \dfrac{2}{1.6 \times 10^{-19}}$

$$= 1.25 \times 10^{19}$$

23. (c) Straight line

Explanation: According to Ohm's law, V = RI, where R is the resistance of the current carrying conductor.

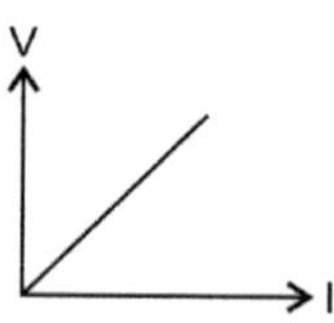

24. (a) 9 : 5

Explanation: For a given V, $P \propto \dfrac{1}{R}$

$$\therefore \qquad \frac{P_1}{P_2} = \frac{R_2}{R_1} = \frac{9}{5}$$

25. (d) B

Explanation: Magnetic field at mid-point M due to current in PQ is,
$$\vec{B}_{PQ} = \frac{\mu_0 \times 2 \times 2}{4\pi d}$$
$$= \frac{4\mu_0}{4\pi d} \qquad \text{...(i)}$$

Magnetic field at mid-point M due to current in RS is,
$$\vec{B}_{RS} = \frac{\mu_0 \times 2 \times 1}{4\pi d}$$
$$= \frac{2\mu_0}{4\pi d} \qquad \text{...(ii)}$$

Net magnetic field at mid-point M is,
$$B = P_{PQ} - B_{RS}$$
$$(\because B_{PQ} \text{ and } B_{RS} \text{ are in opposite direction})$$

or $\qquad B = \dfrac{4\mu_0}{4\pi d} - \dfrac{2\mu_0}{4\pi d}$

$$= \frac{2\mu_0}{4\pi d} \qquad \text{...(iii)}$$

When the current 2A is switched off, the net magnetic field at M is due to only 1A.

$$\therefore \qquad B' = \frac{\mu_0 \times 2 \times 1}{4\pi d} = B \quad \text{[Using eq. (iii)]}$$

26. (c) magnetic flux is maximum

Explanation: Magnetic flux, $\phi_B = BA \cos\theta$

Induced emf, $\varepsilon = BA \sin\theta$

Here $\theta = 0°$

∴ Magnetic flux is maximum and induced emf is zero.

27. (a) Mobility

Explanation: Mobility, $\mu = \dfrac{|v_d|}{E}$

28. (b) $2.5\ \Omega$

Explanation: $\quad r = \left(\dfrac{l_1 - l_2}{l_2}\right) R$

$$= \left(\frac{100 - 80}{80}\right) \times 10 = 2.5\ \Omega$$

29. (a) $6\,\Omega$

Explanation: $\dfrac{P}{Q} = \dfrac{20}{80} = \dfrac{1}{4}$ ...(i)

and, $\dfrac{P+10}{Q} = \dfrac{40}{60} = \dfrac{2}{3}$ ...(ii)

Dividing eq. (i) by (ii), we get

$$\dfrac{P}{P+10} = \dfrac{3}{8}$$

or $8P = 3P + 30$

or $5P = 30$

or $P = 6\,\Omega$

30. (d) $45\,\Omega$

Explanation: For same length and same material,

$$\dfrac{R_2}{R_1} = \dfrac{A_1}{A_2} = \dfrac{2}{1}$$

$\therefore$ $R_2 = 2R_1$

Resistance of thicker wire, $R_1 = 15\,\Omega$

$\therefore$ Resistance of the thinner wire

$$= 2R_1 = 2 \times 15 = 30\,\Omega$$

Total resistance $= 15\,\Omega + 30\,\Omega = 45\,\Omega$

31. (a) Biot-Savart law

Explanation: Ampere's circuital law can be derived from Biot-savart law.

32. (a) $M \propto \omega$

Explanation: Magnetic moment, $M = IA = I(\pi r^2)$

$$= \dfrac{q}{T} \times \pi r^2$$

As, $\omega = \dfrac{2\pi}{T}$

$\therefore$ $M = \dfrac{q}{\left(\dfrac{2\pi}{\omega}\right)} \times \pi r^2$

or $M = \dfrac{q\omega r^2}{2}$

$\therefore$ $M \propto \omega$

33. (c) $5\,A$

Explanation: $B = \dfrac{\mu_0 nI}{l}$

or $I = \dfrac{Bl}{\mu_0 n}$

$$= \dfrac{3.14 \times 10^{-3} \times 2}{(4\pi \times 10^{-7}) \times 1000}$$

$$I = 5A$$

34. (b) increase in both.

Explanation: Two circular loops carrying currents in the same direction will attract each other. If we move them apart, induced currents will try to keep them together by increasing the currents in both the coils.

35. (b) $\vec{E} \times \vec{B}$

Explanation: If $\vec{E}$ and $\vec{B}$ represent electric and magnetic field vectors of an electromagnetic wave, the direction of propagation of the wave is along $\vec{E} \times \vec{B}$.

36. (d) Polarization

Explanation: Polarisation phenomena proved the transverse nature of electromagnetic waves.

37. (b) X-rays

Explanation: Crystal structure can be studied using X-rays.

38. (c) same velocity and different wavelengths.

Explanation: In vacuum, X-rays, gamma rays and microwaves travels with the same velocity *i.e.*, speed of light ($c = 3 \times 10^8$ m/s) but different wavelengths.

39. (i) (b) $15\,V$

Explanation: Potential difference across 1 MΩ resistor

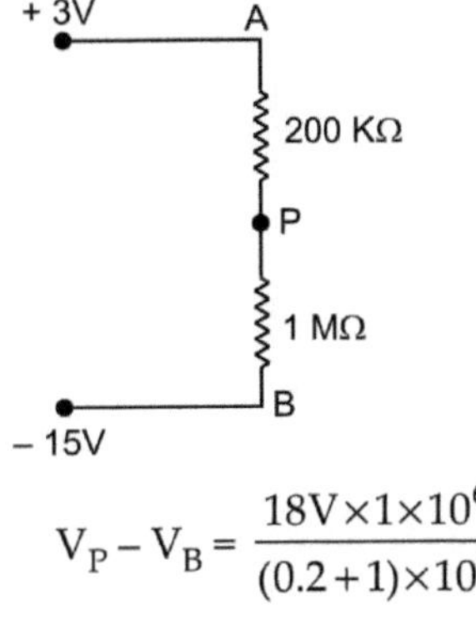

$$V_P - V_B = \dfrac{18V \times 1 \times 10^6\,\Omega}{(0.2 + 1) \times 10^6\,\Omega}$$

$$= \dfrac{18\,V \times 10^6\,\Omega}{1.2 \times 10^6\,\Omega} = 15\ V$$

(ii) (c) $3\,V$

Explanation: Potential difference across 200 kΩ resistor is

$$V_A - V_P = \dfrac{18\ V \times 0.2 \times 10^6\,\Omega}{(0.2 + 1) \times 10^6\,\Omega} = 3\ V$$

40. (i) (a) $450\ \mu J$

Explanation: $q_1 = C_1 V = (1 \times 10^{-6}\ F) \times 30$
$= 30 \times 10^{-6}\ C$

Energy stored in the capacitor,

$$U = \dfrac{1}{2} C_1 V^2$$

$$= \dfrac{1}{2} \times (1 \times 10^{-6}) \times (30)^2$$

$$U = 450\ \mu J$$

(ii) (c) 300 µJ

Explanation: After disconnected from the battery and after connected with a 2 µF capacitor, the equivalent capacitance of the system, is

$$C = C_1 + C_2 = 1 \times 10^{-6}\,F + 2 \times 10^{-6}\,F$$
$$= 3 \times 10^{-6}\,F$$

Energy stored in the system,

$$U' = \frac{1}{2}\frac{Q^2}{C}$$

$$= \frac{1}{2} \times \frac{900 \times 10^{-12}}{3 \times 10^{-6}}$$

$$= 150\ \mu J$$

$$\Delta U = U - U' = (450 - 150)\ \mu J$$
$$= 300\ \mu J$$

41. (i) (b) remains same

Explanation: Resistivity is the property of the material of the wire, thus it will remain same.

(ii) (c) 180 Ω

Explanation: In both cases, volume of the wire is same

$$\therefore \qquad V = A'l' = Al$$

or $$\frac{A'}{A} = \frac{l}{l'} \times \frac{l}{3l} = \frac{1}{3}$$

$$\therefore \qquad \frac{R'}{R} = \frac{\rho \dfrac{l'}{A'}}{\rho \dfrac{l}{A}}$$

$$= \frac{l'}{l} \times \frac{A}{A'}$$

$$= \frac{3}{1} \times \frac{3}{1} = 9$$

$$\therefore \qquad R' = 9R$$
$$= 9 \times 20\ \Omega$$
$$= 180\ \Omega$$

42. (i) (b) $8.7 \times 10^7\ ms^{-1}$

Explanation: Magnetic force on the electron
= Centripetal force on electron

$$qvB = \frac{mv^2}{r}$$

$$\therefore \qquad v = \frac{qBr}{m}$$

$$= \frac{1.6 \times 10^{-19} \times 5 \times 10^{-3} \times 0.1}{9.1 \times 10^{-31}}$$

$$= 8.7 \times 10^7\ ms^{-1}$$

(ii) (c) 21.5 kV

Explanation: If V is the potential difference required to give speed v to the electron, then

$$eV = \frac{1}{2}mv^2$$

$$\Rightarrow \qquad V = \frac{mv^2}{2e}$$

$$= \frac{9.1 \times 10^{-31} \times (8.7 \times 10^7)^2}{2 \times 1.6 \times 10^{-19}}$$

$$\therefore\ V = 21.5\ KV$$

43. (i) (a) $0.96\ Am^2$

Explanation: Here, $l = 8$ cm $= 0.08$ m, $b = 6$ cm $= 0.06$ m

N = 1000, I = 200 mA = 0.2 A and B = 0.2 T
The magnitude of the magnetic dipole moment is given by

$$m = NIA = 1000 \times 0.2 \times (0.08 \times 0.06)$$
$$= 0.96\ Am^2$$

(ii) (d) 0.192 Nm

Explanation: The direction of $\vec{m}$ is normal to area $\vec{A}$ of the coil from S-pole to N-pole. Magnitude of torque on the coil is,

$$\tau = mB \sin \theta$$

For maximum torque, $\vec{m}$ must be perpendicular to $\vec{B}$.

$$\therefore\ \tau_{max} = mB = 0.96 \times 0.2 = 0.192\ Nm$$

44. (i) (b) 60 µA

Explanation: Here, $I_1 = 100$ µA, $\theta_1 = 30°$

$$\theta_2 = \frac{\pi}{10}\ rad = 18°,\ I_2 = ?$$

$$I_1 = \frac{k}{NBA} \cdot \theta_1$$

and $$I_2 = \frac{k}{NBA} \cdot \theta_2$$

$$\therefore \qquad \frac{I_2}{I_1} = \frac{\theta_2}{\theta_1}$$

$$\Rightarrow \qquad I_2 = \frac{\theta_2}{\theta_1} \times I_1$$

$$= \frac{18°}{30°} \times 100 = 60\mu A$$

(ii) (a) 0.3 deg µA^{-1}

Explanation: Current sensitivity $= \dfrac{\theta_2}{I_2}$

$$= \frac{18°}{60\ \mu A} = 0.3\ deg\,\mu A^{-1}$$

45. (i) (a) 2V

Explanation: I

$$\frac{\varepsilon_1}{\varepsilon_2} = \frac{l_2}{l_1}$$

$$\Rightarrow \qquad \varepsilon_2 = \frac{l_2}{l_1}$$

$$\varepsilon_1 = \frac{80}{60} \times 1.5 = 2.0 \text{ V}$$

(ii) (d) cannot be obtained

Explanation: With a driver cell of 1V, the balance point cannot be obtained for a cell of emf 1.5 V, on the wire AB.

(iii) (d) no effect on balance point.

Explanation: The balance point is not affected by the high resistance R because no current flows through the cell at the balance point.

46. (i) (c) $140 \, \pi \text{ rad s}^{-1}$

Explanation: If = 4200 rpm = $\dfrac{4200}{60}$ rps

$$= 70 \text{ rps}$$
$$\omega = 2\pi f = 2\pi \times 70 = 140 \, \pi \text{ rad s}^{-1}$$

(ii) (b) 3520 V

Explanation:
Here, $A = 0.2 \times 0.1 \text{ m}^2 = 2 \times 10^{-2} \text{ m}^2$
$$N = 2000 \text{ and } B = 0.02 \text{ Wb m}^{-2}$$
$$\varepsilon_0 = NBA\,\omega$$
$$= 2000 \times 0.02 \times 2 \times 10^{-2} \times 140 \times \frac{22}{7}$$
$$= 3520 \text{ V}$$

(iii) (c) 1760 V

Explanation: Instantaneous value of induced emf when the coil has turned through 30° is
$$\varepsilon = \varepsilon_0 \sin \omega t$$
$$= 3520 \times \frac{1}{2} = 1760 \text{ V}$$

47. (i) (a) 5 V

Explanation: Potential at B, $V_B = 0$
Potential at C, $V_C = +8V - 3V = 5V$

(ii) (c) 62.5 cm from B

Explanation: Potential difference across wire AB is,
$$V_A - V_B = (8 - 0)V$$
$$= 8V$$

Let x be the position of point D from B.
$$\text{Potential gradient} = \frac{8 \text{ V}}{100 \text{ cm}}$$

Given, $V_C = V_D = 5V$

$$\text{But} \qquad V_D = \left(\frac{8V}{100 \text{ cm}} \right).x = 5V$$

$$\text{or} \qquad x = \left(\frac{5 \times 100}{8} \right) = 62.5 \text{ cm}$$

Hence point D is 62.5 cm from B.

(iii) (d) zero

Explanation: There won't be any current in the resistor connecting C and D points, as potential difference across it is zero *i.e.*, $V_C - V_D = 0$.

48. (i) (b) $5 \times 10^{-6} \text{ T}$

Explanation: Magnetic field at point P due to current in wire AB,

$$B = \frac{\mu_0 I}{2\pi r}$$

$$= \frac{4\pi \times 10^{-7} \times 5}{2\pi \times (0.2)}$$

$$= 5 \times 10^{-6} \text{ T}$$

This field acts on the proton normally into the plane of paper.

(ii) (c) $4 \times 10^{-18} \text{ N}$

Explanation:
$$F = qvB \sin\theta$$
$$= 1.6 \times 10^{-19} \times 5 \times 10^6 \times 5 \times 10^{-6}$$
$$\times \sin 90°$$
$$= 4 \times 10^{-18} \text{ N}$$

(iii) (a) towards right into the plane of paper

Explanation: According to Fleming's left hand rule, the magnetic force acts on the proton towards right into the plane of paper.

49. (i) (b) $7.5 \, \Omega$

Explanation: Inductive reactance,
$$X_L = \omega L = 300 \times 25 \times 10^{-3}$$
$$= 7.5 \, \Omega$$

(ii) (b) $3.3 \, \Omega$

Explanation: Capacitive reactance,
$$X_C = \frac{1}{\omega C}$$
$$= \frac{1}{300 \times 1000 \times 10^{-6}}$$
$$X_C = 3.3 \, \Omega$$

(iii) (a) $6.5 \, \Omega$

Explanation: Impedance,
$$Z = \sqrt{R^2 + (X_L - X_C)^2}$$
$$= \sqrt{(5)^2 + (7.5 - 3.3)^2}$$
$$= 6.5 \, \Omega$$

(iv) (d) 81.6°

Explanation: Phase difference,
$$\phi = \tan^{-1}\left(\frac{X_L - X_C}{R} \right)$$
$$= \tan^{-1}\left(\frac{7.5 - 3.3}{5} \right)$$
$$= \tan^{-1}(6.8)$$
$$\simeq 81.6°$$

50. (i) (a) Mechanical energy to electrical energy

Explanation: AC generator is a device which converts mechanical energy into electrical energy.

(ii) (b) Slip rings with split rings

Explanation: The slip rings in AC generator maintains a connection between the moving rotor and the stationary stator which results in the periodic change of current. However, DC generators consisting of split rings makes the current change direction every half-rotation which causes no change in the direction of current.

(iii) (c) Electromagnetic Induction

Explanation: AC generators works on the principle of electromagnetic induction.

(iv) (c) Metal

Explanation: Slip rings are typically consists of metals.

❑❑

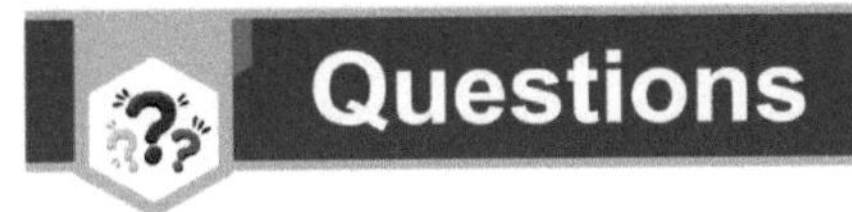

Questions

Question 1

A charge q is placed at the centre of a cube of side l. The electric flux passing through any of its surface is:

(a) $\dfrac{q}{\varepsilon_0}$

(b) $\dfrac{q}{2\varepsilon_0}$

(c) $\dfrac{q}{6\varepsilon_0}$

(d) $\dfrac{6q}{\varepsilon_0}$

Question 2

If a body contains N_1 electrons and N_2 protons, then the total charge on the body will be:

(a) $(N_1 + N_2)$

(b) $\dfrac{N_1 + N_2}{e}$

(c) $(N_1 - N_2)e$

(d) $(N_2 - N_1)e$

Question 3

Three charges q, q and $-q$ are placed at the vertices of an equilateral triangle as shown in figure. Force on the negative charge is:

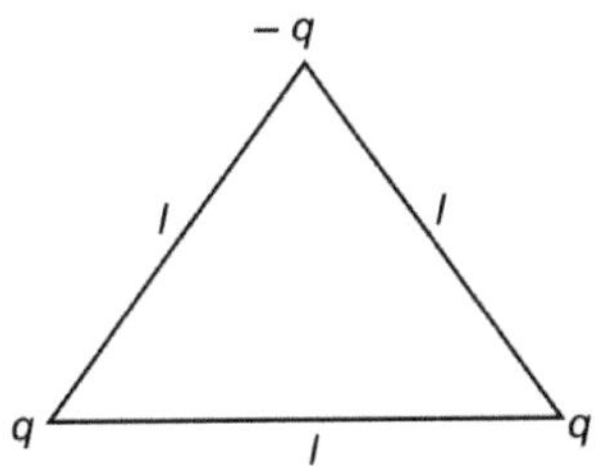

(a) $\dfrac{q^2\sqrt{3}}{4\pi\varepsilon_0 l^2}$

(b) $\dfrac{3q^2}{4\pi\varepsilon_0 l^2}$

(c) $\dfrac{q^2}{4\pi\varepsilon_0 l^2}$

(d) $\dfrac{q^2}{\sqrt{3}.4\pi\varepsilon_0 l^2}$

Question 4

An electric dipole consisting of two opposite charges of magnitude 3×10^{-6} C each, separated by a distance of 0.02 m, is placed in an electric field of 2×10^5 N/C. The maximum torque on the dipole will be:

(a) 12×10^{-2} Nm

(b) 12×10^{-3} Nm

(c) 12×10^{-5} Nm

(d) 12×10^{-7} Nm

Question 5

A solenoid having 400 turns, is 20 cm long and has a cross-section of 4 cm^2. The coefficient of self-induction is approximately:

(a) 4×10^{-1} H

(b) 4×10^{-2} H

(c) 4×10^{-4} H

(d) 4×10^{-6} H

Question 6

In a series LCR circuit, the voltages across R, L and C are as shown in the figure. The voltage of applied source is:

(a) 10 V

(b) 70 V

(c) 100 V

(d) 50 V

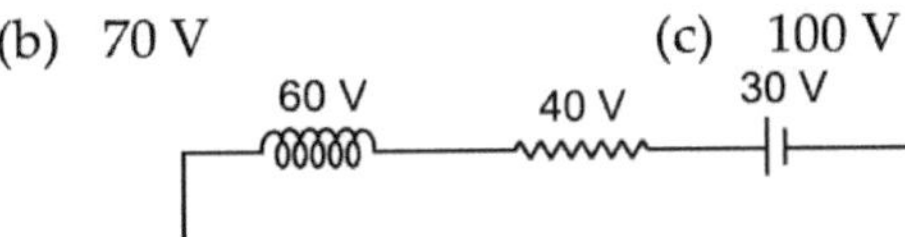

Question 7

Electric lines of force about a positive point charge are:

(a) parallel straight lines. (b) radially outwards.   (c) circular loop.   (d) radially inwards.

Question 8

If work done in bringing a unit positive charge from infinite distance to a point at a distance d from a positive charge Q is W, then the potential at that point is,

(a) $\dfrac{WQ}{d}$ (b) $\dfrac{W}{d}$ (c) W   (d) WQ

Question 9

Potential difference between A and B is 50 V. Then, potential difference across 6 μF capacitor is:

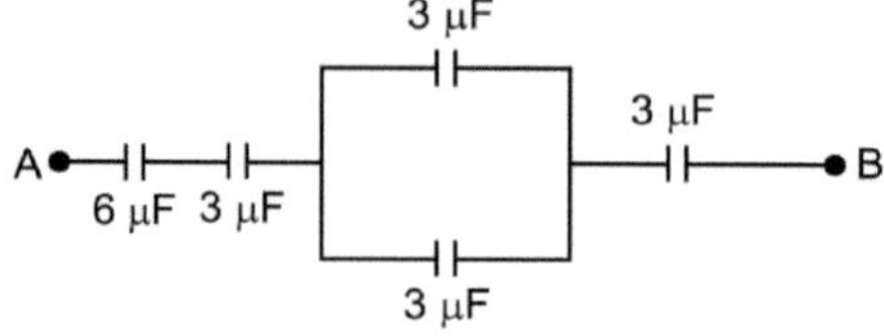

(a) 7.2 V   (b) 8.3 V   (c) 9.2 V   (d) 5.5 V

Question 10

A sphere having surface density σ, is enclosed by a spherical shell. The surface charge density on the spherical shell is:

(a) σ   (b) σ/2   (c) zero   (d) 2σ

Question 11

Four charges are arranged at the corners of a square ABCD as shown in the figure. Force on the positive charge kept at the centre O is:

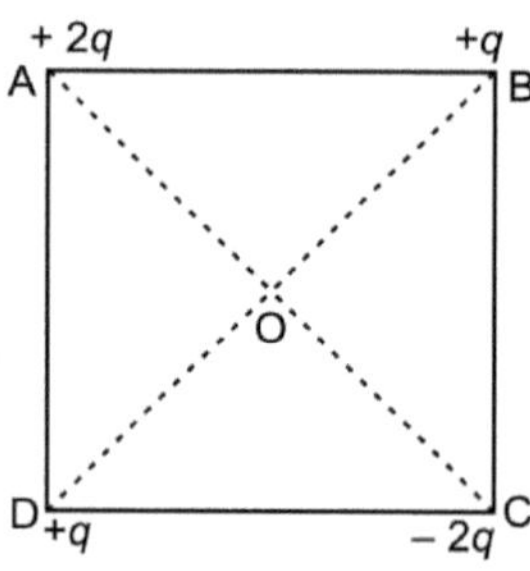

(a) along the diagonal AC   (b) along the diagonal BD

(c) perpendicular to side AB   (d) zero

Question 12

In a uniform electric field of E = 10^4 N/C, an electron is accelerated from rest. The velocity of the electron when it has travelled a distance of 2×10^{-2} m is nearly.

$$\left(\text{Take } \frac{e}{m} \text{ for electron } \approx 1.8 \times 10^{11} \text{C kg}^{-1} \right)$$

(a) 6.5×10^6 ms^{-1} (b) 1.5×10^5 ms^{-1} (c) 7.5×10^6 ms^{-1} (d) 8.5×10^6 ms^{-1}

Question 13

Four charges are placed on the vertices of a square as shown in figure. Let $\vec{E}$ be the electric field and V, the potential at the centre. If the charges at point A and B are interchanged with those on points D and C respectively, then

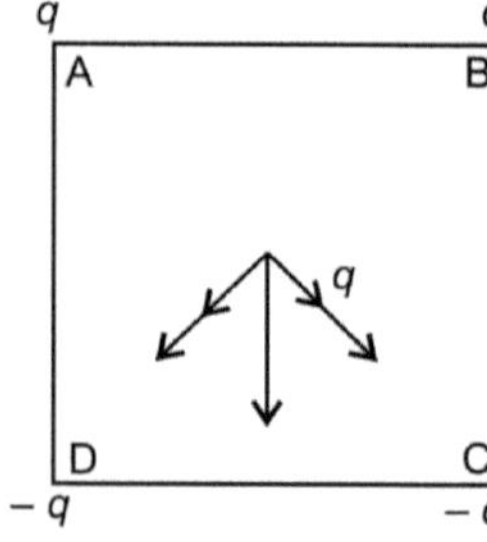

(a) $\vec{E}$ changes, V remains same.

(b) $\vec{E}$ remains same, V changes.

(c) Both $\vec{E}$ and V changes.

(d) $\vec{E}$ and V both remains same.

Question 14

The force between two parallel current carrying wires is independent of:

(a) the length of the wire.

(b) magnitude of currents.

(c) the radii of the wires.

(d) the distance of separation.

Question 15

A wire is placed between the poles of two fixed bar magnets as shown in the figure. A small current flowing in the wire is into the plane of the paper. The direction of the magnetic force on the wire is:

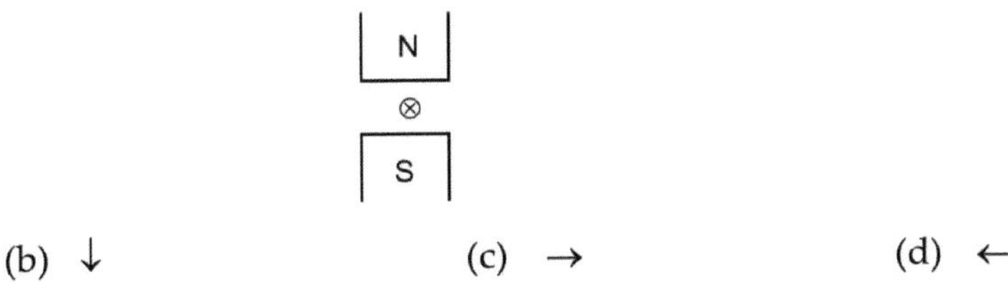

(a) ↑

(b) ↓

(c) →

(d) ←

Question 16

The plot shown in the figure represents the flow of current through a wire at three different times. The ratio of charges flowing through the wire at different times is:

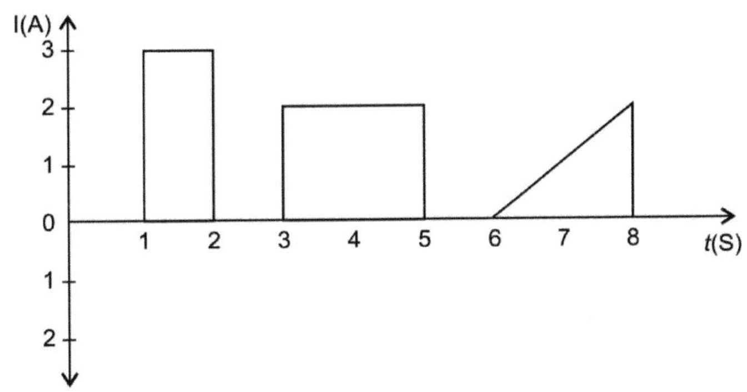

(a) $3:4:2$

(b) $1:2:2$

(c) $1:1:1$

(d) $1:4:2$

Question 17

Two bulbs of 500 W and 250 W are manufactured to operate on a 230 V line. If their resistances are R_1 and R_2 respectively, then R_1/R_2 is:

(a) $\dfrac{1}{2}$

(b) 2

(c) $\dfrac{1}{3}$

(d) $\dfrac{1}{5}$

Question 18

The given figure shows currents flowing in a part of an electric circuit, then the value of current I is:

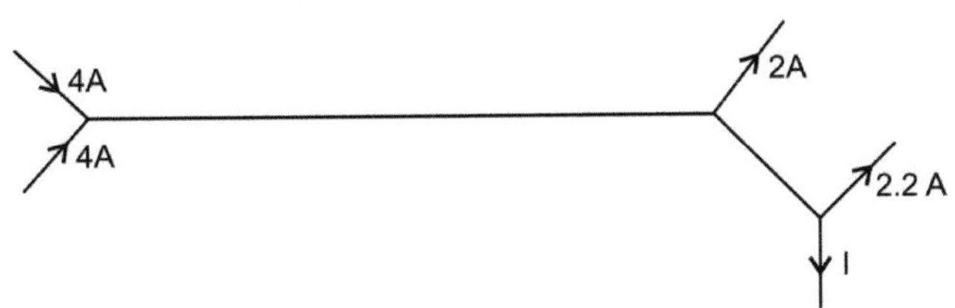

(a) 1.8 A

(b) 3.8 A

(c) 6 A

(d) 3.2 A

Question 19

The resistances in the four arms of a wheatstone network in cyclic order are 4 Ω, 2 Ω, 6 Ω and 15 Ω. If a current of 2 A enters the junction of 4 Ω and 15 Ω, then the current through 2 Ω resistor is:

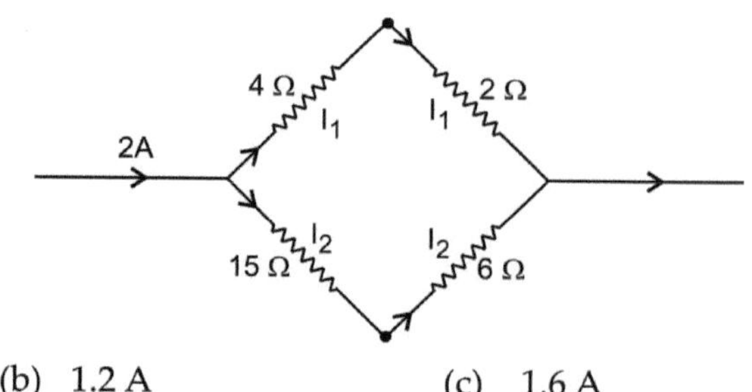

(a) 2.0 A (b) 1.2 A (c) 1.6 A (d) 2.5 A

Question 20

The resistance of 12 Ω each are connected as shown in the figure. Then, the effective resistance between A and B is:

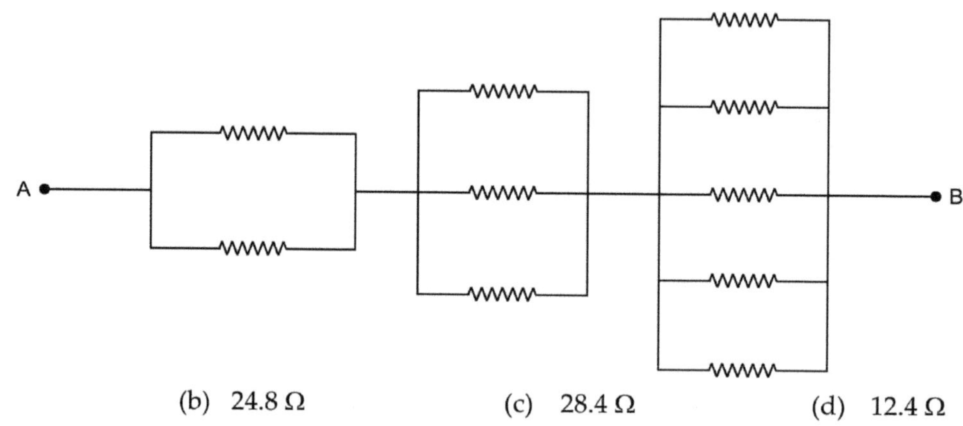

(a) 18.8 Ω (b) 24.8 Ω (c) 28.4 Ω (d) 12.4 Ω

Question 21

The equation of emf in an AC circuit is given by E = 40 sin (100 πt). The minimum time taken for the emf to change from + 20 V to – 20 V is:

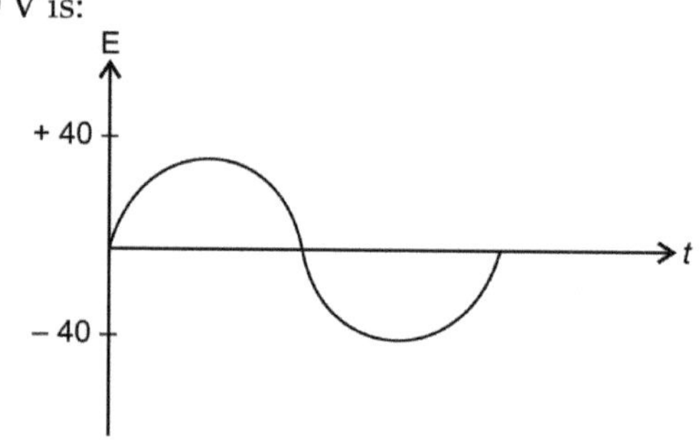

(a) 1/100 S (b) 1/600 S (c) 1/400 S (d) 100 S

Question 22

If the electric current through an electric bulb is 4.8 A, then the number of electrons flowing through it in 2 seconds is

(a) 2×10^{19} (b) 6×10^{19} (c) 3×10^{19} (d) 5×10^{19}

Question 23

A wire of length l is stretched to $4l$ length keeping volume constant. Then, the new resistance becomes

(a) 4 times (b) 2 times (c) 16 times (d) 10 times

Question 24

A silver wire has a resistance of 1.2 Ω at 25.5°C and a resistance of 2.4 Ω at 100°C, then temperature coefficient of resistivity of silver is:

(a) $2.5 \times 10^{-3}\,°C^{-1}$ (b) $3.2 \times 10^{-2}\,°C^{-1}$ (c) $2.04 \times 10^{-2}\,°C^{-1}$ (d) $1.3 \times 10^{-2}\,°C^{-1}$

Question 25

If the resistance of the upper half of a rigid loop is twice to that of the lower half, then the magnitude of the magnetic induction at point O will be:

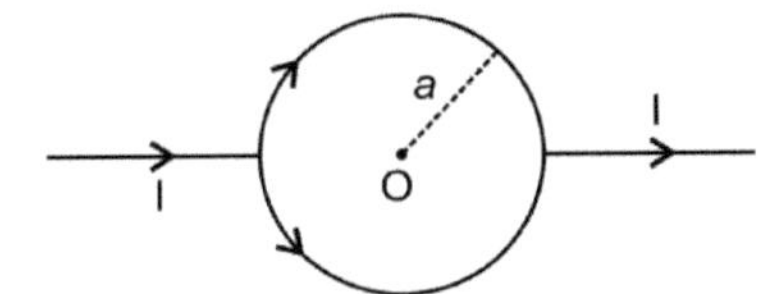

(a) zero
(b) $\dfrac{\mu_0 I}{12a}$
(c) $\dfrac{\mu_0 I}{2a}$
(d) $\dfrac{\mu_0 I}{3a}$

Question 26

A coil having 1000 turns forming square loop of side 10 cm is placed normal to magnetic field which increases at a rate of 1 T s^{-1}. The induced emf is:

(a) 5 V
(b) 10 V
(c) 2 V
(d) 20 V

Question 27

Current flows through a metallic conductor whose area of cross-section increases in the direction of the current. If we move in this direction,

(a) the current will decrease.
(b) the current will increase.
(c) the drift velocity will increase.
(d) the drift velocity will decrease.

Question 28

The validity of Ohm's law lies when:

(a) V is directly proportional to I^2.
(b) V is inversely proportional to I.
(c) V is directly proportional to I^3.
(d) V depends on I linearly.

Question 29

32 cells each of emf 2V and internal resistance 1 Ω are connected in parallel to a load resistor of 10 Ω. Then, the current through the load resistor is:

(a) 5 A
(b) 1 A
(c) 1.5 A
(d) 0.199 A

Question 30

The potential gradient along the length of a uniform wire is 20 V/m. If B and C are the two points at 40 cm and 80 cm on a metre wire along the wire, then the potential difference between B and C will be:

(a) 8 V
(b) 6 V
(c) 16 V
(d) 20 V

Question 31

A closely wound solenoid has 500 turns per metre length of the solenoid. A current of 2 A flows through it. The magnetic induction at the end of the solenoid on its axis is:

(a) $6\pi \times 10^{-4}$ T
(b) $2\pi \times 10^{-4}$ T
(c) $4\pi \times 10^{-4}$ T
(d) $8\pi \times 10^{-4}$ T

Question 32

When a strong magnetic field is applied on a stationary electron, then the electron will:

(a) move in the direction of the field.
(b) move in the direction opposite of the field.
(c) remain stationary.
(d) move perpendicular to the direction of the field.

Question 33

A N turns closely wound circular coil of radius r carries a current I. The magnetic moment of the coil varies as:

(a) $\dfrac{1}{r}$
(b) $\dfrac{1}{r^2}$
(c) r^2
(d) r

Question 34

The amplitude of an alternating voltage is 110 V. Its rms value will be:

(a) 77.8 V
(b) 70.7 V
(c) 102.2 V
(d) 112 V

Question 35

Which of the following have zero average value in a plane electromagnetic wave?

(a) Both magnetic and electric fields
(b) Electric field only
(c) Magnetic field only
(d) Magnetic energy only

Question 36

An electromagnetic wave is propagating along x-axis. At $x = 1$m and $t = 10$s, its electric vector $\vec{E} = 3.6$ V/m. then, the magnitude of its magnetic vector is:

(a) 3×10^{-8} T

(b) 1.2×10^{-8} T

(c) 2×10^{-8} T

(d) 2.8×10^{-8} T

Question 37

Which part of the spectrum of electromagnetic radiation is used for aircraft navigation?

(a) Ultraviolet rays

(b) Radiowaves

(c) X-rays

(d) Infrared waves

Question 38

Which of the following is the correct arrangement of the electromagnetic spectrum in the increasing order of frequency?

(a) Microwaves, radiowaves, visible light, X-rays.

(b) Radiowaves, microwaves, infrared, visible light, X-rays.

(c) X-rays, visible light, infrared, microwaves, radiowaves.

(d) Microwaves, infrared, radiowaves, visible light, X-rays.

Question 39

A potential difference of 100 V is applied to the ends of a copper wire one metre long.

(i) What is the magnitude of electric field produced ?

(a) 100 Vm^{-1}

(b) 20 Vm^{-1}

(c) 10 Vm^{-1}

(d) 25 Vm^{-1}

(ii) What is the average drift velocity of the electrons ? Given that, number of free electrons per unit volume is 8.45×10^{28} m^{-3} and conductivity of copper is 5.81×10^{7} Ω^{-1} m^{-1}.

(a) 1 ms^{-1}

(b) 0.43 ms^{-1}

(c) 0.18 ms^{-1}

(d) 1.3 ms^{-1}

Question 40

Four charges are placed at the vertices of a rectangle as shown in figure. The magnitude of charge q is 50 nC. Assume E and F are the mid points of AB and DC respectively.

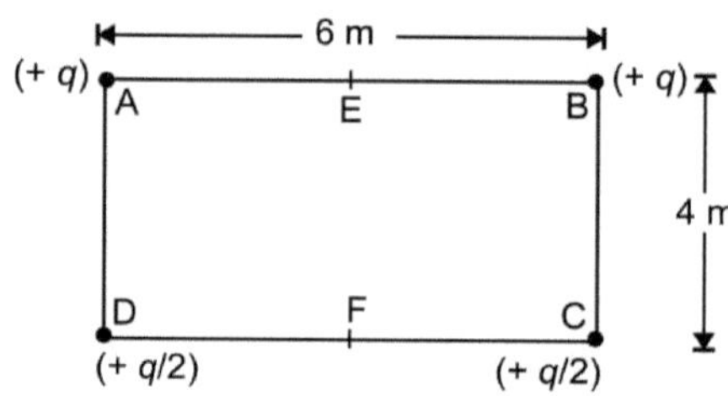

(i) What is the potential at point E?

(a) 390 V

(b) 350 V

(c) 310 V

(d) 300 V

(ii) What is the potential at point F?

(a) 320 V

(b) 310 V

(c) 330 V

(d) 390 V

Question 41

n identical light bulbs each having resistance R are joined in series across a certain voltage supply, V. Each bulb is designed to draw P power from the supply.

(i) What is the current drawn by each bulb?

(a) $\dfrac{nR}{V}$

(b) $\dfrac{V}{nR}$

(c) $n^2 \dfrac{V}{R}$

(d) $\dfrac{V^2}{nR}$

(ii) What is the total power drawn by all bulbs?

(a) $n^2 P$

(b) nP

(c) $\dfrac{P}{n^2}$

(d) $\dfrac{P}{n}$

Question 42

In the circuit shown, the galvanometer G of resistance 60 Ω is connected to a supply voltage of 5.0 V.

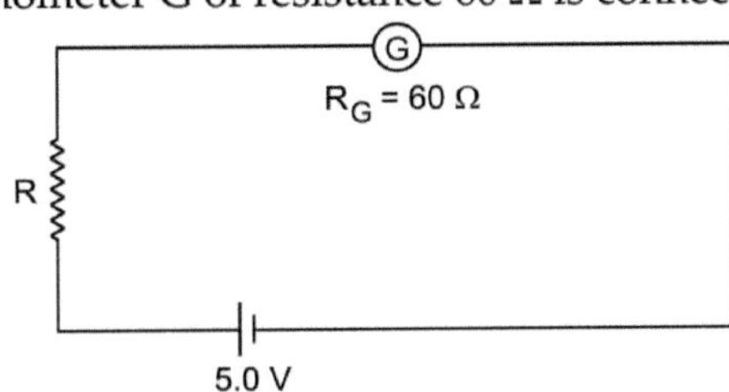

(i) If the galvanometer G is shunted by a resistance $r = 0.02$ Ω, then the effective resistance of the galvanometer will be nearly.

   (a) 2 Ω   (b) 0.02 Ω   (c) 0.2 Ω   (d) 20 Ω

(ii) if current through R is 1 A, then the value of R is nearly:

   (a) 5 Ω   (b) 2 Ω   (c) 50 Ω   (d) 0.5 Ω

Question 43

A current of 2A enters at the corner A of a square frame of side 15 cm and leaves at the opposite corner C. A magnetic field of B = 0.20 T acts in a direction perpendicular to the plane of the paper, as shown in figure.

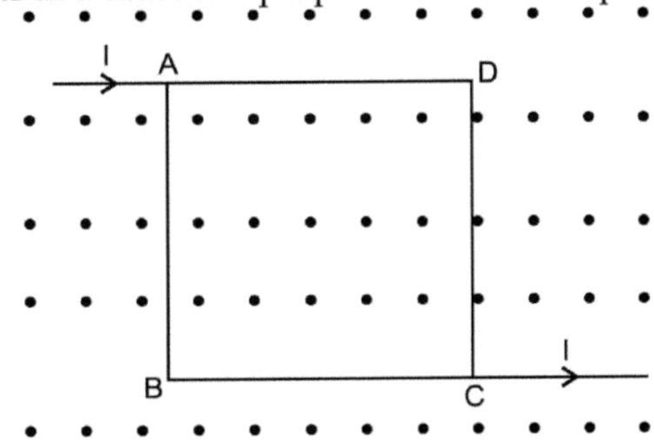

(i) What is the magnitude of magnetic forces acting on the four sides of the frame?

   (a) 0.05 N   (b) 3 N   (c) 0.03 N   (d) 5 N

(ii) Choose the correct statement.

   (a) Force on AB is towards left.   (b) Force on DC is towards right.

   (c) Force on AD is upwards.   (d) Force on BC is upwards.

Question 44

A 100 turn closely wound circular coil of radius 10 cm carries a current of 3.2 A.

(i) What is the magnetic moment of this arrangement?

   (a) 10 Am^2 (b) 20 Am^2 (c) 50 Am^2 (d) 100 Am^2

(ii) The coil is placed in a vertical plane and is free to rotate. A uniform magnetic field of 2T, rotates the coil through an angle of 90°. What is the magnitude of torque acting on the coil?

   (a) 10 Nm   (b) 20 Nm   (c) 50 Nm   (d) 25 Nm

Question 45

A 10 m long wire of uniform cross-section and resistance 20 Ω is used as a potentiometer wire. This wire is connected in series with a battery of 5V along with an external resistance of 480 Ω.

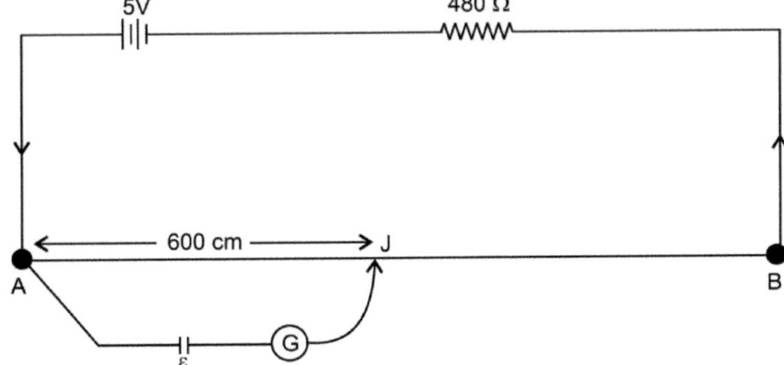

  (i)   What is the potential difference acorss the wire?

     (a) 0.2 V   (b) 0.1 V   (c) 0.02 V   (d) 0.01 V

  (ii) What is the potential gradient of the wire?

     (a) $200\ \text{V cm}^{-1}$ (b) $20\ \text{V cm}^{-1}$ (c) $0.0002\ \text{V cm}^{-1}$ (d) $2\ \text{V cm}^{-1}$

  (iii) If an unknown emf ε is balanced at 600 cm of the potentiometer wire, then what is the value of unknown emf ε?

     (a) 1.2 V   (b) 0.12 V   (c) 1 V   (d) 2 V

Question 46

An air core solenoid 50 cm long having radius 2 cm has 500 number of turns.

  (i)   What is the self-inductance of the solenoid?

     (a) $1.49 \times 10^{-2}\ \text{H}$ (b) $7.89 \times 10^{-4}\ \text{H}$ (c) $1.68 \times 10^{-3}\ \text{H}$ (d) $6.88 \times 10^{-5}\ \text{H}$

  (ii) If a rate of change of current of $4\ \text{As}^{-1}$ induces a current of 20 mV in the solenoid, what is the self inductance of the solenoid?

     (a) 10 mH   (b) 6 mH   (c) 2 mH   (d) 5 mH

  (iii) The inductance in a coil plays the same role as:

     (a) inertia in mechanics   (b) energy in mechanics

     (c) momentum in mechanics   (d) force in mechanics

Question 47

A battery of 6 cells each of emf 2V and internal resistance 0.5 Ω is being charged by DC mains of emf 220 V by using an external resistance of 10 Ω.

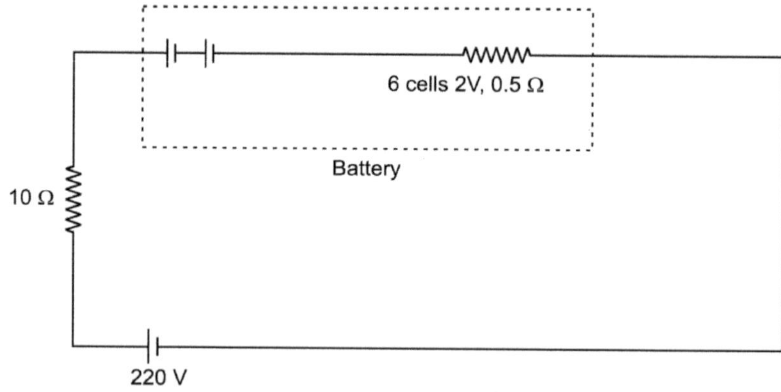

  (i)   What is the net emf and net resistance of the battery?

     (a) 10 V, 2 Ω (b) 12 V, 2 Ω (c) 10 V, 5 Ω (d) 12 V, 3 Ω

  (ii) What is the charging current?

     (a) 10 A   (b) 12 A   (c) 16 A   (d) 2 A

  (iii) What is the potential difference across the battery?

     (a) 60 V   (b) 40 V   (c) 20 V   (d) 50 V

Question 48

A rectangular coil having 100 turns is turned in a uniform magnetic field of $\dfrac{0.05}{\sqrt{2}}\ \hat{j}$ as shown in figure.

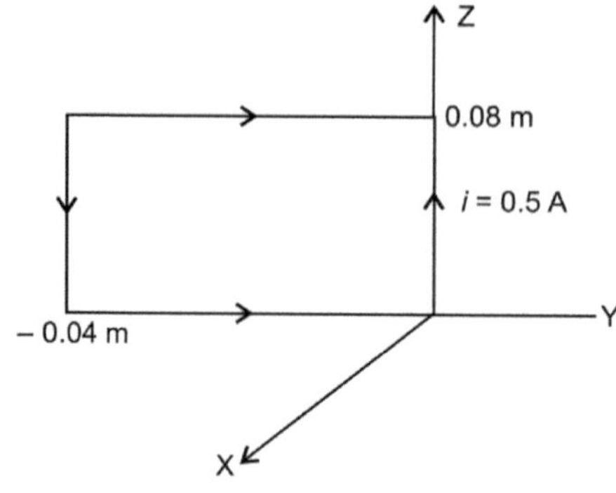

(i) What is the magnetic dipole moment of the current carrying coil?

    (a) $16 \times 10^{-2} \ \hat{j}$ (b) $8 \times 10^{-2} \ \hat{j}$ (c) $16 \times 10^{-2} \ \hat{j}$ (d) $8 \times 10^{-2} \ \hat{j}$

(ii) What is the torque acting on the coil?

    (a) $8.20 \times 10^{-7} \ \hat{j}$ NM   (b) $5.66 \times 10^{-5} \ \hat{k}$ Nm (c) $1.64 \times 10^{-4} \ \hat{j}$ Nm (d) $3.33 \times 10^{-5} \ \hat{k}$ Nm

(iii) What is the amount of work required to turn the coil from a position in which θ equal to zero to θ equal to 180° ?

    (a) 2.5 J   (b) 2 J   (c) 3.3 J   (d) 1.13 J

Question 49

A 2 μF capacitor, 100 Ω resistor and 8H inductor are connected in series with an a.c. source. The peak value of emf of the source is 200 V.

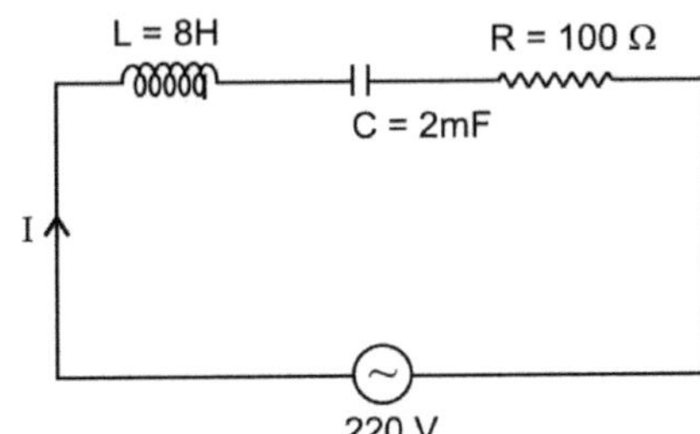

(i) What should be the frequency of the a.c. source for which the current drawn in the circuit is maximum?

    (a) 39.8 Hz   (b) 45 Hz   (c) 25.6 Hz   (d) 20.8 Hz

(ii) What are the inductive and capacitive reactances of the circuit?

    (a) 1000 Ω (b) 2000 Ω (c) 200 Ω (d) 100 Ω

(iii) What is the total impedance of the circuit?

    (a) 100 Ω (b) 1000 Ω (c) 2000 Ω (d) 200 Ω

(iv) What is the peak value of current in the circuit?

    (a) 1 A   (b) 20 A   (c) 2 A   (d) 5 A

Question 50

Anishka was walking by the side of a substation along with her grandfather. Anishka noticed transformers other power system equipments. She asked her grandfather about it. Her grandfather explained her the need of transformers as a power system equipment. Anishka listen to her grandfather very carefully and asked questions to know more about the working and uses of transformers.

(i) Which element is commonly used to make core of a transformer?

    (a) Steel   (b) Copper   (c) Soft iron   (d) Aluminium

(ii) Which quantity remains unchanged in a transformer?

    (a) voltage   (b) current   (c) frequency   (d) none of these

(iii) Why does the core of a transformer is laminated?

    (a) to reduce flux leakage.   (b) to reduce copper loss.

    (c) to reduce hysteresis.   (d) to reduce eddy currents.

(iv) In step-up transformers, what is the relation between number of turns in primary (N_P) and number of turns in secondary (N_S) coils?

    (a) N_S is greater than N_P (b) N_P is greater than N_S

    (c) N_S is equal to N_P (d) $N_P = 2N_S$

Answers

1. (c) $\dfrac{q}{6\varepsilon_0}$

    Explanation: $\phi_E = \dfrac{q_{enclosed}}{\varepsilon_0}$

Since, the charge is at the centre of the cube, net flux would symmetrically and equally distributed through each of the six surfaces of a cube.

$\therefore$ Electric flux passing through any one surface

$$= \frac{1}{6}\frac{q}{\varepsilon_0}$$

2. (d) $(N_2 - N_1)e$

Explanation:

Total charge, $q = N_2 \times e + N_1 \times (-e)$
$$= (N_2 - N_1)\,e$$

3. (a) $\dfrac{q^2\sqrt{3}}{4\pi\varepsilon_0 l^2}$

Explanation: According to Coulomb's law,

$$F = \frac{q^2}{4\pi\varepsilon_0 l^2}$$

$$F_{net} = 2\,F\cos 30°$$
$$= F\sqrt{3}$$

$\therefore \qquad F_{net} = \dfrac{q^2\sqrt{3}}{4\pi\varepsilon_0 l^2}$

4. (b) 12×10^{-3} Nm

Explanation: $\vec{\tau} = \vec{p} \times \vec{E}$

or $\qquad \tau = p\mathrm{E}\sin\theta$

For maximum torque, $\theta = 90°$

$\therefore \qquad \tau_{max} = p\mathrm{E} = q \times l \times \mathrm{E}$

or $\quad \tau_{max} = 3 \times 10^{-6}\ \mathrm{C} \times 0.02\ \mathrm{m} \times 2 \times 10^5\ \mathrm{N/C}$
$$= 12 \times 10^{-3}\ \mathrm{Nm}$$

5. (c) 4×10^{-4} H

Explanation: $L = \dfrac{\mu_0 N^2 A}{l}$

$$= \frac{4\pi \times 10^{-7} \times (400)^2 \times 4 \times 10^{-4}}{0.2}$$

$$\simeq 4 \times 10^{-4}\ \mathrm{H}$$

6. (d) 50 V

Explanation: $V = \sqrt{V_R^2 + (V_L - V_C)^2}$

$$= \sqrt{(40\ \mathrm{V})^2 + (60\ \mathrm{V} - 30\ \mathrm{V})^2}$$

$$= \sqrt{(40)^2 + (30)^2} = 50\ \mathrm{V}$$

7. (b) radially outwards

Explanation: Electric lines of force about a positive point charge are always radially outwards.

8. (c) W

Explanation: The work done in bringing a unit positive charge from infinity to a point which is at a distance d from the positive charge Q is defined as the potential at the given point due to the charge Q. Therefore, potential at that point is W.

9. (b) 8.3 V

Explanation: From the given figure, 3 μF and 3 μF are in parallel and their equivalent capacitance is 6 μF.

The equivalent circuit now reduced to

The equivalent capacitance between A and B is

$$\frac{1}{C} = \frac{1}{6} + \frac{1}{3} + \frac{1}{6} + \frac{1}{3}$$

or $\qquad C = 1$ μF

Now, charge in the circuit,
$$Q = CV = (1\ \mu F) \times (50\ \mathrm{V})$$
$$= 50\ \mu C$$

Potential difference across 6 μF capacitor

$$= \frac{50\ \mu C}{6\ \mu F}$$

$$= 8.3\ \mathrm{V}$$

10. (c) zero

Explanation: The surface charge density on the spherical shell is zero.

11. (a) along the diagonal AC

Explanation: Magnitude and polarity of charges at point B and D are same. Thus, force at O due to these charges cancel each other. Polarities of charges at A and C are opposite, therefore force on charge kept at the centre O is along the diagonal AC.

12. (d) $8.5 \times 10^6\ \mathrm{ms}^{-1}$

Explanation: Force on electron in a uniform magnetic field, $F = e\mathrm{E}$

Acceleration of the electron, $a = \dfrac{F}{m} = \dfrac{e\mathrm{E}}{m}$

where m is the mass of the electron.

Starting from rest, velocity of the electron when it has travelled a distance S is given by

$$v = \sqrt{2aS} = \sqrt{\frac{2e\mathrm{E}}{m}S}$$

Here, $\dfrac{e}{m} = 1.8 \times 10^{11}\ \mathrm{C\ kg}^{-1}$, $\mathrm{E} = 10^4\ \mathrm{N/C}$ and

$S = 2 \times 10^{-2}\ \mathrm{m}$

$\therefore \qquad v = \sqrt{2 \times 1.8 \times 10^{11} \times 10^4 \times 2 \times 10^{-2}}$

$$= 8.5 \times 10^6\ \mathrm{ms}^{-1}$$

13. (a) $\vec{\mathrm{E}}$ changes, V remains same

Explanation: When charges on A and B i.e., $(+q, +q)$ are interchanged with those on D and C i.e., $(-q, -q)$, potential V remains same since it is a scalar quantity (algebraic sum of potentials due to charges on A, B, C and D). However, electric field intensity $\vec{E}$ being a vector quantity, is reversed in direction.

14. (c) the radii of the wires

    Explanation: The force between two parallel current carrying wires is independent of the radii of the wires.

15. (d) $\leftarrow$

    Explanation: According to Fleming's left hand rule, the direction of the magnetic force on the wire is, $\leftarrow$

16. (a) $3:4:2$

    Explanation: Charge for a given time

    = area under the curve of current

    $\qquad$ – time graph for the given time

    $\therefore \qquad q_1 = 3 \times 1 = 3C$

    $\qquad q_2 = 2 \times 2 = 4C$

    $\qquad q_3 = \dfrac{1}{2} \times 2 \times 2 = 2C$

    $\therefore \quad q_1 : q_2 : q_3 = 3 : 4 : 2$

17. (a) $\dfrac{1}{2}$

20. (d) $12.4\,\Omega$

    Explanation:

Explanation: $R = \dfrac{V^2}{P}$

$\Rightarrow \qquad \dfrac{R_1}{R_2} = \dfrac{P_2}{P_1} = \dfrac{250}{500} = \dfrac{1}{2}$

18. (b) 3.8 A

    Explanation: Applying Kirchoff's first law,

    $\qquad I = 4 + 4 - 2 - 2.2 = 3.8\,A$

19. (c) 1.6 A

    Explanation: Resistance of the upper arm $= 6\,\Omega$

    Resistance of the lower arm $= 21\,\Omega$

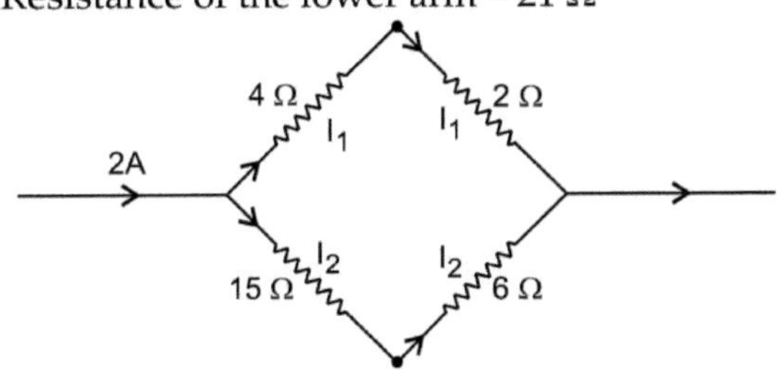

Current through the upper arm

$$I_1 = \dfrac{2A \times 21\Omega}{6\Omega + 21\Omega} = 1.6A$$

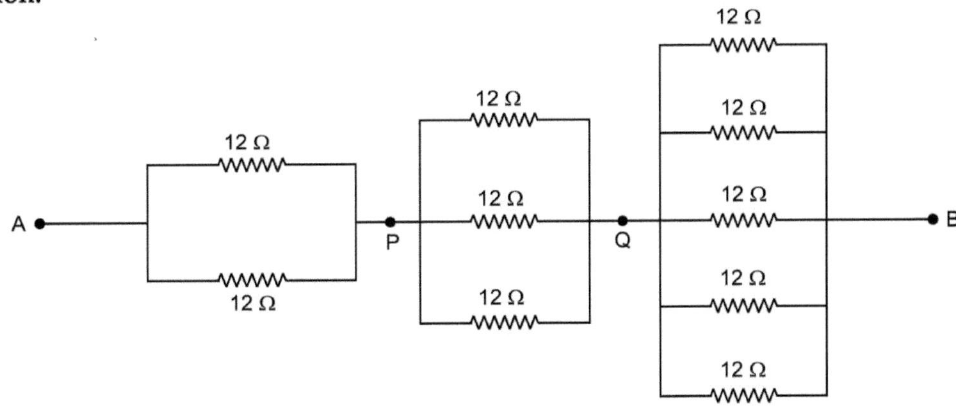

Equivalent resistance between

$$AP = \dfrac{12 \times 12}{12 + 12} = 6\,\Omega$$

Equivalent resistance between

$$PQ = \dfrac{12}{3} = 4\,\Omega$$

Equivalent resistance between

$$QB = \dfrac{12}{5} = 2.4\,\Omega$$

$\therefore$ Equivalent resistance between

$\qquad AB = 6\,\Omega + 4\,\Omega + 2.4\,\Omega$

$\qquad\qquad = 12.4\,\Omega$

21. (a) 1/100 S

    Explanation: $E = 40 \sin (100\,\pi t)$

    $\qquad 20 = 40 \sin (100\,\pi t_1)$

$\Rightarrow \qquad \dfrac{1}{2} = \sin (100\,\pi t_1)$

$\Rightarrow \qquad 100\,\pi t_1 = \dfrac{\pi}{6}$

$\Rightarrow \qquad t_1 = \dfrac{1}{600}\,s$

Similarly,

$\qquad -20 = 40 \sin (100\,\pi t_2)$

$\Rightarrow \qquad -\dfrac{1}{2} = \sin (100\,\pi t_2)$

$\Rightarrow \qquad 100\,\pi t_2 = \dfrac{7\pi}{6}$

$\Rightarrow \qquad t_2 = \dfrac{7}{600}\,s$

$$\therefore \qquad t_2 - t_1 = \frac{7}{600} - \frac{1}{600}$$

$$= \frac{1}{100} \text{ s}$$

22. (b) 6×10^{19}

Explanation: $I = \dfrac{Q}{t}$ or $Q = It$ or $ne = It$

$$\therefore \quad n = \frac{It}{e} = \frac{4.8 \times 2}{1.6 \times 10^{-19}} = 6 \times 10^{19}$$

23. (c) 16 times

Explanation: $R = \rho \dfrac{l}{A}$ or $R = \rho \dfrac{l}{V} \times l \; (\because V = Al)$

$$\therefore \qquad R \propto l^2$$

Now, $\qquad R \propto (4l)^2$

$\therefore$ The new resistance of the wires, $R' = 16\,R$.

24. (c) $2.04 \times 10^{-2}\ ^\circ C^{-1}$

Explanation: Here, $T_1 = 25.5\ ^\circ C$, $T_2 = 100^\circ C$, $R_{T_1} = 1.2\,\Omega$, $R_{T_2} = 2.4\ \Omega$

Temperature coefficient of resistivity

$$\alpha = \frac{R_2 - R_1}{R_1 t_2 - R_2 t_1}$$

$$= \frac{2.4 - 1.2}{1.2 \times 100 - 2.4 \times 25.5}$$

$$= \frac{1.2}{120 - 61.2}$$

$$= \frac{1.2}{58.8} = 0.0204^\circ C^{-1}$$

$$= 2.04 \times 10^{-2\,\circ}C^{-1}$$

25. (b) $\dfrac{\mu_0 I}{12a}$

Explanation:

$\because \qquad I_1 R_1 = I_2 R_2$

$$\therefore \qquad \frac{I_1}{I_2} = \frac{R_2}{R_1} = \frac{R_2}{2R_2} = \frac{1}{2}$$

or $\qquad I_2 = 2I_1$

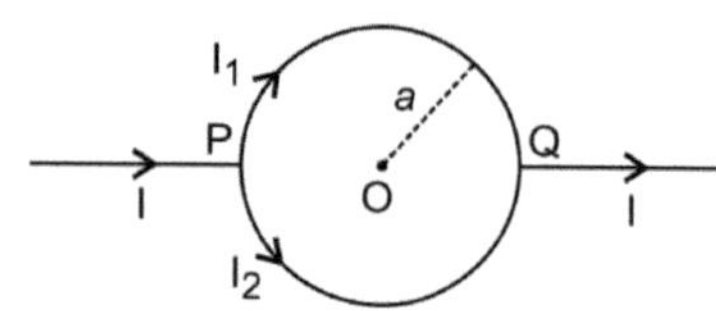

Also, $\qquad I = I_1 + I_2$

$$= I_1 + 2I_1 = 3I_1$$

$$\therefore \qquad I_1 = \frac{I}{3}$$

and $\qquad I_2 = \frac{2I}{3}$

Magnetic field at the centre of the coil is,

$$\vec{B}_0 = B_1 \otimes + B_2 \odot$$

or $\qquad B_0 = -\dfrac{\mu_0 I_1 \pi}{4\pi a} + \dfrac{\mu_0 I_2 \pi}{4\pi a}$ or

$$B_0 = \frac{\mu_0 \pi}{4\pi a}(I_2 - I_1)$$

$$= \frac{\mu_0}{4a}\left(\frac{2I}{3} - \frac{I}{3}\right)$$

$$= \frac{\mu_0}{4a}\left(\frac{I}{3}\right)$$

or $\qquad B_0 = \dfrac{\mu_0 I}{12a}$

26. (b) 10 V

Explanation: Here, $A = 1000 \times (0.1)^2 = 10\ m^2$

$$\frac{dB}{dt} = 1\ Ts^{-1}$$

Induced emf,

$$|\varepsilon| = \frac{d\phi}{dt} = A\frac{dB}{dt}$$

$$= 10 \times 1 = 10\ \text{volt}$$

27. (d) the drift velocity will decrease.

Explanation: $\because$ Whatever be the cross-section, current remains the same. When a steady current flows through a metallic conductor of non-uniform cross-section, then drift velocity is given as

$$v_d = \frac{I}{ne A}$$

or $\qquad v_d \propto \dfrac{1}{A}$

Thus, current remains constant and drift velocity will decrease.

28. (d) V depends on I linearly.

Explanation: According to Ohm's law, $V \propto I$ or $V = RI$, where R is a constant of proportionality called the resistance of the conductor.

29. (d) 0.199 A

Explanation: $I = \dfrac{m\varepsilon}{mR + r}$

Here, $m = 32$, $\varepsilon = 2V$, $r = 1\ \Omega$ and $R = 10\ \Omega$

$$\therefore \qquad I = \frac{64}{320 + 1} = 0.199\ A$$

30. (a) 8V

Explanation: Distance between two points

$$= 80 - 40$$

$$= 40\ cm = 0.4\ m$$

Potential gradient = 20 V/m

$\therefore$ Potential difference

$$= \text{Potential gradient} \times \text{length}$$

$$= 20 \times 0.4 = 8\ V$$

31. (b) $2\pi \times 10^{-4}$ T

Explanation:

$$B = \frac{\mu_0 n I}{2} = \frac{(4\pi \times 10^{-7}) \times 500 \times 2}{2} = 2\pi \times 10^{-4}\,T$$

32. (c) remain stationary

Explanation: $\vec{F} = q(\vec{v} \times \vec{B})$

As, the electron is stationary, velocity $\vec{v} = 0$

$\therefore \qquad \vec{F} = 0$

So, the electron will remain stationary.

33. (c) r^2

Explanation: Magnetic moment, M = NIA
$= NI\pi r^2$

$\therefore \qquad M \propto r^2$

34. (a) 77.8 V

Explanation: Given that, $V_0 = 110$ V

$\therefore \qquad V_{rms} = \frac{V_0}{\sqrt{2}} = \frac{110}{\sqrt{2}} = 77.8$ V

35. (a) Both magnetic and electric fields

Explanation: Both magnetic and electric fields have zero average value in a plane electromagnetic wave.

36. (b) 1.2×10^{-8} T

Explanation: Here, $\vec{E} = 3.6$ V/m

Magnitude of magnetic vector is,

$$|\vec{B}| = \frac{|\vec{E}|}{C}$$

$$= \frac{3.6\ V/m}{3 \times 10^8\ m/s}$$

$$= 1.2 \times 10^{-8}\ T$$

37. (b) Radiowaves

Explanation: For radar systems used in aircraft navigation, radiowaves part of the electromagnetic spectrum is used.

38. (b) Radiowaves, microwaves, infrared, visible light, X-rays.

Explanation: The increasing order of frequencies of the electromagnetic spectrum is

$v_{radio} < v_{micro} < v_{infrared} < v_{visible} < v_{x\text{-}rays}$

39. (i) (a) $100\ Vm^{-1}$

Explanation: V = 100 V and $l = 1$ m

$\therefore$ Electric field $= \frac{v}{l} = \frac{100}{1} = 100\ Vm^{-1}$

(ii) (b) $0.43\ ms^{-1}$

Explanation: $v_d = \frac{\sigma}{ne} E$

$$= \frac{5.81 \times 10^7 \times 100}{8.45 \times 10^{28} \times 1.6 \times 10^{-19}}$$

$$= 0.43\ ms^{-1}$$

40. (i) (a) 390 V

Explanation:

$$DE = CE = \sqrt{(AE)^2 + (AD)^2}$$

$$= \sqrt{(3)^2 + (4)^2} = 5\ m$$

Now, potential at point E,

$$V_E = \frac{1}{4\pi\varepsilon_0}\left[\frac{q}{AE} + \frac{q}{BE} + \frac{q/2}{DE} + \frac{q/2}{CE}\right]$$

$$= \frac{1}{4\pi\varepsilon_0}\left[\frac{q}{3} + \frac{q}{3} + \frac{q/2}{5} + \frac{q/2}{5}\right]$$

$$= \frac{1}{4\pi\varepsilon_0}\left[\frac{2q}{3} + \frac{q}{5}\right]$$

$$= \frac{1}{4\pi\varepsilon_0} \times \frac{13q}{15}$$

$$= \frac{9 \times 10^9 \times 13 \times 50 \times 10^{-9}}{15}$$

$$= 390\ V$$

(ii) (c) 330 V

Explanation: AF = BF

$$= \sqrt{(AD)^2 + (DF)^2}$$

$$= \sqrt{(4)^2 + (3)^2} = 5\ m$$

Now, potential at point F,

$$V_F = \frac{1}{4\pi\varepsilon_0}\left[\frac{q}{AF} + \frac{q}{BF} + \frac{q/2}{DF} + \frac{q/2}{CF}\right]$$

$$= \frac{1}{4\pi\varepsilon_0}\left[\frac{q}{5} + \frac{q}{5} + \frac{q/2}{3} + \frac{q/2}{3}\right]$$

$$\frac{1}{4\pi\varepsilon_0} \times \frac{11q}{15} = \frac{9 \times 10^9 \times 11 \times 50 \times 10^{-9}}{15}$$

$$= 390\ V$$

41. (i) (b) $\dfrac{V}{nR}$

Explanation: Here, V is the supply voltage, and R is the resistance of each bulb.

$$\therefore \qquad R = \frac{V^2}{P}$$

When n bulbs are joined in series across V, current in each bulb will be,

$$I = \frac{V}{nR}$$

(ii) (d) $\dfrac{P}{n}$

Explanation: Power drawn by each bulb
$= I^2 R$

$$= \frac{V^2}{n^2 R^2} \times R$$

$$= \frac{V^2}{n^2 R} = \frac{P}{n^2}$$

$\therefore$ Total power drawn $= n \times \dfrac{P}{n^2} = \dfrac{P}{n}$

42. (i) (b) $0.02\ \Omega$

    Explanation: Here, $R_G = 60\ \Omega$, $r = 0.02\ \Omega$
When the galvanometer is shunted by a resistance r, its effective resistance is

$$R' = \frac{R_G r}{R_G + r}$$

$$= \frac{(60\,\Omega)(0.02\,\Omega)}{60\,\Omega + 0.02\,\Omega} \approx 0.02\ \Omega$$

  (ii) (a) $5\ \Omega$

    Explanation: Total resistance of the circuit

$$= R + R' = R + 0.02$$

$\therefore$ Current in the circuit,

$$I = \frac{5}{R + 0.02}$$

or $\qquad 1 = \dfrac{5}{R + 0.02}$

or $\qquad R + 0.02 = 5$

or $\qquad R = 5 - 0.02$

or $\qquad R \approx 5\ \Omega$

43. (i) (c) $0.03\ N$

    Explanation: Current through each four sides wil be 1 A, due to symmetry.
Given that, $l = 15\ cm = 0.15\ m$ and $B = 0.20\ T$
Magnitude of force on each side is

$$F = Bil \sin 90°$$

$$= 0.20 \times 1 \times 0.15 \times \sin 90°$$

$$= 0.03\ N$$

  (ii) (a) Force on AB is towards left

    Explanation: By Fleming's left hand rule, forces on AB and DC will be towards left and on AD and BC it is downwards.

44. (i) (a) $10\ Am^2$

    Explanation: Here, $N = 100$, $I = 3.2\ A$ and $r = 10\ cm = 0.1\ m$
Magnetic moment associated with the coil,

$$m = NIA = 100 \times 3.2 \times 3.14 \times (0.1)^2$$

$$= 10\ Am^2$$

  (ii) (b) $20\ Nm$

    Explanation: $\quad \tau = mB \sin\theta$

$$= 10 \times 2 \times 1$$

$$= 20\ Nm$$

45. (i) (a) $0.2\ V$

    Explanation: Current through the potentiometer wire is

$$I = \frac{V}{R_{AB} + R}$$

$$= \frac{5V}{(20 + 480)\Omega} = 0.01$$

Resistance of the potentiometer wire,

$$R_{AB} = 20\ \Omega$$

$\therefore$ Potential difference across the wire,

$$V = I R_{AB}$$

$$= 0.01 \times 20$$

$$= 0.2\ V$$

  (ii) (c) $0.0002\ V\ cm^{-1}$

    Explanation: Length of potentiometer wire, $l = 10\ m = 1000\ cm$
Potential gradient,

$$K = \frac{V}{l} = \frac{0.2\ V}{1000\ cm} = 0.0002\ V\ cm^{-1}$$

 (iii) (b) $0.12\ V$

    Explanation: Unknown emf balanced against 600 cm length is

$$\varepsilon = Kl = 0.0002 \times 600 = 0.12\ V$$

46. (i) (b) $7.89 \times 10^{-4}\ H$

    Explanation: Here, $l = 50\ cm = 0.50\ m$
$r = 2\ cm = 2 \times 10^{-2}\ m$
$N = 500$
Self inductance of the solenoid,

$$L = \frac{\mu_0 N^2 A}{l}$$

$$= \frac{\mu_0 N^2 \pi r^2}{l}$$

$$= \frac{4\pi \times 10^{-7} \times (500)^2 \times \pi \times (2 \times 10^{-2})^2}{0.50}$$

$$= 7.89 \times 10^{-4}\ H$$

  (ii) (d) $5\ mH$

    Explanation: $\dfrac{dI}{dt} = 4\ A\ s^{-1}$

and $\quad |\varepsilon| = 20\ mV$

$$= 20 \times 10^{-3}\ V$$

$$|\varepsilon| = L \frac{dI}{dt}$$

$\therefore \qquad L = \dfrac{|\varepsilon|}{dI/dt}$

$$= \frac{20 \times 10^{-3}}{4}$$

$$= 5 \times 10^{-3}\ H$$

$$= 5\ mH$$

(iii) (a) inertia in mechanics

Explanation: The inductance in a coil plays the same role as inertia in mechanics.

47. (i) (d) 12 V, 3 Ω

Explanation: Net emf of the battery = 6 × 2 = 12 V

Net resistance of the battery = 6 × 0.5 = 3Ω

(ii) (c) 16 A

Explanation: Charging current,

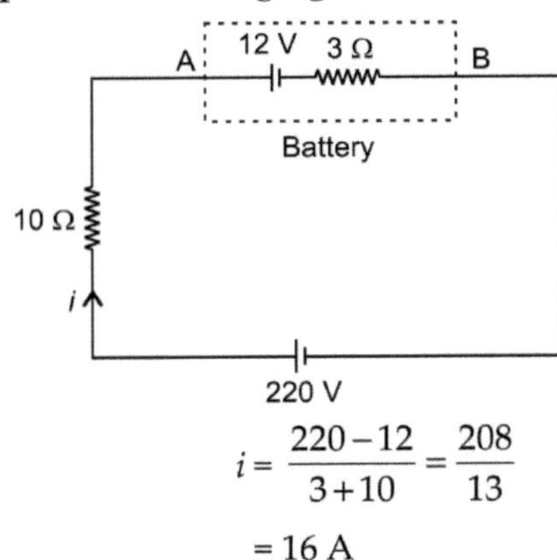

$$i = \frac{220-12}{3+10} = \frac{208}{13}$$

$$= 16 \text{ A}$$

(iii) (a) 60 V

Explanation: $V_A - V_B = 12 + 16 \times 3$

$$= 60 \text{ V}$$

48. (i) (c) $16 \times 10^{-2} \; \hat{j}$

Explanation: Magnetic dipole moment of the current carrying coil is

$$M = NiA\,\hat{n} = 100 \times 0.5 \times (0.08 \times 0.04)\hat{i}$$

or $\qquad M = 16 \times 10^{-2} \; \hat{i} \; \text{Am}^2$

(ii) (b) $5.66 \times 10^{-5} \; \hat{j} \; \text{Nm}$

Explanation: Torque acting on the coil is

$$\tau = M \times B$$

$$= MB(\hat{i} \times \hat{j})$$

$$= 16 \times 10^{-2} \times \frac{0.05}{\sqrt{2}}\hat{k}$$

or $\qquad \tau = 5.66 \times 10^{-5} \; \hat{k} \; \text{Nm}$

(iii) (d) 1.13 J

Explanation: $W = -M.B = -MB \cos\theta$

$$\Delta W = W_f - W_i$$

$$= -(-MB) - (-MB)$$

$$= 2 \text{ MB}$$

$$= 2 \times 16 \times 10^{-2} \times \frac{0.05}{\sqrt{2}} = 1.13 \text{ J}$$

49. (i) (a) 39.8 Hz

Explanation: Current drawn in the circuit will be maximum when the frequency of the a.c. source is equal to the resonant frequency of the circuit.

$$f_r = \frac{1}{2\pi\sqrt{LC}}$$

$$= \frac{1}{2\sqrt{8 \times 2 \times 10^{-6}}}$$

$$= \frac{10^3}{8\pi} = 39.8 \text{ Hz}$$

(ii) (b) 2000 Ω

Explanation: At resonance,

$$X_L = X_C = 2\pi F_r L$$

$$= 2\pi \times 39.8 \times 8$$

$$= 2000 \; \Omega$$

(iii) (a) 100 Ω

Explanation: Total impedance at resonance,

$$Z = R = 100 \; \Omega$$

(iv) (c) 2 A

Explanation: Peak value of current,

$$I_0 = \frac{\varepsilon_0}{Z} = \frac{\varepsilon_0}{R} = \frac{200}{100} = 2A$$

50. (i) (c) Soft iron

Explanation: The core of a transformers is usually made of soft iron.

(ii) (c) frequency

Explanation: A transformer does not change the frequency of ac.

(iii) (d) to reduce eddy currents

Explanation: The core of a transformer is laminated to reduce eddy currents.

(iv) (a) N_S is greater than N_P

Explanation: In step-up transformer, number of turns in secondary coil is greater than the number of turns in primary coil.

❑❑

4 Sample Paper

Questions

Question 1

Relative permittivity of a medium is 27. If ε_m and ε_0 are permittivity of medium and vacuum respectively then:

(a) $\varepsilon_o = 9\,\varepsilon_m$
(b) $\varepsilon_o = 27\,\varepsilon_m$
(c) $\varepsilon_m = 9\,\varepsilon_o$
(d) $\varepsilon_m = 27\,\varepsilon_o$

Question 2

A body has a negative charge of 16×10^{-19} C it has:

(a) an excess of 5 electrons
(b) an excess of 10 electrons
(c) a deficiency of 16 electrons
(d) a deficiency of 8 electrons

Question 3

A positive charge Q kept at the centre O of a square PQRS having four charges are arranged at the corners as shown in the figure. The force on the charge Q.

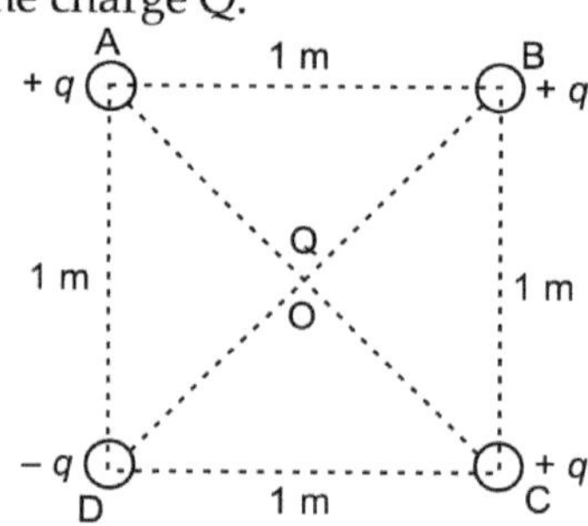

(a) $\dfrac{2Qq}{4\pi\varepsilon_0}$
(b) $\dfrac{Qq}{4\pi\varepsilon_0}$
(c) 0
(d) None of these

Question 4

A negative charge is given to a soap bubble, then its radius:

(a) remains same
(b) increases
(c) decreases
(d) none of these

Question 5

The line charge density of a conductor

(a) is inversely proportional to the length of conductor.
(b) is directly proportional to the length of conductor.
(c) does not depend on length.
(d) none of the above.

Question 6

The dimensional formula for induced emf?

(a) $ML^3T^{-1}A^{-1}$
(b) $MLT^{-2}A^{-1}$
(c) $ML^2T^{-3}A^{-1}$
(d) $MLT^{-3}A^{-1}$

Question 7

The average value of a.c. during a half cycle is:

(a) $\dfrac{2i_o}{\pi}$
(b) 0
(c) $\dfrac{i_o}{\pi}$
(d) 1

Question 8

An electric dipole of dipole moment $\vec{p}$ is placed in an electric field $\vec{E}$ then the maximum amount of work done in rotating the dipole through angle is:

(a) $-mB$ (b) $2\,mB$ (c) $-2\,mB$ (d) mB

Question 9

A charge particle having charge Q placed at a distance r from an electric dipole in the end-on position. If the distance is doubled then the electric field experiences by the charge particle will become:

(a) $\dfrac{E}{4}$ (b) $\dfrac{E}{8}$ (c) $8E$ (d) $4E$

Question 10

Two point charges $(+2q)$ and $(-2q)$ are kept inside a large metallic cube without touching its sides. Electric flux emerging out of the cube is:

(a) $\dfrac{4q}{\varepsilon_0}$ (b) $\dfrac{2q}{\varepsilon_0}$ (c) 0 (d) $\dfrac{q}{\varepsilon_0}$

Question 11

Five capacitors each of capacitance 1 µF, are connected in series. The ratio of capacitance C_p to C_s, where C_p is parallel combination of capacitors and C_s is equivalent capacitance of series combination, is:

(a) $5:1$ (b) $1:5$ (c) $50:1$ (d) $25:1$

Question 12

The S.I. unit of electric dipole moment is:

(a) $C\text{-}m^2$ (b) $C\text{-}m$ (c) C/m (d) C/m^2

Question 13

The work done in taking an electron around a nucleus in a circular path is:

(a) maximum   (b) minimum   (c) 0 (d) none of these

Question 14

Two capacitors $C_1 = 1$ µF, $C_2 = 2$ µF are connected in parallel to a 100 V battery as shown in figure below. The equivalent capacitance of the circuit on point A and B and charge on C_2 will be:

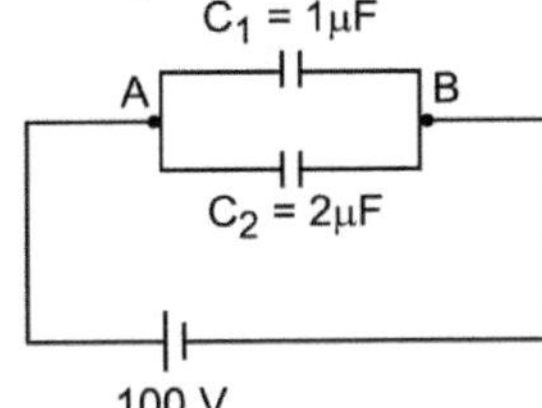

(a) 1 µF, 300 µC   (b) 3 µF, 200 µC   (c) 5 µF, 100 µC   (d) None of these

Question 15

A moving coil galvanometer can be converted into ammeter by connecting:

(a) a low resistance in series with its coil.
(b) a low resistance in parallel with its coil.
(c) a high resistance in parallel with its coil.
(d) a high resistance in series with its coil.

Question 16

An a.c. voltage is applied to a resistance R and inductance L in series. The phase difference between the applied voltage and the current in the circuit, if the resistance R and inductive reactance are both equal to 5Ω, is:

(a) 0 (b) $\dfrac{\pi}{6}$ (c) $\dfrac{\pi}{4}$ (d) $\dfrac{\pi}{2}$

Question 17

A moving electron enters a uniform and perpendicular magnetic field. Inside the magnetic field, the electron travels along:

(a) straight line   (b) parabola   (c) circular   (d) hyperbola

Question 18

The current flowing in the circuit shown in figure below, will be:

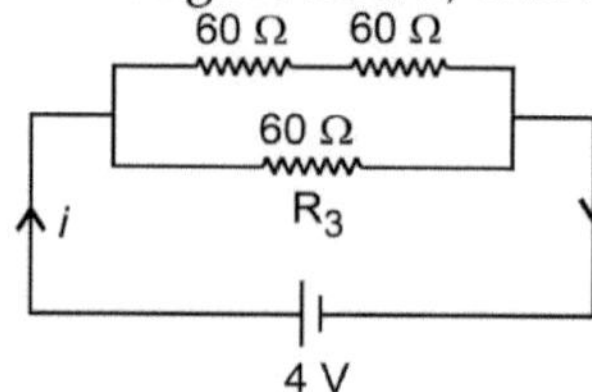

(a) 10 A (b) $\dfrac{1}{20}$ A (c) $\dfrac{1}{10}$ A (d) 20 A

Question 19

A cell of e.m.f. E is connected with an external resistance R, the potential difference across the cell is V. The current flow in the circuit is:

(a) $\dfrac{E-V}{r}$ (b) $(E+v)r$ (c) $\dfrac{E+V}{r}$ (d) $(E-V)r$

Question 20

With the help of Kirchauff current's law, the value of current i is:

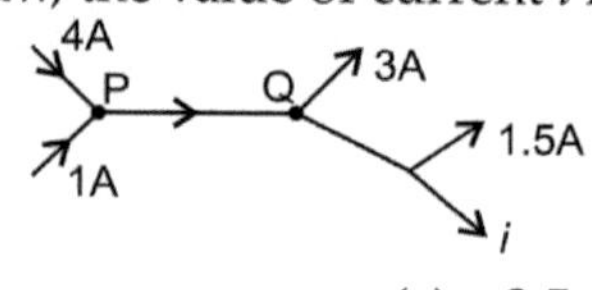

(a) 1.5 (b) 2.5 (c) 3.5 (d) 0.5

Question 21

5 identical cells each of emf 5V and internal resistance 1Ω are connected in series. An external resistance $R = 10\ \Omega$ is connected in series to this combination. The current through R is:

(a) 1.33 A (b) 1.66 A (c) 1.22 A (d) 1.34 A

Question 22

A potentiometer shown in given figure having resistance $0.5\ \Omega$ and $l = 1$ m. The potential gradient will be :

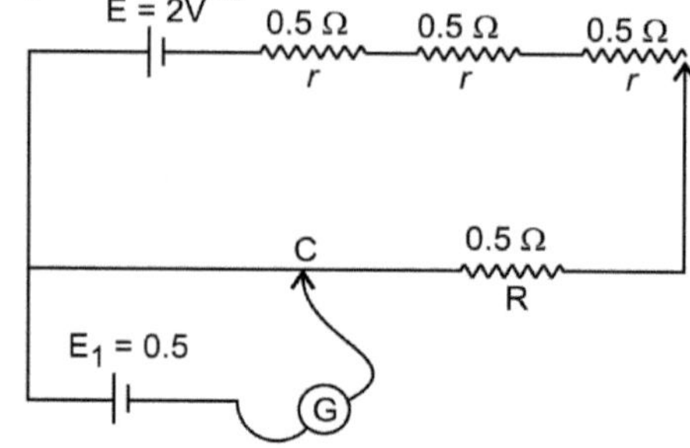

(a) 0.5 volt/cm (b) 0.25 volt-m (c) 0.5 volt/m (d) none of these

Question 23

The emf generated by ac generator is given by $\varepsilon = \varepsilon_0 \sin 210\ \pi t$. What is the frequency of emf?

(a) 115 Hz (b) 100 Hz (c) 105 Hz (d) 110 Hz

Question 24

The drift velocity of a current carrying conductor is V_d if current flowing through the wire is halved then the value of drift velocity is:

(a) remains same (b) four times (c) doubled (d) halved

Question 25

The specific resistance is given by:

(a) $\dfrac{RA}{l}$ (b) $\dfrac{Rl}{A}$ (c) RAl (d) $\dfrac{Al}{R}$

Question 26

If the resistance of wire is $1\ \Omega$. If the radius of wire is halved then the new resistance will be:

(a) 2 R (b) 16 R (c) 8 R (d) 4 R

Question 27

In LCR circuit, L = 1H, R = 10 Ω, C = 1 μF., the resonant frequency is: (in Hz)

(a) $\dfrac{500}{\pi}$　　　(b) 250 π　　　(c) 500 π　　　(d) None of these

Question 28

The Biot-savert law in vector form is:

(a) $\vec{dB} = \dfrac{\mu_0}{4\pi}\dfrac{dl(\vec{I}\times\vec{r})}{r^3}$　　(b) $\vec{dB} = \dfrac{\mu_0}{4\pi}\dfrac{I(\vec{dl}\times\vec{r})}{r^3}$　　(c) $\vec{dB} = \dfrac{\mu_0}{4\pi}\dfrac{I(\vec{r}\times\vec{dl})}{r^3}$　　(d) $\vec{dB} = \dfrac{\mu_0}{4\pi}\dfrac{I(\vec{dl}\times\vec{r})}{r^2}$

Question 29

Five resistance are connected as shown in figure. The equivalent resistance between point A and B is:

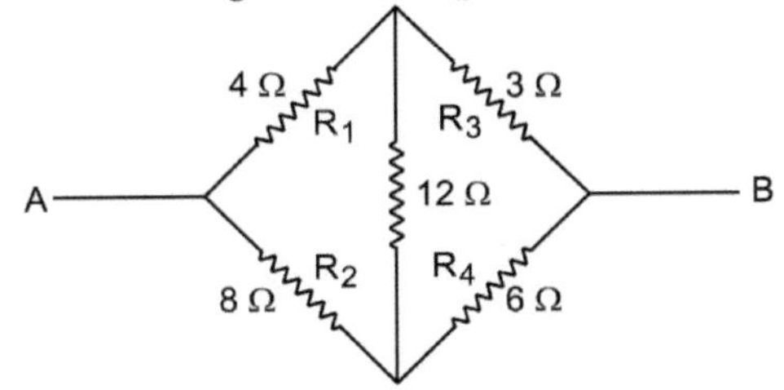

(a) $\dfrac{14}{3\Omega}$　　　(b) 14 Ω　　　(c) $\dfrac{3}{14\Omega}$　　　(d) None of these

Question 30

A potentiometer of length 1 m connected to a 5 Ω resistor and 1 volt battery. If the resistance of potentiometer wire is 5 Ω, then the value of potential gradient is:

(a) 0.05 volt/cm　　(b) 0.5 volt/cm　　(c) 0.005 volt/cm　　(d) 0.5 volt/m

Question 31

In a meter bridge experiment, the ratio of the left gap resistance to right gap resistance is 4 : 1. The balance point from left is:

(a) 20 cm　　(b) 40 cm　　(c) 80 cm　　(d) 60 cm

Question 32

When an electron projected perpendicular to a uniform electric field. The locus of electron is:

(a) Parabola　　(b) Straight line　　(c) Circle　　(d) Right bisector

Question 33

When a charged particle moving parallel to a magnetic field, then the force F is:

(a) qvB　　(b) $qBv/2$　　(c) 0　　(d) None of these

Question 34

The dimension of μ_0:

(a) $MLT^{-2}A^{-2}$　　(b) $ML^{-2}T^{-2}A^{-2}$　　(c) $MLT^{-3}A^{-1}$　　(d) $MLT^{-1}A^{-1}$

Question 35

The rays, which are used for the treatment of cancer:

(a) UV ray　　(b) γ-ray　　(c) IR　　(d) α-ray

Question 36

In transformer, the output power is slightly less than input power due to:

(a) Hysteresis loss　　(b) Flux loss　　(c) Eddy current　　(d) All of these

Question 37

In electromagnetic spectrum, which quantity remains same for all types of wave?

(a) speed of light　　(b) frequency　　(c) wavelength　　(d) none of these

Question 38

Which of the following groups of waves in the electromagnetic spectrum is given in increasing order of frequency?

(a) Radio wave, IR, visible ray, UV　　　　(b) X-ray, visible ray, radio wave, IR

(c) UV, visible ray, IR, Radio wave　　　　(d) IR, UV rays, radiowave, visible rays

Question 39

The resistance of a wire is given by 100 Ω:

(i) The specific resistance of wire of length 1 m and area 2 m^2 is:

   (a) 100 Ω-m   (b) 200 Ω-m   (c) 300 Ω-m   (d) 400 Ω-m

(ii) The specific resistance is proportional to:

   (a) L   (b) R   (c) A   (d) None of these

Question 40

A parallel plate capacitor of plate separation $d = 1$ mm and area 50 cm^2 is connected to a battery of 50 V.

(i) If a dielectric medium, $k = 4$ is filled between plates, then the value of C is:

   (a) 177 μF   (b) 17.7 μF   (c) 177 pF   (d) 17.7 pF

(ii) The magnitude of electric field between plates is:

   (a) 5×10^3 V/m   (b) 5×10^4 V/m   (c) 5×10^2 V/m   (d) 5×10^5 V/m

Question 41

A heater of 1 kW and a tungsten bulb of 100 W both marked for 220 V.

(i) The resistance of heater is:

   (a) 50.4 Ω   (b) 51 Ω   (c) 48.4 Ω   (d) 46 Ω

(ii) Which of the two has greater resistance?

   (a) Both are same   (b) R_b (c) R_h (d) None of these

Question 42

In LCR circuit, the impedance Z is given by $Z = \sqrt{R^2 + \left(\omega L - \dfrac{1}{\omega C}\right)^2}$

(i) The value of Z will be minimum if:

   (a) $\omega L > \dfrac{1}{\omega C}$ (b) $\omega L = \dfrac{1}{\omega C}$ (c) $\omega L < \dfrac{1}{\omega C}$ (d) None of these

(ii) The current in LCR circuit will be maximum if frequency is:

   (a) $Z = R$ (b) $Z < R$ (c) $Z > R$ (d) None of these

Question 43

An a.c. generator generates an e.m.f. 'e' given by: $e = 311 \sin (100\,\pi t)$ volt.

(i) The rms value of emf generated by the generator is:

   (a) 21.99 V   (b) 2.199 V   (c) 219.9 V   (d) None of these

(ii) The frequency of emf generated by a.c. generator is:

   (a) 60 Hz   (b) 55 Hz   (c) 50 Hz   (d) 70 Hz

Question 44

A current 'i' flow through a metallic wire of radius 'r' and area 'A', the free electrons in it drift with a velocity 'v_d':

(i) The drift velocity of the free electron is given by:

   (a) $neAi$ (b) $\dfrac{nei}{A}$ (c) $\dfrac{i}{neA}$ (d) $\dfrac{neA}{i}$

(ii) If the drift velocity is doubled, then the current will become:

   (a) four times   (b) doubled   (c) halved   (d) none of these

Question 45

Three cells, each of e.m.f. 15 V after being connected in series with each other, are connected to the ends of a resistance. The current obtained is 1A. When the cells are connected in parallel with each other and are then connected to the end of the same resistance, the strength of the current through the resistance is 0.36 A.

(i) The value of unknown resistance is:

   (a) 3.50 Ω   (b) 4.125 Ω   (c) 0.125 Ω   (d) 3.125 Ω

(ii) Internal resistance of each cell is:

   (a) 0.125 Ω   (b) 1.525 Ω   (c) 1.125 Ω   (d) None of the these

(iii) The value of current is maximum when: (in series)
    (a) $R > nr$ (b) $R < nr$ (c) $R = nr$ (d) None of these

Question 46

A rectangular coil of 0.25 m × 0.1 m and having 100 turns rotates in a magnetic field of 3×10^{-2} T with a frequency of 2400 rpm about an axis parallel to the longer side and perpendicular to the magnetic field:

(i) The maximum induced e.m.f. is given by:
    (a) 18.58 V   (b) 18.48 V   (c) 18.84 V   (d) 18.28 V

(ii) Instantaneous e.m.f. when the plane of coil is normal to the magnetic field:
    (a) maximum   (b) minimum   (c) 0   (d) 16.32

(iii) If the plane of the coil is making an angle of 30° with magnetic field, then e.m.f.:
    (a) 16.32 V   (b) 18.48 V   (c) 18.84 V   (d) None of these

Question 47

The length of a potentiometer wire is 10 m and carries steady current on connecting the sliding jockey to standard cell of 1.018 volt, the null point is obtained at the distance of 850 cm.

(i) The potential gradient along wire is:
    (a) 1.2×10^{-2} Vm^{-1} (b) 1.2×10^{-2} V/cm   (c) 1.2×10^{-3} V cm^{-1} (d) 1.2×10^{-3} V cm

(ii) The maximum e.m.f. that can be measured is:
    (a) 1.3 volt   (b) 1.2 volt   (c) 1.4 volt   (d) 1.5 volt

(iii) If the length of potentiowire is doubled, then the e.m.f. will be:
    (a) halved   (b) doubled   (c) not change   (d) none of these

Question 48

A circular coil of radius 5 cm, number of turns 200 carries a current of 2A.

(i) The magnetic field at the centre of coil is:
    (a) 5.027×10^{-3} T   (b) 5×10^{-2} T   (c) 5×10^{-4} T   (d) None of these

(ii) At a distance of 10 cm from the center along the axis the magnetic field is:
    (a) 4.5×10^{-3} T   (b) 4×10^{-4} T   (c) 4.5×10^{-4} T   (d) 4.5×10^{-2} T

(iii) If the current increases to 4 times, then the magnetic field is:
    (a) doubled   (b) halved   (c) four times   (d) not change

Question 49

A rectangular coil of dimensions 30 cm × 10 cm having 100 turns rotates about an axis perpendicular to a uniform magnetic field of 0.04 Wbm^{-2}. If the coil makes 2000 revolutions per minute.

(i) The induced e.m.f., when the plane of coil, parallel to B, is:
    (a) 25.132 V   (b) 2.324 V   (c) 0 V   (d) 1.005 V

(ii) If the plane of coil makes an angle of 30° with magnetic field B then the value of e.m.f. is:
    (a) 25.132 V   (b) 1.005 V   (c) 21.76 V   (d) None of these

(iii) If $\theta = 90°$, i.e., plane of coil and magnetic field are p to each other then the induced e.m.f. is:
    (a) 0 V   (b) 24 V   (c) 25.132 V   (d) None of these

(iv) If the coil forms a closed loop of resistance 25 Ω, then the power is dissipated on heat is:
    (a) 23.3 W   (b) 22.3 W   (c) 24.3 W   (d) 25.3 W

Question 50

A pure inductance of 1.0 H is connected across 110 V, 70 Hz. source.

(i) The value of reactance is:
    (a) 330 Ω (b) 450 Ω (c) 440 Ω (d) 400 Ω

(ii) The current flowing through the capacitor is:
    (a) 1 A   (b) 0.25 A   (c) 0.5 A   (d) 0.75 A

(iii) The peak value of current is:
    (a) 0.334 A   (b) 0.1233 A   (c) 0.3535 A   (d) 0.2313 A

(iv) The energy stored in the inductor is:
    (a) 0.013 joule   (b) 0.031 joule   (c) 0.02 joule   (d) none of these

 **Answers**

1. (d) $\varepsilon_m = 27\,\varepsilon_0$

Explanation: We know that the permittivity of medium

$$\varepsilon_m = k\varepsilon_0$$
$$\varepsilon_m = 27\,\varepsilon_0$$

where ε_0 is the permittivity of free space.

2. (b) an excess of 10 electrons

Explanation: $q = ne$

$$n = \frac{q}{e} = \frac{16 \times 10^{-19}\,C}{1.6 \times 10^{-19}\,C}$$
$$= 10 \text{ electron}$$

So, body has an excess of 10 electrons.

3. (a) $\dfrac{2Qq}{4\pi\varepsilon_0}$

Explanation: Forces F_{OA} and F_{OC} are equal and opposite to each other. So they will cancel out.

$$F_{net} = F_{OD} + F_{OB}$$
$$= \frac{1}{4\pi\varepsilon}\left[\frac{Qq}{1^2} + \frac{Qq}{1^2}\right]$$
$$= \frac{2Qq}{4\pi\varepsilon_0}$$

4. (b) increases

Explanation: As the same charge is distributed on the soap bubble. So it causes a repulsive force, which increases the radius of bubble.

5. (a) is inversely proportional to the length of conductor.

Explanation: Line charge density, $\lambda = \dfrac{q}{l}$

6. (c) $ML^2T^{-3}A^{-1}$

Explanation: Work done = e.m.f. × charge

$$emf = \frac{\text{Work done}}{\text{charge}}$$
$$= \frac{ML^2T^{-2}}{AT}$$
$$= ML^2T^{-3}A^{-1}$$

7. (a) $\dfrac{2i_o}{\pi}$

Explanation: The average value of alternating current during half cycle is $i_{ow} = \dfrac{2i_o}{\pi}$

8. (b) 2mB

Explanation:

$$W = mB\,(\cos\theta_1 - \cos\theta_2)$$
$$= mB\,(1 - \cos\theta)$$

when $\theta = 180°$ the work done will be maximum

$$\therefore \quad W = mB\,(1 - \cos 180°)$$
$$= mB\,(2) = 2\,mB$$

9. (b) E/8

Explanation: The electric field at charge Q placed at a distance r from a electric dipole in the end-on position is given by

$$\vec{E} = \frac{1}{4\pi\varepsilon_0} \cdot \frac{2P}{r^3}$$
$$\vec{E} \propto \frac{1}{r^3},$$

if distance is doubled, then $E' = \dfrac{E}{8}$

10. (c) 0

Explanation: The net electric flux $\phi = \dfrac{q_{enc}}{\varepsilon_0}$

$$= \frac{+2q - 2q}{\varepsilon_0} = 0$$

11. (d) 25 : 1

Explanation:

$$\frac{1}{C_{\mu C}} = \frac{1}{1} + \frac{1}{1} + \frac{1}{1} + \frac{1}{1} = 5$$
$$C_{\mu C} = \frac{1}{5}\mu F$$

Again, $C_P = 1 + 1 + 1 + 1 + 1 = 5\,\mu F$

$$\frac{C_p}{C_s} = \frac{5\mu F}{\frac{1}{5}\mu F} = \frac{25}{1} = 25 : 1$$

12. (b) C-m

Explanation: The S.I. unit of electric dipole moment is coulomb-meter.

13. (c) 0

Explanation: Work done by an electron revolving in a circular orbit of radius 'r' around a nucleus is zero because here, force and displacement are at right angles ($\theta = 90°$).

14. (b) 3 μF, 200 μC

Explanation:
$$C_P = C_1 + C_2$$
$$= 1 + 2$$
$$= 3\,\mu F$$
$$\text{Charge Q} = C_P V$$
$$= 3\,\mu F \times 100$$
$$= 300\,\mu C$$

Charge on C_2, $Q_2 = C_2 V = 2 \times 10^{-6} \times 100$
$$= 200\,\mu C$$

15. (b) A low resistance in parallel with its coil.

Explanation: A galvanometer can be converted into ammeter by connecting a low resistance in parallel with its coil.

16. (c) $\dfrac{\pi}{4}$

Explanation: $\tan\phi = \dfrac{X_1}{R} = \dfrac{5}{5} = 1$

phase difference $\phi = \dfrac{\pi}{4}$

17. (c) circular

Explanation: $r = \dfrac{mv}{qB}$ m is the mass and q is charge of electron. r is the radius of path followed by the electron, when projected perpendicular to a magnetic field. The electron moves in a circular path.

18. (c) 1/10 A

Explanation: $R' = 60\ \Omega + 60\ \Omega = 120\ \Omega$

$$R_{eq} = \dfrac{R'R_3}{R' + R_3}$$

$$= \dfrac{120 \times 60}{120 + 60}$$

$$= \dfrac{7200}{180}$$

$$= 40\ \Omega$$

$$i = \dfrac{V}{R}$$

$$= \dfrac{4}{40} = \dfrac{1}{10}\ A$$

19. (a) $\dfrac{E - V}{r}$

Explanation: $E = V + ir$

where V is terminal voltage, E is the emf of cell and r is internal resistance.

$$\therefore \qquad i = \dfrac{E - V}{r}$$

20. (d) 0.5

Explanation: Using KCL, at point P

$$i_1 = 4 + 1 = 5A$$

Again, at point Q, by applying KCL

$$i_1 = 3 + 1.5 + i$$
$$5 = 3 + 1.5 + i \qquad (\because i_1 = 5A)$$
$$i = 0.5\ A$$

21. (b) 1.66 A

Explanation: Given, E = 5V, R = 10 Ω, r = 1Ω

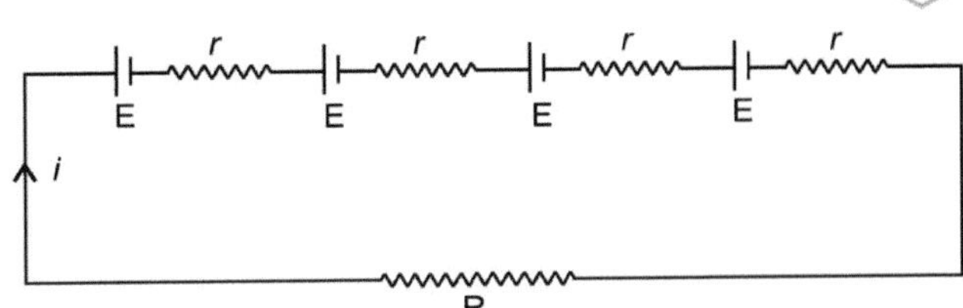

The current $i = \dfrac{nE}{R + nr}$

$$= \dfrac{5 \times 5}{10 + 5(1)}$$

$$= \dfrac{25}{15} = \dfrac{5}{3} = 1.66\ A$$

22. (c) 0.5 volt/m

Explanation:

$$E = i(r + r + r + R)$$
$$2 = i(0.5 + 0.5 + 0.5 + 0.5)$$
$$2i = 2$$
$$i = 1A$$

The potential across the potentiowire resistance $R = V_R = iR = 1 \times 0.5 = 0.5\ V$

Potential gradient, $K = \dfrac{V_R}{l} = \dfrac{0.5}{1} = 0.5$ volt/m

23. (c) 105 Hz

Explanation: $\varepsilon = \varepsilon_0 \sin 210\,\pi t$

By comparing $\varepsilon = \varepsilon_0 \sin \omega t$

$$\omega = 210\,\pi$$
$$2\pi f = 210\,\pi$$
$$f = 105\ Hz$$

24. (d) halved

Explanation: The drift velocity is given by

$$V_d = \dfrac{I}{neA}$$

where, I is current flowing in the conductor, A is the cross-section area.

$$v_d \propto I$$

$\therefore$ If current is halved, the v_d will become halved.

25. (a) $\dfrac{RA}{l}$

Explanation: Resistance of any ohmic conductor,

$$R = \rho \dfrac{l}{A}$$

where ρ is specific resistance, A is the cross-section and l is length of conductor.

$$\rho = \dfrac{RA}{l}$$

26. (b) 16 R

Explanation: $R = \rho \dfrac{l}{A} = \rho \dfrac{l}{\pi r^2}$

$$\therefore \qquad R \propto \frac{l}{r^2}$$

$\because$ Volume of wire remains same.

$$\therefore \qquad \pi r_1^2 l_1 = \pi r_2^2 l_2$$

$$\frac{r_1^2}{r_2^2} = \frac{l_2}{l_1}$$

$$\left(\frac{r_1}{r_2}\right)^2 = \frac{l_2}{l_1}$$

$$\frac{R_{new}}{R} = \frac{l_2}{r_2^2} \times \frac{r_1^2}{l_1}$$

$$= \left(\frac{r_1}{r_2}\right)^2 \times \left(\frac{l_2}{l_1}\right)$$

$$= \left(\frac{r_1}{r_2}\right)^2 \times \left(\frac{r_1}{r_2}\right)^2$$

$$= \left(\frac{r_1}{r_2}\right)^4$$

$$\because \qquad r_2 = \frac{r_1}{2}$$

$$\therefore \qquad \frac{R_{new}}{R} = \left(\frac{r_1}{r_1/2}\right)^4 = (2)^4 = 16$$

$$R_{new} = 16R$$

27. (a) $\dfrac{500}{\pi}$

Explanation: Resonant frequency

$$f = \frac{1}{2\pi\sqrt{C}}$$

$$= \frac{1}{2\pi\sqrt{1\times10^{-6}}}$$

$$= \frac{1}{2\pi\times10^{-3}}$$

$$= \frac{10^3}{2\pi} = \frac{500}{\pi}\,\text{Hz}$$

28. (b) $\vec{dB} = \dfrac{\mu_0}{4\pi}\dfrac{I(\vec{dl}\times\vec{r})}{r^3}$

Explanation: The biot-savart law is given by

$$\vec{dB} = \frac{\mu_0 I}{4\pi}\frac{(\vec{dl}\times\vec{r})}{r^3}$$

29. (a) $\dfrac{14}{3\Omega}$

Explanation: When bridge is balanced, then there is no current flow through $12\,\Omega$ resistance.

$$\because \qquad \frac{R_1}{R_2} = \frac{R_3}{R_4}$$

$$\Rightarrow \qquad \frac{4\Omega}{8\Omega} = \frac{3\Omega}{6\Omega}$$

$$\Rightarrow \qquad \frac{1}{2} = \frac{1}{2}$$

$\therefore$ Bridge is balanced.

Now, R_1 and R_3 are connected in series, R_2 and R_4 are in series combination.

$$\therefore \qquad R' = R_1 + R_3$$
$$= 4 + 3$$
$$= 7\,\Omega$$
$$R'' = R_2 + R_4$$
$$= 8 + 6$$
$$= 14\,\Omega$$

Again, R' and R'' in parallel,

$$\therefore \qquad \frac{1}{R_{AB}} = \frac{1}{R'} + \frac{1}{R''}$$

$$\Rightarrow \qquad R_{AB} = \frac{R'R''}{R'+R''}$$

$$= \frac{7\times14}{14+7} = \frac{98}{21} = \frac{14}{3\Omega}$$

30. (c) 0.005 volt/cm

Explanation: $E = i(5 + 5)$

$$i = \frac{1}{10}A = 0.1A$$

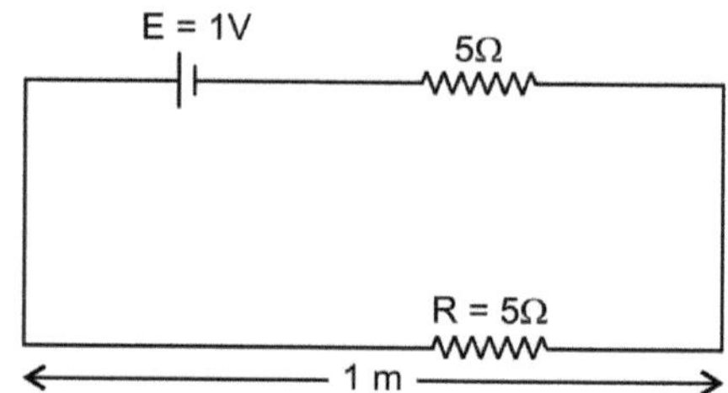

Potential difference across potentiowire

$$E' = iR$$
$$= 0.1 \times 5$$
$$= 0.5\text{ V}$$

Potential gradient, $K = \dfrac{E'}{l}$

$$= \frac{0.5}{100\text{ cm}}$$

$$= 0.005\text{ volt/cm}$$

31. (c) 80 cm

Explanation: In meter bridge,

$$\frac{P}{Q} = \frac{l}{100-l}$$

where l is the length of meter-bridge and P, Q are the left gap resistance and right gap resistance respectively.

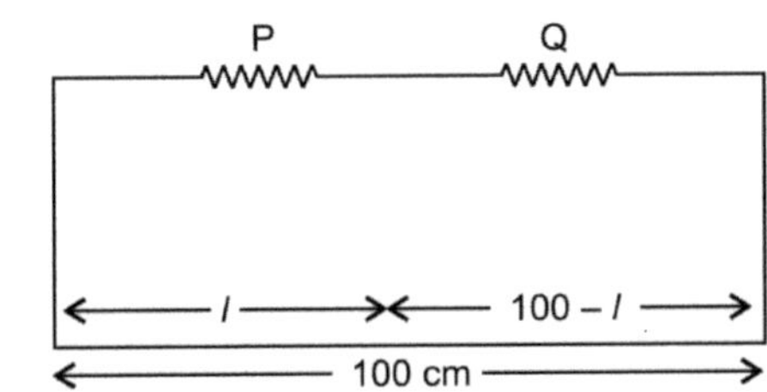

$\because$ Given $\quad P : Q = 4 : 1$

$\therefore \qquad \dfrac{4}{1} = \dfrac{l}{100 - l}$

$$400 - 4l = l$$
$$5l = 400$$
$$l = 80 \text{ cm}$$

The balancing point is 80 cm from left.

32. (a) Parabola

Explanation: An electron moving or follow a parabolic path when it projected perpendicular to a uniform electric field because it experience the electric force in a direction opposite to the field.

33. (c) 0

Explanation: $F = qv\, B \sin\theta$

when $\theta = 0°$ or $v \parallel B$

$$F = qv\, B \sin 0$$
$$= 0$$

34. (a) $MLT^{-2}A^{-2}$

Explanation: Dimension of $\mu_0 = MLT^{-2}A^{-2}$.

35. (b) γ-ray

Explanation: Gamma rays are used in chemotherapy for treatment of cancer.

36. (d) All of those

Explanation: There are some loss of power due to eddy current and hystesis loss, flux losses in the transformer.

37. (a) speed of light

Explanation: The speed of light c is constant for all the waves of electromagnetic spectrum while wavelength and frequency is different.

38. (a) Radio wave, IR, visible ray, UV

Explanation: The increasing order of frequency of waves is

Radio wave < IR < Visible rays < UV rays < X-rays < γ-rays

39. (i) (b) 200 Ω-m

Explanation:

$R = 100\ \Omega$, $l = 1$ m, $A = 2m^2$

$$R = \rho \dfrac{l}{A}$$

$$\rho = \dfrac{RA}{l}$$

$$= \dfrac{100 \times 2}{1}$$

$$= 200\ \Omega\text{-m}$$

(ii) (d) None of these

Explanation: Specific resistance is independent of length L, Area A and resistance R.

40. (i) (c) 177 pF

Explanation: $d = 1$ mm, $A = 50$ cm^2, $V = 50$ V, $K = 4$

Capacitance $C = \dfrac{\varepsilon_0 kA}{d}$

$$= \dfrac{8.85 \times 10^{-12} \times 4 \times 50 \times 10^{-4}}{10^{-3}}$$

$$= 177 \text{ pF}$$

(ii) (b) 5×10^4 V/m

Explanation: $E = \dfrac{V}{d} = \dfrac{50}{10^{-3}} = 5 \times 10^4$ V/m

41. (i) (c) 48.4 Ω

Explanation: $P_1 = 1000$ W (for heater)

$\qquad\qquad\quad P_2 = 100$ W (for bulb)

Resistance of heater,

$$R = \dfrac{V^2}{P_1}$$

$$= \dfrac{220 \times 220}{1000}$$

$$= 48.4\ \Omega$$

(ii) (b) R_b

Explanation: $R_{\text{heater}} = \dfrac{V^2}{P_1}$

$$= \dfrac{220 \times 220}{1000}$$

$$= 48.4\ \Omega$$

$$R_{\text{bulb}} = \dfrac{V^2}{P_2}$$

$$= \dfrac{220 \times 220}{100}$$

$$= 484\ \Omega$$

$$R_{\text{bulb}} > R_{\text{heater}}$$

42. (i) (b) $\omega L = \dfrac{1}{\omega C}$

Explanation:

Impedance $Z = \sqrt{R^2 + \left(\omega L - \dfrac{1}{\omega C}\right)^2}$

When, $\omega L = \dfrac{1}{\omega C}$ then $Z_{\min} = R$

(ii) (a) $Z = R$

Explanation: At resonance, $\omega L = \dfrac{1}{\omega C}$

We get minimum value of $Z = R$

If Z is minimum, the current will be higher.

43. (i) (c) 219.9 V

Explanation: $e = 311 \sin (110 \, \pi t)$

By $\quad e = e_0 \sin (100 \, \pi t)$

$\qquad e_0 = 311$ volt

$$e_{rms} = \frac{e_0}{\sqrt{2}} = \frac{311}{\sqrt{2}}$$

$$= 219.9 \text{ volt}$$

(ii) (c) 50 Hz

Explanation: $\omega = 100 \, \pi$

$\qquad 2\pi f = 100 \, \pi$

$\qquad\quad f = 50$ Hz

44. (i) (c) $\dfrac{i}{ne\text{A}}$

Explanation: The drift velocity $v_d = \dfrac{i}{ne\text{A}}$

(ii) (b) doubled

Explanation: $v_d \propto i \qquad \left(\because v_d = \dfrac{i}{ne\text{A}} \right)$

if drift velocity is doubled then the current will be increases to double.

45. (i) (b) 4.125 Ω

Explanation: Let the e.m.f. of the cell be E_1 internal resistance be r and the external resistance is R.

When the cells are connected in series

$$1 = \frac{n\text{E}}{\text{R} + nr}$$

We have, $n = 3$, $E = 1.5$ V, $I = 1$A

$$1 = \frac{3 \times 1.5}{\text{R} + 3r}$$

$$\text{R} + 3r = 4.5 \qquad\qquad ...(i)$$

When the cells are connected in parallel

$$i = \frac{\text{E}}{\text{R} + \dfrac{r}{m}} = \frac{m\text{E}}{m\text{R} + r}$$

We have I = 0.36 A, $m = 3$, $E = 1.5$ V

$$0.36 = \frac{3 \times 1.5}{3\text{R} + r}$$

$$3\text{R} + r = 12.5 \qquad\qquad ...(ii)$$

By (i) and (ii), we get

$$\text{R} = 4.125 \text{ Ω}, \; r = 0.125 \text{ Ω}$$

(ii) (a) 0.125 Ω

Explanation: By the previous question, on solving equations we get

$$r = 0.125 \text{ Ω}$$

(iii) (c) $\text{R} = nr$

Explanation: The value of current is maximum, when resistance is minimum

$$\text{I} = \frac{n\text{E}}{\text{R} + nr}$$

(for series combination of cell)

at $\text{R} = nr$, I will be maximum.

46. (i) (c) 18.84 V

Explanation: Here, B = 3×10^{-2} Wb/m^2,

A = $0.25 \times 0.1 = 0.025$ m^2, $n = 100$

Maximum induced e.m.f. is given by

$$\text{E}_0 = \text{BA}n\omega$$

$$\text{E}_0 = 3 \times 10^{-2} \times 0.025 \times 100 \times 80 \, \pi$$

$$\left(\because \omega = 2\pi f = \frac{2\pi.2400}{60} \text{ rps} \right) = 80\pi$$

$$= 18.84 \text{ V}$$

(ii) (c) 0

Explanation: When the coil is normal to the field

$\phi = \omega t = 0$, induced e.m.f., $\text{E} = \text{E}_0 \sin \omega t = 0$

(iii) (a) 16.32 V

Explanation: When the plane of the coil makes an angle 30° with the field,

$\omega t = \phi = 90° - 30° = 60°$

$$\text{E} = \text{E}_0 \sin \omega t$$

$$= 18.84 \times \sin 60°$$

$$= 16.32 \text{ V}$$

47. (i) (c) 1.2×10^{-3} V cm^{-1}

Explanation: Given: $l_1 = 10$ m,

$l_2 = 850$ cm $= 8.5$ m, $E_2 = 1.018$ V

$$\text{Potential gradient} = \frac{\text{E}_2}{l} = \frac{1.018}{850}$$

$$= 1.2 \times 10^{-3} \text{ V/cm}^{-1}$$

(ii) (b) 1.2 volt

Explanation:

$$\frac{\text{E}_1}{\text{E}_2} = \frac{l_1}{l_2}$$

$$\frac{\text{E}_1}{1.018} = \frac{10}{8.5}$$

$$\text{E}_1 = \frac{10 \times 1.018}{8.5} = 1.2 \text{ V}$$

(iii) (b) doubled

Explanation: $\text{E} = kl$

$\text{E} \propto l$ *i.e.* if length is doubled then E is also doubled.

48. (i) (a) 5.027×10^{-3} T

Explanation: Field at the centre of the coil

$$\text{B} = \frac{\mu_0 \text{N}_i}{2a}$$

$$= \frac{4\pi \times 10^{-7} \times 200 \times 2}{2 \times 5 \times 10^{-2}}$$

$$= 5.027 \times 10^{-3} \text{ T}$$

(ii) (c) 4.5×10^{-4} T

Explanation: Field at a distance x

$$B = \frac{\mu_0 N a^2 i}{2(a^2 + x^2)^{3/2}}$$

$$= \frac{4\pi \times 10^{-7} \times 200 \times (5 \times 10^{-2})^2 \times 2}{2[(5 \times 10^{-2})^2 + (10 \times 10^{-2})^2]^{3/2}}$$

$$= 4.5 \times 10^{-4} \text{ T}$$

(iii) (c)   four times

Explanation: $B \propto i$

The magnetic field will become four times.

49. (i)   (a)   25.132 V

Explanation: Given $B = 0.04$ Wb/m^2,

$A = 30 \times 10 \times 10^{-4}$ m^2, $N = 100$ turns,

$f = \dfrac{2000}{60}$ rev/sec

Peak value of e.m.f. generated

$$E_0 = BAN\omega$$

$$= 0.04 \times 30 \times 10 \times 10^{-4} \times 100$$

$$\times \left(2\pi \times \frac{2000}{60} \right)$$

$$= 25.132 \text{ V}$$

$\because \quad \theta = (90 - 0)^\circ = 90^\circ$

$$E = E_0 \sin \theta$$

$$= 25.132 \sin 90^\circ$$

$$= 25.132 \text{ V}$$

(ii) (c) 21.76 V

Explanation: $\theta = (90 - 30)^\circ = 60^\circ$

$$E = E_0 \sin 60^\circ$$

$$= 25.132 \times \frac{\sqrt{3}}{2}$$

$$= 21.76 \text{ V}$$

(iii) (a)   0 V

Explanation: $\theta = (90^\circ - 90^\circ) = 0^\circ$

$$E = E_0 \sin 0 = 0 \text{ V}$$

(iv) (d)   25.3 W

Explanation: $I_0 = \dfrac{E_0}{R}$

$$= \frac{25.132}{25} = 1.005 \text{ A}$$

Power dissipated as heat

$$= E_0 I_0 = 25.132 \times 1.005$$

$$= 25.3 \text{ W}$$

50. (i)   (c)   440 Ω

Explanation: $L = 1$H, $f = 70$ Hz

$$X_L = 2\pi f L$$

$$= 2\pi \times 70 \times 1$$

$$= 140 \pi$$

$$= 440 \ \Omega$$

(ii) (b)   0.25 A

Explanation: $I = \dfrac{V}{X_L}$

$$= \frac{110}{440} = \frac{1}{4} = 0.25 \text{ A}$$

(iii) (c)   0.3535 A

Explanation:

$$I_0 = I_{rms} \times \sqrt{2} = 0.25\sqrt{2} = 0.3535 \text{ A}$$

(iv) (a)   0.013 joule

Explanation: $U = \dfrac{1}{2} L I^2$

$$= \frac{1}{2} \times 1 \times (0.25)^2$$

$$= \frac{1}{2} \times \frac{1}{16}$$

$$= \frac{1}{32} \text{ Joule}$$

$$= 0.013 \text{ Joule}$$

❑❑

Question 1

The force between two charges q_1 and q_2 at a distance r, when a metal plate is placed between them.

(a) Decreases (b) Increases (c) remain same (d) Zero

Question 2

27 charges of equal values are combined together to make a large charge. It the potential of each charge is 5 V, then the potential of the big charge will be:

(a) 40 V (b) 45 V (c) 50 V (d) 55 V

Question 3

The SI unit of surface integral of electric field is:

(a) V (b) N/C (c) Vm (d) C/m^2

Question 4

Choose the correct statement:

(a) The electric force is attractive while gravitational force is repulsive.

(b) The electric force is repulsive while gravitational force is attractive.

(c) The electric force is either attractive or repulsive while gravitational force is always attractive.

(d) The electric force is always repulsive while the gravitational force may be repulsive or attractive.

Question 5

Choose the correct relation:

(a) $q = V/C$ (b) $C = V \times q$ (c) $V = q/C$ (d) $V = Cq$

Question 6

In a parallel plate capacitor, the capacity increases if:

(a) Area of the plate is decreased.

(b) Distance between the plates is increasesd.

(c) Area of the plate is increased.

(d) Dielectric constantly decreases.

Question 7

A cloth is rubbed with wool is found to have a negative charge of 4×10^{-8} C. The no. of electron transferred is:

(a) 1.5×10^{11} (b) 2.5×10^{11} (c) 3.5×10^{11} (d) 4.5×10^{11}

Question 8

An infinite line charge produce a field of 3×10^4 N/C at a distance of 3 cm. The linear charge density is:

(a) $0.5 \, \mu$ C/m (b) $1 \, \mu$ C/m (c) $1.5 \, \mu$ C/m (d) $2 \, \mu$ C/m

Question 9

The potential at point P due to charge of 4×10^{-7} C, located 9 cm away is:

(a) 1×10^4 V (b) 2×10^4 V (c) 3×10^4 V (d) 4×10^4 V

Question 10

Graph shows the variation of electric field E due to a hollow spherical conductor of radius R as a function of distance from centre of the sphere.

(a) 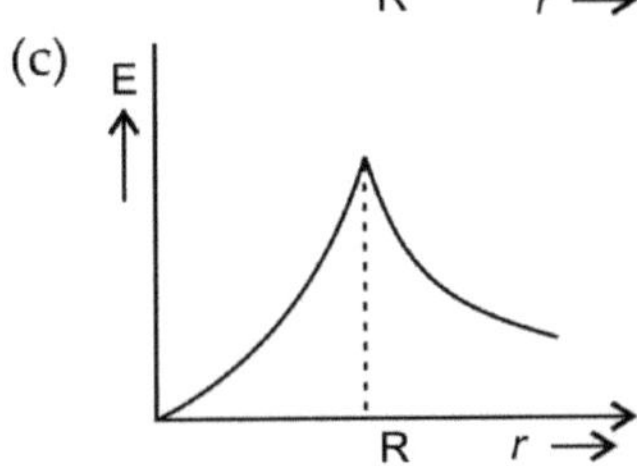

(b) 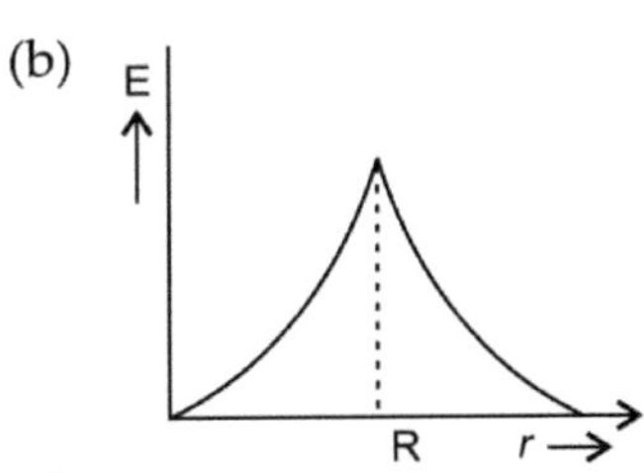

(c) 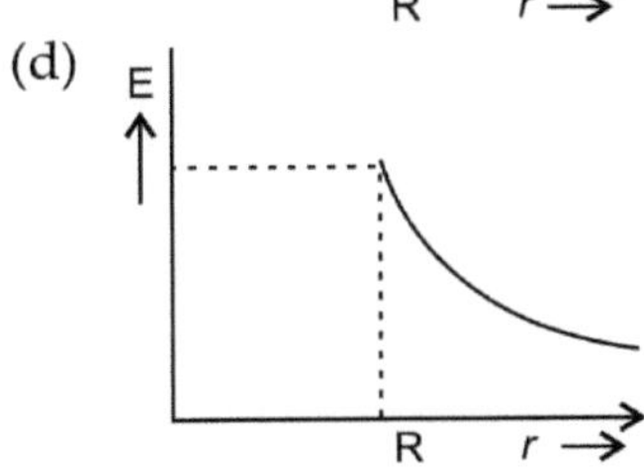

Question 11

A charge q is divided into two parts such that force between resulting to charges is maximum when separated to through distances r. The division of charges would be:

(a) $\dfrac{3q}{8}, \dfrac{5q}{8}$ (b) $\dfrac{2q}{4}, \dfrac{2q}{4}$ (c) $\dfrac{q}{2}, \dfrac{q}{2}$ (d) $\dfrac{3q}{6}, \dfrac{3q}{6}$

Question 12

Choose the correct answer for this figure:

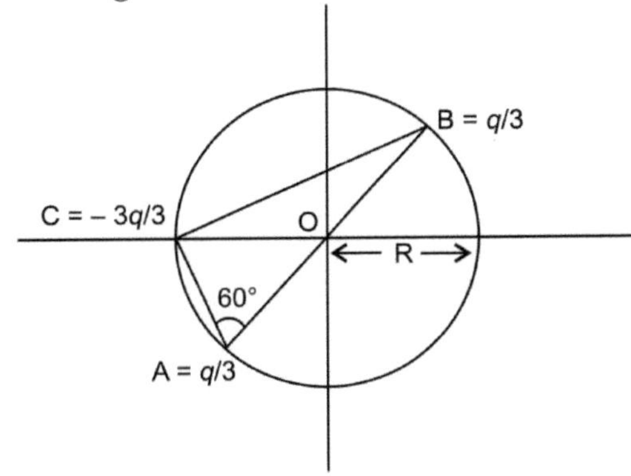

(a) The electric field at a O is $q/8\pi\,\varepsilon_0 R^2$.

(b) The magnitude of the force between the charges at C and B is $q^2/54\,\pi\varepsilon_0 R^2$.

(c) The PE of system is zero.

(d) The PE at 0 is $q/12\pi\varepsilon_0 R$.

Question 13

Choose the correct option for these two statement given:

(A) The force with which two charges interact is not changed by the presence of the other charges.

(B) Electric force experienced by the charged particle due to no. of fixed point charges is vector resultant of forces experiences due to individual charges.

(a) A & B both are correct   (b) Ony A is correct

(c) Only B is correct   (d) A & B both are wrong

Question 14

Choose the correct form of Gauss law:

(a) $\phi_E = q/\varepsilon_0$ (b) $\phi_E = \oint \vec{E}.\vec{dA}$ (c) (a) and (b) both   (d) None of these

Question 15

Current in the wire, when the charge of 20C is flowing for 2 hrs:

(a) 0.03 A   (b) 0.3 A   (c) 0.003 A   (d) 3A

Question 16

A galvanometer coil has a resistance of 10 Ω and the metre show full scale deflection for a current of 3 mA. The galvanometer will be converted into voltmeter by:

(a) connecting a resistance in series

(b) connecting a resistance in parallel

(c) connecting a shunt wire

(d) by connecting a battery

Question 17

The resistance of the wire of potentiometer is 4 Ω and its length is 1 m. It is then connected to a cell of emf 2 V and internal resistance 1 Ω. Potential difference across the potentiometer wire is:

(a) 1.2 V

(b) 1.6 V

(c) 0.8 V

(d) 2.0 V

Question 18

Find condutivity of material of the wire of length 30 cm, when the p.d. of 4V is applied and current density is 10^{-7} Am^{-2} is given?

(a) 0.75 Ω^{-1}m^{-1}

(b) 0.075 Ω^{-1}m^{-1}

(c) 0.0075 Ω^{-1}m^{-1}

(d) 7.5 Ω^{-1}m^{-1}

Question 19

Value of current in circuit is:

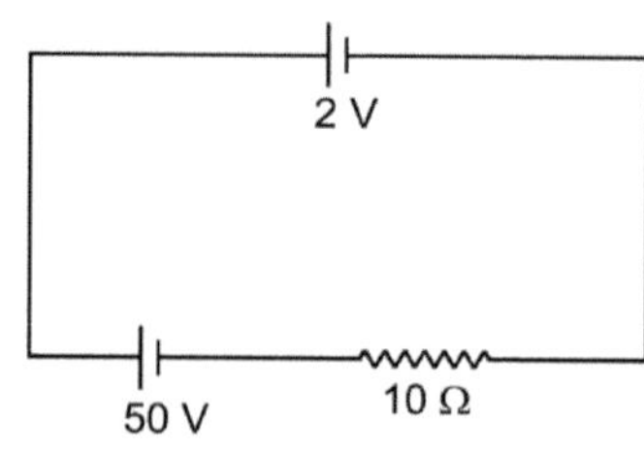

(a) 4A

(b) 4.2 A

(c) 4.6 A

(d) 4.8 A

Question 20

On rising the temperature, the drift velocity will:

(a) increase

(b) decrease

(c) not affected

(d) zero

Question 21

Two conductors with resistance R and 2R respectively connected to a dc source. Ratio of their heat will be:

(a) 1:1

(b) 2:1

(c) 1:2

(d) 2:2

Question 22

If the electron is drifting from lower potential to higher potential then all the free electrons are moving in same direction.

(a) True

(b) False

(c) Not related

(d) None of these

Question 23

A resistor is marked as 98 Ω-0.5 W, the largest voltage can be put in this is:

(a) 3V

(b) 5V

(c) 7V

(d) 9V

Question 24

Ratio of current flowing through the wire. If both the wire have same area and the ratio between their length is 4 : 1.

(a) 1 : 1

(b) 1 : 4

(c) 4 : 1

(d) 4 : 4

Question 25

Energy consumed by heater in 5 min, when the current flowing through heater is 5A and resistance is 44 Ω.

(a) 4.5×10^5 J

(b) 3.0×10^5 J

(c) 4×10^5 J

(d) 3.3×10^5 J

Question 26

A wire has resistance 2Ω at 60°C and a resistance of 3Ω at 70°C. Temperature coefficient of resistance of wire is:

(a) 0.3 (°C)$^{-1}$

(b) 0.03 (°C)$^{-1}$

(c) 0.5 (°C)$^{-1}$

(d) 0.05 (°C)$^{-1}$

Question 27

The equivalent resistance in the following circuit:

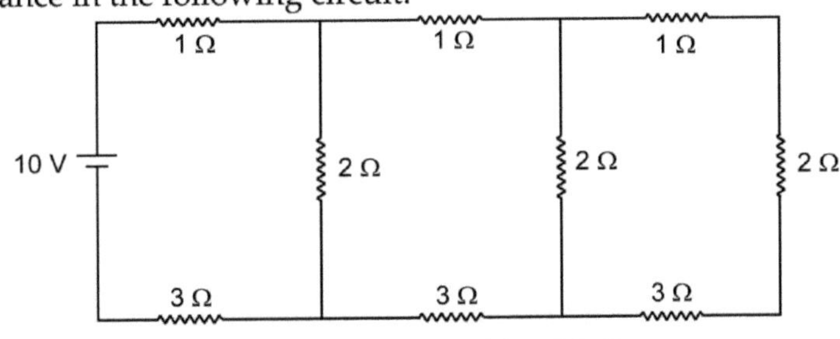

(a) $5.47\,\Omega$ (b) $1.47\,\Omega$ (c) $1.5\,\Omega$ (d) $5.5\,\Omega$

Question 28

Correct form of Biot-Savart law is:

(a) $dE = \dfrac{1}{4\pi\varepsilon_0}\dfrac{dq}{r^2}$ (b) $dB = \dfrac{\mu}{4\pi_0}\dfrac{dq}{r^2}$ (c) $dE = \dfrac{\mu_0}{4\pi}\dfrac{i\,dl\sin\theta}{r^2}$ (d) $dB = \dfrac{\mu_0}{4\pi}\dfrac{i\,dl\sin\theta}{r^2}$

Question 29

$\oint \vec{B}.d\vec{I}^{-1} = \mu_0 \hat{i}$, equation is form of:

(a) Biot-Savart law (b) Maxwell equation
(c) Ampere's circuital law (d) None of these

Question 30

If the no. of turns in a circular coil of radius 4 cm are 80 and the current flows in that is 2A, the magnitude of magnetic field at the centre will be:

(a) 0.25 T (b) 0.025 T (c) 0.0025 T (d) 25T

Question 31

The charge appearing on capacitor B, long time after the switch S is closed, is:

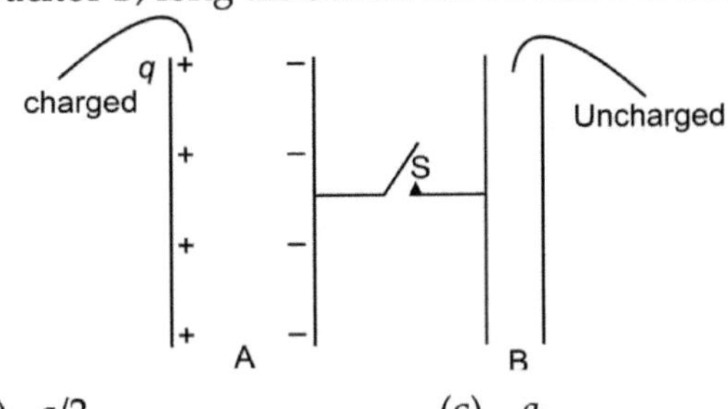

(a) zero (b) $q/2$ (c) q (d) $2q$

Question 32

A parallel plate capacitor is made of two circular plates separated by a distance of 5 mm and with a dielectric of dielectric constant 2.2 between them. When the electric field in the dielectric is 3×10^4 V/m, the charge density of the positive plate will be close to:

(a) 6×10^{-7} C/m^2 (b) 3×10^{-7} C/m^2 (c) 3×10^4 C/m^2 (d) 6×10^4 C/m^2

Question 33

Two capacitors C_1 and C_2 are charged to 120 V and 200 V respectively. It is found that by connecting them together the potential on each one can be made zero, then:

(a) $5C_1 = 3C_2$ (b) $3C_1 = 5C_2$ (c) $3C_1 + 5C_2 = 0$ (d) $9C_1 = 4C_2$

Question 34

The energy required to charge a parallel plate capacitor of plate separation d and plate area of cross-section A, such that the uniform electric field E between the plates is:

(a) $1/2\ \varepsilon_0 E^2/Ad$ (b) $\varepsilon_0 E^2/Ad$ (c) $\varepsilon_0 E^2 Ad$ (d) $1/2\ \varepsilon_0 E^2 Ad$

Question 35

Find the magnetic flux linked with each coil having 200 turns and self induction 20 mH. If current flowing through the coil is 4 mA.

(a) 2×10^{-7} Wb (b) 4×10^{-7} Wb (c) 6×10^{-7} Wb (d) 20×10^{-7} Wb

Question 36

A bar magnet is placed with its axis at 60° with uniform external magnetic field of 0.25 T, if $\tau = 4.5 \times 10^{-2}$ J. The magnitude of magnetic moment of the magnet is:

(a) 0.16 J/T (b) 0.20 J/T (c) 0.26 J/T (d) 30 J/T

Question 37

The current due to orbital motion of e^- which is moving around hydrogen atom of radius 0.51×10^{-10} m with velocity 2×10^5 m/s, is:

(a) 10^{-1} A (b) 10^{-2} A (c) 10^{-3} A (d) 10^{-4} A

Question 38

If the equivalent current due to orbital motion of an electron is 10^{-6} A, the value of magnetic moment associated with orbiting electron is (the radius of atom is 30×10^{-7} m).

(a) 2.8×10^{-10} Am^2 (b) 2.8×10^{-15} Am^2 (c) 2.8×10^{-17} Am^2 (d) 2.8×10^{-19} A/m^2

Question 39

(i) Equivalent resistance between A and D in the following figure.

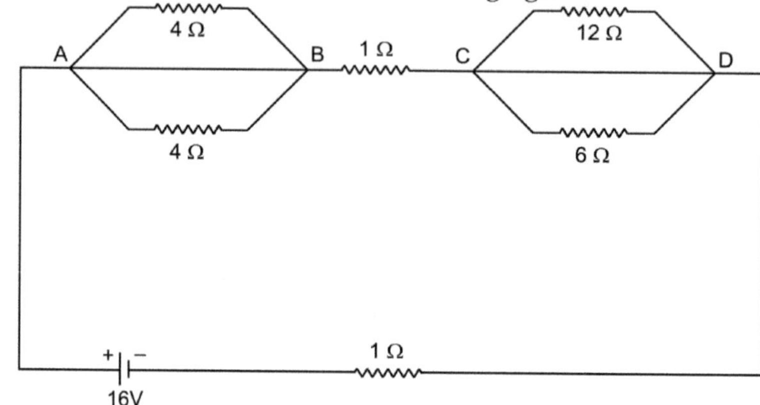

(a) 3 Ω (b) 5 Ω (c) 7 Ω (d) 9 Ω

(ii) Total current in the circuit:

(a) 1A (b) 2A (c) 3A (d) 4A

Question 40

Answer the following question about the graph shown below:

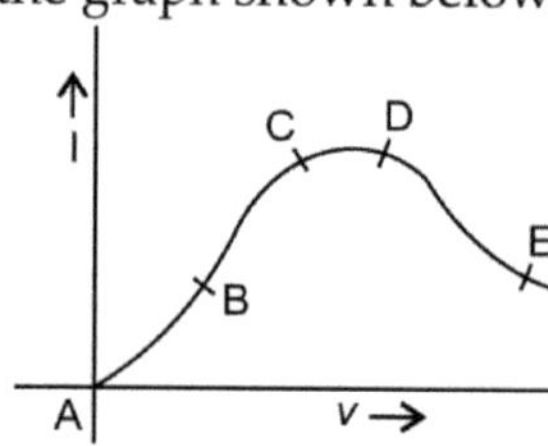

(i) Region of negative resistance

(a) AB (b) BC (c) CD (d) DE

(ii) Region of positive resistance

(a) AB (b) BC (c) CD (d) DE

Question 41

$V = 200 \sin 314\, t$ is applied to 10Ω resistance:

(i) frequency and peak voltage:

(a) 50 Hz, 200 V (b) 200 Hz, 50 V (c) 141 V, 50 Hz (d) 200 V, 14 Hz

(ii) rms voltage and rms current:

(a) 14 V, 141 A (b) 141 V, 14 A (c) 40 V, 40 A (d) 40 V, 4A

Question 42

A current of 2 ampere is passing in an aluminium wire whose cross-section is 4×10^{-3} m^2.

(i) The current density in the wire is given by

(a) $j = iA$ (b) $j = i/A$ (c) $j = A/i$ (d) None of these

(ii) The value of current density in (A/m^2) is:
  (a) 2×10^2 Am^{-2}
  (b) 5×10^2 Am^{-2}
  (c) 4×10^2 Am^{-2}
  (d) None of these

Question 43

In the meter bridge, give answer to the following:

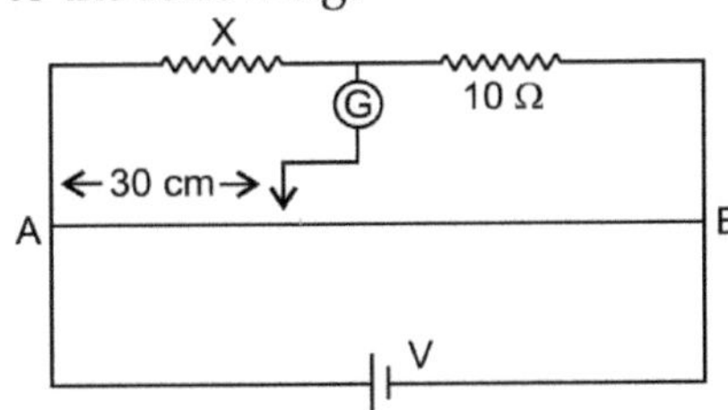

(i) Value of X:
  (a) $3\,\Omega$
  (b) $4.29\,\Omega$
  (c) $4\,\Omega$
  (d) $5.88\,\Omega$
(ii) Balance point, if X is interchanged with $10\,\Omega$:
  (a) 30 cm
  (b) 70 cm
  (d) 60 cm
  (d) 40 cm

Question 44

An electron is accelerated through the potential difference of 3000 V.
(i) Energy acquire by electron :
  (a) 4.86×10^{-16} J
  (b) 4.3×10^{-16} J
  (c) 1.6×10^{-19} J
  (d) 3.2×10^{-16} J
(ii) Speed gain by electron:
  (a) 2×10^7 m/s
  (b) 3.2×10^{-7} m/s
  (d) 2.5×10^{-7} m/s
  (d) 3.2×10^7 m/s

Question 45

A cell has a emf of 2V and internal resistance is 4Ω. Connected to a resistance and the current flowing in the circuit is 1A. Answer the following for this:
(i) Rate of energy dissipation inside the cell:
  (a) 2W
  (b) 3W
  (c) 4W
  (d) 5W
(ii) Rate of chemical energy consumption of cell is:
  (a) 2W
  (b) 3W
  (c) 4W
  (d) 5W
(iii) Rate of energy dissipation in the resistor is:
  (a) -2W
  (b) -3W
  (c) -4W
  (d) -5W

Question 46

A closely wound solenoid of 2000 turns and area of cross-section 1.6×10^{-4} m^2, carrying a current of 4A is suspended through its centre allowing it to turn in a horizontal plane.

(i) Magnetic moment associated with the axis of the solenoid is:
  (a) 1.6 J/T
  (b) 4.0 J/T
  (c) 1.28 J/T
  (d) 1.40 JT

(ii) Force on solenoid if a uniform horizontal magnetic field of 7.5×10^{-2} T is setup at an angle of 30° with the axis of the solenoid:
  (a) 30N
  (b) 40 N
  (c) 0
  (d) None

(iii) Torque for the same condition, given in (ii):
  (a) 1.28×10^{-2} Nm
  (b) 7.5×10^{-2} Nm
  (c) 4.8×10^{-2} Nm
  (d) None

Question 47

Assume the electric field to be a part of an electromagnetic wave in vacuum

$E = 3.1$ N/C cos $[(1.8$ rad/m$)y + (5.4 \times 10^8$ rad/sec$)t]\ \hat{j}$

Answer the following:

(i) Direction of motion:
  (a) X direction
  (b) Y direction
  (c) $-$X direction
  (d) $-$Y direction

(ii) Wavelength λ :
  (a) 2 m
  (b) 2.5 m
  (c) 3 m
  (d) 3.5 m

(iii) Frequency (v) :
  (a) 86 MHz
  (b) 85 MHz
  (c) 84 MHz
  (d) 83 MHz

Question 48

For the following figure, answer the given question:

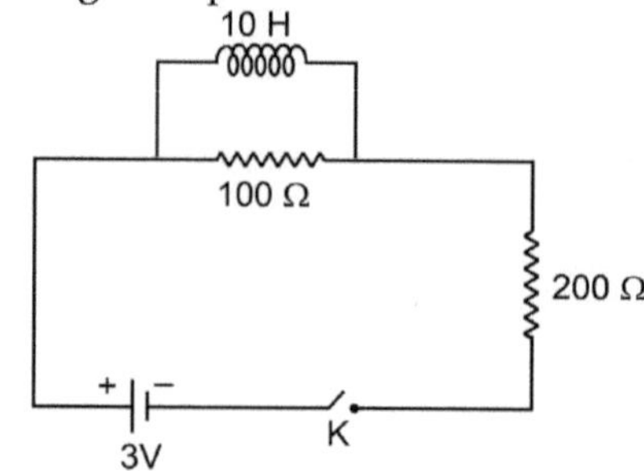

(i) Initial current drawn from battery.

(a) 1A (b) 0.1A (c) 0.01 A (d) 0.001A

(ii) Initial potential drop across the inductor:

(a) 1V (b) 0.1V (c) 0.01V (d) 0.001V

(iii) Current drawn from battery:

(a) 15A (b) 0.15 A (c) 0.015A (d) 0.0015A

Question 49

Choose the correct energy of photon (eV) for following ray :

(a) γ rays:

(a) 1.24×10^6 (b) 1.24×10^{-6} (c) 4.125 (d) 2.475

(ii) UV rays:

(a) 2.475 (b) 4.125 (c) 1.24×10^6 (d) 4.125×10^{-5}

(iii) Micro waves:

(a) 1.24×10^6 (b) 4.125 (c) 4.12×10^{-5} (d) 2.475

(iv) Radiowaves:

(a) 4.125 (b) 1.24×10^6 (c) 1.24×10^6 (d) 4.12×10^5

Question 50

A circuit having an inductor of 80 mH and a capacitor of 60 μF connected in series with a supply of 230 V – 50Hz. Resistance is negligible. Answer the following :

(i) Impedance of circuit:

(a) 28 Ω (b) 26 Ω (c) 20 Ω (d) 18 Ω

(ii) Current amplitude:

(a) 11.6 A (b) 10.5 A (c) 9.5 A (d) 3.5 A

(iii) rms current:

(a) 7.21 A (b) 8.21 A (c) 5.2 A (d) 3.1 A

(iv) rms voltage across inductor :

(a) 106 V (b) 102 V (c) 202 V (d) 206 V

Answers

1. (b) Increases
2. (b) 45 V

   Explanation:

   $$27 \, V_{small} = V_{large}$$
   $$27 \times \frac{4}{3} \pi r^3 = \frac{4}{3} \pi R^3$$
   $$3r = R$$
   $$V_{small} = Kq/r$$

   $$V_{large} = \frac{K \times 27q}{R}$$
   $$V_{large} = 27 \, kg/3r$$
   $$V_{large} = 9 \, V_{small}$$
   $$V_{large} = 9 \times 5 = 45 \, V$$

3. (c) Vm
4. (c) The electric force is either attractive or repulsive white gravitational force is always attractive.
5. (c) $V = q/C$

6. (c) Area of the plate is increased.

Explanation: Area of the plate is increased on increasing the capacity of parallel plate capacitor.

$$\left[\because C = \frac{k\varepsilon_0 A}{d} \; i.e., \; C \propto A\right]$$

7. (b) 2.5×10^{11}

Explanation: $q = -4 \times 10^{-8}$ C

$$n = \frac{4 \times 10^{-8}}{1.6 \times 10^{-19}}$$

$$= 2.5 \times 10^{11}$$

8. (a) $0.5 \, \mu$ C/m

Explanation: $E = \dfrac{\lambda}{2\pi\varepsilon_0 r}$

$$\Rightarrow \qquad \lambda = E \times 2\pi\varepsilon_0 r$$

$$\lambda = \left(\frac{4\pi\varepsilon_0}{2}\right) r.E$$

$$= \frac{1}{9 \times 10^9} \times \frac{3 \times 10^{-2} \times 3 \times 10^4}{2}$$

$$= 0.5 \times 10^{-7}$$

$$= 0.5 \, \mu \, c/m$$

9. (d) 4×10^4 V

Explanation: $V = \dfrac{1}{4\pi\varepsilon_0} \dfrac{Q}{r}$

$$= 9 \times 10^9 \times \frac{4 \times 10^{-7}}{9 \times 10^{-2}}$$

$$= 4 \times 10^4 \text{ volt}$$

10. (a) a uniformly charged conducting sphere electric field

inside E = 0 No charge enclose inside the conducting

outside $E = Kq/r^2$ Outside it decreases uniformly. So graph (a) is correct.

11. (c) $\dfrac{q}{2}, \dfrac{q}{2}$

Explanation: Let one part of charge is q_1, and second part is $(q - q_1)$. Therefore,

$$F = \frac{1}{4\pi\varepsilon_0} \frac{q_1(q - q_1)}{r^2}$$

For F to be maxima, $\dfrac{dF}{dr} = 0 \Rightarrow q_1 = q/2$

12. (b) The magnitude of the force between the charges at C and B is $q^2/ 54 \, \pi\varepsilon_0 R^2$.

Explanation:
$$F = \frac{1}{4\pi\varepsilon_0} \frac{(2q/3)(q/3)}{(2R \sin 60°)^2}$$

$$= \frac{q^2}{54\pi\varepsilon R^2}$$

13. (a) A and B both are correct.

14. (c) (a) and (b) both

15. (c) $i = \dfrac{\theta}{t} = \dfrac{20 \text{ C}}{2 \times 3600} = 0.003$A

16. (a) connecting a resistance in series

17. (b) 1.6 V

Explanation: $I = \dfrac{E}{R + r}$

$$= \frac{2}{4 + 1} = 0.4 \text{ A}$$

$$V = I \times R = 0.4 \times 4 = 1.6 \text{ V}$$

18. (b) $0.075 \, \Omega^{-1} m^{-1}$

Explanation: $\sigma = \dfrac{J}{v/d} = \dfrac{10^{-7}}{(4/0.3)}$

$$= \frac{10^{-7} \times 0.3}{4}$$

$$= 0.075 \, \Omega^{-1} \, m^{-1}$$

19. (d) 4.8 A

Explanation: $E_1 = 2$ V, $E_2 = 50$ V, $R = 10 \, \Omega$

E = 50 − 2 = 48 V

$$I = \frac{E}{R} = \frac{48}{10} = 4.8 \text{ A}$$

20. (b) On rising the temperature the drift velocity will decrease.

21. (b) 2:1

Explanation:
$$Q = \frac{V^2}{R} t$$

$$\frac{Q_1}{Q_2} = \frac{V^2 t / R_1}{V^2 t / R_2} = \frac{R_2}{R_1}$$

$$= \frac{2R}{R} = 2 : 1$$

22. (b) False.

23. (c) 7V

Explanation: $V = \sqrt{PR}$

$$= \sqrt{0.5 \times 98}$$

$$= \sqrt{49} = 7$$

24. (c) 4 : 1

Explanation: $\dfrac{I_A}{I_B} = \dfrac{R_B}{R_A} = \dfrac{l_A}{l_B} = \dfrac{4}{1}$

25. (d) 3.3×10^5 J

Explanation: $\omega = i^2 R t$

$$\omega = (5 \times 5) \times 44 \times (5 \times 60)$$

$$= 3.3 \times 10^5 \text{ J}$$

26. (d) 0.05 $(°C)^{-1}$

Explanation: $R_1 = 2\Omega$, $t_1 = 60°C$, $R_2 = 3\Omega$, $t_2 = 70°C$

$$\alpha = \frac{R_2 - R_1}{R_1(t_2 - t_1)}$$

$$= \frac{3-2}{2(70-60)}$$

$$= \frac{1}{2\times10}$$

$$= \frac{0.5}{10}$$

$$= 0.05 \; (°C)^{-1}$$

27. (a) $5.47 \, \Omega$

Explanation:

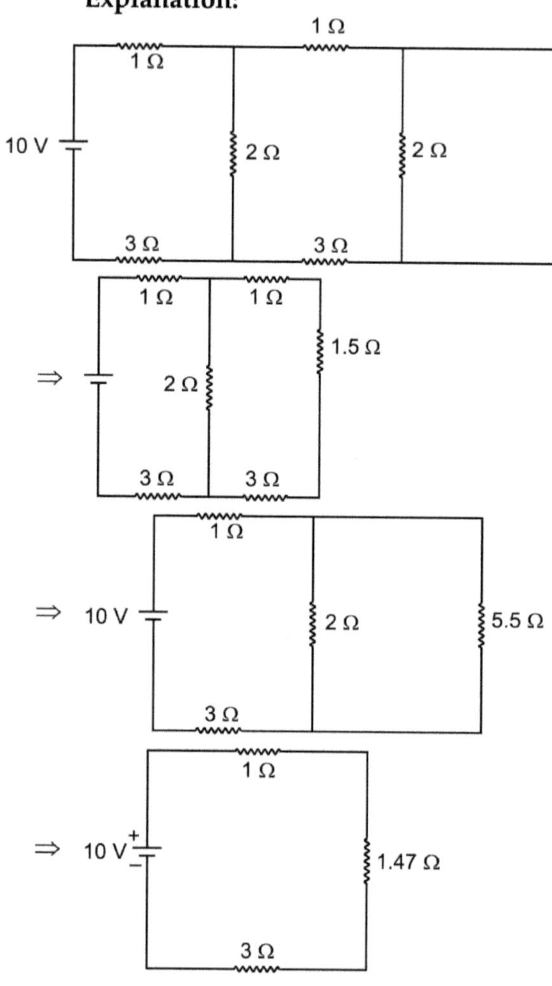

$$R = 1\,\Omega + 3\,\Omega + 1.47\,\Omega$$
$$= 5.47\,\Omega$$

28. (d) $dB = \dfrac{\mu_0}{4\pi} \dfrac{i\,dl\sin\theta}{r^2}$

The correct form of Biot-savart law is option (d).

29. (c) Ampere's circuital law

30. (c) $0.002t$ T

Explanation: $n = 80$, $i = 2A$, $r = 4 \times 10^{-2}$ m

$$B = \frac{\mu_0}{2} \cdot \frac{ni}{r}$$

$$\Rightarrow 10^{-7} \times 4 \times \frac{22}{7} \times \frac{80\times2}{2\times4\times10^{-2}}$$

$$= 4 \times \frac{22}{7} \times 10^{-7} \times 20 \times 10^2$$

$$= 251.43 \times 10^{-5} = 0.0025 \text{ T}$$

31. (a) zero

Explanation: The charges on capacitor A are locked due to mutual attraction of position and negative charges. Thus after switch S is closed, no current flows through it.

32. (a) 6×10^{-7} C/m^2

Explanation: $E = \dfrac{\sigma}{k\varepsilon_0}$

$$\sigma = EK\varepsilon_0$$
$$= 3 \times 10^4 \times 2.2 \times 8.85 \times 10^{-12}$$
$$= 6 \times 10^{-7} \text{ c/m}^2$$

33. (b) $3C_1 = 5C_2$

Explanation: $V = \dfrac{q_1 - q_2}{C_1 + C_2}$

$$= \frac{C_1 V_1 - C_2 V_2}{C_1 + C_2}$$

But $V_1 = 120$ V, $V_2 = 200$ V, $V = 0$ and $C_1 + C_2 \neq \infty$

$$C_1 V_1 - C_2 V_2 = 0$$
$$C_1 V_1 = C_2 V_2$$
$$120 \, C_1 = 200 \, C_2$$
$$3C_1 = 5C_2$$

34. (d) $\dfrac{1}{2}\varepsilon_0 E^2 Ad$

Explanation: The energy per unit volume

$$= \frac{1}{2}\varepsilon_0 E^2$$

Volume of space between plates = Ad

Total energy stored = $\dfrac{1}{2}\varepsilon_0 E^2 Ad$

35. (b) 4×10^{-7} Wb

Explanation: $\phi_B = \dfrac{Li}{N} = \dfrac{20\times10^{-3}\times4\times10^{-3}}{200}$

$$= 4 \times 10^{-7} \text{ Wb}$$

36. (b) 0.20 J/T

Explanation: $m = \dfrac{\tau}{B\sin\theta}$

$$= \frac{4.5\times10^{-2}}{0.25\times\sin 60°}$$

$$= 0.20 \text{ J/T}$$

37. (d) 10^{-4} A

Explanation: $i = e \times n$

$$= \frac{eV}{2\pi r}$$

$$= \frac{1.6\times10^{-9}\times2\times10^5}{2\times3.14\times0.51\times10^{-10}}$$

$$= 10^{-4}\,\text{A}$$

38. (c) $2.8 \times 10^{-17}\,\text{Am}^2$

Explanation: $m = i\text{A} = \iota \times \pi r^2$
$$= 10^{-6}\,\text{A} \times 3.14 \times (30 \times 10^{-7})^2$$
$$= 2,826 \times 10^{-20}$$
$$= 2.8 \times 10^{-17}\,\text{Am}^2$$

39. (i) (c) $7\,\Omega$

Explanation:

$$R_{AB} = \frac{4\times4}{4+4} = \frac{16}{8} = 2\Omega$$

$$R_{BC} = 1\,\Omega$$

$$R_{CD} = \frac{12\times6}{12+6} = \frac{12\times6}{18} = 4\Omega$$

$$R_{eq} = R_{AB} + R_{BC} + R_{CD}$$
$$= 2 + 1 + 4 = 7\,\Omega$$

(ii) (b) 2A

Explanation: $I = \dfrac{E}{R+r} = \dfrac{16V}{(7+1)} = 2A$

40. (i) (d) DE

(ii) (a) AB

41. (i) (a) $\quad f = \dfrac{\omega}{2\pi} = \dfrac{314}{2\times3.14} = 50\,\text{Hz}$

$$V_0 = 200\,\text{V}$$

(ii) (b) $\quad v_{rms} = \dfrac{V_0}{\sqrt{2}}$

$$= \frac{200}{1.414} = 141.4V$$

$$I_{rms} = \frac{V_{rms}}{R} = \frac{141.4}{10} = 14.14\,\text{A}$$

42. (i) (b) $j = i/A$

Explanation: The current density $j = \dfrac{i}{A}$

(ii) (b) $5 \times 10^2\,\text{Am}^{-2}$

Explanation: $j = \dfrac{i}{A}$

$$= \frac{2}{4 \times 10^{-3}} = 0.5 \times 10^3$$

$$j = 5 \times 10^2\,\text{Am}^{-2}$$

43. (i) (b) $\quad \dfrac{X}{10} = \dfrac{30}{(100-30)}$

$$\Rightarrow \quad X = \frac{30\times10}{70}$$

$$= 4.29\,\Omega$$

(ii) (b) $\quad 100 - 30 = 70$ cm (New balance point)

44. (i) (a) $4.86 \times 10^{-16}\,\text{J}$

Explanation: K.E. $= q$V
$$= 1.6 \times 10^{-19} \times 3000$$
$$= 4.8 \times 10^{-16}\,\text{J}$$

3.2×10^7 m/s

(ii) (d) 3.2×10^7 m/s

Explanation: $\quad v = \sqrt{\dfrac{2\text{K.E.}}{m}}$

$$= \sqrt{\frac{2\times4.8\times10^{-16}}{9.1\times10^{-31}}}$$

$$= \sqrt{1.05\times10^{15}}$$

$$= \sqrt{10.5\times10^{14}}$$

$$= 3.2 \times 10^7\,\text{m/s}$$

45. (i) (c) Rate of energy dissipation inside the cell
$$= i^2 r = 1 \times 1 \times 4 = 4\,\text{W}$$

(ii) (a) $\quad Ei = 2 \times 1a = 2\,\text{W}$

(iii) (a) $\quad Ei - i^2R = 2W - 4W = -2W$

46. (i) (c) $1.28\,\text{J/T}$

Explanation: $m = \text{NiA}$
$$= 2000 \times 4 \times 1.6 \times 10^{-4}$$
$$= 1.28\,\text{JT}^{-1}$$

(ii) (c) Net force on solenoid is zero.

(iii) (c) $4.8 \times 10^{-2}\,\text{Nm}$

Explanation: $\tau = mB\sin\theta$
$$= 1.28 \times 7.5 \times 10^{-2} \times \sin 30°$$
$$= 1.28 \times 7.5 \times 10^2 \times 1/2$$
$$= 4.8 \times 10^{-2}\,\text{Nm}$$

47. (i) (d) Y direction

Explanation: From the equation, it is clear that the direction of motion of EM wave is along $-y$ direction.

(ii) (d) 3.5 m

Explanation: $E = E_0 \cos(ky + wt)$
On comparing $k = 1.8$
$$\lambda = \frac{2\pi}{K} = \frac{2\times22/7}{1.8} = 3.492\,\text{m}$$

(iii) (a) 86 MHz

Explanation: $\quad v = \dfrac{\omega}{2\pi}$

$$= \frac{5.4\times10^8}{2\times3.14}$$

$$= 0.86 \times 10^8\,\text{Hz}$$

$$\approx 86\,\text{MHz}$$

48. (i) (c) $\quad i = \dfrac{3V}{(100+200\,\Omega)} = 0.01A$

(ii) (a) $\text{V} = 0.01\,\text{A} \times 100\,\Omega = 1V$

(iii) (c) $\quad i = \dfrac{3V}{200\,\Omega} = 0.015\,\text{A}$

49. (i) (a) 1.24×10^6

    (ii) (b) 4.125

    (iii) (c) 4.12×10^{-5}

    (iv) (b) 1.24×10^{-6}

50. (i) (a) $28\ \Omega$

     Explanation: Given $L = 80\ \text{mH} = 80 \times 10^{-3}\ \text{H}$

$$C = 60 \times 10^{-6}\ \text{F}$$

$$E_{rms} = 230\ \text{V}$$

$$E_0 = \sqrt{3}E_{rms} = 325\ \text{V}$$

$$f = 50\ \text{Hz}$$

$$\omega = 2\pi f$$

$$= 314\ \text{rad/sec as } R \to 0$$

$$Z = \sqrt{R^2 + \left(\omega L - \frac{1}{\omega C}\right)^2}$$

$$X_L = \omega L = 314 \times 80 \times 10^{-3} = 25.12\ \text{W}$$

$$X_C = 1/\omega C = 1/314 \times (60 \times 10^{-6}) = 53.08\ \Omega$$

$$Z = \sqrt{0 + \left(\omega L - \frac{1}{\omega C}\right)^2}$$

$$Z = \omega L - \omega C$$

$$= 25.12 - 53.08$$

$$= 28\ \Omega$$

(ii) (a) $\quad i_0 = \dfrac{E_0}{Z} = \dfrac{325\ \text{V}}{28.0\ \Omega} = 11.6\ \text{A}$

(iii) (b) $\quad i_{rms} = \dfrac{E_{rms}}{Z}\ \dfrac{230\ \text{V}}{28\ \text{V}} = 8.21\ \text{A}$

(iv) (d) $\quad V_L = i_{rms} \times W_L = 8.21\ \text{A} \times 25.12\ \Omega = 206\ \text{V}$

❏❏

Chemistry

Specimen Question Paper

Chemistry

Maximum Marks: 70
Time allowed: One and a Half hours

Questions

Question 1. [1]

Na and Mg crystallise in bcc and fcc structures respectively. The value of Z (number of atoms) for their crystals is:

(a) 8 and 14　　　　(b) 2 and 4　　　　(c) 14 and 8　　　　(d) 6 and 4

Question 2. [1]

Colligative properties depend on:

(a) The nature of solute particles in solution　　(b) The number of solute particles in solution

(c) The nature of solute and solvent particles　　(d) The physical properties of solute particles in solution

Question 3. [1]

On dilution, the specific conductance of a solution:

(a) Remains unchanged　　　　　　　　(b) Increases

(c) Decreases　　　　　　　　　　　　(d) First increases then decreases

Question 4. [1]

The flux used in the extraction of iron from haematite ore is:

(a) Limestone　　　　　　　　　　　(b) Silica

(c) Coke　　　　　　　　　　　　　(d) Calcium phosphate

Question 5. [1]

Which of the following xenon fluoride of xenon cannot be formed?

(a) XeF_2　　　　(b) XeF_4　　　　(c) XeF_6　　　　(d) XeF_3

Question 6. [1]

The gas obtained on heating iodoform with silver powder is:

(a) Propane　　　　(b) Ethane　　　　(c) Ethyne　　　　(d) Ethene

Question 7. [1]

Boiling point of ethyl alcohol is greater than diethyl ether due to:

(a) Vander Waals forces　　　　　　(b) London forces

(c) Polarity　　　　　　　　　　　(d) Hydrogen bonding

Question 8. [1]

In a face centred cubic lattice, atom 'A' occupies the corner positions and atom 'B' occupies the face centred positions. If one atom of 'B' is missing from one of the face centred points, the formula of the compound will be:

(a) AB_2　　　　(b) A_2B_3　　　　(c) A_2B_5　　　　(d) A_2B

Question 9. [1]

The standard reduction potential values of three metallic cations X, Y and Z are 0.52 V, – 3.03 V and –1.18 V respectively. The order of reducing power of the corresponding metals is:

(a) $Y > Z > X$

(b) $X > Y > Z$

(c) $Z > Y > X$

(d) $Z > X > Y$

Question 10. [1]

If molality of the dilute solution of a non-volatile, non-dissociating and non-associating electrolyte is doubled, the value of molal elevation constant or Ebullioscopic constant (K_b) will be:

(a) Doubled

(b) Halved

(c) Tripled

(d) Unchanged

Question 11. [1]

Extraction of zinc from zinc blende is achieved by :

(a) Electrolytic reduction

(b) Roasting, followed by reduction with carbon

(c) Roasting, followed by reduction with another metal

(d) Roasting, followed by self-reduction

Question 12. [1]

The most powerful oxidizing agent is:

(a) Fluorine

(b) Chlorine

(c) Bromine

(d) Iodine

Question 13. [1]

During the course of S_N^1 reaction, the intermediate species formed is:

(a) A free radical

(b) A carbanion

(c) A carbocation

(d) An intermediate complex

Question 14. [1]

Which type of defect has the presence of cations in the interstitial sites?

(a) Schottky defect

(b) Vacancy defect

(c) Frenkel defect

(d) Metal deficiency defect

Question 15. [1]

Reaction between acetone and methyl magnesium chloride, followed by hydrolysis will give:

(a) tert-butyl alcohol

(b) iso-butyl alcohol

(c) iso-propyl alcohol

(d) sec-butyl alcohol

Question 16. [1]

If 5.85 g of NaCl are dissolved in 90 g of water, the mole fraction of solute is:

(a) 0.2632

(b) 0.0102

(c) 0.0196

(d) 0.1045

Question 17. [1]

When zinc granule is dipped into copper sulphate solution, copper is precipitated because:

(a) Both copper and zinc have a positive reduction potential.

(b) Both copper and zinc have a negative reduction potential.

(c) Reduction potential of zinc is higher than that of copper.

(d) Reduction potential of copper is higher than that of zinc.

Question 18. [1]

The optically active compound is:

(a) Butan-1-ol

(b) Butan-2-ol

(c) Propan-1-ol

(d) 2-methyl-propan-1-ol

Question 19. [1]

Chlorine reacts with cold and dilute NaOH under ordinary conditions to give:

(a) NaCl and Cl_2O

(b) NaCl and ClO_2

(c) NaCl and NaClO

(d) NaCl and $NaClO_3$

Question 20. [1]

Solutions which distil without any change in composition and temperature are called:

(a) Ideal

(b) Super saturated

(c) Azeotropic

(d) Isotonic

Question 21. [1]

The reaction: Sodium alkoxide + alkyl halide $\rightarrow$ Ether + Sodium halide is called:

(a) Wurtz reaction

(b) Kolbe's reaction

(c) Perkin's reaction

(d) Williamson's synthesis

Question 22. [1]

Benzene diazonium chloride on hydrolysis gives:

(a) Benzene

(b) Phenol

(c) Chlorobenzene

(d) Benzyl alcohol

Question 23. [1]

The vacant space in body centred cubic lattice unit cell is:

(a) 32%

(b) 26%

(c) 48%

(d) 68%

Question 24. [1]

For a spontaneous reaction ΔG° and E° cell will be respectively:

(a) −ve and −ve

(b) +ve and +ve

(c) +ve and −ve

(d) −ve and +ve

Question 25. [1]

A liquid is mixed with ethanol and few drops of conc. H_2SO_4 is added. A compound with a fruity smell is formed. The liquid is:

(a) HCHO

(b) CH_3CHO

(c) CH_3COOH

(d) CH_3COCH_3

Question 26. [2]

The chief ore of copper is copper pyrite ($CuFeS_2$)

(i) How is the sulphide ore concentrated?

    (a) By Gravity separation process

    (b) By Froth-floatation process

    (c) By Electromagnetic separation process

    (d) By Leaching process

(ii) Copper is purified by electrolytic refining of blister copper. The correct statement about this process is:

    (a) Impure copper strip is used as cathode

    (b) Impurities do not settle as anode mud

    (c) Pure copper deposits at cathode

    (d) Acidified silver nitrate is used as electrolyte

Question 27. [2]

The reaction: $CH_3Br + OH^- \rightarrow CH_3OH + Br^-$

(i) The expected mechanism of the above reaction is:

    (a) S_N^1 mechanism

    (b) S_N^2 mechanism

    (c) S_E^1 mechanism

    (d) S_E^2 mechanism

(ii) The above reaction is:

    (a) Elimination reaction

    (b) Nucleophilic addition reaction

    (c) Nucleophilic substitution reaction

    (d) Electrophilic substitution reaction

Question 28. [2]

For the extraction of metal, answer the following:

(i) The smelting of iron ore in blast furnace involves all the processes except:

    (a) Combustion   (b) Reduction

    (c) Slag formation   (d) Sublimation

(ii) Which of the following metal is obtained by leaching the concentrated ore with dilute sodium cyanide solution, followed by treatment with zinc?

    (a) Aluminium   (b) Iron

    (c) Copper   (d) Silver

Question 29. [2]

Phenol is heated with alcoholic KOH and chloroform:

(i) What is the name of the reaction?

    (a) Cannizzaro reaction   (b) Gattermann reaction

    (c) Reimer –Tiemann reaction   (d) Kolbe reaction

(ii) What is the main product formed in this reaction?

    (a) Salicylaldehyde   (b) Salicylic acid

    (c) Aniline   (d) Phenyl isocyanide

Question 30. [2]

For IF_7 molecule:

(i) The structure of the given molecule is:

    (a) Octahedral   (b) Tetrahedral

    (c) Trigonal bipyramidal   (d) Pentagonal bipyramidal

(ii) The type of hybridization of the given molecule is:

    (a) sp^3 hybridisation   (b) sp^3d^3 hybridisation

    (c) sp^3d^2 hybridisation   (d) sp^3d hybridisation

Question 31. [2]

Ethyl alcohol when reacts with PCl_5 gives a compound (A). When compound (A) is treated with alc. KOH, compound (B) is formed along with KCl and H_2O.

(i) The compound (A) is:

    (a) $C_2H_4Cl_2$ (b) CH_3CHO

    (c) C_2H_5Cl (d) CH_3OH

(ii) The compound (B) is:

    (a) C_2H_2 (b) C_2H_4

    (c) C_2H_6 (d) C_2H_5OH

Question 32. [2]

Copper pyrite or chalcopyrite ($CuFeS_2$) is the main ore of copper. The extraction of copper from its ore involves, concentration, partial roasting, removal of iron and self-reduction.

(i) On heating the mixture of Cu_2O and Cu_2S, which one of the following will be obtained?

    (a) Cu_2SO_3 (b) $Cu + SO_3$

    (c) $CuO + CuS$ (d) $Cu + SO_2$

(ii) Iron is removed during the extraction of copper as:

    (a) FeO (b) FeS (c) $FeSiO_3$ (d) Fe_2O_3

Question 33. [2]

Conversion of chlorobenzene into phenol.

(i) Which of the following statements is correct for the above conversion?

    (a) Heating it with alc. KOH at room temperature

    (b) Heating it with aqueous NaOH at 623 K under pressure followed by acidification with dilute HCl

    (c)   Heating it with CuCN followed by acidification with dilute HCl

    (d)   Heating it with sodium metal in the presence of dry ether

  (ii) What is the name of the above reaction?

    (a)   Dow process   (b)   Wurtz reaction

    (c)   Sandmeyer's reaction   (d)   Kolbe's reaction

Question 34.   **[2]**

With reference to XeF_6 molecule, answer the following questions.

  (i)   What is the hybridisation of Xe atom in the given molecule?

    (a) sp^3d^3 (b) sp^3d^2

    (c) sp^3 (d) sp^3d

  (ii) What is the geometry of this molecule?

    (a)   Distorted octahedral   (b)   Square planer

    (c)   Pyramidal   (d)   Tetrahedral

Question 35.   **[2]**

An unknown alcohol is treated with Lucas reagent to determine whether the alcohol is primary, secondary or tertiary.

  (i)   Which alcohol reacts fastest and by what mechanism?

    (a)   Tertiary alcohol by S_N2 (b)   Secondary alcohol by S_N1

    (c)   Tertiary alcohol by S_N1 (d)   Secondary alcohol by S_N2

  (ii) What is the chemical composition of the Lucas reagent used above?

    (a)   Anhydrous zinc chloride in concentrated HCl

    (b)   Anhydrous aluminium chloride in concentrated HCl

    (c)   Anhydrous lead chloride in concentrated HCl

    (d)   Anhydrous barium chloride in concentrated HCl

Question 36.   **[2]**

Ozone is prepared from oxygen:

  (i)   Which method is used in the above preparation?

    (a)   Oxidation at high temperature   (b)   Oxidation using catalyst

    (c)   Silent electric discharge   (d)   Reduction at high temperature

  (ii) The ozone obtained above acts as a:

    (a)   reducing agent   (b)   oxidising agent

    (c)   decomposer   (d)   dehydrating agent

Question 37.   **[2]**

Copper metal crystallises with face centred cubic unit cell. If the edge length of copper atom is 361.5 pm. (Atomic weight of Cu = 63.5, N_A = 6.02 × 10²³ mol⁻¹)

  (i)   The density of copper metal is:

    (a)   7.86 g/cm³   (b)   8.93 g/cm³

    (c)   9.76 g/cm³   (d)   10.5 g/cm³

  (ii) The radius of copper metal is:

    (a)   180.75 pm   (b)   156.53 pm

    (c)   127.79 pm   (d)   104.86 pm

Question 38.   **[2]**

An aqueous solution containing one gram of urea (molecular weight = 60) boils at 100.25°C. The same solution freezes at –0.894 °C. The aqueous solution containing 3 gram of glucose (Molecular weight = 180) in the same volume of solution:

  (i)   What is the boiling point of glucose?

    (a)   100.75 °C   (b)   100.50 °C   (c)   100.25 °C   (d)   100.08 °C

(ii) What is the freezing point of glucose?

    (a) +0.894 °C   (b) –0.894 °C

    (c) +0.447 °C   (d) –0.447 °C

Question 39. [2]

When two Faradays of electricity is passed through an aqueous solution of $CuSO_4$ and an aqueous solution of $AgNO_3$. (Atomic weight of Cu = 63.5 g mol^{-1}, Ag = 108 g mol^{-1})

(i) The mass of copper deposited at the cathode is:

    (a) 127.02 g   (b) 63.50 g

    (c) 31.75 g   (d) 15.87 g

(ii) The mass of silver deposited at the cathode is:

    (a) 54 g   (b) 108 g

    (c) 216 g   (d) 270 g

Question 40. [2]

Gold has cubic crystal whose unit cell has an edge length of 407.9 pm. Density of gold is 19.3 g cm^{-3}. Atomic weight of gold is 197 g mol^{-1}. (N_A = 6.02 × 10^{23} mol^{-1})

(i) The number of atoms (Z) in a unit cell of gold is:

    (a) 1   (b) 2

    (c) 3   (d) 4

(ii) The type of crystal structure of gold is:

    (a) Simple cubic unit cell   (b) Body centred cubic unit cell

    (c) Face centred cubic unit cell   (d) Side centred cubic unit cell

Question 41. [2]

A solution of sucrose (molecular weight 342 g mol^{-1}) has been prepared by dissolving 68.4 g of sucrose in 1000 g of water.

(K_f for water = 1.86 K kg mol^{-1})

(i) The freezing point of the solution obtained will be:

    (a) –0.52 °C   (b) +0.52 °C

    (c) –0.372 °C   (d) +0.372 °C

(ii) The molality of sucrose solution will be:

    (a) 0.1   (b) 0.2

    (c) 0.3   (d) 0.4

Question 42. [2]

The standard electrode potential for the reaction is:

(I) $Ag^+ + e^- \rightarrow Ag_{(s)}$; $E°Ag^+/Ag$ = +0.80 V

(II) $Sn^{2+} + 2e^- \rightarrow Sn_{(s)}$; $E°Sn^{2+}/Sn$ = –0.14 V

(i) The E°cell will be:

    (a) 0.66 V   (b) 0.88 V

    (c) 0.94 V   (d) 1.08 V

(ii) The value of standard Gibbs energy (ΔG°) will be:

    (F = 96,000 C mol^{-1})

    (a) –181.42 kJ   (b) –90.71 kJ

    (c) –45.36 kJ   (d) –22.68 kJ

Question 43. [2]

A metal has face centred cubic lattice. The edge length of the unit cell is 404 pm. The density of the metal is 2.72 g/cm^3. (N_A = 6.023 × 10^{23} mol^{-1})

(i) The molar mass of the metal is:

    (a) $20\ g\ mol^{-1}$ (b) $27\ g\ mol^{-1}$

    (c) $30\ g\ mol^{-1}$ (d) $40\ g\ mol^{-1}$

(ii) The radius of the metal atom in centimetre (cm) is:

    (a) $103.29 \times 10^{-10}\ cm$ (b) $125.63 \times 10^{-10}\ cm$

    (c) $142.81 \times 10^{-10}\ cm$ (d) $175.76 \times 10^{-10}\ cm$

Question 44.   **[2]**

A binary solution contains 92 g ethyl alcohol and 72 g water.

(Atomic weight of C = 12, H =1, O =16)

(i) Mole fraction of ethyl alcohol is:

    (a)   0.40   (b)   0.80

    (c)   0.66   (d)   0.33

(ii) Mole fraction of water is:

    (a)   0.33   (b)   0.66

    (c)   0.20   (d)   0.80

Question 45.   **[2]**

The limiting molar conductivities $(\wedge^{\infty}_{m})$ for NaCl, KBr and KCl are 126, 152 and 150 $ohm^{-1}\ cm^{2}\ mol^{-1}$ respectively.

(i) The molar conductivity at infinite dilution for NaBr is:

    (a) $128\ ohm^{-1}\ cm^{2}\ mol^{-1}$ (b) $176\ ohm^{-1}\ cm^{2}\ mol^{-1}$

    (c) $278\ ohm^{-1}\ cm^{2}\ mol^{-1}$ (d) $302\ ohm^{-1}\ cm^{2}\ mol^{-1}$

(ii) The law applied to determine the molar conductivity of infinite dilution is known as:

    (a)   Faraday's Law   (b)   Avogadro's Law

    (c)   Kohlrausch's Law   (d)   Ohm's Law

Question 46.   **[1]**

Assertion: Haloalkanes when treated with alcoholic KCN forms alkane nitrile as a major product.

Reason: Potassium cyanide is a covalent compound.

(a) Assertion is false but reason is true.

(b) Assertion is true but reason is false.

(c) Both assertion and reason are false.

(d) Both assertion and reason are true and reason is the correct explanation of the assertion.

Question 47.   **[1]**

Assertion: Iron is found free in nature.

Reason: Iron is highly reactive element.

(a) Assertion is false but reason is true.

(b) Assertion is true but reason is false.

(c) Both assertion and reason are true but reason is not correct explanation of the assertion.

(d) Both assertion and reason are true and reason is the correct explanation of the assertion.

Question 48.   **[1]**

Assertion: Ethers are more volatile than alcohols having the same molecular formula.

Reason: Alcohols have intermolecular hydrogen bond.

(a) Assertion is false but reason is true.

(b) Assertion is true but reason is false.

(c) Both assertion and reason are true but reason is not correct explanation of the assertion.

(d) Both assertion and reason are true and reason is the correct explanation of the assertion.

Question 49. [1]

Assertion: SO_2 decolorises pink colour of acidified $KMnO_4$ solution.

Reason: SO_2 is an oxidising agent

(a) Assertion is false but reason is true.

(b) Assertion is true but reason is false.

(c) Both assertion and reason are true but reason is not the correct explanation of the assertion.

(d) Both assertion and reason are true and reason is the correct explanation of the assertion.

Question 50. [1]

Assertion: Sulphide ores are concentrated by froth floatation process.

Reason: Sulphide ores are wetted by pine oil forming the froth while impurities are vetted by water.

(a) Both assertion and reason are correct and reason is the correct explanation of the assertion.

(b) Both assertion and reason are correct but reason is not the correct explanation of the assertion.

(c) Assertion is correct and the reason is wrong.

(d) Both assertion and reason are wrong.

Answers

1. (b) 2 and 4

   Explanation: In bcc unit cell:

   8 corners × 1/8 per corner atom + 1 body center atom(1 × 1) = 2 atoms

   In fcc unit cell:

   8 corners × 1/8 per corner atom + 6 face centred atom × ½ atom per unit cell = 4 atoms

2. (b) The number of solute particles in solution

   Explanation: All the colligative properties depend on the number of solute particles irrespective of their nature relative to the total number of particles present in the solution.

3. (c) Decreases

   Explanation: Specific conductivity is the conductance by an electrolytic solution of unit volume kept between two platinum electrodes of unit length .It depends upon concentration of the solution. On dilution, volume increases, so number of ions per unit volume carrying the current decreases. Hence, specific conductivity also decreases.

4. (a) Limestone

   Explanation: The flux used in the extraction of iron from haematite ore is limestone. This flux is added for the removal of silica impurities from the haematite ore. The reactions are as follows:

   $$CaCO_3 \rightarrow CaO + CO_2$$
   $$CaO + SiO_2 \rightarrow CaSiO_3$$
   $$\text{(slag)}$$

5. (d) XeF_3

   Explanation: Xenon is an inert gas with electronic configuration $[Kr]4d^{10}5s^25p^6$.

   When one, two or three electrons are promoted from $5p$ (filled) to $5d$ (empty) orbitals, two, four and six half-filled orbitals are formed.

   Xenon can combine with even number of F atoms to form XeF_2, XeF_4 or XeF_6. It cannot combine with odd number of F atoms.

   Thus, from the given options formation of XeF_3 is not possible.

6. (c) Ethyne

   Explanation: When 2 moles of iodofrom reacts with 6 moles of silver powder, it forms ethyne gas and silver iodide is formed as a by-product.

   $$CHI_3 + 6Ag + CHI_3 \rightarrow CH \equiv CH + 6AgI$$
   $$\text{Ethyne}$$

7. (b) Hydrogen bonding

Explanation: The boiling point of ethanol is higher than diethyl ether due to extensive intermolecular hydrogen bonding. Hydrogen bonding increases the boiling point because a lot of energy is required to break the hydrogen bond. In case of ethanol, from the functional group -OH, one hydrogen atom is attached to a very electronegative oxygen atom directly. Due to which both hydrogen and oxygen become polar and results in the formation of hydrogen bond. whereas, in case of diethyl ether, oxygen is not directly attached to the oxygen, due to the formation of hydrogen bond is not possible in diethylether. Thus, ethanol has higher boiling point than diethylether.

While in diethyl ether, there is no hydrogen bonding and the intermolecular attraction present is weaker than intermolecular forces *i.e,* due to hydrogen bonding between molecules of ethyl alcohol. Hence, ethanol has a higher boiling point than diethyl ether.

8. (c) A_2B_5

Explanation: In fcc cubic lattice

A at corners = 8 corners × 1/8 per corner atom = 1

B at face centres = 5 centres × ½ per face centre atom= 5/2

Ratio of A : B = 1:5/2 = 2:5

Formula = A_2B_5

9. (a) Y > Z > X

Explanation: We know, $E^{\circ}_{OP} = -E^{\circ}_{RP}$

Higher the oxidising potential, higher is the tendency to lose an electron and higher is the reducing nature. Thus, smaller the reduction potential of a substance, more is its reducing power (Y > Z > X).

10. (d) Unchanged

Explanation: $\Delta T_b = K_b \times m$

$\Delta T_f = K_f \times m$

Where, m = molality

K_b and K_f are the proportionality constant which depends on the nature of solvent, not on molality i.e., they are independent of molality.

11. (b) Roasting, followed by reduction with carbon

Explanation: The extraction of zinc from zinc blende is carried out by first roasting and then reduction with carbon. The reactions are as follows:

$$ZnS + O_2 \rightarrow ZnO + SO_2 \qquad \text{Roasting}$$

$$ZnO + C \xrightarrow{\Delta} Zn + CO\uparrow \quad \text{Carbon reduction}$$

12. (a) Fluorine

Explanation: Strong oxidising agents have high tendency to oxidise other element and itself get reduced. Flourine is a strong oxidising agent as compared to chlorine, bromine and iodine because it has high electronegativity and reduction potential. Thus, out of the given options fluorine is a powerful oxidising agent.

13. (c) A carbocation

Explanation: In the $S_N{}^1$ reaction mechanism, the carbocation species is a reaction intermediate.

14. (d) Frenkel defect

Explanation: Frenkel defect arises when an ion (usually cation) is missing from its lattice site and occupies an interstitial position in the crystal. Some examples include AgBr, ZnS, AgCl, and AgI.

15. (a) tert. butyl alcohol

Explanation: Reaction of acetone whith methyl magnesium bromide (Grignard reagent) forms a complex which on hydrolysis to gives tert. butyl alcohol.

$$CH_3-\underset{\underset{O}{\|}}{C}-CH_3 \xrightarrow[\text{(ii) } H_3O^+]{\text{(i) } CH_3MgCl} CH_3-\underset{\underset{OH}{|}}{\overset{\overset{CH_3}{|}}{C}}-CH_3 + Mg\underset{Cl}{\overset{OH}{<}}$$

16. (c) 0.0196

$$\text{Explanation:} \quad \text{Moles of NaCl} = \frac{5.85\text{gm NaCl in solution}}{58.5}$$

$$= 0.1 \text{ mol}$$

$$\text{Moles of H}_2\text{O} = \frac{90\text{gm of H}_2\text{O}}{18}$$

$$= 5 \text{ mol}$$

$$\text{Mole fraction of NaCl} = \frac{0.1}{5+0.1} = 0.0196$$

17. (d) Reduction potential of copper is higher than that of zinc.

Explanation: when zinc granules are dipped in copper sulphate solution, having higher reduction potential of copper (0.34 V) than zinc (–0.76 v), zinc easily displaces copper from its copper sulphate solution and make its own salt.

18. (b) Butan-2-ol

Explanation: A compound to be optically active requires atleast 1 chiral carbon.

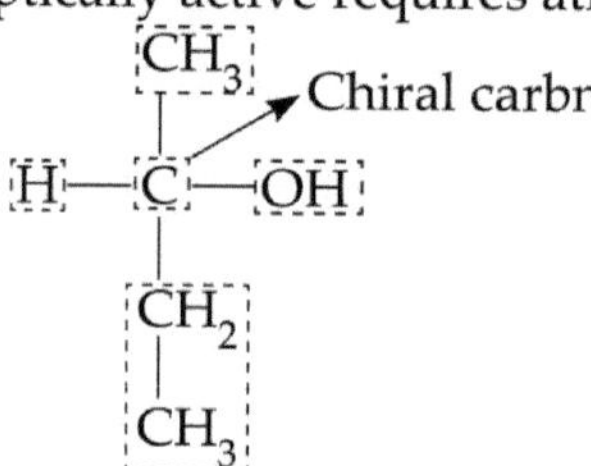

19. (c) NaCl and NaClO

Explanation: When chlorine reacts with dilute and cold NaOH, sodium chloride and sodium hypochloride.

$$2\text{NaOH}_{(aq)} + \text{Cl}_{2(g)} \longrightarrow \text{NaCl}_{(aq)} + \text{NaOCl}_{(aq)} + \text{H}_2\text{O}_{(l)}$$

Cold Dilute   Sodium chlorate(i)

20. (c) Azeotropic

Explanation: A constant boiling mixture in which the composition of the mixture remains same throughout the boiling is an azeotropic mixture. For such solution, the composition of vapour is same as that of liquid solution at its boiling point. Thus, such mixtures distill without change in composition or temperature.

21. (d) Williamson's synthesis

Explanation:

$$R{-}O^{\ominus}\,Na^{\oplus} \;+\; R{-}Cl \longrightarrow R{-}O{-}R \;+\; \text{NaCl}$$

Sodium alkoxide   Ether

22. (b) Phenol

Explanation: Benzene diazonium chloride on hydrolysis gives phenol and nitrogen gas.

$$\underset{}{\overset{+}{N_2}}\overset{-}{Cl} + H_2O \longrightarrow N_2 + \text{(phenol, OH)} + \text{NaCl}$$

23. (a) 32%

Explanation: 68% of the available volume is occupied by spheres. Thus, vacant space is 32%.

24. (d) –ve and +ve

Explanation:

$$\Delta G^\circ < 0$$

For spontaneous reaction $\Delta E^\circ > 0$

$\because \qquad \Delta G^\circ = n\text{FE}^\circ_{\text{cell}}$

Thus, both have opposite signs.

25. (d) CH_3COCH_3

Explanation: when A liquid is mixed with ethanol and few drops of conc. H_2SO_4 is added. A compound with a fruity smell is formed and is called as ethyl acetate. This process is known as esterification.

$$CH_3COOH + C_2H_5OH \xrightarrow{\text{Conc. } H_2SO_4} CH_3\overset{\displaystyle O}{\overset{\|}{C}} - OC_2H_5 + H_2O$$

Ethyl acetate
(Fruity smell)

26. (i) (b) By Froth-floatation process

Explanation: Copper pyrite is sulphide ore. Sulphide ores are first concentrated by froth floatation method.

(ii) (c) Pure copper deposits at cathode

Explanation: Anode is made of impure copper.

Pure copper during electrolytic refining deposit at cathode.

Impurities such as Ag, Au settle down as anode mud.

Acidified $CuSO_4$ aqueous solution is used to increase conduction.

27. (i) (b) S_N2 mechanism

Explanation: : S_N2 reaction is second order reaction and its rate depends on the concentration of the substrate as well as the nucleophile.

Thus, the rate of conversion of methyl bromide to methanol is given by the expression rate $= k[CH_3Br]$ $[OH^-]$.

(ii) (c) Nucleophilic substitution reaction

Explanation: In this reaction, nucleophile Br^- is replaced by another nucleophile OH^-. So, it is a nucleophilic substitution reaction.

28. (i) (d) Sublimation

Explanation: Sublimation is the transition of a substance directly from the solid to the gas phase without passing through the intermediate liquid phase.

(ii) (d) Silver

Explanation: Silver is obtained by leaching its ore with dilute cyanide solution.

29. (i) (c) Reimer –Tiemann reaction

(ii) (a) Salicylaldehyde

Explanation: When phenol is treated with chloroform in the presence of alcoholic potassium hydroxide, salicylaldehye is formed and this reaction is known as Reimer-Tiemann reaction.

Salicylaldehyde

30. (i) (d) Pentagonal bipyramidal

(ii) (b) sp^3d^3 hybridisation

Explanation:

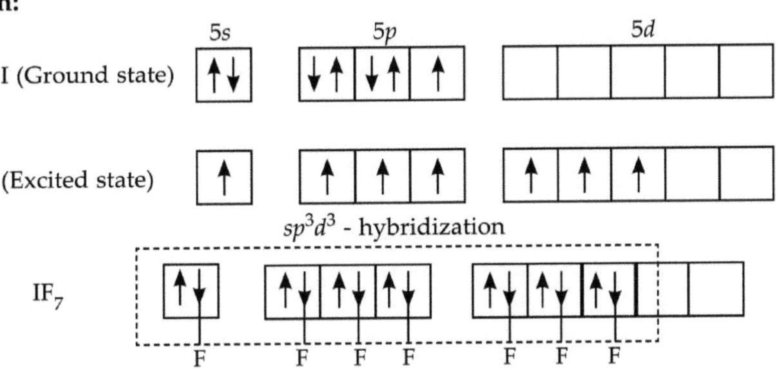

Formation of IF_7 molecule involving sp^3d^3 hybridization

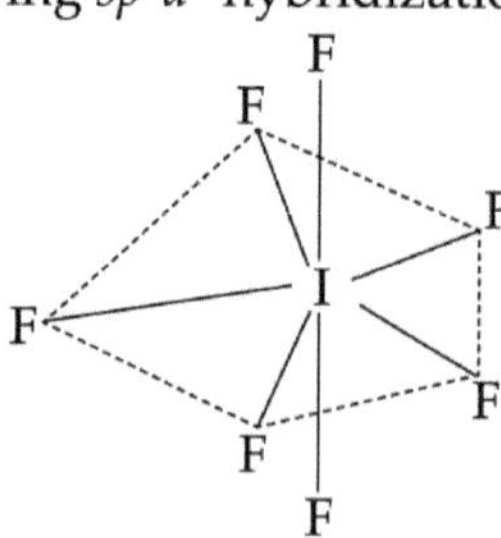

Pentagonal bipyramidal geometry of IF_7 molecule and is has sp^3d^3 hybridisation

31. (i) (c) C_2H_5Cl

   (ii) (b) C_2H_4

      Explanation: $C_2H_5OH + PCl_5 \rightarrow C_2H_5Cl + POCl_3 + HCl$

$$C_2H_5Cl \xrightarrow[\text{(alc.KOH)}]{\Delta} C_2H_4 + KCl + H_2O$$

32. (i) (d) $Cu + SO_2$

   (ii) (c) $FeSiO_3$

      Explanation: On heating the mixture of Cu_2O and Cu_2S, Cu and SO_2 is obtained. Iron is removed during the extraction of copper as $FeSiO_3$

$$2CuS + 3O_2 \rightarrow 2CuO + SO_2 \qquad \text{Roasting}$$
$$Cu_2O + C \rightarrow 2Cu + CO \qquad \text{Carbon reduction}$$
$$FeO + SiO_2 \rightarrow FeSiO_3 \qquad \text{Slag formation}$$

33. (i) (b) Heating it with aqueous NaOH at 623 K under pressure followed by acidification with dilute HCl.

   (ii) (a) Dow process

      Explanation: By the Dow's process . When chlorobenzene is heated with NaOH at 623K under 300 atm and it forms sodium phenoxide which upon acidification gives phenol.

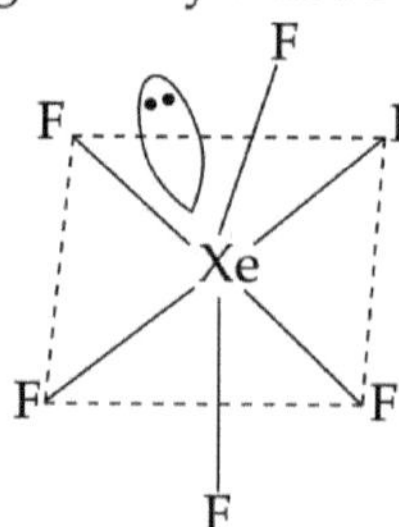

34. (i) (a) sp^3d^3

   (ii) (a) Distorted octahedral

      Explanation: Due to the presence of one lone pair of electrons, there will be lone-pair –bond-pair repulsion in the molecule and the geometry will be distorted octahedral.

35. (i) (c) Tertiary alcohol by $S_N{}^1$

      Explanation: Tertiary alcohol reacts faster because of the formation of tertiary carbocation during the reaction which is very stable carbocation.

   (ii) (a) Anhydrous zinc chloride in concentrated HCl

      Explanation: Lucas' reagent is a solution of anhydrous zinc chloride in concentrated hydrochloric acid.

36. (i) (c) Silent electric discharge

Explanation: Ozone is prepared in laboratory by passing silent electric discharge through dry oxygen. By passing the electric current some of the oxygen molecules dissociate and then atomic oxygen combines with oxygen molecules to form ozone.

(ii) (b) Oxidising agent

Explanation: Ozone is an oxidizing agent: Ozone serves as a strong oxidizing agent as an atom of nascent oxygen that is more reactive than oxygen and will quickly decompose to give oxygen.

37. (i) (b) 8.93 g/cm^3

(ii) (c) 127.79 pm

Explanation: Given,

$$a = 361.5 \text{ pm} = 3.61 \times 10^{-8} \text{ cm}$$

$$a = 2\sqrt{2}r$$

$$\therefore \quad r = \frac{361.5}{2\sqrt{2}} = 127.79 \text{ pm}$$

$$M = 63.5 \text{ g/mol}$$

Number of atoms in unit cell of fcc, $Z = 4$

$$\therefore \quad \text{Density} = \frac{Z \times M}{a^3 N_A} = \frac{4 \times 63.5}{(3.61 \times 10^{-8})^3 \times 6.023 \times 10^{23}}$$

$$= 8.92 \text{ g/cm}^3$$

38. (i) (c) 100.25 °C

(ii) (b) -0.894 °C

Explanation: Moles of urea $= \dfrac{1}{60}$ mol

Moles of glucose $= \dfrac{3}{180} = \dfrac{1}{60}$ mol

When moles are same, then molality is also similar and Kb and Kf will remain unchanged. Thus, temperature will also remain unchanged.

39. (i) (b) 63.50 g

Explanation: Cathode reaction: $Cu^{2+}_{(aq.)} + 2e^- \rightarrow Cu$

According to the above equation, 2 mol of electrons, *i.e,* 2 faradays of electricity will deposit 1 mol of Cu.

1 mol Cu = 63.5gm

(ii) (c) 216 gm

Explanation: Cathode reaction: $Ag^+ (aq.) + 1e^- \rightarrow Ag$

According to the above equation, 1 mol of electrons, *i.e,* 2 faradays of electricity will deposit 2 mol of Ag.

2mol Ag = 2 x 108 gm = 216gm

40. (i) (d) 4

(ii) (c) face centred cubic unit cell

Explanation:

$$\text{Density} = \frac{z \times M}{a^3 \times N_A}$$

$$z = \frac{\rho \times a^3 \times N_A}{M}$$

$$z = \frac{(19.3 \, gcm^{-3}) \times (407.9 \times 10^{-10} \text{ cm})^3 \times (6.022 \times 10^{23}) \text{mol}^{-1})}{197 \, g \, \text{mol}^{-1}}$$

$$z = 4$$

Hence, structure is face centred cubic lattice.

41. (i) (d) +0.372 °C

(ii) (b) 0.2

Explanation: Depression in freezing point,

$$\Delta T_f = K_f \times m$$

where,

$$m = \text{molality} = \frac{W_B \times 1000}{M_B \times W_A}$$

$$m = \frac{68.4 \times 1000}{342 \times 1000} = 0.2$$

$$\Delta T_f = 1.86 \times 0.2 = 0.372 \text{ °C}$$

$$T_f = T°_f - \Delta T_f = 0 - 0.372 = 0.372 \text{ °C}$$

42. (i) (c) 0.94 V

(ii) (a) –181.42 kJ

Explanation: $Ag^+_{(aq)} + e^- \rightarrow Ag_{(s)}$

$Sn^{2+}_{(aq)} + 2e^- \rightarrow Sn_{(s)}$

$Sn[Sn^{2+} (1M | | Ag^{2+} (1M) | Ag$ is :

$$E°_{Ag} = 0.80V$$

$$E°_{Sn} = -0.14 \text{ V}$$

$$E°_{cell} = E°_{Cathode} - E°_{Anode}$$

$$\Delta G° = -nFE°_{cell}$$

$$= 0.80 - (-0.14) \text{ Vz } 0.94 \text{ V}$$

$$\Delta G° = -2 \times 96,000 \times 0.94 \text{J}$$

$$\Delta G° = -181.42 \text{ kJ}$$

43. (i) (b) 27g mol^{-1}

(ii) (c) 142×10^{-10} cm

Explanation: Edge length of fcc unit cell :

$$a = 2\sqrt{2}r$$

$$\therefore r = \frac{a}{2\sqrt{2}} = \frac{404 \times 10^{-10}}{2\sqrt{2}} \text{ cm} = 142.81 \times 10^{-10} \text{ cm}$$

Density of unit cell is given as :

$$d = \frac{\text{mass of unit cell}}{\text{volume of unit cell}} = \frac{z \times M}{a^3 \times N_A}$$

$$M = \frac{d \times a^3 \times N_A}{z}$$

$$M = \frac{(2.72g / cm^3) \times (4.4 \times 10^{-10} cm)^3 \times (6.02 \times 10^{23} mol^{-1})}{4}$$

$$M = 26.9g \text{ mol}^{-1} \approx 27g \text{ mol}^{-1}$$

44. (i) (d) 0.33

(ii) (b) 0.66

Explanation: Number of moles $= \dfrac{\text{Given mass}}{\text{Molar mass}}$

$$\text{Moles of ethyl alcohol} = \frac{92}{46} = 2 \text{ mol}$$

$$\text{Moles of water} = \frac{72}{18} = 4 \text{ mol}$$

$$\therefore \quad \text{Mole fraction of ethanol} = \frac{2}{2+4} = \frac{1}{3} \approx 0.33$$

$$\text{Mole fraction of water} = \frac{4}{2+4} = \frac{2}{3} \approx 0.66$$

45. (i) (a) 128 s cm^3

Explanation: we have,

$$\Lambda^{\circ}_{NaCl} = 128 \text{s cm}^3$$
$$\Lambda^{\circ}_{KBr} = 152 \text{s cm}^3$$
$$\Lambda^{\circ}_{KCl} = 150 \text{s cm}^3$$

As,

$$\Lambda^{\circ}_{NaCl} = \Lambda^{\circ}_{Na^+} + \Lambda^{\circ}_{Cl^-} \quad\quad ....(i)$$
$$\Lambda^{\circ}_{KBr} = \Lambda^{\circ}_{K^+} + \Lambda^{\circ}_{Br^-} \quad\quad ....(ii)$$
$$\Lambda^{\circ}_{KCl} = \Lambda^{\circ}_{K^+} + \Lambda^{\circ}_{Cl^-} \quad\quad ....(iii)$$

Including all equations as (i) + (ii) − (iii)

$$\because \quad \Lambda^{\circ}_{NaCl} = \Lambda^{\circ}_{Na^+} + \Lambda^{\circ}_{Br^-}$$
$$\Lambda^{\circ}_{NaBr} = 126 + 152 - 150 = 128 \text{s cm}^3$$

(ii) (c) Kohlrausch's Law

Explanation: Kohlrausch's law states that the equivalent conductivity of an electrolyte at infinite dilution is equal to the sum of the conductance of the anions and cations.

46. (i) (b) Assertion is true but reason is false.

Explanation: For example : Alkyl halide (Bromoethane) react with alc. KCN to give Alkyl cyanide. Alkyl halide reacts with alcoholic KCN to form alkyl cyanide (alkane nitrile)

$$CH_3 - CH_2 - Br + \text{alc. KCN} \longrightarrow CH_3 - CH_2 - CN + KBr$$

Bromoethane or ethyl bromide   Ethyl cyanide propane nitrile

KCN is predominantly ionic compound. The attack takes place through the carbon atom and not through nitrogen atom because the C-C bond is more stable than C-N bond. Thus, assertion is true but reason is false.

47. (a) Assertion is false but reason is true.

Explanation: Iron is not found freely in nature because it is highly reactive. Thus, assertion is false but reason is true.

48. (d) Both assertion and reason are true and reason is the correct explanation of the assertion.

Explanation: Alcohols are less volatile than ether because alcohols contain a hydrogen atom attached to the strongly electronegative oxygen atom. Therefore they form intermolecular hydrogen bonding. Thus, both assertion and reason are true but reason is not the correct explanation of assertion.

49. (b) Assertion is true but reason is false.

Explanation: Sulphur dioxide (SO_2) is passed through an acidified solution of potassium permagnate ($KMnO_4$) which is purple in colour. On doing so, sulphur dioxide being a strong reducing agent, reduces the purple coloured solution to form a colourless solution.

$$2KMnO_4 + 5SO_2 + 2H_2O \rightarrow K_2SO_4 + 2MnSO_4 + 2H_2SO_4$$

(purple)   (colourless)

Moist sulphur dioxide behaves as a reducing agent, as it reduces MnO^{4-} to Mn^{2+}. Thus, assertion is true but reason is false.

50. (a) Both assertion and reason are correct and reason is the correct explanation of the assertion.

Explanation: Froth floatation method is used to concentrate sulphide ores. Wet pine oil is used in froth flotation process because it does not have an affinity towards water. It attracts impurities which can be washed away. Thus, both and assertion and reason are true and reason is the correct explanation of assertion.

❑❑

Questions

Question 1

Arrange the types of arrangement in terms of decreasing packing efficiency.

(a) BCC > Simple cubic > CCP

(b) HCP > CCP > BCC

(c) HCP > BCC > Simple cubic

(d) CCP > BCC > HCP

Question 2

Of the following terms used for denoting concentration of a solution, the one which does not gets affected by temperature is :

(a) Molarity

(b) Molality

(c) Normality

(d) Formality

Question 3

Electrolysis involves oxidation and reduction respectively at :

(a) Anode and cathode

(b) Cathode and anode

(c) At both the electrode

(d) None of these

Question 4

Purest form of iron is:

(a) Cast iron

(b) Hard Steel

(c) Stainless steel

(d) Wrought iron

Question 5

Which of the following mainly exhibits (– 2) oxidation state ?

(a) S

(b) O

(c) Se

(d) Te

Question 6

Carbylamine test involves heating a mixture of :

(a) Alcoholic KOH, methyl iodide, and sodium metal

(b) Alcoholic KOH, methyl iodide, and primary amine

(c) Alcoholic KOH, chloroform, and primary amine

(d) Alcoholic KOH, methyl alcohol, and primary amine

Question 7

The ionisation constant of phenol is higher than that of ethanol because :

(a) Phenoxide ion is a stronger base than ethoxide ion

(b) Phenoxide ion is stabilised through delocalisation

(c) Phenoxide ion is less stable than ethoxide ion

(d) Phenoxide ion is bulkier than ethoxide ion

Question 8

Which of the following is most acidic ?

(a) H_2O

(b) CH_3OH

(c) C_2H_5OH

(d) $CH_3CH_2CH_2OH$

Question 9

When chloroform is heated with aqueous NaOH, it gives :

(a) Formic acid   (b) Sodium formate   (c) Acetic acid   (d) Sodium acetate

Question 10

Which of the following is not an interhalogen compound ?

(a) ICl_4^- (b) ClF_5 (c) IPO_4 (d) ClF_3

Question 11

Which of the following ore is best concentrated by froth floatation process ?

(a) Magnetite   (b) Cassiterite   (c) Galena   (d) Malachite

Question 12

The electrode Pt, Hg (g) /HCl is reversible with respect to :

(a) Cl^- ions   (b) HCl

(c) H^+ ions   (d) Both H^+ and Cl^- ions

Question 13

Electrochemical equivalent is the amount of substance which gets deposited from its solution on passing electrical charge equal to :

(a) 96,500 coulomb   (b) 1 coulomb   (c) 60 coulomb   (d) 965 coulomb

Question 14

Solution that obeys Raoult's law :

(a) Normal solution   (b) Molar solution   (c) Ideal solution   (d) Saturated solution

Question 15

A substance A_xB_y crystallizes in a face centered cubic (*fcc*) lattice in which atoms 'A' occupy each corner of the cube, atom 'B' occupy the centres of each face of the cube. Identify the correct composition of the substance A_xB_y :

(a) AB_3 (b) A_4B_3

(c) A_3B (d) Composition cannot be specified

Question 16

In a rock salt structure each Cl^- ion is surrounded by :

(a) $4\,Na^+$ ions   (b) $6\,Na^+$ ions

(c) $8\,Na^+$ ions   (d) $12\,Na^+$ ions

Question 17

Determination of correct molecular mass from Raoult's law is applicable to :

(a) An electrolyte in solution   (b) A non-electrolyte in dilute solution

(c) A non-electrolyte in conc. Solution   (d) An electrolyte in a liquid solvent.

Question 18

Which of the following aqueous solutions should have the highest boiling point?

(a) 1.0 M NaOH   (b) 1.0 M Na_2SO_4

(c) 1.0 M NH_4NO_3 (d) 1.0 M KNO_3

Question 19

The standard electrode potentials of four elements A, B, C and D are -3.05, 1.66, -0.40 and 0.80 volts respectively. The highest chemical activity will be shown by :

(a) A   (b) B   (c) C   (d) D

Question 20

Heating Cu_2O and Cu_2S will give :

(a) $Cu + SO_2$ (b) $Cu + SO_3$ (c) $CuO + CuS$ (d) Cu_2SO_3

Question 21

The high viscosity and high boiling point of HF is due to :

(a) Low dissociation energy of F_2 molecule

(b) Associated nature due to hydrogen bonding

(c) Ionic character of HF

(d) High electronegativity of fluorine

Question 22

When phenol is treated with excess of bromine water, it gives :

(a) *m*-bromophenol

(b) *o*-and *p*-bromophenol

(c) 2, 4-dibromophenol

(d) 2, 4, 6-tribromophenol

Question 23

Shape of ClF_3 is :

(a) Trigonal planar

(b) Tetrahedral

(c) T-Shaped

(d) Distorted octahedral

Question 24

Which of the following compound has been suggested as causing depletion of the ozone layer in the upper stratosphere ?

(a) CH_4

(b) CCl_2F_2

(c) CF_4

(d) CH_2Cl_2

Question 25

Zn/Zn^{2+} ($a = 0.1M$) $\|$ Fe^{2+} ($a = 0/1M$)/Fe. The e.m.f. of the above cell is 0.290 V. Equilibrium constant for the cell reaction is:

(a) $10^{0.32/0.0991}$

(b) $10^{0.32/0.0295}$

(c) $10^{0.26/0.0295}$

(d) $e^{0.32/0.295}$

Question 26

(i) Which of the following 0.1 M aqueous solution will have the lowest freezing point ?

(a) Potassium sulphate

(b) Sodium chloride

(c) Urea

(d) Glucose

(ii) Which of the following is an example of a non-ideal solution showing positive deviation?

(a) Acetone + Carbon disulphide

(b) Chlorobenzene + Bromobenzene

(c) Chloroform + Benzene

(d) Acetone + Aniline

Question 27

(i) Copper has the face centered cubic structure. The coordination number of each ion is :

(a) 4

(b) 12

(c) 14

(d) 8

(ii) Gold crystallizes in a face-centred unit cell. What is its atomic radius if the edge length of the gold unit cell is 0.407×10^{-9} m? (Gold atomic mass = 197 u)

(a) 0.115 nm

(b) 0.144 nm

(c) 0.235 nm

(d) 0.156 nm

Question 28

(i) Molar conductivities of the weak electrolyte at infinite dilution is evaluated through:

(a) Kohlrausch Law　(b) Ostwald dilution　(c) Arrhenius Concept　(d) none of these

(ii) The limiting molar conductivities for NaCl, KBr, KCl are 126, 152 and 150 S cm^2mol^{-1} The limiting conductivity for NaBr is:

(a) 128 S cm^2mol^{-1}

(b) 278 S cm^2mol^{-1}

(c) 976 S cm^2mol^{-1}

(d) 302 S cm^2mol^{-1}

Question 29

(i) When an atom has 'N' octahedral voids, the number of tetrahedral voids are:

(a) 8N

(b) 1/2N

(c) 6N

(d) 2N

(ii) The number of tetrahedral void in the unit cell of a face centered cubic lattice of similar atom is:

(a) 6

(b) 8

(c) 4

(d) 2

Question 30

(i) Which of the following element has highest Ionization enthalpy?

    (a) As   (b) Sb   (c) P   (d) N

(ii) Which element possess highest electron gain enthalpy in the periodic table?

    (a) F   (b) Cl   (c) Br   (d) I

Question 31

(i) Molar conductivity of 0.15 M solution of KCl at 298 K, if its conductivity of 0.0152 S cm^{-1} will be:

    (a) $124\ \Omega^{-1}$ cm² mol^{-1} (b) $204\ \Omega^{-1}$ cm² mol^{-1}

    (c) $101\ \Omega^{-1}$ cm² mol^{-1} (d) $300\ \Omega^{-1}$ cm² mol^{-1}

(ii) Electrical conductance through metals is called metallic or electronic conductance and is due to the movement of electrons. The electronic conductance depends on:

    (a) The nature and structure of the metal   (b) The number of valence electrons per atom

    (c) Change in temperature   (d) All of these

Question 32

(i) AgCI is crystallized from molten AgCI containing a little $CdCI_2$. The solid obtained will have:

    (a) Cationic vacancies equal to number of Cd^{2+} ions incorporated

    (b) Cationic vacancies equal to double the number of Cd^{2+} ions

    (c) Anionic vacancies

    (d) Neither cationic nor anionic vacancies.

(ii) Which of the following gives both Frenkel and Schottky defect?

    (a) AgCl   (b) KCl   (c) AgBr   (d) NaCl.

Question 33

(i) Partial pressure of a solution component is directly proportional to its mole fraction. This is known as:

    (a) Henry's law   (b) Raoult's law

    (c) Distribution law   (d) Ostwald's dilution law

(ii) The relative lowering in vapour pressure is proportional to the ratio of number of:

    (a) Solute molecules to solvent molecules

    (b) Solvent molecules to solute molecules

    (c) Solute molecules to the total number of molecules in solution

    (d) Solvent molecules to the total number of molecules in solution

Question 34

(i) Faraday's law of electrolysis is related to:

    (a) Atomic number of cation   (b) Speed of cation

    (c) Speed of anion   (d) Equivalent weight of electrolyte

(ii) How much electricity in terms of Faraday is required to produce 100 g of Ca from molten $CaCl_2$?

    (a) 1F   (b) 2F   (c) 3F   (d) 5F

Question 35

A dihalogen derivative (A) of hydrocarbon having two carbon atom reacts with alcoholic potash and forms another hydrocarbon which gives red precipitate with ammonical solution of cuprous chloride. Compound A gives an aldehyde when treated with aqueous KOH.

(i) What is (A) compound?

    (a) Dichloroethane   (b) Dibromoethane   (c) Diiodoethane   (d) Difluoroethane

(ii) An aldehyde formed when A is treated with aq. KOH

    (a) Propanal   (b) Methanal   (c) Ethanal   (d) None of the above

Question 36

(i) Arrange the following in decreasing Lewis acid strength - PF_3, PCI_3, PBr_3, PI_3

    (a) $PI_3 > PBr_3 > PCl_3 > PF_3$ (b) $PF_3 > PCl_3 > PBr_3 > PI_3$

    (c) $PCl_3 > PBr_3 > PI_3 > PF_3$ (d) $PBr_3 > PI_3 > PF_3 > PCl_3$

  (ii) Arrange the following hydrides of group 16 elements in order of increasing stability.

    (a) $H_2S < H_2O < H_2Te > H_2Se$ (b) $H_2O < H_2Te < H_2Se < H_2S$

    (c) $H_2O < H_2S < H_2Se < H_2Te$ (d) $H_2Te < H_2Se < H_2S < H_3O$

Question 37

  (i) The significance of leaching in the extraction of aluminium is:

    (a) It helps removing the impurities like SiO_2, Fe_2O_3 etc. from the bauxite ore

    (b) It converts the ore into oxide

    (c) It reduces melting point of the ore

    (d) It eliminates water from bauxite

  (ii) Which of the following metals cannot be obtained by reduction of its metal oxide by aluminium ?

    (a) Cr   (b) Mn   (c) Fe   (d) Mg

Question 38

  (i) The density of a metal which crystallises in bcc lattice with unit cell edge length 300 pm and molar mass 50 g mol^{-1} will be:

    (a) 10 g cm^{-3} (b) 14.2 g cm^{-3} (c) 6.15 g cm^{-3} (d) $9.3\,2 \text{ g cm}^{-3}$

  (ii) Which of the following will have metal deficiency defect?

    (a) NaCl   (b) FeO   (c) KCl   (d) ZnO

Question 39

A compound (A) reacts with thionyl chloride to give compound (B). (B) reacts with magnesium to form Grignard reagent which is treated with acetone and the product is hydrolysed to give 2-methyl-2- butanol.

  (i) What is (A) compound?

    (a) Butanol   (b) Propanol   (c) Methanol   (d) Ethanol

  (ii) What is (B) compound?

    (a) Butyl chloride   (b) Propyl chloride   (c) Ethyl chloride   (d) Methyl chloride

Question 40

A compound (A) with molecular formulae $C_4H_{10}O$ on oxidation form compound (B). The compound (B) gives positive iodoform test and on reaction with CH_3MgBr followed by hydrolysis gives (C),

  (i) The compound A is:

    (a) 2-Butanol   (b) Diethylether   (c) 2-Butanal   (d) None of these

  (ii) The compound C is:

    (a) 2-methyl-2 butanol   (b) 2-methyl butan-3-ol

    (c) 3-methyl butan-2-ol   (d) Pentanol

Question 41

  (i) During the process of electrolytic refining of copper, some metals present as impurity settle as 'anode mud'. These are:

    (a) Pb and Zn   (b) Sn and Ag   (c) Fe and Ni   (d) Ag and Au

  (ii) Extraction of zinc from zinc blende is achieved by

    (a) Electrolytic reduction

    (b) Roasting followed by reduction with carbon

    (c) Roasting followed by reduction with another metal

    (d) Roasting followed by self-reduction

Question 42

  (i) In a simple cubic, body-centred cubic and face-centred cubic structure, the ratio of the number of atoms present is respectively

    (a) $8:1:6$ (b) $1:2:4$ (c) $4:2:1$ (d) $4:2:3$

  (ii) Na and Mg crystallize in crystals of bcc and fcc form respectively and then the amount of Na and Mg atoms present in their respective crystal unit cells is:

    (a) 4 and 2   (b) 9 and 14   (c) 14 and 9   (d) 2 and 4

Question 43

(i) S-S bond is present in which of the ion pairs?

(a) $S_2O_7^{2-}, S_2O_3^{2-}$ (b) $S_4O_6^{2-}, S_2O_7^{2-}$ (c) $S_2O_7^{2-}, S_2O_8^{2-}$ (d) $S_4O_6^{2-}, S_2O_3^{2-}$

(ii) P_4O_{10} has ______ bridging O atoms.

(a) 4 (b) 5 (c) 6 (d) 2

Question 44

(i) C–Cl bond of chlorobenzene in comparison to C–Cl bond in methyl chloride is

(a) Longer and weaker (b) Shorter and weaker

(c) Shorter and stronger (d) Longer and stronger

(ii) Identify the reagent used in the following chemical reaction to for a diazonium salt.

$C_6H_5-NH_2 \xrightarrow[273-278\ K]{NaNO_2 + \text{`Y'}} C_6H_5-N_2^+Br^-$

(a) NaBr (b) HBr (c) HCl (d) Cu_2Br_2

Question 45

(i) What should be the correct IUPAC name for diethylbromomethane?

(a) 1-Bromo-1,1-diethylmethane (b) 3-Bromopentane

(c) 1-Bromo-1-ethylpropane (d) 1-Bromopentane

(ii) Molecules whose mirror image is non-superimposable over them are known as chiral. Which of the following molecules is chiral in nature?

(a) 2-Bromobutane (b) 1-Bromobutane

(c) 2-Bromopropane (d) 2-Bromopropan-2-ol

Question 46

Assertion: 2,4-Dinitrophenol is less acidic than phenol

Reason: Lower alcohols are more soluble in water than higher alcohols

(a) Assertion is false but reason is true

(b) Assertion is true but reason is false

(c) Both assertion and reason are true, but reason is not a true explanation for assertion

(d) Both assertion and reason are true and reason is the correct explanation for assertion

Question 47

Assertion: Nitration of chlorobenzene leads to the formation of m- nitrochlorobenzene

Reason: NO_2 group is a m-directing group.

(a) Assertion is false but reason is true

(b) Assertion is true but reason is false

(c) Both assertion and reason are true, but reason is not a true explanation for assertion

(d) Both assertion and reason are true and reason is the correct explanation for assertion

Question 48

Assertion: The heavier p-block elements do not form strong π bonds.

Reason : The heavier elements of p-block form $d\pi - p\pi$ or $d\pi - d\pi$ bonds..

(a) Assertion is false but reason is true

(b) Assertion is true but reason is false

(c) Both assertion and reason are true, but reason is not a true explanation for assertion

(d) Both assertion and reason are true and reason is the correct explanation for assertion

Question 49

Assertion: Bond angle of H_2S is smaller than H_2O.

Reason : Electronegativity of the central atom increases, bond angle decreases.

(a) Assertion is false but reason is true

(b) Assertion is true but reason is false

(c) Both assertion and reason are true, but reason is not a true explanation for assertion

(d) Both assertion and reason are true and reason is the correct explanation for assertion

Question 50

Assertion: Limestone is added to blast furnace during extraction of iron.

Reason: Limestone decomposes to calcium oxide and carbon dioxide.

(a) Assertion is false but reason is true

(b) Assertion is true but reason is false

(c) Both assertion and reason are true, but reason is not a true explanation for assertion

(d) Both assertion and reason are true and reason is the correct explanation for assertion

Answers

1. (c) HCP > BCC > Simple cubic

    Explanation:

Packing efficiency	Crystal arrangement
74%	CCP
68%	BCC
52.4%	Simple cubic

2. (b) Molality

    Explanation: Molality is the ratio of number of moles to weight of the solvent molecule, independent of temperature whereas other have term volume which is temperature dependent.

3. (a) Anode and cathode

    Explanation: Oxidation is loss of electron, which makes electron travel to anode which is positively charged while reduction is process of gain of electron which occurs at cathode which is negatively charged.

4. (a) Wrought iron

5. (b) O

    Explanation: All others have vacant d-orbital whereas O does not possess vacant d-orbital.

6. (c) Alcoholic KOH, chloroform and primary amine

7. (b) Phenoxide ion is stabilised through delocalisation

8. (a) H_2O

    Explanation: This is due to –I effect of the alkyl group, which donates electrons and stabilizes charges hence makes removal H^+ difficult.

9. (b) Sodium formate

    Explanation: Chloroform when boiled with aqueous solution of caustic soda, first it forms formic acid which reacts further and form sodium formate.

This is hydrolysis of chloroform.

$$CHCl_3 + 3NaOH \rightarrow CH(OH)_3 \xrightarrow{H_2O} HCOOH$$
$$- (NaOH) \rightarrow HCOONa$$

10. (c) IPO_4

    Explanation: Interhalogen compound are those which are formed by the combination of halogens wherein P and O are not halogen elements.

11. (c) Galena

    Explanation: Froth flotation process is best suited with sulphur based ores, hence galena lies under the category of sulphide ores.

12. (c) H^+ ions

13. (a) 96,500 coulomb

14. (c) Ideal solutions

15. (a) AB_3

    Explanation: A occupies corner, so the contribution to unit cell is of one atom whereas B at face centered the contribution to six faces shared between two is 3.

16. (b) 6 Na^+ ions

    Explanation: Coordination number is 6 which is satisfied by Na^+ ions.

17. (b) A non-electrolyte in dilute solution

18. (b) 1.0 M Na_2SO_4

    Explanation: As $i = 3$

    $\Delta T_b \propto i$, Boiling point $\propto \Delta T_b$

19. (a) A

    Explanation: Standard electrode potential of A is minimum, thus, its oxidation potential is maximum means highly reactive than others. The trend of electrode potential is B>D>C>A and hence reactivity would be in order A>C>D>B *i.e.,* electrode potential is inversely proportional to electrode potential.

20. (a) $Cu + SO_2$

Explanation: $2Cu_2O + Cu_2S \xrightarrow{\Delta} 6Cu + SO_2$

21. (b) Associated nature due to hydrogen bonding

22. (d) 2, 4, 6-tribromophenol

Explanation: The phenol is highly activated in presence of aqueous bromine and all ortho and para positions are substituted in the same molecule.

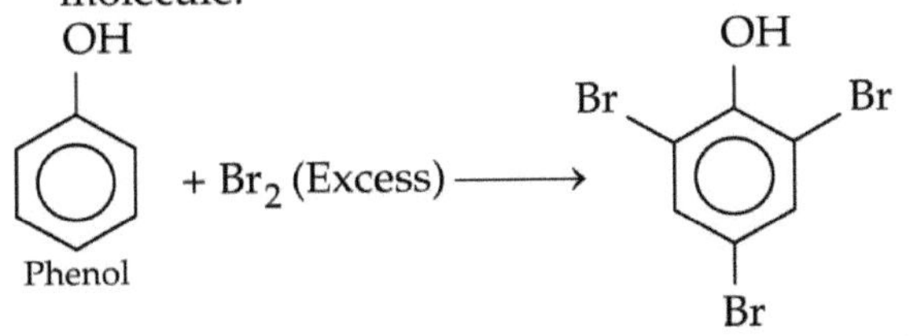

23. (c) T-shaped

Explanation: Hybridisation: sp^2

Shape: T shaped

$$F-Cl-F$$
$$|$$
$$F$$

24. (b) CCl_2F_2

25. (b) $10^{0.32/0.0295}$

Explanation: The half-cell reactions are

(i) $\qquad Zn(s) \rightarrow Zn^{2+}(aq) + 2e^-$

(ii) $\dfrac{Fe^{2+}(aq) + 2e^- \rightarrow Fe(s)}{Zn(s) + Fe^{2+}(aq) \rightarrow Zn^{2+}(aq) + Fe(s)}$

On applying the Nernst equation

$E_{cell} = E^0_{cell} - 0.0591/n \log10[Zn^{2+}]/[Fe^{2+}]$

$0.2905 = E^0_{cell} -- 0.0591/n \log10\ 0.1/0.01$

$E^o_{cell} = 0.32V$

$E_{cell} = E^o_{cell} - 0.0591/n \log10\ K_c$

$\log_{10} K_c = 0.32/0.02955$

$K_c = 100.32/0.02955$

26. (i) (a) Potassium sulphate

Explanation: Urea and glucose do not dissociate in the solution whereas others dissociate in 2 ions of Na^+ Cl^- and 3 ions of K^+ SO_4^{2-} in the solution. Higher number of ions favour more depression in freezing point.

(ii) (a) Acetone + Carbon disulphide

27. (i) (b) 12

(ii) (b) 0.144nm

Explanation: Edge length of the Gold unit cell

$(a) = 0.407 \times 10^{-7}$ m

For FCC unit cell, the atomic radius (r)

$= a/(2\sqrt{2})$

$= 0.407 \times 10^{-9}/2\sqrt{2})$

$= 0.144$ nm

28. (i) (a) Kohlrausch's law

(ii) (a) 128 S cm^{2}mol^{-1}

Explanation:

$\lambda_{NaBr} = \lambda NaCl + \lambda KBr - \lambda KCl$

$\lambda_{NaBr} = 126+152-150=128$ Scm^{2}mol^{-1}

29. (i) (d) 2N

Explanation: No. of tetrahedral voids are twice the octahedral voids.

(ii) (b) 8

30. (i) (d) N

Explanation: As we go down in the group, atomic size increases and ionization enthalpy is low for the last element in group, N being first element of the group has the highest I.E.

(ii) (b) Cl

Explanation: Electron gain enthalpy decreases the group whereas Cl has the highest as because size of F is small and it leads to electron-electron repulsion.

31. (i) (c) 101 Ω^{-1} cm^2 mol^{-1}

Explanation:

$\Lambda_m = K \times 1000/M$

$=1.52 \times 10^{-2} \times 10000/15$

$=101\ \Omega^{-1}$ cm^2 mol^{-1}

(ii) (d) All of these

32. (i) (a) cationic vacancies equal to number of Cd^{2+} ions incorporated

(ii) (a) AgCl

33. (i) (b) Raoult's law

(ii) (c) Solute molecules to the total number of molecules in solution

Explanation: One mole of electron charge is equivalent to one Faraday.

Given reaction,

$$CaCl_2 \rightarrow Ca^{2+} + 2Cl^-$$

Ca is undergoing oxidation *i.e.,* $Ca^{2+} + 2e^- \rightarrow Ca$

We can observe that 40g of Ca takes $2e^-$ charge,

So,1 mole of Ca(40g) ≡ 2F

Now, 100g of Ca ≡ 5F

34. (i) (d) Equivalent weight of electrolyte

(ii) (d) 5F

Explanation: One mole of electron charge is equivalent to one Faraday.

Given reaction,

$$CaCl_2 \rightarrow Ca^{2+} + 2Cl^-$$

Ca is undergoing oxidation *i.e.,* $Ca^{2+} + 2e^- \rightarrow$ Ca

We can observe that 40g of Ca takes $2e^-$ charge,

So, 1 mole of Ca(40 g) = 2F

Now, 100 g of Ca = 5F

35. (i) (a) Dichloroethane

(ii) (c) Ethanal

36. (i) (a) $PI_3 > PBr_3 > PCl_3 > PF_3$

Explanation: The sequence for the Lewis acid strength for:

$$PF_3 > PCl_3 > PBr_3 > PI_3$$

Lewis acids have a tendency to accept electrons. As mentioned above, phosphorous has empty d orbital in its valence shell to accept electrons. Also, the electronegativity of the halides decreases as F > Cl > Br > I. So, fluorine has stronger affinity towards electrons making PF_3 stronger lewis acid while making PI_3 weakest lewis acid.

(ii) (d) $H_2Te < H_2Se < H_2S < H_3O$

Explanation: The stability of hydrides of group 16 decreases down the group.

37. (i) (a) it helps removing the impurities like SiO_2, Fe_2O_3 etc. from the bauxite ore

(ii) (d) Mg

38. (i) (c) 6.15 g cm^{-3}

Explanation: Theoretical density of crystal, $\rho = ZxM/Nxa^3 \text{ g/cm}^3$

Given for bcc Z = 2; $a = 300 \times 10^{-10}$ cm, M = 50 g

$\therefore \quad \rho = 2 \times 50/6.022 \times 10^{23} \times (300)^3 \times (10^{-10})^3$

$= 6.15 \text{ g/cm}^3$

(ii) (b) FeO

39. (i) (d) ethanol

Explanation: $CH_3 - CH_2 - OH \rightarrow CH_3CH_2Cl$ $\rightarrow CH_3CH_2MgCl \rightarrow CH_3C(OH)(CH_3)CH_2CH_3$

(ii) (c) Ethyl chloride

40. (i) (a) 2-Butanol

Explanation: A : Butan-2-ol

B : Butan-2-one

C : 2 methylbutan-2-ol

Butan-2-ol undergoes oxidation in presence of mild oxidising agent to convert into butan-2-one. it give iodoform test since it has a methyl ketogroup.

CH_3MgBr acts as nucleophile and attack the carbonyl group to give compound C.

(ii) (a) 2-methyl-2 butanol

41. (i) (d) Ag and Au

(ii) (b) roasting followed by reduction with carbon

42. (i) (b) $1:2:4$

Explanation: $Z_{SC} = 8 \times 1/8 = 1$ [Atoms are only at the corners]

$Z_{BCC} = 8 \times 1/8 + 1 = 1 + 1$ [Atoms are at the corners and at the body centre]

$Z_{FCC} = 8 \times 1/8 + 6 \times 1/2 = 1 + 3 = 4$ [Atoms are at the corners and at the face centres]

Here, Z = effective number of atoms in the unit cell.

$$Z_{SC} : Z_{BCC} : Z_{FCC} = 1 : 2 : 4$$

(ii) (d) 2 and 4

Explanation: BCC cell consists of 8 atoms at the corners and one atom at center.

$\therefore$ Number of atoms $(n) = (8 \times 1/8) + 1 = 2$.

The fcc cell consists of 8 atoms at the eight corners and one atom at each of the six faces. This atom at the face is shared by two unit cells.

$\therefore$ Number of atoms $(n) = 8 \times 1/8 + (6 \times 1/2) = 4$.

43. (i) (d) $S_4O_6^{2-}$, $S_2O_3^{2-}$

(ii) (c) 6

44. (i) (c) Shorter and stronger

(ii) (b) HBr

Explanation: The chemical reaction is diazotisation reaction where an aromatic amine in aqueous mineral acid (HBr) is treated with $NaNO_2$ at cold temperature to form respective diazonium salts.

45. (i) (a) 1-Bromo-1, 1-diethylmethane

(ii) (a) 2-Bromobutane

46. (b) Assertion is true but reason is false

Explanation: Phenol is more acidic than aliphatic alcohol due to the stabilisation of phenoxide ion through resonance. So, phenol is more acidic than ethanol and methanol.

ERG (like $-CH_3$) destabilizes the phenoxide ion and hence, acidity decreases but an EWG (like $-NO_2$ group) stabilizes the phenoxide ion and hence increases the acidity.

So, 2,4 dinitrophenol is more acidic than phenol.

Higher alcohols are less soluble in water due stearic hindrance.

47. (a) Assertion is false but reason is true.

Explanation: The assertion is incorrect but the reason is correct as the chlorination of nitrobenzene (not the nitration of chlorobenzene) leads to the formation of *m*-nitrochlorobenzene because $-NO_2$ group deactivates the ring because it is meta-directing.

48. (d) Both assertion and reason are true and reason is the correct explanation for assertion.

Explanation: The presence of the *d*-orbitals influences the chemistry of the heavier elements in a number of other ways. The combined effect of size and availability of *d*-orbitals considerably influences the ability of these elements to form π bonds.

The heavier elements do form π bonds but this involves d orbitals ($d\pi - p\pi$ or $d\pi - d\pi$). As the *d* orbitals are of higher energy than the *p* orbitals, they contribute less to the overall stability of molecules than does $p\pi - p\pi$ bonding of the second row elements.

49. (b) Assertion is true but reason is false

Explanation: Bond angle of H_2S ($92°$) < H_2O ($104°31$). As the electronegativity of the central atom decreases, bond angle decreases.

In the present case, S is less electronegative than oxygen. Thus bond pairs in H_2S are more away from the central atom than in H_2O and thus repulsive forces between bond pairs are smaller producing smaller bond angle.

50. (c) Both assertion and reason are true.

Explanation: Limestone is added to blast furnace as flux and sulphur, silicon and phosphorous are oxidized and passed into slag. The metal is removed and free from slag by passing through rollers.

❑❑

Question 1

The packing efficiency of simple cubic structure, body centered cubic structure and face centered cubic structure respectively is:

(a) 52·4%, 74%, 68%

(b) 74%, 68%, 52·4%

(c) 52·4%, 68%, 74%

(d) 68%, 74%, 52·4%

Question 2

Molecular weight of non-volatile solute can be determined by:

(a) Victor-Mayer's method

(b) Graham's law of diffusion

(c) Gay Lussac's law

(d) Raoult's law

Question 3

Conductivity of a solution is directly proportional to:

(a) Dilution

(b) Number of ions

(c) Current density

(d) Volume of the solution

Question 4

The process of zone refining is used in the purification of:

(a) Al

(b) Ge

(c) Cu

(d) Ag

Question 5

Aqua regia is a mixture of :

(a) Conc. HNO_3 and conc. H_2SO_4

(b) Conc. HCl and conc. H_2SO_4 in the ratio of 3 : 1

(c) Conc. HCl and conc. HNO_3 in the ratio of 3 : 1

(d) None of these

Question 6

Alkyl halides undergo :

(a) Electrophilic substitution reactions

(b) Electrophilic addition reactions

(c) Nucleophilic substitution reactions

(d) Nucleophilic addition reactions

Question 7

The correct order of boiling points for primary (1°), secondary (2°) and tertiary alcohol (3°) is:

(a) $1° > 2° > 3°$

(b) $3° > 2° > 1°$

(c) $2° > 1° > 3°$

(d) $2° > 3° > 1°$.

Question 8

Phenol is heated with $CHCl_3$ and alcoholic KOH when salicylaldehyde is produced. This reaction is known as :

(a) Rosenmund's reaction

(b) Reimer-Tiemann reaction

(c) Friedel-Craft's reaction

(d) Sommelet reaction

Question 9

Halogenation of alkane gives :

(a) Only required alkyl halide

(b) Alkyl halide and unreacted halogen

(c) A mixture of mono-, di-, tri- and tetra-halogen derivatives

(d) Alkyl halide and unreacted alkane

Question 10

The geometry of XeF_6 molecule and the hybridisation of Xe atom in the molecule is :

(a) Distorted octahedral and sp^3d^3
(b) Square planar and sp^3d^2
(c) Pyramidal and sp^3
(d) Octahedral and sp^3d^3

Question 11

In aluminothermic process, Al is used as :

(a) Reducing agent
(b) Oxidising agent
(c) Catalyst
(d) Electrolyte

Question 12

The reaction is spontaneous if the cell potential is :

(a) Positive
(b) Negative
(c) Zero
(d) Infinite

Question 13

For a dissociated solute in solution the value of van't Hoff factor is :

(a) Zero
(b) One
(c) Greater than one
(d) Less than one.

Question 14

How many kinds of space lattice are possible in a cubic crystal ?

(a) 23
(b) 7
(c) 30
(d) 14

Question 15

Which one is called oleum ?

(a) Liq. NH_3
(b) $H_2SO_4 + SO_3$
(c) Conc. HNO_3
(d) Dilute solution of H_2O_2

Question 16

In the extraction of chlorine by electrolysis of brine ____________.

(a) Oxidation of Cl^- ion occur to chlorine gas
(b) Reduction of Cl^- ion occur to chlorine gas
(c) For overall reaction $\Delta G°$ has negative value
(d) A displacement reaction takes place

Question 17

The number of moles of solute present in 1000 gm of the solvent is known as :

(a) Molarity
(b) Molality
(c) Normality
(d) Mole fraction.

Question 18

In a compound, atoms of element Y forms ccp lattice and those of element X occupy 2/3 rd of tetrahedral voids, the formula of the compound will be :

(a) X_4Y_3
(b) X_2X_3
(c) X_2Y
(d) X_3X_4

Question 19

The quantity of electricity required to deposit 1·15 g of sodium from molten NaCl (Na = 23, Cl = 35·5) is :

(a) 1 F
(b) 0·5 F
(c) 0.05 F
(d) 1·5 F

Question 20

The reaction in presence of dry ether,

$2C_2H_5Br + 2Na \rightarrow C_2H_5 - C_2H_5 + 2NaBr$ is an example of :

(a) The Wurtz reaction
(b) Sandmeyer's reaction
(c) Aldol condensation
(d) Williamson's reaction

Question 21

Which of the following is simple ether ?

(a) $C_2H_5OCH_3$
(b) CH_3OCH_3
(c) $C_6H_5OCH_3$
(d) All of these

Question 22

Which of the following alcohol is least soluble in water ?

(a) *n*-Butyl alcohol

(b) *Iso*-Butyl alcohol

(c) *Tert*-Butyl alcohol

(d) *Sec*-Butyl alcohol

Question 23

Which one contains both iron and copper ?

(a) Cuprite   (b) Chalcocite   (c) Malachite   (d) Copper pyrites

Question 24

Osmotic pressure of a dil. solution is given by :

(a) $P = P0x$ (b) $\pi V = nRT$ (c) $p = VRT$ (d) None of these

Question 25

The unit of equivalent conductance is :

(a) $ohm^{-1} cm^2 equiv^{-1}$

(b) $ohm^{-1} cm^2 gm^{-1}$

(c) $ohm\ cm^2 equiv^{-1}$

(d) $ohm^{-1} mole^{-1}$

Question 26

(i) In a solid lattice the cation has left a lattice site and is located at an interstitial position, the lattice defect is :

    (a) Interstitial defect

    (b) Valency defect

    (c) Frenkel defect

    (d) Schottky defect

(ii) In NaCl structure:

    (a) All octahedral and tetrahedral sites are occupied

    (b) Only octahedral sites are occupied

    (c) Only tetrahedral sites are occupied

    (d) Neither octahedral nor tetrahedral sites are occupied

Question 27

(i) Grignard's reagent is prepared by the action of magnesium metal on:

    (a) Alcohol   (b) Phenol   (c) Alkyl halide   (d) Benzene

(ii) When ethanol reacts with PCl_5, it gives three products which include chloroethane and hydrochloric acid. What is the third product?

    (a) Phosphorus acid

    (b) Phosphoric acid

    (c) Phosphorus trichloride

    (d) Phosphoryl chloride

Question 28

(i) Molar ionic conductivities of a bivalent electrolyte are 57 and 73. The molar conductivity of solution will be:

    (a) $130\ S\ cm^2 mol^{-1}$

    (b) $65\ S\ cm^2 mol^{-1}$

    (c) $260\ S\ cm^2 mol^{-1}$

    (d) $187\ S\ cm^2 mol^{-1}$

(ii) In the cell reaction:

$$Cu(s) + 2Ag^+ \rightarrow Cu^{2+}(aq) + 2Ag(s)$$

$E^\circ_{cell} = 0.46$ V. By doubling the concentration of Cu^{2+}, E_{cell} is:

    (a) Decrease by small fraction

    (b) Doubled

    (c) Unchanged

    (d) Decrease by small fraction

Question 29

(i) The coordination number of a metal crystallizing in hexagonal closed packed structure is:

    (a) 8   (b) 4   (c) 6   (d) 12

(ii) The coordination number of sodium in sodium oxide is:

    (a) 6   (b) 8   (c) 4   (d) 2

Question 30

With respect to lanthanoid series:

(i) Lanthanide contraction is due to increase in:

    (a) Atomic radius   (b) Atomic number

    (c) Shielding by $4f$ electrons   (d) Effective nuclear charge

(ii) Across the lanthanide series, the basicity of lanthanide hydroxides:

    (a) Increases   (b) First increases than decreases

    (c) Decreases   (d) Remain same

Question 31

(i) In a hydrogen –oxygen fuel cell, combustion of hydrogen occurs to:

    (a) Produce high purity water

    (b) Create potential difference between two electrode

    (c) Generates heat

    (d) Removes adsorbed oxygen from electrode

(ii) The electricity needed to liberate one gram equivalent of Cu^{2+} is:

    (a) 1C   (b) 2F   (c) 96500 C   (d) 96500 F

Question 32

(i) The crystal system of a compound with unit cell dimensions, $a = 0.387$, $b = 0.387$ and $c = 0.504$ nm and $\alpha = \beta = 90°\ \gamma = 120°$ is:

    (a) Triclinic   (b) Orthorhombic   (c) Cubic   (d) Hexagonal

(ii) Among 7 crystal which one is unsymmetrical:

    (a) Triclinic   (b) Orthorhombic   (c) Cubic   (d) Hexagonal

Question 33

(i) The amount of solute required to prepare 10 L of decimolar solution is:

    (a) 0.01 mole   (b) 0.2 mole   (c) 0.05 mole   (d) 1 mole

(ii) The molarity of pure water is

    (a) 18 M   (b) 5.56 M   (c) 55.6 M   (d) 100 M

Question 34

(i) Specific conductance of 0.1M NaCl solution is 1.06×10^{-2}ohm^{-1}cm^{-1}. Its molar conductance in ohm^{-1}cm^{2}mol^{-1}:

    (a) 1.06×10^2 (b) 1.06×10^3 (c) 1.06×10^4 (d) 53

(ii) The emf of the cell :

$Cu(s)\,|\,Cu^{2+}(1M)\,|\,|\,Ag^{+}(1M)\,|\,Ag$

is 0.46V. The standard reduction potential for Ag^{+}/Ag is 0.80V. The standard reduction potential of Cu^{2+}/Cu is:

    (a) -0.34V   (b) 1.26V   (c) 0.34V   (d) -1.26V

Question 35

A compound(A) reacts with thionyl chloride to give compound (B). (B) reacts with magnesium to form Grignard reagent which is treated with acetone and the product is hydrolysed to give 2-methyl-2- butanol.

(i) What is (A) compound?

    (a) Butanol   (b) Propanol   (c) Methanol   (d) Ethanol

(ii) What is (B) compound?

    (a) Butyl chloride   (b) Propyl chloride   (c) Ethyl chloride   (d) Methyl chloride

Question 36

With respect to d block elements:

(i) The 3d block element that exhibits maximum number of oxidation states:

    (a) Mn   (b) Sc   (c) Ti   (d) Zn

(ii) Which one of the following forms a colourless solution in aq. medium?

(a) Cr^{3+} (b) Ti^{3+} (c) Sc^{3+} (d) V^{3+}

Question 37

(i) Smelting involves reduction of metal oxide with:

(a) Carbon   (b) Carbon Monoxide   (c) Magnesium   (d) Aluminium

(ii) Electromagnetic separation is used in the concentration of:

(a) Bauxite   (b) Copper pyrites   (c) Casseiterite   (d) Cinnabar

Question 38

(i) The number of atoms in BCC arrangement is:

(a) 1   (b) 2   (c) 8   (d) 4

(ii) In *hcp* arrangement, each atom at the corner contributes to the unit cell equal to:

(a) 1/2   (b) 1/8   (c) 1/6   (d) 1/4

Question 39

A compound(A) reacts with thionyl chloride to give compound (B). (B) reacts with magnesium to form Grignard reagent which is treated with acetone and the product is hydrolysed to give 2-methyl-2- butanol.

(i) What is(A) compound?

(a) Butanol   (b) Propanol   (c) Methanol   (d) Ethanol

(ii) What is (B) compound?

(a) Butyl chloride   (b) Propyl chloride   (c) Ethyl chloride   (d) Methyl chloride

Question 40

Phenol reacts with chloroform in the presence of aq. KOH at 340 K followed by hydrolysis of the resulting product giving salicyladehdye

(i) The above reaction is called:

(a) Reimer-Tiemann reaction   (b) Wurtz Reaction

(c) Fries Rearrangement   (d) Kolbe's Synthesis

(ii) The electrophile in this electrophilic substitution reaction is:

(a) $^-:CCl_3$ (b) $:CCl_2$ (c) $CHCl_2^+$ (d) Cl^-

Question 41

(i) Roasting results in the production of metal in the case of:

(a) Cinnabar   (b) Iron pyrites   (c) Bauxite   (d) Galena

(ii) During roasting of Zinc blende, it converts to:

(a) Zinc oxide   (b) Zinc Sulphate   (c) Zinc carbonate   (d) Zinc

Question 42

In context to imperfection in solids

(i) The appearance of colour in solid alkali metal halides is generally due to:

(a) Schottky defects   (b) Frenkel defects

(c) Interstial effect   (d) F- position

(ii) Schottky defect in crystal is observed when:

(a) Density in crystal increase

(b) Unequal number of cation and anion are missing from the lattice

(c) Equal number of cations and anions are missing from the lattice

(d) Density of the crystal is increased

Question 43

There are two series of *f*-block elements as 4*f* and 5*f*, hence

(i) The atomic number of three lanthanide elements X, Y, Z are 65,68,70 respectively. The basic character of their hydroxide will decrease:

(a) $X > Y > Z$ (b) $Z > Y > X$ (c) $Y > X > Z$ (d) $Z > X > Y$

(ii) Terbium has electronic configuration configuration: [Xe] $4f^9 6s^2$, Oxidation state will be:

    (a) +3,+4   (b) +2, +3,+4   (c) +3,+4, +5   (d) +2,+3,+4, +5

Question 44

A chloro compound(A) on reduction with Zn-Cu and ethanol give hydrocarbon (B) with 5 carbon atoms. When(A) is dissolved dry ether and treated with sodium metal it gave 2, 2, 5, 5 tetra methyl hexane. The treatment of A as A'C (in presence of alcoholic KCN)

(i) The compound A is:

    (a) 1-chloro-2,2 dimethyl propane   (b) 1-chloro-2,2 dimethyl propane

    (c) 1-chloro-2 methyl butane   (d) 2-chloro-2 methyl propane

(ii) The reaction of A with aq. KOH will preferably favour:

    (a) SN_1 Mechanism   (b) E_1 Mechanism   (c) SN_2 Mechanism   (d) E_2 Mechanism

Question 45

Alkyl halide undergoes nucleophilic substitution reaction in which halogen atom is replaced by other atom.

$$RX + Nu:^- \rightarrow Nu - R + X^-$$

(i) Which of the following is least reactive towards SN_2 mechanism?

    (a) $(CH_3)_3CCH_2Br$ (b) $(CH_3)_2CHCH_2Br$ (c) CH_3CH_2Br (d) $(CH_3)_2CHBr$

(ii) Which of the following has highest nucleophilicity?

    (a) SH^- (b) H_2O (c) OH^- (d) F^-

Question 46

Assertion: 1-Iodopropane and 2-Iodopropane are chain isomers

Reason: These differ in the position of Iodine in the carbon chains

(a) Assertion is false but reason is true

(b) Assertion is true but reason is false

(c) Both assertion and reason are true, but reason is not a true explanation for assertion

(d) Both assertion and reason are true and reason is the correct explanation for assertion

Question 47

Assertion: Ether molecule is linear

Reason: Ether can be prepared from alkyl halide by Wurtz reaction

(a) Assertion is false but reason is true

(b) Assertion is true but reason is false

(c) Both assertion and reason are true, but reason is not a true explanation for assertion

(d) Both assertion and reason are true and reason is the correct explanation for assertion

Question 48

Assertion: Xenon forms fluorides

Reason: Because $5d$-orbitals are available for valence shell expansion.

(a) Assertion is false but reason is true

(b) Assertion is true but reason is false

(c) Both assertion and reason are true, but reason is not a true explanation for assertion

(d) Both assertion and reason are true and reason is the correct explanation for assertion

Question 49

Assertion: Gold and platinum occur in native state.

Reason: Gold and platinum are expensive metals

(a) Assertion is false but reason is true

(b) Assertion is true but reason is false

(c) Both assertion and reason are true, but reason is not a true explanation for assertion

(d) Both assertion and reason are true and reason is the correct explanation for assertion

Question 50

Assertion: Copper glance, zinc blende and Anglesite are sulphide ores.

Reason: Silica is basic flux used in metallurgy

(a) Assertion is false but reason is true
(b) Assertion is true but reason is false
(c) Both assertion and reason are true, but reason is not a true explanation for assertion
(d) Both assertion and reason are true and reason is the correct explanation for assertion

Answers

1. (c) 52.4%, 68%, 74%

2. (d) Raoult's law

3. (b) Number of ions

4. (b) Ge

5. (c) Conc. HCl and conc. HNO_3 in the ratio of 3 : 1

6. (c) Nucleophilic substitution reactions
Explanation: Alkyl halides form new bonds with nucleophile that replaces halogen from α-carbon.

7. (a) $1° > 2° > 3°$
Explanation: The order of bp is 1 > 2 > 3. This is because the surface area decreases and the van Der waals forces decreases. And another reason is the increase in molecular mass which leads to increase in boiling point.

8. (b) Reimer-Tiemann reaction

9. (c) A mixture of mono-, di-, tri- and tetra-halogen derivatives

10. (a) Distorted octahedral and sp^3d^3
Explanation: The geometry of XeF_6 molecule and the hybridization of Xe atom in the molecule are distorted octahedral and sp^3d^3 respectively. Xe has 6 bond pairs of electrons and one lone pair of electrons.
In XeF_6, Xe undergoes sp^3d^3 hybridisation which results in the electronic geometry of pentagonal bipyramidal and molecular geometry of distorted octahedral.

11. (a) Reducing agent

12. (a) Positive
Explanation: Gibbs free energy
$\Delta G°_{cell} = -nFe°_{cell}$
Spontaneous reaction
Condition: $\Delta G°_{cell} < 0$
$\therefore E°_{cell} > 0$

13. (c) Greater than one

14. (d) 14

15. (b) $H_2SO_4 + SO_3$

16. (a) oxidation of Cl^- ion to chlorine gas occur
Oxidation: $2Cl^- - 2e^- \rightarrow Cl_2$

17. (b) Molality

18. (a) X_4Y_3
Explanation: Y occupies ccp lattice, it contributes at corner as 1 atom in unit cell and atom at corner is equal to number of octahedral voids. Tetrahedral voids are twice that of octahedral voids and hence
No. of Octahedral voids N
No. of atoms at corner N
No of tetrahedral voids 2N
It occupies 2/3 of tetrahedral voids, contribution to the unit cell $2/3 \times 2N = 4N/3$.

$$X : Y$$
$$N : 4N/3$$
$$3 : 4$$

Formula is X_3Y_4

19. (c) 0.05 F
Explanation: Number of moles of Na = 1.15/23 = 0.05 moles.
$$Na^+ + e \rightarrow Na$$
Thus, deposition of 1 mole of Na will require 1 mole of electrons which corresponds to 1 Faraday of electricity. The, deposition of 0.05 moles (1.15 g) of Na will require 0.05 moles of electrons which corresponds to 0.05 Faraday of electricity.

20. (a) The Wurtz reaction

21. (b) CH_3OCH_3

22. (a) n-Butyl alcohol

23. (d) Copper pyrites

24. (b) $\pi V = nRT$

25. (a) $ohm^{-1} cm^2 equiv^{-1}$

26. (i) (c) Frenkel defect
   (ii) (b) only octahedral sites are occupied

27. (c) Alkyl halide
Explanation: Grignard reagent is prepared by:
$$R - X + Mg \xrightarrow{\text{dry ether}} RMgX$$

   (ii) (d) Phosphoryl chloride
   Explanation:
   $CH_3CH_2.OH + PCl_5 \rightarrow CH_3CH_2.Cl$
   $\qquad\qquad\qquad + POCl_3 + NCl$

28. (i) (a) $130 \text{ S cm}^2 \text{ mol}^{-1}$

Explanation: According to kohlrausch law of independent migration of ions, the molar conductivity of an electrolyte at infinite dilution is equal to the sum of the contributions of the molar conductivities of its ions.

Hence,

$$\Lambda_{AB} = \lambda_A^{2+} + \lambda_B^{2-}$$
$$= 57 + 73$$
$$= 130 \text{ S cm}^2\text{mol}^{-1}$$

(ii) (a) Decrease by small fraction

Explanation:

Nernst equation:

$$E_{cell} = E^o_{cell} - RT/nF \ln Q \qquad ...(i)$$

$E_{cell} \rightarrow$ Emf of cell.

$E_{cell} \rightarrow$ Standard reduction potential.

$R \rightarrow$ Universal gas constant.

$T \rightarrow$ Temperature in Kelvin.

$n \rightarrow$ moles of electrons.

$F \rightarrow$ Faraday's constant.

$Q \rightarrow$ Reaction Quotient.

$$2Ag^+ (aq) + Cu(s) \rightarrow Cu^{2+} (aq) + 2Ag(s)$$
$$...(ii)$$

$Q = [\text{Products}]^a/[\text{Reactants}]^b$

a and $b \rightarrow$ stoichiometric co-efficient of product and reactant respectively.

For pure state concentration is taken as unity

$$\Rightarrow E_{cell} = E_{cell} \rightarrow RT/nF \ln [Cu^{2+}_{aq}]/[Ag^+_{aq}]^2$$
$$...(iii)$$

$\Rightarrow$ From Equation 4, it is observed that $E_{(cell)}$ depends on the concentration of both Cu^{2+} and Ag^+. It increases with increase in concentration of Ag^+.

29. (i) (d) 12

(ii) (c) 4

30. (i) (d) effective nuclear charge

(ii) (c) decreases

Explanation: $M(OH)_3$ is a lanthanoid hydroxide. In lanthanoid series, ionic radii decreases and increasing covalent character. Thus, basicity decreases.

31. (i) (b) create potential difference between two electrode

(ii) (c) 96500 C

32. (i) (d) Hexagonal

(ii) (d) triclinic

33. (i) (d) 1 mole

Explanation: Decimolar solution = 0.1 M

$$V = 10 \text{ L}$$

$$M = n/V$$
$$0.1 = n/10/10$$
$$\Rightarrow \qquad n = 1 \text{ mole}$$

(ii) (c) 55.6 M

34. (i) (a) 1.06×10^2

Explanation: Molar conductivity is defined as the conductivity of an electrolyte solution divided by the molar concentration of electrolyte.

Specific Conductance $(\kappa) = 1.06 \times 10^{-2}$ $\text{ohm}^{-1}\text{cm}^{-1}$

Molarity $(M) = 0.1$M

$$\Lambda m = \kappa \times 1000/M$$
$$= (1.06 \times 10^{-2} \times 1000)/0.1$$
$$= 1.06 \times 10^{-2} \text{ ohm}^{-1} \text{ cm}^2 \text{ mol}^{-1}$$

(ii) (c) 0.34 V

Explanation: The standard potential of the reaction is calculated as:

$$E_{cell} = E_{red} - E_{ox}$$
$$0.463 = 0.800 - E_{Cu}$$
$$E_{Cu} = 0.337 \text{ V}$$

35. (i) (c) enol

Explanation: Enol $C = C(OH)$ is an organic compound that contains a hydroxyl group bonded to a carbon atom having a double bond.

Enols produce violet colour with $FeCl_3$ solution.

(ii) (c) Ethyl chloride

Explanation:

$$CH_3 - CH_2 - OH \xrightarrow{SO_2Cl_2} CH_3CH_2Cl$$
$$\xrightarrow{Mg} CH_3CH_2MgCl \rightarrow CH_3C(OH)(CH_3)$$
$$CH_2CH_3$$

36. (i) (a) Mn

(ii) (c) Sc^{3+}

37. (i) (a) Carbon

(ii) Casseiterite

38. (i) (b) 2

(ii) (c) 1/6

39. (i) (d) ethanol

(ii) (c) Ethyl chloride

40. (i) (a) Reimer-Tiemann reaction

(ii) (b) $:CCl_2$

41. (i) (a) cinnabar

(ii) (a) Zinc oxide

Explanation: Roasting of zinc blend:

$$\underset{\text{Zinc blend}}{ZnS} + O_2 \xrightarrow{>850°C} \underset{\text{Zinc oxide}}{ZnO} + SO_2$$

42. (i) (a) Schottky defects

(ii) (b) equal number of cations and anions and missing from the lattice

43. (i) (a) X > Y > Z

(ii) (a) +3, +4

44. (i) (a) 1-chloro-2, 2 dimentyl propane

Explanation: Since A, a five carbon atom chloro compound, on reaction with sodium in ether (Wurtz reaction) gives 2, 2, 5, 5-tetramethylhexane, therefore, A must be neopentyl chloride or 1-chloro-2,2-dimethylpropane

$$2CH_3 - C(CH_3)_2 - CH_2 - Cl + 2Na$$

1-Chloro-2,2-dimethylpropane (A)

$$\xrightarrow{\text{Dry Ether}} CH_3 - C(CH_3)_2 - CH_2CH_2C(CH_3)_2CH_3 + 2NaCl$$

2,2,5,5-Tetramethylhexane

Since A on reduction with Zn–Cu Couple and alcohol gives a hydrocarbon (B), therefore, B must be neopentane or 2,2-dimethylpropane

$$2CH_3 - C(CH_3)_2 - CH_2 - Cl + 2[H]$$

1-Chloro-2, 2-dimethylpropane (A)

$$\xrightarrow{\text{Zn-Cu couple+alcohol}} CH_3 - C(CH_3)_2 - CH_3 + HCl$$

2, 2-Dimethylpropane (B)

(ii) SN$_1$ Mechanism

Explanation: SN$_1$ Mechanism is followed as no change in orientation of the compound is observed.

45. (i) (a) $(CH_3)_3CCH_2Br$

Explanation: Since SN$_2$ reaction requires the approach of the nucleophile to the carbon-bearing the leaving group, the presence of bulky substituents on or near the carbon atom have a dramatic inhibiting effect. Of the simple alkyl halides, methyl halides react most rapidly in SN$_2$ reactions because there are only three small hydrogen atoms.

A primary alkyl halide will prefer a SN$_2$ reaction.

Thus the order of reactivity followed is:

Primary halide > Secondary halide > Tertiary halide.

(ii) (a) SH$^-$

Explanation: Lesser the electronegativity of the donor atom, more is its tendency to donate a pair of electron and stronger is the nucleophile.

46. (a) Assertion is false but reason is true.

Explanation: Chain isomers have the same molecular formula but different types of chains as; linear or branched. The least number of carbon atoms required in a hydrocarbon to show chain isomerism is 4.

47. (c) Both assertion and reason are true, but reason is not a true explanation for assertion.

Explanation: Ether has tetrahedral geometry only symmetrical alkanes can be prepared with the help of wurtz reaction.

48. (d) Both assertion and reason are true and reason is the correct explanation for assertion.

Explanation: Xenon belongs to noble gases which are considered to be very unreactive. In xenon atom, the ionisation potential of Xe to lose one electron. Also, due to the presence of empty 5d-orbitals, electrons can be excited and higher valency of xenon can be produced. e.g., XeF$_2$, XeF$_4$, XeF$_6$ etc.

49. (c) Both assertion and reason are true, but reason is not a true explanation for assertion.

50. (a) Assertion is false but reason is true.

❑❑

Questions

Question 1

Cubic close packing arrangement is also known as :

(a) Hexagonal close packing

(b) Face centered cubic

(c) Body centered cubic

(d) None of these

Question 2

The solubility of a gas varies directly with pressure of the gas, is based upon :

(a) Raoult's law

(b) Henry's law

(c) Nernst's distribution law

(d) None of these

Question 3

When zinc granule is dipped into copper sulphate solution, copper is precipitated because :

(a) Both, copper and zinc have a positive reduction potential

(b) Reduction potential of copper is higher than that of zinc

(c) Reduction potential of zinc is higher than that of copper

(d) Both, zinc and copper have a negative reduction potential

Question 4

When lime stone is heated, CO_2 is given off. The metallurgical operation is :

(a) Smelting   (b) Reduction   (c) Calcination   (d) Roasting

Question 5

Which of the following reagent does not give O_2 gas on reaction with Ozone?

(a) $KMnO_4$ (b) $SnCl_2/HCl$ (c) $FeSO_4/H_2SO_4$ (d) PbS

Question 6

Which alkyl halides react most readily by nucleophilic substitution ?

(a) CH_3CH_2Cl (b) CH_3CH_2I (c) CH_3CH_2Br (d) CH_3CH_2F

Question 7

Lucas test is used for distinction of :

(a) Alcohols   (b) Phenols   (c) Alkyl halides   (d) Aldehydes

Question 8

Sodium methoxide on heating with bromoethane gives ___________.

(a) Methoxymethane

(b) Methoxyethane

(c) Ethoxyethane

(d) Diethyl ether

Question 9

When acetone is treated with Grignard's reagent, followed by hydrolysis, the product formed is:

(a) Secondary alcohol

(b) Tertiary alcohol

(c) Primary alcohol

(d) Aldehyde

Question 10

Which one absorbs U.V. radiation in stratosphere ?

(a) CO_2　　　　(b) N_2　　　　(c) O_3　　　　(d) H_2

Question 11

Which one of the following is an oxide ore ?

(a) Malachite　　　(b) Copper glance　　　(c) Haematite　　　(d) Zinc blende

Question 12

The cell reaction is spontaneous or feasible when e.m.f. of the cell is:

(a) Negative　　　　　　　　　　(b) Positive

(c) Zero　　　　　　　　　　　　(d) Either positive or negative

Question 13

The molal elevation constant is the ratio of the elevation in boiling point to :

(a) Molarity　　　　　　　　　　(b) Molality

(c) Mole fraction of solute　　　　(d) Mole fraction of solvent

Question 14

In a crystal, the atoms are located at the position of :

(a) Maximum P.E.　　(b) Minimum P.E.　　(c) Zero P.E.　　(d) Infinite P.E.

Question 15

Designation of the pattern as AB, AB, AB…… etc., of successive vertical layers of identical atoms gives the arrangement called as :

(a) Hexagonal close packing (hcp)　　　(b) Cubic close packing (ccp)

(c) Face centered cubic (fcc)　　　　　(d) Body centered cubic (bcc)

Question 16

Which of the following is not a colligative property ?

(a) Depression in freezing point　　　(b) Elevation in boiling point

(c) Osmotic pressure　　　　　　　(d) Modification of refractive index

Question 17

Conductivity of a solution is directly proportional to :

(a) Dilution　　　　　　　　　　(b) Number of ions

(c) Current density　　　　　　　(d) Volume of the solution

Question 18

Identify the alloy containing a non-metal as a constituent in it.

(a) Invar　　　　(b) Steel　　　　(c) Bell metal　　　　(d) Bronze

Question 19

Which of the following has lowest reducing character ?

(a) H_2O　　　　(b) H_2S　　　　(c) H_2Te　　　　(d) H_2Se

Question 20

Alkyl halides undergo :

(a) Electrophilic substitution reactions　　　(b) Electrophilic addition reactions

(c) Nucleophilic substitution reactions　　　(d) Nucleophilic addition reactions

Question 21

When acetaldehyde is treated with Grignard reagent, followed by hydrolysis the product formed is :

(a) Primary alcohol　　　　　　　(b) Secondary alcohol

(c) Carboxylic acid　　　　　　　(d) Tertiary alcohol.

Question 22

When oxalic acid is heated with glycerol we get :

(a) Formic acid　　　(b) Acetic acid　　　(c) Lactic acid　　　(d) Tartaric acid

Question 23

Which of the following reagent cannot be used to prepare an alkyl chloride from an alcohol ?

(a) $HCl + ZnCl_2$ (b) $SOCl_2$ (c) $NaCl$ (d) PCl_5

Question 24

Which of the following element is present as the impurity to the maximum extent in the pig iron ?

(a) Manganese   (b) Carbon   (c) Silicon   (d) Phosphorus

Question 25

The number of Faradays required to reduce one mol of Cu^{+2} to metallic copper is :

(a) One   (b) Two   (c) Three   (d) Four

Question 26

(i) Which solution is isotonic to the blood ?

    (a) 0.75% by weight of NaCl approximately   (b) 0.99% by weight of NaCl approximately

    (c) 0.90% by weight of NaCl approximately   (d) None of these

(ii) Which of the following statements regarding Ideal solutions is false?

    (a) Ideal solutions obey Raoult's law under all conditions of temperature and concentrations

    (b) There will be some change in volume on mixing the components, *i.e.*, $\Delta V_{mixing} \neq 0$

    (c) There will be no change in enthalpy when the two components are mixed, *i.e.*, $\Delta H_{mixing} = 0$

    (d) There will be no change in volume on mixing the components, *i.e.*, $\Delta V_{mixing} = 0$

Question 27

(i) A solid has a structure in which 'W' atoms are located at the corners of a cubic lattice, 'O' atoms at the centre of edges and 'Na' atoms at the centre of the cube. The formula for the compound is :

    (a) $NaWO_2$ (b) $NaWO_3$ (c) Na_2WO_3 (d) $NaWO_4$

(ii) Voids in two-dimensional hexagonal close packed structure are ___________.

    (a) Circular shape   (b) Rectangular shape

    (c) Triangular shape   (d) Hexagonal shape

Question 28

(i) P_4O_{10} has ______ bridging O atoms.

    (a) 4   (b) 5   (c) 6   (d) 2

(ii) Diethyl ether on heating with conc. HI gives two moles of:

    (a) Ethanol   (b) Iodoform   (c) Ethyl iodide   (d) Methyl iodide

Question 29

(i) A *p*-type material is electrically:

    (a) Concentration dependent   (b) Negative

    (c) Positive   (d) Neutral

(ii) The *p* type material have maximum concentration of:

    (a) Electrons   (b) Holes

    (c) Both electrons and holes   (d) None of these

Question 30

(i) The geometry of $XeOF_2$:

    (a) Pentagonal   (b) Pyramidal   (c) Octahedral   (d) T-shape

(ii) Shape of XeF_4 molecule:

    (a) Tetrahedral   (b) Distorted   (c) Square planar   (d) Square pyramidal

Question 31

(i) Cell reaction is spontaneous, when:

    (a) E^0_{red} is negative   (b) $\Delta G°$ is negative   (c) E^0_{oxid} is Positive   (d) $\Delta G°$ is positive

(ii) Equilibrium constant K is related to E^0_{cell} and not E_{cell} because:

    (a) E^0_{cell} is easier to measure than E_{cell}

    (b) E_{cell} becomes zero at equilibrium point but E^0_{cell} remains constant under all conditions

(c) At a given temperature, Ecell changes hence value of K can't be measured

(d) Any of the terms E_{cell} or E^0_{cell} can be used

Question 32

(i) In which of the following structure, the coordination number of both ions are same?

(a) Cesium Chloride (b) Sodium Chloride   (c) Zinc Chloride   (d) All of these

(ii) The coordination number of anion is four in:

(a) Sodium chloride (b) Zinc chloride   (c) Calcium fluoride   (d) Both (b) and (c)

Question 33

(i) The colligative properties of a dilute solution depends on:

(a) Nature of solute   (b) Nature of solvent

(c) Number of solute particles   (d) Number of solvent particles

(ii) The boiling point of a solvent containing a non -volatile solute:

(a) Depressed   (b) Elevated   (c) Does not change   (d) None of these

Question 34

(i) S.I. unit of molar conductivity is $ohm^{-1}cm^2mol^{-1}$:

(a) $S\,m^2\,mol^{-1}$ (b) $S\,m^{-1}\,mol^{-1}$ (c) $S\,m^{-2}\,mol$ (d) $S\,m^3\,mol^{-1}$

(ii) The unit of cell constant is:

(a) $ohm^{-1}cm^{-1}$ (b) cm   (c) $ohm^{-1}cm$ (d) cm^{-1}

Question 35

(i) The molecular formula of ether is:

(a) $C_nH_{2n+1}O$ (b) $C_nH_{2n}O$ (c) $C_nH_{2n}OC_nH_{2n}$ (d) $C_nH_{2n+2}O$

(ii) The compound which is not isomeric with diethyl ether is:

(a) n-propyl methyl ether   (b) 2-methyl propan-2-ol

(c) Butanone   (d) Butan-1-ol

Question 36

(i) Out of all the halogen hydracids , the weakest hydracid is:

(a) HI   (b) HBr   (c) HF   (d) HCl

(ii) Which halogen acid has highest acidic strength (in water)?

(a) HCl   (b) HF   (c) HBr   (d) HI

Question 37

(i) For which ore of the metal, froth floatation process is used:

(a) Hematite   (b) Bauxite   (c) Cinnabar   (d) Horn silver

(ii) Which of the following is magnetite?

(a) Fe_2CO_3 (b) Fe_2O_3 (c) Fe_3O_4 (d) $Fe_2O_3.3H_2O$

Question 38

(i) The number of atoms in hcp unit cell is:

(a) 4   (b) 6   (c) 8   (d) 12

(ii) Which of the following statement is/not true about hexagonal close packing?

(a) It has 26% empty space   (b) Coordination number is 6

(c) Third layer is identical to first layer   (d) None of these

Question 39

(i) Phenol is more acidic than:

(a) Acetic acid   (b) p-methoxy phenol

(c) Ethyl alcohol   (d) p-nitrophenol

(ii) Phenol reacts with bromine water in CS_2 at low temperature:

(a) o-Bromophenol   (b) o and p-bromophenol

(c) p-bromophenol   (d) 2, 4, 6 Tribromophenol

Question 40

(i) Compound (A) $C_4H_{10}O$ is found to be soluble in sulphuric acid. (A) does not react with sodium metal or potassium permanganate. When (A) is heated with excess of HI, it is converted into single alkyl halide. What is the structural formula of (A)?

    (a) Diethyl ether   (b) Acetone   (c) Butanol   (d) Butanal

(ii) After heating A with excess of HI, the product formed is:

    (a) Butyl Iodide   (b) Ethyl Iodide   (c) Iodobutanal   (d) Butane

Question 41

(i) The method of zone refining of metal is based on the principle of:

    (a) Greater solubility of the impurity in the molten state than in the solid

    (b) Greater mobility of the pure metal than that of the Impurity

    (c) Higher melting point of the impurity

    (d) Greater noble character of solid metal than the impurity

(ii) The reduction of iron in blast furnace involves all the steps except:

    (a) Fusion   (b) Sublimation   (c) Reduction   (d) Roasting

Question 42

(i) In a fcc arrangement of P and Q atoms, where P atom are at the corners of the unit cell. Q atom at the face centres and two atom are missing from two corners in each unit cell, the formula of the compound is:

    (a) PQ_4 (b) P_4Q_5 (c) P_2Q_3 (d) P_4Q_5

(ii) A metal crystallizes in fcc lattice and the edge of the unit cell is 620 pm. The radius of the metal atom is:

    (a) 265.5 pm   (b) 310 pm   (c) 219.2 pm   (d) 438.6 pm

Question 43

(i) The correct order of the acidic strength is:

    (a) $HClO_4 < HClO_3 < HClO_2 < HClO$ (b) $HClO < HClO_2 < HClO_3 < HClO_4$

    (c) $HClO < HClO_3 < HClO_2 < HClO_4$ (d) $HClO_4 < HClO_2 < HClO < HClO_3$

(ii) The basicity of phosphorous acid is:

    (a) 2   (b) 3   (c) 1   (d) 0

Question 44

An organic compound A with molecular formula C_4H_9Br on treatment with alcoholic KOH gave two isomeric compound B and C with formula C_4H_8. On ozonolysis, B gave only one product CH_3CHO while C gave two different products. Identify the compounds A,B.

(i) Compund A is:

    (a) 2-Bromobutane   (b) 3-Bromobutane   (c) 2-Bromobutene   (d) 3-Bromobutene

(ii) Compound B is:

    (a) But-1-ene   (b) But-2-ene   (c) Butane   (d) None of these

Question 45

(i) Isopropyl chloride undergoes hydrolysis by:

    (a) SN_1 Mechanism   (b) SN_2 Mechanism

    (c) SN_1 & SN_2 Mechanism   (d) Neither SN_1 & SN_2 Mechanism

(ii) Which of the following undergoes nucleophilic substitution exclusively by SN_1 mechanism?

    (a) Benzyl Chloride   (b) Ethyl chloride

    (c) Chloro benzene   (d) Isopropyl chloride

Question 46

Assertion: Benzyl bromide when kept in acetone- water, it produces benzyl chloride

Reason: The reaction follows SN_2 mechanism

(a) Assertion is false but reason is true

(b) Assertion is true but reason is false

(c) Both assertion and reason are true, but reason is not a true explanation for assertion

(d) Both assertion and reason are true and reason is the correct explanation for assertion

Question 47

Assertion: Alcohols are stronger acids than water

Reason: Reactivity of ethanol is less with sodium than that of isopropyl alcohol

(a) Assertion is false but reason is true

(b) Assertion is true but reason is false

(c) Both assertion and reason are true, but reason is not a true explanation for assertion

(d) Both assertion and reason are true and reason is the correct explanation for assertion

Question 48

Assertion: $HClO_4$ is less acidic than $HBrO_4$

Reason: $HClO_4$ ionises less in water than $HBrO_4$

(a) Assertion is false but reason is true

(b) Assertion is true but reason is false

(c) Both assertion and reason are true, but reason is not a true explanation for assertion

(d) Both assertion and reason are true and reason is the correct explanation for assertion

Question 49

Assertion: F_2 has low reactivity

Reason: F-F bond has low bond dissociation enthalpy

(a) Assertion is false but reason is true

(b) Assertion is true but reason is false

(c) Both assertion and reason are true, but reason is not a true explanation for assertion

(d) Both assertion and reason are true and reason is the correct explanation for assertion

Question 50

Assertion: Oxides and carbonates ores are concentrated by froth floatation process.

Reason: In froth flotation pine oil is used because prefentially wets the ore particels

(a) Assertion is false but reason is true

(b) Assertion is true but reason is false

(c) Both assertion and reason are true, but reason is not a true explanation for assertion

(d) Both assertion and reason are true and reason is the correct explanation for assertion

Answers

1. (b) Face centered cubic
2. (b) Henry's law
3. (b) Reduction potential of copper is higher than that of zinc
4. (c) Calcination
5. (b) $SnCl_2/HCl$
6. (b) CH_3CH_2I
7. (a) Alcohols
8. (b) methoxyethane

Explanation: Williamson synthesis of unsymmetrical ether, where CH_3ONa is reacted with CH_3CH_2Br to form $CH_3CH_2OCH_3$, which is ethyl methyl ether.

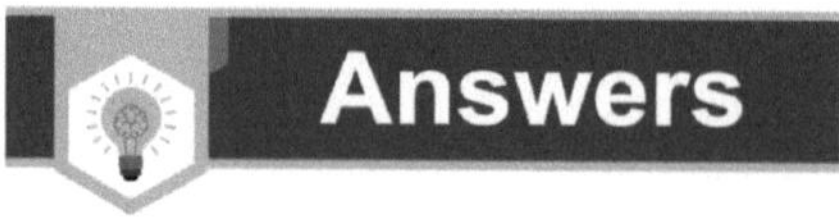

$$CH_3-O^-Na^+ \xrightarrow[-\frac{1}{2}H_2\uparrow]{CH_3CH_2-Br}$$

Sodium methoxide

$$CH_3-O-CH_3CH_2 + NaBr$$

Methoxyethane   Sodium bromide

9. (b) Tertiary alcohol

Explanation: $CH_3 - \overset{\overset{\displaystyle O}{\|}}{C} - CH_3 + CH_3MgBr \rightarrow$

$CH_3 - \overset{\overset{\displaystyle \overset{+}{O^-}MgBr}{|}}{\underset{\underset{\displaystyle CH_3}{|}}{C}} - CH_3 \xrightarrow{H_3O^+} CH_3 - \overset{\overset{\displaystyle OH}{|}}{\underset{\underset{\displaystyle CH_3}{|}}{C}} - CH_3$

(3° Alcohol)

10. (c) O_3

11. (c) Haematite

12. (b) positive

13. (b) Molality

14. (b) Minimum P.E.

15. (a) Hexagonal close packing (hcp)

16. (d) Modification of refractive index

17. (b) Number of ions

18. (b) Steel

19. (a) H_2O

Explanation: Reducing character is directly related to the ease of losing hydrogen. Due to decrease in bond dissociation enthalpy, stability also decrease down the group, increasing the reducing character.

20. (c) Nucleophilic substitution reactions

21. (b) Secondary alcohol

22. (a) Formic acid

Explanation: When glycerol is heated with crystalline oxalic acid at 100-110°C, we get formic acid.

23. (c) NaCl

Explanation: And NaCl cannot be used for the preparation of alkyl chlorides from alcohols. Lucas' reagent is a solution of anhydrous zinc chloride in concentrated hydrochloric acid. This solution is used to classify alcohols of low molecular weight. Thionyl chloride phosphorous chloride yield alkyl halide.

24. (b) Carbon

25. (b) Two

26. (i) (c) 0.90% by weight of NaCl approximately

(ii) **(b)** There will be some change in volume on mixing the components, *i.e.,* $\Delta V_{mixing} \neq 0$.

27. (i) (b) $NaWO_3$

(ii) **(c)** Triangular shape

28. (i) (c) 6

(ii) **(c)** ethyl iodide

29. (i) (d) neutral

(ii) **(b)** holes

30. (i) (d) T-shape

Explanation:

Geometry $XeOF_2$

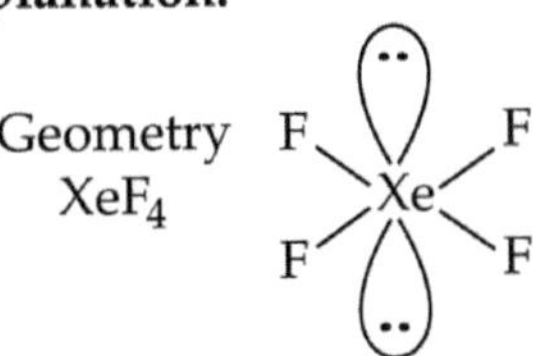

(ii) **(c)** square planar

Explanation:

Geometry XeF_4

31. (i) (b) $\Delta G°$ is negative

(ii) at a given temperature, E_{cell} changes hence value of K cannot be measured

Explanation: According to the Nernst equation:

$$E_{cell} = E°_{cell} - \frac{RT}{nF} \ln Q$$

At equilibrium, $E_{cell} = 0$ and $Q = K$

$$0 = E°_{cell} - \frac{RT}{nF} \ln K$$

$$\ln K = \frac{nFE°_{cell}}{RT}$$

This relation shows (K) rate constant is related to standard cell potential ($E°_{cell}$).

32. (i) (d) All of these

Ion	Coordination no.
Cs^+ ion	8
Cl^- ion	8
Na^+	6
Cl^-	6
Zn^{+2}	4
S^{-2}	4
Ca^{+2}	8
F^-	4

(ii) **(d)** Both (b) and (c)

33. (i) (c) Number of solute particles

(ii) **(b)** Elevated

34. (i) (a) $S\ m^2\ mol^{-1}$

(ii) **(d)** cm^{-1}

35. (i) (a) $C_nH_{2n+1}O$

(ii) **(c)** Butanone

36. (i) (c) HF

Explanation: As we go down in the group, the size of the halogen increases, so size of halogen increases so HX bond becomes weaker.

(ii) (d) HI

Explanation: As we go down in the group, the size of the halogen increases, so size of halogen increases so HX bond becomes weaker.

37. (i) (a) Hematite

(ii) (c) Fe_3O_4

38. (i) (b) 6

Explanation: The hCP unit cell arrangement has coordination number of 12 and contain 6 atom per unit cell.

(ii) (b) Coordination number is 6

39. (i) (c) ethyl alcohol

Explanation: Electron withdrawing group increases acidity while the electron-donating group decreases acidity so phenol is more acidic than p methoxyphenol.

In phenol. In the p-position (4-methoxy-phenol), only resonance will be at play and because it donates electron by resonance, this will decrease acidity compared to phenol.

(ii) (b) o and p-bromophenol

Explanation:–OH is ring activating group because it is electron-donating so it is ortho and para director with compound o- and p-bromophenols

$$2\ \text{C}_6\text{H}_5\text{OH} + 2Br_2 \xrightarrow[273\ K]{CS_2}$$

o-bromophenol (20%) + p-bromophenol (80%) + 2HBr

40. (i) (a) Diethyl ether

Explanation: (i) As compound A does not react with sodium metal or potassium permanganate, it cannot be alcohol.

(ii) As compound A dissolves in cons. H_2SO_4, it may be an ether.

(iii) As compound A on heating with an excess of HI gives a single alkyl halide, therefore, compound A must be a symmetrical ether.

(iv) The only symmetrical ether having molecular formula $C_4H_{10}O$ is diethyl ether. Thus compound 'A' is diethyl ether, $CH_3-CH_2-O-CH_2-CH_3$

(ii) (b) Ethyl Iodide

41. (i) (a) greater solubility of the impurity in the molten state than in the solid

(ii) (b) Sublimation

42. (i) (a) PQ_4

(ii) (c) 219.2 pm

Explanation: It crystallizes in FCC lattice $r = a/2\sqrt{2}$ where r is radius of an atom and a is the edge length.

$r = 620/(2\sqrt{2})$

$r = 219.2$ pm

43. (i) (b) $HClO < HClO_2 < HClO_3 < HClO_4$

Explanation: Higher the oxidation state lesser is the acidic strength Cl has +1 in HClO, +2 in $HClO_2$, +3 in $HClO_3$ and +4 in $HClO_4$

(ii) (a) 2

44. (i) (a) 2-bromobutane

Explanation: CH_3–CH_2–CH(Br)–CH_3 $\xrightarrow{\text{alc. KOH}}$

$$CH_3CH = CHCH_3 \xrightarrow{\text{Ozonolysis}} 2CH_3CHO$$

A: 2 BROMOBUTANE

B: ETHANAL

(ii) (b) But-2-ene

45. (i) (c) SN_1 & SN_2 mechanism

(ii) (a) Benzyl chloride

46. (c) Both assertion and reason are true, but reason is not a true explanation for assertion.

Explanation: On keeping benzyl bromide in acetone water, it produces benzyl alcohol because benzyl bromide is hydrolysed easily by acetone-water. Also, this reaction proceeds by SN_2 mechanism.

C–Br bond is replaced with C–O bond.

$$PhCH_2Br \xrightarrow[\text{water hydrolysis}]{\text{acetone}} PhCH_2OH$$

47. (c) Both assertion and reason are true, but reason is not a true explanation for assertion.

48. (c) Both assertion and reason are true, but reason is not a true explanation for assertion.

Explanation: A : $HClO_4$ is a stronger Brønsted acid than $HBrO_4$, but HCl is a weaker acid than HBr. In Group 17 oxyacids, electron density is drawn away from the O atom as the electronegativity of the halogen increases. This in turn draws electron density away from the O–H bond and weakens it.

R : $HClO_4$ is a stronger Brønsted acid than $HBrO_4$, but HCl is a weaker acid than HBr. In Group 17 oxyacids, electron density is drawn away from the O atom as the electronegativity of the halogen increases. This in turn draws electron density away from the O–H bond and weakens it Facts are false.

49. (b) Assertion is true but reason is false.

Explanation: Fluorine have the highest electronegativity of all the elements because it has the largest nuclear charge and the least atomic shell, so it has the largest nuclear pull force. In other words, fluoride has the strongest ability to pull or catch an electron to form negative ion (that is, electronegativity). Bond dissociation energy of F_2 is fairly low due to the lone pair-lone pair repulsions of the two flourine atoms, which are placed so close to each other due to small size of the atom.

50. (a) Assertion is false but reason is true.

❑❑

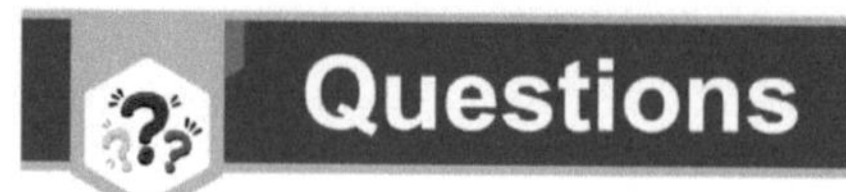

Questions

Question 1

Zinc is converted from its melted state to its solid state. It possess *hcp* structure. The nearest number of atoms will be ___________.

(a) 6   (b) 8   (c) 12   (d) 4

Question 2

The boiling points of C_6H_6, CH_3OH, $C_6H_6-NH_2$ and $C_6H_5-NO_2$ are 80°C, 65°C, 184°C and 212° respectively. Which of the following will have highest vapour pressure at room temperature?

(a) $C_6H_5NO_2$ (b) $C_6H_5NH_2$ (c) CH_3OH (d) C_6H_6

Question 3

Salt-bridge contains :

(a) Calomel   (b) Corrosive sublimate   (c) H_2O (d) agar-agar gel

Question 4

Which of the following metallic pair does not form an alloy ?

(a) Fe, Hg   (b) Fe, C   (c) Zn, Cu   (d) Hg, Na

Question 5

Nobel gases do not occur in ___________.

(a) Sea water   (b) atmosphere   (c) Ores   (d) Natural gas

Question 6

Which of the following exchange reaction will occur?

(a) $R - I + NaCl$ (b) $R - F + KCl$

(c) $R - Cl + NaI$ (d) $CH_3F + AgBr$

Question 7

Fermentation is ___________.

(a) Endothermic reaction   (b) Exothermic reaction

(c) Reverse reaction   (d) None of these

Question 8

The number of Bravis lattice is ___________.

(a) 12   (b) 14   (c) 7   (d) 16

Question 9

During the evaporation of liquid ___________.

(a) The temperature remains unaffected   (b) May rise or fall depending on the nature

(c) The temperature of the liquid will fall   (d) The temperature of the liquid will rise

Question 10

The method of protecting a metal from corrosion by connecting it to another easily oxidisable metal is known as ___________.

(a) Anodic protection   (b) Galvanisation   (c) Amalgamation   (d) Cathodic protection

Question 11

Which of the following is used as white pigment ?

(a) $ZnCO_3$ (b) $Zn(OH)_2$ (c) ZnS (d) ZnO

Question 12

Nuclear fusion produces ___________.

(a) Argon   (b) Deuterium   (c) Helium   (d) Krypton

Question 13.

In one step, ethyne can be obtained from ___________.

(a) ethanol   (b) ethanal   (c) chloroform   (d) ethyl bromide

Question 14.

Which of the following products is produced during the given chemical reaction?

$$CO(g) + H_2(g) \xrightarrow[ZnO,\ Cr_2O_3]{575\ K} ?$$

(a) Ethanol   (b) Methanal   (c) Methanol   (d) Ethanal

Question 15.

Cations are present in the interstitial sites in ___________.

(a) Frenkel defect   (b) Schottky defect

(c) Vacancy defect   (d) Metal deficiency defeat

Question 16.

The vapour pressure of water depends upon ___________.

(a) Temperature   (b) Volume of container

(c) Surface area of container   (d) All of these

Question 17.

Among the following quantities mentioned below, which is temperature independent?

(a) Emf of cell   (b) Cell constant   (c) Conductivity   (d) Resistivity

Question 18.

A colourless gas with smell of rotten fish is ___________.

(a) H_2S (b) PH_3 (c) SO_2 (d) None of these

Question 19.

Chlorobenzene on treatment with sodium in dry ether gives diphenyl. This reaction is known as ....

(a) Wurtz-fittig reaction (b) Fittig reaction   (c) Gattermann reaction (d) Wurtz reaction

Question 20.

In India, ethanol is mainly manufactured by:

(a) Catalytic hydrogenation of CO   (b) Fermentation of molasses

(c) Hydration of ethylene   (d)   Destromativedistillationofwood

Question 21.

The spin only magnetic moment of Fe^{+2} ion:

(a) 4 BM   (b) 5 BM   (c) 6 BM   (d) 7 BM

Question 22.

Edge length of a cube is 347 pm. Its body diagonal will be ___________.

(a) 263.3 pm   (b) 336.5 pm   (c) 601 pm   (d) 436.5 pm

Question 23.

Among the following substances, the lowest vapour pressure is exerted by ___________.

(a) Rectified spirit   (b) Kerosene   (c) Mercury   (d) Water

Question 24.

The conductance of electrolytes decreases due to :

(a) Interionic attraction at higher concentration   (b) Increase in temperature

(c) Dilution   (d) None of these

Question 25.

Separation of silver from lead is done by :

(a) filtration   (b) addition of zinc

(c) amalgamation   (d) fractional crystallisation

Question 26.

(i) The least stable hydroxide of 15th group element is ___________.

    (a) NH_3 (b) PH_3 (c) AsH_3 (d) BiH_3

(ii) The non-existant species is ___________.

    (a) PF_5 (b) BrF_5 (c) XeF_5 (d) SbF_5

Question 27.

(i) Which of the following possess highest melting point ?

    (a) Chlorobenzene   (b) o-dichlorobenzene   (c) m-dichlorobenzene (d) p-dichlorobenzene

(ii) What should be the correct IUPAC name for diethyl bromomethane?

    (a) 1-Bromo-l, 1-diethylmethane   (b) 3-Bromopentane

    (c) 1-Bromo-l-ethylpropane   (d) 1-Bromopentane

Question 28.

(i) Which is most viscous ?

    (a) CH_3OH (b) C_2H_5OH (c) $\underset{\displaystyle CH_2OH}{CH_2OH}$ (d) None of these

(ii) Which of the following process do not yield alcohols?

    (a) Acid catalysed hydration of alkenes   (b) Hydroboration-oxidation of alkenes

    (c) Reduction of aldehydes   (d) Free radical halogenation of alkanes

Question 29.

(i) In a cubic cell, the contribution of an atom at the face of a unit cell is ___________.

    (a) 3   (b) $\dfrac{1}{2}$ (c) 1   (d) 2

(ii) Aluminium crystallizes in a face-centred cubic lattice. The edge length of the unit cell of aluminium atom involved in lattice is 4.05×10^{-10} m. What is the density of aluminium? (Atomic mass of Al = 27)

    (a) 2700 kg m^{-3} (b) 3000 kg m^{-3} (c) 2400 kg m^{-3} (d) 2100 kg m^{-3}

Question 30.

(i) Which will have largest ΔT_b ?

    (a) 65 g urea in 1 kg water   (b) 18 g glucose in 100 g water

    (c) 342 g sucrose in 1000 g water   (d) 180 g glucose in 1 kg water

(ii) Which of the following is not an example of an Ideal solution?

    (a) Benzene + Toluene   (b) n-Hexane + n-Heptane

    (c) Ethyl alcohol + Water   (d) Ethyl bromide + Ethyl chloride

Question 31.

(i) A half-cell (quinhydrone) electrode may be reversible if it is in presence of ___________.

    (a) quinol   (b) quinone   (c) H^+ (d) None of these

(ii) Which metal cannot be obtained by electrolysis ?

    (a) Al   (b) Ca   (c) Mg   (d) Cr

Question 32.

(i) The stability of Mn^{2+}, Fe^{2+}, Cr^{2+}, Co^{2+} in order of (Atomic Number of Mn = 25, Fe = 26, Cr = 24, Co = 27) is:

    (a) $Mn^{2+} > Fe^{2+} > Cr^{2+} > Co^{2+}$ (b) $Fe^{2+} > Mn^{2+} > Co^{2+} > Cr^{2+}$

    (c) $Co^{2+} > Mn^{2+} > Fe^{2+} > Cr^{2+}$ (d) $Cr^{2+} > Mn^{2+} > Co^{2+} > Fe^{2+}$

(ii) Out of Mn_2O_7 V_2O_3, V_2O_5, CrO, Cr_2O_3, the basic oxides are:

    (a) Mn_2O_7, V_2O_3 (b) V_2O_3, V_2O_5

    (c) V_2O_5, CrO (d) V_2O_3 and CrO

Question 33.
 (i) Extraction of gold and silver involves leaching with CN^-. Silver is later recovered by:
   (a) Distillation   (b) Zone refining
   (c) Displacement by Zn   (d) Liquation
 (ii) The chemical composition of copper matte is:
   (a) $Cu_2S + FeS$ (b) $Cu_2S + Cu_2O$ (c) $Cu_2S + FeO$ (d) $Cu_2O + FeS$

Question 34.
 (i) SN^1 reaction of optically active alkyl halides leads to __________.
   (a) Inversion of configuration   (b) Retention of configuration
   (c) Racemisation   (d) None of these
 (ii) Which of the following structure is enantiomeric with the molecule given in the figure?

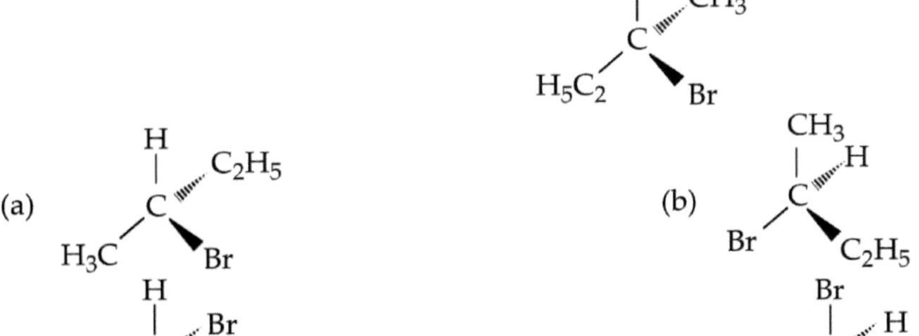

Question 35.
 (i) Which of the following produces violet colour with $FeCl_3$ solution?
   (a) Alkyl halides   (b) Ethanal   (c) Enols   (d) Ethanol
 (ii) Identify the catalyst in the hydration of alkenes to produce alcohols.
   (a) HCl   (b) $FeCl_3$ (c) Pt   (d) Ni

Question 36.
 (i) The ratio of cationic radius to anionic radius in an ionic crystal is greater than 0.732. Its co-ordination number is __________.
   (a) 1   (b) 4   (c) 6   (d) 8
 (ii) The ratio of close parcel atoms to tetrahedral holes in cublic close packing is __________.
   (a) $1:1$ (b) $1:2$ (c) $1:3$ (d) 2

Question 37.
 (i) A solution containing 8.6 g urea in one litre was found to be isotonic with 5% (wt/vol) solution of an organic non-volatile solute. The molecular weight of latter is __________.
   (a) 861.2   (b) 3489   (c) 34.89   (d) 348.9
 (ii) Which law specifically governs the relative lowering of vapor pressures in solutions?
   (a) van't Hoff law   (b) Boyle's law   (c) Raoult's law   (d) Amagat's law

Question 38.
 (i) Forth floatation process is used for __________.
   (a) Bauxite   (b) Haematite   (c) Hoom silver   (d) Cinnabar
 (ii) Which of the following are collectors used in the froth floatation process?
   (a) Aniline   (b) Pine oil
   (c) Ethyl xanthate   (d) Potassium ethyl xanthates

Question 39.
 (i) There is no S–S bond in __________.
   (a) $S_2O_7^{2-}$ (b) $S_2O_5^{2-}$ (a) $S_2O_4^{2-}$ (a) $S_2O_3^{2-}$

(ii) Which is not oxidised by MnO_2^-?

    (a) I_2 (b) F   (c) I   (d) Cl

Question 40.

(i) When Zn reacts with dil. HNO_3, the product (without nitrate) obtained is __________.

    (a) NH_4NO_3 (b) NO_2 (c) NO   (d) H_2

(ii) Which of the following reacts with PCl_3 to form PCl_5?

    (a) O_2 (b) N_2 (c) S   (d) Cl_2

Question 41.

(i) Pt, H_2/H_2O, this half cell behaves as SHE, if pressure is __________.

    (a) 1 bar   (b) 2 bar   (c) 10^7 bar   (d) 10^{-13} bar

(ii) Criteria for equilibrium are __________.

    (a) $\Delta G° = 0$, $E_{cell}^0 = 0$ (b) $\Delta G° = 0$, $E_{cell} = 0$

    (c) Both (a) and (b) are correct   (d) None of these

Question 42.

(i) Reaction of chlorobenzene with chloral in presence conc. H_2SO_4 gives __________.

    (a) Gammazene   (b) Hexachloroethane

    (c) Freon   (d) DDT

(ii) Freon 12 is manufactured from which of the following compound in the Swart's reaction?

    (a) Dichloromethane   (b) Trichloromethane

    (c) Tetrachloromethane   (d) Dichlorodifluoromethane

Question 43.

(i) What is the value of universal gas constant in Nernst equation when the potential is given in volts?

    (a) $8.314 \, J \, mol^{-1}K^{-1}$ (b) $0.0821 \, L \, atm \, mol^{-1}K^{-1}$

    (c) $8.205 \, m^3 \, atm \, mol^{-1}K^{-1}$ (d) $1.987 \, cal \, mol^{-1}K^{-1}$

(ii) Calculate the equilibrium constant for the reaction $Fe + CuSO_4 \rightleftharpoons FeSO_4 + Cu$ at 25°C. (Given $E°(OP/Fe) = 0.5 \, V°$, $E°(OP/Cu) = -0.4 \, V$)

    (a) 3.46×10^{30} (b) 3.46×10^{26} (c) 3.22×10^{30} (d) 3.22×10^{26}

Question 44.

(i) Which one a gem-dihexane?

    (a) Ethylidene dichloride   (b) Benzyl chloride

    (c) Ethylene dichloride   (d) None of these

(ii) The strongest acid among the following aromatic compounds is __________.

    (a) Meta-nitrophenol   (b) Ortho-nitrophenol

    (c) Para-chlorophenol   (d) Para-nitrophenol

Question 45.

(i) Diethyl ether on heating with conc. HI gives two moles of __________.

    (a) Methyl iodide   (b) Ethyl iodide   (c) Ethanol   (d) Ethyl iodide

(ii) Action of diazomethane on phenol liberates __________.

    (a) H_2 (b) O_2 (c) CO_2 (d) N_2

Question 46.

Assertion: HI cannot be prepared by the reaction of KI with concentrated H_2SO_4.

Reason: HI has lowest H–X bond strength among halogen acids.

(a) Assertion is false but reason is true

(b) Assertion is true but reason is false

(c) Both assertion and reason are true, but reason is not a true explanation for assertion

(d) Both assertion and reason are true and reason is the correct explanation for assertion

Question 47.

Assertion: The α-hydrogen atom in carbonyl compounds is less acidic.

Reason: The anion formed after the loss of α-hydrogen atom is resonance stabilized.

(a) Assertion is false but reason is true
(b) Assertion is true but reason is false
(c) Both assertion and reason are true, but reason is not a true explanation for assertion
(d) Both assertion and reason are true and reason is the correct explanation for assertion

Question 48.
Assertion: E_{cell} should have a positive value for the cell to function.
Reason: $E_{cathode} < E_{anode}$

(a) Assertion is false but reason is true
(b) Assertion is true but reason is false
(c) Both assertion and reason are true, but reason is not a true explanation for assertion
(d) Both assertion and reason are true and reason is the correct explanation for assertion

Question 49.
Assertion: When NaCl is added to water a depression in freezing point is observed.
Reason: The lowering of vapour pressure of a solution causes depression in the freezing point.

(a) Assertion is false but reason is true
(b) Assertion is true but reason is false
(c) Both assertion and reason are true, but reason is not a true explanation for assertion
(d) Both assertion and reason are true and reason is the correct explanation for assertion

Question 50.
Assertion: Alkali halides do not show Frenkel defect
Reason: Ions of alkali halides have almost equal in size

(a) Assertion is false but reason is true
(b) Assertion is true but reason is false
(c) Both assertion and reason are true, but reason is not a true explanation for assertion
(d) Both assertion and reason are true and reason is the correct explanation for assertion

Answers

1. (c) 12
   Explanation: In hCP lattice, coordination number is 12.

2. (c) CH_3OH
   Explanation: Vapour pressure increases with decrease in boiling point.

3. (d) agar-agar gel.
   Explanation: These inert electrolytes are chosen in such a way that they do not react with chemicals used in half cells.

4. (a) Fe, Hg

5. (a) Sea water

6. (c) $R - Cl + NaI$

7. (b) Exothermic reaction

8. (b) 14
   Explanation: Bravias lattice refers to 14 different 3-dimensional configuration in which atoms can be arranged in crystals.

9. (c) The temperature of liquid will fall
   Explanation: During evaporation high energy modulus leave the surface of the leading to fall in average kinetic energy and temperature of the liquid.

10. (d) Cathodic protection

11. (d) ZnO

12. (c) Helium
   Explanation: Nuclear fusion chemical reaction:
   $$_1^2H + {}_1^3H \longrightarrow He_2^4 + {}_0^1n + \text{Energy}$$

13. (c) Chloroform

14. (c) Methanol
   Explanation:
   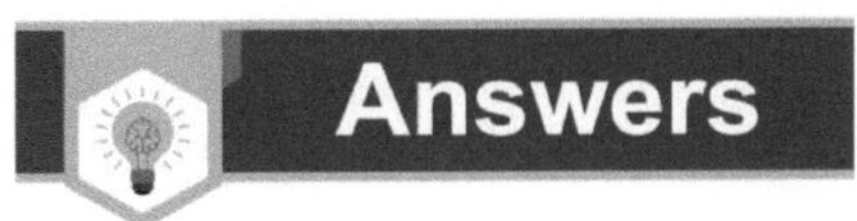
   $$\underbrace{CO + H_2}_{\text{Water gas}} + H_2 \xrightarrow[673\,K,\,300\,atm]{Cr_2O_3\,/\,ZnO} CH_3OH$$

15. (a) Frenkel defect

16. (a) Temperature
17. (b) Cell constant
18. (b) PH_3
19. (b) Fittig reaction
    Explanation:

$$C_6H_5\text{-Cl} + 2Na + \text{Cl-}C_6H_5 \xrightarrow{\text{ether}} C_6H_5\text{-}C_6H_5$$

20. (b) Fermentation of molasses
21. (b) No. of unpaired electron = 4.
$$r = \sqrt{4(4+2)} \text{ BM}$$
$$= \sqrt{24} \text{ BM}$$
$$= 5 \text{ BM}$$

22. (c) 601 pm
    Explanation: $d = (3)^{1/2} \times a$
    a = edge length
23. (c) Mercury
24. (c) Dilution
25. (b) Agb more soluble in zinc then lead forming Zn-Ag alloy which separates on coding.
26. (i) (d) Due to inert pair effect Bi^{+5}, more stable than Bi^{+3} and hence Bi forms trihalides rather than pentahalides.
    (ii) (c) XeF_5
27. (i) (d) p-dichlorobenzene
    (ii) (b) 3-Bromopentane
        Diethyl bromomethane structure

$$\overset{5}{H_3C}-\overset{4}{H_2C}-\overset{3}{CH}-\overset{2}{CH_2}-\overset{1}{CH_3}$$
with Br on carbon 3

Its IUPAC name is 3-bromopentane.

28. (i) (c) CH_2OH
        |
        CH_2OH

    (ii) (d) Free radical halogenation of alkanes
        Explanation: Alcohols can be prepared from alkenes by acid catalysed Hydration and Hydroboration-oxidation or from reduction of aldehydes.
        Alkanes on free radical halogenation produce a mixture of haloalkanes and not alcohols.

29. (i) (b) $\dfrac{1}{2}$

    (ii) (a) 2700 kg m^{-3}
        Explanation: Density of Aluminium
        $$\rho = \frac{Z \times M}{a^3 \times N_o}$$

$$= \frac{4 \times 27}{(4.05 \times 10^{-10})^3 \times 6.02 \times 10^{23}}$$
$$= 2700 \text{ kg m}^{-3}$$

30. (i) (a) Because 65 g were contains 1.0833 moles which is largest among others.
    (ii) (c) Ethyl alcohol + Water

31. (c) benzoquinone $+ 2H^+ + 2e \longrightarrow$ hydroquinone, $K = \dfrac{1}{[H^+]^2}$ and E depends on $[H^+]$

    (ii) (d) Cr
32. (i) (a) $Mn^{2+} > Fe^{2+} > Cr^{2+} > Co^{2+}$
        Explanation: Based on the electronic configuration : Mn^{2+} ($3d^5$) is most stable, Fe^{2+} ($3d^6$), $Cr^{2+}(3d^4)Co^{2+}(3d^1)$ least stable.
    (ii) (d) V_2O_3 and CrO
        Explanation: V_2O_3 and CrO are basic oxides due to lower oxidation states.
33. (i) (c) Displacement by Zn
        Explanation: Silver recovery:
        $$2[Ag(CN)_2]^- \rightarrow [Zn(CN)_4]^{2-} + 2Ag$$
    (ii) (a) $Cu_2S + FeS$
34. (i) (c) Racemisation
        Explanation: In S_N^1 reaction, carbocations are the intermediates. A 50 : 50 mixture of two enantiomer is obtained, this is called racemisation.
    (ii) (a) Compound (a) is enantiomer of compound (A) because the configuration of two groups, *i.e.*, CH_3 and C_2H_5 in them is reversed at the chiral carbon.
35. (i) (c) Enols
    (ii) (a) HCl
        Explanation: Alkenes react with water in the presence of a mineral acid as a catalyst to form alcohols. The H^+ ion from the acid helps to form a carbocation for nucleophilic attack.
36. (i) (d) 8
        Explanation : Body centred cubic lattice, coordination number = 8.
    (ii) (a) 1 : 2
        Explanation: In CCP lattice atoms
        $$= \left(\frac{1}{8} \times 8\right) + \left(6 \times \frac{1}{2}\right)$$
        $$= 1 + 3 = 4$$
        and tetrahedral voids = $4 \times 2 = 8$
        Ratio = 4 : 8 $\Rightarrow$ 1 : 2

37. (i) (d) 348.9

Explanation: No. of moles of urea = 8.6/60

5% of unknown solution = 5g/100ml

50g/1000 ml

= 5g/litre

No. of moles of unknown solute = 50/m

8.6/60 = 50/m

$m = (50 \times 60)/8.6$

$m = 348.9 \ (349)$

(ii) (c) Raoult's law

38. (i) (d) Cinnabar HgS is a sulphide ore.

(ii) (a) Aniline

39. (i) (a) $S_2O_7^{2-}$

Explanation:

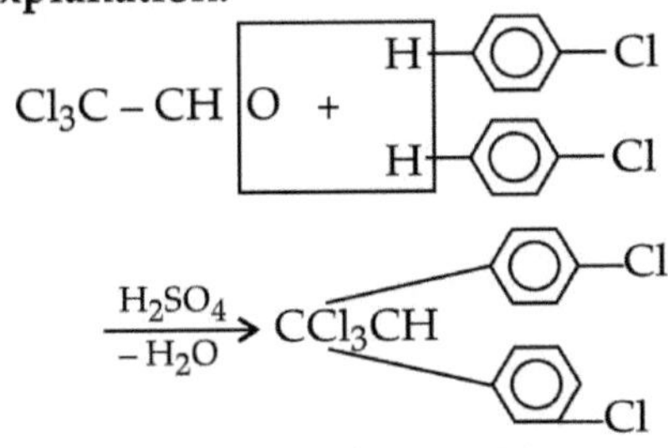

here S–O–S connection

(ii) (b) F

40. (i) (a) NH_4NO_3

Explanation:

$4Zn + 10HNO_3 \rightarrow 4Zn(NO_3)_2 + NH_4NO_3$
(Cold Dilute) $+ 3H_2O$

(ii) (d) Cl_2

Explanation: Phosphorus trichloride (PCl_3) reacts with chlorine gas (Cl_2) to form phosphorus pentachloride (PCl_5).

$$PCl_3(g) + Cl_2(g) \rightarrow PCl_5(g)$$

41. (i) (d) 10^{-14} bar

(ii) (c) Both (a) and (b) are correct

42. (i) (d) DDT

Explanation:

$Cl_3C – CH \mid O \ +$
H—⟨○⟩—Cl
H—⟨○⟩—Cl

$\xrightarrow[-H_2O]{H_2SO_4}$ CCl_3CH ⟨○⟩—Cl ⟨○⟩—Cl

1, 1, 1-trichloro-
2, 2 bis (*p*-chlorophenyl)
ethane or DDT

(ii) (a) Tetrachloromethane

Explanation: Freon 12 (CCl_2F_2) is obtained by heating CCl_4 with antimony fluoride in the presence of antimony pentachloride by Swart's reaction.

43. (i) (a) $8.314 \, J \, mol^{-1}K^{-1}$

(ii) (c) 3.22×10^{30}

Explanation: The cell reaction shows oxidation of Fe and reduction of Cu^{2+}

$$Fe + CuSO_4 \rightleftharpoons FeSO_4 + Cu$$
$$E^{\circ}_{(cell)} = E^{\circ}_{(OP/Fe)} + E^{\circ}_{(RP/Cu)}$$
$$E^{\circ}_{(cell)} = 0.5 + 0.4 = 0.9 \text{ V}$$

We have, $E^{\circ} = 0.0592 \log_{10} K_c$

$0.9 = 0.0592 \log 10 \, K_c$

$K_c = 3.22 \times 10^{30}$

44. (i) (a) Ethylidene dichloride

(ii) (d) para-nitrophenol

Explanation: Conjugate base of *p*-nitrophenol is highly stabilized through resonance.

45. (i) (b) Ethyl iodide

Explanation:

$$2C_2H_5O – C_2H_5 + 2HI \xrightarrow{\Delta} 2C_2H_5I + H_2O$$

(ii) (d) N_2

Explanation:

OH ⟨○⟩ $+ CH_2N_2 \xrightarrow{HBF_4}$ OCH$_3$ ⟨○⟩ $+ N_2$

46. (c) Both assertion and reason are true, but reason is not a true explanation for assertion.

Explanation: HI gets oxidised to I_2 as H_2SO_4 (conc.) is oxidising agent.

47. (a) Assertion is false but reason is true.

Explanation: The α-hydrogen atom in carbonyl compounds is highly acidic in nature due to anion formed after removal of H^+ is highly stable due to resonance.

48. (b) Assertion is true but reason is false.

Explanation: For the cell reaction to be feasible $E_{cathode}$ should be positive $\Delta_r G^{\circ} = - nF. E_0$ cell for the value of E_0 cell to be positive $E_{cathode} > E_{anode}$.

49. (d) Both assertion and reason are true and reason is the correct explanation for assertion.

Explanation: On addition of nonvolatile solute (viz. NaCl) to water NaCl solution is formed. Due to relatively lesser number of water molecules at the surface of liquid, the solution exerts a lower vapour pressure as compared to that of pure water. It is because of this lowering of vapour pressure that a depression in freezing point of water is observed.

50. (d) Both assertion and reason are true and reason is the correct explanation for assertion.

❏❏

Questions

Question 1

The most unsymmetrical and symmetrical system are ___________ respectively.

(a) Tetragonal, cubic
(b) Triclinic, cubic
(c) Rhombohedral, hexagonal
(d) Orthorombic, cubic

Question 2

The concentration units independent of temperature would be:

(a) Normality
(b) Molarity
(c) Molality
(d) Mass-volume percent

Question 3

The standard electrode potential for Pb^{2+}/Pb and Zn^{2+}/Zn are $-0.126V$ and $-0.763V$ respectively. The e.m.f of the cell $Zn \mid Zn^{2+}(0.1M) \parallel Pb^{2+}(0.1M) \mid Pb$ is:

(a) 0.637 V
(b) < 0.637V
(c) > 0.637 V
(d) 0.889V

Question 4

The ores that are concentrate by floatation method are:

(a) Carbonates
(b) Sulphides
(c) Oxides
(d) Phosphates

Question 5

The geometry of $XeOF_2$ is:

(a) Pyramidal
(b) T-Shaped
(c) Octahedral
(d) Tetrahedral

Question 6

Formation of alkanes by the action of zinc on alkyl halide is called:

(a) Wurtz reaction
(b) Canninzzaro's reaction
(c) Claisen reaction
(d) Frankland Reaction

Question 7

Phenol is more acidic than ethyl alcohol because:

(a) Phenoxide ion is more resonance stabilized than alcohol
(b) There is more hydrogen bonding in phenol than ethyl alcohol
(c) Ethoxide ion is less resonance stabilized than ethyl alcohol
(d) Phenol has higher boiling point than ethyl alcohol

Question 8

Close packing is maximum in which of the following crystal lattice?

(a) BCC
(b) FCC
(c) Simple cubic
(d) All of these

Question 9

The number of moles of NaCl in 3 litres of 3M solution is:

(a) 1
(b) 3
(c) 9
(d) 27

Question 10

The e.m.f of the cell : $Cu(s) \mid Cu^{2+}(1M) \parallel Ag^{+}(1M) \mid Ag$ is 0.46V. The standard reduction potential of Ag^{+}/Ag is 0.80V. The standard reduction potential of Cu^{2+}/Cu is:

(a) -0.34
(b) 1.26
(c) -1.26
(d) 0.34

Question 11

Copper pyrites are concentrated by:

(a) Electromagnetic Method

(b) Froth Floatation Process

(c) Gravity Method

(d) All of these

Question 12

In compound, OF_2, the oxidation state for 'O' is:

(a) +2

(b) –2

(c) +4

(d) +6

Question 13

Which of the following is not correct about White Phosphorous (P_4)?

(a) Six P-P single bonds

(b) Four P-P single bonds

(c) Four lone pair of electrons

(d) PPP angle is 60^0

Question 14

Vicinal and gem dihalides can be distinguished by:

(a) aq. KOH

(b) Zn dust

(c) alc. KOH

(d) Br_2 water

Question 15

Reimer Tiemann reaction is useful for the preparation:

(a) Benzaldehyde

(b) Salicylaldehyde

(c) Toluene

(d) Acetophenone

Question 16

In fcc arrangement of P and Q atoms, where P atom are at the corners of the unit cell, Q atom at the face centres and two atom are missing from two corners in each unit cell, then the formula of the compound is

(a) P_2Q_3

(b) P_4Q

(c) P_4Q_5

(d) PQ_4

Question 17

In depression in freezing point experiment, it is observed that:

(a) Vapour pressure of the solution is less than that of pure solvent

(b) Vapour pressure of the solution is more than that of pure solvent

(c) Only solute molecule solidifies at freezing point

(d) Only solvent molecules solidifies at freezing point

Question 18

E°_{cell} and ΔG^0 are related as:

(a) $\Delta G^0 = nFE^{\circ}_{cell}$

(b) $\Delta G^0 = - nFE^{\circ}_{cell}$

(c) $\Delta G^0 = - nFE^{\circ}_{cell}$

(d) $\Delta G^0 = nFE^{\circ}_{cell} = 0$

Question 19

Coke is used in metallurgical process chiefly are:

(a) Flux

(b) Reducing Agent

(c) Slag

(d) Oxidising agent

Question 20

Out of all halogen hydracids, the weakest is:

(a) HI

(b) HBr

(c) HF

(d) HCl

Question 21

The IUPAC name of $CH_3\text{-}CH=CHCH_2Br$ is:

(a) 1-Bromo-2 butene

(b) 1-Bromo-2 butene

(c) 2-Butene-1-bromide

(d) Fittig reaction

Question 22

Glycerol reacts with $KHSO_4$ to give:

(a) Acrolein

(b) Tartonic acid

(c) Oxalic acid

(d) Formaldehyde

Question 23

Schottky defects in the crystal is observed when:

(a) Equal number of cations and anions are missing from the lattice

(b) Equal number of cations and anions are missing from the lattice

(c) Ions leaves its normal site and occupies an interstitial site

(d) Density of crystal is increased

Question 24

The osmotic pressure of equimolar solution of glucose, sodium chloride and barium chloride will be in order:

(a) $BaCl_2 >NaCl >$ glucose

(b) $BaCl_2 >$ glucose $>$ NaCl

(c) glucose $> BaCl_2 >$ NaCl

(d) NaCl $> BaCl_2 >$ glucose

Question 25

The correct order of bond angles (smallest first) in:

(a) $H_2S < NH_3 < SiH_4 < BF_3$

(b) $NH_3 < H_2S < SiH_4 < BF_3$

(c) $H_2S < SiH_4 < NH_3 < BF_3$

(d) $H_2S < NH_3 < BF_3 < SiH_4$

Question 26

(i) 1, 2 dichloroethene is known to exhibit:

   (a) Optical isomerism

   (b) Geometrical isomerism

   (c) Metamerism

   (d) Tautomerism

(ii) Which of the following is not correctly matched with its IUPAC name?

   (a) $CHF_2CBrClF$ 1-Bromo-1-chloro-1, 2, 2-trifluoroethane

   (b) $(CCl_3)_3CCl$ 2-(Trichloromethyl)-1, 1, 2, 3, 3-heptachloropropane

   (c) $CH_3C\,(p\text{-}ClC_6H_4)_2CH(Br)CH_3$ 2-Bromo-3, 3-bis (4- chlorophenyl) butane

   (d) $o\text{-}BrC_6H_4CH(CH_3)CH_2CH_3$ 2-Bromo-l- methylpropylbenzene

Question 27

(i) Benzenediazonium chloride on reaction with phenol in weakly basic medium gives:

   (a) Diphenyl ether

   (b) p-hydroxyazobenzene

   (c) Chlorobenzene

   (d) Benzene

(ii) 1-Propanol and 2-propanol can be best distinguished by:

   (a) Oxidation with $KMnO_4$ followed by reaction with Fehling solution

   (b) Oxidation with acidic dichromate followed by reaction with Fehling solution

   (c) Oxidation by heating with copper followed by reaction with Fehling solution

   (d) Oxidation with cone. H_2SO_4 followed by reaction with Fehling solution

Question 28

(i) A concentration cell involving a metal M is:

$M(s)\,|\,M^+ (aq;0.05\,molar)\,|\,|\,M^+(aq;1\ molar)\,|\,1M\ (s)$

For the above electrolytic cell, the magnitude of cell potential $|E_{cell}| = 70mV$.

For the above cell

(a) $E_{cell} < 0;\ \Delta G > 0$ (b) $E_{cell} > 0;\ \Delta G < 0$ (c) $E_{cell} < 0;\ \Delta G^0 > 0$ (d) $Ecell > 0;\ \Delta G^0 < 0$

(ii) If the 0.05 molar solution of M+ is replaced by a 0.0025 molar M+ solution, the magnitude of the cell potential would be:

   (a) 35 mV   (b) 70 mV   (c) 140mV   (d) 700mV

Question 29

(i) The maximum radius of sphere that can be fitted in the octahedral hole of cubical closed packing of sphere of radius r is:

   (a) 0.732r   (b) 0.155r   (c) 0.235r   (d) 0.414r

(ii) The structure of Na_2O crystal is:

   (a) $ZnCl_2$ type   (b) NaCl type   (c) Antiflourite   (d) CsCl type

Question 30

(i) Ionic radii (in Å) of As^{3+}, Sb^{3+} and Bi^{3+} follow the order:

   (a) $As^{3+} > Sb^{3+} > Bi^{3+}$ (b) $Sb^{3+} > Bi^{3+} > As^{3+}$ (c) $Bi^{3+} > As^{3+} > Sb^{3+}$ (d) $Bi^{3+} > Sb^{3+} > As^{3+}$

(ii) Which one of the following elements is most metallic ?

   (a) P   (b) As   (c) Sb   (d) Bi

Question 31

(i) An increase in the conductivity equivalent of a solid electrolyte with dilution is primarily due to:

   (a) Increased ionic mobility of ions

   (b) 100 percent electrolyte ionisation with natural dilution

   (c) Increase in both ion numbers and ionic mobility

   (d) A rise in ion counts

(ii) The aqueous solution of which of the following compounds is the best conductor of electric current?

   (a) Acetic acid   (b) Hydrochloric acid   (c) Ammonia   (d) Fructose

Question 32

(i) How many space lattices are obtainable from the different crystal systems?

   (a) 32   (b) 230   (c) 14   (d) 7

(ii) The structure of MgO is similar to NaCl. What would be the coordination number of magnesium?

   (a) 6   (b) 12   (c) 8   (d) 10

Question 33

(i) Saturated solution of KNO_3 is used to make 'salt bridge' because:

   (a) Velocity of K^+ is more than NO_3^- (b) Velocity of K^+ is less than NO_3^-

   (c) Velocity of K^+ is equal to NO_3^- (d) KNO_3 is soluble in water

(ii) Which of the following electrolytic solutions has the least specific conductance?

   (a) 0.2N   (b) 0.02N   (c) 2N   (d) 0.002N

Question 34

(i) Which of the following is not correct ?

   (a) Gibb's energy is an extensive property

   (b) Electrode potential or cell potential is an intensive property

   (c) Electrical work $= -\Delta G$

   (d) If half reaction is multiplied by a numerical factor, the corresponding E_0 value is also multiplied by the same factor.

(ii) The highest electrical conductivity of the following aqueous solutions is of :

   (a) 0.1 M acetic acid   (b) 0.1 M chloroacetic acid

   (c) 0.1 M fluoroacetic acid   (d) 0.1 M difluoroacetic acid

Question 35

(i) Phosgene is commonly known as:

   (a) Thionyl chloride   (b) Carbonyl chloride

   (c) Carbon dioxide and phosphine   (d) Phosphoryl chloride

(ii) The reaction of tert butyl bromide with sodium methoxide produces mainly:

   (a) Isobutane   (b) Isobutylene

   (c) Tert-butyl methyl ether   (d) Sodium tert butoxide

Question 36

(i) Choose the correct order of acidity:

   (a) *p*-nitrophenol > *p*-cresol > phenol > *p*-chlorophenol

   (b) *p*-nitrophenol < *p*-cresol < phenol < *p*-chlorophenol

   (c) phenol > *p*-cresol > *p*-nitrophenol > *p*-chlorophenol

   (d phenol > *p*-chlorophenol > *p*-nitrophenol > *p*-cresol

(ii) The best reagent to convert pent-3-en-2-ol into pent-3-en-2-one is:

   (a) Acid permagnate   (b) Acidic dichromate

   (c) Chromic anhydride   (d) None of these

Question 37

(i) The significance of leaching in the extraction of aluminium is:

(a) It helps removing the impurities like SiO_2, Fe_2O_3 etc. from the bauxite ore

(b) It converts the ore into oxide

(c) It reduces melting point of the ore

(d) It eliminates water from bauxite

(ii) Which of the following metals cannot be obtained by reduction of its metal oxide by aluminium ?

(a) Cr   (b) Mn   (c) Fe   (d) Mg

Question 38

(i) The density of a metal which crystallises in BCC lattice with unit cell edge length 300 pm and molar mass 50 g mol^{-1} will be

(a) 10 g cm^{-3} (b) 14.2 g cm^{-3} (c) 6.15 g cm^{-3} (d) 9.3 2 g cm^{-3}

(ii) Which of the following will have metal deficiency defect?

(a) NaCl   (b) FeO   (c) KCl   (d) ZnO

Question 39

(i) 1- propanol and 2 propanol can be distinguished by:

(a) Oxidation with alkaline $KMnO_4$

(b) Oxidation with acidic dichromate

(c) Oxidation by heating with copper

(d) Oxidation with sulphuric acid

(ii) Propanone is obtained by dehydrogenation of:

(a) 2-propanol   (b) Propyl chloride   (c) Ethyl chloride   (d) Methyl chloride

Question 40

(i) Butane nitrile may be prepared by heating:

(a) Propyl chloride with KCN

(b) Propyl alcohol with KCN

(c) Butyl chloride with KCN

(d) Butyl alcohol with KCN

(ii) 1 chlorobutane on reaction with alcoholic potash gives:

(a) But-1-ene   (b) But -2-ene   (c) Butan-1-ol   (d) Butan-2-ol

Question 41

(i) In the extraction of chlorine by electrolysis of brine:

(a) Oxidation of Cl^- ion to chlorine gas occurs.

(b) Reduction of Cl– ion to chlorine gas occurs.

(c) For overall reaction ∆G V has negative value.

(d) A displacement reaction takes place

(ii) In the metallurgy of aluminium ____________ .

(a) Al^{3+} is oxidised to Al (s).

(b) Graphite anode is oxidised to carbon monoxide and carbon dioxide.

(c) Oxidation state of oxygen changes in the reaction at anode.

(d) Oxidation state of oxygen changes in the overall reaction involved in the process.

Question 42

(i) The number of second nearest Na^+ ion in NaCl structure is:

(a) 12   (b) 6   (c) 8   (d) 4

(ii) The coordination number of ccp and hcp arrangement of metal atom are ____________ respectively.

(a) 6, 6   (b) 8, 6   (c) 12, 6   (d) 12, 12

Question 43

(i) Which of the following has regular tetrahedral structure?

(a) BF_4^- (b) SF_4 (c) XeF_4 (d) $[Ni(CN)_4]^{2-}$

(ii) Which of the following forms salt like KHX_2?

(a) HF   (b) HCl   (c) HCl   (d) HI

Question 44

(i) Diethyl ether on heating with conc. HI gives two moles of:

    (a) Ethanol   (b) Iodoform   (c) Ethyl iodide   (d) Methyl iodide

(ii) Ethers are quite stable towards:

    (a) Oxidising Agent (b) Grignard reagent   (c) Sodium metal   (d) Base

Question 45

(i) Which of the following solutions shows positive deviation from Raoult's law?

    (a) Acetone + Aniline   (b) Acetone + Ethanol

    (c) Water + Nitric acid   (d) Chloroform + Benzene

(ii) The osmotic pressure of a solution can be increased by:

    (a) Increasing the volume   (b) Increasing the number of solute molecules

    (c) Decreasing the temperature   (d) Removing semipermeable membrane

Question 46

Assertion: p-Nitrophenol is stronger acid than o- phenol.

Reason: Intramolecular hydrogen bonding makes o-isomer weaker than p-isomer.

(a) Assertion is false but reason is true

(b) Assertion is true but reason is false

(c) Both assertion and reason are true, but reason is not a true explanation for assertion

(d) Both assertion and reason are true and reason is the correct explanation for assertion

Question 47

Assertion: SN_2 reactions proceed with inversion of configuration.

Reason: SN_2 reactions occur in one step.

(a) Assertion is false but reason is true

(b) Assertion is true but reason is false

(c) Both assertion and reason are true, but reason is not a true explanation for assertion

(d) Both assertion and reason are true and reason is the correct explanation for assertion

Question 48

Assertion: Xenon form fluorides.

Reason: Because $5d$ orbitals are available for valence shell expansion.

(a) Assertion is false but reason is true

(b) Assertion is true but reason is false

(c) Both assertion and reason are true, but reason is not a true explanation for assertion

(d) Both assertion and reason are true and reason is the correct explanation for assertion

Question 49

Assertion: $HClO_4$ is stronger acid than $HClO_3$

Reason: Oxidation state of Cl in $HClO_4$ is +5 and in $HClO_3$ is +7

(a) Assertion is false but reason is true

(b) Assertion is true but reason is false

(c) Both assertion and reason are true, but reason is not a true explanation for assertion

(d) Both assertion and reason are true and reason is the correct explanation for assertion

Question 50

Assertion: Hydrometallurgy involves dissolving the ore in suitable reagent followed by precipitation by a more electropositive metal

Reason: Copper is extracted by hydrometallurgy

(a) Assertion is false but reason is true

(b) Assertion is true but reason is false

(c) Both assertion and reason are true, but reason is not a true explanation for assertion

(d) Both assertion and reason are true and reason is the correct explanation for assertion

Answers

1. (b) Triclinic, cubic

   Explanation: In triclinic system all edge length and interfacial angles are unequal.

2. (c) Molality

   Explanation: Molality is term which is independent of volume.

3. (d) 0.889 V

   Explanation: $E^o_{cell} = E^o_{cell} - \dfrac{0.059}{n} \log(K)$

   For chemical reaction, $n = 2$

   $$Zn + Pb^{2+} \rightarrow Zn^{2+} + Pb$$

   $$E^o_{cell} = E_{cathote} - E_{anode}$$

   $$= 0.126 - (-0.763)$$

   $$= 0.889 \text{ V}$$

   $$E_{cell} = 0.889 - \dfrac{0.059}{2} \log(0.1)$$

   $$= 0.889 \text{ V}$$

4. (b) sulphides

5. (b) T-Shaped

6. (d) Frankland reaction

7. (a) phenoxide ion is more resonance stabilized than alcohol.

8. (b) FCC

   Explanation: FCC has 74% of packing efficiency.

9. (c) 9

   Explanation: M = No. of moles/Volume of solution (in L)

   No. of Moles = $3 \times 3 = 9$

10. (d) 0.34

    Explanation: $E_{cell} = E_{red} - E_{ox}$

    $$0.463 = 0.800 - E_{Cu}$$

    $$E_{Cu} = 0.337 \text{ V}$$

11. (b) Froth Floatation Process

12. (a) +2

13. (b) Four P-P single bonds

14. (a) aq. KOH

    Explanation: $ClCH = CHCl + aq.KOH$

    Vicinal

    $$\rightarrow HOCH = CHOH$$

    Vicinal alcohol

15. (b) salicylaldehyde

16. (d) PQ_4

Explanation: Contribution of P atom at the corner is 1 per unit cell and that of Q occupies fcc postion which is equal to 4 (3 faces+ 1 corner) hence PQ_4.

17. (a) Vapour pressure of the solution is less than that of pure solvent.

18. (d) $\Delta G° = nFE°_{cell} = 0$

19. (d) Oxidising agent

20. (c) HF

    Explanation: Due to small size of F, the bond between H and F is the strongest which is difficult to break makes HF as weakest acid.

21. (a) 1-Bromo-2 butene

22. (a) acrolein

23. (a) Equal number of cations and anions are missing from the lattice

24. (a) $BaCl_2 > NaCl >$ glucose

    Explanation: Van't hoff factor is greater for barium chloride as 3 and NaCl is 2 whereas glucose is zero. Higher the value of I grater is the colligative property.

25. (a) $H_2S < NH_3 < SiH_4 < BF_3$

    Explanation: Bond angle of H_2S (Hydrogen sulfide) is 90 degrees. Bond of angle of NH_3 (Ammonia) is 107 degrees. Bond angle of BF_3 (Boron trifluoride) is 120 degrees. Bond angle of SiH_4 (Silicon hydride) is 109.5 degrees.

26. (i) (d) tautomerism

    (ii) (b) $(CCl_3)_3CCl$ - 2-(Trichloromethyl)-1, 1, 2, 3, 3-heptachloropropane

27. (i) (b) p-hydroxyazobenzene

    (ii) (c) Oxidation by heating with copper followed by reaction with Fehling solution

28. (i) (b) $E_{cell} > 0; \Delta G < 0$

    (ii) (c) 140 mV

    Explanation: $E_{cell} = 0$, for every concentration cell

    $E = 0"0.059/n \log [M^+]$anode $//[M^+]$cathode

    $= -0.059/1 \log[0.0025]$

    $= +153 \text{ mV}$

    It is close to 140 mV

29. (i) (d) 0.414r

    (ii) (c) Antiflourite

30. (i) (d) $Bi^{3+} > Sb^{3+} > As^{3+}$

    Explanation: As we go down in the group the ionic radii increase due to increase in the atomic radii.

(ii) (d) Bi

Explanation: As we go down in the group the ionic radii increase due to increase in the atomic radii.

31. (i) (c) increase in both ion numbers and ionic mobility.

(ii) (b) Hydrochloric acid

32. (i) (c) 14

(ii) (a) 6

33. (i) (c) Velocity of K^+ is equal to NO_3^-

(ii) (d) 0.002N

Explanation: Specific conductance of an electrolyte decreases with dilution. So, 0.002N solution has least specific conductance.

34. (i) (d) If half reaction is multiplied by a numerical factor, the corresponding E^o value is also multiplied by the same factor.

(ii) (d) 0.1 M difluoroacetic acid

Explanation: Difluoroacetic acid is stronger than fluoroacetic acid or chloroacetic acid or acetic acid. Therefore, 0.1M difluoroacetic acid will have highest electrical conductivity.

35. (i) (b) carbonyl chloride

(ii) (d) sodium tert butoxide

36. (i) (a) p-nitrophenol > p-cresol > phenol > p-chlorophenol

Explanation: Nitro group increases the acidity whereas methyl group decreases the acidity of the phenol.

(ii) (c) chromic anhydride

37. (i) (a) it helps removing the impurities like SiO_2, Fe_2O_3 etc. from the bauxite ore

(ii) (d) Mg

38. (i) (c) 6.15 g cm^{-3}

Explanation: Theoretical density of crystal,
$\rho = Z \times M/Nxa^3$ g/cm^3
Given for BCC Z = 2; $a = 300 \times 10^{-10}$ cm, M = 50 g
∴ $\rho = 2 \times 50/6.022 \times 1023 \times (300)^3 \times (10^{-10})^3$
= 6.15 g/cm^3

(ii) (b) FeO

39. (i) (c) oxidation by heating with copper

(ii) (a) 2-propanol

40. (i) (a) propyl chloride with KCN

(ii) (a) But-1-ene

41. (i) (b) reduction of Cl^- ion to chlorine gas occurs

(ii) (b) graphite anode is oxidised to carbon monoxide and carbon dioxide.

Explanation: The oxidation state of O does not change in either the reaction.

42. (i) (a) 12

(ii) (d) 12, 12

Explanation : A CCP arrangement has a total of 4 spheres per unit cell and an HCP arrangement has 8 spheres per unit cell. However, both configurations have a coordination number of 12.

43. (i) (a) BF_4^-

Explanation:

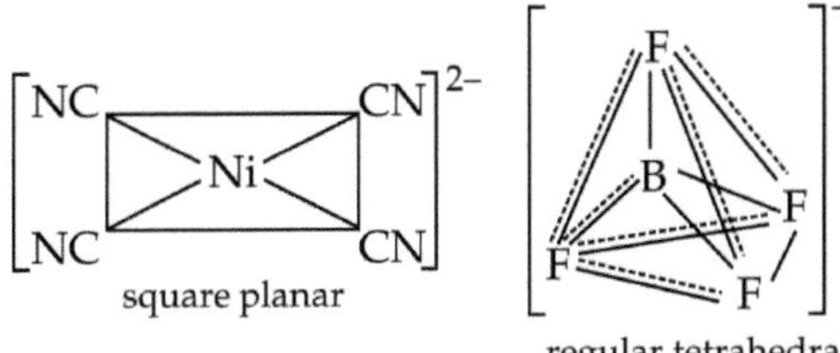

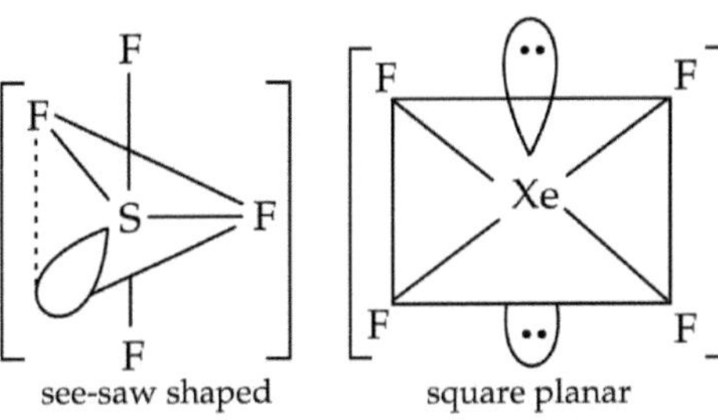

(ii) (a) HF

Explanation: Due to highest electronegativity of fluorine the anion [F—H—F] – exists as a result of strong hydrogen bond by which K^+ associate to form KHF_2.

44. (i) (c) ethyl iodide

(ii) (a) Oxidising Agent

45. (i) (b) Acetone + Ethanol

(ii) (b) increasing the number of solute molecules

Explanation: Osmotic pressure is affected by concentration and temperature. Concentration of solute and temperature each affect the amount of pressure created by the movement of water across a membrane. Higher concentrations and higher temperatures increase osmotic pressure.

46. (d) Both assertion and reason are true and reason is the correct explanation for assertion.

Explanation: p-nitrophenol is more acidic than phenol because the deactivating nature of nitro group and after loosing the proton it makes more resonance stabilization as nitro group has strong deactivating nature so it attracts electron towards it and intra molecular hydrogen bonding makes o isomer weaker.

47. (b) Both assertion and reason are true, but reason is not a true explanation for assertion.

Explanation: S_N^2 reaction takes by inversion of configuration and no intermediate is formed in the reaction and it is a single step reaction.

48. (c) Both assertion and reason are true, but reason is not a true explanation for assertion.

Explanation: Xenon belongs to noble gases which are considered to be very unreactive.

In xenon atom, the ionisation potential of Xe to lose one electron. Also, due to the presence of empty $5d$-orbitals, electrons can be excited and higher valency of xenon can be produced. e.g., XeF_2, XeF_4, XeF_6 etc.

49. (b) Assertion is true but reason is false.

Explanation: Oxidation state for Cl in $HClO_4$ is +7 and that for $HClO_3$ is +5.

50. (b) Assertion is true but reason is false.

❑❑

Biology

Specimen Question Paper

Biology

Maximum Marks: 70
Time allowed: One and a Half hours

General Instructions

*(Candidates are allowed additional **15 minutes** for **only** reading the paper.)*
ALL QUESTIONS ARE COMPULSORY.
*Each Question / Subpart of a question carries **one** mark.*
Select the correct option for each of the following questions.

Questions

Answer the questions given below by choosing the correct option.

Question 1.

Which of the following steps in transcription is catalysed by RNA polymerase?

(a) Initiation   (b) Elongation   (c) Termination   (d) All of these

Question 2.

In a DNA strand the nucleotides are linked together by

(a) glycosidic bonds   (b) phosphodiester bonds

(c) peptide bonds   (d) hydrogen bonds

Question 3.

If the sequence of nitrogen bases of the coding strand of DNA in a transcription unit is: 5′ – ATGAATG – 3′, the sequence of bases in its RNA transcript would be

(a) 5′ – AUG A AUG – 3′   (b) 5′ – UACUU AC – 3′

(c) 5′ – CAUUCAU – 3′   (d) 5′ – GUAAGUA – 3′

Question 4.

In *E. coli* the lac operon gets switched on when

(a) lactose is present and it binds to the repressor

(b) repressor binds to operator

(c) RNA polymerase binds to the operator

(d) lactose is present and it binds to RNA polymerase

Question 5.

The amino acid attaches to the tRNA at its

(a) 5′ – end   (b) 3′ – end   (c) anticodon site   (d) DHU loop

Question 6.

Which of the following provides the most satisfactory evidence in the favour of the organic evolution?

(a) Fossils   (b) Neoteny

(c) Connecting links   (d) None of above

Question 7.

Which era is dubbed as the age of prokaryotic microbes?

(a) Phanerozoic　　　　(b) Proterozoic　　　　(c) Precambrian　　　　(d) Archeozoic

Question 8.

The presence of gill slits in the embryos of all vertebrates supports the theory of:

(a) Recapitulation　　　　　　　　(b) Organic evolution

(c) Metamorphosis　　　　　　　　(d) Biogenesis

Question 9.

In Miller's experiment, the gaseous mixture in the flask contained:

(a) Methane, ammonia, carbon dioxide and helium

(b) Carbon dioxide, hydrogen, water vapour and ammonia

(c) Ammonia, methane, hydrogen and water vapour

(d) Hydrogen, ammonia and methane and helium

Question 10.

Neo–Darwinism is:

(a) Natural selection theory　　　　　(b) Modern mutation theory

(c) Modern synthetic theory　　　　　(d) Population theory

Question 11.

Trichoderma, free living fungi, present in root ecosystem are useful as:

(a) Biofertilizer　　　　　　　　(b) Biopesticides

(c) Methanogens　　　　　　　　(d) Vector for genetic engineering

Question 12.

During spermatogenesis, the second maturation division results in the formation of:

(a) 8 haploid spermatids　　　　　(b) 2 diploid spermatids

(c) 4 haploid spermatids　　　　　(d) 4 haploid spermatids

Question 13.

What is the effect of high pH on sperm?

(a) High activity leading to early death　　　(b) Sluggish, longer life

(c) High activity, longer life　　　　　　　(d) No effect

Question 14.

If temperature is reduced to $0°C$, what will happen to spermatozoa?

(a) All will die　　　　　　　　(b) No change

(c) Shedding of tail　　　　　　(d) Temporary inactivation

Question 15.

Select the incorrect statement about gametes:

(a) Sperm begin developing before puberty　　(b) Sperm do not develop successfully at $37°C$

(c) Sperm are made in the seminiferous tubules　(d) Sperm are capable of movement

Question 16.

In industries, citric acid is obtained from which of the following the microbe?

(a) *Aspergillus niger*　　　　　　(b) *Clostridium botulinum*

(c) *Saccharomyces cerevisiae*　　　(d) *Trichoderma polysporum*

Question 17.

Statins are used as:

(a) Clot busters　　　　　　　　(b) Clearing of fruit juices

(c) Blood cholesterol lowering agents　　(d) Meat tenderisers

Question 18.

Biological name of the common yeast used in baking industry is:

(a) *Saccharomyces cerevisiae* (b) *Clostridium butylicum*

(c) *Trichoderma polysporum* (d) *Propionibacterium shermanii*

Question 19.

Which of the following microbes is used in the production of Swiss cheese?

(a) *Aspergillus niger* (b) *Mucor*

(c) *Monascus purpureus* (d) *Penicillium notatum*

Question 20.

Which of the following can be used as biofertilizer?

(a) Anabaena (b) Nostoc

(c) Oscillatoria (d) All of these

Question 21.

The abbreviation 'HIV' stands for:

(a) Human immune virus (b) Hepatitis virus

(c) Human Immuno deficiency virus (d) Highly infectious virus

Question 22.

The abbreviation snRNA stands for:

(a) Small nuclear RNA (b) Small nucleus and RNA

(c) Small nucleolar RNA (d) Sub-nuclear RNA

Question 23.

The fact that DNA is the genetic material was proved by:

(a) Meselson and Stahl (b) Sutton and Boveri

(c) Watson and Crick (d) Hershey and Chase

Question 24.

The term biodiversity was coined by:

(a) Wilson (b) R. Mishra

(c) Rio de Janeiro (d) Oparin

Question 25.

Bt cotton is a/an __________ resistant variety of cotton.

(a) insecticide (b) pest

(c) insect (d) disease

Question 26.

Bt cotton has been produced by transferring genes of __________ into the cotton plant.

(a) *Escherichia coli* (b) *Pseudomonas putida*

(c) *Bacillus tumorigenes* (d) *Bacillus thuringiensis*

Question 27.

The enzyme pectinase is obtained from:

(a) *Bacillus aureus* (b) *Bacillus cereus*

(c) *Trichoderma* (d) *Claviceps*

Question 28.

The enzyme __________ is used to remove the turbidity and clear the fruit juices:

(a) Zymase (b) Pectinase

(c) Amylase (d) Papain

Question 29.

Secondary sewage treatment is mainly a __________ process:

(a) chemical (b) biological

(c) mechanical (d) physical

Question 30.

Corpus luteum has _________ function:

(a) Reproductive

(b) Endocrine

(c) Excretory

(d) All of these

Question 31.

The hormone __(A)__, released by __(B)__ helps in the release of milk from the mammary glands.

(a) Oxytocin, placenta

(b) Prolactin, posterior pituitary

(c) Prolactin, ovary

(d) Oxytocin, posterior pituitary

Question 32.

If the mother is homozygous for blood group B, and the father is heterozygous for blood group A, their offspring will be of _____ and _____ blood groups:

(a) A, B

(b) O, B

(c) B, AB

(d) A, AB

Question 33.

The vermiform appendix is _________ organ in humans.

(a) A homologous

(b) An analogous

(c) A vestigial

(d) An over-specialised

Question 34.

The sperm of *Drosophila* contains _________ number of chromosomes:

(a) 4

(b) 46

(c) 23

(d) 8

Question 35.

Which of the following is not correct regarding vasectomy?

(a) It is irreversible

(b) It causes loss of secondary sexual characters in males

(c) It leads to absence of sperm in the semen

(d) This process involves bilateral cutting and ligating of the sperm ducts

Question 36.

Which of the following statements is correct?

(a) Down's syndrome is caused due to trisomy of 22nd chromosome

(b) Haemophilia is an autosomal recessive disorder

(c) The life on the Earth appeared about 3.5 million years ago

(d) In angiosperms, the endosperm is triploid

Question 37.

Identify the correct match from the columns and mark the correct option:

A	Leydig cells	p	Extra embryonic mesoderm	i.	ABP
B	Primordial germ cell	q	Interstitial space	ii.	Upto puberty no development
C	Spermatogonia	r	Germ cell of testis	iii.	During embryonic life
D	Sertoli cell of testis	s	Nurse cell	iv.	Testosterone

(a) A-q-iv, B-p-iii, C-r-ii, D-s-i

(b) A-s-iv, B-p-iii, C-q-ii, D-r-i

(c) A-q-i, B-r-ii, C-s-iii, D-p-iv

(d) A-q-iv, B-r-ii, C-p-i, D-s-iii

Question 38.

Match Column-I with Column-II and select the correct option from the choices given below:

	Column – I (Microbe)	Column – II (Product)
(a)	*Saccharomyces cerevisiae*	Ethanol
(b)	*Monascus purpureus*	Lipase
(c)	*Clostridium*	Statins
(d)	*Penicillium*	Butyric acid

Matching codes:

(a) A-3, B-1, C-2, D-4
(b) A-1, B-4, C-3, D-2
(c) A-2, B-1, C-4, D-3
(d) A-4, B-3, C-2, D-1

Question 39.

Which of the following is odd one out with reference to evolution?

(a) Flippers of whale
(b) Wings of pigeon
(c) Forelimbs of rabbit
(d) Wings of butterfly

Question 40.

Which of the following is odd one out with reference to geological time scale?

(a) Proterozoic
(b) Mesozoic
(c) Jurassic
(d) Coenozoic

Question 41.

Assertion: All the plants belonging to a single clone are phenotypically identical.

Reason: All the plants within a clone are derived from vegetative cells through mitosis and have the same genetic constitution.

(a) Both assertion and reason are true, and reason is the correct explanation of assertion.

(b) Both assertion and reason are true, but reason is not the correct explanation of assertion.

(c) Assertion is true, but reason is false.

(d) Both assertion and reason are false.

Question 42.

Assertion: Autosomal disease is transferred from father to both son and daughter.

Reason: Autosomes are transferred only from father to son.

(a) Both assertion and reason are true, and reason is the correct explanation of assertion.

(b) Both assertion and reason are true, but reason is not the correct explanation of assertion.

(c) Assertion is true, but reason is false.

(d) Both assertion and reason are false.

Question 43.

Assertion: Tropical latitudes have greater biological diversity temperate latitudes.

Reason: Tropical regions remain relatively undisturbed for millions of years.

(a) Both assertion and reason are true, and reason is the correct explanation of assertion.

(b) Both assertion and reason are true, but reason is not the correct explanation of assertion.

(c) Assertion is true, but reason is false.

(d) Both assertion and reason are false.

Question 44.

Assertion: Methane component of greenhouse gases contributing to global warming is about 20%.

Reason: Introduction of multi-point fuel injection increase methane production. engines in automobiles has decreased methane content in the exhausts.

(a) Both assertion and reason are true, and reason is the correct explanation of assertion.

(b) Both assertion and reason are true, but reason is not the correct explanation of assertion.

(c) Assertion is true, but reason is false.

(d) Both assertion and reason are false.

Question 45.

Assertion: Mendel conducted his experiments on *Pisum sativum*.

Reason: *Pisum sativum* belongs the family *Solanaceae*.

(a) Both assertion and reason are true, and reason is the correct explanation of assertion.

(b) Both assertion and reason are true, but reason is not the correct explanation of assertion.

(c) Assertion is true, but reason is false.

(d) Both assertion and reason are false.

Question 46.

Study the diagram given below and answer the questions that follow:

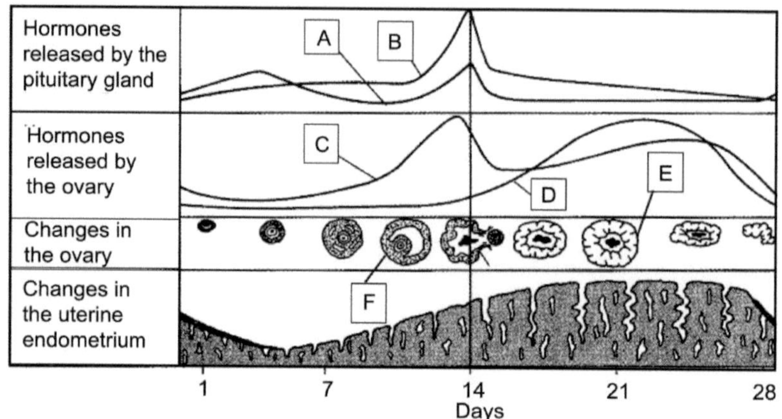

(i) The alphabet 'A' represents __________ hormone.

    (a) Oestrogen   (b) Progesterone

    (c) FSH   (d) LH

(ii) The alphabet 'D' represents __________ hormone.

    (a) Progesterone   (b) Oestrogen

    (c) LH   (d) FSH

(iii) The structure marked 'E' is __________.

    (a) Corpus luteum   (b) Secondary follicle

    (c) Graafian follicle   (d) Corpus albicans

(iv) Ovulation occurs on day __________ of a typical menstrual cycle.

    (a) 12   (b) 14

    (c) 22   (d) 28

(v) Menstrual cycle operates in __________.

    (a) All vertebrates   (b) All mammals

    (c) Only primates   (d) Only apes

Question 47.

The pedigree chart given below represents the pattern of inheritance of haemophilia in a family. Study it carefully and answer the following questions:

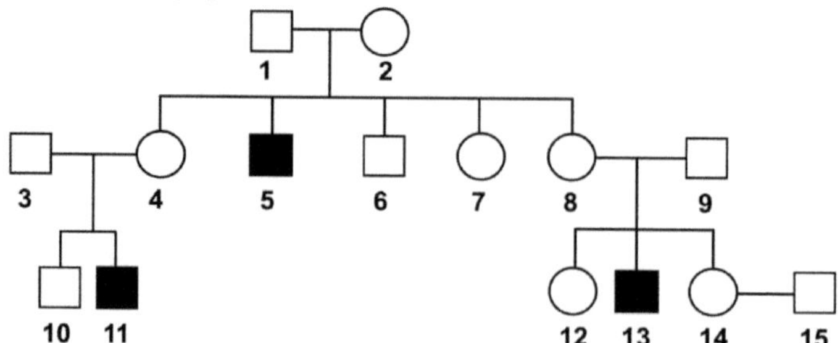

(i) Identify the correct statement with respect to member '4':

    (a) He is a carrier male   (b) She is a carrier female

    (c) He is haemophilic   (d) She is a homozygous female

(ii) The possible genotype of member '5' is:

    (a) $X^H X^H$ (b) $X^H Y$

    (c) $X^h Y$ (d) None of these

(iii) The possible genotype(s) of member '6' is/are:

    (a) $X^H X^H, X^H X^h$ (b) $X^H Y$

    (c) $X^h X^h$ (d) None of these

(iv) Haemophilia is a/an _________ trait

    (a) Dominant   (b) Autosomal

    (c) X-linked   (d) Y-linked

(v) Assuming that member '14' is heterozygous for haemophilia, the probability of the son of this couple to be haemophilic is:

    (a) 25%   (b) 50%

    (c) 75%   (d) 100%

Question 48.

The diagram of the organs of female reproductive system is given below. Study it carefully and answer the questions that follow:

(i) The place where fertilisation takes place is:

    (a) A   (b) B

    (c) C   (d) D

(ii) The place where the embryo is implanted:

    (a) A   (b) B

    (c) C   (d) D

(iii) The ovum is released by:

    (a) A   (b) B

    (c) C   (d) D

(iv) The hormone testosterone is released by:

    (a) A   (b) B

    (c) C   (d) None of these

(v) The _________ layer of the organ 'C' undergoes a cyclic change every month:

    (a) Outermost   (b) Innermost

    (c) Middle   (d) Both (b) and (c)

Question 49.

Read the passage given below, and answer the questions that follow:

The cotton bollworm is considered a major pest, all over the world. Due to its destructive feeding nature and continuous consumption of the same chemicals, it evolved resistant against many insecticides. To overcome this problem, scientists introduced a virus which selectively infects and kills the bollworm.

(i) The virus used in this process was:

    (a) Baculovirus   (b) Tobacco mosaic virus

    (c) Bacteriophage   (d) All of these

(ii) In scientific terms, this method of pest control is an example of:

    (a) Bioremediation   (b) Chemical control

    (c) Biological control   (d) All of these

(iii) The advantage of this process is that it helps in:

    (a) Controlling pollution   (b) Evolution of new chemicals

    (c) Improving the quality of cotton   (d) None of these

(iv) The virus used in this process can also be used to control some mosquito-borne diseases like:

    (a)   Malaria   (b)   Filaria

    (c)   Dengue   (d)   None of these

(v) From the statements given below, select the correct statement with respect to this process:

    (a)   The viruses are specific to insect host species

    (b)   The viruses are not specific to individual insect host species

    (c)   The same virus can be used to control corn-borer also

    (d)   The insect host never develops resistance against the virus

Question 50.

Read the passage given below, and answer the questions that follow:

Some students wanted to investigate the pattern of inheritance of flower colour in snapdragon. They selected some plants which were homozygous for red flowers and some other plants which were homozygous for white flowers. These plants were labelled as Parental Plants (P_1). These plants (red-flowered and white-flowered), were cross-pollinated. The seeds obtained from these plants were planted in a separate field. These seeds germinated to produce the plants which were labelled as the plants of F_1-generation.

Based on the above experiment, answer the following questions:

(i) Select the statement which correctly predicts the phenotype of the plants of F1 generation.

    (a)   All the plants will bear red flowers

    (b)   All the plants will bear white flowers

    (c)   50% plants will bear red flowers and 50% will bear white flowers

    (d)   100% plants will bear pink flowers.

(ii) If the plants of F_1-generation are allowed to self-pollinate, then in F_2-generation.

    (a)   All of the resulting plants will have pink flowers.

    (b)   75% plants will have red flowers and the remaining 25% plants will have white flowers.

    (c)   25% plants will have red flowers, 25% plants will have pink flowers and 25% will have white flowers.

    (d)   25% plants will have red flowers and the remaining 75% plants will have white flowers.

(iii) The genotypic ratio of the plants of F2-generation will be:

    (a)   1: 2: 3   (b)   9: 3: 3: 1

    (c)   1: 2: 1   (d)   3:1

(iv) This type of inheritance can be described as:

    (a)   Polygenic inheritance   (b)   Incomplete dominance

    (c)   Co-dominance   (d)   Pleiotropism

(v) The biological name of snapdragon is:

    (a)   *Antirrhinum majus*   (b)   *Pisum sativum*

    (c)   *Lathyrus odoratus*   (d)   *Rhizobium leguminosarum*

1. (d) All of these

    Explanation: RNA polymerase is a DNA-dependent enzyme. It binds to the promoter to initiate transcription. After initiation it continues polymerization of ribonucleotides to form RNA. Once it reaches the termination region of DNA, it separates from the DNA-RNA hybrid and ends the process.

2. (b) phosphodiester bonds

    Explanation: Two nucleotides are joined through 3′–5′ phosphodiester linkage.

3. (b) 5′ – UACUU AC – 3′

    Explanation: The process of converting DNA to RNA is known as translation.

It consists of coding and template strands of DNA, with the template strand becoming RNA and following the base pairing rule except in the RNA strand, where uracil replaces thymine.

We have coding strand- 5' ATGAATG 3'

So, template strand- 3' TACTTAC 5'

Therefore, RNA strand- 5' AUGAAUG 3'

4. (a) lactose is present and it binds to the repressor

   Explanation: Lactose acts as an inducer in the lac operon. It binds to the repressor and leaves the operator region open for RNA polymerase

5. (b) 3' – end

   Explanation: tRNA has an amino acid acceptor end to which the amino acid binds. The anticodon loop on tRNA has bases that are complementary to the coding, and the amino acid acceptor end binds to amino acids. In tRNAs, the site is located at the 3' end opposite the anticodon and is unique to each amino acid.

6. (a) Fossils

   Explanation: The best and most direct evidence in support of the favour of organic evolution comes from fossils. Fossils are the dead remains of plants and animals that have been preserved in ancient rocks.

7. (b) Proterozoic

   Explanation: The age of prokaryotic bacteria is known as the proterozoic. During the Archaeozoic, Precambrian, and Phanerozoic Eras, microbes were not dominating. As a result, they are not classified as prokaryotic microbes.

8. (a) Recapitulation

   Explanation: According to the Recapitulation Theory, embryological growth follows the same evolutionary path. Gill slits can be found in fish and aquatic amphibians, and reptiles and mammals have evolved from them over time.

9. (c) Ammonia, methane, hydrogen and water vapour

   Explanation: The Miller and Urey experiment was a chemical test that demonstrated the genesis of life on Earth in its most rudimentary state. Water (H_2O), methane (CH_4), ammonia (NH_3), and hydrogen (H_2) were utilised in the experiment.

10. (c) Modern synthetic theory

    Explanation: Neo-Darwinism is a recent synthetic theory that extends Darwin's theory of evolution. It's the result of a mix of mutations and natural selection. Mutation and population genetics are at the heart of both Darwinian and synthetic theories. The majority of biologists agree with this theory.

11. (b) Biopesticides

    Explanation: *Trichoderma* sps. are free-living fungi which act against several plant pathogens and are useful as biopesticides.

12. (c) 4 haploid spermatids

    Explanation: The haploid secondary spermatocytes undergo second meiotic division to produce four spermatids.

13. (c) High activity, longer life

    Explanation: An alkaline pH increases sperm motility and activity.

14. (d) Temporary inactivation

    Explanation: At 0 degree Celsius the sperms retain their viability but lose their mobility.

15. (a) Sperm begin developing before puberty

    Explanation: Sperm formation (Spermatogenesis) begins at the age of puberty.

16. (a) *Aspergillus niger*

    Explanation: Citric acid is obtained from the fungus *Aspergillus niger*.

17. (c) Blood cholesterol lowering agents.

    Explanation: Statins are a class of drugs used to treat high cholesterol levels. They function by lowering blood cholesterol levels, particularly low-density lipoprotein (LDL) or "bad" cholesterol. People who have a high LDL cholesterol level are more likely to acquire cardiovascular disease.

18. (a) *Saccharomyces cerevisiae*

    Explanation: *Saccharomyces cerevisiae* is also called baker's yeast.

19. No correct option is present

    Explanation: *Propionibacterium sharmanii* is the bacterium used in the production of Swiss cheese.

20. (d) All the above

    Explanation: All of them fix atmospheric nitrogen and increase organic matter in the soil.

21. (c) Human Immuno deficiency virus

    Explanation: HIV stands for Human Immuno Deficiency Virus. It is a sexually transmitted disease.

22. (a) Small nuclear RNA

    Explanation: Small nuclear RNA (snRNA) is a type of non-coding RNA that is found in the nucleus. Because these molecules play critical roles in RNA metabolism, such as pre-mRNA splicing and ribosomal RNA processing, their transcription in eukaryotic cells must be strictly regulated.

23. (d) Hershey and Chase

    Explanation: Hershey and Chase experimented on bacteriophages to prove that DNA is the genetic material. Alfred Hershey and Martha Chase conducted a series of studies in 1952 that helped to prove that DNA is genetic material.

24. No correct option is present

    Explanation: Walter Rosen coined the term biodiversity in 1985.

25. (c) Insect

    Explanation: Bt cotton produces proteins which kill some insects like lepidopterans.

26. (d) *Bacillus thuringiensis*

    Explanation: Bt cotton is an insect-resistant cotton variety produced by a genetically modified organism (GMO) *Bacillus thuringiensis* that produces an insecticide to combat bollworm.

27. (b) *Bacillus cereus*

    Explanation: Pectinase can be extracted from bacteria, fungi and plants.

28. (b) Pectinase

    Explanation: Pectinases are enzymes that break down the polysaccharide pectin present in plant cell walls. In bottled fruit juices, it removes turbidity.

29. (b) biological

    Explanation: By flowing through a water hyacinth pond, trickling filter method, or activated sludge method, organic waste is degraded by microbes and sewage fungus in biological process of secondary sewage treatment. Sludge oxidation is aided by aeration.

30. (b) Endocrine

    Explanation: The corpus luteum (CL) is a dynamic endocrine gland located within the ovary that regulates the menstrual cycle and the early stages of pregnancy.

31. (b) Prolactin, posterior pituitary

    Explanation: The principal hormonal signal responsible for stimulating milk synthesis in the mammary glands is prolactin (PRL), which is released by the anterior pituitary gland in response to suckling by the offspring.

32. (b) O, B

    Explanation: If the mother is homozygous for blood group B, genotype of mother will be $I^B I^B$. The father is heterozygous for blood group A, his genotype will be I^A. So the cross between them will be:

	I^A	i
I^B	$I^A I^B$ (AB)	$I^B i$ (B)
I^B	$I^A I^B$ (AB)	$I^B i$ (B)

33. (c) a vestigial

Explanation: The organs present in organisms which have no functional use are called vestigial organs. For example: vermiform appendix.

34. (d) 8

Explanation: *Drosophila* has a total of 8 chromosomes. *Drosophila* (fruit flies) are frequently studied by scientists because they have large chromosomes with easily visible genes. A fruit fly's body cell has eight chromosomes. There are four chromosomes in each gamete (sperm or egg) of *Drosophila.*

35. (b) It causes loss of secondary sexual characters in males

Explanation: Vasectomy is the surgical process of cutting vas deferens and tying them up so that sperms are not released in the semen. It has no side effects on the body.

36. (d) In angiosperms, the endosperm is triploid

Explanation: Endosperm develops from the primary endosperm nucleus which is the result of triple fusion.

37. (a) A-q-iv, B-p-iii, C-r-ii, D-s-i

38. (a) A-3, B-1, C-2, D-4

39. (c) Forelimbs of rabbit

Explanation: All the others are analogous organs.

40. (c) Jurassic

Explanation: All the others are era.

41. (a) Both assertion and reason are true, and reason is the correct explanation of assertion.

42. (c) Assertion is true but reason is false.

Explanation: Autosomal diseases are not sex-dependent. These are caused in the autosomal chromosomes and both son and daughter have equal probability of inheriting them.

43. (a) Both assertion and reason are true, and reason is the correct explanation of assertion.

Explanation: Tropical regions have a longer evolutionary time for developing species diversity.

44. (a) Both assertion and reason are true, and reason is the correct explanation of assertion.

45. (c) Assertion is true but reason is false.

Explanation: *Pisum sativum* belongs to the family Fabaceae.

46. (i) (c) FSH

Explanation: Follicle stimulating hormone (FSH) secreted from anterior pituitary regenerates the endometrium.

(ii) (a) Progesterone

Explanation: Progesterone levels rise in the luteal phase of the menstrual cycle.

(iii) (a) Corpus luteum

Explanation: The ruptured follicle develops into corpus luteum during the luteal phase of the menstrual cycle.

(iv) (b) 14

Explanation: Ovulation occurs at around 14th day of the menstrual cycle and lasts for 48 hours.

(v) (c) Only primates

Explanation: Menstrual cycle is the rhythmic series of changes occurring in reproductive organs of female primates.

47. (i) (b) She is a carrier female

Explanation: Since the next generation (member 11) is haemophilic and the member 3 is not haemophilic, member 4 will be a carrier female.

(ii) (b) $X^H Y$

Explanation: Member 5 is a male who is affected by the disease.

(iii) (d) None of these

Explanation: The genotype will be XY.

(iv) (c) X-linked.

Explanation: The gene for haemophilia is present on X chromosome.

(v) (a) 25%

48. (i) (a) A

Explanation: Fertilisation takes place in ampullary-isthmic junction.

(ii) (c) C

Explanation: The embryo gets implanted in the uterus.

(iii) (b) B

Explanation: The ovary releases the ovum at the time of ovulation.

(iv) (b) B

Explanation: Ovaries are secretory organs which release hormones.

(v) (b) Innermost

Explanation: The innermost lining of uterus, endometrium, undergoes cyclic changes.

49. (i) (a) Baculovirus

Explanation: Baculoviruses are pathogens that attack insects and some arthropods.

(ii) (c) Biological control

Explanation: Controlling plant diseases and pests using biological methods is called biocontrol.

(iii) (c) Improving the quality of cotton

Explanation: Biocontrol methods do not have any chemical side effects on the crops.

(iv) (c) Dengue

(v) (a) The viruses are specific to insect host species

50. Following cross will be made for the given experiment:

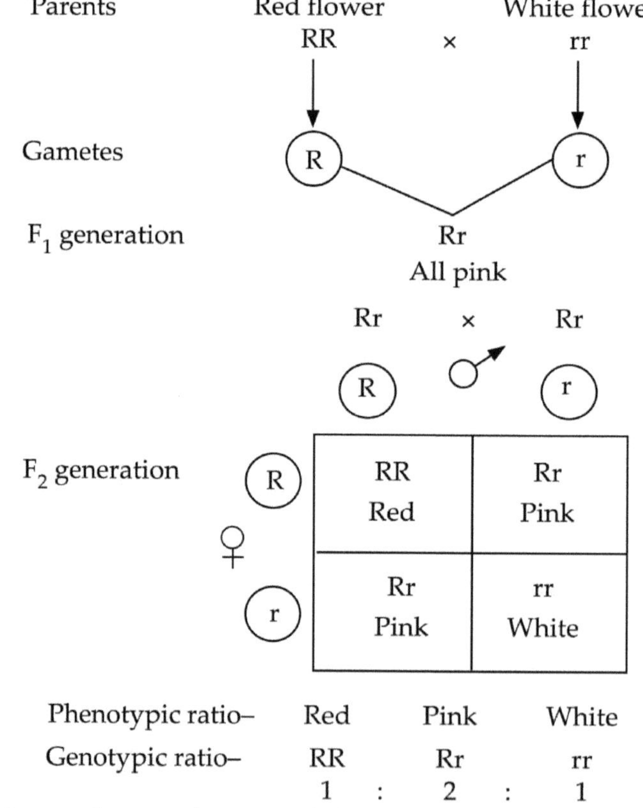

Monohybrid cross in snapdragon, where one allele is incompletely dominant over the other allele

(i) (d) 100% plants will bear pink flowers.

Explanation: Snapdragon exhibits incomplete dominance.

(ii) No option is correct.

Explanation: 25% will have red flowers, 50% will have pink flowers and 25% will have white flowers

(iii) (c) 1 : 2 : 1

(iv) (b) Incomplete dominance

Explanation: None of the allele is dominant in such condition.

(v) (a) *Antirrhinum majus*

Answer the questions given below by choosing the correct option.

Question 1

Prostate gland and seminal vesicle perform the function of:

(a) Secretion of pregnancy hormone:

(b) Nutrition and fluid medium for sperm movement.

(c) Penetration of ovum

(d) All of these

Question 2

Which of the following hormone attains a peak level in the middle of the menstrual cycle (around the 14th day)?

(a) LH   (b) Progesterone   (c) Oxytocin   (d) GnRH

Question 3

Parturition is the process of expelling the fully formed young one from the mother's uterus. It is controlled by which of the following hormones?

(a) Relaxin   (b) Oxytocin   (c) Prolactin   (d) hCG

Question 4

Head of epididymis is called as:

(a) Cauda epididymis   (b) Hammer head   (c) Corpus epididymis   (d) Caput epididymis

Question 5

Endosperm is meant for:

(a) protection   (b) transduction   (c) nourishment   (d) respiration

Question 6

One of two protective envelope in each ovule is called:

(a) Micropyle   (b) Integument   (c) Hilum   (d) Chalaza

Question 7

Usually, how many embryo sacs are present in an ovule?

(a) 1   (b) 3   (c) 2   (d) Many

Question 8

Which of the following undergoes meiosis II?

(a) Second polar body   (b) Spermatogonia   (c) Secondary oocyte   (d) Both (a) and (c)

Question 9

Zona pellucida is synthesised by:

(a) Follicle cell   (b) Oocyte   (c) Granulosa cells   (d) Both (a) and (b)

Question 10

During the first two months of pregnancy the basic structures are formed. During this period, the developing stage is called as:

(a) Child   (b) Young one   (c) Foetus   (d) Infant

Question 11

Infertility cases due to inability of male partner to inseminate the female is corrected by:

(a) ZIFT (Zygote intra fallopian transfer)
(b) GIFT (Gamete intra fallopian transfer)
(c) ICSI (Intra cytoplasmic sperm injection)
(d) AI (Artificial insemination)

Question 12

Couple unable to produce children in spite of unprotected sexual co-habitation is termed as:

(a) STD (Sexually transmitted diseases)
(b) PID (Pelvic inflammatory disease)
(c) Impotency
(d) Infertility

Question 13

Which of the following are included in barrier method?

(a) Condoms
(b) Cervical caps and vault
(c) Diaphragms
(d) All of these

Question 14

It was found that sometimes phenotype of F_1 does not resemble either of the parents and was in between the two. This is the case of :

(a) Dominance
(b) Co dominance
(c) Pleiotropism
(d) Incomplete dominance

Question 15

The unmodified allele is equivalent to modified allele when it produces:

(a) Normal enzyme
(b) A non functional enzyme
(c) No enzyme at all
(d) Inactive enzyme

Question 16

Which symbol of pedigree is correctly matched?

(a) ◇ —Female

(b) ⟨5⟩ — Affected offsprings

(c) ▨ —Affected male of autosomal recessive disorder

(d) □⊨○ —Marriage between relatives

Question 17

Negative charge on DNA is due to which of the following constituent:

(a) Sugar
(b) Nitrogenous base
(c) Phosphoric acid
(d) Hydroxyl group (– OH) present on sugar

Question 18

Select the correct one in reference to direction of DNA replication.

(a) $5' \to 3'$ Template $\to$ continuous synthesis
(b) $3' \to 5'$ Template $\to$ discontinuous synthesis
(c) $3' \to 5'$ Template $\to$ continuous synthesis
(d) $3' \to 5'$ Template $\to$ leading strand synthesis

Question 19

Which of the following cell cycle event is responsible for aneuploidy based chromosomal disorder ?

(a) Failure of G_1 phase
(b) Failure of DNA replication in S-phase
(c) Failure of segregation or disjunction of chromosome
(d) Failure of movement of chromosomes

Question 20

Which of the folllowing methodology is used to identify all the genes that are expressed as RNA in Human Genome Project (HGP)?

(a) Sequence Annotation
(b) Expressed Sequence Tags
(c) Karyotyping
(d) Ammonification

Question 21

Hugo de vries called the single step large mutation as:

(a) Mutation
(b) Sports
(c) Microevolution
(d) Saltation

Question 22

Pouched mammals survived in Australia due to :

(a) Divergent evolution
(b) Continental drift
(c) Adaptive radiation
(d) Convergent evolution

Question 23

Forelimbs of whale, bat, cheetah and human are examples of:

(a) Analogous organs
(b) Homologous organs
(c) Homoplastic organs
(d) Vestigial organs

Question 24

The animals which evolved into the first amphibian that lived on both land and water, were:

(a) Jawless fish
(b) Lobefins
(c) Ichthyosaurus
(d) Shrew

Question 25

Which was absent in Miller's experiment?

(a) Vacuum pump
(b) Electrodes
(c) Condenser
(d) None of these

Question 26

What is a placenta?

(a) Cells
(b) Parenchymatous cushion
(c) Layers
(d) Ovary

Question 27

Find out the incorrect statement:

(a) Cucurbits are monoecious plants.
(b) Papaya is a dioecious plant.
(c) Meiocytes are haploid.
(d) Male gametes are transferred through pollen tube in spermatophytes.

Question 28

What does the stigma do?

(a) Compatibility test
(b) Support
(c) Connection
(d) Reproduce

Question 29

Enclosed within the integuments is a mass of cells called:

(a) Micropyle
(b) Nucellus
(c) Chalaza
(d) Embryo sac

Question 30

Perisperm is present in:

(a) Mango
(b) Guava
(c) Black pepper
(d) Pea

Question 31

Stellar distance is measured in:

(a) Kilometer
(b) Light years
(c) Per second
(d) None of these

Question 32

What is the regulation of a lac operon by a repressor known as?

(a) Neutral regulation
(b) Positive regulation
(c) Mixed regulation
(d) Negative regulation

Question 33

Short stretches of DNA used to identify complementary sequence in a sample are called:

(a) probes   (b) markers   (c) VNTRs   (d) primers

Question 34

The mode of action of the copper ions in an IUD is to :

(a) increase the movement of sperms

(b) decrease the movement of the sperms

(c) make the uterus unsuitable for implantation

(d) make the cervix hostile to the sperms

Question 35

Where do the ovules grow?

(a) Flower   (b) Gynoecium   (c) Stigma   (d) Placenta

Question 36

Pollen grains are preserved as fossils due to the presence of:

(a) Sporopollenin   (b) Cellulose   (c) Lignocellulose   (d) Pectocelluose

Question 37

The thalamus contributes to the fruit formation in:

(a) banana   (b) orange   (c) strawberry   (c) guava

Question 38

Which of the following beverage is produced without distillation ?

(a) Whiskey   (b) Brandy   (c) Wine   (d) Rum

Question 39

Bacillus thuringiensis show their inhibitory effect on which part of the insect body?

(a) Gut   (b) Respiratory tract   (c) Nervous system   (d) Circulatory system

Question 40

Use of biofertilizer is the part of:

(a) Inorganic farming   (b) Organic farming   (c) Energy cropping   (d) Energy plantation

Question 41

Assertion : Only the sense strand of DNA is copied into RNA.

Reason   : The antisense strand plays a role in replication.

(a) Both assertion and reason are true and reason is the correct explanation of assertion.

(b) Both assertion and reason are true, but reason is not the correct explanation of assertion.

(c) Assertion is true, but reason is false.

(d) Both assertion and reason are false.

Question 42

Assertion : DNA fingerprinting is very well known for its application in paternity testing in case of disputes.

Reason   : It employs the principle of polymorphism in DNA sequence as the polymorphism is inheritable from parent to offsprings.

(a) Both assertion and reason are true and reason is the correct explanation of assertion.

(b) Both assertion and reason are true, but reason is not the correct explanation of assertion.

(c) Assertion is true, but reason is false.

(d) Both assertion and reason are false.

Question 43

Assertion : The person heterozygous for sickle-cell trait produces both normal and abnormal haemoglobin.

Reason   : The normal allele and sickle cell allele are codominant.

(a) Both assertion and reason are true and reason is the correct explanation of assertion.

(b) Both assertion and reason are true, but reason is not the correct explanation of assertion.

(c) Assertion is true, but reason is false.

(d) Both assertion and reason are false.

Question 44

Assertion : Cross pollination results in healthy and stronger offspring.

Reason   : This happens due to phenomenon of hybrid vigour.

(a) Both assertion and reason are true and reason is the correct explanation of assertion.

(b) Both assertion and reason are true, but reason is not the correct explanation of assertion.

(c) Assertion is true, but reason is false.

(d) Both assertion and reason are false.

Question 45

Assertion : Disadvantages of synthetic pesticides can be overcome by the use of natural or biopesticides.

Reason   : Biopesticides are harmless agents which are used to control weeds and pest without causing any damage.

(a) Both assertion and reason are true and reason is the correct explanation of assertion.

(b) Both assertion and reason are true, but reason is not the correct explanation of assertion.

(c) Assertion is true, but reason is false.

(d) Both assertion and reason are false.

Read the following and answer the following questions:

Question 46

Cleavage is the series of rapid mitotic divisions in zygote and forms blastula. The 2, 4, 8, 16 daughter cells are called blastomere. Embryo with 64 blastomere is known as blastocyst and has blastocoel cavity. Blastocyst gets implanted in uterine wall and leads to pregnancy.

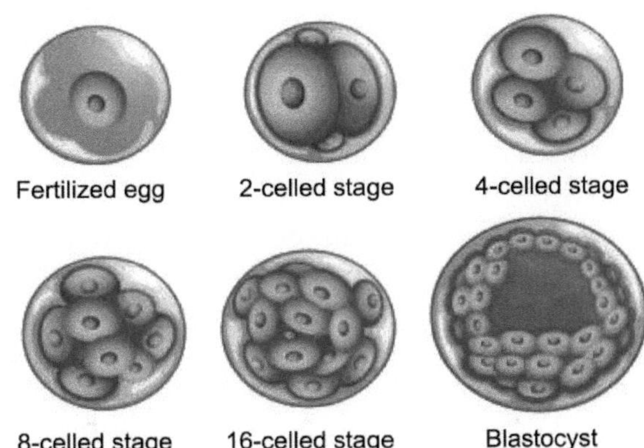

(i) Solid mass of cells with 16 blastomere is called:

(a) Morula   (b) Blastula   (c) Gastrula   (d) Zygote

(ii) The cells within the inner cell mass that possess the ability to give rise to the entire organism are called:

(a) placental cells   (b) stem cells   (c) mother cells   (d) zygote

(iii) Site of implantation is:

(a) Endometrium of uterus   (b) Cervix

(c) Uterine fundus   (d) Infundibulum of oviduct

(iv) Correct sequence of various structures formed during embryonic development:

(a) Morula → Embryo → Gastrula → Blastula

(b) Zygote → Embryo → Morula → Blastula

(c) Blastula → Morula → Gastrula → Zygote

(d) Zygote → Morula → Blastula → Gastrula

(v) The solid mass of 8-16 cells formed from zygote after successive mitotic division is called:

    (a) Blastula   (b) Gastrula   (c) Morula   (d) None of these

Question 47

Apomixis is a mode of reproduction which does not involve formation of zygote through genetic fusion. In plants, apomixis commonly mimics sexual reproduction but produces seeds without fertilization. There are several methods of apomictic development in seeds. Apomixis can be observed in hawthorns, shadbush, Sorbus, brambles, and blackberries, meadow grasses, mat grass, hawkweeds, etc.

(i) Apomixis is a type of reproduction in plants in which:

    (a) Fertilisation does not take place

    (b) Male nucleus takes part in fertilisation

    (c) Pollen fusion takes place

    (d) Generative nucleus takes part in fertilisation

(ii) If the hybrids are made into apomicts, there is no segregation of characters in the hybrid progeny.

    (a) False   (b) True   (c) cannot say   (d) None of these

(iii) Adventive embryony is found in:

    (a) Citrus   (b) Opuntia   (c) Apple   (d) Both (a) and (b)

(iv) Formation of embryo directly from diploid egg without fertilisation is called:

    (a) apospory   (b) polyembryony

    (c) diplospory   (d) parthenogenesis

(v) ______________ produces seeds without fertilisation.

    (a) Hibiscus   (b) Rafflesia   (c) Asteraceae   (d) Familiceae

Question 48

In human beings gene I controls the ABO blood groups. The gene I has three alleles I^A, I^B, i. Since there are three different alleles, six different genotypes are possible. If two persons with `AB' blood group marry and have many children, there children can be categorised as `A' blood group, `B' blood group and `AB' blood group in 1 : 1 : 2 ratio. Modern technique of protein electrophoresis reveals presence of both `A', and `B' type protein in `AB' blood group individuals.

(i) How many types of phenotypes can occur in ABO blood group?

    (a) Six   (b) Two   (c) Three   (d) Four

(ii) If a man of `A' blood group marries a woman of AB blood group. Which type of progeny indicates that man is heterozygous?

    (a) O   (b) B   (c) A   (d) AB

(iii) ABO blood groups in human beings is an example of:

    (a) Incomplete dominance   (b) Co-dominance

    (c) Multiple allelism   (d) Both (b) and (c)

(iv) Presence of both `A' and `B' type proteins in `AB' blood group individuals is an example of:

    (a) Partial dominance   (b) Incomplete dominance

    (c) Co-dominance   (d) Complete dominance

(v) Complete the following table:

Genotypes	Blood Groups
$I^A I^B$	1
$I^B i$, 2	B
3	O
$I^A I^A$, 4	I^A

        1   2   3   4

  (a)   O $I^B I^B$ $I^B i$ $I^A i$

  (b)   AB $I^A i$ $I^A I^B$ $I^B i$

  (c)   AB $I^B I^B$ ii $I^A i$

  (d)   O $I^A I^A$ ii $I^A i$

Question 49

Villagers in a place near chamber started planning to make power supply for agricultural purpose from cow dung. They have started a biogas plant for the purpose. Study the flow chart for biogas production given below and answer the questions:

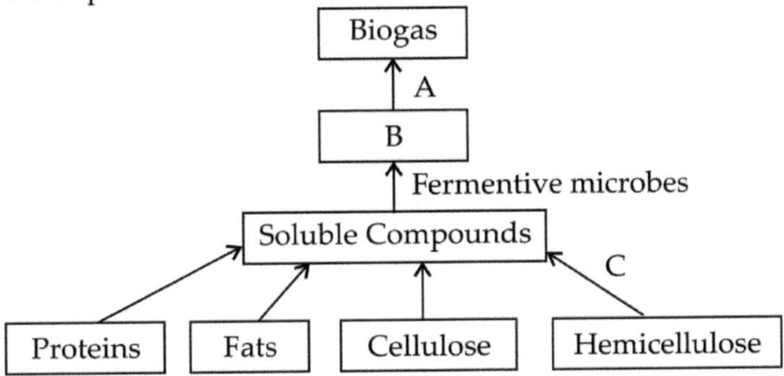

(i) Biogas is composed of:

    (a) methane, CO_2 and O_2 (b) Methane, CO_2

    (c) CO_2, H_2S and CH_4 (d) H_2S, H and O_2

(ii) In the given flowchart 'A' denotes:

    (a) Aerobic bacteria   (b) Methanogenic bacteria

    (c) Cellulose degrading bacteria   (d) Yeast and protozoa

(iii) What is represented by 'B' in flow chart ?

    (a) Carbohydrates   (b) Protein polymers

    (c) Organic acids   (d) Fat globules

(iv) 'C' in the flow chart causes

    (a) aerobic breakdown of complex organic compounds

    (b) anaerobic digestion of complex organic compounds

    (c) fermentation of organic compounds

    (d) fermentation of monomers

(v) If 'A' is not added :

    (a) Methane will not be formed

    (b) CO_2 will not be formed

    (c) Organic compound will not be converted to H_2S

    (d) O_2 will not be formed

Question 50

Overpopulation causes number of family problems. Strategies like birth control measures help to control population explosion. Natural methods of birth control do not involve medication or devices to prevent pregnancy but rather rely on behavioural practices and making observation about menstrual cycle.

(i) Which method helps in contraception of temporary absence of sex?

    (a) Coitus interruptus   (b) Withdraw method

    (c) Rhythm method   (d) Lactational amenorrhea method

(ii) Why is lactational amenorrhea effective for about 4-5 months after parturition?

    (a) Ovulation occurs on about the 14th day of menstruation

    (b) Ovulation does not occur during intense lactation

    (c) This method inhibits mobility of sperms

    (d) Both (b) and (c)

(iii) Which fact is not the basis of periodic abstinence method of birth control?

    (a) Ovum remains alive for about 1-2 days

    (b) Ovulation occurs on about 14th day of menstruation

    (c) Sperms survive for about 3 days

    (d) Alteration in uterine endometrium

(iv) On which days of menstrual cycle coitus should be avoided to prevent fertillisation?

(a) 10-17   (b) 6-13   (c) 1-5   (d) 15-28

(v) Emergency contraceptives are effectively used within:

(a) 72 hrs of coitus   (b) 72 hrs of ovulation

(c) 72 hrs of menstruation   (d) 72 hrs of implantation

Answers

1. (b) Nutrition and fluid medium for sperm movement.

   Explanation: Seminal vesicle and the prostate glands add their secretions so that the sperm is in a fluid state that makes their transport easier and provides nutrition.

2. (a) LH

   Explanation: When the level of estrogen is sufficiently high, it produces a sudden rise in concentration of LH which triggers a set of complex events in the follicle resulting in maturation of eggs.

3. (b) Oxytocin

   Explanation: Oxytocin is secreted from pituitary gland. This hormone cause vigorous uterine contractions and leads to delivery of foetus.

4. (d) Caput epididymis

   Explanation: The epididymis is a narrow tube that connects efferent ducts from the testis to the vas deferens and the head part is called caput epididymis.

5. (d) nourishment

   Explanation: The cells of this tissue are filled with reserve food materials and are used for the nutrition of the developing embryo. Endosperm is the food laden tissue which is meant for nourishing the embryo in seed plants.

6. (b) Integument

   Explanation: Integument is the protective layer of cells covering the ovule.

7. (a) 1

   Explanation: The embryo sac or which is also called as the female gametophyte is an oval structure which is situated in the ovule of flowering plants. There is only one egg in an embryo sac. Number of embryo sacs present in an ovule is one.

8. (c) Secondary oocyte

   Explanation: Each secondary oocytes undergoes meiosis II to generate four oocytes.

9. (b) Oocyte

   Explanation: Zona pellucida is thick glycoprotein layer between oocyte and granulosa cells synthesised by oocytes.

10. (c) foetus

    Explanation: After embryonic stage, the fetal stage begins which runs till birth and the baby is called foetus.

11. (c) ICSI

    Explanation: ICSI (Intracytoplasmic sperm injection) helps achieve fertilisation for couples with severe male infertility.

12. (d) Infertility

    Explanation: Infertility is inability to produce children inspite of having unprotected sexual co-habitation.

13. (d) All of these

    Explanation: Barrier methods include the diaphragm, cervical cap, male condom, and female condom and spermicidal foam, sponges, and film. Unlike other methods of birth control, barrier methods are used only when you have sexual intercourse.

14. (d) Incomplete dominance

    Explanation: In incomplete dominance heterozygotes have an intermediate phenotype in between two homozygous phenotypes.

15. (a) Normal enzyme

    Explanation: A gene is responsible for the appearance of a specific trait. In diploid organisms, a gene is represented by a pair of alleles. When these two alleles are not identical, one of alleles is different with modified allele. Normal allele will form normal enzyme. Changed or modified allele can form three types of enzymes i.e. normal enzyme, non-functional enzyme, no enzyme at all. Enzyme is always required for the formation of substrate say 'S'. Modified allele is almost similar to normal allele and forms the same enzyme and produces same phenotypic trait i.e., leads to the formation of substrate'S'. But sometimes allele formed are from non-functional enzyme or no enzyme and phenotypic trait depends on functioning of unmodified allele. Functional or unmodified allele will form the original normal phenotypic trait (due to dominant allele) and modified allele will be known as recessive allele.

16. (d) ☐▭○ —Marriage between relatives

Explanation: In human genetics, the pedigree study provides a strong tool, which is utilized to trace the inheritance of a specific trait, abnormality or disease wherein some of the important symbols used in the pedigree analysis are shown.

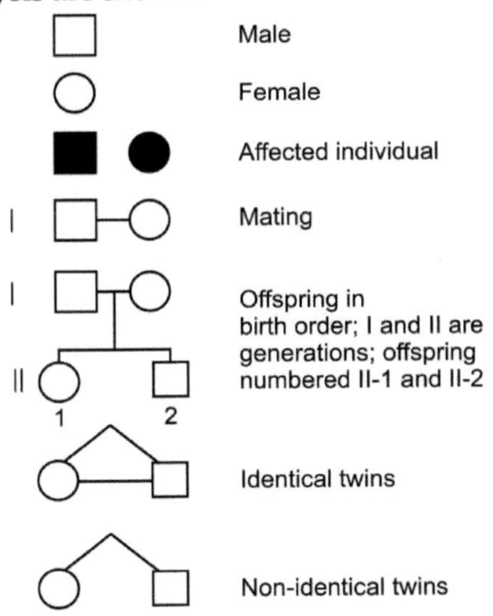

17. (c) Phosphoric acid

Explanation: Each phosphate group has one negatively charged oxygen atom.

18. (c) 3′ → 5′ Template → continuous synthesis

Explanation: During DNA replication, new strand is synthesised, catalysed by DNA polymerase enzyme called leading strand.

19. (c) Failure of segregation or disjunction of chromosome

Explanation: Error in chromosome segregation leads to aneuploidy.

20. (c) Expressed Sequence Tags

Explanation: The methodologies for the HGP are involved in some major processes. One among them is ESTs (Expressed Sequence Tags). It is used to identify all the genes that are expressed as RNA in HGP.

21. (d) Saltation

Explanation: A single step large mutation that leads to speciation is known as saltation.

22. (b) Continental drift

Explanation: In prehistoric time Australia was a part of Asian continent. After the evolution of protherians from reptiles Australia got separated from mainland of Asia (continental drift). Later on eutherian mammals developed in Asia which were carnivorous in nature and they destroyed protherians and marsupials from Asia. But pouched mammals (marsupials) from Australia survived because of lack of competition from any other mammals.

23. (b) Homologous organs

Explanation: The structure of these animals are the same but the function is different.

24. (b) Lobefins

Explanation: Lobefins were the first animals to be declared as amphibians.

25. (d) None of these

26. (b) Parenchymatous cushion

Explanation: The ovule bearing parenchymatous tissue is known as the placenta. It is also the part of the ovary where the funiculus attaches itself. Just like in humans, the placenta provides nutrition to the growing ovules.

27. (c) Meiocytes are haploid

Explanation: Through meiosis, the diploid meiocyte divides into four different haploid gametes.

28. (c) Compatibility test

Explanation: Stigma acts as a landing place for the pollen grains from where the style carries it to the ovaries for the fertilization. Stigma also checks whether the pollen grain is compatible or not.

29. (b) Nucellus

Explanation: Nucellus is the central part of ovule in which embryo sac is present. It is a mass of parenchymatous cells and forms the major part of the ovule.

30. (c) Black pepper

Explanation: In some angiosperms, the perisperm is a layer of nutritive tissue derived from the nucellus that surrounds the embryo of the seed. It is a diploid food storing tissue. Examples of seeds containing persistent perisperm are black pepper, castor, coffee, cardamom, etc.

31. (b) Light years

32. (d) Negative regulation

Explanation: The regulation of a lac operon by the repressor is known as negative regulation. At rare occasions, lac operons are also observed to be under the control of positive regulation. In negative regulation, the operon is turned off by the repressor molecule.

33. (a) probes

Explanation: A probe is a single stranded DNA used to search complementary sequence in a sample genome.

34. (b) decrease the movement of the sperms

Explanation: IUD's release copper ions to suppress the activity or the mobility of sperm inside the female reproductive tract.

35. (d) Placenta

Explanation: The ovules grow and mature on the parenchymatous cushion in the ovary, also known as the placenta. Placenta is the medium through which young ovules get nutrition. The ovules may appear singly or in a cluster.

36. (a) Sporopollenin

Explanation: Sporopollenin is one of the most chemically inert biological polymer.

37. (c) strawberry

Explanation: Thalamus contributes in the formation of fruit known as false fruit. For example, apple, strawberry, peer, cucumber, etc.

38. (c) Wine

Explanation: The alcoholic drinks formed without distillation is wine prepared by fermentation of fruit juice by yeast.

39. (a) Gut

Explanation: Toxins produced by *Bacillus thuringiensis* in the mid gut cause cell swelling and lysis resulting in the death of the insect.

40. (b) Organic farming

Explanation: Biofertilizers add nutrients to the soil through natural process.

41. (b) Both assertion and reason are true, but reason is not the correct explanation of assertion.

Explanation: Strand of DNA which has $3' \rightarrow 5'$ polarity is called template strand or antisense, or (–) strand. The other strand which has a polarity of $5' \rightarrow 3'$ is displaced during transcription. This non-template strand which does not take part in transcription is also called sense or coding strand or plus (+) strand because genetic code present in this strand is similar to genetic code (based on *m*RNA) except that uracil is replaced by thymine. Thus, both assertion and reason are correct but reason is not the correct explanation for assertion.

42. (a) Both assertion and reason are true and reason is the correct explanation of assertion.

Explanation: DNA fingerprinting involves identifying differences in some specific regions in DNA sequence called as repetitive DNA, because in these sequences, a small stretch of DNA is repeated many times. These sequence show high degree of polymorphism and form the basis of DNA fingerprinting. As the polymorphisms are inheritable from parents to children, DNA fingerprinting is the basis of paternity testing in case of disputes. Thus, both assertion and reason are correct and reason is the correct explanation for assertion.

43. (a) Both assertion and reason are true and reason is the correct explanation of assertion.

Explanation: The altered form of hemoglobin that causes sickle-cell anaemia is inherited as a co-dominant trait. Specifically, heterozygous individuals express both normal and sickle hemoglobin, so they have a mixture of normal and sickle red blood cells. Thus, both assertion and reason are correct and reason is the correct explanation for assertion.

44. (a) Both assertion and reason are true and reason is the correct explanation of assertion.

Explanation: Cross pollination is helpful in making strong and sturdy progeny. It ensures the mixing of genes in the gene pool and thus, results in the mixing up of characters. New varieties are produced by the method of cross-pollination. In this case, the pollinators like insects, birds, water, air etc., will cause the pollen grains to fall on the stigma of a different type of flower in some cases and thus causes variation. Thus, both assertion and reason are correct and reason is the correct explanation for assertion.

45. (b) Both assertion and reason are true, but reason is not the correct explanation of assertion.

Explanation: Disadvantages of synthetic pesticides can be overcome by the use of natural or biopesticides. Biopesticides are harmless agents which are used to control weeds and pest without causing any damage. Thus, both assertion and reason are true but reason is not the correct explanation of assertion

46. (i) (a) Morula

(ii) (b) stem cells

Explanation: The stem cells are a population of cells within the inner cell mass that possess the ability of giving rise to an entire organism.

(iii) (a) Endometrium of uterus

(iv) (d) Zygote → Morula → Blastula → Gastrula

(v) (c) Morula

47. (i) (a) Fertilisation does not take place

(ii) (b) True

Explanation: True, it helps the farmers to keep on using the hybrid seeds to raise new crop year after year and he does not have to buy hybrid seeds every year. Because of the importance of apomixis in hybrid seed industry, active research is going on in many laboratories around the world to understand the genetics of apomixis and to transfer apomictic genes into hybrid varieties.

(iii) (d) Both (a) and (b)

(iv) (d) parthenogenesis

(v) (c) Asteraceae

Explanation: Apomixis occurs in certain plants such as grasses and species of Asteraceae and they produce seeds without fertilization. The plants that show apomixis are called apomictic plants.

48. (i) (d) Four

(ii) (b) B

(iii) (d) Both (b) and (c)

(iv) (c) Co-dominance

(v) (c)

	1	2	3	4
	AB	$I^B I^B$	ii	$I^A i$

49. (i) (c) CO_2, H_2S and CH_4

(ii) (b) Methanogenic bacteria

(iii) (c) Organic acids

(iv) (b) anaerobic digestion of complex organic compounds

(v) (a) Methane will not be formed

50. (i) (c) Rhythm method

(ii) (b) Ovulation does not occur during intense lactation

(iii) (d) Alteration in uterine endometrium

(iv) (a) 10-17

(v) (a) 72 hrs of coitus

❑❑

Questions

Answer the questions given below by choosing the correct option.

Question 1

The technique called Gamete Intra Fallopian Transfer (GIFT) is recommended for those females:

(a) Who cannot produce an ovum

(b) Who cannot retain foetus inside uterus

(c) Who cannot provide suitable environment for fertilisation

(d) All of these

Question 2

In a population increased IMR and decreased MMR will:

(a) not cause significant change in growth rate

(b) cause rapid growth rate increase

(c) result in decline of growth rate

(d) result in population explosion

Question 3

What is the genotype of the person suffering from Klinefelter's syndrome?

(a) 44 + XXX (b) 42 + XXX (c) 44 + XXY (d) 42 + XXY

Question 4

What are the finger-like projections of trophoblast called?

(a) Endometrium (b) Placenta (c) Chorionic villi (d) Fetus

Question 5

Which of the following is not the function of a placenta?

(a) Supply of nutrients to the fetus (b) Removal of excretory products from the fetus

(c) Supply of carbon dioxide to the fetus (d) Supply of oxygen to the fetus

Question 6

In the event of pregnancy, the corpus luteum persists under the influence of:

(a) LH (b) FSH

(c) Chorionic gonadotropin (d) progesterone

Question 7

Exine of pollen grain is formed of:

(a) Callose (b) Pectocellulose (c) Lignocellulose (d) Sporopollenin

Question 8

A dicotyledonous plant bears flowers but never produces fruits and seeds. The most probable cause for the above situation is:

(a) Plant is monoecious

(b) Plant is dioecious and bears only pistillate flowers

(c) Plant is dioecious and bears only staminate flowers

(d) Plant is dioecious and bears both pistillate and staminate flowers

Question 9

In _________, female gametophytes stop their growth at 8 nucleate stages.

(a) cleistogamous　　(b) chasmogamous　　(c) gymnosperms　　(d) angiosperms

Question 10

Offspring produced by sexual reproduction exhibit more variation than those produced by asexual reproduction because–

(a) sexual reproduction is a lengthy process.

(b) gametes of parents have qualitatively different genetic composition.

(c) genetic material comes from parents of two different species.

(d) greater amount of DNA is involved in sexual reproduction.

Question 11

Number of chromosome pairs in human beings:

(a) 23　　　　(b) 26　　　　(c) 24　　　　(d) 22

Question 12

What is the duration of juvenile phase in bamboo and interflowering period of *Strobilanthes kunthiana* respectively:

(a) 25-300 years and 12 years　　　　(b) 3-120 years and 12 years

(c) 50-100 years and 12 years　　　　(d) 50-100 years and 21 years

Question 13

The law of co-dominance is used to explain the expression of only one of the parental characters in a monohybrid cross in _________ and the expression of both in _________ .

(a) F_1 and F_2　　(b) F_2 and F_3　　(c) F_1 and F_3　　(d) F_2 and F_1

Question 14

Which of the following is a recessive trait in pea plants?

(a) Dwarf stem height　　(b) Violet flowers　　(c) Axial flowers　　(d) Inflated pod

Question 15

Experimental verification of chromosomal theory of inheritance was proposed by:

(a) Tshermark　　(b) De Vries　　(c) Sutton　　(d) Morgan

Question 16

Study of family history about inheritance of a particular trait in several generations of a family is called:

(a) Phylogeny　　(b) Ontogeny　　(c) Pedigree　　(d) Cladistics

Question 17

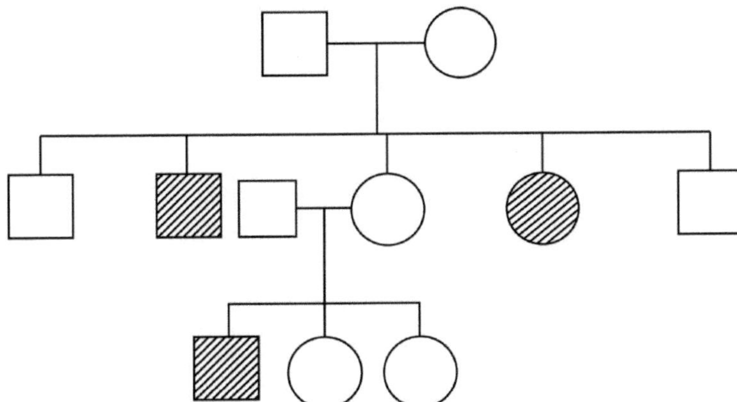

What is the mode of inheritance in the given pedigree?

(a) Autosomal dominant　　　　(b) Autosomal recessive

(c) X-linked dominant　　　　(d) X-linked recessive

Question 18

What approach used by Mendel was utterly new?

(a) Mathematics to study biological phenomena

(b) Crossing of plants

(c) Growing garden pea plants

(d) Emasculation

Question 19

During replication large amount of energy gets exhausted. The source of this energy is:

(a) Deoxyribonucleotide triphosphate

(b) Deoxyribonucleoside monophosphate

(c) Deoxyribonucleoside triphosphate

(d) Both (a) and (b)

Question 20

A transcription unit in DNA is defined primarily by three regions in DNA. These regions are :

(a) Promoter, regulator and structural genes

(b) Promoter, regulator and terminator

(c) Promoter, regulator and operator genes

(d) Promoter, structural genes, terminator

Question 21

Which of the following rRNA shows structural as well as functional role in bacteria ?

(a) 16 s rRNA   (b) 23s rRNA   (c) 5s rRNA   (d) 28s rRNA

Question 22

In eukaryotes as well as prokaryotes those DNA sequences that appear in mature or processed RNA are known as

(a) Introns   (b) Exons   (c) Cistrons   (d) Mutons

Question 23

Change in a single base pair of DNA can be termed as:

(a) Chromosomal

(b) Point mutation

(c) Genomic mutation

(d) Frame shift mutation

Question 24

Name the island where Darwin visited and discovered adaptive radiation.

(a) Archipelago   (b) Galapagos   (c) Port Blair   (d) Lakshadweep

Question 25

Which of the following represents the Hardy Weinberg equation?

(a) $p^2 + q^2 = 1$ (b) $p^2 + 2pq + q^2 = 1$ (c) $p^2 + q^2 = 0$ (d) $(p^2 + q^2)^2 = 1$

Question 26

In which type of natural selection the peak gets higher and narrower?

(a) Stabilising selection (b) Directional selection (d) Disruptive selection (d) None of these

Question 27

The industrial melanism phenomenon demonstrates:

(a) Gene mutation   (b) Genetic drift   (d) Natural selection   (d) Migration

Question 28

A nitrogen fixing microbe associated with the fern (Azolla) in rice fields is:

(a) Frankia   (b) Rhizobium   (c) Spirulina   (d) Anabaena

Question 29

Which of the following is a non-symbiotic biofertiliser :

(a) VAM   (b) Azotobacter   (c) Anabaena   (d) Rhizobium

Question 30

BOD of waste water is estimated by measuring the amount of:

(a) total organic matter

(b) biodegradable organic matter

(c) oxygen evolution

(d) oxygen consumption

Question 31

Which of the following organism has higher number of chromosomes?

(a) Housefly (b) Butterfly (c) Onion (d) Ophioglossum

Question 32

If a butterfly has chromosome number 360 in its meiocytes ($2n$). What will be the chromosome number in its gametes?

(a) 95 (b) 90 (c) 190 (d) 760

Question 33

Strobilanthes kunthiana differs from bamboo in:

(a) being polycarpic (b) length of juvenile phase
(c) being monocarpic (d) none of these

Question 34

During the process of fertilisation the pollen tube of the pollen grain usually enters the emrbyo sac through:

(a) integuments (b) nucellus (c) chalaza (d) micropyle

Question 35

____________ may be defined as occurrence of two or more embryos in one ovule.

(a) Polyembryony (b) Nucellus (c) Parthenocarpy (d) Embryogenesis

Question 36

What is the function of germ pore?

(a) Emergence of radicle

(b) Absorption of water in seed germination

(c) Initiation of pollen tube

(d) All of these

Question 37

Endosperm is completely consumed by the developing embryo in:

(a) Castor and groundnut (b) Maize and castor
(c) Pea and groundnut (d) Maize and pea

Question 38

Urine test during pregnancy determines the presence of:

(a) human chorionic gonadotropin hormone (b) LH
(c) estrogen (d) progesterone

Question 39

Acrosome is a type of:

(a) flagella (b) lysosome (c) ribosome (d) basal body

Question 40

Confirmatory test for STDs is:

(a) ELISA (b) PCR (d) DNA hybridisation (d) All of these

Question 41

Assertion : Zygote is the only vital link between two generations of an organism.

Reason : Male and female gametes fuse to form a zygote.

(a) Both assertion and reason are true and reason is the correct explanation of assertion.

(b) Both assertion and reason are true, but reason is not the correct explanation of assertion.

(c) Assertion is true, but reason is false.

(d) Both assertion and reason are false.

Question 42

Assertion : A drop of temperature does not effect spermatogenesis.

Reason : During temperature drop the smooth muscles contacts and bring the testes closer to the pelvic cavity

(a) Both assertion and reason are true and reason is the correct explanation of assertion.

(b) Both assertion and reason are true, but reason is not the correct explanation of assertion.

(c) Assertion is true, but reason is false.

(d) Both assertion and reason are false.

Question 43

Assertion : Nucleopolyhedrovirus used as biocontrol agent.

Reason : It kills insects and pests.

(a) Both assertion and reason are true and reason is the correct explanation of assertion.

(b) Both assertion and reason are true, but reason is not the correct explanation of assertion.

(c) Assertion is true, but reason is false.

(d) Both assertion and reason are false.

Question 44

Assertion : Trichoderma, found in root system causes biological control of many pathogens.

Reason : The enzymes released by Trichoderma inhibits growth of many disease causing pathogens.

(a) Both assertion and reason are true and reason is the correct explanation of assertion.

(b) Both assertion and reason are true, but reason is not the correct explanation of assertion.

(c) Assertion is true, but reason is false.

(d) Both assertion and reason are false.

Question 45

Assertion : In co-dominance, F_1 generation resembles both the parents.

Reason : An example is different type of red blood cells that determine ABO blood grouping in humans.

(a) Both assertion and reason are true and reason is the correct explanation of assertion.

(b) Both assertion and reason are true, but reason is not the correct explanation of assertion.

(c) Assertion is true, but reason is false.

(d) Both assertion and reason are false.

Read the following and answer the following questions:

Question 46

In testis, the immature male germ cells produces sperms by spermatogenesis that begins at puberty. It occurs in the seminiferous tubules of the testis. Seminiferous tubules are linked by germinal epithelium. Study the diagrammatic representation below and answer the following questions:

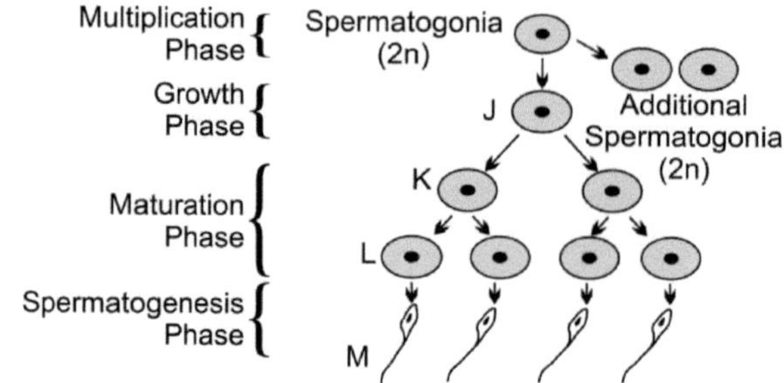

(i) Which cell division occurs during multiplication phase?

   (a) Mitosis   (b) Meiosis I   (b) Meiosis II   (d) Both (b) and (c)

(ii) What is the number of chromosome of secondary spermatocyte and spermatid respectively?

    (a) 46, 23   (b) 46, 46   (c) 23, 23   (d) 23, XY

(iii) Transformation of L into M is known as :

    (a) Spermatogenesis   (b) Spermiation

    (c) Spermiogenesis   (d) None of these

(iv) Select the correct option:

    (a) Larger primary spermatocyte is obtained from type A spermatogonia.

    (b) One spermatogonium forms two spermatids.

    (c) Spermiation is the release of sperms from seminiferous tubules.

    (d) Secondary spermatocytes are formed from primary spermatocytes after mitosis.

(v) Which hormone is responsible for sperm production?

    (a) Insulin   (b) GnRH   (c) ABP   (d) FSH

Question 47

The endosperm makes the main source of food for the embryo. Generally the endosperm nucleus divides after the division of the oospore. There are many cases when endosperm is formed even before division of oospore. There are three general types of endosperm formations: (a) nuclear type, (b) cellular type, (c) helobial type. The endosperm is usually triploid but haploid endosperm is also found. Endosperm may either be completely consumed by developing embryo before seed maturation or it may persist in the mature seed.

endosperm

Free nuclei   endosperm

(a) Nuclear endosperm   (b) Cellular endosperm   (c) Helobial endosperm

(i) Coconut water is _________________ endosperm.

    (a) free-nuclear   (b) cellular   (c) PEN   (d) nuclei

(ii) Persistent endosperm is found in:

    (a) Bean   (b) Castor   (c) Pea   (d) Groundnut

(iii) If an endosperm cell of a gymnosperm consists of 12 chromosomes, number of chromosomes in each root cell will be:

    (a) 4   (b) 24   (c) 32   (d) 16

(iv) In angiosperms, normally after fertilisation:

    (a) the zygote divides earlier than the primary endosperm nucleus

    (b) the primary endosperm nucleus divides earlier than zygote

    (c) both the zygote and primary endosperm nucleus divide simultaneously

    (d) both the zygote and primary endosperm nucleus undergo resting period

(v) White kernel of tender coconut is:

    (a) free nuclear endosperm   (b) helobial endosperm

    (c) cellular endosperm   (d) nuclear endosperm

Question 48

Enzymes are best known for their ability to catalyse biochemical reactions without undergoing any change. A large number of enzymes are being used in biotechnological industry. Most of them are obtained from microbes. Proteases degrade proteins and polypeptides. Most of the commercially applicable proteases are alkaline and are biosynthesised mainly by bacteria such as *Pseudomonas, Bacillus* and some fungi like,

Aspergillus. These enzymes are used in clearing beer, softening of bread and meat, degumming of silk, etc. Alkaline serine proteases have the largest applications in bio-industry. Alkaline proteases have shown their capability to work under high pH, temperature and in presence of inhibitory compounds. Another important group of enzymes is amylases. Amylolytic enzymes act on starch. These are obtained from *Aspergillus, Rhizopus* and *Bacillus* species. These are used in softening and sweetening of bread, production of alcoholic beverages from starchy materials, clearing of turbidity in juices caused by starch, etc.

(i) Polypeptides are degraded by

    (a) amylases   (b) proteases   (c) pectinases   (d) lipases

(ii) Amylolytic enzymes are not obtained from

    (a) *Aspergillus*   (b) *Rhizopus*   (c) *Mucor*   (d) *Bacillus*

(iii) Clearing of turbidity in juices is achieved by

    (a) amylases   (b) pectinases   (c) rennet   (d) both (a) and (b)

(iv) Select the incorrect option from the following:

    (a) Enzymes are proteinaceous substances.

    (b) Enzymes are substrate specific.

    (c) Enzymes are large sized molecules.

    (d) Microbial enzymes can work only in normal temperature and pH.

(v) A farmer harvests corns and prepares corn starch. He wants to prepare some corn syrup from this. For the conversion he needs to use enzyme ___________ .

    (a) amylase   (b) glucoamylases   (c) glucoisomerases   (d) all of these

Question 49

Translation process of polymerisation of amino acids forms a polypeptide. The order and sequence of amino acids are defined by the sequence of bases in the *m*RNA. The amino acids are joined by a bond called peptides. Ribosome is the site of protein synthesis.

(i) What is the process of activation of amino acids in the presence of ATP and its linkage to their cognate *t*RNA known as?

    (a) Charging of *t*RNA   (b) Charging of ATP

    (c) Aminoacetylation of *t*RNA   (d) Aminoacetylation of ATP

(ii) Which of the following is the start codon?

    (a) UAA   (b) UAG   (c) AUG   (d) UGA

(iii) Which part of *m*RNA contains untranslated region (UTR)?

    (a) 3′ end   (b) 5′ end

    (c) either 3′ or 5′ end   (d) Both 5′ end and 3′ end

(iv) Name the enzyme that helps in combining amino acids to its particular *t*RNA:

    (a) Activating enzyme   (b) Amino-acyl *t*RNA synthetase

    (c) Peptidyl transferase   (d) Both (a) and (b)

(v) From the given list, select the translation machinery:

    (i) *m*RNA   (ii) Ribosomes

    (iii) Amino acids   (iv) *t*RNA's

    (v) Peptidyl transferase   (vi) Amino acyl *t*RNA synthelase

    (vii) Pyrophosphatase

    (a) (i), (ii), (iii), (iv) and (vi)   (b) (i), (ii), (iii), (iv) and (v)

    (c) (i), (ii), (iii), (iv), (v), (vi)   (d) (i), (ii), (iii), (iv), (v), (vi), (vii)

Question 50

Human male reproductive system comprises of a pair of testes, primary sex organs associated with formation of gametes and production of sex hormone. Study the given figure of human male reproductive system and answer the following questions.

(i) Which of the following is correct for labelled part P?

(a) P is rete testis which transports sperms to outside

(b) P is epididymis which secretes fluid that nourishes the sperms

(c) P is epididymis that carries sperms and secretion from seminal vesicles

(d) P is rete testes which lies along inner side of each testis and stores the sperms

(ii) Identify the correctly matched pair:

(a) Q—Vasa efferentia

(b) R—Ejaculatory duct

(c) S—Seminal vesicle

(d) T—Cowper's gland

(iii) Which statements is incorrect for Q?

(a) It carries spermatozoa from epididymis to ejaculatory duct

(b) Q are only 2 in number

(c) It arises from rete testis

(d) It constitutes male sex accessory duct

(iv) Which structure passes through the prostate gland and carries sperms and secretion of seminal vesicle?

(a) P
(b) T
(c) S
(d) R

(v) The function of the secretion of prostate gland is to:

(a) inhibit sperm activity

(b) attract sperms

(c) stimulate sperm activity

(d) none of these

Answers

1. (a) Who cannot produce an ovum

Explanation: GIFT is a technique used against infertility in couples. GIFT is an assisted reproductive technology. It is known as gamete intrafallopian transfer. The eggs are retrieved from the ovaries of the female. The male provides a sperm sample the same day that the eggs are retrieved. The eggs are then mixed with the sperm in a catheter and implanted in the uterus.

2. (a) not cause significant change in growth rate

Explanation: Increased IMR and decreased MMR will not cause any significant change in the growth rate as they are inversely proportional.

3. (c) 44 + XXY

Explanation: The genotype of the person suffering from Klinefelter's syndrome is 44 + XXY. This deviation from a normal person's genotype is due to the additional copy of the X-chromosome.

4. (c) Chorionic villi

Explanation: The trophoblast of the blastocyst sends finger-like projections into the uterine cell wall to derive nutrition. These projections are called chorionic villi.

5. (c) Supply of carbon dioxide to the fetus

Explanation: Placenta connects the maternal system to the fetal system. It provides nutrients for the fetus. It also removes the excretory products that would be harmful to it. It also provides a gaseous exchange by providing oxygen and removing carbon dioxide.

6. (c) Chorionic gonadotropin

Explanation: During pregnancy, human chorionic gonadotropin hormone is released by trophoblastic cells which pass out in urine. Thus, if this hormone appears in urine test, it means the woman is pregnant. This hormone maintains the corpus luteum and stimulates it to secrete progesterone which is required for the maintenance of the uterus.

7. (d) Sporopollenin

Explanation: Exine is made of sporopollenin while intine is made of cellulose.

8. (c) Plant is dioecious and bears only staminate flowers

Explanation: Fruits can develop from a single ovary of a single flower(simple fruit) or from several free carpels of a single flower (aggregate). In total, fruits develop from ovaries. This is why, a dioecious plant (unisexual) bearing only staminate (male) flowers will not produce fruits, whereas monoecious plants (bisexual) or dioecious plants bearing only pistillate (female) flowers or pistillate and staminate both can bear fruits.

9. (d) angiosperms

Explanation: Double fertilization occurs only in angiosperms. The female gametophyte in angiosperms abruptly stops their growth at 8 nucleate stages.

10. (b) gametes of parents have qualitatively different genetic composition.

Explanation: In sexual reproduction, male and female gametes produced by different individuals of the opposite sex fuse to form the zygote which develops into an offspring. So, the offspring possesses DNA from two different individuals thus, is genetically different from the parents. On the contrary, in asexual reproduction, offspring is produced from the single parent and possesses parental DNA thus, is genetically and morphologically similar to each other and to their parents.

11. (a) 23

Explanation: In humans, each cell normally contains 23 pairs of chromosomes, for a total of 46. 22 of these pairs, called autosomes, look the same in both males and females. The 23rd pair, the sex chromosomes, differ between males and females.

12. (b) 3-120 years and 12 years

Explanation: Neelakurinji -- also known as *Strobilanthes kunthiana* -- bloom once every 12 years, and belong to a shrub found in the Shola forests of the Western Ghats in the states of Kerala, Karnataka and Tamil Nadu. The *Strobilanthes kunthiana* differs from bamboo in the length of the juvenile phase. The juvenile phase of *Strobilanthes kunthiana* varies from 8-16 years, whereas the juvenile phase of bamboo varies from 3-120 years.

13. (a) F_1 and F_2

Explanation: In co-dominance both dominant and recessive alleles are expressed.

14. (a) Dwarf stem height

Explanation: Recessive traits are the ones that require both alleles to be present to result in the expression of the gene product. Of the mentioned traits, only dwarf stem height is a recessive trait.

15. (d) Morgan

Explanation: Experimental verification of the Chromosomal Theory of Inheritance was done by Thomas Hunt Morgan and his colleagues. Morgan observed two genes under consideration did not segregate independently as in the case of Mendel's study.

16. (c) Pedigree

Explanation: A pedigree is genetic representation of a family tree.

17. (b) Autosomal recessive

Explanation: In autosomal recessive disorder two mutated genes are inherited one from each parent, passed on by two carriers.

18. (a) Mathematics to study biological phenomena

Explanation: People had performed crosses on garden pea plants before Mendel. But no one had applied a statistical and probabilistic approach to unveil the underlying phenomena. Mendel was the first to do so.

19. (c) Deoxyribonucleoside triphosphate

Explanation: Deoxynucleoside triphosphate provides the energy source for the reaction.

20. (d) Promoter, structural genes and terminator

Explanation: A transcription unit is a segment of DNA that takes part in transcription.

21. (b) 23s $rRNA$

Explanation: 23s $rRNA$ shows peptidyl transferase activity which catalyses peptide bond formation in proteins or amino acid chains.

22. (b) Exons

Explanation: The functional coding sequences are called exons.

23. (b) Point mutation

Explanation: A point mutation is when a single base pair is altered.

24. (b) Galapagos

Explanation: During the voyage of Darwin, he visited the Galapagos island. There, he came across different varieties of species. He saw the variations in the modification of beaks of finches.

25. (b) $p^2 + 2pq + q^2 = 1$

Explanation: The Hardy Weinberg equation is $p^2 + 2pq + q^2 = 1$. Here, p^2 denotes the allele of AA and q^2 denotes the allele aa. This shows that p, q and A, a are related in multiplication. So, $2pq$ represent Aa.

26. (a) Stabilising selection

Explanation: Stabilising selection act against individuals in the middle of the trait distribution.

27. (c) Natural selection

Explanation: Natural selection is a mechanism of evolution.

28. (d) Anabaena

Explanation: Anabaena azollae, a cyanobacterium that lives in symbiotic association with the free floating water fern.

29. (b) Azotobacter

Explanation: Azotobacter is free living nitrogen fixing bacteria.

30. (d) oxygen consumption

Explanation: BOD is measured by amount of oxygen that would be consumed when all the organic matter.

31. (d) Ophioglossum

32. (c) 190

Explanation: In case of Butterfly:

Chromosome numbers in meiocytes (diploid, $2n$) = 360

Gametes (haploid, n) = 190

33. (b) length of juvenile phase

Explanation: The *Strobilanthes kunthiana* differs from bamboo in the length of the juvenile phase. The juvenile phase of *Strobilanthes kunthiana* varies from 8-16 years, whereas the juvenile phase of bamboo varies from 3-120 years.

34. (d) micropyle

35. (a) Polyembryony

Explanation: Polyembryony is defined as occurrence of two or more embryos in an ovule. In a seed with several embryos, generally one embryo matures and rest degenerate during the course of its development.

36. (c) Initiation of pollen tube

Explanation: Germ pore is the place on pollen grains exine, where the sporopollenin is absent. It helps in formation of pollen tube by intine.

37. (c) Pea and groundnut

38. (a) human chorionic gonadotropin hormone

Explanation: The human chorionic gonadotropin (hCG) test is done to measure the amount of the hormone hCG in blood or urine to see if a woman is pregnant. hCG may also be measured to see if cancer of the ovaries or testicles is present.

39. (b) lysosome

Explanation: The acrosome is a large lysosome-like vesicle overlying the sperm nucleus. This spermatid specific organelle, derived from the Golgi during spermatogenesis, contains both unique acrosomal enzymes and common enzymes associated with lysosomes in somatic cells.

40. (d) All of these

41. (b) Both assertion and reason are true, but reason is not the correct explanation of assertion

Explanation: Fusion of male and female gametes results in the formation of zygote which is the end product of sexual reproduction. It further develops into next generation so, it forms a vital link between two generations of a species. Thus, both assertion and reason are true but reason is not the correct explanation of assertion.

42. (a) Both assertion and reason are true and reason is the correct explanation of assertion

Explanation: The normal temperature of the testes in the scrotum is about 2°–2.5°C lower than the internal body temperature. When the body is chilled, the smooth muscle contracts and brings the testes closer to the pelvic cavity. This movement towards the pelvic cavity allows the testes to absorb heat from the rest of the body so that the sperm cells do not become chilled and get optimum temperature for spermatogenesis. Thus, both assertion and reason are correct and reason is the correct explanation for assertion.

43. (a) Both assertion and reason are true and reason is the correct explanation of assertion

Explanation: The nucleopolyhedrovirus (NPV), part of the family of Baculovirus, is a virus affecting insects, predominantly moths and butterflies. It has been used as a pesticide. It kills insects and pests. Thus, both assertion and reason are true and reason is the correct explanation of assertion.

44. (a) Both assertion and reason are true and reason is the correct explanation of assertion

45. (a) Both assertion and reason are true and reason is the correct explanation of assertion

Explanation: In *Mirabilis jalapa*, red and white-coloured flowers are seen. When they are crossed, in the F_1 generation, all flowers are pink coloured. This is because of the incomplete dominance of red-coloured flowers. Thus, both assertion and reason are true and reason is the correct explanation of assertion.

46. (i) (a) Mitosis

(ii) (c) 23, 23

(iii) (c) Spermiogenesis

Explanation: The transformation of spermatids into spermatozoa is called spermiogenesis.

(iv) (c) Spermiation is the release of sperms from seminiferous tubules.

(v) (d) FSH

47. (i) (a) free-nuclear

Explanation: Coconut water in tender coconuts, is a free nuclear endosperm that is made of many nuclei and the surrounding white center is the cellular endosperm.

(ii) (b) Castor

Explanation: All the cereals have persistent endosperm. Examples of such plants are- rice, mustard, wheat, maize, castor. In the case of mustard, the thin fruit wall is fused to the seed coat. Thus, the nutritious part of the grain is the seed and its endosperm.

(iii) (b) 24

Explanation: Root of gymnosperm is diploid which thus has 2n equals 24 chromosomes. Endosperm in gymnosperm is haploid in nature with 12 chromosomes. Triploid endosperms are seen in angiosperms, formed as a result of double fertilisation.

(iv) (b) primary endosperm nucleus divides earlier than zygote

(v) (c) cellular endosperm

48. (i) (b) proteases

Explanation: Proteases are enzymes that degrade proteins and polypeptides.

(ii) (b) *Rhizopus*

(iii) (b) Pectinases

Explanation: Pectinases are enzymes that breaks down pectin found in plant cell walls. It clears the turbidity in bottled fruit juices.

(iv) (b) Enzymes are substrate specific

(v) (a) amylase

49. (i) (a) Charging of tRNA

Explanation: In order to form a peptide bond, a certain quantity of energy is required. The first phase in this process is known as charging of tRNA. It is also known as aminoacylation of tRNA. In this process, the amino acids are activated in the presence of ATP and are linked to their cognate tRNA.

(ii) (c) AUG

Explanation: An amino acid usually possesses different codons. It also has a start and a stop codon. The stop codons are UAA, UAG and UGA. The start codon is AUG.

(iii) (d) Both 5′ end and 3′ end

(iv) (d) Both (a) and (b)

(v) (a) (i), (ii), (iii), (iv) and (vi)

50. (i) (b) P is epididymis which secretes fluid that nourishes the sperm

(ii) (b) R—Ejaculatory duct

(iii) (c) It arises from rete testis

(iv) (d) R

(v) (c) stimulate sperm activity

❑❑

Answer the questions given below by choosing the correct option.

Question 1

It is usually seen that when an orange seed is squeezed many embryos of different shapes and sizes are revealed. This happen because of the phenomenon

(a) Polyembryony   (b) Parthenogenesis   (c) Apomixis   (d) Parthenocarpy

Question 2

The unique flowering phenomenon exhibited by *Strobilanthus kunthiana* (neelkurinji) is that it

(a) reproduces by parthenocarpy   (b) flowers once in 12 years

(c) is a unisexual flower   (d) flowers annually

Question 3

Name the event during cell division cycle that results in the gain or loss of chromosome.

(a) Failure of segregation of chromosomes   (b) Crossing over

(c) Formation of spindle fibres   (d) Formation of recombinants

Question 4

_________ is used as an atmospheric pollution indicator.

(a) Lepidoptera   (b) Lichens   (c) Lycopersicon   (d) Lycopodium

Question 5

In humans, fertilization takes place in:

(a) Ampulla   (b) Isthmus   (c) Infundibulum   (d) Uterine cavity

Question 6

The theory of survival of the fittest was given by—

(a) Charles Darwin   (b) Hardy Weinberg   (c) Hugo de Vries   (d) S.L. Miller

Question 7

The bones of forelimbs of whale, bat, cheetah, and man are similar in structure, because _________.

(a) one organism has given rise to another   (c) they perform the same function

(b) they share a common ancestor   (d) they have biochemical similarities

Question 8

Which of the event are not required for the conversion of hnRNA to mRNA?

(a) Splicing   (b) Tailing   (c) Capping   (d) Translation

Question 9

Select the odd one out.

(a) AUG   (b) UAA   (c) UAG   (d) UGA

Question 10

A genetic disease is transferred from a phenotypically normal but carrier female to only some of the male progeny. What kind of disease is this?

(a) Autosomal dominant   (b) Autosomal recessive

(c) Sex-linked dominant   (d) Sex-linked recessive

Question 11

It is known that the total sum of all the frequencies of the allele is _____.

(a) one　　　　　(b) two　　　　　(c) three　　　　　(d) four

Question 12

Identify the cyanobacterium that can fix atmospheric nitrogen.

(a) Spirulina　　　　　(b) Azospirillum　　　　　(c) Oscillatoria　　　　　(d) Spirogyra

Question 13

Spermiation is the process of the release of sperms from:

(a) Seminiferous tubules　　　　　(b) Vas deferens

(c) Epididymis　　　　　(d) Prostate gland

Question 14

Which one of the following is not a male accessory gland?

(a) Seminal vesicle　　　　　(b) Ampulla

(c) Prostate　　　　　(d) Bulbourethral gland

Question 15

Which of the following is a mass of finger like projections on the synergid wall?

(a) Egg　　　　　(b) Chalaza　　　　　(c) Micropylar　　　　　(d) Filiform apparatus

Question 16

How many chromosomes do drones of honeybee possess?

(a) 12　　　　　(b) 16　　　　　(c) 24　　　　　(d) 32

Question 17

A typical angiospermic anther possesses

(a) 4 lobes, 2 sporangia　(b) 4 lobes, 4 sporangia　(c) 2 lobes, 2 sporangia　(d) 2 lobes, 4 sporangia

Question 18

Which of the following statements is correct about a cistron?

(a) It is the non-coding DNA segment.

(b) It contains repetitive DNA sequences.

(c) It is a segment of DNA coding for a polypeptide.

(d) It is a segment of DNA that codes for a monopeptide.

Question 19

Which part of the flower do the tassels of the corn-cob represent?

(a) Petals　　　　　(b) Stigma

(c) Style　　　　　(d) Both style and stigma

Question 20

The transcriptionally active region of chromatin in a nucleus is:

(a) intron　　　　　(b) exon　　　　　(c) heterochromatin　　　　　(d) all of these

Question 21

At which stage of cell division does segregation of an independent pair of chromosomes occurs?

(a) Anaphase-I of Meiosis-I　　　　　(b) Prophase – I of Meiosis –I

(c) Anaphase-II of Meiosis-II　　　　　(d) Prophase-II of Meiosis-II

Question 22

Moss plants produce very large number of male gametes. These gametes are called

(a) Heterogametes　　　　　(b) Antherozoids　　　　　(c) Isogametes　　　　　(d) Egg

Question 23

A pea plant homozygous for axial flowers and constricted pods (AAii) is crossed with the pea plant homozygous for terminal flowers having inflated pods (aaII). The genotype of the parents would be

(a) Aaii x aaii　　　　　(b) aaIi x AaIi　　　　　(c) AAii x aaII　　　　　(d) AAII x aaii

Question 24

What type of sex-determination mechanisms the following cross show?

Female ZW and Male ZZ

(a) Male heterogamety
(b) Male homogamety
(c) Female homogamety
(d) Female heterogamety

Question 25

Sporopollenin is found in

(a) Integuments of ovule
(b) Intine
(c) Exine
(d) Anther

Question 26

At which ends do 'capping' and 'tailing' of mRNA occur respectively?

(a) 5′ and 3′
(b) 5′ and 5′
(c) 3′ and 3′
(d) 3′ and 5′

Question 27

Consider the template strand given below:

----A T G C A T G C A T A C-----

Write the sequence of RNA that will be transcribed from the above transcription unit along with its polarity.

(a) 3′ - U A C G U A C G U A U G –5′
(b) 5′ - U A C G U A C G U A U G – 3′
(c) 5′ - T A C G T A C G T A T G – 3′
(d) 3′ - T A C G T A C G T A T G – 5′

Question 28

Sexual reproduction in flowering plants was discovered by —

(a) Camerarius
(b) Nawaschin
(c) Strasburger
(d) Maheshwari

Question 29

Marchantia is a :

(a) Monoecious plant
(b) Homothallic plant
(c) Dioecious plant
(d) Bisexual plant

Question 30

The bacterium *Streptococcus* produces the enzyme

(a) Streptokinase
(b) Statin
(c) Lipase
(d) Chitin

Question 31

Which of the following is a better mode of reproduction?

(a) Sexual
(b) Asexual
(c) Both sexual and asexual
(d) Parthenocarpy

Question 32

Tendrils of Cucurbita and thorns of Bougainvillea are

(a) Analogous structures
(b) Homologous structures
(c) Vestigial organs
(d) Connecting links

Question 33

Who proposed the concept of Central Dogma?

(a) Meselson and Stahl
(b) Frederich Meischer
(c) Watson and Crick
(d) Francis Crick

Question 34

Which of the following is the terminal method to prevent pregnancy in humans?

(a) Condoms
(b) Saheli pills
(c) Tubectomy
(d) CuT

Question 35

Transcription of hnRNA is catalysed by

(a) DNA polymerase
(b) RNA polymerase
(c) DNA ligase
(d) Gyrase

Question 36

The phase that all organisms have to pass through before they can reproduce sexually is

(a) Juvenile phase
(b) Senescent phase
(c) Reproductive phase
(d) Menopausal phase

Question 37

Cucurbits are categorized as

(a) Dioecious   (b) Monoecious   (c) Hermaphrodites   (d) Parthenogenetic

Question 38

Which embryonic stage gets implanted in the uterine wall of a human female?

(a) Blastocyct   (b) Morula   (c) Blastomere   (d) Zygote

Question 39

Which of the following is a post-fertilisation event in flowering plants?

(a) Transfer of pollen grains   (b) Embryo development

(c) Formation of flower   (d) Formation of pollen grains

Question 40

Which of the following gases is not included in biogas?

(a) CH_4 (b) H_2S (c) CO_2 (d) H_2O

Question 41

Assertion : Fertilization is the fusion of male and female gametes.

Reason : Fertilization is followed by division of zygote multiple times to form the blastocyst.

(a) Both assertion and reason are true and reason is the correct explanation of assertion.

(b) Both assertion and reason are true, but reason is not the correct explanation of assertion.

(c) Assertion is true, but reason is false.

(d) Both assertion and reason are false.

Question 42

Assertion : Pollen grains are well preserved as fossils.

Reason : Exine of the pollen grain contains sporopollenin.

(a) Both assertion and reason are true and reason is the correct explanation of assertion.

(b) Both assertion and reason are true, but reason is not the correct explanation of assertion.

(c) Assertion is true, but reason is false.

(d) Both assertion and reason are false.

Question 43

Assertion : Pills contain a combination of estrogen and progesterone.

Reason : Pills are not safe to take.

(a) Both assertion and reason are true and reason is the correct explanation of assertion.

(b) Both assertion and reason are true, but reason is not the correct explanation of assertion.

(c) Assertion is true, but reason is false.

(d) Both assertion and reason are false.

Question 44

Assertion : Meiosis results in formation of two daughter cells.

Reason : Both the daughter cells are exactly same.

(a) Both assertion and reason are true and reason is the correct explanation of assertion.

(b) Both assertion and reason are true, but reason is not the correct explanation of assertion.

(c) Assertion is true, but reason is false.

(d) Both assertion and reason are false.

Question 45

Assertion : If dsDNA has 28% of cytosine, the amount of guanine will also be 28%.

Reason : According to Chargaff's rule, amount of guanine is always equal to amount of cytosine.

(a) Both assertion and reason are true and reason is the correct explanation of assertion.

(b) Both assertion and reason are true, but reason is not the correct explanation of assertion.

(c) Assertion is true, but reason is false.

(d) Both assertion and reason are false.

Question 46

Study the diagram given below and answer the questions that follow.

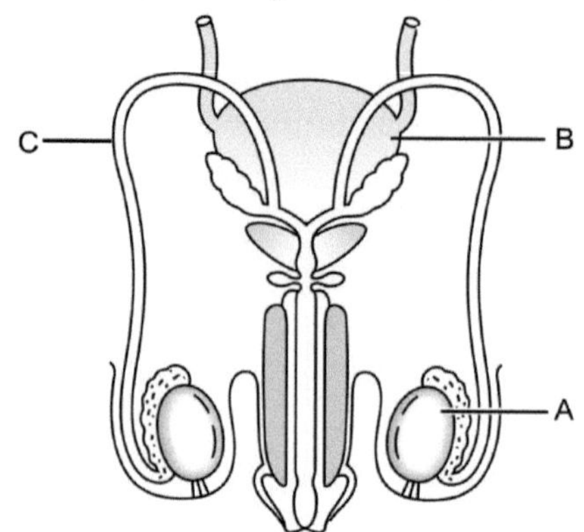

(i) 'A' represents

    (a) Seminal vesicle   (b) Vas deferens   (c) Epididymis   (d) Testis

(ii) Name the accessory gland 'B'.

    (a) Seminal vesicle   (b) Vas deferens   (c) Epididymis   (d) Testis

(iii) Name the organ 'C'.

    (a) Seminal vesicle   (b) Vas deferens   (c) Epididymis   (d) Testis

(iv) Which of the following hormone regulates Sertoli cells?

    (a) GH   (b) Oxytocin   (c) LH   (d) FSH

(v) Sertoli cells are present

    (a) outside seminiferous tubules   (b) in epididymis

    (c) in the lining of seminiferous tubules   (d) in the lining of epididymis

Question 47

Study the pedigree analysis given below and answer the questions that follow:

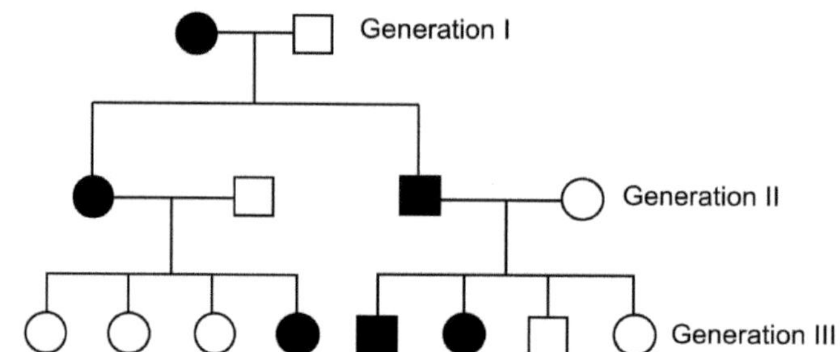

(i) The type of inheritance depicted here is:

    (a) Sex-linked dominant   (b) Sex-linked recessive

    (c) Autosomal dominant   (d) Autosomal recessive

(ii) The possible genotype of parents is

    (a) female – $X^d X^d$ and male – $X^d Y$ (b) female – $X^d X$ and male – $X^d Y$

    (c) female – $X^d X^d$ and male – $X Y$ (d) female – $X X$ and male – $X^d Y$

(iii) Which of the following disease shows this type of inheritance?

    (a) Down's syndrome   (b) Thalassemia

    (c) Sickle-cell anaemia   (d) Hemophilia

(iv) Sickle-cell anaemia is a result of ___________ mutation.

    (a) frameshift   (b) chromosomal   (c) point   (d) base

(v) A son receives X-chromosome from—

    (a) The mother   (b) The father

    (c) Both mother and father   (d) Either mother or father

Question 48

Study the diagram of biogas plant given below and answer the questions that follow.

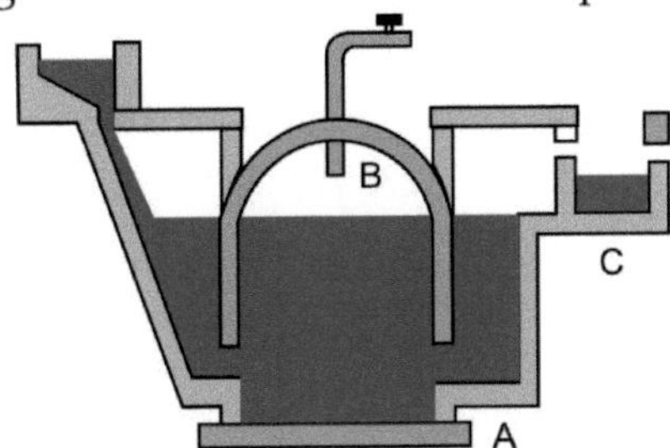

(i) The major constituents of biogas are:

(a) CH_4, CO_2 (b) C_2H_6, O_2 (c) CH_4, O_2 (d) C_2H_6, CO_2

(ii) The component labeled as 'A' is—

(a) Gas tank (b) Digester (c) Outlet (d) Inlet

(iii) The biogas plant is constructed—

(a) Under the ground (b) Above the ground

(c) On top of a building (d) Near a water source

(iv) The spent slurry is

(a) used as fuel (b) used as fertilizer

(c) is a waste (d) is reused to produce biogas

(v) The component labeled as 'B' is—

(a) Gas tank (b) Digester (c) Outlet (d) Inlet

Question 49

Read the passage given below and answer the questions that follow.

A couple cannot decide whether to have children or not since many members in the husband's family have been suffering from a debilitating genetic condition. They consult a doctor and he refers them to a geneticist. The geneticist asks them about their entire family history up to 5 generations and gives them the advice.

(i) The method that the geneticist used was—

(a) Blood tests (b) Pedigree analysis (c) Test crosses (d) Chromosomal tests

(ii) Which of the following symbols represents marriage?

(a) draw two circles joined by two lines (b) draw two squares joined by two lines

(c) draw a circle and a square joined by a line (d) draw a circle and square joined by two lines

(iii) The advantage of this method is—

(a) helps in genetic counselling

(b) shows origin of trait in family

(c) predicts harmful effects of marriage between close relatives

(d) All of these

(iv) The characters studied in this type of test is equivalent to—

(a) Quantitative trait (b) Mendelian trait

(c) Polygenic trait (d) Maternal trait

(v) A pair of contrasting characters is called—

(a) Phenotype (b) Genotype (c) Homozygosity (d) alleles

Question 50

Read the following passage and answer the questions that follow.

Urey & Miller tried to create in the laboratory the similar conditions which might have existed in early primitive atmosphere. A mixture of water vapours, methane, ammonia & hydrogen is exposed to electric discharge in a closed chamber, this fluid thus formed is allowed to stand for several week as a result, amino acids e.g. glycerine & alanine are formed from fluid. They suggested that electric discharge produced during lightening in primitive atmosphere of earth might have resulted in formation of organic compound.

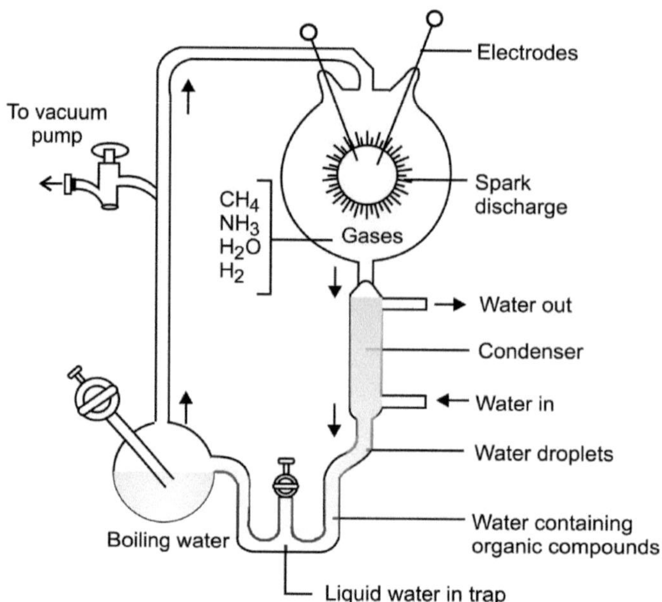

(i) Who were the two scientists that conducted an experiment to synthesise organic molecule abiotically?

   (a) Urey   (b) Miller   (c) Both (a) and (b)   (d) Stanley

(ii) The conclusion of this experiment by scientists was

   (a) Life originated through spontaneous generation

   (b) Life came from pre-existing life

   (c) Life came from pre-existing organic molecules

   (d) Life was created by God

(iii) The concept of this experiment is based on

   (a) Interaction of water, air and clay under intense heat

   (b) Effect of solar radiation on chemicals

   (c) Possible origin of life by combination of chemicals under suitable environmental conditions

   (d) Crystallization of chemicals

(iv) This experiment created primitive earth conditions. These conditions include

   (a) Low temperature, volcanic storms, atmosphere rich in oxygen

   (b) Low temperature, volcanic storms, reducing atmosphere

   (c) High temperature, volcanic storms, non-reducing atmosphere

   (d) High temperature, volcanic storms, reducing atmosphere

(v) Miller in his experiment, synthesized simple amino acid from _____________.

   (a) methane, ammonia, oxygen, nitrogen

   (b) hydrogen, methane, ammonia, water

   (c) ammonia, methane, carbon dioxide, oxygen

   (d) hydrogen, water, oxygen, helium

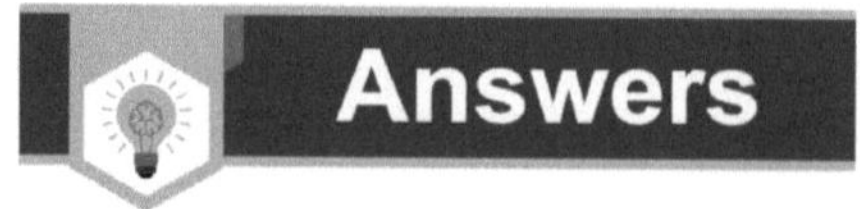

Answers

1. (a) Polyembryony

Explanation: Polyembryony is a situation in which a single fertilsed egg produces two or more embryos, resulting in identical twins in humans. Polyembryony is a common phenomena in many plant and animal species, and it happens frequently in the nine-banded armadillo, which normally has four identical offspring.

2. (b) flowers once in 12 years

Explanation: *Strobilanthes kunthiana* flowers once in 12 years.

3. (a) Failure of segregation of chromosomes

Explanation: In Anaphase stage of division, chromosomes are pulled by spindle fibres to opposite poles. This stage ensures equal segregation of chromosomes in the dividing cells. Failure of segregation would result in loss or gain of chromosomes.

4. (b) Lichens

Explanation: Lichens are the association between specific ascomycetes and certain genera of either green algae or cyanobacteria. Lichens can be used as an atmospheric pollution indicator. As they are sensitive (especially phycobiont) to oxides of nitrogen and sulphur, they do not grow in areas that are polluted, hence unable to synthesise organic food and do not grow well. Lepidoptera is an insect order. *Lycopersicon* is the scientific name of tomato. Lycopodium is a pteridophyte.

5. (a) Ampulla

Explanation: Fertilization can only take place when ovum and sperm are simultaneously transported to the ampulla of the fallopian tube.

6. (a) Charles Darwin

Explanation: Darwin noticed that all the life forms which exist have gradually evolved to themselves a fit for the natural conditions.

7. (b) they share a common ancestor

Explanation: The bones of forelimbs of whale, bat, cheetah, and man are similar in structure, but are different in functions. Such structures are called homologous organs.

8. (d) Translation

Explanation: *m*RNA is converted to *m*RNA after the process of transcription. The events that take place are collectively called post-transcriptional modifications. These include splicing, tailing and capping.

9. (a) AUG

Explanation: AUG is a start codon whereas others are stop codons.

10. (d) Sex-linked recessive

Explanation: Since female is a carrier, it means that only one X chromosome carries the defective gene. Hence, it is a recessive disorder. Also, since the males having defective X chromosome will be affected, it is sex-linked recessive disorder.

11. (a) one

Explanation: According to Hardy Weinberg principle, the total sum of all the frequencies of the allele is one. It shows that the gene pool remains the same or constant, i.e. one. Hence, it can be also termed as genetic equilibrium.

12. (c) Oscillatoria

Explanation: Oscillatoria fixes atmospheric nitrogen and adds organic matter to the soil.

13. (a) Seminiferous tubules

Explanation: The process of spermatogenesis (formation of sperm cells) takes place in the seminiferous tubules. After the sperms are formed (spermiogenesis), their heads get embedded in the sertoli cells present inside the seminiferous tubules. Spermiation is the process of release of sperms from seminiferous tubules.

14. (b) Ampulla

Explanation: The seminal vesicle, prostate and bulbourethral gland are the accessory glands of male while ampulla is a part of female oviducts/fallopian tubes which is a female accessory duct.

15. (d) Filiform apparatus

Explanation: Filiform apparatus is a mass of finger like projections of the wall of the synergid cells into the cytoplasm. It may or may not be present. It guides the male gametophytes during fertilization.

16. (b) 16

Explanation: Drones possess 16 chromosomes. The process of mitosis is involved in the production of sperms.

17. (d) 2 lobes, 4 sporangia

Explanation: Anther is composed of two anther sacs or lobes. Each lobe consists of two theca. In each lobe two microsporangia are present.

18. (c) It is a segment of DNA coding for a polypeptide

Explanation: A cistron is a segment of DNA coding for a polypeptide

19. (d) Both style and stigma

Explanation: The tassels of corn cob represent the female part of the flower which is style and stigma. The corn cob plant has female flower clusters arranged on the stem which means it only blooms female flowers. These flowers are covered with spath. The style of these flowers is very long hence this overhang from the flowers in the form of a bunch which are known as tassels. The tassels are present at the terminal or end point (apex) of the corn stalk. These tassels have stigma on their terminal point. The tassels are long as they are involved in the production of large no. of pollen grains. These help to trap the pollen in the wind flow for a wider dispersion and future progeny.

20. (b) exon

Explanation: Exons are the coding regions of RNA which are present along with the non-coding regions called the introns. Heterochromatin are the regions of chromatin that are densely packed. These contain inactive genes.

21. (a) Anaphase-I of Meiosis-I

Explanation: Anaphase-I begins when the two chromosomes of each bivalent (tetrad) separate and start moving towards opposite poles of the cell as a result of the action of the spindle. This results in the independent segregation of the pair of chromosomes.

22. (b) The gametes are called antherozoids

Explanation: Mosses are bryophytes and they need water for fertilisation. During the transfer of male gametes, many of them are destroyed or lost. Thus, moss plants produce very large number of male gametes to compensate for the loss during transport. These male gametes are called antherozoids.

23. (c) AAii × aaII

Explanation :

Parents	Axial flowers and constricted pods	×	Terminal flowers and inflated pods
Genotype	AAii		aaII
Gametes	Ai		aI
F1 generation genotype		AaIi	
Phenotype	All are axial flowers with inflated pods		

24. (d) Female heterogamety

Explanation: In such type of sex determination mechanism the females have one Z and one W chromosome whereas males have a pair of Z chromosomes.

25. (c) Exine

Explanation: Sporopollenin is the most resistant organic material in nature. It is present in the exine of pollen grains.

26. (a) 5′ and 3′

Explanation: Capping takes place at the 5′ end and tailing takes place at the 3′ end of the mRNA transcript.

27. (b) 5′ - U A C G U A C G U A U G – 3′

Explanation: The RNA product is complementary to the template strand and is almost identical to the other DNA strand, called the nontemplate (or coding) strand. However, there is one important difference: in the newly made RNA, all of the T nucleotides are replaced with U nucleotides.

28. (c) Strasburger

Explanation: Strasburger first discovered syngamy and monosporic embryo sac in angiosperms.

29. (c) Dioecious plant

Explanation: Marchantia can reproduce sexually or asexually. In sexual reproduction, sperm from the antheridia fertilizes an egg in the archegonia. These antheridia and archegonia are the special gametophyte stalks which are present on the separate thalli. So, Marchantia is considered as a heterothallic plant because these plants are dioecious.

30. (a) Streptokinase

Explanation: *Streptococcus* bacterium produces streptokinase. It is used for removing clots from the blood vessels in a patient suffering from myocardial infarction or in a heart patient.

31. (a) Sexual

Explanation: The sexual mode of reproduction is better because it involves two parents. This introduces variations in the offspring which help in evolution and survival in the changing environment.

32. (b) Homologous structures

Explanation: Tendrils of Cucurbita and thorns of Bougainvillea are both stem modifications. They both arise from the axillary positions of the stem but perform different functions – tendrils help in climbing and thorns help in protection. Thus, they are considered homologous structures.

33. (d) Francis Crick

Explanation: Central dogma of life describes the flow of information from the DNA to protein through RNA. It was discovered by Francis Crick.

34. (c) Tubectomy

Explanation: In tubectomy, a small part of the fallopian tubes is cut and tied up through a small incision in the abdomen or the vagina.

35. (b) RNA polymerase

Explanation: The enzyme RNA polymerase II transcribes *hn*RNA. *hn*RNA stands for heterogenous nuclear RNA. The process it undergoes before processed into *m*RNA is capping. The *hn*RNA needs to undergo changes for converting into functional RNA. It contains both exons and introns. The exons are coding segments whereas the introns are non- functional sequences.

36. (a) Juvenile phase

Explanation: To sexually reproduce, all the organisms have to grow and become mature. This phase is called juvenile phase.

37. (b) Monoecious

Explanation: Monoecious or homothallic organisms bear both male and female gametes in one individual. Dioecious or heterothallic are those organisms in which male and female gametes are carried by different individuals.

38. (a) Blastocyct

Explanation: The morula divides continuously to form a large mass of cells called blastocyst. It has an outer layer called the trophoblast and inner cell mass. The trophoblast gets attached to the endometrium and the inner cell mass develops into the embryo.

39. (b) Embryo development

Explanation: Events in sexual reproduction after the fertilization are called post-fertilization events. After fertilization, a diploid zygote is formed in all sexually reproducing organisms. Zygote divides by mitosis and gives rise to the proembryo and subsequently to the globular, heart shaped mature embryo. The process of development of an embryo from the zygote is called embryogenesis.

40. (d) H_2O

Explanation: Certain bacteria produce a mixture of gases such as methane, hydrogen sulphide and carbon dioxide. These gases form biogas and can be used as a source of energy as it is inflammable.

41. (b) Both assertion and reason are true, but reason is not the correct explanation of assertion.

Explanation: Fertilization is important for sexual reproduction. The male gamete reaches the female reproductive system and fuses with it to form the zygote. Zygote, then, undergoes mitotic division multiple times to form the blastocyst. Thus, both assertion and reason are true, but reason is not the correct explanation of assertion.

42. (a) Both assertion and reason are true and reason is the correct explanation of assertion.

Explanation: Sporopollenin is one of the most resistant organic material. It can withstand high temperature, strong acids and alkali. Thus, both assertion and reason are true and reason is the correct explanation of assertion.

43. (c) Assertion is true, but reason is false.

Explanation: Birth control pills contain a combination of estrogen and progesterone. These work by preventing ovulation. These pills have few side-effects but are safe to take. Thus, assertion is true but reason is false.

44. (d) Both assertion and reason are false.

Explanation: Meiosis results in formation of four haploid daughter cells which differ from each other. This is because crossing over during division leads to recombination. Thus, both assertion and reason are false.

45. (a) Both assertion and reason are true and reason is the correct explanation of assertion.

Explanation: According to Chargaff's rule, [A + T] = [G + C]. Thus, both assertion and reason are true and reason is the correct explanation of assertion.

46. (i) (d) Testis

(ii) (a) Seminal vesicle

(iii) (b) Vas deferens

(iv) (d) FSH

Explanation: Follicle stimulating hormone (FSH) stimulates Sertoli cells to secrete factors which help in spermiogenesis.

(v) (c)   in lining of seminiferous tubules

Explanation: Each seminiferous tubule is lined on its inside by Sertoli cells and spermatogonia.

47. (i) (b)   Sex-linked recessive

Explanation: Since the female, having XX chromosomes, is a carrier it is implied that only one of the X chromosome carries the defective gene. So, the disease is recessive as it does not express itself in heterozygous condition. Some of the males which will have this defective X chromosome will be affected as males have only one X chromosome (XY). Thus, the disease is sex-linked recessive.

(ii) (a)   female – $X^d X^d$ and male – $X^d Y$

Explanation: Since both the progenies of Generation 1 are affected, both the parents must have the defective gene. Also, the male is not affected, the defective gene must be present on the X chromosome. The female is affected so, both the X chromosomes are defective.

(iii) (d)   Hemophilia

Explanation: Hemophilia is also a sex-linked recessive disorder.

(iv) (c)   Point

Explanation: Sickle cell anaemia is due to point mutation at the sixth codon of the beta-globin chain of haemoglobin. This leads to the substitution of valine in place of glutamic acid.

(v) (a)   The mother

Explanation: Males have the sex chromosomes XY. The Y chromosome is passed on by the father and the X chromosome is passed on by the mother.

48. (i) (a) CH_4, CO_2

Explanation: Biogas is a mixture of inflammable gases like methane, carbon dioxide, etc.

(ii) (b)   Digester

Explanation: The digester contains the microbes, methanogens, which act on the cow dung in the slurry to release biogas.

(iii) (a)   Under the ground

Explanation: The biogas plant has a concrete tank which is fixed 10-15 feet deep in the ground. Only the inlet and outlet ports are made above the ground.

(iv) (b)   used as fertilizer

Explanation: The spent slurry collected in the outlet port is used as fertilizer as it is rich in organic substances.

(v) (a)   Gas tank

Explanation: The tank of the biogas plant has a floating cover which rises on production of gas in the tank.

49. (i) (b)   Pedigree analysis

Explanation: Pedigree analysis is the study of inheritance of genetic traits over the generations in families. It predicts the occurrence of genetic disorders in future generations.

(ii) (c)   draw a circle and a square joined by a line

Explanation: A box represent the male and a circle represents the female in pedigree chart. When they are linked with a line, it depicts mating between the two.

(iii) (d)   All of these

(iv) (b)   Mendelian trait

Explanation: Pedigree analysis is based on mendelian form of inheritance. It follows the three Mendelian laws: Law of dominance, Law of independent assortment and Law of segregation.

(v) (d)   alleles

Explanation: Alleles are a pair of contrasting traits. Mendel called them 'factors' before the term was coined.

50. (i) (c)   Both (a) and (b)

Explanation: Urey & Miller tried to create in the laboratory the similar conditions which might have existed in early primitive atmosphere.

(ii) (c)   Life came from pre-existing organic molecules

Explanation: Urey and Miller had concluded that life originated from pre-existing non-living organic molecules and their formation was preceded by chemical evolution.

(iii) (c) Possible origin of life by combination of chemicals under suitable environmental conditions

(iv) (d) High temperature, volcanic storms, reducing atmosphere

(v) (b) Hydrogen, methane, ammonia, water

Explanation: Hydrogen, methane, ammonia and water was kept in a closed flask with electrical discharge. He produced a small living atmosphere in a lab experiment. The flask was maintained at 800°C.

❑❑

4 Sample Paper

Biology

Answer the questions given below by choosing the correct option.

Question 1

What is phase when the organism is old enough to reproduce known as?

(a) Juvenile phase

(b) Vegetative phase

(c) Senescence

(d) Reproductive phase

Question 2

Sexual reproduction in flowering plants was discovered by—

(a) Camerarius
(b) Nawaschin
(c) Strasburger
(d) Maheshwari

Question 3

What should be the phenotype of the F_1 progeny produced by a cross between tall and dwarf true-breeding garden pea plants?

(a) Tall plants

(b) Dwarf plants

(c) Intermediate plants

(d) Mixed population of tall and dwarf plants

Question 4

Clitoris in females is—

(a) homologous to penis

(b) analogous to penis

(c) functional penis in female

(d) non-functional

Question 5

Wings of bat and bird are—

(a) Homologous but not analogous

(b) Neither homologous nor analogous

(c) Analogous but not homologous

(d) Vestigial

Question 6

Coacervates were experimentally produced by—

(a) Oparin and Sidney Fox

(b) Fischer and Huxley

(c) Jacob and Monod

(d) Urey and Miller

Question 7

Yeast is used in the production of—

(a) Citric acid and Lactic acid

(b) Lipase and Pectinase

(c) Beer

(d) Cheese and Butter

Question 8

What is the most important event in sexual reproduction?

(a) Fusion of gametes

(b) Secondary sexual organs

(c) Temperature

(d) Environmental factors

Question 9

In which of the following highest number of chromosomes found?

(a) Dog
(b) Human
(c) Rice
(d) Ophioglossum

Question 10

Analogous organs arise due to—

(a) Divergent evolution

(b) Artificial selection

(c) Genetic drift

(d) Convergent evolution

Question 11

The permissible use of the technique amniocentesis is for—

(a) detecting any genetic abnormality

(b) detecting sex of the unborn foetus

(c) artificial insemination

(d) transfer of embryo into the uterus of a surrogate mother

Question 12

Corpus luteum secretes—

(a) LH

(b) Estrogen

(c) Progesterone

(d) FSH

Question 13

The unit of natural selection is—

(a) an individual

(b) a species

(c) a germ

(d) a population

Question 14

The first genetic material is—

(a) Protein

(b) Carbohydrates

(c) DNA

(d) RNA

Question 15

Synergids are—

(a) Haploid

(b) Diploid

(c) Triploid

(d) Tetraploid

Question 16

In the absence of acrosome, the sperm—

(a) Cannot get food

(b) Cannot swim

(c) Cannot penetrate the egg

(d) Cannot get energy

Question 17

Which of the following genotypes show the heterozygous condition ?

(a) Rr

(b) RR

(c) rr

(d) None of these

Question 18

Epidermis, endothecium, middle layers, tapetum are:

(a) Pollen sac layers

(b) walls of anther

(c) Pollen grain layers

(d) epidermal layers

Question 19

Which one of the following is the most widely accepted method of contraception in India at present ?

(a) Cervical caps

(b) Tubectomy

(c) Diaphragms

(d) IUD's (Intra Uterine Devices)

Question 20

The sugar present in milk is—

(a) Glucose

(b) Lactose

(c) Fructose

(d) Sucrose

Question 21

Identify the odd from the following—

(a) Labia minora

(b) Fimbriae

(c) Infundibulum

(d) Isthmus

Question 22

Genotypic ratio of a monohybrid cross is—

(a) 5 : 1

(b) 3 : 1

(c) 1 : 2 : 1

(d) 1 : 1

Question 23

Meiosis occurs in—

(a) endosperm cells

(b) intercalary meristems

(c) apical meristems

(d) spore mother cells

Question 24

Theory of spontaneous generation was proposed by—

(a) Spallanzani

(b) Aristotle

(c) F. Redi

(d) Louis Pasteur

Question 25

Abiogenesis occurred about __________ billion years ago.

(a) 1.2

(b) 1.5

(c) 2.5

(d) 3.5

Question 26

Chromosomal basis of inheritance was established by __________ .

(a) McClung

(b) Henking

(c) Morgan

(d) Sutton and Boveri

Question 27

Methanogens do not produce—

(a) oxygen

(c) hydrogen sulphide

(b) methane

(d) carbon dioxide

Question 28

In angiosperms __________ lead to the formation of a mature male gametophyte from a pollen mother cell.

(a) two meiotic divisions

(b) one meiotic and two mitotic division

(c) one mitotic and two meiotic division

(d) a single mitotic division

Question 29

The word gene for Mendelian factor was introduced by __________ in 1909.

(a) Watson and Crick

(b) Sutton and Boveri

(c) Johannsen

(d) Punnett

Question 30

__________ comprises the egg apparatus.

(a) Polar nuclei

(b) Antipodal cells

(c) Egg cell and synergids

(d) Male gametes

Question 31

What is each copy of the duplicated chromosome called?

(a) Chromatid

(b) Chromomere

(c) Kinetochore

(d) Chromonema

Question 32

__________ is the phenomenon wherein, the ovary develops into a fruit without fertilisation.

(a) Parthenocarpy

(b) Apomixis

(c) Sexual reproduction

(d) None of these

Question 33

__________ carried out experiments to study linkage in *Drosophila*.

(a) Morgan

(b) Correns

(c) Boveri and Brauer

(d) Flemming

Question 34

Larger nucleus in a pollen grain is called __________ .

(a) callus

(b) generative nucleus

(c) vegetative nucleus

(d) none of these

Question 35

Which one is the correct statement amongst the following ?

(a) Dioecious (hermaphrodite) organisms are found only in animals.

(b) Dioecious organisms are found only in plants.

(c) Dioecious organisms are found in both plants and animals.

(d) Dioecious organisms are found only in vertebrates.

Question 36

Diaphragms are contraceptive device used by females. Which one is the correct option from the statement given below?

(i)   They are introduced into the uterus.

(ii) They are placed to cover the cervical region.

(iii) They act as physical barrier for sperm entry.

(iv) They act as spermicidal agents.

(a) (i) and (ii)

(b) (i) and (iii)

(c) (ii) and (iii)

(d) (iii) and (iv)

Question 37

Match the following and choose the correct options:

Column I	Column II
(A) Trophoblast	(i) Embedding of blastocyst in the endometrium
(B) Cleavage	(ii) Group of cells that would differentiate as embryo
(C) Inner cell mass	(iii) Outer layer of blastocyst attached to the endometrium
(D) Implantation	(iv) Mitotic division of zygote

Options:

(a) A-(ii), B-(i), C-(iii), D-(iv)

(b) A-(iii), B-(iv), C-(ii), D-(i)

(c) A-(iii), B-(i), C-(ii), D-(iv)

(d) A-(ii), B-(iv), C-(iii), D-(i)

Question 38

Match the contraceptive methods given under column I with their examples given under column II and select the correct option.

	Column I (Contraceptive methods)		Column II (Examples)
A	Barriers	(i)	Tubectomy and vasectomy
B	IUDs	(ii)	Spermicidal jelly and foam
C	Chemical	(iii)	Vaults and cervical cap
D	Sterilisation	(iv)	Multiload 375

(a) A-(ii), B-(iv), C-(i), D-(iii)

(b) A-(iii), B-(iv), C-(i), D-(ii)

(c) A-(iii), B-(iv), C-(ii), D-(i)

(d) A-(ii), B-(i), C-(iii), D-(iv)

Question 39

Identify the odd one.

(a) Vaults

(b) Condoms

(c) Diaphragms

(d) Periodic abstinence

Question 40

Find the odd one out.

(a) Clitoris

(b) Mons pubis

(c) Lactiferous duct

(d) Labia majora

Question 41

Assertion : Gynoecium consists of pistil.

Reason   : It represents the male reproductive part in flowering plants.

(a) Both assertion and reason are true and reason is the correct explanation of assertion.

(b) Both assertion and reason are true, but reason is not the correct explanation of assertion.

(c) Assertion is true, but reason is false.

(d) Both assertion and reason are false.

Question 42

Assertion : Corpus luteum is produced by Graafian follicle after ovulation.

Reason   : It secretes oestrogen which is necessary to maintain pregnancy.

(a) Both assertion and reason are true and reason is the correct explanation of assertion.
(b) Both assertion and reason are true, but reason is not the correct explanation of assertion.
(c) Assertion is true, but reason is false.
(d) Both assertion and reason are false.

Question 43

Assertion : A person should be considered reproductively healthy if he or she has healthy reproductive organs but is emotionally imbalanced.

Reason : This statement about reproductive health was not given by the WHO.

(a) Both assertion and reason are true and reason is the correct explanation of assertion.
(b) Both assertion and reason are true, but reason is not the correct explanation of assertion.
(c) Assertion is true, but reason is false.
(d) Both assertion and reason are false.

Question 44

Assertion : Test cross is the cross between the F_1 progeny and either of the parent types.

Reason : Back cross is the cross between F_1 progeny and one of its parent plants.

(a) Both assertion and reason are true and reason is the correct explanation of assertion.
(b) Both assertion and reason are true, but reason is not the correct explanation of assertion.
(c) Assertion is true, but reason is false.
(d) Both assertion and reason are false.

Question 45

Assertion : Nuclear endosperm is formed by subsequent nuclear division without wall formation.

Reason : Coconut is an example of such endosperm where the endosperm remains nuclear throughout the development of the fruit.

(a) Both assertion and reason are true and reason is the correct explanation of assertion.
(b) Both assertion and reason are true, but reason is not the correct explanation of assertion.
(c) Assertion is true, but reason is false.
(d) Both assertion and reason are false.

Question 46

Study the diagram given below and answer the questions that follow:

An assignment on sewage treatment plant (STP) to study the microbial load. It was assigned to Saurin, a M.Sc. Student. He made of simplified figure of the STP for his project after visiting such plant in his locality.

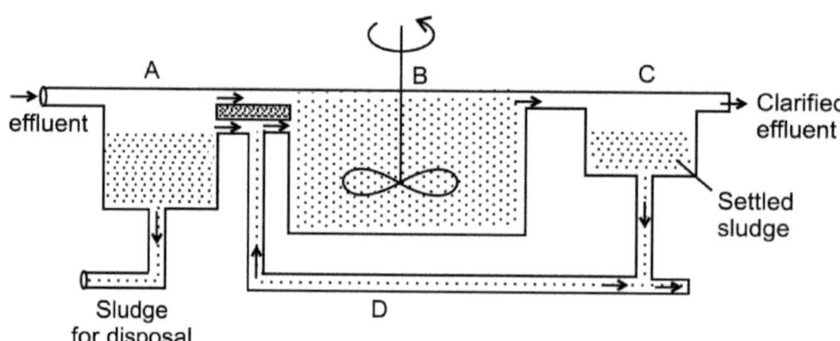

(i) A denotes:
  (a) aeration tank
  (b) primary settling tank
  (c) secondary settling tank
  (d) sludge digester

(ii) What does D denotes in the figure?
  (a) Primary sludge
  (b) Primary effluent
  (c) Activated sludge
  (d) Secondary effluent

(iii) Which of the following is correct regarding the sludge release from A?
  (a) It is formed after primary treatment
  (b) It does not require aeration
  (c) It possess flocs of decomposer microbes
  (d) It is used in landfills

(iv) What are flocs?

(a) Masses of fungi   (b) Masses of algae   (c) Masses of animals   (d) Masses of bacteria

(v) Which of the following is not considered as microorganisms?

(a) Bacteriophage   (b) *Streptococcus*   (c) Porphyra   (d) *Staphylococcus*

Question 47

Read the details and answer the questions that follow:

A technique known as amniocentesis is used to determine fetal abnormalities. This test is based on the chromosomal pattern in amniotic fluid. However, this technique is legally banned now.

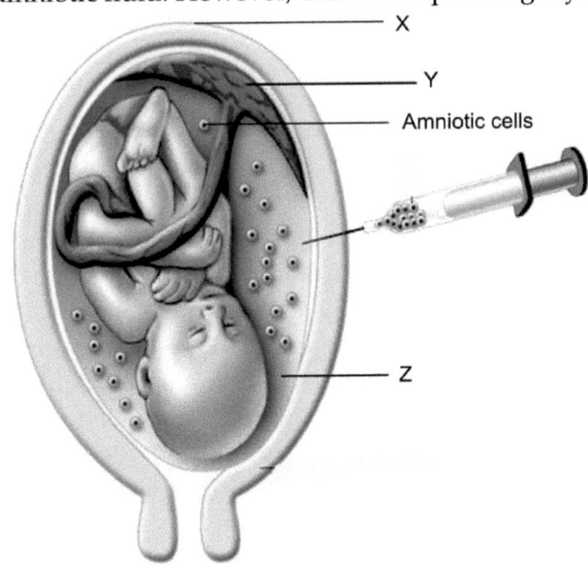

(i) Identify X and Y.

	X	Y
(a)	Amnion	Chorion
(b)	Uterine wall	Placenta
(c)	Placenta	Uterine wall
(d)	Uterine wall	Amnion

(ii) What is the function of Z?

(a) Z is an amniotic fluid which prevents dessication of an embryo.

(b) Z is yolk sac which functions as site of early blood cell formation.

(c) Z is amnion which takes part in placenta formation.

(d) None of these

(iii) Which of the following disease cannot be diagnosed by amniocentesis?

(a) Down's syndrome   (b) Turner's syndrome

(c) Jaundice   (d) Klinefelter's syndrome

(iv) Which of these is a non invasive technique of detecting fetal disorder?

(a) Fetoscopy   (b) Amniocentesis

(c) Chorionic villi sampling   (d) Ultrasound imaging

(v) Abortion can be safely done for about ___________ weeks of pregnancy.

(a) 4   (b) 12   (c) 8-10   (d) 15-18

Question 48

Observe the diagram given below and answer the questions that follows:

P	i	P	o	z	y	a

(i) Lac operon is an example of

(a) only positive regulation   (b) only negative regulation

(c) both positive and negative regulation   (d) cometines positive sometimes negative

(ii) What does the structural gene (y) of a lac operon code for?
  (a) β-galactosidase (b) Transacetylase   (c) Permease   (d) Glucagon

(iii) The sequence of the structural gene in the lac operon is
  (a) Lac Z–Lac Z–Lac Y   (b) Lac Z–Lac Y–Lac A
  (c) Lac Z–Lac A–Lac Y   (d) Lac A–Lac Y–Lac Z

(iv) Lac operon will be turned on when
  (a) Lactose is less than glucose   (b) Lactose is less in the medium
  (c) Lactose is more than glucose   (d) Glucose is enough in the medium

(v) In Lac operon, the gene product of Lac A gene is:
  (a) Beta-galactoside permease   (b) Beta-galactosidase transacetylase
  (c) Beta galactosidase   (d) Beta-galactosidase isomerase

Question 49

Read the following and answer the following questions:

An operon is a cluster of bacterial genes along with an adjacent promoter that controls the transcription of those genes.

In *E. coli*, and many other bacteria, genes encoding several different proteins may be located on a single transcription unit called an operon. The genes in an operon share the same transcriptional regulation, but are translated individually. Eukaryotes generally do not group genes together as operons (exception is *C. elegans* and a few other species). *E. coli* encounters many different sugars in its environment. These sugars, such as lactose and glucose, require different enzymes for their metabolism. Whenever glucose is present, *E. coli* metabolizes it before using alternative energy sources such as lactose, arabinose, galactose, and maltose. Only when the supply of glucose has been exhausted does RNA polymerase start to transcribe the lac genes efficiently, which allows E. coli to metabolize lactose. Three of the enzymes for lactose metabolism are grouped in the lac operon: *lacZ, lacY,* and *lacA*. In the presence of lactose and absence of glucose, cyclic AMP (cAMP) joins with a catabolite activator protein that binds to the lac promoter and facilitates the transcription of the lac operon.

(i) How many structural genes are present in a lac operon?
  (a) One   (b) Five   (c) Three   (d) Seven

(ii) In the presence of lactose, how long does it take for the lac operon to be expressed?
  (a) When lactose equals glucose concentration
  (b) When glucose is more than lactose concentration
  (c) As long as lactose is more than glucose concentration
  (d) As long as lactose is more than galactose concentration

(iii) Which of these acts as an inducer of the lac operon?
  (a) Allolactose   (b) Lactose   (c) Galactose   (d) Glucose

(iv) In a cell as per the Operon Concept, the regulator gene governs the chemical reactions by:
  (a) Inhibiting the substrate in the reaction   (b) Inhibiting migration of mRNA into cytoplasm
  (c) mRNA transcription inhibited   (d) Enzyme-reaction inactivation

(v) The following statements are drawn as conclusions from the graph given below:

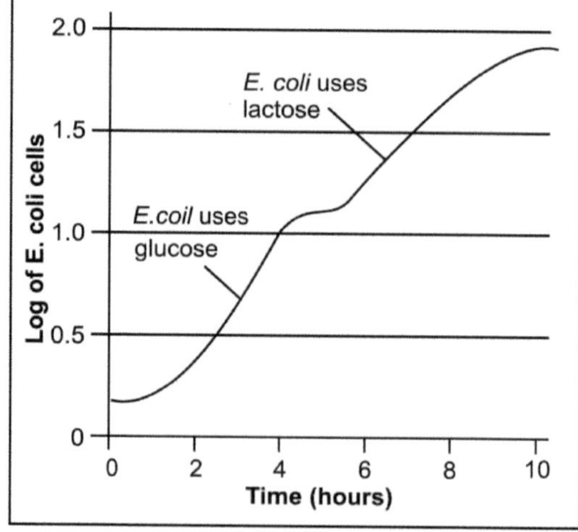

I. When grown in the presence of two substrates, *E. coli* uses the preferred substrate (in this case glucose) until it is depleted. Then, enzymes needed for the metabolism of the second substrate are expressed and growth resumes, although at a slower rate

II. When grown in the presence of two substrates, *E. coli* uses both the substrates equally.

III. When grown in the presence of two substrates, *E. coli* uses the less preferred substrate (in this case glucose) until it is depleted. Then, enzymes needed for the metabolism of the second substrate are expressed and growth resumes, although at a faster rate.

IV. When grown in the presence of two substrates, *E. coli* uses only one substrate.

Choose from below the correct alternative.

(a) Only I is true

(b) I, and IV are true

(c) III and II are true

(d) I and III are true

Question 50

Read the following and answer the following questions:

Gregor Johann Mendel proposed the law of inheritance or Mendel's law of inheritance after conducting several experiments on the garden pea plants. This includes three laws that are the law of dominance, the law of segregation and the law of independent assortment. More and more studies and discoveries were made on genetics after Mendel's studies. However, regularities of his experiment are applied only to the organisms he consciously chose for his experiments. These laws do not explain some pattern of genetic inheritance. Apart from these laws, there are several deviations. The principle of independent assortment doesn't apply if the genes are close together (or linked) on a chromosome. Also, alleles do not always interact in a standard dominant/recessive way, particularly if they are co-dominant or have differences in expressivity or penetrance.

(i) Mendel used _______________ for his experiments.

(a) *Pisum sativum*   (b) *Pisum album*   (c) *Oryza sativa*   (d) *Oryza orientalis*

(ii) In what mode of inheritance, the F_1 progeny exhibit characteristics of both the parents?

(a) Complete dominance

(b) Incomplete dominance

(c) Co-dominance

(d) Multiple allelism

(iii) ABO blood grouping in humans is an instance of________ .

(a) complete dominance

(b) incomplete dominance

(c) co-dominance

(d) pseudoscience

(iv) In incomplete dominance____________________ .

(a) Phenotype of both allele is expressed

(b) Phenotype of only one allele is expressed

(c) Phenotype of neither of the alleles are expressed

(d) Phenotype of both allele is partially expressed

(v) Unlike Mendel's pea plants, humans don't come in two clear-cut "tall" and "short" varieties. In fact, they don't even come in four heights, or eight, or sixteen. Instead, it's possible to get humans of many different heights, and height can vary in increments of inches or fractions of inches.

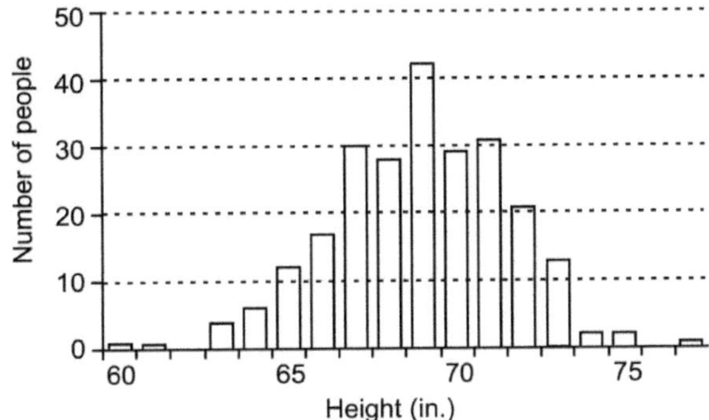

Figure: Histogram showing height in inches of male high school seniors in a sample group.

Skin colour, eye colour, and adult height are examples of ....in humans.

(a) Polygenic traits

(b) Co-dominance

(c) Incomplete dominance

(d) Complete dominance

Answers

1. (d) Reproductive phase

   Explanation: The phase when it is growing is known as the juvenile phase or the vegetative phase (in plants). The phase after that when the reproductive organs in the organism matures is known as the reproductive phase. Senescence is the phase when the plant starts deteriorating as it grows old and finally dies.

2. (a) Camerarius

   Explanation: Camerarius – He first discovered sexual reproduction in plants.

   Nawaschin – He first discovered triple fusion and double fertilization in angiosperms.

   Strasburger – He first discovered syngamy and monosporic embryo sac in angiosperms.

   Maheshwari – He first discovered the lab to land habit in plants.

3. (a) Tall plants

   Explanation: Tall plants are dominant over dwarf plants. Being true-breeding parents, the offsprings will all be heterozygous. Moreover, hence phenotypically, all of them will be tall.

4. (a) homologous to penis

   Explanation: A small erectile organ, the clitoris, lies at the anterior junction of the labia minora. It is homologous to the penis in the male but is very small and solid, having no passage through it. It consists of a short shaft with erectile tissue.

5. (c) Analogous but not homologous

   Explanation: Birds and bats did not inherit wings from a common ancestor with wings, but they did inherit forelimb from a common ancestor with forelimbs.

6. (a) Oparin and Sidney Fox

   Explanation: Oparin and Sidney Fox held that large organic molecules synthesized abiotically on primitive earth later came together spontaneously and due to intermolecular attraction, formed large colloidal aggregates called coacervates.

7. (c) Beer

   Explanation: Yeast (*Sacchromyees cerevisae*) is used to produce beer as it does fermentation of extract of barley.

8. (b) Fusion of gametes

   Explanation: Fertilization is the most important event in sexual reproduction. It is the process of fusion of two haploid gametes of different sex, forming one single diploid zygote. It is also known as syngamy.

9. (d) Ophioglossum

   Explanation: Ophioglossum has 1,440 chromosomes, the highest number of any organism known to science.

10. (d) Convergent evolution

    Explanation: The organs which have similar functions but are different in their structure and origin are known as analogous organs, which is the result of convergent evolution.

11. (a) detecting any genetic abnormality

    Explanation: Amniocentesis is a technique in which the amniotic fluid can be analysed to detect any genetic abnormality. An unfortunate and illegal use is analysis of amniotic fluid to detect sex of unborn child.

12. (c) Progesterone

    Explanation: Corpus leuteum secretes a large amount of progesterone for the proliferation and maintenance of the endometrium for the implantaion of fertilised ovums.

13. (a) an individual

    Explanation: Natural selection is gradual, a non-random process by which biological traits become either more or less common. The term was popularised by Charles Darwin. The unit of natural selection is an individual since genes work at an individual level.

14. (d) RNA

    Explanation: RNA was considered to be the first genetic material and there is a variety of evidence that suggests that the essential life processes revolve around RNA like metabolism, translations all use RNA as a catalyst. Being the catalyst it was reactive and hence unstable to be served as the genetic material, therefore, DNA evolved from RNA with structural and chemical modification to make it more stable.

15. (a) Haploid

Explanation: Synergids are haploid in nature as it is formed from the mother gametophyte by the meiosis.

16. (c) Cannot penetrate the egg

Explanation: Acrosome reaction is to help the sperm get through the egg's protective coat and to allow the plasma membranes of the sperm and egg to fuse.

17. (a) Rr

Explanation: Two different alleles show heterozygous condition (Rr).

18. (b) walls of anther

19. (d) IUD's (Intra Uterine Devices)

Explanation: Intra Uterine Devices (IUD), are inserted in the uterus through vagina which increases phagocytosis of sperm and Cu^{2+} ions suppress sperm mobility and their fertilisation capacity.

20. (b) Lactose

Explanation: Lactose is the milk sugar which make up around 2-8% of milk by weight.

21. (a) Labia minora

Explanation: Labia minora is the part of female genital while rest are the parts of oviduct or fallopian tube.

22. (c) 1 : 2 : 1

Explanation: 1 : 2 : 1 is a monohybrid genotypic ratio.

3 : 1 is monohybrid phenotypic ratio

1 : 1 is monohybrid test cross ratio

23. (d) spore mother cells

Explanation: In meiosis single cell divides two times to produce four haploid cells, genetically distinct from parent cell.

24. (b) Aristotle

Explanation: The Greek philosopher Aristotle was one of the earliest recorded scholars to articulate the theory of spontaneous generation, the notion that life can arise from non-living matter. Aristotle proposed that life arose from non-living material if the material contained pneuma ("vital heat").

25. (d) 3.5

Explanation: Abiogenesis, the idea that life arose from non-living more than 3.5 billion years ago on Earth. Abiogenesis proposes that the first life-forms generated were very simple and through a gradual process became increasingly complex.

26. (d) Sutton and Boveri

Explanation: Walter Sutton and Theodor Boveri are credited with developing the Chromosomal Theory of Inheritance, which states that chromosomes carry the unit of heredity (genes).

27. (a) oxygen

Explanation: Methanogens are obligate anaerobes, which produce methane, hydrogen sulfide and carbon dioxide but do not produce oxygen.

28. (b) one meiotic and two mitotic division

Explanation: Meiosis produces pollen grains which divides mitotically to produce generative nucleus and tube cell. Generative nucleus undergoes another mitotis to form two male gametes.

29. (c) Johannsen

Explanation: Johannsen coined the word gene to describe the Mendelian units of heredity.

30. (c) Egg cell and synergids

Explanation: The egg apparatus is a group of three cells in the 7-celled embryo sac of an angiosperm. It consists of an egg cell and two synergids.

31. (a) Chromatid

Explanation: The chromosomes duplicate during the G_2 phase of the cell cycle. Each copy of the chromosome is identical and is hence called a chromatid. The G_2 phase is followed by M phase or meiotic phase, where the chromatids align together at the metaphase plate followed by segregation during the anaphase.

32. (a) Parthenocarpy

33. (a) Morgan

Explanation: Linkage and recombination are phenomena that describe the inheritance of genes. A linkage is a phenomenon where two or more linked genes are always inherited together in the same combination for more than two generations. The phenomenon of linkage was studied by the scientist T.H. Morgan using the common fruit fly or *Drosophila melanogaster.*

34. (c) vegetative nucleus

Explanation: The larger nucleus is in the vegetative cell that helps in development of pollen grains while smaller in generative cells, which fuse with egg. The tube nucleus guides or controls the growth of pollen tube and cells follow the path of the tube nucleus.

35. (d) Dioecious organisms are found only in vertebrates

36. (c) (ii) and (iii)

37. (b) A-(iii), B-(iv), C-(ii), D-(i)

Explanation: A. The blastomeres in the blastocyst are arranged into an outer layer called trophoblast and an inner group of cells attached to trophoblast called the inner cell mass. The trophoblast layer gets attached to the endometrium.

B. Cleavage is the repeated mitotic division of cells in the early embryo.

C. Inner cell mass gets differentiated as the embryo.

D. Implantation is the process of attachment and invasion of the uterus endometrium by the blastocyst and it leads to pregnancy.

38. (c) A-(iii), B-(iv), C-(ii), D-(i)

Explanation: There are various different methods that can be used in birth control. Spermicidal jelly and foam are the chemical forms of birth control. IUDs are intrauterine devices that are placed in the uterine cavity. This consists of the copper-T and loop. Condom and cervical cap are mechanical barriers. This prevents the entry of the sperm in the vaginal canal. Tubectomy and vasectomy are surgical methods. These methods are permanent forms of birth control.

39. (d) Periodic abstinence

Explanation: Periodic abstinence also known as fertility awareness, natural family planning, and the rhythm method, this approach entails not having sexual intercourse on the days of a woman's menstrual cycle when she could become pregnant or using a barrier method (such as a condom, the diaphragm or a cervical cap) for birth control.

40. (c) Lactiferous duct

Explanation: Clitoris, mons pubis, and labia majora are the parts of the female external genitalia whereas lactiferous duct is the part of mammary glands.

41. (c) Assertion is true, but reason is false.

Explanation: The gynoecium represents the female reproductive part of the flower consisting of pistil. Thus, assertion is true but reason is false.

42. (c) Assertion is true, but reason is false.

Explanation: After ovulation, the granulosa cells within the empty Graafian follicle turns into the yellow body called corpus luteum. It becomes a temporary endocrine gland secreting progesterone which helps in implantation. Oestrogen is the hormone which helps to maintain the secondary sexual characters in the female. Thus, assertion is true but reason is false.

43. (d) Both assertion and reason are false.

Explanation: A person is reproductively healthy if he or she is capable of producing offsprings. This statement was given by WHO. Thus, both assertion and reason are false.

44. (d) Both assertion and reason are false.

Explanation: A test cross is a cross which involves the breeding of an individual with a phenotypically recessive individual, in order to determine the zygosity of the former by analyzing proportions of offspring phenotype and not the parent types. Back cross is the crossing of a hybrid with one of its parents or an individual genetically similar to its parent, in order to achieve offspring with a genetic identity which is closer to that of the parent. Thus, both assertion and reason are false.

45. (c) Assertion is true, but reason is false.

Explanation: In nuclear endosperm, first and further divisions of primary endosperm nucleus are not followed by cytokinesis or wall formation and thus these free nuclear divisions lead to formation of a large number of free nuclei in embryo sac. Endosperm of coconut is unique in sense that it is both nuclear and cellular. Here the primary endosperm nucleus undergoes a number of free nuclear divisions. Thus, assertion is true but reason is false.

46. (i) (b) primary settling tank

(ii) (c) Activated sludge

(iii) (c) It possess flocs of microbe decomposers

(iv) (d) Masses of bacteria.

(v) (c) Porphyra

Explanation: Porphyra is a cold water seaweed belongs to red algae.

47. (i) (b) Uterine wall   Placenta

(ii) (a) Z is an amniotic fluid which prevents dessication of an embryo.

(iii) (c)   Jaundice

(iv) (d)   Ultrasound imaging.

(v) (b)   12

Explanation: MTP is comparatively safe upto 12 weeks of pregnancy.

48. (i) (c)   both positive and negative regulation

(ii) (c)   Permease

Explanation: The structural gene (z) of the lac operon codes for β-galactosidase. It is responsible for the hydrolysis of polysaccharides. The 'y' genes code for permease. It increases the permeability of a cell to β-galactosidase. The 'a' gene codes for transacetylase.

(iii) (b)   Lac Z—Lac Y—Lac A

(iv) (c)   Lactose is more than glucose

(v) (b)   Beta-galactosidase transacetylase

49. (i) (c)   Three

Explanation: A lac operon consists of one regulatory gene (i) and three structural genes (z, y and a). The "i" in regulatory gene is derived from the word "inhibitor".

(ii) (c)   As long as lactose is more than glucose concentration

(iii) (a)   Allolactose

(iv) (d)   Enzyme-reaction inactivation

(v) (a)   Only 1 is true

50. (i) (a)   *Pisum sativum*

(ii) (c)   Co-dominance

(iii) (c)   co-dominance

(iv) (d)   Phenotype of both allele is partially expressed

(v) (a)   polygenic traits

❏❏

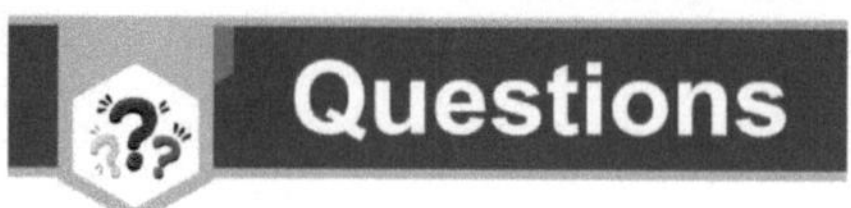

Answer the questions given below by choosing the correct option.

Question 1

There are various types of reproduction. The type of reproduction adopted by an organism depends upon—

(a) The habitat and morphology of the organism

(b) Morphology of the organism

(c) Morphology and physiology of the organism

(d) The organism's habitat, physiology and genetic makeup

Question 2

Double fertilisation involve—

(a) Fertilisation of the egg by two male gametes

(b) Fertilisation of two eggs in the same embryo sac by two sperms brought by one pollen tube

(c) Fertilisation of the egg and the central cell by two sperms brought by different pollen tubes

(d) Fertilisation of egg and central cell by two sperms brought by the same pollen tube

Question 3

Common test to find genotype of hybrid is by—

(a) Studying sexual behaviour of F_1 progeny

(b) Crossing F_1 individuals with recessive parents

(c) Crossing one F_2 progeny with male parent

(d) Crossing one F_2 progeny with female parent

Question 4

Morula resembles a—

(a) Mulberry fruit   (b) Football   (c) Hollow ball   (d) None of these

Question 5

Which of the following was likely to have been absent in a free molecule state, in the primitive atmosphere of the earth ?

(a) Carbon   (b) Oxygen   (c) Hydrocarbon   (d) Nitrogen

Question 6

Genetic drift operates only in—

(a) Island population   (b) Smaller population

(c) Larger population   (d) Mendelian population

Question 7

Mycorrhiza does not help the host plant in—

(a) Enhancing its phosphorus uptake capacity   (b) Increasing its tolerance to drought

(c) Enhancing its resistance to root pathogens   (d) Increasing its resistance to insect

Question 8

Which of the following statement support the view that elaborate sexual reproductive process appeared much later in the organic evolution ?

(i) Lower group of organisms have simpler body design

(ii) Asexual reproduction is common in lower groups of organisms

(iii) Asexual reproduction is common in higher groups of organisms

(iv) The high incidence of sexual reproduction in angiosperms and vertebrates

Choose the *correct* answer from the options given below —

(a) (i) and (ii)   (b) (i) and (iii)   (c) (ii) and (iv)   (d) (ii) and (iii)

Question 9

Study of pollen grains is called —

(a) Ethnology   (b) Palynology   (c) Paleobotany   (d) Co-taxonomy

Question 10

Darwin's finches are good example of —

(a) Connecting link   (b) Adaptive radiation

(c) Convergent evolution   (d) Industrial melanism

Question 11

Amniocentesis is a technique used to —

(a) Determine

(b) Pinpoint specific cardiac ailments in embryo

(c) Determine any hereditary/genetic abnormality in embryo

(d) All of these

Question 12

Signals for parturition originate from —

(a) Both placenta as well as fully developed foetus

(b) Placenta only

(c) Oxytocin released from maternal pituitary

(d) Fully developed foetus only

Question 13

Cause of speciation is —

(a) Random mating   (b) Hybridisation

(c) Geographic Isolation   (d) Migration

Question 14

In the Lac operon system, β-galactosidase is encoded by —

(a) a-gene   (b) i-gene   (c) y-gene   (d) z-gene

Question 15

Seedless banana is —

(a) Parthenocarpic fruit   (b) Multiple fruit   (c) Drupe fruit   (d) Tree fruit

Question 16

1st polar body is formed at which stage of oogenesis —

(a) 1st meiosis   (b) 2nd mitosis   (c) 1st mitosis   (d) Differentiation

Question 17

The term genetics was proposed by —

(a) Mendel   (b) Bateson   (c) Morgan   (d) Johannsen

Question 18

The largest unit in which gene flow is possible is —

(a) Organism   (b) Population   (c) Species   (d) Genes

Question 19

The test tube baby programme employs which one of the following technique ?
(a) Intra Cytoplasmic Sperm Injection (ICSI)   (b) Intra Uterine Insemination (IUI)
(c) Gamete Intra Fallopian Transfer (GIFT)   (d) Zygote Intra Fallopian Transfer (ZIFT)

Question 20

Lactic Acid is formed by the process of —
(a) Fermentation   (b) Glycolysis   (c) HMP pathway   (d) None of these

Question 21

Eyelids in human embryo separate in :
(a) 14 weeks   (b) 16 weeks   (c) 24 weeks   (d) 40 weeks

Question 22

A monohybrid for qualitative trait is crossed with homozygous recessive individual of its type, the phenotype ratio is—
(a) $1:2:1$ (b) $3:1$ (c) $1:1$ (d) $9:7$

Question 23

Embryo sac is also called —
(a) microspore   (b) megaspore
(c) megagametophyte   (d) microgametophyte

Question 24

Theory of chemical origin of life was given by —
(a) Miller and Fox   (b) Oparin and Haldane
(c) Miller and Watson   (d) Watson and Melvin

Question 25

Birbal Sahni Institute of Palaeobotany is located at __________ .
(a) Delhi   (b) Lucknow   (c) Dehradun   (d) Kolkata

Question 26

In the given pedigree chart, the trait shown is __________ .

(a) Autosomal dominant   (b) Autosomal recessive
(c) X-linked   (d) Y-linked

Question 27

Which of the following is maintained for optimum production of Vinegar?
(a) Anaerobic condition   (b) Temperature of 65ºC
(c) Aerobic condition   (d) Microaerophilic condition

Question 28

The further growth of embryo takes place when the __________ has been formed.
(a) pollen   (b) ovule   (c) zygote   (d) pistil

Question 29

The chromosomal theory of inheritance was proposed by __________ in 1902.
(a) Mendel   (b) Sutton and Boveri
(c) Bateson and Punnett   (d) Watson and Crick

Question 30

Endosperm cell of an angiosperm has 36 chromosomes. The number of chromosomes in the gametes would be __________ .

(a) 11   (b) 12   (c) 8   (d) 9

Question 31

__________ is the exchange of chromosome segments between the non-sister chromatids.

(a) Crossing over   (b) Recombination

(c) Both (a) and (b)   (d) Linkage

Question 32

__________ among the following is triploid.

(a) Megaspore   (b) Embryo   (c) Endosperm   (d) Microspore

Question 33

__________is the graphic representation of a linkage group.

(a) Gene map   (b) Chromosome map   (c) Pedigree chart   (d) Karyotype

Question 34

Sporopollenin occurs in __________ .

(a) female gametophyte   (b) male gametophyte

(c) vegetative cells of pollen grain   (d) exine of pollen wall

Question 35

In spermatogenesis, reduction division of chromosomes occur during conversion of:

(a) Spermatognoia is primary spermatocytes

(b) Primary spermatocytes to secondary spermatocyte

(c) Secondary spermatocytes to spermatides

(d) Spermatids to sperms

Question 36

Which of the following is the component of oral pills ?

(a) Progesterone   (b) Oxytocin   (c) Relaxin   (d) None of these

Question 37

Match the structures of male reproductive system given in column I with their features given in column II and select the correct match from the options given below.

	Column I (Structures)		Column II (Features)
A	Rete testis	(i)	Facilitates insemination
B	Leydig cells	(ii)	Meiosis and sperm formation
C	Seminiferous tubules	(iii)	Connects seminiferous tubules to vasa efferentia
D	Penis	(iv)	Secrete androgens

(a) A-(ii), B-(i), C-(iii), D-(iv)   (b) A-(iii), B-(iv), C-(ii), D-(i)

(c) A-(iii), B-(i), C-(ii), D-(iv)   (d) A-(ii), B-(iv), C-(iii), D-(i)

Question 38

Match column I with column II and select the correct option from the given codes.

	Column I		Column II
A	Integuments	(i)	A mass of cells
B	Chalaza	(ii)	Stalk of ovule
C	Funicle	(iii)	Protective envelopes
D	Nucellus	(iv)	Basal part of the ovule

(a) A-(iii), B-(ii), C-(i), D-(iv)   (b) A-(iv), B-(iii), C-(ii), D-(i)

(c) A-(i), B-(ii), C-(iv), D-(iii)   (d) A-(iii), B-(iv), C-(ii), D-(i)

Question 39

Find the odd one out.

(a) Clitoris   (b) Mons pubis   (c) Lactiferous duct   (d) Labia majora

Question 40

Identify the odd one from the following:

(a) Labia minora   (b) Fimbriae   (c) Infundibulum   (d) Isthmus

Question 41

Assertion : In a microsporangium, the tapetal cells possess little cytoplasm and generally have a single prominent nucleus.

Reason : During microsporogenesis, the microspore mother cells undergo mitotic divisions to produce haploid microspore tetrads.

(a) Both assertion and reason are true and reason is the correct explanation of assertion.

(b) Both assertion and reason are true, but reason is not the correct explanation of assertion.

(c) Assertion is true, but reason is false.

(d) Both assertion and reason are false.

Question 42

Assertion : During pregnancy, development of foetus occurs in stages.

Reason : In second month of pregnancy, limbs, most of the organs and external genitalia are formed.

(a) Both assertion and reason are true and reason is the correct explanation of assertion.

(b) Both assertion and reason are true, but reason is not the correct explanation of assertion.

(c) Assertion is true, but reason is false.

(d) Both assertion and reason are false.

Question 43

Assertion : MTPs can be performed by unqualified quacks.

Reason : MTPs are not considered relatively safe during the second trimester.

(a) Both assertion and reason are true and reason is the correct explanation of assertion.

(b) Both assertion and reason are true, but reason is not the correct explanation of assertion.

(c) Assertion is true, but reason is false.

(d) Both assertion and reason are false.

Question 44

Assertion : Behaviour of chromosome is parallel to gene.

Reason : Genes are located on the chromosome.

(a) Both assertion and reason are true and reason is the correct explanation of assertion.

(b) Both assertion and reason are true, but reason is not the correct explanation of assertion.

(c) Assertion is true, but reason is false.

(d) Both assertion and reason are false.

Question 45

Assertion : Emasculation is the first step of artificial hybridisation in unisexual flowers.

Reason : It does not involve the dusting of stigma of desired female parent with desired pollen grains.

(a) Both assertion and reason are true and reason is the correct explanation of assertion.

(b) Both assertion and reason are true, but reason is not the correct explanation of assertion.

(c) Assertion is true, but reason is false.

(d) Both assertion and reason are false.

Question 46

Read the following and answer the following questions:

India was amongst the first countries in the world to initiate action plans and programmes at a national level to attain total reproductive health as a social goal. These programmes called 'family planning' were initiated in 1951 and were periodically assessed over the past decades. Improved programmes covering wider reproduction-related areas are currently in operation under the popular name 'Reproductive and Child Health Care (RCH) programmes'. Creating awareness among people about various reproduction related aspects and providing facilities and support for building up a reproductively healthy society are the major tasks under these programmes. With the help of audio-visual and the print-media governmental and non-governmental agencies have taken various steps to create awareness among the people about reproduction-related aspects. Introduction of sex education in schools should also be encouraged to provide right information to the young so as to discourage children from believing in myths and having misconceptions about sex-related aspects. Proper information about reproductive organs, adolescence and related changes, safe and hygienic sexual practices, sexually transmitted diseases (STD), AIDS, etc., would help people, especially those in the adolescent age group to lead a reproductively healthy life.

(i) Which among the following is the 1st country in the world to initiate action plan to attain total reproductive health ?

    (a) Indonesia   (b) Britain   (c) India   (d) USA

(ii) In which year was 'Family Planning' progamme launched?

    (a) 1905   (b) 1925   (c) 1947   (d) 1951

(iii) Under reproductive health programme, what is the full form of RCH ?

    (a) Regeneration Child HealthCare Centre   (b) Reproduction Children Health Care

    (c) Rehabilitation Centre for Child Care   (d) Reproductive and Child Health Care

(iv) What is full form of STDs ?

    (a) Sexually Treated Diseases   (b) Sexually Transmitted Diseases

    (c) Sexually Transformation of Diseases   (d) Sexual Transmission of Diseases

(v) Which of the following causes AIDS ?

    (a) Bacillus bacteria (b) HIV   (c) Cyanobacteria   (d) Detrimental fungus

Question 47

DNA fingerprinting is a technique of determining nucleotide sequences of certain areas of DNA which are unique to each individual. Each person has a unique DNA fingerprint. Each fingerprint is the same for every cell, tissue and organ of a person. DNA fingerprinting is the basis of paternity testing in case of disputes.

(i) The technique developed to identify a person with the help of DNA restriction analysis is known as

    (a) DNA profiling (b) DNA fingerprinting (c) RFLP   (d) both (a) and (b)

(ii) For DNA fingerprinting, DNA is obtained from

    (a) blood   (b) hair root cells   (c) semen   (d) all of these

(iii) During DNA fingerprinting, the radioactive probes

    (a) hybridise with DNA sample to form double stranded structure

    (b) degrade and DNA

    (c) create positive charge on DNA

    (d) cut the DNA sample at various sites

(iv) In India, DNA fingerprinting technique was developed by

    (a) Dr. Lalji Singh   (b) Alec Jeffreys

    (c) Dr. Khurana   (d) None of these

(v) Which of the following is true about DNA fingerprinting?

    (a) VNTR is used to probe

    (b) DNA samples are loaded on agarose gel electrophoresis

    (c) It is based on identification of nucleotide sequence present on the DNA molecule

    (d) All of these

Question 48

The mature ovum or a female gamete is spherical in shape. The human ovum is almost free of yolk and is said to be alecithal. Human ovum loses its ability to be fertilised about 24 hours after ovulation. Refer to the given structure of ovum and answer the following questions.

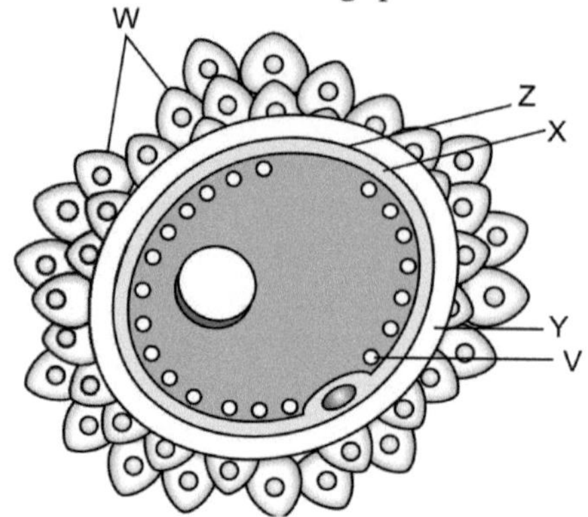

(i) Thick cellular layer formed of radially elongated follicular cells is:

    (a) zona pellucida   (b) plasma membrane

    (c) perivitelline membrane   (d) corona radiata

(ii) In humans, at which stage does ovum get released from ovary?

    (a) Secondary oocyte   (b) Oogonium

    (c) Primary oocyte   (d) First polar body

(iii) Cytoplasm of an ovum is enveloped by ____________ .

    (a) zona pellucida   (b) corona radiata   (c) cell membrane   (d) perivitelline space

(iv) Select the correct option.

	V	W	X
(a)	Cytoplasm	Zona pellucida	Plasma membrane
(b)	Cortical granules	Corona radiata	Zona pellucida
(c)	Cortical granules	Plasma membrane	Corona radiata
(d)	Cytoplasm	Corona radiata	Zona pellucida

(v) Which of the following is not a characteristic of an ovum?

    (a) Nucleus of an ovum has prominent nucleolus.

    (b) Only one ovum formed from one oogonium.

    (c) It lacks centrioles.

    (d) It has very small amount of ooplasm.

Question 49

Read the following and answer the following questions:

The genetic code may be defined as the exact sequence of DNA nucleotides read as three letter words or codons, that determines the sequence of amino acids in protein synthesis. In other words, the genetic code is the set of rules by which information encoded in genetic material (DNA or RNA sequences) is translated into proteins (amino acid sequences) by living cells. Genetic code is the full set of relationships between codons and amino acids (or stop signals). It is basically the way through which the A, C, G and T are strung together.

(i) Which of the following is not a feature of the genetic code?

    (a) Triplet   (b) Degenerate   (c) Non – overlapping   (d) Ambiguous

(ii) Which of the following is not a termination codon?

    (a) UGA   (b) UAG   (c) UAA   (d) UAC

(iii) The codon is a ______________ .

    (a) Singlet   (b) Duplet   (c) Triplet   (d) Quadruplet

(iv) The first amino acid added by the tRNA is added to the anticodon ______________ .

    (a) AUG   (b) UAC   (c) ACG   (d) UGC

(v) Which of the following statement can be concluded from the graph below?

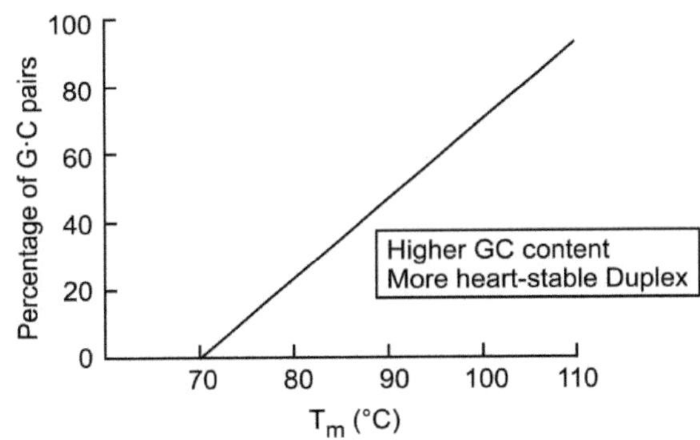

    (a) GC pairings are more stable because they have 3 hydrogen bonds, so they require a higher temperature to break.

    (b) GC pairings are more stable because they have 2 hydrogen bonds, so they require a higher temperature to break.

    (c) AT pairings are more stable because they have 3 hydrogen bonds, so they require a higher temperature to break.

    (d) AT pairings are more stable because they have 2 hydrogen bonds, so they require a higher temperature to break.

Question 50

Read the following and answer the questions that follow:

Chromosomal abnormalities, alterations and aberrations are at the root of many inherited diseases and traits. Chromosomal abnormalities often give rise to birth defects and congenital conditions that may develop during an individual's lifetime. Examining the karyotype of chromosomes (karyotyping) in a sample of cells can allow detection of a chromosomal abnormality. The normal human chromosome contains 23 pairs of chromosomes, giving a total of 46 chromosomes in each cell, called diploid cells. Aneuploidy refers to the presence of an extra chromosome or a missing chromosome and is the most common form of chromosomal abnormality. Down syndrome, Turner syndrome, and Klinefelter's syndrome constitute the most common chromosomal abnormalities.

(i) Chromosomal disorders are based on—

    (a) Mutant allele and their defective products

    (b) Imbalance in chromosome number and chromosome arrangement

    (c) Mutant allele and chromosome arrangement

    (d) Mutant allele and imbalance in chromosome number

(ii) Which of the following is not a characteristic feature of Down's syndrome?

    (a) Very tall   (b) Small round head

    (c) Furrowed tongue   (d) Partially open mouth

(iii) What is the genotype of the person suffering from Klinefelter's syndrome?

    (a) 44 + XXX   (b) 42 + XXX   (c) 44 + XXY   (d) 42 + XXY

(iv) Which of the following is incorrect with respect to Klinefelter's syndrome?

    (a) The fusion of an abnormal egg with a normal sperm

    (b) The fusion of a normal egg with an abnormal sperm

    (c) The fusion of a normal egg with a normal sperm

    (d) An additional copy of X-chromosome

(v)

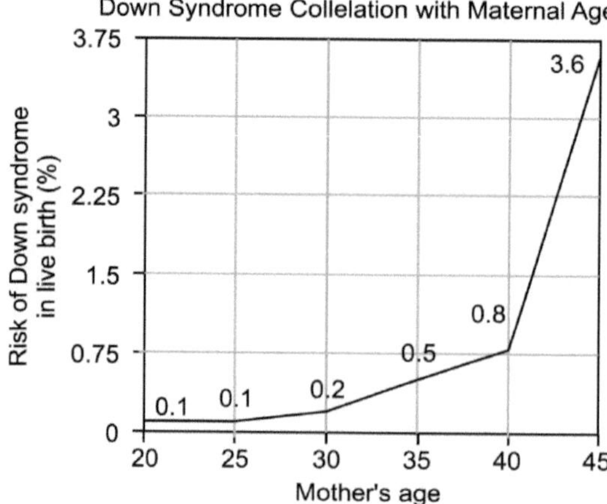

Which of the following statement is true in reference to graph?

(a) The incidence of Down syndrome is correlated with maternal age; older women are more likely to become pregnant with fetuses carrying the trisomy 21 genotype.

(b) The incidence of Down syndrome is correlated with maternal age; younger women are more likely to become pregnant with fetuses carrying the trisomy 21 genotype.

(c) The incidence of Down syndrome is correlated with maternal age; older women are more likely to become pregnant with fetuses carrying the trisomy 23 genotype.

(d) The incidence of Down syndrome is correlated with maternal age; younger women are more likely to become pregnant with fetuses carrying the trisomy 23 genotype.

Answers

1. (d) The organism's habitat, physiology and genetic makeup

2. (d) Fertilisation of egg and central cell by two sperms brought by the same pollen tube

3. (b) Crossing F_1 individuals with recessive parents

   Explanation: In order to determine the genotype of a hybrid, a test cross is done in which a dominant phenotype organism is crossed with the recessive parent rather than selfing. The progenies of such a hybrid can be simply analysed to predict the test organism's genotype.

4. (a) Mulberry fruit

   Explanation: The morula is produced by a series of cleavage division of the early embryo, starting with the single celled zygote. Once the embryo has divided into 6 cells, it resembles a mulberry fruit.

5. (c) oxygen

   Explanation: The atmosphere of earth at the time of origin of life was without free oxygen

atoms. The primitive atmosphere consists of methane, ammonia, water vapour, hydrogen gas, nitrogen gas and some carbon dioxide. Hydrogen atoms were most numerous and reactive. They combined with all available oxygen atoms and formed water.

6. (b) Smaller population

   Explanation: The evolution was caused due to the random change in the allele frequencies of a population over generations. It is mainly caused in small isolated populations due to chance rather than natural selection. It may cause the change in the gene pool by random sampling of a particular allele which may incur in deleting a particular gene.

7. (c) Enhancing its resistance to root pathogens

8. (c) (ii) and (iv)

   Explanation: Asexual reproduction has been found in most primitive animals like Hydra but over the evolutionary time as the higher or advanced organisms came into existence they restored the sexual reproduction as it ensures the genetic recombination that results in variation.

9. (b) Palynology

10. (b) Adaptive radiation

 Explanation: Darwin's finches have a wide variety of beak forms and structures. Adaptive radiation occurs as a result of differences in eating habits and habitat. Adaptive radiation is the process through which organisms diverge from their ancestral species as a result of changes in habitat, eating habits, and other factors.

11. (c) Determine any hereditary/genetic abnormality in embryo

12. (a) Both placenta as well as fully developed foetus

 Explanation: Foetal ejection reflex are mild uterine contractions. This stimulates the posterior pituitary to release oxytocin, which induces uterine contractions.

13. (c) Geographic Isolation

 Explanation: Scientists think that geographic isolation is a common way for the process of speciation to begin: rivers change course, mountains rise, continents drift, organisms migrate, and what was once a continuous population is divided into two or more smaller populations.

14. (d) z-gene

 Explanation: Lac operon is required for transport and metabolism of lactose in *E.coli*. It has three adjacent structural genes Z, Y and A. The genes encode β-galactosidase, lactose permease and thiogalactoside transacetylase respectively.

15. (a) Parthenocarpic fruit

 Explanation: Parthenocarpy is the phenomenon of formation of fruit without fertilization. Usually these parthenocarpic fruits are seedless, .e.g., seedless banana.

16. (a) 1st meiosis

 Explanation: The larger cell is known as the secondary oocyte, while the smaller cell formed is known as the polar body. The formed polar body does not posses any specific function and dies soon after the formation. Thus polar body is formed during Meiosis I.

17. (b) Bateson

18. (b) Population

 Explanation : Gene flow is the passing over of genes from one population to another population. There are various factors that affect the gene flow. The largest unit of population in which gene flow is readily possible is biological species. In species, successful interbreeding is possible which results in the successful reproduction and hence the gene flow.

19. (d) Zygote Intra Fallopian Transfer (ZIFT)

 Explanation : Test-tube baby refers to in vitro fertilisation and embryo transfer. This is accomplished using a technique known as ZIFT (zygote intra fallopian transfer). The oocyte and sperm are taken out of the body and fertilisation takes place in vitro, outside of the female's body. The fallopian tube receives an early embryo with more than 8 blastomeres.

20. (a) Fermentation

 Explanation : In homolactic fermentation, one molecule of glucose is converted to two molecules of lactic acid while in heterolactic fermentation CO_2 and ethanol is produced.

21. (c) 24 weeks

 Explanation: The eyelids are first evident as folds at 7 weeks of development, and they are expanded during the eighth week by rapidly proliferating mesenchymal tissue. The upper and lower eyelids fuse with each other around Week 9, and they separate again at around 6 months or 24 weeks.

22. (c) 1 : 1

 Explanation: A cross between an organism with an unknown genotype and a recessive parent is known as a test cross. So, the given condition can be considered as a test cross.

 A monohybrid testcross gives a 1 : 1 ratio indicating that the two pairs of factors are segregating and assorting independently.

23. (c) megagametophyte

 Explanation: The embryo sac is nothing but the female gametophyte which is also called the megagametophyte. The egg cells are produced inside this embryo sac. The embryo sac also consists of synergids, antipodal cells and central cells.

24. (b) Oparin and Haldane

Explanation: Chemical evolution involves chemical reactions of inorganic compounds to form organic compounds. In the year 1992, Haldane and Oparin proposed the chemical theory of origin of life in which he stated that formation of organic materials take place from abiogenic material in presence of an external source of energy.

25. (b) Lucknow

26. (b) Autosomal recessive

Explanation: Autosomal recessive inheritance is a way a genetic trait or condition can be passed down from parent to child. A genetic condition can occur when the child inherits one copy of a mutated (changed) gene from each parent. The parents of a child with an autosomal recessive condition usually do not have the condition. Unaffected parents are called carriers because they each carry one copy of the mutated gene and can pass it to their children.

27. (a) Anaerobic condition

Explanation: While in the second stage of fermentation, the ethanol formed after the product of the first stage is oxidized aerobically into acetic acid with the help of microorganisms such as Acetobacter. The presence of oxygen promotes the acceleration of the process. This condition must be maintained for optimum production of vinegar.

28. (c) zygote

Explanation: Further growth of embryo sac occurs only when the zygote has been formed and primary endosperm nucleus has been created by triple fusion.

29. (b) Sutton and Boveri

30. (b) 12

Explanation: Number of chromosomes in diploid plant is 36 *i.e.* $3n = 36$

So, $n = 12$

Since gametes are haploid, its ploidy level is n.

Thus, the number of chromosomes in the gametes will be $n = 12$.

31. (c) Both (a) and (b)

Explanation: Crossing over, or recombination is the exchange of chromosome segments between non-sister chromatids in meiosis. Crossing over creates new combinations of genes in the gametes that are not found in either parent, contributing to genetic diversity.

32. (c) Endosperm

Explanation: Each ovule receives a pollen tube that delivers two sperm cells to the embryo sac. One male gamete fertilizes the egg cell, generating the diploid zygote, while the other male gamete fertilizes the central cell giving rise to endosperm that is usually triploid.

33. (b) Chromosome map

34. (d) exine of pollen wall

35. (b) Primary spermatocytes to secondary spermatocyte

Explanation: The germ cells of seminiferous tubules present near the capsule serve as spermatogonia, which divide and produce more cells by mitosis. Some of these new cells serve as primary spermatocytes that undergo meiosis, meiosis I produce two secondary spermatocytes (n), which is followed by meiosis II that produces four spermatids. Spermatids then differentiate into sperm where only morphological changes take place and no cell division occurs during differentiation of spermatids into sperms.

36. (a) Progesterone

Explanation: Oral pills contain either progesterone alone or a combination of progesterone and estrogen. Progesterone inhibits the LH production. Example of progesterone pills is i-Pills and Unwanted-72.

37. (b) A-(iii), B-(iv), C-(ii), D-(i)

Explanation: Rete testis carries sperms from the seminiferous tubules (where sperms are produced through meiosis) of the testes into the vasa efferentia. Leydig cells synthesise and secrete testicular hormones called androgens. The penis is the male external genitalia that facilitates insemination.

38. (d) A-(iii), B-(iv), C-(ii), D-(i)

Explanation: Funicle is the stalk through which the ovule is attached to the placenta, integuments are the protective envelopes of an ovule, chalaza represents the basal part of the ovule opposite to the micropyle, and nucellus is the mass of cells enclosed within the integuments.

39. (c) Lactiferous duct

Explanation: Clitoris, mons pubis, and labia majora are the parts of the female external genitalia whereas lactiferous duct is the part of mammary glands.

40. (a) Labia minora

Explanation: Fimbriae, infundibulum, isthmus and ampulla are the parts of fallopian duct while labia minora is the female external genitalia.

41. (d) Both assertion and reason are false.

Explanation: Tapetum is the innermost wall layer of a microsporangium. It nourishes the developing pollen grains. The tapetal cells enlarge radically and become filled with dense protoplasmic contents as well as nutrients. Microsporogenesis refers to the process of formation of haploid microspores mother cell or pollen mother cell through meiosis. Thus, both assertion and reason are false.

42. (c) Assertion is true, but reason is false.

Explanation: A typical pregnancy lasts 40 weeks. It is divided into three stages, called trimesters: first trimester, second trimester, and third trimester. The foetus undergoes many changes throughout maturation. Hence during pregnancy, development of the foetus occurs in stages. By the end of the third month of pregnancy, limbs, most of the organs and external genitalia are formed. Thus, assertion is true but reason is false.

43. (d) Both assertion and reason and false.

Explanation: MTP is the termination of pregnancy before the foetus becomes viable. It is done to get rid of unwanted pregnancies. It is comparatively safe up to first trimester (12 weeks) of pregnancy. After the first trimester, MTP becomes more risky as the foetus becomes intimately associated with the maternal tissues. Thus, both assertion and reason are false.

44. (a) Both assertion and reason are true and reason is the correct explanation of assertion.

Explanation: During Anaphase of meiosis I, the two chromosome pairs can align at the metaphase plate independently of each other. Sutton and Boveri argued that the pairing and separation of a pair of chromosomes would lead to the segregation of a pair of factors they carried.

45. (d) Both assertion and reason are false.

Explanation: In the artificial hybridisation programme selection of parents is done first. In case of female parent producing unisexual female flowers emasculation step is not needed. During emasculation in bisexual female flower anthers are removed from flower bud before the anther dehisces. Thus, both assertion and reason are false.

46. (i) (c) India

(ii) (d) 1951

(iii) (d) Reproductive and Child Health Care

(iv) (b) Sexually Transmitted Diseases

(v) (b) HIV

47. (i) (d) Both (a) and (b)

(ii) (d) all of these

Explanation: For DNA fingerprinting, DNA is obtained from blood, semen, hair roots, tissue samples, nuclei of white blood cells or of spermatozoa, body secretions, etc.

(iii) (a) hybridise with DNA sample to form double stranded structure

Explanation: In DNA fingerprinting, during hybridisation the bands are flooded with single stranded radioactive DNA probe. This single stranded DNA probe and sample DNA hybridise to form double stranded structure due to natural affinity.

(iv) (b) Alec jeffreys

Explanation: DNA fingerprinting technique was developed by Alec Jeffreys.

(v) (d) All of these

48. (i) (d) corona radiata

Explanation: In humans, ovum is released from the ovary as secondary oocyte.

(ii) (a) Secondary oocyte

(iii) (c) cell membrane

(iv) (b) Cortical granules, Corona radiata, Zona pellucida

Explanation: V–Cortical granules

W–Cells of corona radiata

X–Zona pellucida

Y–Perivitelline space

Z–Plasma membrane

(v) (d) It has very small amount of cytoplasm called ooplasm.

49. (i) (d) Ambiguous

(ii) (d) UAC

(iii) (c) Triplet

(iv) (b) UAC

(v) (a) GC pairings are more stable because they have 3 hydrogen bonds, so they require a higher temperature to break.

50. (i) (b) Imbalance in chromosome number and chromosome arrangement

(ii) (a) Very tall

(iii) (c) 44 + XXY

(iv) (c) The fusion of a normal egg with a normal sperm

(v) (a) The incidence of Down syndrome is correlated with maternal age; older women are more likely to become pregnant with fetuses carrying the trisomy 21 genotype.

❑❑

9 789391 184407

Printed by Libri Plureos GmbH in Hamburg,
Germany